THE PSYCHOLOGY OF LEARNING

McGRAW–HILL SERIES IN PSYCHOLOGY

Consulting Editors

NORMAN GARMEZY

HARRY F. HARLOW

LYLE V. JONES

HAROLD W. STEVENSON

BEACH, HEBB, MORGAN, AND NISSEN / *The Neuropsychology of Lashley*
VON BÉKÉSY / *Experiments in Hearing*
BERKOWITZ / *Aggression: A Social Psychological Analysis*
BERLYNE / *Conflict, Arousal, and Curiosity*
BLUM / *Psychoanalytic Theories of Personality*
BROWN / *The Motivation of Behavior*
BROWN AND GHISELLI / *Scientific Method in Psychology*
BUCKNER AND MC GRATH / *Vigilance: A Symposium*
COFER / *Verbal Learning and Verbal Behavior*
COFER AND MUSGRAVE / *Verbal Behavior and Learning: Problems and Processes*
CRAFTS, SCHNEIRLA, ROBINSON, AND GILBERT / *Recent Experiments in Psychology*
DAVITZ / *The Communication of Emotional Meaning*
DEESE / *The Psychology of Learning*
DEESE AND HULSE / *The Psychology of Learning*
DOLLARD AND MILLER / *Personality and Psychotherapy*
ELLIS / *Handbook of Mental Deficiency*
EPSTEIN / *Varieties of Perceptual Learning*
FERGUSON / *Statistical Analysis in Psychology and Education*
FORGUS / *Perception: The Basic Process in Cognitive Development*
GHISELLI / *Theory of Psychological Measurement*
GHISELLI AND BROWN / *Personnel and Industrial Psychology*
GILMER / *Industrial Psychology*
GRAY / *Psychology Applied to Human Affairs*
GUILFORD / *Fundamental Statistics in Psychology and Education*
GUILFORD / *The Nature of Human Intelligence*

THE PSYCHOLOGY OF LEARNING

JAMES DEESE
Professor of Psychology
The Johns Hopkins University

STEWART H. HULSE
Associate Professor of Psychology
The Johns Hopkins University

68293

THIRD EDITION

MC GRAW-HILL BOOK COMPANY
New York   St. Louis   San Francisco
Toronto   London   Sydney

THE PSYCHOLOGY OF LEARNING

PREFACE

The chief objective of the first two editions of this book was to bring together the various aspects of the study of learning. That is also the aim of this edition, though once again a new strategy has been adopted. The first edition was intended to be a survey of all topics in learning, general and specific, theoretical and applied. The second edition pruned away the applied topics and the topics of marginal concern to the study of learning. In this edition, that pruning process has continued so that only matters of central concern to the psychology of learning remain. Furthermore, this edition has been reorganized to bring together into the individual chapters processes rather than topics. The present edition, then, covers a range of topics restricted to the core of the psychology of learning. As in the previous editions, however, the book is meant to provide for the student as representative a picture as possible of the contemporary concern with the psychology of learning.

The early chapters stress the basic processes of conditioning and learning. For their substantive material, they rely heavily, though by no means exclusively, upon information derived from the animal laboratory. Chapter 1 provides a general introduction to the psychology of learning. While the opening sections of the chapter may be review for some students, the last sections include material which will be new to all students. Two chapters on reinforcement follow, the first emphasizing data and definition of basic concepts, the second showing in a purposely selective way how data have been handled by theory. Succeeding chapters treat extinction, patterns of reinforcement, generalization and discrimination, and the roles of emotion and motivation in the learning process. The chapter on patterns of reinforcement fits the traditional topics of partial reinforcement and schedules of reinforcement into a broader view of the effects of changing conditions of reward upon learning.

Beginning with the eighth chapter, topics of peculiar concern to human learning are treated. Verbal learning and the learning of skills provide the major topics, and various processes are allotted to the individual chapters. Chapter 8 introduces problems and methods in the study of acquisition. It presents the traditional tools of the laboratory as well as the newer concern with grammatical structures and the like. The succeeding chapters deal with special theoretical problems, such as mediation, transfer, retention, and concept learning. A final chapter built around the topic of learning of skills introduces some matters of basic theoretical importance that have arisen in the study of perceptual-motor skills.

The authors have approached their field empirically. Theory is introduced in the interests of solving particular problems, not as a presentation of the "system" of a particular individual or school. The early chapters present a theoretical discussion of the definition of learning itself and go on to examine theoretical problems in the areas of reinforcement, extinction, and discriminative learning. In several instances, theory is introduced in historical perspective, and the student is shown how an older theory has fared under the impact of new ideas and, above all, new data. In the later chapters, mediation theory, mathematical learning theory, interference theory, and various structural theories are represented in the context of particular problems and analyses.

Like the earlier editions, this revision of the book is intended primarily for junior and senior students in psychology and for graduate students in psychology or educational psychology. However, the text is self-sufficient, and a student can study it with profit without a particular background in psychology.

Several persons have read all or portions of the manuscript, and the authors are grateful to these readers for important corrections and useful suggestions. The manuscript was typed and in some instances corrected by Mrs. Leonora C. Hunner and Mrs. Reva Diffenderfer, to whom the authors are truly grateful. Thanks are also due to students, colleagues, and families for their help and patience.

Permission has been granted by many publishers and individuals for the reproduction of illustrations and tables. The authors gratefully acknowledge permissions from the following: Academic Press Inc.; American Association for the Advancement of Science; *American Journal of Psychology;* American Psychological Association; Appleton-Century-Crofts, Inc.; Georgetown University Press; J. B. Lippincott Company; Journal Press; *Psychological Reports;* Psychometric Society; Society for the Experimental Analysis of Behavior; Society of the Sigma Xi; University of California Press; John Wiley and Sons, Inc.; and Yale University Press.

JAMES DEESE
STEWART H. HULSE

CONTENTS

1

INTRODUCTION

Most human behavior is learned. This fact in itself makes clear why the study of learning is one of the most important parts of psychology. It is impossible to understand the behavior of human beings and that of most animals without knowing something about the basic principles of learning. In order to have a thorough understanding of almost any problem in psychology, we should know what effect learning and different learning experiences have upon the problem we are studying. For example, if we were interested, as personality theorists are, in the effects of traumatic experiences upon adult personality, we would find that we could understand this problem only to the extent that we understood the basic principles of learning. If we knew as much about learning as we would like to know, we could answer questions about the extent to which traumatic experiences during infancy, or other times of life, affect different segments of adult behavior. By the same token, a thorough understanding of the learning process would enable us to settle questions about the most effective way to teach, to train personnel to do a certain job, and to write books such as the one you are reading. In short, it is not difficult to show the importance of learning as part of the science of psychology.

It is probably more difficult to convince the student that *learning theory* is of enough general importance to warrant study. Theory, even to the fairly sophisticated student of psychology, often means fussy disputes about matters of little or no consequence. We must admit that there is a certain justice to this criticism, particularly when it is leveled at an area within a relatively young science such as psychology. Theories within the domain of learning tend to be narrow, based on scanty evidence involving few, if any, mathematical constants, and wrong more often than not. This should not blind us, however, to the importance of theory construction as an *approach* to an understanding of the phenomena of learning. Ultimately, it is to be hoped, this approach will provide broad laws of great usefulness and power.

Theories, even limited ones, serve several valuable functions. First, they guide research. They supply hypotheses about unsolved problems and serve to integrate and lend coherence to a scientific discipline. Second, they help to organize factual information and to generalize this information to other areas. For example, it is generally more profitable to formulate a hypothesis about how to program a teaching machine from a well-established theory of learning than from a simple factual rule. This is true because a theory frequently suggests why a particular application should be made, while the extension of a factual rule, more often than not, is simply a guess. Third, theories help to tell us when we are pursuing a profitable or an unprofitable line of thinking about a problem. This is true because a well-constructed theory is capable of proof or disproof. In short, it is testable. If we find that our latest theoretical hunch is going to lead to no reasonable laboratory check of its validity, then we are best off if we discard our notion and move on to something else.

There is no better way to appreciate the value of theory than to read a survey of the experimental literature about some aspect of learning. If you do this, you will find hundreds of experiments which overlap, duplicate, and frequently contradict one another. If you were to memorize the contents of such a survey, you would have at your command a mass of highly specific information limited to narrow examples of behavior. Most general principles are established through theory of some sort. Therefore a theory can be used to lift us beyond the confines of isolated experiments into an awareness of general principles about learning and behavior.

As we have noted, there are very few theoretical principles in the psychology of learning that are both unequivocal and widely accepted, because very few existing theories are supported by a wide variety of evidence. We must therefore be cautious about the extent to which we apply theory. It is necessary to strike a balance between the simple factual information at our disposal and the general principles we develop to explain and extend it. Complete devotion to a particular theory is almost certainly dangerous, given our present ignorance about the facts of psychology. So we should be cautious in accepting a universal set of explanatory principles that can be applied to all problems in learning. Therefore, we shall study some limited aspects of certain theories, *microtheories* if you will, and their applications to specific problems. Some of the grand sweep of a really systematic theory is lost in this way, but considering the limitations of our factual knowledge, this approach is more realistic.

SOME METHODOLOGICAL BACKGROUND

Before we go farther, we need to establish some ground rules about finding evidence and discovering or inventing theoretical principles. We shall now look briefly at the nature of experiments and the logic of scientific method as they apply to some of the problems we shall examine later.

EXPERIMENT AND OBSERVATION

A scientific observation occurs when one looks at an event and records it in such a way that any other competent observer, given the same conditions, would make the same report. An experiment, in the simplest sense, is an observation made under conditions that are to some extent of the observer's own devising. In an experiment the investigator actually changes and controls the events that occur. Thus, watching squirrels retrieve buried nuts from the ground could be a scientific observation, but to turn this into an experiment, we should have to control some of the conditions of observation (such as the place where the nuts are buried).

Most of the factual information in the psychology of learning has been gathered in experiments, because, whenever possible, investigators prefer to experiment rather than simply to observe. This preference is well founded; it is always easier to infer *causal* relations when the events under study are controlled. The kind and extent of the control in the observation limits the adequacy and generality of the causal inferences the investigator may make. If only one condition is varied systematically, we can be a good deal more certain of the cause than if all conditions were allowed to vary haphazardly. Since we are usually interested in making causal inferences from our observations, it will be worthwhile to look at some of the rules for conducting experiments.

INDEPENDENT AND DEPENDENT VARIABLES. In the simplest kind of experiment, all conditions are held constant but one, and this one is allowed to vary in known ways. For example, we may want to study the effects of different kinds of rewards upon the speed with which monkeys can learn a new habit. To do this, we would systematically vary the nature of the reward given to different monkeys and try to keep constant in all monkeys the effects of motivation, previous history, testing conditions, and so forth. Since we had controlled all the variables but reward, we would be safe in making inferences from our results about the effects of quality of reward upon speed of learning.

In this example, kind of reward is an *independent variable* because it is independently controlled and varied by the experimenter. The changes in behavior that result from changes in reward provide the *dependent variable*. Speed of learning, in this example, is the dependent variable because changes in it depend upon changes in the independent variable, reward. Independent variables, then, are the conditions that are systematically varied by the experimenter; dependent variables are the consequent changes in behavior.

MORE THAN ONE INDEPENDENT OR DEPENDENT VARIABLE. In the example just mentioned, all the variables but kind of reward were controlled; they were held constant or they were allowed to vary at random from animal to animal. In some experiments, however, we may use more than one independent variable and measure more than one dependent variable.

Experiments with more than one independent variable are quite common. Investigators frequently use this method because they suspect that the two independent variables somehow modify each other's influence on the dependent variable. In these circumstances, we speak of the result as an *interaction* between the two variables. For example, Hull (1951) proposed that motivation and reward interact in their effect upon behavior. He suggested that when motivation is low, the amount of reward that is given an animal will have relatively little effect on the speed, say, with which the animal will run a maze. A large reward should produce about the same speed as a small reward. When motivation is high, however, large rewards should produce clearly faster speeds than small rewards. Other theorists (e.g. Spence, 1956) have made different assumptions, but the important point here is that in Hull's system, the effect of reward on behavior was to be *modified* by the effect of motivation on behavior; the experimental literature is full of examples of interaction between two or more variables. Indeed, it would be extraordinary if the host of variables we know are involved in the learning process were truly independent of one another.

Sometimes, too, we may use more than one dependent variable in an experiment. We may be interested in the influence of reward upon both speed of learning and general activity. In this case we obtain information that we could not get by doing two separate experiments, one on speed of learning and one on general activity level. The additional information is not quite in the same form as that achieved in the case of two independent variables; usually it comes in the form of a *correlation* between the two dependent variables. Speed of learning and general activity may be so highly correlated, for example, under the influence of different kinds of reward or motivation, that we would suspect there is some underlying factor that accounts for the changes in *both* speed of learning and general activity.

FUNCTIONAL RELATIONSHIPS. When the dependent variable shows change as a result of variation in the independent variable, we say that the dependent variable is a *function* of the independent variable. In the example discussed above, Hull hypothesized that running speed was a function of amount of reward and of strength of motivation. More specifically, he hypothesized that running speed was a *joint* function of both these variables, since they were assumed to interact in their effects upon behavior. Functional relationships are very important in the psychology of learning, because many of the results of experiments are quantitative and can sometimes be expressed as simple mathematical functions.

More frequently a functional relationship between one or more independent and dependent variables is presented in the form of a graph. Graphs are useful because they show at a glance the nature of a functional relationship. In graphic presentation the independent variable is always placed on the horizontal axis (the abscissa) and the dependent variable on the vertical axis (the ordinate). A good example of such a graph is Figure 2.4 on page 35. Here, the magnitude of a conditioned response (dependent variable) is plotted as a function of the number of trials of training (independent variable).

DEFINITIONS IN THE PSYCHOLOGY OF LEARNING

Someone who comes upon the psychology of learning for the first time is generally struck by the psychologist's concern over the definition of the terms he uses in his science. At times, this concern seems to border on the picayune. There is a good reason for this, a reason which can be made abundantly clear in a few minutes. Ask several friends to define the term *reward*. The chances are that you will get almost as many different definitions for the term as the number of friends that you ask. The reason for this is that common definitions of a term, the kinds of definition that enable us to get along very well in everyday discourse, depend upon casual observation, tradition, and the opinion of authorities. These definitions are the sort that wind up in good dictionaries, but they are rarely of much use to someone who wants to build an experimental science based upon the concepts implied by words such as *reward, motive,* and the like. The scientist requires something much more exact. He will generally look for a definition that eventually refers to unequivocal measurable facts—concrete objects that he can point to directly, conditions that he can duplicate with great precision time after time. Much is lost in the process; the definition of a term that will satisfy the experimental psychologist may seem rather sterile and barren to the person who is not a psychologist. But much is gained as well. Given a good scientific definition of the term *reward,* for example, the psychologist knows that all his colleagues will understand *precisely* what he means when he uses the term, and he has gained a corresponding ability to *communicate* the meaning of the terms he introduces into his science.

OPERATIONAL DEFINITIONS. How do we decide when we have a hungry rat? In other words, how can we arrive at a rule which will define for us the term *hunger?* We might require, as many psychologists do, that the rat first be accustomed to a daily schedule of feeding and then be deprived of food for some specified period of time. We might then watch to see if the rat would eat when some food was presented to it. Notice that we have done essentially two things: We have taken food away from the rat for a period of time, and then we have made a simple measurement of behavior. We have watched to see if, given the first condition, the rat would eat when we provided some food. If both these conditions are satisfied, we could state quite arbitrarily that the rat is "hungry," and we shall have established a set of rules which define, for us, the term *hunger.* Note very well that in order to satisfy ourselves that we have met the conditions required for our definition of hunger, our rules require that we *do something* in a way which is closely prescribed, repeatable, and—above all—directly observable. We are not sure we have a hungry rat, for example, until we actually give the rat some food and watch it eat. In other words, our definitional rules require that we perform "operations" upon the environment to establish that certain criteria are met, and for this reason we call our definition an *operational definition.*

To give another example, an operational definition of the term *reward* usually states that it is some change in the environment which increases the likelihood of an organism repeating the behavior that immediately preceded the reward. Our preset criterion of a change in the environment could be satisfied by presenting the rat with a piece of food, for example. Our criterion that a piece of food presented in this way will increase the likelihood that the rat will repeat his behavior could be checked by the operations of watching, or otherwise measuring, what the rat does. Notice there is no mention of "something that the animal likes" or "something that it wants to get"; rather, the definition is explicitly stated in terms of things that can always be observed and agreed upon. We may all disagree about what animals "like" (unless we operationally define "like"), but most of us can agree that sometimes animals repeat what they have done before when their behavior was followed by a reward. We can agree because we can watch and measure them doing it.

INTERVENING VARIABLES AND HYPOTHETICAL CONSTRUCTS. An intervening variable is a convenient label for a *number* of independent and dependent variables which we have some reason to believe are closely related. For example, we might do an experiment in which we deprived one group of rats of water for a certain period of time and injected a second group of rats with a hypertonic salt solution. If we gave rats in both these groups a chance to drink water, we would probably find that their water intake would be greater than if they had not been through our initial experimental procedures. We might then conveniently summarize our work by saying that both our independent variables affect *strength of thirst*. To give another example, we might have some reason to believe that the taste of a reward we use would have a similar effect upon two dependent variables: the probability that a particular response would be repeated in the future, and the magnitude or amplitude of the response. If this were so, we could use the single term *strength of response* to cover changes both in the probability of occurrence of the response and in its magnitude.

Intervening variables like strength of thirst and strength of response have some important things in common. First, they are not independent or dependent variables themselves. Instead, they are labels or abstractions for conditions which we establish by manipulating independent variables, and which we then measure by examining changes in dependent variables (hence the term *intervening*). Second, intervening variables are always reducible to independent and dependent variables which can be talked about in terms of experimental operations. You cannot see, hear, feel, point to, or otherwise measure directly a particular strength of thirst, a particular level of anxiety, or a particular strength of response. These are abstractions which cannot be directly observed. Thus, when the psychologist uses a term such as strength of response—and we shall use this particular intervening variable a great deal in this book—he always refers to things or to variables which he can see or measure directly: changes in the speed with which a rat runs a maze, changes in the probability that a response will occur, and so forth. Finally (and this point will become clearer in a moment), when a psychologist uses an intervening variable as a label, he does not intend it to connote any special theoretical meaning. In a sense, intervening variables are merely terms which provide a convenient shorthand, and when a psychologist uses them, he is generally talking rather specifically about experimental operations that he uses in the laboratory.

Sometimes a psychologist will use terms in developing his science which cannot, like intervening variables, be reduced completely to collections of experimental operations. He is most apt to do this when he is offering a hypothesis or a theory about some aspect of behavior, or when he is attempting to relate the terms of his science to some other science, such as neurophysiology or physics. Such terms—based in part on operational definitions, but also partly on some shrewd theoretical guesses about a psychological process—are called *hypothetical constructs* (MacCorquodale & Meehl, 1948).

Let us look at some examples of hypothetical constructs. *Reward* is often used as a hypothetical construct rather than as a simple operationally defined term (though in this case, the term *reinforcement* is generally substituted for it). We might assert that reinforcement is a "slight decrement in the level of neural excitability" or that it results from a "sudden reduction in the strength of a motive." Similarly, we might say that strength of response is ultimately defined in terms of the "arrangement of graded electrical potentials at a particular set of synapses in the central nervous system." In each of these cases, the operations by which we would establish the basic criteria for using the terms reward and response strength are taken for granted (go back and check our operational definition of the term reward, for example), and we have added something else —some hypothesis, some theoretical "surplus meaning"—to the concepts.

At the time we introduce hypothetical constructs, our science may not be sufficiently developed to permit us to perform the actual experimental operations we would need to check the validity of our theoretical assertions. Sometimes we may even find ourselves in the awkward position of being uncertain if we can *ever* find a set of operations which will unequivocally assure us about the validity of a particular hypothetical construct. Psychology abounds with constructs that are potentially explanatory but are only really so if we are willing to accept a great many dubious assumptions or a great deal of conflicting evidence. But in using these terms, we deliberately suggest the way we feel theory should be developed, and of more importance perhaps, we suggest the choice of experiments that should be done on a particular problem. If we choose a hypothetical construct which implies that the critical locus of the reinforcement process lies in the nervous system, for example, we are going to do experiments that will be quite different from the ones we would carry out if we made the perhaps rash assertion that the reinforcement process does not involve the nervous system at all. In other words, hypothetical constructs can help guide us to explanations of the manner in which psychological processes work. They can help us discover *why* behavior changes under a particular set of conditions.

Keep in mind the distinction between intervening variables and hypothetical constructs, as well as the distinction between these and simple operational definitions. If you do, you will find it much easier to keep fact and theory separate and to evaluate theory against available factual evidence.

The remainder of this chapter discusses some important operational distinctions between several types of behavior and between at least two types of learning. Since there is a question whether or not these distinctions involve theoretical as well as operational matters, the importance of keeping theoretical and operational terms separate should be apparent at the outset.

OPERATIONALLY DEFINED TYPES OF LEARNING

Learning to typewrite is different from learning to ski, if for no other reason than that different movements and muscles are involved. Learning to typewrite and learning to ski, however, are both examples of the same process of learning. In both cases, initial attempts are corrected in response to information the learner receives about their success. Most psychologists, however, are now convinced that not all learning involves the same process, although they do not agree about how many processes should be distinguished. This disagreement has led to a theoretical controversy which has raged with greater or lesser intensity for some time. We shall return to this controversy at the end of this chapter.

Now, however, we wish to develop some additional groundwork that we shall need for our study of learning. We shall be introducing some terms and some standard laboratory procedures which will be used and to which we shall refer throughout much of the remainder of the book. Of greatest importance, we shall develop a classificatory scheme for some of the experimental operations that a psychologist uses in studying simple learning processes. The vast majority of the facts that we shall be discussing in the next few chapters have been obtained using one or another of these experimental paradigms.

CLASSICAL OR PAVLOVIAN CONDITIONING

Every student of psychology is familiar with the famous experiments on conditioning made by Ivan P. Pavlov, the Russian physiologist. Because Pavlov's experiments are both well known and fundamental to some of the problems we shall be discussing, we can use one of them to illustrate one type of experimental operation that is used in the study of learning.

CONDITIONED SALIVATION. In this experiment (Pavlov, 1927), small openings were made in the cheeks of dogs, so that the duct of the parotid salivary gland could be directed outward; this allowed the saliva to be collected and measured as it was secreted. The dog was placed in a soundproof room which had a small window that permitted the experimenters to watch the dog. A tuning fork was sounded in the room, and a few seconds later, small amounts of powdered meat were presented for the dog to eat. The tuning fork, of course, did not produce saliva, but the sight of meat and its presence in the mouth did. After a few pairings of the tuning fork and the meat powder, the tuning fork was sounded in the room *without* being followed by the meat powder, and the dog salivated. It was apparent that the sound of the tuning fork had acquired the ability to elicit the salivary response that was initially limited to the meat powder.

Pavlov referred to the meat powder as an *unconditioned stimulus,* often abbreviated UCS. An unconditioned stimulus is any stimulus that has the ability to elicit a response without prior training.[1] Thus, when meat powder is placed in the mouth of a dog, a salivary reflex is immediately produced. This is called an *unconditioned response,* a UCR. The tuning fork was referred to by Pavlov as a *conditional stimulus,* a CS. Conditional stimuli, in Pavlovian conditioning, are those which initially do not elicit the response under study but which come to do so by being paired with the UCS. Likewise, the salivary response produced by the tuning fork is called a *conditioned response,* a CR, because it is a learned response conditional upon the presentation of the CS and upon the previous pairing of the CS with the UCS.

This basic experiment of Pavlov's has had an enormous influence upon the psychology of learning, and the terms conditional and unconditioned stimuli and conditioned and unconditioned responses are part of the basic vocabulary of the psychology of learning. Now, however, let us look at some operationally defined types of learning which differ in a number of important respects from the one studied by Pavlov.

INSTRUMENTAL CONDITIONING

One of the major operational features which characterizes Pavlovian conditioning—and there are others, as we shall see—is that the organism plays a purely passive role in so far as the delivery of the conditional and unconditioned stimuli is concerned. In the example we just discussed, for instance, the dog had absolutely no control over the delivery of the meat powder. Instead, the experimenter decided when this stimulus was to be presented. A second operationally defined type of learning can be distinguished when we let the organism assume some active role in the learning situation. In particular, we can set things so that the organism is not rewarded or cannot escape from punishment of some kind until it some-

---

[1] The ability of the unconditioned stimulus to elicit a response may be because of learning that took place before the animal came to the laboratory. Operationally, however, the "unconditioned" ability of a stimulus refers to the state of things at the beginning of an experiment. Obviously, if one wishes to state that a particular unconditioned stimulus has an innate eliciting tendency, he must carefully control the life history of the animal.

how makes the response we want it to make. This is a method which is essentially the one that animal trainers use in teaching animals to do tricks. In cases such as this, where reward is made deliberately *contingent* on the prior occurrence of the response we want the organism to learn, we speak of *instrumental conditioning*. As the name implies, the organism quite literally plays an *instrumental* role in producing rewards for itself, or in escaping from or avoiding some punishment.

In general, psychologists have been satisfied to use a surprisingly small number of basic experimental arrangements in their study of the simple processes of instrumental conditioning. At the risk of some over-simplification, but not too much, we can identify three basic features that characterize most instrumental conditioning experiments. First of all, the typical experimental plan will use experimental procedures that involve *reward* or *punishment*. For example, we reward a hungry dog with a piece of food, or we punish an animal by subjecting it to some unpleasant stimulus like electric shock. The general operational term for the specific operations of reward or punishment is *reinforcement,* and particular kinds of rewards or punishment are called *reinforcers* or *reinforcing stimuli*. Second, our experimental plan can lead an organism to either *produce* or *withhold* some specified response. An animal may have to do something actively, or the animal may have to withhold or inhibit a response before we give it a bit of food, for example. Third, a *discriminative cue* will be used in some experimental plans, but not used in others. A discriminative cue is a stimulus of some sort that tells the organism, in effect, when reinforcement can be obtained and when it cannot be obtained. Generally, the instrumental response will be reinforced if it occurs when the discriminative cue is present, but the response will not be reinforced if it occurs when the discriminative cue is absent. In other words, a discriminative cue, if it is used in an experiment, "sets the appropriate occasion" for the behavior that leads to reinforcement.

A little reflection will show that eight experimental plans, or paradigms, can be specified by appropriate combinations of the types of reinforcement, response, and reinforcement cue that we have mentioned (Kimble, 1961; Grant, 1964). Table 1.1 summarizes the basic operations that are involved in these paradigms.

We now have a convenient classification of some operationally defined types of instrumental conditioning. Let us look at some examples of experiments or experimental situations which fit these types of conditioning.

REWARD TRAINING. A white rat is placed in a 12-inch-square box that is relatively soundproof. At one end of this box is a small lever that projects from the wall. The lever is connected to an automatic recording

TABLE 1.1 Operational Types of Instrumental Conditioning

OPERATIONAL TYPE	DISCRIMINATIVE CUE AVAILABLE?	RESPONSE COMES TO BE:	REINFORCE-MENT BASED ON:
Reward training	No	Produced	Reward
Discrimination training	Yes	Produced	Reward
Escape training	No	Produced	Punishment
Avoidance training	Yes	Produced	Punishment
Omission training	No	Withheld	Reward
Punishment training	No	Withheld	Punishment
Discriminated omission training	Yes	Withheld	Reward
Discriminated punishment training	Yes	Withheld	Punishment

device and to an electrically operated magazine filled with pellets of rat food. When the lever is pressed, the magazine automatically delivers a pellet of food into a small cup near the bar. This device is often called a Skinner box after B. F. Skinner, who first described its use (but it is not called this by Skinner himself nor many of his associates, who prefer to use the term "experimental space").

If the rat is hungry when it is placed in the box, it will explore the box quite readily. It will sniff the air, paw the walls, and bite here and there. Eventually, it will stumble against the lever. Sooner or later, it will depress the lever enough to release a pellet of food. The rat may not discover the food immediately, but when it does, it will certainly eat the food. There is a fair certainty also that the rat will press the lever a second time. This time, perhaps, it will discover the pellet of food immediately. At this point, the behavior of the rat will change dramatically. Instead of resuming its casual exploration of the box, it will now proceed to press the lever repeatedly. As a matter of fact, if it is hungry enough, it will press the lever at a rate which is limited only by the time it takes the rat to put its nose down and eat the food from the cup.

DISCRIMINATION TRAINING. Let us use the same apparatus that we have just described, but let us add a discriminative cue—a small white light located in the wall of the box so that the rat can easily see it. Let us turn the light on, place the rat in the box, and use reward training to a point where the rat is pressing the lever in a rapid and consistent fashion. Now we shall turn off the light and, at the same time, disconnect the food magazine from the lever so that lever presses no longer produce pellets of food. After a minute or two, we turn the light back on and reconnect the food magazine so that lever presses are once again reinforced when they occur. We continue to alternate periods of light-on with reinforcement and light-off with no reinforcement, choosing time intervals for these periods which are not consistently of the same length.

The first time that we omit the discriminative cue of the light, the rat will probably continue pressing the lever for a considerable period of time, but since presses of the lever are not rewarded, the rat will eventually press the lever much less frequently than before. As a matter of fact if we withheld reinforcement indefinitely, the rat would stop pressing the lever altogether (a process known as *experimental extinction*). Consequently, when the light is turned back on, we may have to wait a while for the rat to return to the lever. When the rat does this and reward is forthcoming, however, the rat will return to pressing the lever just about as frequently as before. Eventually, after a number of periods in which the light is turned on and off—and reinforcement is delivered or withheld accordingly—the rat will reserve most of its lever presses for the period of time in which the light is on, and it will make very few lever presses when the light is off. The discriminative cue of the light has come to set the occasion for lever pressing. It tells the rat, in effect, when to behave in order to obtain reinforcement.

ESCAPE TRAINING.   A dog is placed in one compartment of a two-compartment box. The two compartments are separated by a door. The door is arranged in such a way that it can be dropped through a slot in the floor so that the dog can move from the first compartment into the second. Both compartments are equipped with floors made of stainless steel bars through which an electric current can be passed. The bars are wired in such a way that when current is passed through them, a shock of moderate intensity is delivered to the dog through the dog's feet. The bars are also wired so that when current is on in one compartment, it is off in the other. At some time determined by the experimenter, the door drops and, at the same instant, current is turned on in the first compartment. The shock continues until the dog passes through the door and reaches the "safe" compartment in which shock is not present. The door closes, and the dog then "rests" until the experimenter again drops the door and turns on the shock in the second compartment. The dog must then move through the door back to the original compartment, which is now "safe." The process of shock in one compartment followed by escape to the other compartment then continues for as many trials as the experiment may call for.

It is easy to imagine what the reaction of the dog will be the first time that it feels the punishing stimulus of the shock in such a "shuttle box." There will be a good deal of yelping, some urination and defecation, and a great deal of agitated activity. Eventually, however, the dog will stumble through the door and reach the safe compartment. The second time the shock comes on, the dog will show much less agitation and will move through the door much more rapidly than on the first trial. After a few trials, the dog will escape through the door with a very short latency.

At this point we should stop and ask a pertinent question about the nature of reinforcement in escape training. We might guess that the actual process of reinforcement depends on the fact that shock stops when the dog moves from one compartment to the next. It might seem reasonable to think of escape training as a rather special case of reward training, on the assumption that escaping a noxious stimulus like shock is rewarding. There is, of course, much intuitive merit to this point of view. The important point at the moment, however, is that the paradigm for escape training in instrumental conditioning depends upon a reinforcement *operation* which involves a punishing stimulus like electric shock, and an active response which gets the organism away from the punishing stimulus. Right now, we wish to make no theoretical guesses about the precise nature of the process which underlies or which actually produces the strengthening of the instrumental response in the situation. We shall have a good deal to say about that later on.

AVOIDANCE TRAINING. We can describe the avoidance-training paradigm by using the same apparatus that we used for escape training. We shall modify the apparatus in one respect by adding a light in each compartment that the dog can easily see when it is turned on. The dog is placed in one compartment of the shuttle box with the light turned off. At some appropriate moment, we provide the dog with a discriminative cue by turning on the light and dropping the door which separates the first compartment from the second. Ten seconds later, we apply current to the floor in the first compartment and shock the dog. However, the dog can *avoid* the punishing stimulus of the shock by running through the door to the "safe" compartment during the ten-second interval between the onset of the discriminative cue and the onset of the shock. Again, the discriminative cue "sets the occasion" for the dog's response. When the dog goes to the second compartment, we close the door, and the dog rests. The next trial begins when we again deliver the discriminative cue and, ten seconds later, turn on the shock.

As with discrimination training, the discriminative cue will have essentially no effect on the behavior of the dog on the first trial. The first time we deliver the cue and follow it with shock, the dog will behave in essentially the same way that it would behave in an escape-training situation. As a matter of fact, early trials in avoidance training actually involve simple escape training so long as the dog fails to respond to the discriminative cue within the prescribed time interval, takes the shock, and then runs to the safe compartment. However, after a few trials during which the latency of the response to the shock may decrease considerably, the dog will begin to respond to the discriminative cue and run to the second compartment before the shock comes on. If the strength of the shock is sufficiently great, the dog may never again take a shock once a trial occurs in which it successfully avoids the shock.

OTHER OPERATIONAL TYPES. Another glance at Table 1.1 will show that, thus far, we have been discussing operational types of instrumental conditioning that involve the active *production* of a response by the organism in conjunction with reinforcement operations of reward or punishment. Most of the experimental literature dealing with simple instrumental conditioning describes procedures which involve one or another of the corresponding methods of training we have outlined in some detail. Curiously enough, with the possible exception of punishment training, the remaining four types of instrumental conditioning outlined in Table 1.1 have received relatively little attention in the laboratory. Consequently, it is not possible to describe fairly standard laboratory situations in which these types have been used, although it is easy to imagine some simple arrangements in which a response must be *withheld* in order to obtain a reward or to avoid some punishment.

With our Skinner box apparatus, we can quite simply describe some operations that could be used for *omission training* and *punishment training*. Assume that we have used reward training to a point where a rat is pressing a lever for food pellets in a consistent, stable fashion. Now let us suddenly change things so that (1) lever presses are no longer reinforced, but (2) *failure* to press the lever *is* reinforced. The latter could be done in some arbitrary way, perhaps by dropping a food pellet into the food cup at the end of each five-second period that the rat fails to press the lever. Under these conditions, the rat must learn to *withhold* or *omit* an already established response in order to assure a continued flow of food pellets. Similarly, we could change things so that, instead of producing food pellets, lever presses suddenly begin to produce electric shocks to the rat's feet. The original response is now punished, and the rat must learn to *omit* this response if punishment is to be avoided. If we add some kind of discriminative cue to our experimental situation, we can easily establish the conditions for *discriminated* omission or punishment training. Thus, if we choose a light as a discriminative cue, we could arrange things so that light onset sets the occasion for omitting lever presses in order to obtain rewards or to avoid punishments. In the absence of the discriminative cue—that is, when the light is off—we could reintroduce simple reward training, and lever presses could once again produce food pellets.

Operations of these kinds are by no means confined to the sequestered world of Skinner boxes, food pellets, and electric shock. Parents learn, for example, that rewards given when children withhold some kind of unwanted behavior can sometimes (though not always!) prevent the recurrence of the unwanted behavior. They can also, of course, punish undesirable behavior with hopes that it will be abandoned. And they sometimes use discriminative cues—often in the form of verbal commands—that set the occasion for the omission of the behavior in question. In the case of discriminated punishment training, for example, a parent may *warn* a child that unless some kind of unwanted behavior is omitted, punishment will ensue. Of course, the child may very well learn to omit the response in the presence of the discriminative cue represented by the parent, but go right ahead with things when the parent is absent. Such are the things that exasperate parents! Our general point, however, is that there are many occasions where responses must be withheld in order to satisfy some sort of reinforcement contingency supplied by the environment.

FREE VERSUS CONTROLLED RESPONDING. We have described some apparatus and some procedures in developing our scheme for instrumental conditioning which differ from each other along a very basic dimension that we have not yet identified. In the case of avoidance training, for example, we used an experimental procedure where the determination of the start and end of a particular trial was left *to the experimenter*. In the case of simple reward training, on the other hand, we used an experimental procedure where the initiation of the first lever press and the frequency of subsequent lever presses were left *to the rat*. If we had wished, however, we could have described a procedure for reward training—such as running the rat one trial at a time in a maze—which, in fact, would leave to the experimenter to decide when to start and to terminate a trial.

The important point is this: Instrumental conditioning can involve either *free-responding* or *controlled-responding* procedures. The distinction is based on whether the *subject* or the *experimenter* controls the opportunity to make the instrumental behavior in question, and the distinction is an important one to keep in mind. First of all, the decision to use one as opposed to the other of the procedures may well determine the kind of measure of behavior that can be used in the experiment. With a free-responding procedure such as that typically used in the Skinner box, for example, a frequently used measure of behavior will be the *rate* at which a number of responses are produced, i.e., their frequency per unit time. Obviously, in a controlled-responding situation, where the opportunity to respond is under the rigid control of the experimenter, it is not possible to use the rate at which a number of responses occur as an index of the effect of some variable on behavior. Instead, the experimenter is more apt to record some feature of an *individual* response each time it occurs, such as the time that a rat takes to leave the start box of a maze, or the time that a dog takes to get from one side of a shuttle box to the other. Then, the psychologist will often make the assumption that, for a particular independent variable, measures of behavior that are obtained in free-responding and controlled-responding situations will be closely correlated. Indeed, they often are. Sometimes, however, the simple principles of learning which are developed from data obtained in free-responding situations may not generalize very well to controlled-responding situations (we shall see a particularly good example of this when we discuss the topic of *partial reinforcement*). This is obviously a problem of some importance, to which psychologists are now beginning to devote considerable attention.

PRINCIPLES DISTINGUISHING CLASSICAL AND INSTRUMENTAL CONDITIONING

OPERATIONAL DISTINCTIONS

We have now looked at the details of the operations that are used in the laboratory to establish a classically conditioned response and to establish an instrumentally conditioned response. Are there any general features of these two collections of operations that distinguish them? The answer, of course, is yes.

When we first introduced the concept of instrumental conditioning, we noted that the organism is required to do something—to produce or to withhold a response—before the experimenter provides reinforcement. This was contrasted with the procedure in classical conditioning, where the organism has no control over the delivery of the UCS. In the former case, the experimenter must pay close attention to what the organism is doing so as to be sure to provide reinforcement and so on at the proper time. In the case of classical conditioning, however, the necessary operations are performed entirely independently of what the organism happens to be doing. Given the onset of the CS, the onset of the UCS, say, is determined not by the organism's behavior but by the fact that a clock has run a certain period of time. So our first distinction arises in this sense: The operations for instrumental conditioning depend critically upon what the organism does, while for those involved in classical conditioning, behavior can be essentially ignored.

The next distinction appears when we try to use Pavlov's terms for simple classical conditioning to describe the things we did in our example of instrumental reward training. Our first problem arises when we try to identify the UCS in the reward-training paradigm. Now, it is clear that the unconditioned response must be pressing the lever during the course of exploration. But what was the stimulus that elicited this response? We can guess, but we can never know with any certainty what the stimulus actually was. It might have been the sight of the lever or the tactual stimulation obtained by sniffing along the walls of the box, but we cannot be sure. In other words, in a classical conditioning experiment, there is always a readily identifiable stimulus, the UCS, which elicits the response we wish to condition, while in an instrumental conditioning experiment, a comparable stimulus cannot be identified. As Skinner (1938) has pointed out, the to-be-conditioned response in classical conditioning is *elicited* by a stimulus supplied by the experimenter. In instrumental conditioning, however, we must wait for the response we want to condition to occur spontaneously; we must wait for the organism to *emit* the response.

Similarly, what is the CS to which lever pressing is conditioned in our example of instrumental reward training? In other words, what leads the rat to press the lever after it has "discovered the connection" between the lever and food? Again we are reduced to a guess. Though the response may be occurring with considerable regularity after the rat has obtained several reinforcing stimuli, there is still no identifiable stimulus in instrumental conditioning which we can say with absolute certainty *elicits* the instrumental response. In this connection, do not confuse a discriminative cue, such as the one we described for discrimination training or for avoidance training, with a CS. As we have seen, the function of the discriminative cue is to *set the occasion* for some rather complex instrumental behavior, not to elicit a response reflexively. As Skinner (1935) has pointed out, the experimental operations that are involved in establishing a functional discriminative cue in instrumental conditioning are quite different from those that are used to establish a functional CS in classical conditioning. For instance, the discriminative cue in discrimination training acquires its unique control over behavior when we reinforce a response when the cue is present, but withhold reinforcement when the cue is absent. In classical conditioning, on the other hand, the CS is *always* present, and it is *always* followed by the UCS.

Probably the most important operational distinction between classical and instrumental conditioning concerns the role of reinforcement in the two situations. Pavlov used the terms reinforcement and unconditioned stimulus interchangeably. This usage has caused some confusion, though in a sense it is justified. The UCS is a reinforcer in Pavlovian conditioning because without it no conditioning would occur;

it literally *reinforces* or *strengthens* conditioning. The two terms, reinforcement and unconditioned stimulus, are not generally synonymous, however, for we have just learned that we cannot use the term unconditioned stimulus to apply to reinforcement in instrumental conditioning. The reinforcement operation in this case is to provide a stimulus, like food, *after* the response takes place. We do not know what stimulus actually causes the response to be produced in the first place, but when the response is finally emitted by the organism, then we can reinforce it and thus "strengthen" it. Therefore, another difference between classical and instrumental conditioning is that in classical conditioning, the UCS simultaneously elicits and reinforces the response, while in instrumental conditioning reinforcement occurs only when—and if—the response occurs.

THEORETICAL DISTINCTIONS

Earlier in this chapter, we noted that psychologists do not agree about how many *theoretical* processes or types of learning—as opposed to experimental operations that are used to study learning—should be identified. Should we assume, for example, that each set of operations noted in Table 1.1 involves a truly different process of learning? Should we increase the list in some way by two sets? Ten sets? Fifty sets? Or should we assume that all the operational types we can distinguish are simply special instances of a single basic process of learning, and that an organism is going to learn by this process regardless of which operational procedure we choose to use?

Intuition tells us that there might be almost as many processes which could be used in acquiring a new response as there are responses to be acquired. We hope intuition is wrong in this instance! But many things sometimes seem to force upon us the notion that organisms learn in a great many different ways. Is the same process of learning involved when a teacher uses the phonics method, as opposed to the sight method, in teaching first graders to read? Learning to read is a much more complex sort of task than the simple kinds of learning tasks we shall be discussing in the first chapters of this book, but we could ask with equal cogency if a rat and a monkey learn to solve some sort of simple discrimination problem in exactly the same way. If for no other reason than the fact that the monkey's brain is an infinitely more elegant structure than the rat's, it would be surprising if *precisely* the same learning process were used by the two organisms in solving the problem. Nevertheless, many psychologists have thus far been satisfied to account for essentially all simple learning phenomena with theoretical systems that distinguish exactly *two* basic processes of learning. This has been done by attaching some theoretical significance to the distinction between classical and instrumental conditioning and to the different things that happen when the two procedures are used.[2]

The operational distinction between instrumental and classical conditioning is already before you. That the two sets of operations might refer to theoretically distinguishable processes of learning has been noted by a number of people, e.g., Schlosberg (1937), Skinner (1938), Hilgard and Marquis (1940), Mowrer (1947, 1960), Konorski (1950), and Stephens (1942). Skinner, in a long series of papers and in his book, *The Behavior of Organisms* (1938), has singled out the most important reasons for maintaining that classical and instrumental conditioning involve truly different theoretical processes of learning. An excellent general discussion of the problem has also been provided by Kimble (1961).

OPERANT VERSUS RESPONDENT BEHAVIOR. Skinner's theoretical distinction rests upon the basic notion that *different kinds of responses* are conditionable with the techniques of classical and instrumental conditioning (or, in Skinner's terms, respondent and operant conditioning). *Respondents,* the kinds of behavior that are supposed to be most typically conditionable with Pavlovian techniques, are classes of responses that are directly elicited by stimuli. They obey the classical physiological laws of reflexes, and, indeed, the terms respondent and reflex are identical for all practical purposes. Examples of respondents are salivation, the knee jerk, the eye blink, the heartbeat, and the galvanic skin response. *Operants,* the kinds of behavior that are supposed to be most typically conditionable with the techniques of instrumental conditioning, are responses for which there are no readily observable external stimuli. Examples of operants are the familiar ones of spontaneous, emitted behavior in animals and men, the kinds of behavior that we have already discussed in some detail —dogs moving from one side of a shuttle box to the other, rats pressing levers, and so forth. Although, as we have seen, we cannot identify a prior stimulus that produces such behavior, we do not assume that the behavior is truly spontaneous. We simply recognize that we generally cannot observe, much less produce, the necessary stimuli.

Skinner, together with Schlosberg (1937), have further pointed out that respondents are mediated by the autonomic nervous system, while operants are mediated by the skeletal somatic nervous system. The correlation is far from perfect, for the familiar knee jerk, which is under the

---

[2] Some psychologists, e.g., Hull (1943), think of classical conditioning as a special case of instrumental conditioning and distinguish only one type. Tolman (1949), on the other hand, at one point suggested six types of learning; many psychologists would consider his types reducible, basically, to either classical or instrumental conditioning.

control of the somatic nervous system, is best characterized as a respondent, and so is the eye blink. The correlation of these two types of behavior with different parts of the peripheral nervous system is a theoretically important one, however, because of the role of the autonomic nervous system in emotion. As one might expect, respondents are especially important in learning based on emotional motivation, and principles of classical or respondent conditioning play an important role in the theoretical account of such learning.

How well does Skinner's theoretical distinction fare when put to experimental test? Like most theories in psychology, it handles some parts of the data well, some parts with more difficulty. Skinner's approach, strictly speaking, would require that operants not be conditionable with classical techniques and that respondents not be conditionable with instrumental techniques. Yet there are a number of instances in which responses that are normally classed as respondents, such as the eye blink, have been conditioned with instrumental procedures (e.g., Kimble, Mann, & Dufort, 1955). However, and this would be critical from Skinner's point of view, an eye blink that has been classically conditioned differs in a number of ways—in its latency, for example—from an eye blink that has been instrumentally conditioned. In short, when it is possible to make some kind of comparison, the two training procedures appear to produce conditioned responses that are not at all the same. Skinner's approach is also strongly supported by the fact that there is apparently no instance of successful instrumental conditioning of a respondent, such as the human heartbeat, which is clearly under autonomic, "involuntary" control (but see Fowler & Kimmel, 1962).

Although there does seem to be a strong indication that at least two types of learning can be distinguished, it would be misleading to give the impression that new behavior is always acquired with one type to the exclusion of the other. Even a relatively simple response, like a food-reinforced lever press, is almost certainly a vast complex of smaller bits of behavior, some conditioned instrumentally, some conditioned classically. It would also be misleading to imply that classical and instrumental conditioning lead to radically different principles of learning. In fact, quite the opposite is the case; phenomena such as stimulus and response generalization, inhibition, extinction, discrimination—and many others—can all be demonstrated with both procedures, as we shall see. So keep in mind that, while a theoretical distinction between two types of learning and their corresponding types of behavior seems justified and is useful in developing certain theoretical accounts of learning, the types are in many respects more similar than dissimilar.

THE STUDY OF SIMPLE LEARNING

We have examined two instances of elementary kinds of learning. Such examples are usually called conditioning. There is no special way in which conditioning can be differentiated from learning, and we shall probably find ourselves occasionally slipping into the habit of using the terms interchangeably. When we use the term conditioning, however, we intend to refer to cases of learning in which simple responses are acquired under simple and relatively restricted conditions, conditions which minimize previous or concurrent learning that would either help or interfere with the response under study. These elementary examples are extremely interesting to the psychologist, because with them he can examine basic processes of learning that may be obscured in more complicated cases.

VARIABLES THAT DETERMINE THE NATURE OF CONDITIONING.   In the next few chapters, we shall look at some of the variables that determine the course of simple learning. These generally operate in more complicated examples of learning as well, but usually in ways that make them more difficult to study. These conditions include such things as the kind and level of motivation, the relevance of the response and the reinforcement to that motivation, the scheduling of reinforcement (whether or not reinforcements are given for every response), time relations between stimuli and between stimuli and responses, and so forth.

THEORIES ABOUT CONDITIONING.   As we discuss the way in which these various factors determine the course of conditioning, we shall also examine the role that theories play in interpreting or predicting the results of experiments which use these variables. So far as it is possible, we shall try to evaluate the success of some selected theories in making such predictions; in practice this is difficult to do, since theories are frequently not stated clearly enough to make unequivocal predictions about behavior. In one sense, the mark of a good theory is that it is easy to prove wrong; it will make clear and unequivocal predictions that are easy to test. Unfortunately, psychology is saddled with many poor theories that endure because they are so vaguely stated that it is impossible to prove them wrong and to discard them.

A WORD ABOUT THE RAT

Much of what we have to say in the next few chapters will be based on information obtained from the white rat and from his laboratory cohorts, the dog, the pigeon, and the monkey. Later we shall be paying particular attention to human learning and to human behavior. It is always difficult to understand why so many of the basic facts and theories of learning are developed with creatures lower than man, and as a result, the person who first comes upon the psychology of learning sometimes develops a skeptical attitude about the usefulness of these facts and theories. They seem far removed from most of the human behavior that he sees going on around him. Such skepticism is sometimes justified, and many times it is shared by people who have worked with the psychology of learning for a long time. But there is a very good reason why psychologists depend so much upon lower animals for basic information about conditioning. The reason is this: *Lower animals can't talk.* This distinguishing characteristic is very important to the psychologist. It is much more important than many of the good reasons that are also cited for using lower animals, such as the facts that they breed rapidly, are genetically "pure," can be easily maintained in the laboratory, can have a controlled past history, and so forth. Language provides a means for encoding information that can be stored, digested, and used later in an infinite number of ways. If we want to study conditioning and simple learning, we must start, so far as we can, with simple responses and with an organism that does not have a capacity for introducing the extraordinary complications that language introduces into the learning process. This is so important that our book has been organized around what might be termed two psychologies of learning: that excluding language, and that including it.

It should not be assumed that these two "psychologies" are in any sense irrevocably separate. As things have turned out, a great deal of information that we have obtained with nonverbal lower animals has generalized—at least roughly, and sometimes amazingly well—to human behavior. This fact makes it clear that skepticism about the usefulness of animals in the study of learning is generally unjustified. And, of course, we are here simply identifying one problem among many that a general psychology of learning must solve. So, while caution is always appropriate in using some relatively simple experiments carried out with lower animals to make assumptions about the effect of some variable on human behavior, it would be folly to discard or to disregard the wealth of valuable information that has been obtained from organisms lower than man.

2

REINFORCEMENT AND
LEARNING:
BASIC PRINCIPLES

Since the time of Thorndike (1898, 1911), the notion that behavior can be strengthened or weakened by its own consequences, by reward or punishment, has occupied a central position in the psychology of learning. An enormous amount of experimental information has been compiled about the intricate effects of rewarding or punishing a response, and psychologists can now state with considerable confidence some general principles involving these effects. Yet while a great deal is known at the present time, a great deal remains to be learned. This chapter, which introduces some of the basic variables that are known to be involved in the processes of reward and punishment, will reflect the current state of affairs. Where there are holes in our present knowledge, little more can be done than to admit them. Often we will have to do this explicitly, and you will have a chance to share the frustrations that the experimental psychologist encounters as he attempts to add further information to his science. Sometimes gaps in our knowledge are implicit, and it is to be hoped that you will be challenged to discover them and, perhaps, to seek some answers for yourself.

While the terms reward and punishment are familar in everyday use, psychologists generally prefer to use the more exact term *reinforcement*. One reason for this is that there is some question whether terms like reward and punishment—in their ordinary meaning—can be applied to the phenomenon of classical conditioning. Another reason for using an exact, abstractly defined term is that the concept of reinforcement often plays a pivotal role in the development of theories of learning. In a very real sense, theoretical discussions of the means by which organisms learn new things may hinge upon the way in which the theoretician treats the concept of reinforcement. As we shall see in detail in the next chapter, some theories place great emphasis on the notion that reinforcement is necessary if new responses are to be learned. Other theories state that reinforcement is not necessary at all in the learning process.

THE DEFINITION OF REINFORCEMENT

Recall, for a moment, the example of instrumental reward training given in the first chapter. In that example, a rat learned to press a lever, and this response was reinforced with a pellet of food. The food was clearly responsible for an increase in the rate with which the rat pressed the lever, for we know that without it the rat would only occasionally have pressed the lever. Having worked for a few pellets in this way, however, the rat pressed the lever just about as rapidly as it could, pausing between responses only to eat the pellets.

If we had followed the lever-pressing response with the sound of a buzzer instead of a pellet of food, would the rat have learned to press the lever? Probably not, our common experience with rewards would tell us. (Sometimes our common experience can lead us to wrong conclusions. As Roberts, Marx, and Collier [1958] have shown, rats *will* learn to press a lever when the response is followed by the onset of a dim light!) Here, however, our common experience would be right; in this situation food is a reinforcer and a buzzer is not. Food is a reinforcer because it produces an increase in the frequency of the response that it follows. Obviously, because the buzzer cannot produce such an increase, it is not a reinforcer.

REINFORCERS AND REINFORCEMENT

With these thoughts in mind, we can now look at a formal definition of reinforcers and reinforcement. *A reinforcer is a stimulus event which, if it occurs in the proper temporal relation with a response, tends to maintain or to increase the strength of a response or of a stimulus-response connection.* In the case of instrumental or operant conditioning, the reinforcer is contingent upon the occurrence of the response and thus follows the response in time. In the case of classical conditioning, the reinforcer is the stimulus, the UCS, that elicits the unconditioned reflex, the UCR. Barring delays that are imposed by the speed with which impulses can be conducted in the nervous system and translated into effector activity, the UCS and the UCR occur simultaneously. The operations of using stimulus events in the manners described are known, collectively, as *reinforcement* (Meehl, 1950).

POSITIVE AND NEGATIVE REINFORCERS.   In the case of instrumental or operant conditioning, it turns out to be convenient if we distinguish two subclasses of reinforcing stimuli: *positive* reinforcers and *negative* reinforcers (Skinner, 1938; Keller & Schoenfeld, 1950). The concept of positive reinforcement is clear enough from earlier discussion and from the general definition of reinforcement we have just given. In common terms, a positive reinforcer is a reward. It is a stimulus, like a piece of food, that we give to an organism after the organism has done something we want it to learn to do. But what of negative reinforcers? How, literally, can a response be *negatively* reinforced? The word *reinforce* connotes that a response is strengthened, while the word *negative* seems to add the implication that the response is somehow weakened at the same time. The use of the term negative reinforcer clearly raises some semantic problems, but these can be easily straightened out if we keep an operational definition in mind. Negative reinforcers are stimuli which strengthen a response when they are *removed* if the response occurs. Recall our example of simple escape training. In this instance, the dog's response of leaping from one side of the shuttle box to the other was reinforced by *removing* electric shock when the response occurred.

As you can easily infer, negative reinforcement involves the use of a stimulus event which has aversive properties, a stimulus event that an organism will ordinarily avoid if it can. And, as we saw in the last chapter, such stimulus events can also be used to *punish* a response. Thus, in the case of simple punishment training, a lever-pressing response that a rat had learned to make initially in order to obtain food pellets was punished by changing things so that lever presses began to produce electric shocks instead of morsels of food. And we noted that a procedure of this type would ordinarily tend to make the rat omit or withhold the lever-pressing response.

Since aversive, noxious stimuli like electric shock can be used operationally to produce two very different effects, reinforcement and punishment, we had better be explicit about the experimental operations that will lead to one effect as compared with the other. Noxious stimulation can be used to *reinforce* a response when we supply noxious stimulation independently of anything the organism does, and when we set things so that the occurrence of the response we want the organism to learn *removes* or *turns off* the noxious stimulation. Noxious stimulation can be used to *punish* a response when the occurrence of the response *supplies* or *turns on* the noxious stimulation. In everyday terms, people tend to stop doing things that expose them to punishing, traumatic events, but if they are plunged into the middle of a traumatic situation owing to circumstances beyond their control, responses that get them away from trauma will be reinforced and learned.

The concepts of positive and negative reinforcement cannot be applied very meaningfully to classical conditioning. It is true that food, a substance that can function very efficiently as a positive reinforcer in instrumental conditioning, can be used as a UCS to elicit salivation, and thus, to establish a classically conditioned salivary response. It is also true, however, that a weak acid solution injected into the mouth of a dog does the job just as well (Pavlov, 1927), and it is doubtful that weak acid solutions would function very well as positive reinforcers for instrumental conditioning. Offhand, we might guess that acid would be apt to have properties more closely akin to a negative rather than to a positive reinforcer. In the case of classical conditioning, the critical feature of a UCS that makes it function to reinforce a reflex is its ability to reliably *elicit* the reflex. And two stimuli, for example, that could be used interchangeably to elicit the same reflex in a classical conditioning situation might have effects as different as those associated with positive and negative reinforcers if they were used as stimulus events to reinforce instrumental behavior.

WEAK VERSUS STRONG DEFINITIONS OF REINFORCEMENT.   Our definitions of reinforcers and reinforcement are strictly operational. They are phrased in terms of the things that experimenters see, do, and measure. Psychologists have labeled this kind of definition the "weak" form of a definition of reinforcement; it simply describes the kinds of things that are done and the kinds of things that are supposed to happen if the concept of reinforcement is to be applied. Such a definition makes no assertions about the underlying mechanism by which a positive reinforcer like food, for example, strengthens some kind of response like pressing a lever. But it would be most reasonable to ask why food does, in fact, act this way. Is it because the food reduces some kind of motive or drive like hunger? Or is it because the food has some particular stimulus quality, like a special taste? If we were to ask questions like these, we would be on the road, via a hypothetical construct, to a "strong" definition of the concept of reinforcement. That is, we would be asking *why* or *how* reinforcers, in fact, produce the increase or decrease in strength of response which we measure when we use them. We shall have a great deal to say about the various forms of a "strong" definition of reinforcement in the next chapter.

TRANS-SITUATIONAL REINFORCERS.   The definition of reinforcement that has been given is open to the charge of being circular—it is only a definition, not a law. There are laws about reinforcement, however, and one of them is that most reinforcers for operant behavior are trans-situational (Meehl, 1950). This means that most reinforcers will strengthen *all* or *most* learnable responses in a given species. In other words, if a particular stimulus is reinforcing for a lever-pressing response in a rat, it ought to be reinforcing for other responses, such as running a maze.

Respondents are trans-situational in the sense that one can use almost any given *conditional* stimulus for a given response so long as it meets the usual requirements for conditional stimuli, such as being detectable by the organism. However, a given *unconditioned* stimulus can generally be used for only a few closely related respondents, those reflexes that can be triggered by the same stimulus. Thus, respondents are trans-situational with respect to conditional stimuli, but are trans-situational only in a very limited sense with respect to unconditioned stimuli.

Meehl (1950) proposes that all reinforcers (at least for operants) are trans-situational and that every increase in strength of response which occurs when reinforcers are used involves the use of a trans-situational reinforcer. This is probably not exactly true, for later in this book there are examples of operant reinforcers which are specific to certain responses, but it is probably true that most of the reinforcers of everyday life are trans-situational. This means that it is possible to use almost any reinforcer to teach almost any response; the success of the reinforcement for a particular response will not depend upon that particular response-reinforcer connection, but upon the general adequacy of the reinforcer. If some stimulus is not reinforcing for lever pressing, it will not be reinforcing for learning a maze.

THE CONCEPT OF RESPONSE STRENGTH

The phrase *response strength* has been used in the definition of reinforcement and in much of the discussion which followed that definition, but we have not yet made explicit what the phrase means or how the strength of a response is measured. Let us turn to this problem now.

Response strength is properly an intervening variable (Chapter 1), something that cannot be directly observed. As a result, we infer the strength of a response from some aspect of a response that we can measure. Thus, in order to specify the formal definition of reinforcement completely, we need to state exactly what dependent variables can be used to indicate the strength of a response.

The most important indicator of strength of response is a measure ordinarily called probability of response. This is the likelihood that a response will occur in a given unit of time or when a particular stimulus is presented. Thus, if a response occurs frequently in a given unit of time, it is a strong one. For rats in a Skinner box, a strong tendency to press the lever might be indicated by a rate of 10 responses per minute, while a relatively weak tendency would be 1 response per minute.

Some investigators prefer to limit the measurement of strength of response to probability (Skinner, 1938), and still others try to reduce all other possible indicators of strength of response to some form of probability of occurrence (Estes, 1950, 1964; Mueller, 1950). In practice, however, many other indicators are used. Some of these are reaction time or latency, response duration, response speed, and amplitude or magnitude of response. Generally speaking, these measures tend to be well correlated with each other; if a response has a short latency, for example, it will probably also have a large amplitude. This is not always the case, and we shall have occasion to look at some learning variables which do not produce consistent correlations among different measures of response strength. For the time being, however, we shall not be too concerned with problems, like this one, which are raised by recognizing several indicators of strength of response.

TESTING THE EFFECTS OF REINFORCEMENT ON RESPONSE STRENGTH

In the case of operant behavior and instrumental conditioning, the methods of assessing the effects of reinforcement are quite simple. Usually the response before reinforcement is very low in strength; the probability of occurrence is very small or the amplitude is very low. After a few reinforcements, however, the probability of occurrence per unit time changes rapidly. Figure 2.1 shows this effect taking place. In the figure the cumulative frequency of responses is plotted against time. Thus when the frequency of responses per unit time is low, as it is at the outset of the experiment, the responses cumulate very slowly; the result is a nearly horizontal line with occasional bumps that show the occurrence of responses. As the response becomes conditioned, however, the response occurs much more frequently, so that the line goes up rapidly. The actual learning itself, in this example, is shown by the change in the slope of the curve.[1]

[1] See Estes (1959) for some examples of cumulative curves for lever pressing which show a much more gradual shift from a very low to a very high rate of response.

FIG. **2.1** A cumulative curve of instrumental conditioning. All responses were reinforced. There is no evidence of learning following the first three responses, but the fourth is followed by a rapid change in rate of responding. (Skinner, 1938.)

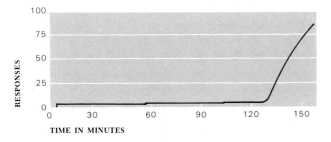

In classical conditioning the situation is usually more complicated. As we have seen, the reinforcing stimulus in the classical conditioning of a respondent is the unconditioned stimulus. Thus, the stimulus that elicits the response in the first place also provides the reinforcement. The conditioned or learned response, however, occurs to the conditional stimulus, and because the conditional stimulus usually precedes the unconditioned stimulus, the conditioned response often "anticipates" the occurrence of the unconditioned response.

The conditioned response does not always anticipate the unconditioned response, however, for it is quite possible to condition a respondent when the unconditioned and conditional stimuli occur simultaneously. If they occur simultaneously, then we must use special "test" trials to find out whether any conditioning has taken place. Without these trials we would have no way of knowing whether a particular response was the result of the conditional or unconditioned stimulus. If we make the two stimuli simultaneous and then test for a conditioned response by omitting the unconditioned stimulus on some trial, we can determine whether or not we have a conditioned response. If we run a number of test trials during the course of an experiment, we can calculate the probability that a conditioned response will be obtained for a particular experimental variable by noting the frequency with which the conditioned response appears. When a conditioned response is obtained on a test trial for 9 out of 10 subjects, for example, the probability of obtaining a conditioned response for any given subject is .90. Care must be used when a test-trial procedure is employed to check for conditioning, however. According to the definition of reinforcement, prior association of the conditioned stimulus-response connection with the unconditioned stimulus is necessary, so that if we omit the unconditioned stimulus on too many successive test trials, the conditioned response will disappear.

THE INFERENCE OF LEARNING FROM CHANGES IN RESPONSE STRENGTH

How do we decide when an organism has "learned" something, and how can we describe the course of such "learning"? The first thing that must be done is to recognize that "learning" itself cannot be observed directly. It is quite properly an intervening variable which must be inferred from some observable aspect of behavior. Generally speaking, psychologists infer the concept of learning on the basis of two things. First, they assume that the necessary independent variable which must be manipulated to produce learning is something that is akin to practice of, experience with, or repetition of a response. In order to learn, organisms must practice or have experience with things. For simple learning, a

commonly accepted index of such practice is *number of reinforced trials.*
Second, psychologists require the specification of a dependent variable
which will reflect the results of practice or experience. Psychologists are
by no means in agreement about what particular sort of independent
variable is the best one to use, but they do agree that the dependent
variable must be some measure of the overt performance of the response
that is practiced by the organism. The kinds of measures that we have
identified under the heading of *response strength* are quite commonly
used, at least for relatively simple responses. Generally speaking, then,
learning will be inferred if there is some change in the strength of a
response with the practice of that response.

The exact shape of the fundamental learning curve—the one relating response strength to number of reinforced practice trials—has occupied the interest of many theoretical psychologists. Investigators have
tried to predict the shape of simple learning curves from mathematical
assumptions and then tried to apply these predictions, in turn, to more
complicated relationships in psychology. We shall now examine one
widely accepted attempt to characterize the basic properties of the fundamental learning curve.

At the outset, we can think of some things that we know our
learning curve must reflect. Here are three basic properties that must be
expressed in any mathematical or theoretical learning equation:

1. Strength of response increases as the number of reinforced
practice trials increases. In instrumental conditioning, at least, we have
to assume that the strength of a response is never actually zero, or else the
response would never occur so that we could reinforce it and raise the
probability that it be repeated. But for all practical purposes, we can
think of response strength at the beginning of learning as essentially nil.

2. There is some upper limit beyond which response strength cannot increase. This upper limit, the *asymptote* of response strength, will be
determined by many things, such as the nature of the species, the nature
of the response that is to be learned, and the particular conditions of reinforcement, motivation, and the like that we impose. As these things
change, so will the upper limit of response strength, but if they are held
constant, the upper limit of response strength will be a constant.

3. Experience with a wide variety of responses in a wide variety
of learning situations shows that the biggest additions to response strength
occur early in learning; as the number of practice trials increases, smaller
and smaller increments of response strength are added to the total strength
of the response.

Let us put these three basic properties of learning curves into
mathematical form. First, we shall designate the strength R, of a response
after some training trial n as R_n. We want an expression which will tell

us how much response strength increases from one practice trial to the next. That is, as we go from trial n to trial $(n+1)$, we want to find the relation between R_n and $R_{(n+1)}$. Our first principle tells us that $R_{(n+1)}$ should be greater than R_n, thus:

$$R_{(n+1)} = R_n + \Delta R_n \qquad (1)$$

where Δ means an increase or increment.

Our second principle tells us that response strength will approach some limit beyond which it cannot go for a given set of experimental conditions. Let us call this limit M.

Our third principle tells us that, as number of trials increases, the increase in response strength per trial becomes smaller. That is, the closer R_n is to the limit M, the smaller ΔR_n will be. We can satisfy this condition (in one of many possible ways) if we make the assumption that the size of ΔR_n which is contributed by a practice trial is a constant fraction k of the total amount of response strength that remains to be acquired until learning is complete. At the beginning of trial $(n+1)$, for example, the total amount of response strength that remains to be acquired can be obtained by subtracting the amount of response strength that has already been acquired, R_n, from the total that can be acquired, M. This gives the expression $(M - R_n)$. Thus, the *increment* in response strength that will occur with practice trial $(n+1)$ will be

$$\Delta R_n = k(M - R_n) \qquad (2)$$

If we substitute Equation (2) in Equation (1), we can find the *total* amount of response strength that will exist after trial $(n+1)$ occurs. Thus

$$R_{(n+1)} = R_n + k(M - R_n) \qquad (3)$$

If we add another practice trial, the total response strength will be

$$R_{(n+2)} = R_{(n+1)} + k(M - R_{(n+1)})$$

and so on for as many practice trials as we wish to use.

Figure 2.2 shows four learning curves that were derived by the above reasoning. Two curves were derived on the assumption that the limit of response strength was 100 arbitrary units, but for one, $k = .10$, and for the other, $k = .50$. Two other curves were derived with the same values for k, but with M set at 300 arbitrary units of response strength. It is easy to see from the figure that all curves start with large increments to response strength during early practice trials, but the increments become smaller as trials increase. Also, when $k = .50$, response strength approaches its limit much more quickly than when $k = .10$.

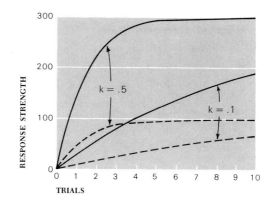

FIG. 2.2 Some hypothetical learning curves derived by reasoning discussed in the text. The solid curves are heading toward an asymptote of 300 units of response strength, while the dashed curves are heading toward an asymptote of 100 units of response strength. Note that the curves approach these limits faster when $k = 0.5$ than when $k = 0.1$.

Learning curves based on the kinds of assumptions we have outlined here are basic to many theories of psychology (Hull, 1943; Estes, 1950; Bush & Mosteller, 1955). Sometimes the assumptions which are involved may be elaborated to take into account the fact that early trials may not always produce the greatest increases in response strength; early trials may involve something akin to a warm-up period, so that the greatest increments in response strength come after the first few trials (Spence, 1956). In cases such as this, the learning curve will be S-shaped. Sometimes, modifications may be introduced when the behavior that is being measured involves a choice between one or more alternative responses (Estes, 1959). Here, the basic equations that are developed will be expressed in terms of the probabilities that one response as compared with another will be made, and changes in the strength of a response will be expressed in terms of changes in these probabilities. But the basic nature of the assumptions that lie behind theoretical learning curves remains much the same in all cases.

BASIC REINFORCEMENT VARIABLES

Thus far in this chapter, we have been examining in a very general way the concept of reinforcement and how the use of reinforcement affects the strength of a response. Now we wish to consider in detail how certain specific things that we can do with reinforcers affect the way in which a response is acquired by an organism. Since reinforcement is such an essential mechanism in the behavior of organisms, it is possible to look upon the rest of the chapter as a fundamental introduction to the psychology of learning.

NUMBER OF REINFORCEMENTS

One of the simplest and most straightforward ways to vary a reinforcement condition in an experiment is to vary the number of times that a response is reinforced and to measure the concomitant changes in response strength which occur. Since a good deal has already been said about the theoretical relation between number of reinforcements and response strength, this section will be used to give some examples of experiments in which number of reinforcements was varied. As we go, compare the conclusions reached in the theoretical discussion with the results that come from the laboratory.

AMPLITUDE OF RESPONSE. Let us begin with an example from the classical conditioning literature in which amplitude of response was used as an index of response strength for a respondent. The respondent was the galvanic skin response in man. This response is a change in the electrical resistance of the skin due to the activity of some effectors in the skin, probably the sweat glands. It is an autonomic response which is not subject to voluntary control. In the experiment (Hovland, 1937c) the investigator gave some subjects a mild electric shock (UCS) at about the same time that he applied a vibrator to the skin (CS). Originally, the vibrator did not elicit much response, though the electric shock did. After a few pairings of the vibrator and electric shock, however, the vibrator alone came to elicit a good-sized response. As the number of reinforcements increased, the magnitude of the response to the vibrator increased. This can be seen in Figure 2.3.

Hovland's experiment shows that the first reinforcement contributes the greatest increment to the strength of the galvanic skin response. Each successive reinforcement adds less to the increase in amplitude, however, and the curve gradually approaches a limit. The general

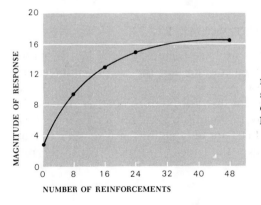

FIG. 2.3 Amplitude of the galvanic skin response (GSR) as a function of number of reinforcements. (Hovland, 1937c.)

shape of the curve compares quite well with those presented earlier in Figure 2.2.

SPEED OF RESPONSE. For a second example, let us look at an experiment that involved an instrumental running response for the rat. In this experiment (Bacon, 1962), an L-shaped enclosed runway was used. Rats were confined in a start box at one end of the long arm of the L; when the start-box door was raised, they ran 5 feet down the long arm and made a right turn into the short arm of the L, which was the goal box. As rats reached the turn, they intercepted a photobeam which stopped a clock that had started when the start-box door went up. The running response was reinforced by letting the rats drink a sweet saccharine solution in the goal box. Different groups of rats received different numbers of reinforced trials in the runway; one group had 10 trials, while the others had 30, 100, and 300 trials. Each day 10 trials were run, with one minute between trials. Figure 2.4 shows the speeds with which the rats ran, at the end of their allotted number of trials.

LATENCY OF RESPONSE. The latency of a response is the time between the presentation of a stimulus and the beginning of a response. Latency is inversely related to response strength; that is, the shorter the time which elapses after a signal is presented before a response begins, the greater the response strength.

An experiment by Felsinger, Gladstone, Yamaguchi, and Hull (1947) provides a good example of a study in which response latency was examined as a function of number of reinforced practice trials. In this experiment, a modified Skinner box was used. The device that the subject manipulated in order to obtain a pellet of food was a bar inserted

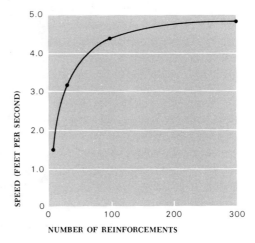

FIG. 2.4 Speed of running as a function of number of reinforcements. (Data from Bacon, 1962.)

through one wall of the box. The bar could be quickly withdrawn through the wall as soon as it was moved a short distance to one side by the rat. A shutter was located inside the box in such a way that it covered the bar as the rat was placed in the box; the shutter could be lifted out of the way by the experimenter. Raising the shutter constituted the stimulus which signalled the beginning of a trial. Note that since moving the bar is an operant, the stimulus in this case did not elicit the response; the stimulus in reality was a discriminative cue. The latency of the response was the difference between the time the shutter was raised and the time the bar was moved at least 1/16 inch by the rat. After the response occurred and the rat had consumed the food pellet, the rat was removed from the apparatus to wait for the next trial given the next day. Note that this experiment is an example of one in which a controlled rather than a free-responding procedure was used in the Skinner box. The results of the experiment are shown in Figure 2.5.

As the figure shows, the experimenters report their results in two ways. The top curve is based on *mean* latency scores, while the bottom curve is based on *median* latency scores. The top curve begins at a higher point than the bottom one because a mean score tends to overweight occasional very long latencies that are apt to occur early in learning, while a median score does not. With both measures, however, the general

FIG. 2.5 Latency of response as a function of number of reinforcements. (Felsinger, Gladstone, Yamaguchi, & Hull, 1947.)

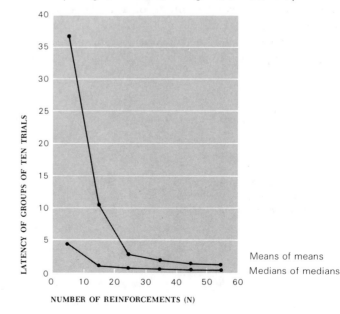

NUMBER OF REINFORCEMENTS (N)

course of learning follows the same pattern. There is the familiar rapid increase in response strength as a result of the initial reinforcements, followed by a much slower rate of increase to the limit of response strength.

GENERAL CONCLUSIONS. We could cite many other examples of experiments in which response strength was measured in different ways as a function of number of reinforced practice trials. If we did, we would find many experiments which yield learning curves similar to the ones we have looked at, but we would find some exceptions as well. Where exceptions occur, they can often be attributed to the kind of response that is being learned, or to some other factor. Spence (1956) has argued, for example, that many learning curves, particularly when they involve an index of response strength that is based on the *frequency* with which conditioned responses occur, are S-shaped. That is, they show a period of positive acceleration in response strength during the first few trials, and then begin to show the negative acceleration we have identified as characteristic of most learning curves. Other investigators—Estes, for example —have obtained data which strongly suggest that the increase in response strength as a function of number of reinforcements is essentially an all-or-none affair. Response strength was shown to jump from a chance level almost to its maximum after *one* reinforced trial (Estes, 1960; Estes, Hopkins, & Crothers, 1960). However, the Estes et al. experiment involved the use of human subjects and a verbal learning task (the learning of an association between a group of three consonant letters and a number), so this experiment may contain the complications that beset the study of learning in verbal organisms. The data we have presented in this section are probably considerably better than first approximations to the general relation between number of reinforcements and response strength—for relatively simple responses made by nonverbal animals.

AMOUNT OF REINFORCEMENT

A second basic thing that is done to vary the conditions which are used to reinforce a response is to vary the amount or magnitude of the reinforcer that follows the response. With positive reinforcers, and with relatively simple learning tasks like training rats to run alleys or to press levers, this can be accomplished by varying things like the weight, volume, or taste of a reward, in short, by varying the *quantity* or *quality* of a reward. With negative reinforcers, a commonly used method of varying amount of reinforcement is to vary the intensity of some noxious stimulus, like electric shock, that is given when the response which is under study occurs. In this section, we shall limit the discussion to data involving positive reinforcers; negative reinforcers will be dealt with later.

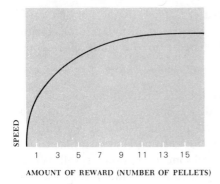

SPEED

1 3 5 7 9 11 13 15

AMOUNT OF REWARD (NUMBER OF PELLETS)

FIG. **2.6** Hypothetical curve showing the relationship between response speed and amount of reinforcement (number of food pellets, in this case). The curve is typical of data from a number of experiments. (Logan, 1960.)

QUANTITY OF REINFORCEMENT AND RESPONSE STRENGTH. A large number of experiments have varied the weight of a food reinforcer, or the number of food pellets that animals find in a goal box, and shown that response strength increases as quantity of reinforcement increases. Crespi (1942), for example, trained groups of rats to run a 20-foot straight runway and rewarded the rats in each group with one of a number of weights of food in the goal box. The speed with which the animals ran after 20 training trials increased as the weight of the food reward increased. Zeaman (1949) measured the latency with which rats ran from a start box at the beginning of a runway and provided different groups of rats with one of five amounts of reinforcement. Zeaman's reinforcers were, appropriately, pieces of cheese that varied in weight from .05 to 2.40 grams. Again, response strength increased as amount of reinforcement increased; the larger the piece of cheese, the shorter the latency of the running response at the end of training. Logan (1960) has summarized data such as these, together with data from a large number of experiments of his own, by means of the relationship between quantity of reinforcement (number of food pellets) and response strength shown in Figure 2.6.

The figure indicates that amount of reinforcement, like number of reinforcements, is related to response strength according to an increasing, negatively accelerated function. That is, if we deal with very small quantities of reinforcement, it does not take much of an increase in amount to produce a rather large increase in response strength. As a response is reinforced with larger and larger quantities of reinforcement, however, the net addition to response strength becomes smaller and smaller.

QUALITY OF REINFORCEMENT AND RESPONSE STRENGTH. Certain substances, like sucrose (common table sugar), seem to have an innate taste appeal for animals as well as people, and these substances can be used very effectively as reinforcing stimuli. Thus, the *qualitative* characteristics of a stimulus furnish another dimension which can be used to manipulate response strength in a way that seems to fit best under the heading of amount of reinforcement. An experiment by Hutt (1954), which used a technique first introduced by Guttman (1953), shows the relation between several qualities of reinforcement and response strength. This experiment is particularly interesting in that it also incorporated different quantities of reinforcement. Hutt was thus able to determine if quantity and quality of reinforcement would *interact* (see Chapter 1) in their effect on response strength. For his reinforcing substance Hutt chose a liquid food which, if used as a complete diet, would provide proper nutrition for rats. This food was used in pure form in the experiment (the *basic* reinforcer), or else it was adulterated with citric acid or with saccharin to give it a sour or sweet taste (the *citric* and *saccharin* reinforcers). The quantity of these substances that was used for each reward was 3, 12, or 50 milligrams. In all, 9 groups of rats were required in the experiment in order to test response strength for each combination of quality and quantity of reinforcement.

Hutt used a Skinner box for his experiment. Rats were required to press a lever to obtain a reinforcer, and the reinforcers were automatically delivered to the rat by a dipper mechanism which measured out the appropriate quantity of the reinforcing substance. To prevent satiation of the rats as they pressed the lever during a long experimental session, and to assure that one rat could not obtain a larger number of reinforcers than another, Hutt used a *fixed-interval schedule* of reinforcement. With this schedule, a lever press produced a reinforcer only if a certain amount of time had elapsed since the rat last obtained a reinforcer—one minute, in this case. The rat was free to respond during the one-minute interval, but these responses were not reinforced.[2] Figure 2.7 shows the rates at which the rats responded on the last day of training, after they had received 150 reinforcements (but had made a great many more responses because of the schedule of reinforcement).

In general, the figure shows that rate of responding, and hence response strength, was highest for the saccharin reinforcer and lowest for the citric reinforcer, with the basic reinforcer coming somewhere between these extremes. Also, response strength increased as the quantity of the reinforcer increased.

[2] With fixed-interval schedules, the rat's best strategy is to make a single response just after the interval of time that the experimenter sets between reinforcers has elapsed. For understandable reasons, rats are not able to respond with this precision. Their ability to "hold off" their responding until the proper moment will be affected by a number of things, e.g., their state of motivation and, of particular interest at the moment, the amount of reinforcement that is used. We shall have a great deal to say about schedules of reinforcement in Chapter 5.

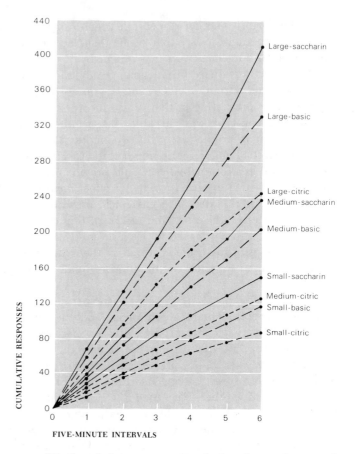

FIG. 2.7 Cumulative response records for three volumes and three qualities of reinforcement. The curves were computed from responses cumulated over six succesive 5-minute intervals of responding. (Hutt, 1954.)

Hutt's data reveal no indication of an interaction between quantity and quality of reinforcement. That is, the effect of the quality variable is generally the same regardless of the particular quantity of reinforcement which is used. However, if quality is redefined to mean different concentrations of the same substance, such as different concentrations of sucrose (Guttman, 1953), interactions between quantity and quality occur. Collier and Myers (1961) showed, for example, that the rate with which a rat presses a lever at the *beginning* of an experiment will increase with the volume of a sucrose solution that is used as a reinforcer, and with its concentration (up to a 64 percent concentration, a syrupy substance indeed). As an experimental session progresses, however, interactions occur between concentration, volume, and the time between reinforcements (that is, the duration of the interval in a fixed-interval schedule of reinforcement).

The exact pattern of the interactions between these variables is a very complicated one, but in general, the rate with which the rat responds toward the end of a session of lever pressing depends to a large extent upon how much fluid the rat has been receiving during the course of a number of lever presses. If volumes of reinforcement are large, or if the time between reinforcements is short, response rates at the end of a session will be much lower than they were at the beginning. Moreover, the extent of this decline in rate depends critically on the concentration of the sugar solution that is used. A very high concentration, a large volume, and a short interval between reinforcements produces the highest rate of responding at the *beginning* of a session, but the *lowest* rate at the end of a session. This change probably occurs because of complicated interactions between taste and osmotic effects in the rat's digestive system (Mook, 1963). Hutt's experiment, in contrast to that of Collier and Myers, was designed to minimize effects such as these, but they are certainly present if they are looked for.

We should not leave the impression that quality of reinforcement has its effects only in free-responding situations, or with the lever-pressing response. For example, similar effects as a function of sweetness can be shown in controlled responding situations which involve responses like running alleys (Young & Shuford, 1954, 1955; Snyder, 1962).

MORE COMPLICATED LEARNING SITUATIONS. Are the kinds of relations between amount of reinforcement and response strength that we have been talking about best reserved for rather "simple" responses such as running alleys or pressing levers? What happens if we use a more "complicated" learning task such as giving an organism some kind of discrimination problem to learn, or requiring that the organism learn a succession of right and left turns in a maze? From the experimenter's point of view, at least, the latter kinds of task are more "complicated" because he can measure two potentially different aspects of an organism's behavior if he uses them: whether the organism makes an error or not, and how quickly (in terms of latency or speed) the correct or incorrect response occurs. We might guess, for example, that amount of reinforcement would affect only the vigor with which an animal pursues *some* path through the maze—whether it is the correct one or not. A small amount of reinforcement might be just as effective as a large amount in teaching the animal the *correct* path.

For a time, it appeared that a distinction between the effects of amount of reinforcement on these two aspects of behavior was justified.

Reynolds (1949), for example, rewarded one group of rats with a 30-milligram pellet of food and another group with a 160-milligram pellet of food if they went to the white end box in a discrimination apparatus. If the rats went to the black end box, they received nothing. Rats were run until they chose the white box on 18 out of 20 successive trials. The results showed that rats who received the large reward required just as many trials to reach this particular criterion of learning as rats who received the small reward. However, the rats rewarded with the large amount took *less time* to make a response than the rats rewarded with the small amount. Similar results were obtained by Maher and Wickens (1954). These experiments thus appear to lend weight to the notion that amount of reinforcement has independent effects upon learning the "correct" response and upon the alacrity with which responses are made in a complex learning task.

The great weight of more recent experimentation has, however, shown that amount of reinforcement can affect the learning of correct versus incorrect responses in complex learning tasks (e.g., Hughes, 1957; Leary, 1958; Hill, Cotton, & Clayton, 1962). These experiments typically involve a feature that was not incorporated in the Reynolds or the Maher and Wickens experiments. Specifically, they permit the organism to become familiar at different times with *all* the amounts of reinforcement that are used in the experiment. For example, Schrier (1958) trained monkeys on a series of very simple discrimination problems. On each problem, the monkeys had to learn to choose one of two objects in order to receive a reward. For four groups of monkeys, the amount of reward was constant during a pretraining period, which was used to familiarize the monkeys with the apparatus, and throughout the series of discrimination problems that followed. For one group, the reward was always 1 pellet, while for the other three groups, it was always 2, 4, or 8 pellets. For a fifth group (the "shift" group), the amount of reward was shifted during the pretraining period and as the monkeys went from one discrimination problem to the next. On the first discrimination problem, for example, the monkeys might receive 1 pellet of food, but on the next, they would receive 8 pellets, and so on. The "shift" group thus had extensive experience with all four of the amount-of-reinforcement conditions by the time the experiment had ended. The results are very clear-cut: For subjects that experienced only one amount of reinforcement during the course of the experiment (it did not matter which one), just about the same percentage of correct responses were made on the discrimination problems. A monkey that got 1 pellet did just about as well as a monkey that got 8. For the "shift" group that experienced all four amounts of reward, however, the percentage of correct responses on a problem increased as the amount of reward which was used with the problem increased. The monkeys made more correct responses on problems that involved an 8-pellet reward than they did on problems that involved a 1-pellet reward, for example.

THE DEFINITION OF AMOUNT OF REINFORCEMENT: SOME PROBLEMS. Offhand, from the research we have just examined, it would seem that psychologists do not have much trouble identifying a characteristic of a simple reinforcing stimulus that defines its amount or magnitude. At this point, however, let us introduce some of the confusing frustration that you were warned about at the beginning of this chapter.

In all the experiments discussed thus far, the experimenter defined amount of reinforcement in terms of some simple physical scale: weight, volume, concentration, and so on. And animals can clearly differentiate *something* about different points along these scales, since differences in a physical dimension such as weight of food or volume of sucrose solution can, in fact, produce appropriate differences in response strength. But what is it, specifically, about a big heavy piece of food, for example, that makes the rat respond to it as a larger amount of reinforcement than a small light piece of food? As yet, psychologists do not know for sure. Big pieces of food take longer to eat, require more bites, may look bigger, and are very likely eaten in bigger chunks than small pieces of food (Kling, 1956; Spence, 1956; Pubols, 1960). Which one of these variables, or which combination of several of them, is actually correlated with amount of reinforcement—from the rat's point of view—remains an unanswered question.

For example, Snyder and Hulse (1961) did an experiment which was designed to analyze the effects on response strength of two variables they thought might be good indices of amount of reinforcement. One variable was the *total volume* of water that thirsty rats got to drink from a drinking tube in the goal box after they ran down a straight runway. The second variable was the *number of licks* the rats had to make in order to get their particular allotment of water. Three groups of rats received 0.75, 1.50, or 2.65 cubic centimeters of water as reinforcement in the goal box at the end of each trial. Some rats within each group had to make only 295 licks to get their appropriate total amount; others had to make 450 or 675 licks. A special pump system was used to adjust the size of the water drop that the rats got with each lick so that these experimental conditions could be satisfied. For example, rats who obtained 2.65 cubic centimeters in 295 licks got a bigger drop of water than rats who received the same amount in 675 licks. The results of the experiment were clear—and distressing. It did not matter which condition of reinforcement prevailed; after 34 training trials all rats in the experiment ran down the alley at just about the same speed. In the face of data such as these, it is perhaps not surprising that psychologists often have to be satisfied with pragmatic definitions of amount of reinforcement. Although the "why" of the matter has not been settled, it is a simple fact that amounts of reinforcement chosen from some simple physical scale of amount, like weight of food or number of food pellets, generally *do* produce orderly differences in response strength.

It is also true that you can choose different amounts of reinforcement according to even the simplest of physical scales and find that their effect on response strength can depend upon things which do not seem to be directly related to the variable of amount of reinforcement at all. For example, Schrier's (1958) experiment, if you will recall, showed that amount of reinforcement had no differential effect on behavior unless the organism was taught something about the *range* of amounts of reinforcement which could occur when a correct response was made. In another experiment, Lewis (1964) varied the amount of *effort* that had to be expended in order to obtain a reward. He attached a harness to hungry rats and, during a preliminary phase, trained them to pull against different weights to get at a food reward of *constant* amount (20 Rice Krispies). Then, on test trials, he removed the weights and measured how fast rats would run an alley for the same amount of reinforcement, 20 Rice Krispies. He also measured how fast the rats ate the Rice Krispies in the goal box. The results of the experiment show that the heavier the weight the rats had to pull during the preliminary phase, the faster they ran and ate on test trials. One possible way of looking at these data would be to conclude that the reward appeared to be larger (from the rat's point of view) if a relatively great deal of effort had to be expended to get it—even though the size of the reward was constant in terms of a physical scale of amount.

We could go on in this vein at great length. If we were to do so, we would be carried quickly beyond the scope of this section and, perhaps, beyond the scope of this book. For the moment, the important point is that a reinforcing stimulus never exists in a vacuum; the manner in which an organism responds to different amounts of reinforcement can depend profoundly upon the conditions under which the organism is exposed to them, and upon what the organism has to do to get them.

CONDITIONED REINFORCEMENT

Food pellets and sucrose solutions are examples of *primary* reinforcing stimuli. That is, they will operate as simple reinforcers even though the organism has had little, if any, previous experience with them. Generally speaking, primary reinforcers are tied pretty closely to some basic physiological system or mechanism of an organism: taste, hunger, thirst, and so on. It is obvious that most behavior, particularly that of human beings, is learned on the basis of reinforcement which is quite different from such simple primary reinforcement. Money is an excellent example of something that is a reinforcing stimulus for most people, but a stimulus which is certainly not tied in any direct fashion to a basic physiological system. Consequently, many psychologists have found it not only convenient but absolutely necessary to add a concept to the basic principles of learning which will account for the fact that organisms can learn in the absence of anything that could be called primary reinforcement. This concept is that of secondary or *conditioned* reinforcement. Again, we shall confine our discussion here to conditioned reinforcement based on positive primary reinforcement. Similar considerations that involve negative reinforcers will be dealt with later.

THE DEFINITION AND MEASUREMENT OF CONDITIONED REINFORCEMENT. A conditioned reinforcer is *a neutral stimulus that acquires the functional properties of a primary reinforcer by being paired in time with a primary reinforcer or with another conditioned reinforcer.* In other words, conditioned reinforcers are stimuli that acquire the power to reinforce by being paired with other stimuli that already possess the power to reinforce. In this sense, conditioned reinforcers are stimuli that acquire their reinforcing properties through *learning.*

According to a straightforward interpretation of our definition of conditioned reinforcement, we could establish a conditioned reinforcer quite simply. We could, for example, pair a neutral stimulus with a primary reinforcer by turning on a light for a moment or two just as we presented a pellet of food to a hungry rat. After a few pairings of the light with the food, the light ought to acquire some of the *functional* properties of the food; that is, the light—in its own right—should be usable as a reinforcing stimulus. However, we would not be sure about this unless we went on to demonstrate specifically that the light, by itself, could function in the same way that we would expect any reinforcing stimulus to function. In practice, psychologists have used three general techniques to do this. Let us look briefly at these techniques and examine some experiments that furnish examples of each technique—and the principle of conditioned reinforcement—at work.

The first technique involves pairing a stimulus with primary reinforcement in one situation and with one response, and then testing to see if the stimulus has become a conditioned reinforcer by using it—and it alone—to reinforce a *new* response in a *new* situation. If the stimulus which we think is a conditioned reinforcer can, in fact, produce new learning, then we have demonstrated that it is a conditioned reinforcer.

The second technique is to use *resistance to extinction* as a measure of the establishment of a conditioned reinforcer. We cannot develop the concept of resistance to extinction here; that will take a good portion of Chapter 4. However, we can say—with considerable oversimplification —that resistance to extinction is a measure of the extent to which an organism is willing to *persist* in the performance of some response when we stop reinforcing the response. For example, when one rat makes more responses on a lever than another rat after the experimenter stops giving food pellets for lever presses, we say that the first rat is more resistant to extinction than the second rat. With respect to conditioned reinforcers, we would expect a stimulus that had acquired some value as a conditioned reinforcer to increase resistance to extinction if we followed lever presses during extinction with the stimulus. Even though we have withdrawn primary reinforcement, we would still be giving *some,* albeit learned, reinforcement for lever-pressing behavior.

The third technique is to study conditioned reinforcement as it operates in a *chain* of behavior. A chain of behavior is a *sequence* of different responses, each response paired with a different stimulus, that eventually leads to some primary reinforcement like food. The concept of a chain of behavior, and the role that conditioned reinforcement plays in such a chain, are best explained by means of an example from the experimental literature, so we shall return to this point in a moment. First, let us look at experiments that are representative of our first two techniques.

Saltzman (1949) trained rats to run down a straight runway to a goal box that contained food. The goal box was either black or white. In one condition, the goal box always contained food when it was black, but did not when it was white. After this training, the rats were taught a simple maze in which they had to choose between two pathways, one leading to a black goal box and the other to a white one. The rats learned to go to the black goal box, *even though it was never baited with food.* Thus it is clear that the black goal box itself was a stimulus complex that was reinforcing because it had been paired with primary reinforcement, food, in another situation. The black goal box was thus a conditioned reinforcer.

Miles (1956) did an experiment in which resistance to extinction was used to measure the strength of a conditioned reinforcer. His experiment incorporated two variables: the number of times that a conditioned reinforcer was paired with a food-reinforced lever press, and the strength of hunger drive at the time extinction began. Let us look in some detail at the part of the experiment in which number of pairings of conditioned reinforcer with primary reinforcement was the independent variable. Different groups of rats had the delivery of a food pellet paired with both a flash of light and an audible click (the conditioned reinforcer) following 0, 10, 20, 40, 80, or 160 lever presses. Then the food-delivery apparatus

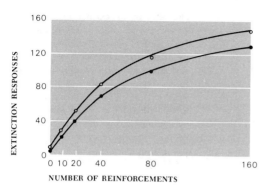

FIG. 2.8   Effect of a conditioned reinforcer on resistance to extinction as a function of number of reinforcements. (Adapted from Miles, 1956.)

was turned off, and the rats pressed the lever without primary reinforcement. For half the rats, lever presses during extinction produced the conditioned reinforcer; for the other half, the conditioned reinforcer was omitted. Figure 2.8 shows part of the results. As you can see, resistance to extinction increased as number of reinforcements increased, but the group which was extinguished with the conditioned (secondary) reinforcer made more lever presses than the group which was extinguished without the conditioned reinforcer.

Another important question to ask of the same data is this: *How much* of an increase in resistance to extinction did the conditioned reinforcer add as a function of the number of times it was paired with primary reinforcement? The answer to this question is obtained by subtracting the number of lever presses made by the group which was extinguished without the conditioned reinforcer from the number of lever presses made by the group which was extinguished with the conditioned reinforcer. If we do this for each value of the independent variable that Miles used, we get the function shown in Figure 2.9. You can see from the figure that if the conditioned reinforcer was paired with the food-reinforced lever press just a few times, the use of the conditioned reinforcer during extinction did not produce many extra responses. After 40 pairings, however, use of the conditioned reinforcer added about 15 extra responses, and the function appears to approach an asymptote of about 20 extra responses after 160 pairings. As you may have noted already, this function looks very much like many we have seen before that show the relationship between response strength and variables such as number of reinforced trials or amount of reinforcement.

Before we leave Miles's experiment, we should note that the effect of the conditioned reinforcer on resistance to extinction also depended

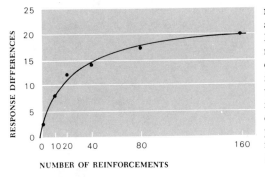

NUMBER OF REINFORCEMENTS

FIG. **2**.9 Extra extinction responses added by a conditioned reinforcer. Each point shows the difference in number of responses between a group extinguished with a conditioned reinforcer and a group extinguished without one. The conditioned reinforcer adds more responses during extinction the greater the number of primary reinforcements during original training. (Adapted from Miles, 1956.)

upon the strength of the hunger drive under which the rats entered extinction. Generally speaking, the conditioned reinforcer added more extra responses the longer the rats were deprived of food. The function relating number of extra responses to hours of food deprivation looks very much like that shown in Figure 2.9.

Let us now return to our third technique and examine the concept of conditioned reinforcement as it can be shown to operate in a chain of behavior. To do this, let us look at an experiment by Napalkov (1959) cited in Kelleher and Gollub (1962). Napalkov first trained pigeons to peck a lever (response 1) in order to obtain a primary reinforcer, food. Then he reinforced pecks only if they occurred when a white light (stimulus 1) was turned on. You will recognize that this procedure made a discriminative cue out of the light. After the pigeon had learned to confine most of its pecks to the time that the light was on, the pigeon was required to jump onto a platform (response 2) in order to turn on the light. But the light could only be turned on if the jumping response was made in the presence of another discriminative cue, a rotating black air vane (stimulus 2). This procedure was carried on until the pigeon had learned a sequence of responses, a chain of behavior, that involved 7 component responses, each response correlated with a different discriminative cue. The whole experiment is outlined in Table 2.1. Note that the chain was established in reverse order; the response closest to primary reinforcement was established first, then earlier components were added, response by response.

Now it is clear that the first component of the chain, pecking the lever, was reinforced with a primary reinforcer, food. But what was the reinforcing stimulus for the second component response, jumping on the platform? Clearly, it must have been the discriminative cue of the white light. In other words, the jumping response was reinforced by a previously neutral stimulus that acquired its reinforcing power by being paired—as a discriminative cue—directly with primary reinforcement. Similarly, the third response, jumping onto the floor of the apparatus, was reinforced

TABLE 2.1   **Summary of Napalkov's Experiment**
(From Kelleher & Gollub, 1962)

RESPONSE	DISCRIMINATIVE CUE	REINFORCING STIMULUS	NO. OF TRIALS FOR RESPONSE TO OCCUR TO DISCRIMINATIVE CUE
1. Peck lever	White light (S_1)	Food	14–18
2. Jump on platform	Black air vane rotating (S_2)	White light	12–20
3. Jump onto floor of apparatus	Whistle (S_3)	Black air vane	20–30
4. Jump down onto a platform	Blue light (S_4)	Whistle	18–36
5. Jump onto rod	Horn (siren) (S_5)	Blue light	31–45
6. Jump into right section of apparatus	Bell (S_6)	Horn	40–55
7. Jump into left section of chamber and up onto a shelf	Large white air vane (S_7)	Bell	42–61

by the discriminative cue of the rotating black air vane. Thus the black air vane was also a conditioned reinforcer, but it acquired its reinforcing power by being paired, not with primary reinforcement, but with another *conditioned* reinforcer. So this experiment demonstrates that conditioned reinforcers can be developed by pairing stimuli, as discriminative cues, not only with primary reinforcers, but also with other conditioned reinforcers.

Another thing that the Napalkov experiment shows is that in a long chain of behavior, it takes a larger number of trials for a discriminative cue to acquire the properties of a conditioned reinforcer the farther away the cue is in the chain from primary reinforcement. For different birds, it took only 14 to 18 trials for the response of jumping onto the platform (response 2) to occur when it was reinforced by the white light, but it took 42 to 61 trials to get the initial response of the chain (response 7) to occur when the bell was the reinforcing stimulus.

SOME THINGS THAT AFFECT THE STRENGTH OF CONDITIONED REIN-FORCERS.   Since conditioned reinforcers are developed through a learning process, we would expect that their strength might be correlated with variables which have been shown to affect the strength of a learned association. Miles's (1956) experiment, if you will recall, demonstrated that the strength of a conditioned reinforcer was a function of the number of times the conditioned reinforcer had been paired with primary reinforcement as well as a function of the strength of hunger motivation during extinction test trials. Other experiments have shown that the strength of a conditioned reinforcer increases as the amount of primary reinforcement with which it is paired increases (D'Amato, 1955; Butter & Thomas, 1958). Also, the strength of a conditioned reinforcer depends upon the amount of time that elapses between onset of the conditioned reinforcer and the delivery of the primary reinforcer. Jenkins (1950) found that conditioned reinforcers were most effective if this interval was on the order of 0.5 to 1.0 seconds. As we shall see in the next section, the interval of time that elapses between two stimuli, or between a stimulus and a response, can be of profound importance in determining the strength of a response or of a learned association.

Another thing that can affect the apparent strength of a conditioned reinforcer is the technique which is used to see if a stimulus has acquired the properties of a conditioned reinforcer. The first two techniques we looked at—that of using a conditioned reinforcer to establish a new response, and that of testing by measuring resistance to extinction —have an important drawback. As Kelleher and Gollub (1962) have cogently pointed out, both involve the *removal* of the primary reinforcer when the test for conditioned reinforcement is made. Since learning tends to weaken—through experimental extinction—in the absence of primary reinforcement, and since the properties of a conditioned reinforcer evolve through learning and can presumably extinguish, a very "strong" conditioned reinforcer may be required if its effects are to be detected at all.

This particular problem, at least, can be avoided by using the third technique we looked at, that of establishing conditioned reinforcers in a *chain* of responses. This is true because, under the experimental conditions that characterize a chain, the chain *always* leads to *primary* reinforcement at its end. Consequently, as the chain develops, the strengths of its components are constantly increasing rather than decreasing. This, it would seem, should provide not only a very sensitive way to test for the reinforcing power of cues associated with different components of the chain, but also a means for watching the progressive development of a neutral cue into a conditioned reinforcer while the development is actually taking place. Certainly the Napalkov experiment, together with a great many others (Kelleher & Gollub, 1962), suggests that the chaining approach to conditioned reinforcement can be a useful one.

THE NECESSARY CONDITIONS FOR ESTABLISHING A CONDITIONED REINFORCER. What experimental operations should we choose in order to *guarantee* that a particular stimulus will become a conditioned reinforcer? While psychologists have some good hunches about the answer to this question, they still must deal with it much as they have had to deal with the problem of selecting a variable that will properly describe different amounts of reinforcement. The choice of a technique remains pretty much a pragmatic affair. One of the best, in the sense that it does work most consistently, is to make a discriminative cue out of the neutral stimulus which is to acquire some reinforcing value. This technique, first described by Skinner (1938), is characteristic of the Napalkov experiment as well as a great many others (Keller & Schoenfeld, 1950; Myers, 1958; Kelleher & Gollub, 1962).

But there is abundant evidence which shows that, while making a discriminative cue out of a stimulus may be a sufficient condition for establishing a conditioned reinforcer, it is not a *necessary* one. Often a simple, simultaneous pairing of a neutral stimulus with a primary reinforcer each time that the reinforcer occurs will work perfectly. Miles's (1956) experiment and those of Stein (1958) and Autor (1960) are cases in point—among many others that could be mentioned. Like many problems in psychology, the specification of all the necessary *and* sufficient conditions for establishing a conditioned reinforcer depends upon a good deal of additional theoretical and experimental work.

TIME RELATIONS IN CONDITIONING AND LEARNING

So far in our examination of basic reinforcement variables, we have postponed discussion of a very important set of relationships in the conditioning and learning of simple responses. This has to do with the way in which stimuli, responses, and reinforcers are related in time. Such matters are important because they are directed explicitly at a very general problem that has interested psychologists—and philosophers—for a great many years. The basic question is this: How should two or more events be arranged in time so that an organism will associate them with each other? For example, can we expect a stimulus and a response to be associated when the stimulus preceeds the response by one second, one week, one year? Similarly, suppose a response occurs, but we withhold reinforcement for a period of time. How long can we postpone the reinforcement and still obtain an increase in the strength of the response? Or, to put it the other way around, what is the *optimum* interval of time that should elapse between stimuli, responses, and reinforcers if response strength is to grow to a maximum level?

In practice, psychologists have sought answers to these questions in two domains. First, classical conditioning techniques have been used to study the strength of a conditioned response when the interval varies between the CS and the UCS. Second, instrumental conditioning techniques have been used to study the strength of a response when the interval varies between the occurrence of the response and the delivery of the reinforcing stimulus. Both of these problem areas have been closely woven into theoretical discussions of the learning process, and though we shall treat them here as if they were separate topics for experimental study, we shall have occasion to return to them in other ways later on.

THE CS-UCS INTERVAL IN CLASSICAL CONDITIONING

There is now a large number of experiments which demonstrate the strength of a classically conditioned response as a function of the relation of the CS and UCS in time. It is hardly surprising that Pavlov was the first to devote some attention to this problem, and we shall now have a look at some of the things he did.

PAVLOV'S STUDIES ON TIME RELATIONS IN CONDITIONING. Pavlov (1927) used two different techniques in the study of time relations in classical conditioning. In one, the CS and the UCS overlapped each other in time. Either the CS came before the UCS, or the two were simultaneous; but the essential condition was that they overlapped. In the other technique, the CS and the UCS did not overlap. Usually, the CS was presented first and turned off. Then, after an interval, the UCS was turned on.

Pavlov thought that the simultaneous presentation of the CS and UCS produced the most rapid conditioning, and in all the experiments in his laboratory, they were presented initially in this way. Following this, he would gradually lengthen the interval between the CS and UCS, or would allow longer exposures of the CS before he presented the UCS.

When the UCS was delayed, Pavlov found that animals could learn to delay the onset of the CR for long periods of time. They would delay giving a CR until just before the UCS was about to appear. Pavlov took this to mean that the CR was actively inhibited. He used the delayed conditioned response as an example of what he called "internal inhibition." He also found that animals could delay the onset of the CR when the CS was presented and then withdrawn before the UCS appeared. Pavlov called this the "trace" conditioned response, and he considered it also to be an example of internal inhibition. He found, moreover, that it was more difficult to establish the trace CR than the delayed CR.

These observations are important because they indicate that associations between a CS and a CR are extraordinarily flexible. Such associations do not have to be based on simultaneity or even upon close temporal association between the stimuli involved. Pavlov found that he could introduce delays of many minutes in the conditioning procedure and still produce a conditioned response. The CS would come on and then, after a wait, the CR would appear. For the production of such delays, however, it is apparently essential that nothing else occur between the CS and the subsequent response. Pavlov's experiments were performed in sound-deadened rooms so that the animal would not be stimulated in any way between the occurrence of the CS and the time for the CR. Such an absolutely controlled environment seems to be necessary for very long delays. Also, the animals themselves came to inhibit activity in the time interval and, in some instances, appeared to go to sleep.

RESPONSE STRENGTH AND THE CS-UCS INTERVAL. At present there are some 20-odd experiments available which were designed to show specifically how response strength changes when the CS-UCS interval varies (Kimble, 1961). Three representative studies with human subjects (Spooner & Kellogg, 1947; Moeller, 1954; Kimble, Mann, & Dufort, 1955) used conditioned responses which were, variously, a hand movement, a galvanic skin response, and an eyelid blink. These experiments, and most like them, are consistent in showing that conditioning is most rapid and terminal response strength is greatest when the CS *precedes* the UCS by approximately half a second. Figure 2.10 gives the data on the conditioned hand movement, together with some data from earlier studies of the same response (Wolfle, 1930, 1932).

FIG. **2.10** Results of the Spooner and Kellogg (1947) and the Wolfle (1930, 1931) studies on the time interval between conditional and unconditioned stimuli. The curve labeled "present study" is from the data of Spooner and Kellogg. Notice that the maximum frequency of conditioned responses occurs when the conditional stimulus precedes the unconditioned stimulus by about half a second. Backward conditioned responses rarely occur. (Spooner & Kellogg, 1947).

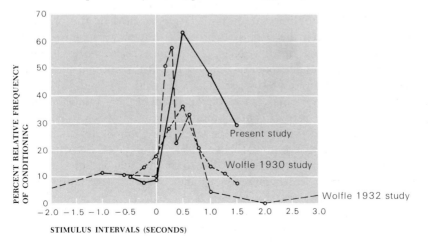

STIMULUS INTERVALS (SECONDS)

One curious case of the time relation between the CS and the UCS is shown in Figure 2.10. This is *backward* conditioning, so called because in backward conditioning, the UCS precedes the CS. Pavlov thought that conditioning could not take place in this case; however, the data presented in Figure 2.10 provide some evidence for backward conditioning. It is probably not true conditioning, however, but more likely a sensitization of the whole response system. The UCS (often an electric shock or some other noxious stimulus in the cases in which backward conditioning is found) sensitizes the subject so that he will give a response to almost any stimulus. This implies, of course, that the stimulus in question need not even be paired with the UCS. Such an interpretation agrees quite well with the data of Spooner and Kellogg (1947), who found that the number of backward conditioned responses was high early in training, but decreased during it. Presumably this happened because the subjects readily adapted to stimuli other than the shock. Incidentally, the fact that such "pseudoconditioned" responses sometimes appear suggests an important thing to keep in mind when designing classical conditioning experiments. A well-designed experiment, particularly if it involves a response or a UCS that has not received much previous experimental attention, will have a control group that does not receive the CS, but only the UCS. After the UCS has been presented by itself for a number of times, a test for sensitization is made by turning on the CS for the *first* time. If a response appears under these conditions, the experimenter would do well to wonder if the "conditioned" responses obtained when the CS is paired with the UCS in conventional fashion might be contaminated by sensitization due to the simple presentation of the UCS alone.

All studies show that conditioning is less efficient when stimuli are presented together than when the CS precedes the UCS by a brief interval. This fact implies that the association learned by the organism is not always between the stimuli themselves, but may be between one stimulus and the *trace,* or aftereffects, of another. Just why asynchrony is best is not yet fully understood, but the brevity of the optimal time interval between the CS and UCS suggests clearly that this effect has to do with the timing of events in the central nervous system. The important fact, however, is that the rate of conditioning of many kinds of respondents drops rapidly as the time interval between the CS and the UCS is increased to even a few seconds (Moeller, 1954). In delayed CR conditioning, this interval can be extended, but only through tedious training under conditions in which there is minimal external stimulation. Also, there are some kinds of respondents, such as classically conditioned "fear" (which we will have a good deal to say about later on), for which it is possible to obtain good levels of conditioning at CS-UCS intervals well beyond a few seconds. But for most respondents, an interval of half a second appears to be best.

DELAY OF REINFORCEMENT IN INSTRUMENTAL CONDITIONING

Suppose we somehow coaxed a dog to make a response and then rather fiendishly failed to give the dog some appropriate reward until an hour or so had passed. Would the dog learn the response? Psychologists can say with considerable confidence that under most conditions, and with animals such as dogs, the response will be learned with great difficulty, if it is learned at all. On the other hand, suppose we made the dog wait only a few seconds before we reinforced the response. Under these conditions, psychologists can say—with equal confidence—that the response will be learned with facility. But what is the general functional relation between learning and the extent to which a reward is *delayed* following a response? Let us now turn our attention to this problem.

We shall begin by looking at two of the initial experiments that dealt with delay of reinforcement. Wolfe (1934) trained rats to go to one arm of a T-shaped maze. The goal box at the end of this arm contained food, and the identical goal box in the other arm did not. The maze had doors just before the goal boxes, so that the animals could be retained in the arms of the T before they were allowed to enter the goal box. Thus the arms of the T served as retention chambers. Wolfe's rats were able to learn to turn into the correct arm of the T when they were delayed in the retention chambers for as long as 20 minutes.

Perin (1943) trained rats in a Skinner box that was modified so that movement of a rod to either the right or the left would produce a food pellet. Immediately after the rod was moved, it was withdrawn from the box until the next trial. After the rats had learned to move the rod in both directions and had displayed their preference for one direction, the apparatus was changed so that a movement of the rod in the preferred direction would produce no food. A movement of the rod in the other direction, however, would cause the food pellet to be delivered. Also, at this point, the apparatus was changed so that correct movement of the rod produced the food pellets for different rats after 0, 2, 5, 10, 20, or 30 seconds. Perin ran the rats under these conditions for 120 trials and measured the frequency with which the rats made the correct response, i.e., moved the rod in the new direction. He then calculated the *slope* of the learning curve associated with each of the delay periods at the point where the rats were making 50 percent correct responses—that is, at the point where the problem was "half learned." Perin's rationale was that if delay of reinforcement affected the facility with which the correct response would be acquired, rats who were learning the problem faster would show a greater *rate* of improvement (a steeper slope on the learning

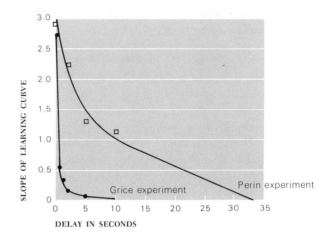

FIG. 2.11 Delay-of-reinforcement gradients obtained by Perin (1943) and Grice (1948). Note that Grice's procedure, which presumably reduced conditioned reinforcement, set things so that there was little learning beyond a delay of five seconds. (Grice, 1948.)

curve) than rats who were having more difficulty with the problem. A plot of the slopes as a function of delay of reinforcement, a *gradient of reinforcement,* is shown by the upper function in Figure 2.11.

It is very clear in this figure that the shorter the delay of reinforcement, the steeper the slope of the learning curve. Rats with short delays learned the problem at a much faster rate than rats with long delays. Looking at the curve, it would be predicted that no learning at all would occur (that is, the slope of the learning curve would be 0) if reinforcement were delayed for about 35 to 40 seconds. As a matter of fact, about half the rats in the 30-second group extinguished during the course of the 120 learning trials; the delay was so long that they stopped moving the rod altogether.

How are Perin's data, which showed the gradient of reinforcement to extend for roughly 40 *seconds,* to be reconciled with Wolfe's data which showed the gradient to extend for as much as 20 *minutes?*

CONDITIONED REINFORCEMENT AND THE GRADIENT OF REINFORCEMENT. A paper by Spence (1947) and an experiment by Grice (1948) provide one approach to a solution of the problem.[3] Spence argued that experiments which had shown a long gradient of reinforcement had used

[3] Related material can be found in Kimble (1961), Mowrer (1960), Kelleher and Gollub (1962), and Perkins (1947).

procedures which assured the presence of *conditioned* reinforcers during the delay period. In the Wolfe experiment, for example, the retention chamber in one arm of the T immediately preceded food, and it could thus acquire the properties of a conditioned reinforcer. Similarly, the proprioceptive stimuli coming from a turn into the correct arm of the T could acquire some value as conditioned reinforcers, and these could be distinguished from the proprioceptive cues associated with a turn into the incorrect arm (on the assumption that the rat could tell the difference in the muscular "feel" of making a correct as compared with an incorrect turn). Thus, while a correct response in the Wolfe experiment was followed by *delayed primary* reinforcement, it was in fact associated with *immediate conditioned* reinforcement, which could have produced the learning that Wolfe observed. In the Perin experiment, some attempt was made to control for conditioned reinforcement by removing, immediately after a response occurred, one of the most likely candidates for a cue that could acquire value as a conditioned reinforcer—the rod that the rat moved to produce food pellets. And, Spence's argument would run, the removal of this cue should shorten the gradient of reinforcement, as it did. But since Perin's rats were still exposed to a host of other cues in the Skinner box which could acquire value as conditioned reinforcers, some learning should have still taken place even when delays were of appreciable length. Spence notes, however, that if it were possible to remove *all* conditioned reinforcers during the delay period, the gradient of reinforcement ought to almost vanish!

Grice's (1948) experiment provided strong support for Spence's point of view. Grice set out to remove from the delay period as many cues with potential value as conditioned reinforcers as he could and predicted that if any gradient of reinforcement were obtained at all, it would be a very short one. He conditioned rats in a black-white discrimination apparatus in which they were trained to leave a start box and to choose between one of two straight alleys. The initial portion, the "discrimination section," of one alley was painted white, while the initial portion of the other was painted black. After choosing a discrimination section (the white one was always correct), the rat ran into a gray delay section and then into a gray goal box, where food was available after a correct response. With this procedure, the white and black cues provided by the discrimination sections—the brightness cues the rats had to use to solve the problem—were never paired directly in time with primary reinforcement and should therefore have acquired little value as conditioned reinforcers. Further, the black and white cues were shifted randomly from side to side on different trials, so that the rats could not solve the problem by simply learning to go to the right or left. This assured that no particular pattern of proprioceptive cues could acquire differential value as a conditioned reinforcer by being paired consistently with primary reinforcement. Different delays of reinforcement for correct responses were introduced for different rats by reinforcing them directly in the discrimination section (0 delay), by varying the length of the delay section through which they ran, and for long delays, by confining rats in the delay section before permitting them to run into the goal box. With these techniques, delays of 0, 0.5, 1.2, 2.0, 5.0, and 10.0 seconds were used. The rats were considered to have learned the problem when they made 18 correct choices during 20 consecutive trials. Grice calculated the slopes of the learning curves for his rats in a manner which was essentially the same that Perin used, and obtained the bottom function shown in Figure 2.11. Clearly, Grice's results demonstrate that rats would not have been able to learn the problem if reinforcement were delayed much longer than 5 seconds; three out of five rats in the 10-second group did not learn at all. This is a striking confirmation of Spence's assertion.

Though the Spence-Grice approach appears to handle the problem very well, other data suggest that this is by no means the only possible approach. Let us—once again—introduce some confusing frustration by looking at an experiment of Lawrence and Hommel (1961). What would happen in a discrimination problem, these experimenters asked, if control for conditioned reinforcement was maintained during the delay period, but the goal boxes into which the rats ran after a correct or incorrect choice were highly discriminable from each other? To answer this question, three groups of rats were trained in an apparatus which was basically the same that Grice used.

For all groups, a response to the white discrimination section was correct, and following both correct and incorrect choices, all animals were confined for 10 seconds in a gray delay section. Then they were permitted to run into a goal box. For group C, both goal boxes were identical in structure and were painted gray—the conditions Grice used. For group DG, both goal boxes were also gray, but they differed in shape and in floor texture. For group BW, one goal box was white and the other was black; however, the black goal box was used with the white discrimination section, and the white goal box was used with the black discrimination section. Note that, since choice of the white discrimination section was correct, food was presented in the black goal box. Thus "black" as a cue presumably acquired the properties of a conditioned reinforcer. But note also that if "black" was a conditioned reinforcer, responses to the *black* discrimination section would be the ones that would receive immediate conditioned reinforcement, and *these were incorrect responses not followed by food.* So if conditioned reinforcement were at work in the situation, it would operate *against* mediation of the delay and solution of the discrimination problem.

The results of the experiment show that for group C, only 2 of 10 rats reached the learning criterion of 18 correct choices in 20 successive trials during 300 learning trials. These results are quite comparable to those of Grice. For group DG, however, 7 of 9 rats reached the criterion in a median of 169 trials, and for group BW, all of 10 rats reached the criterion in a median of 119.5 trials. Further, when delays for the BW group were subsequently increased from 10 to as much as 60 seconds, the rats maintained the discrimination. Taken as a whole, the results indicate clearly that rats can solve a discrimination problem involving delay of reinforcement on some basis other than that of conditioned reinforcement alone. Lawrence and Hommel feel that when food appears in one place and not in another, and when the rat can distinguish between the two places, the rat will search for and attend selectively to other cues—notably those in the discrimination sections—that lead to primary reinforcement. In a sense, the rat is provided with some information which enables it to recognize that it does, in fact, have a discrimination problem to solve: it has to find its way to that unique place where food is consistently available and to avoid that unique place where food is never found.

In Grice's experiment, on the other hand, both correct and incorrect responses (from the experimenter's point of view) lead to the *same* place, a gray goal box (from the rat's point of view). Though the experimenter has a discrimination problem in mind, the problem for the rat may never become a discrimination problem at all. Rather, as Lawrence and Hommel point out, delays in identical gray sections followed by runs into identical gray goal boxes may simply leave the rat to ponder for 300 or so trials why gray goal boxes sometimes contain food and sometimes do not. From the rat's point of view, an appropriate solution to the problem, since it at least would pay off half the time, would be to develop a "position preference," a consistent choice of one alley of the apparatus. This is precisely what some rats in group C did.

While the use of the concept of conditioned reinforcement as an explanatory tool must be hedged—in the case of discrimination learning, at least—there is some evidence that stimuli best classified as conditioned reinforcers can function to mediate long delays of reinforcement in other types of experimental situations. *Token reward* experiments provide a case in point. Chimpanzees can be trained to insert poker chips into a device in order to obtain food from it. After they have learned to do this, it can be shown that the poker chips, as "tokens for food," have acquired the properties of a conditioned reinforcer. For example, Wolfe (1936) found that chimps would work at a weight-pulling task, which required considerable expenditure of effort, in order to obtain poker chips that could be exchanged for food only after a delay interval. The experimenter increased the delay interval from trial to trial until it was so long that the chimps refused to pull the lever. Under these conditions, Wolfe found that the delay interval could be increased to as much as an hour or more, and the chimps would still work for the poker chips. In similar experiments, Kelleher (1956, 1957) showed that the delay interval could be extended to as much as two hours. Both Wolfe and Kelleher made an informal observation which further suggests that the poker chips were effective conditioned reinforcers that helped to mediate the delay of reinforcement period: during the delay interval, the chimps frequently put the chips into their mouths and manipulated them as if they were food.

WHAT DO ORGANISMS DO DURING A DELAY INTERVAL? From our discussion thus far, you might think that animals simply luxuriate during the delay interval in the array of conditioned reinforcers coming from the environment, confident that primary reinforcement will soon arrive. The facts indicate otherwise. Further, they remind us that the central, and more general, problem here is how organisms go about bridging the interval of time that elapses between a response and its associated primary reinforcement. As we have seen, the principle of conditioned reinforcement, defined and used operationally, represents one conceptual approach to the problem, but psychologists know about some other things that may also play an important role in mediating delays of reinforcement. One of these is a class of events of which *superstitious behavior* is an example. The other is *language*. First, let us look at the phenomenon of superstitious behavior.

Suppose a hungry pigeon is put in a Skinner box, and an experimenter arranges to present some grain to the pigeon once every minute. The experimenter does not require that the pigeon do anything in particular in order to get the grain; rather than watching the pigeon, the experimenter watches a clock. What will pigeons do under these conditions? Skinner (1948) found that most pigeons rapidly developed some kind of consistent behavior during the wait between the deliveries of grain. One pigeon, for example, developed a response of "circling to the left," while another spent a great deal of time poking its beak into one corner of the box. Though reinforcement was not contingent upon any particular response from the experimenter's point of view, the pigeon seemed to supply one anyway! In this sense, the pigeon's behavior was superstitious; it was very much like the contortions some baseball players go through as they walk from the dugout to the plate for their turn at bat. In neither case does the behavior have any direct effect on the ultimate outcome of the event in question, but the behavior and some successful outcome have probably been accidentally associated in the past.

The next question is whether superstitious behavior will appear in an experimental arrangement designed around a delay-of-reinforcement paradigm. If so, superstitious behavior could be playing some role in helping the pigeon to bridge the span of time between operant response and primary reinforcement. Ferster (1953) trained pigeons to peck at a lighted key on a variable-interval schedule of reinforcement.[4] However, a peck which was to produce a reinforcer turned out the light behind the key and started a clock which introduced a delay period of one minute before grain was actually made available to the pigeon. If the pigeon pecked on the dark key during the delay interval, the clock reset, and the pigeon had to wait an additional minute. Pigeons emitted superstitious behavior at a great rate during the delay interval. One pigeon, for example, developed a circling response and, on one occasion, made approximately forty turns during an 80-second delay period. It is not unreasonable, at least, to suppose that the pigeon's behavior was functioning in addition to (or perhaps in spite of) conditioned reinforcement to "time" the delay interval by filling it with a highly stereotyped pattern of behavior.

It is important to recognize that superstitious behavior is rather a special case of the use of any general kind of *overt behavior* to span gaps of time between events. Though he couples the notion with conditioned reinforcement, Skinner (1938) has proposed that any *chain* of behavior can function to mediate delays between events (recall the Napalkov experiment, for example). And we are all familiar with the sometimes ritual-like things that people do when, after the occasion has been set, some outcome must be awaited. Though the example is admittedly far removed from an occasion that involves pure delay of reinforcement, conjure the image of the hospital waiting room and the pacing expectant father for a case in point.

Of course, expectant fathers can do other things besides pace to fill intervals of time. Though animals are probably left to depend upon conditioned reinforcement and superstitious behavior—or the like—to mediate spans of time between response and reinforcer, or between other events, there is no question that people have a much more powerful, comprehensive, and unique mechanism for doing the same thing. That mechanism is, of course, *language.* While organisms lower than man can mediate spans of time that are probably no longer than a few hours, even under the very best of conditions, it is clear that for people, the comparable span of time is almost limitless. People can do things for which they may have to wait years before appropriate outcomes take place. Writing books, obtaining college degrees, and contributing to pension funds are

[4] A variable-interval schedule is similar to the fixed-interval schedule we mentioned earlier, except that a response will produce reinforcement only after intervals of time have elapsed that *vary* from reinforcement to reinforcement. See Chapter 5 for further discussion of schedules of reinforcement.

obvious examples. Further discussion along these lines now would carry us into problems of verbal learning, retention, and forgetting—and into much later chapters of the book. But it is important to recognize that there is potentially a vast difference between the way lower organisms and men cope with delays of reinforcement.

THE DISTINCTION BETWEEN LEARNING AND PERFORMANCE

Common experience tells us that organisms do not always go around performing the things which they have learned just to please curious psychologists. If a rat, for example, has had some extensive practice learning a complicated maze in a highly motivated state, we might find that the rat was perfectly content to sit at the beginning of the maze if we suddenly reduced the level of motivation. But should we state, when confronted with such an uncooperative beast, that the rat has suddenly forgotten what it once knew, i.e., that learning has simply and suddenly disappeared? Or should we state that we have perhaps failed to supply the necessary conditions which are required before the rat will demonstrate in overt behavior what it really knows? Prudence suggests the latter alternative. Thus, we are led to make a distinction between *learning* (what the rat knows from its past experience) and *performance* (what the rat is willing to show us about what it knows at any particular moment in time). In short, learning must always be inferred from overt performance. But sometimes we may have good reason to believe that an organism is simply not demonstrating what it has learned because we have not chosen the proper conditions which will assure the overt display of the appropriate behavior.

Let us underline the distinction between learning and performance by looking at two areas where the distinction has been usefully applied. The first is the phenomenon of *latent learning,* while the second has to do with the effects of some of the basic reinforcement variables upon the development and maintenance of a habit.

LATENT LEARNING

The latent-learning experiments grew out of the theories of E. C. Tolman (1932, etc.). One of Tolman's principal ideas was that reinforcement—or reward—affected performance but had little or nothing to do with learning. The latent-learning experiments were designed to test this idea, and one of the earliest was made by Blodgett (1929).

Blodgett allowed one group of hungry rats to explore a maze that did not have food in the goal box. This group of rats, therefore, was not reinforced, argued Blodgett (though this argument is suspect, as we shall see). The rats in a second group explored a maze with food in the goal box, and therefore they received conventional reward training.

As you might expect, the group which was reinforced with food learned the maze in straightforward fashion, but the unreinforced rats showed little improvement. After seven days, the rats in this group were entering almost as many blind alleys as they had on the first day. At this time, however, Blodgett put food into the goal box for these rats. Their performance suddenly and dramatically improved, so that almost immediately they made as few errors as did the rats who had been reinforced throughout the experiment.

These results can be seen in Figure 2.12. They show us that the rats which did not receive the food as reinforcement were able to profit from their experience in the maze, though the results of such experience did not show up until a reward was provided. Because the learning that apparently took place during the unreinforced trials was not evident until food was introduced, the learning was said to be "latent."

Many investigators have repeated this or similar experiments (Thistlethwaite, 1951), and while most have found the same general effect that Blodgett obtained, not all have been able to do so. A careful repetition of Blodgett's study (Reynolds, 1945), for example, showed that the absence of food in the goal box does not necessarily mean the absence of *all* reinforcement, for in this repetition, animals that were not reinforced

FIG. **2.12** Number of errors during reinforced and non-reinforced trials in maze learning. When reinforcement is introduced, errors drop to a level comparable to that of animals reinforced from the beginning of training. (Data from Blodgett, 1929.)

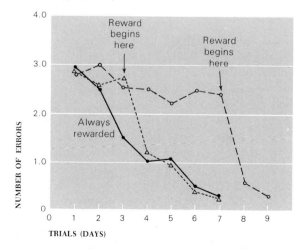

with food nevertheless showed improvement during the "latent" period, albeit less than those animals that were reinforced (see also Tolman & Honzik, 1930). Actually, as you can see in Figure 2.12, Blodgett's animals, too, improved their performance a bit as they explored the maze for seven trials without food. Nevertheless, while the phenomenon is often subtle, and while we are still uncertain about all the conditions that produce it (Kimble, 1961), there is little question that animals can learn quite complicated responses in the absence of anything that we could call primary reinforcement. The important thing, from our point of view of the moment, is that in the case of latent learning, animals clearly learn something during early nonreinforced trials that does not appear in overt performance until we supply the proper conditions—the sudden introduction of reward in this case.

AMOUNT OF REINFORCEMENT AND LEARNING VERSUS PERFORMANCE

While psychologists have assessed the relative effect of a number of basic reinforcement variables upon learning and performance, let us look at just one: the amount of reinforcement. In general, the way in which this variable has been treated is quite representative of others we could also examine (Kimble, 1961).

Two investigators (Crespi, 1942, 1944; Zeaman, 1949) did experiments which set the proper stage and indicate the general sort of question that is asked about the problem. In each, the effects of amount of reinforcement upon learning and performance were separated by (1) training different groups of rats to run a simple runway under various amounts of food reinforcement, and (2) switching the amount of reinforcement when the rats had reached a stable level of performance. The results of these initial studies are well defined, though as we shall see, the conclusions to be drawn from them must be modified in the light of results from later work.

Both Crespi and Zeaman found that the amount of reinforcement has no effect upon the *rate* with which animals approach the final level of performance, but it does affect the final level they achieve. In other words, after learning is complete, animals that have received different amounts of reinforcement do perform at different levels; but they do not learn at different rates. Thus, to return to the language of our earlier discussion of learning curves, the limit of response strength, M, is affected by the amount of reinforcement, but the rate at which this limit is reached, k, is not. The results of Crespi and Zeaman also indicate that if one trains a rat with a given amount of reinforcement and then shifts suddenly to a larger amount, the change in performance is almost instantaneous. The rat does not have to *learn* to behave in the way appropriate for the new amount of reinforcement—the shift, in this case, to a larger amount of reinforcement produces an *abrupt* increase in level of performance. If amount of reinforcement had an effect upon learning, we would expect that it might take a fairly large number of trials for the rat to adjust its behavior when shifted from one amount to another; but under the conditions of these experiments, this does not seem to be the case.

More recent work indicates, however, that under experimental conditions which are a bit different from those of Crespi and Zeaman, amount of reinforcement can be shown to have an effect upon behavior that is quite characteristic of the permanent effects we would associate with learning. Collier and Marx (1959), for example, trained three groups of rats to find and drink a drop of fluid from a mechanically driven dipper in a Skinner box. One group got a drop of a 4 percent sucrose solution, while the others got drops of 11.3 and 32 percent solutions, respectively. Then, after the animals had had an opportunity to obtain 160 reinforcements from the dipper, all groups were trained to press a lever for a reward that consisted of a drop of 11.3 percent solution. The three groups differed markedly in their performance on the lever—in spite of the fact that all were now getting a reinforcer of exactly the same amount. Furthermore, the differences showed no sign of diminishing over a 10-day period. These results indicate, it would seem, that the effects of dipper training with different concentrations of sucrose were not the momentary, fleeting sorts of effects we would expect with a variable that was simply producing an effect on the performance of the moment. Rather, as they went about learning the lever-pressing response, the rats behaved as if they had carried with them some permanent, *learned* effect of their prior experience with different amounts of reinforcement.

Why should such different conclusions be indicated by the data of Crespi and of Zeaman as compared with those of Collier and Marx? There are many possible reasons, not the least of which is that both Crespi and Zeaman used runways and a controlled-responding procedure, while Collier and Marx used a free-responding procedure where the rats were asked to transfer what they had learned about amount of reinforcement from one sort of behavior (licking from a dipper) to another sort of behavior (pressing a lever).

Hulse (1962) has suggested, too, that if a training procedure is used which leads the rat to, in a sense, "pay attention" to the reinforcer, then learning effects may occur. He conditioned rats to lick from a drinking tube for different concentrations of a saccharin solution, but not all licks were reinforced with a drop of fluid. This procedure, Hulse reasoned, ought to single out the reinforcer as a rather special stimulus, since sometimes it was there following a response, but sometimes it was not. Consequently, the rats ought to be oriented toward the reinforcing stimulus in a way they would not be if it were always there after every response (the procedure that both Crespi and Zeaman used), and perhaps a reinforcer of a particular concentration might have relatively more permanent effects on behavior. In any event, Hulse found that if rats were trained under these conditions on one concentration and were then suddenly switched to another concentration, their behavior on the new concentration seemed permanently modified by their experience on the old. If, for example, a group of rats had been trained initially on a low concentration and then was switched to a high one, rate of responding increased—but never to the level of a control group that had been reinforced on the high concentration throughout the experiment. Furthermore, the increase was not a very abrupt one.

Perhaps these experiments remind you of Schrier's (1958), in which amount of reinforcement was shown to produce differential effects upon behavior only under conditions where the animal had an opportunity to learn that amount of reinforcement was, in fact, a relevant variable in the experiment. In any event, it now seems clear that if we choose the proper conditions, a basic reinforcement variable like amount of reinforcement can be shown to produce permanent modifications of behavior which are characteristic of the particular amount of reinforcement that is used. It remains for future research to identify precisely what all the proper conditions may be, but there seems little question that we can no longer defend strongly the proposition that a variable like amount of reinforcement has an effect upon momentary performance, but no effect upon the way in which a response is learned. Nevertheless, until all the necessary information is in, a distinction between learning and performance can be quite useful and is valid for many purposes. In the next chapter, we shall see that psychologists have incorporated the distinction as an important factor in their theories of learning.

3

REINFORCEMENT AND LEARNING: SOME THEORETICAL ISSUES

Why is it that certain classes of events function as reinforcers but others do not? In the last chapter we avoided questions like this, for the most part, and worked with reinforcement as an operationally defined concept and empirically determined principle. In this chapter we shall adopt a different approach. Our task will be to see how psychologists have fitted the concept of reinforcement into their theories about the learning process and to see some of the consequences of one theoretical strategy as opposed to another. In reality, this one task quickly becomes two. On the one hand, there is the problem of identifying the logical role that is assigned the concept of reinforcement within a particular theory. On the other hand, there is the task of specifying the precise mechanism that is assumed to operate when a reinforcer strengthens new learning. The latter problem carries us from an operational, "weak" definition of reinforcement to a "strong" definition of reinforcement in which the theorist commits himself to some precise statement about *how* reinforcers work.

At the outset, it must be ruefully admitted that much work—both theoretical and experimental—needs to be done before the concept of reinforcement can be assigned its proper place in the psychology of learning. As we shall see, psychologists cannot agree if reinforcement is actually *necessary* for learning to occur, though most agree that operations of reward and punishment, in the sense in which they were discussed in the last chapter, have considerable practical utility. And the psychologists who do fit reinforcement into their theories of learning as a necessary part of a general plan often disagree about the precise form that a strong definition of reinforcement should assume. Consequently, any attempt to single out some particular theoretical approach to the problem of reinforcement as "correct" would be most misleading. So we shall not make the attempt. However, it would also be misleading to give the impression that psychologists—in spite of their disagreement about many aspects of the reinforcement problem—do not agree about other aspects. If nothing else, it is often possible to state in unequivocal terms some of the questions to which answers must be obtained; and as we shall see, there has been no hesitancy to appeal to that ultimate arbiter, experimental data, to settle questions of fact and theory.

Before we proceed to an examination of some specific approaches to the problem of reinforcement per se, we must pause and have a look at some of the things that broadly characterize one theory of learning as compared with another. Then we shall have a general framework into which we can fit precisely some of the theoretical and empirical comments that have been made about the reinforcement process. It is beyond the scope of our discussion at the present time to give detailed elaborations of the many attempts that have been made to organize the phenomena of learning into theoretical schemas.[1] But there are some basic questions to which any theory of learning should provide answers, whether or not the answers are stated in broad, general terms or in precise, mathematically defined terms. We shall look at these questions now.

WHAT IS LEARNED?

What does an organism actually acquire as a function of practice or experience in a particular learning situation? Does the organism learn an association between a stimulus and a response, for example, and should we adopt a stimulus-response or *S-R* theory of learning (Spence, 1951)? Perhaps learning is to be conceived of as a new association between one or more stimuli (a stimulus-stimulus, or *S-S* theory of learning), where the basic function of practice or experience is to provide a kind of "restructuring" of the way in which an organism perceives the world in which it lives. Or does learning, in fact, involve both *S-R* and *S-S* processes, with one process applicable at one time or in one situation, and the other applicable at other times or in other situations? More generally, should the learning process even be expressed in terms like stimulus and response, terms that have been borrowed from reflex physiology? Perhaps we should talk about learning in terms more cognitively tinged, as Tolman (1932) has done and as Miller, Galanter, and Pribram (1960) do when they introduce and define images, plans, and feedback loops and use them to build a model of behavior that leans heavily upon principles of computer programing and computer operation.

---

[1] Excellent discussions of theories of learning have been provided by Hilgard and Bower (1966), and Hill (1963). Also, the interested reader may consult Skinner (1950) for a point of view that questions, in general, the necessity for any theory of learning.

Questions such as these, and the arguments that have raged about them, have been with us for many years and will probably be with us for an indefinite number of years to come. Thus, for example, John Dewey's paper, "The Reflex Arc Concept in Psychology," and James Gibson's paper, "The Concept of the Stimulus in Psychology," which share in part a concern about the notions of stimulus and response and their use in models of behavior, are equally relevant to modern learning theory. Yet Dewey wrote in 1896, and Gibson wrote in 1960.

While the basic question of what is learned remains to be settled in the indefinite future, there is one important thing that happens if a particular stand is taken, however informally, on this problem. If we adopt the point of view, for example, that learning consists basically of strengthening an association between a stimulus and a response, we are apt to go into the laboratory with some problems in mind that are quite different from those we would choose if we thought that learning was basically a process of perceiving new relationships among stimuli. The result will be that new information will be obtained—and further problems will be raised—which might not have been generated by one approach alone. And these are necessary things for the fruitful development of any science.

IS REINFORCEMENT NECESSARY FOR LEARNING?

A problem of central importance in this chapter has to do with the role that reinforcement is assumed to play when new learning occurs. Some theorists, Hull (1943) for example, say that whatever the fundamental nature of the learning process, experience or practice in a new situation has no effect—learning will not occur—unless practice is reinforced. For a *reinforcement theory* of this sort, there exists the problem of specifying the precise mechanism by which a reinforcer does, in fact, reinforce. Does food, for example, reinforce because it stimulates certain taste receptors on the tongue as it is eaten, or because its ingestion reduces the intensity of some motive or drive like hunger? In other words, when a theorist makes a reinforcement operation a necessary integral part of the conditions under which learning occurs, he often goes on to adopt some "strong" definition of the concept of reinforcement.

Other theorists, Guthrie (1935, 1959) for example, postulate that reinforcement is not necessary for learning to occur. Generally, the only requirement is that the elements which are to constitute the new learning (whether they are stimuli, responses, or whatever) be contiguous—be closely paired or related to each other in time. Psychologists who maintain a *nonreinforcement* position of this sort must face the demonstrable fact that operations of reward and punishment are powerful tools to use in the control of behavior. So if the theorist maintains that reinforcement is not actually necessary for learning to occur, and if he satisfies himself with an operational, "weak" definition of reinforcement, we can ask what position he then assigns the concept of reinforcement in his theory.

There was a time, in the 1940s and early 1950s, when a true controversy existed regarding the relative merits of a reinforcement as opposed to a nonreinforcement approach to learning. As time has passed, however, the sharp lines of battle drawn by reinforcement theorists such as Hull (1943, 1951) and Miller and Dollard (1941) and by nonreinforcement theorists such as Guthrie (1935, 1959) have blurred. This has happened in part because of the constant flow of new information that has come from the laboratory about the processes of reinforcement and learning, and because theorists have, happily, been quick to change their positions in the face of such new evidence. Undoubtedly the "reinforcement-nonreinforcement controversy," to the extent that it is still with us at all, will continue to fade as the years go on. Keep this important fact in mind as we now examine some specific approaches to learning and reinforcement.

SOME BASIC APPROACHES TO LEARNING AND REINFORCEMENT

LEARNING BY CONTIGUITY

We owe to Aristotle the notion that two events will be associated when they occur closely together. To make this statement intelligible, as we have seen, we have to state what kinds of things become associated and under what conditions associations will occur. In learning theory, one of the most common ideas is that stimuli and responses are the associated factors, and that simple contiguity in time is all which is required for an association to occur.

According to an *S-R contiguity* view, stimuli come to elicit responses that they had not previously elicited because, perhaps quite by accident, these stimuli occur simultaneously with certain responses. The model for this process is the classically conditioned response. Here we elicit an unconditioned response by using an appropriate unconditioned stimulus at the same time that we present a conditional stimulus. Because the conditional stimulus is simultaneous with the response (or nearly so, if you remember the discussion in Chapter 2 on time relations in conditioning), it comes—through association—to elicit the response.

An *S-R* contiguity theory can be applied directly to classically conditioned responses. It also applies to instrumentally conditioned responses, even though we cannot always produce, or control experimentally, stimuli that are properly related in time with the response to be conditioned. Let us see how a contiguity theory says the process occurs.

One of the early advocates of an *S-R* contiguity theory of learning was E. R. Guthrie, who had this to say about the learning process: "A combination of stimuli which has accompanied a movement will on its recurrence tend to be followed by that movement" (Guthrie, 1935, 1952). Later, Guthrie (1959) modified his position a bit to require that an organism be "paying attention" to a particular combination of stimuli before learning occurs by contiguity, and he spends some time wrestling with the problem of defining the concept "paying attention," but the essence of his approach remains essentially the same. For Guthrie, the classically conditioned response is the model for all learning processes.

In most cases of instrumental conditioning, however, we cannot observe conditional stimuli (remember, for example, our discussion of the rat pressing the lever in the Skinner box); and so in Guthrie's theory they take on the character of hypothetical constructs. That is to say, we invent some conditional stimuli for a particular set of learned responses. In the case of lever pressing, some of the conditional stimuli are presumed to be kinesthetic, according to Guthrie. In other words, the rat makes a series of movements, these stimulate the sense organs of the muscles, and this combination of muscular sensations serves as one primary source of conditional stimuli. Another important source of conditional stimuli, again chiefly internal, comes from sensations associated with a particular condition of motivation such as hunger or thirst; these are called *maintaining stimuli*. Maintaining stimuli have the important characteristic that they remain relatively constant throughout the learning of a long sequence of responses such as that required to traverse a maze or to run off a long chain of behavior. This, as we shall see, turns out to be a useful construct to have at hand when the role of reinforcement in *S-R* contiguity theory must be specified.

Thus, according to *S-R* contiguity theory, the distinction between classical and instrumental conditioning becomes purely a matter of convenience. Guthrie believes that this distinction may even be a bit pernicious, since it tends to make us accept instrumental behavior as purely "spontaneous" and prevents us from looking for stimuli which might cause the behavior.

Strangely enough, however, the only major experimental study with which Guthrie's name is associated is on instrumental conditioning. Guthrie is dissatisfied with the typical experiment on instrumental behavior because, he claims, it examines the *results* of behavior, not the behavior itself. Take the lever-pressing case, for example. In the Skinner box we find out how many times per minute the rat presses the lever; ordinarily we are not interested in the *way* in which the lever is pressed by the animal. Guthrie objects to this approach, for he believes that it is the association of particular *movements* of the animal with stimuli that is really important and that the *result* of the movements is only secondary. Consequently, in an experimental situation, Guthrie and Horton (1946) studied the way in which cats learned to escape from a puzzle box. Instead of merely recording the time it took the cats to escape or the number of times they got out of the box, Guthrie and Horton took motion pictures of the cats in action. One of the things that impressed them was the degree of behavioral stereotypy. In many cases, the cats' movements were almost identical from trial to trial. This indicated to Guthrie that there was a close association between the cues and the movements involved.

One of the implications of Guthrie's notion of association of stimulus and response through contiguous exposure is that it takes only one pairing for conditioning to occur. This seems to go against everything we have said so far, since curves show that learning is a gradual process (recall from the last chapter the functional relation between number of practice trials and response strength, for example). Guthrie has a good answer for this: An ordinary instrumental act (such as lever pressing or escaping from a puzzle box) involves many different movements. Thus, it may take many trials for the animal to perfect a *pattern* of movements that is eventually successful in performing the act in question. Most behavior involves the association of many stimulus-response units. We are constantly learning and unlearning these associations, so that there is a continuous fluctuation in our behavior. Therefore, it takes time to perfect a series of movements that accomplish a particular result.

STATISTICAL LEARNING THEORY. Guthrie's initial statements about the learning process have led to the development of some important theories of learning which have in common the property of describing the learning process by means of *models* based on the mathematics of *variability* or *randomness*. One of these, a theory that stems in basic format quite directly from Guthrie's parent theory of learning by contiguity, is that of Estes (Estes, 1950, 1959, 1964a; Estes & Burke, 1953).

The basic notion behind any statistical theory is that the events one measures in the laboratory are the result of the influence of a whole population of elementary random events. These are events which cannot be predicted if they are taken one by one; a good example is the unbiased toss of a coin. If we toss a penny enough times, it will come out heads about 50 percent of the time and tails about 50 percent of the time. We can think of the percentage of heads as the "result" measured in the laboratory and each individual toss of the coin as one of the elementary events that goes to make up the result. In statistical learning theory, the basic strategy is to state postulates about the distribution of elementary random events and to predict measurable results from a mathematical development of these postulates.

In one form of his theory (Estes, 1950, 1959; Estes & Burke, 1953), Estes assumed that on any given trial the response that is to be learned is conditioned to a *sample* of all possible stimulus elements that could impinge upon the organism over a number of successive trials. We can think of the sample as a group of stimulus elements that manage to get through the sensory input of the organism at the time a particular response occurs. Like Guthrie, Estes assumed that learning is an all-or-none affair, in the sense that the response which occurs on any given trial is conditioned completely to all the stimulus elements present on that particular trial. According to this form of the theory, the reason why learning curves increase gradually and irregularly in practice is that different sets of stimulus elements will be sampled from trial to trial. The elements in the sample will overlap to some extent, so that after an initial trial, some of the stimulus elements will already be conditioned. Others will not, but these become conditioned on the next and succeeding trials. We can see that if the total population of stimulus elements were a limited one, eventually so many elements would be conditioned that none would be left to condition. Thus, conditioning approaches a limit of 100 percent. An intuitive idea of how learning cumulates according to this theory can be derived from Figure 3.1.

One especially characteristic feature of this *stimulus sampling model* of Estes, as well as of other similar statistical models (e.g., Bush & Mosteller, 1955), is that, while a response is completely conditioned to a stimulus *sample* in one trial, additional trials add by bits and pieces to the strength of a relation between the response and the total population of stimuli. In other words, learning progresses by relatively small *increments*. Evidence has accumulated, however, which shows that for certain kinds of learning tasks, at least, the strength of such a learned relation can go from some low, perhaps chance, level to its maximum after just *one* trial (Estes, 1964a; Estes, Hopkins, & Crothers, 1960; Bower, 1961). The same data show that if this does not happen—that is, if a subject does

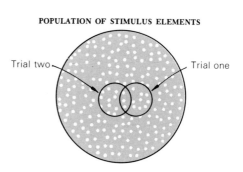

FIG. 3.1 An illustration of two successive trials according to one form of statistical learning theory. Each dot represents one of the "elements" of the learned act. The dots enclosed by trial 1 are present and hence conditioned on the first trial. The dots enclosed by trial 2 are present on the second trial. Notice that some of these dots represent elements which are already conditioned, so that the second trial adds fewer elements to the strength of conditioning.

POPULATION OF STIMULUS ELEMENTS

Trial two

Trial one

not demonstrate complete learning in a single trial—the probability that he will make a correct response on the next trial remains at the initial chance level. Thus, learning is once again an all-or-none affair, though in a somewhat different sense; the subject either learns completely on a trial or he does not learn at all. In effect, the subject behaves as if he were associating a response with *one* stimulus element instead of sampling sets of different stimulus elements from trial to trial.

Let us look at some further reasoning (Estes, 1964a) to see in better detail how the process is presumed to work. Suppose we choose a task that involves the learning of *paired associates*. With a task of this sort, subjects are first presented with a pair of items—two English words like BALL-HOUSE, for example. The subjects are asked to associate the two so that on a subsequent test, they will be able to give the response word HOUSE when the stimulus word BALL is shown to them by itself. A typical experiment will use a list of paired items so that the subject has a number of stimulus items and a number of response items which he must learn to associate in proper fashion. Let us suppose that, in addition to the response word HOUSE in our example, the subject has three other response words from which he might select when he is given the stimulus word BALL. In this case the probability *by chance alone* of making the correct response, HOUSE, will be 0.25. Assume further, however, that there is some fixed probability, say 0.50, that the subject will *learn* the correct association on a given trial; if he does, the probability that he will give the correct response shifts from the initial chance level of 0.25 to a probability of 1.0. For several subjects, the process is like that diagrammed in Figure 3.2.

You can see from the example shown in the figure that different subjects learn the correct response on different trials; this happens because the probability is only 0.5 that any given subject will learn on any

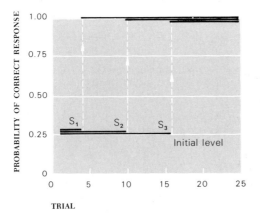

FIG. 3.2 Learning "curves" for individual subjects according to a one-element learning model. For each subject (S_1, S_2, or S_3) the probability of a correct response goes from a chance level to 1.0 in just one trial, but this happens on different trials for different subjects. (Estes, 1964a.)

given trial. Note also that if a subject *learns* on a given trial, the probability of a correct response on all subsequent trials remains at 1.0. However, if a subject does *not* learn on a given trial, it is assumed that the probability of his giving a correct response on the next trial remains at the chance level, i.e., it remains at 0.25. Thus, with respect to individual subjects, learning is truly an *all-or-none* and *not* an incremental affair; a subject either learns completely or not at all on a given trial. But what happens if the data from a *group* of subjects are *pooled* so that the probability of a correct response on a given trial is averaged across a number of subjects? The result is shown in Figure 3.3.

The horizontal dashed line labeled $P(C_{n+1}|N_n)$ is to be read "the probability that subjects will be correct on trial $n + 1$, given that they were *not* correct on trial n." This value, 0.25, corresponds to the value we would expect for subjects who had *not* learned but who were simply correct now and then by chance guessing. As trials progress, however, more and more subjects will learn, that is, their probabilities of being correct will jump on a given trial from 0.25 to 1.0 and stay there. As we have seen, the probability that this will happen on a given trial for a given subject is 0.50. The net effect is that the proportion of subjects who have learned, as compared with those who have not, will increase steadily as number of trials increases. This fact is reflected in the solid curve in Figure 3.3 which gives the mean proportion of correct responses per trial. It is quite apparent that this curve has the same characteristics as other

FIG. **3.3** A learning function based on data *pooled* across a number of subjects according to a one-element learning model. As trials progress, the proportion of subjects who have learned as compared with those who have not changes so that the overall probability of a correct response increases. For those subjects who have not learned, the probability of a correct response remains at the chance level. (Adapted from Estes, 1964a.)

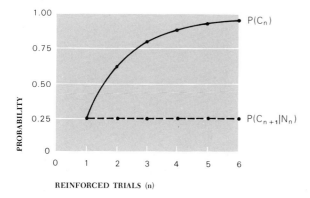

learning curves we have examined. It is important to remember, however, that it has been generated by pooling data from a *group* of subjects, a group composed of some subjects who have learned completely, and some who have not learned at all—a process which is quite different from that used to produce learning curves we have seen earlier.

THE ROLE OF REINFORCEMENT IN LEARNING BY CONTIGUITY.   By now it may be obvious that in an *S-R* contiguity theory, reinforcement does not have to occur in order for particular stimulus and response events to become associated; mere contiguity can bring that about. In Guthrie's parent theory, for example, reinforcement operations are assigned two rather simple mechanical functions. First and foremost, a reinforcing stimulus provides an end to the particular sequence of stimuli and responses that the experimenter wants the organism to learn. Reward serves to prevent the organism from unlearning what it has already learned by keeping it from reacting in other ways to the stimuli that lead to the desired response pattern. Food at the end of a maze for a hungry rat, for example, keeps the rat there instead of allowing it to wander through the maze unlearning proper turns and learning new turns into blind alleys. Thus, the rat eventually does learn the maze.

Second, the *consummatory behavior* that a particular reward evokes will be associated through contiguity with the *maintaining stimuli* characteristic of the motivational state of the organism. If food is used for a reward, for example, and an animal is hungry, it is almost certain that the animal will seize, chew, and swallow the food once it has been discovered in the goal box of a maze. This consummatory activity will be associated with the maintaining stimuli characteristic of hunger, such as internal stimulation arising from stomach contractions. Now, maintaining stimuli are present when the animal is at the *beginning* as well as at the end of the maze. So once an association has been learned between a pattern of maintaining stimuli and the responses elicited by the reinforcing stimulus—and this association, too, should be learned in one trial—a mechanism is available by which the animal, theoretically, can "anticipate" the reward before the goal box is entered. As Guthrie (1935) puts it: "When the rat runs the maze he is ready for whatever reward has been received in the past."

Estes' thoughts concerning reinforcement are, very generally, much the same as those of Guthrie. For Estes (1959), reinforcers constitute a class of stimulus events which are merely another part of the general pattern of stimuli to which an organism responds when learning occurs. Thus, they are ultimately like any other set of stimuli in a learning situation. To the extent that they tend (perhaps innately) to evoke approach movements, they might increase the probability that a stimulus pattern of which they are a part will be sampled. Also, Estes—like Guthrie—states that reinforcers may function to mark the end of a particular stimulus-response sequence and preserve it as a unit. That is, reinforcing events may protect a newly formed association from the interference that might occur if the organism were left to associate additional, perhaps wrong or incompatible, responses with a particular stimulus pattern. However, while Estes has speculated in this fashion about the basic underpinnings of the reinforcement process, he has avoided any theoretical commitment to a specific, precisely defined mechanism of reinforcement. He notes, for example, that experimental operations as different as giving rewards, removing noxious stimuli, and saying the word "correct" can all function in one experimental situation or another to change behavior in the manner we demand when we wish to apply the term reinforcement. For this reason, Estes opts for a weak definition of the concept of reinforcement—for the time being, at least.

COGNITIVE OR SIGN LEARNING

Let us now look at a second general theory of learning, an approach closely associated with the name of E. C. Tolman. Tolman (1932, 1951, 1959) developed and expanded what he called a "purposive" theory of learning. His theory deemphasizes classical conditioning as the prime model for the learning process and replaces that model with what he calls "sign learning." This means that animals usually learn (when running a maze, for example) the succession of stimuli or "signs" that lead to or "signify" the goal. In contrast to Guthrie's approach, Tolman's theory stresses the notion that organisms learn relations among *stimuli* rather than relations among stimuli and responses per se. In a characteristically epigrammatical phrase, Tolman (1948) says that rats develop "cognitive maps" of the maze.

One of the chief characteristics of Tolman's theory is that it was subject to frequent change. Throughout a metamorphosis that lasted twenty years or so, however, Tolman consistently emphasized the importance of *purpose* in the learning of new behavior. Learned behavior is always directed and oriented toward some end, some *goal*.

In his last statement (Tolman, 1959), the chief learning construct for Tolman was the *means-end-readiness*. One form of a means-end-readiness can be diagrammed $S_1R_1 \rightarrow S_2$. This says that if an organism is exposed to a stimulus pattern, S_1, it acquires a "belief" that the performance of some behavior, R_1, will lead to a second stimulus pattern, S_2. The S_2 stimulus pattern can be a pattern characteristic of the next choice point in a maze, for example, or it can be a pattern characteristic of a goal object such as food. A second form of a means-end-readiness can be diagrammed $S_1 \rightarrow S_2$. This signifies that an organism learns that the presence of one stimulus pattern, S_1, will be accompanied or followed shortly by the occurrence of a second stimulus pattern, S_2. This type of means-end-readiness is reserved for events associated with classical conditioning and conditioned reinforcement, for example, where learning is presumed to be an essentially pure association between stimuli. Both types of means-end-readiness increase in strength as a function of practice. That is, for example, the more frequently an organism experiences an $S_1 \rightarrow S_2$ sequence, the stronger the "belief" that S_1 will be followed by S_2. To summarize in Tolman's words: "Means-end-readinesses are to be thought of as acquired cognitive dispositions resulting directly from previous trials or from other, related, previous training."

A second important construct in Tolman's theory is that of *expectancy*. While a means-end-readiness is a general sort of "belief" acquired over a relatively long past history of an organism, an expectancy is a state aroused when a means-end-readiness is evoked on a particular single occasion. Again in Tolman's words: "When an *instance* of an S_1 is presented, there tends to be released an expectancy that an instance of the kind of performance symbolized by R_1 will lead to an instance of S_2 (or else simply that the presentation of an instance of S_1 will by itself lead to, or be accompanied by, an instance of S_2)." For example, when a rat is placed in the start box of a runway on, say, the 24th learning trial, the stimuli of the start box arouse an expectancy that a particular goal object such as food can be obtained in the goal box if the rat runs the runway. The expectancy elicited on trial 24 is due, however, to the fact that the rat has been placed in the start box on 23 preceding trials. From this previous experience, the rat has developed a means-end-readiness that start-box stimuli, followed by running the runway, will lead to food.

Two other things which distinguish Tolman's approach are his notions concerning the concepts of stimulus and response. Both are quite different from, say, Guthrie's. For Tolman, a stimulus is a *perception;* it is an environmental event that is *processed* by the organism and thus colored by the organism's past history. For example, the way in which an animal perceives the lights and sounds of the start box of a maze depends upon what has happened in the start box before, what has happened as the rat has run the maze on other occasions, what has happened previously in the goal box, and so on. Similarly, Tolman does not think of a response as a collection of muscle twitches or glandular secretions, the general approach Guthrie adopted. Rather, learned behavior is composed of *performances*. Performances are classes of behavior that are defined in terms of some end result or goal; they are "patterns of organism-environment rearrangements." Tolman notes, for example, that rats in a Skinner box adopt all sorts of methods of pressing the lever, sometimes using their noses, sometimes their paws, and so on. For him, these are all the same performances because they all accomplish the same end result.[2] For Guthrie, however, they represent different responses because they involve different patterns of motor movements, each associated with its own unique set of conditional stimuli.

SIGN LEARNING AND REINFORCEMENT. For Tolman, as we have seen, learning lies in the development of means-end-readinesses. Tolman's approach, strictly speaking, does not require that practice be reinforced for the means-end-readiness to develop; nor does Tolman advocate some particular strong definition of the concept of reinforcement. Yet he does attempt to account for the fact that positive and negative reinforcing stimuli (in their operational sense) have powerful effects upon behavior. This he does through the concepts of *value* and *valence*.

If a motive such as hunger is induced by depriving an animal of food, then food as a goal object has positive *value* for the animal in the sense that it is needed to repair internal deficits produced by starvation. Whether food, in fact, does have positive value for a particular animal could be determined objectively by finding out if the animal will eat food when given the opportunity, or, more generally, by finding out if the animal will repeat behavior that leads to food. In addition to their value, however, goal objects also have a *valence*. Valence, in Tolman's terms, reflects the "goodness" or "badness" of the particular goal object that the animal expects to find at the end of a maze on some particular occasion. If a hungry animal has been rewarded on a number of past occasions with positively valued food, for example, the animal expects something of the particular "goodness" associated with food to be in the goal box when it begins to run the maze on a new occasion. This expectancy constitutes the valence of the goal object of food on that particular trial.

At first glance, the concept of valence, and the distinction between value and valence, may seem somewhat peculiar. But Tolman has a particular class of facts in mind when he uses these terms. It so happens (Tinklepaugh, 1928; Cowles & Nissen, 1937) that if an animal is trained to do something with one kind of reward, and a different, perhaps less preferred, reward is substituted (unknown to the animal) on some particular learning trial, behavior toward the goal object can be markedly disrupted when the animal discovers the substitution. Tinklepaugh (1928), for example, trained monkeys on a simple discrimination problem, using bananas as a reward. Then he substituted a piece of lettuce, a less preferred food, for the bananas. On the trial in which the switch occurred, the monkeys would have nothing to do with the lettuce and appeared to be "searching" for the missing bananas. Tolman takes this *dis-*

---

[2] Skinner (1935) discusses a similar approach.

ruption of behavior as evidence that the monkeys were expecting a goal object with the particular positive valence associated with bananas. This happened in spite of the fact that both bananas and lettuce have positive value; each can function to restore or maintain a proper physiological state of affairs.

OTHER COMMENTS. It is almost impossible to give the true flavor of Tolman's approach in a few paragraphs. In some respects, his injection into learning theory of so many cognitively tinged constructs—loaded with surplus meaning—and his predilection for stringing together with hyphens the words which label the constructs (viz., sign-gestalt-expectation, means-end-readiness) casts, for some, a bothersome aura about his point of view. Besides, as Hill (1963) notes, Tolman consistently wrote with a chuckle lurking somewhere in the background, always called his theory programmatic, and was ready to shift a point of view at a moment's notice. Tolman's concern with seemingly loose concepts like "cognitive maps" has also bothered many psychologists. With good humor, but with some exasperation, Guthrie once accused Tolman of leaving his rats "buried in thought" at the choice point of a maze. Yet despite the whimsical tone of much of what he wrote, Tolman knew what he was up to. There is little doubt that he deliberately named constructs as he did in order to emphasize his cognitive, purposive approach to learning and to set this approach apart from the more mechanistic positions of theorists such as Guthrie.

EFFECT OR REINFORCEMENT THEORY

We have just had a broad look at two general approaches to learning which say that, in fine, reinforcement is unnecessary for learning to occur. Let us know look at a different kind of theory. This position, broadly conceived, is closely associated with the names of Thorndike (1898), Hull (1943, 1952), and Miller (1959). While these psychologists have developed accounts of the learning process which differ considerably in matters of detail, sometimes important detail, they have all assumed somewhere in their theories that learning cannot occur at all unless behavior is *reinforced* during the learning process. Simple contiguity between stimulus and response, for example, is not enough. In general, there must also be some consequence or *effect* of the new behavior before new learning will occur, a reinforcement operation in particular.

As we have noted before, once a theorist takes the initial step of adopting an effect, or reinforcement, approach to learning, he is generally impelled to take the additional step of specifying some underlying mechanism by which reinforcers do, in fact, reinforce. This leads to a number of related questions. Why, for example, do some stimuli function very

well as reinforcers while others do not? Why, too, do some stimuli function as reinforcers for certain species, but not for other species? For example, it is fairly clear that there are only a limited number of stimuli that
are reinforcing for every animal. Animal trainers know this, of course, and
they are careful to reward the behavior they want to teach their animals
with the proper reinforcement. If we are teaching tricks to dogs, a simple
pat on the head will reinforce a great deal of the time, though food is
probably better. With the domestic cat, a pat on the head is usually not
enough, and often food does not work either. Indeed, it is possible that
the difficulty people have in teaching cats as compared with dogs may be
due in part to the fact that cats are sensitive to a far more limited class
of reinforcing stimuli.

THE ORIGINS OF EFFECT THEORY.   The origins of modern effect
theory and of many of our notions about the things characteristic of
stimuli that reinforce probably come from Darwin and the theory of
natural selection. Darwin and his successors tried to explain the process
of species evolution in terms of natural selective breeding. The adaptive
characteristics of organisms survive, said Darwin, and the unadaptive
ones die out. Naturalists have pointed out many examples of anatomical
and physiological characteristics that are adaptive and that seem to be
perpetuated through selective breeding. Thus, in evolution, biological
changes in organisms have "good" and "bad" effects, and, according to
the theory of natural selection, only the changes with "good" effects
survive.

It was apparent to many early workers in evolution that behavioral patterns also provide good examples of the survival of adaptive
mechanisms. Furthermore, in the lifetime of an individual of a species
there appears to be a process of selective adaptation. Organisms seem to
learn those things which are useful—they learn the location of food supplies, water, hiding places, and so forth.

Thus, the argument goes, adaptive behavior (that which preserves the animal from harm and keeps it fed and sheltered) survives and
becomes learned, but unadaptive behavior does not. This concept was
combined with the hedonistic ideas of utilitarianism. Pleasure, it was
held, is associated with adaptive behavior and pain with nonadaptive
behavior. Thus pleasure and pain were brought into an adaptive theory.
These notions—a behavioral hedonism combined with the survival of
adaptive traits—have had an enormous influence on the theory of learning
and behavior. It is hard to find theorists who deny that reinforcing
stimuli are connected with adaptive mechanisms in the animal—though,
as we have indicated already, theorists often disagree about the exact
nature of the relationship.

THORNDIKE AND HULL. E. L. Thorndike (1898, 1911) was one of the first experimental psychologists to explore the relation between reinforcement and adaptive mechanisms, and it is to him that we owe the term *principle of effect*. Thorndike had worked with animals and their ways of learning for many years and was struck by the extent to which a particular bit of behavior was shaped and fixated by its effects or consequences. His principle of effect states, in general, that behavior is *stamped in,* or increased in strength, when it is followed by a "satisfying state of affairs" (reward). Correspondingly, behavior is weakened when it is followed by an "annoying state of affairs" (punishment). As Hilgard (1956) notes, Thorndike defines "satisfiers" and "annoyers" in terms that we would consider today to be quite operational. Thus, a satisfying state of affairs was "one which the animal does nothing to avoid, often doing things which maintain or renew it," while an annoying state of affairs was "one which the animal does nothing to preserve, often doing things which put an end to it."

Later, Thorndike modified his principle of effect somewhat by altering the role assigned to punishment. Some experiments had led him to believe that annoyers sometimes did not *weaken* a learned connection, though they did tend to make behavior more variable in the situation in which the punishment was given. Consequently, he deemphasized the importance of punishment as a variable in the process of changing learned associations. As we shall see in Chapter 7, however, not all psychologists would agree today that Thorndike was right in relegating punishment to a place of less importance than that assigned to reward. There is still considerable controversy over the relative merits of reward and punishment in the learning of new associations.

Thorndike's work was of tremendous significance in providing a bridge between Darwin's theories of natural selection and adaptive behavior and the young experimental psychology of learning. He was also the first to identify many concepts—not only reinforcement, but many others —which appear as major components of present-day psychologies of learning. It remained for Clark L. Hull (1943, 1951, 1952), however, to take a Darwinian-Thorndikian approach and turn it into a truly systematic and elegant theory of learning.

Hull's approach to science in general, and to the science of psychology in particular, was Newtonian. The learning process was to be described by means of postulates and corollaries, and the business of the experimental psychology of learning was to arrive at testable hypotheses about behavior by a process of logical *deduction* from the postulates and corollaries. If hypotheses turned out to be in error when put to experimental test, then the elements of the theory were to be changed accordingly. A second general characteristic of Hull's approach was that the relationships among the elements which composed the system were expressed in quantitative mathematical terms. To see examples of this characteristic, let us look at Hull's constructs of *habit strength* and *reaction potential.*

HABIT STRENGTH $(_sH_r)$. For Hull, the elements that combined during learning to form new associations were stimuli and responses. A stimulus was "physical energy falling on a receptor" (light, sound, and so forth), while a response was an "effector mechanism" (muscular movements, glandular secretions, and the like). Hull (1952, postulate 4) said that $_sH_r$, *the tendency for a particular stimulus to evoke a particular response,* increased in strength as a function of the number of times that the stimulus and response occurred together, *so long as each pairing of the stimulus and response was reinforced.* Hull said further that habit strength was related to number of reinforced trials according to the mathematical expression, $_sH_r = 1 - 10^{-.03N}$, where N is number of reinforced trials and 0.03 is an empirically determined constant. This expression was determined by fitting a curve to some data obtained by Williams (1938) and Perin (1942). In these experiments, the investigators measured the total number of nonreinforced lever presses rats would emit (experimental extinction) after they had been reinforced for different numbers of training trials. As you might expect, the greater the number of reinforced responses during training, the more lever presses that were emitted during extinction, and as you can see, the equation of $_sH_r$ is of the general form that we described in Chapter 2 in our discussion of learning curves. Initial increments to $_sH_r$ are large during early reinforced practice, but they become progressively smaller as training proceeds.

Habit strength is the sole learning construct in Hull's system. His definition of $_sH_r$ is his single statement regarding the things that combine to form new learning and the conditions under which such learning occurs. Note that Hull does not differentiate between classical and instrumental conditioning in his postulate; he presumes that the laws of learning for these two sets of experimental operations are basically the same. And finally, Hull's definition of habit strength places him squarely in the camp of learning theorists who hold an *S-R* reinforcement point of view.

REACTION POTENTIAL $(_sE_r)$. The output variable in Hull's system is specifically defined; it is reaction potential, $_sE_r$. This is an intervening variable which is presumed to be correlated directly with measures of response strength such as reaction latency or amplitude of response. The magnitude of reaction potential is determined by a number of variables, but chief among these are habit strength and *drive, D.* Drives, at least primary drives like hunger and thirst, are intervening variables tied to the length of time that an organism has been deprived of food and water. The greater the time of deprivation, the greater the strength of D—to the point, at least, where the organism weakens through starvation or dehydration. Hull assumed that reaction potential is related to habit strength and to drive according to the function $_sE_r = {_sH_r} \times D$. What this says, in effect, is that habits are displayed in overt behavior with measurable response strength when they are activated by drives.

Note that the relationship between $_sH_r$ and D is assumed to be multiplicative: the magnitude of reaction potential is determined by strength of habit *times* strength of drive. This assumption is quite useful because it means that reaction potential will be greater than 0 only under those conditions where *both* habit strength and drive are greater than 0. Thus, for example, $_sH_r$ for a particular response system might be quite high, say 0.80 on an arbitrary scale ranging from 0 to 1.00. But if D were 0, reaction potential would also be 0, since $_sE_r = {_sH_r} \times D = 0.80 \times 0 = 0$. In terms of our familiar Skinner box example, a hungry rat may have been trained so that it has emitted a great many food-reinforced lever presses; this means that the magnitude of $_sH_r$ is great. But if the experimenter satiates the rat with food, the rat fails to press the lever—not because the strength of the habit has become weaker, but because, on that particular occasion, the rat is not motivated to do so.

For simplicity, we have chosen to introduce the concept of $_sE_r$ in terms of only two of its components, $_sH_r$ and D. In its complete form, reaction potential is given by the expression $_sE_r = {_sH_r} \times D \times V \times K$, where V (stimulus-intensity dynamism) and K (incentive motivation) are intervening variables tied with mathematical functions, respectively, to the intensity of the stimulus that evokes a reaction and to the amount of reinforcement that is used. In Hull's system, V and K are like D in that they are performance variables which have their effects directly on reaction potential. As you can see from the equation, they multiply with $_sH_r$ to produce the response latency or response amplitude that the experimenter will measure when a stimulus evokes a response on some particular occasion. The V and K variables are also like D in that they do not affect the strength of the associative factor, $_sH_r$. For example, if K is relatively large, $_sE_r$ will be great, and the response strength measured by the experimenter will also be great. But this does not mean that $_sH_r$ is growing any faster than it would if K were small (so long, of course, as K is not actually 0, in which case responses would not be reinforced at all). The magnitude of $_sH_r$, as we have seen before, depends only upon N, the *number* of reinforced learning trials.

REINFORCEMENT IN HULL'S SYSTEM. Earlier, we noted that Hull's postulate concerning the development of habit strength specified reinforcement to be necessary for learning. Given that the origin of much of Hull's thinking was rooted in a functional Darwinian approach to behavior, it is not hard to guess the basic nature of the reinforcement mechanism upon which he settled. Hull said first about this matter that primary reinforcement consisted of the reduction of physiological needs or drives of the organism. Later, he amended this statement somewhat (for reasons we shall discuss shortly), so that primary reinforcement consisted of the *rapid reduction or diminution of motivational stimuli, S_D,* a definition that we have paraphrased slightly from Hull (1952).

It is interesting to note that in spite of this definition, Hull's theory would stand just as well in a formal, logical sense if the notion that reinforcement is necessary for learning were dropped altogether. Thus, for example, we have seen that Hull postulated $_sE_r$ to be equal to the product of $_sH_r$ and D. Though Hull assumed and made part of his postulate regarding the development of $_sH_r$ that $_sH_r$ would not increase in magnitude unless practice trials, N, were reinforced, the relationship between $_sE_r$, $_sH_r$, and D need not be changed a bit if the reinforcement assumption were eliminated completely. As a matter of fact, Spence (1956) has offered a theory that does precisely this. Spence postulates for instrumental learning a relationship between habit strength, drive, and reaction potential that is identical to Hull's (in basic format, at least), but goes on to add the proposition that the magnitude of habit strength is a function simply of the number of times that a stimulus evokes the response in question. And Spence states specifically that reinforcement is not necessary in the process. As you can see, a Hullian sort of approach is, in the final analysis, by no means distantly removed from a simple contiguity theory of learning.

While it is all very well to say that the formal structure of Hull's system does not require that behavior be reinforced for learning to occur, we must not forget that Hull did, after all, state in his postulate regarding $_sH_r$ that reinforcement was necessary for $_sH_r$ to develop. So keep this in mind as we turn now to a closer look at some theories of reinforcement.

CONDITIONS FOR SIMPLE REINFORCEMENT

In this section, we shall look in some detail at two general attempts to specify the necessary and sufficient conditions for reinforcement. In doing this, we leave a weak, empirical definition of reinforcement (which all psychologists accept) and move on to strong, theoretical definitions of reinforcement and the attempts that have been made to assess the relative ability of one theory as opposed to another to handle the facts that come from experimentation. First, we shall examine the drive-reduction approach initiated by Hull and see how psychologists have attempted to buffer this general theory with experimental data. Next, we shall look at systems that emphasize the *incentive,* or drive-*inducing* properties of reinforcing stimuli. In all cases, we shall be dealing with situations in which psychologists have attempted to reduce the reinforcement process to its most basic terms, and we shall have frequent occasion to call upon our old friend, the laboratory rat, for experimental facts. As you will see, the reinforcement process, even in its most elementary form, is by no means simple. Though we know much, we are a long way from fully understanding it.

DRIVE REDUCTION AND REINFORCEMENT

The drive-reduction theory of reinforcement states, in its most general form, that reinforcers are always related to specific motives in animals and men. Events which reinforce are always those which reduce organic needs. The needs themselves are produced initially by operations such as food or water deprivation, or by the onset of painful stimuli like electric shock. Thus, food is reinforcing for a hungry animal, just as water is reinforcing for a thirsty one, and organisms tend to do things that will reduce the intensity of painful stimuli—or that will remove them altogether.

NEED, DRIVE, AND DRIVE STIMULUS.   When an animal is deprived of some substance such as food for a period of time, there are a number of things about the animal that change. Various kinds of tissue deficiencies arise, changes in the endocrine system occur, and the pattern of neural activity in certain areas of the hypothalamus is altered (Teitelbaum & Epstein, 1962; Morgan, 1965). These changes, resulting from lack of food, constitute a physiological condition that we call a *need.* Hull presumed that needs tend to induce a generalized state of tension (measurable by an increase in general activity, for example), and in the case of needs established by food deprivation, lead to food-seeking behavior. According to a simple need-reduction point of view, responses which eventually lead to food and to eating will be reinforced and thus learned, because the ingestion of food reduces or eliminates the need state. And here is the germ of the problem that led Hull and others to modify the notion of simple *need* reduction as the necessary condition for reinforcement.

The problem is this: It takes *time* for food, once it has been eaten, to be digested and thus to begin returning the internal environment toward its normal "need-free" state. From what you know about delay of reinforcement, you can see that this would place serious strain on a theory that postulated the reduction of actual physiological *needs* as the essential reinforcement mechanism. It is problematical, for example, if a rat would ever learn to press a lever for a food reward if the response were not actually reinforced until sufficient time had elapsed for the food to be digested in the rat's stomach.

For Hull (1943), the way out of this dilemma was to introduce the concepts of *drive, D,* and *drive stimulus, S_D.* Drives, as we have seen earlier in this chapter, are intervening variables tied to operations like food or water deprivation, or to the administration of a painful stimulus like electric shock. Thus, drives tend to be *correlated* with operations that produce physiological needs, though strictly speaking, they are defined in terms like the amount of time that an organism has been without food or the intensity, in physical units, of an electric shock. Hull assumed further that a particular need state had associated with it a characteristic stimulus quality, that is, a characteristic pattern of *drive stimuli.* In the case of hunger, for example, food deprivation would produce an increase in the frequency and intensity of stomach contractions. These could, theoretically, provide an organism with an internal pattern of stimuli unique to the hunger drive produced by lack of food. Furthermore, the intensity of the internal stimuli would vary with the length of time the organism had been without food.[3]

With the hypothetical construct of drive stimulus at hand, Hull had little trouble handling the problem of delay of reinforcement raised by a pure need-reduction approach to reinforcement. Thus, to return to our example of the rat learning to press a lever, the ingestion of a pellet of food following a lever press could reduce the intensity of the drive stimuli associated with food deprivation in rapid fashion—compared, at least, with the amount of time that would have to elapse before the physiological need itself could be repaired. So food pellets as *drive-stimulus-reducing* objects could have their effects well within the limits imposed by delays of reinforcement. In short, though food pellets will eventually repair needs, it is their property of producing quick reductions in the intensity of drive stimuli that give them their power to reinforce.

Hull was never very consistent in his use of the concepts of need reduction, drive reduction, and drive-stimulus reduction, as Kimble (1961, pp. 239f) has pointed out. Nor did Hull himself ever embark on any extensive experimental analysis of basic mechanisms of reinforcement. A broad experimental program cast in drive-reduction terms has, however, been undertaken by Neal Miller (Miller & Dollard, 1941; Miller, 1951, 1959).

---

[3] Hull's concept of drive stimulus implies that different drives have different patterns of stimuli associated with them, and, therefore, that organisms ought to be able to discriminate among the drive stimuli characteristic, say, of hunger as compared with thirst. Bolles and Petrinovich (1954), among others, have shown that this in fact is true. With other stimulus conditions constant, rats could learn to do one thing when hungry and another thing when thirsty.

For Miller (1941), a drive can be produced by *any* stimulus if it is made strong enough to "impel action." Thus, food deprivation produces hunger drive because it arouses strong internal stimuli and, presumably, initiates food-seeking behavior. Strong electric shocks and loud sounds can also function as drive stimuli. Like Hull, Miller presumes that drives are often *correlated* with internal physiological needs of the organism, but in the end, the necessary operation for producing a drive is to assure that an organism is subjected to intense stimulation of some sort. And it is the concept of drive, rather than that of need, which enters into Miller's explicit definition of reinforcement. Thus, Miller says that a reinforcing state of affairs is simply that which produces a rapid reduction in the intensity of a drive stimulus.

With the general drive-reduction theory before us, we can now see how it has fared when put to experimental test. The two types of experimental approach we shall look at by no means exhaust the attempts that have been made in the laboratory to check the validity of a general drive-reduction point of view. We shall have frequent occasion throughout the remainder of the book to see how drive-reduction theory, and other alternative theories of reinforcement, can account for and predict the things that happen in the laboratory and in other places where learning can be studied. The experiments that we shall now examine are, however, representative of the host that have been inspired by the thinking of Hull, Miller, and other proponents of the drive-reduction point of view.

MOUTH VERSUS STOMACH EFFECTS AND REINFORCEMENT BY DRIVE REDUCTION.   Let us take hunger as an example of a basic sort of drive that provides "strong internal stimuli" and food as an example of a substance that reduces hunger-drive stimuli and so, according to drive-reduction theory, functions to reinforce the learning of new behavior. Food has two properties that are of special interest to us at the moment. First of all, once eaten, it enters the stomach, where the processes of digestion begin to occur. Correlated with this will be a number of things: changes in stomach distension, changes in the frequency of stomach contractions, changes in a host of other internal physiological conditions. Some of these changes occur rather quickly; others take longer; but all fall into the general class of events that are presumed to constitute a reduction in hunger drive.

Food has a second property, however, which—in an intact organism—always goes along with the process of ingestion: food has taste, and in the process of eating, food is tasted. Furthermore, as we saw in Chapter 2, sugar (which is a sweet-tasting food) can function very well as a reinforcer for learning. Given these two properties of food, a problem is raised that is critical for drive-reduction theory: Does food function as a rein-forcer because it reduces the intensity of hunger-drive stimuli, or because it has certain *stimulus* properties that trigger the sense of taste or smell in some special way, perhaps in a way that is innately "pleasant"? According to the latter view (about which we will have a great deal to say later), food as a reinforcing stimulus might function as a highly valued *incentive* and, if anything, *produce* drive in the learning situation rather than reduce it. Thus, it becomes crucial from a pure drive-reduction point of view to separate "mouth factors," like taste, from "stomach factors," like stomach distension, and to show that the latter—alone—can mediate the process of reinforcement.

The experiments that have been done on this problem have adopted the general strategy of feeding food to rats under one of two conditions: Food is eaten by mouth in the normal way, or the mouth is bypassed, and food is injected directly into the stomach through a surgi-cally placed gastric tube. Then a comparison is made between the relative efficiency of these two procedures in reducing hunger drive, on the one hand, and reinforcing the learning of a new response, on the other. If drive-reduction theory is correct, we would expect that direct injection of food into the stomach would be sufficient to produce both of these effects.

Kohn (1951) trained rats in a Skinner box to push a panel with their noses in order to obtain a drop of milk that was delivered auto-matically by a dipper mechanism. Then he operated on the rats and made a stomach fistula by sewing a tube directly into the rats' stomachs. The tube ran out through the skin on the rats' backs. The outside opening of the tube was located in such a way that a hypodermic syringe could be attached to it and the stomach loaded directly with fluid. After the rats had recovered from the operation, Kohn did the following experiment. First, rats in one group were injected with 14 cubic centimeters of milk, and those in another with 14 cubic centimeters of isotonic salt solution. The salt solution was, of course, nonnutritive; it could not reduce hunger in any physiological way. It did, however, distend the stomach just as much as the milk. Rats in a third group drank 14 cubic centimeters of milk with their mouths in the normal manner. Then all rats were re-turned immediately to the Skinner box and permitted to push the panel for milk rewards, as they had before. Kohn reasoned that the amount of panel pressing the rats now emitted would reflect the extent to which their hunger drive had been reduced by the different preloading techniques; the greater the reduction in hunger drive, the less the rats should work for additional food.

The results of the experiment are these: The rats preloaded with saline pressed an average of 13.02 times per minute during the 30-minute test, those preloaded with milk pressed 7.34 times per minute, and those that had drunk milk by mouth pressed only 5.64 times per minute. As you can see, milk drunk by mouth, and thus tasted, reduced hunger by the greatest amount, but milk injected directly into the stomach also reduced hunger relative to the base line provided by the isotonic salt solution. Another important point is that, since the panel-pressing test was essentially complete 30 minutes after the various preloading operations had occurred, the effects of Kohn's procedures must have been upon something other than the physiological *needs* of the organism. This is so because it takes considerably longer than 30 minutes for food, once it is in the stomach, to produce any significant change in the general need state of the rat. Thus, Kohn's results support a distinction between need reduction and drive reduction—so long, at least, as it is assumed that need reduction cannot take place until after a significant amount of digestion has taken place.

Other experiments (Epstein, 1960; Epstein & Teitelbaum, 1962) add further evidence to the notion that substances placed directly into the stomach can reduce drives. Epstein and Teitelbaum, for example, used Kohn's basic approach of placing a small plastic tube directly into the rat's stomach. However, they ran the tube up the esophagus, out the nose, and under the skin of the snout, then attached the outside end to a pedestal fixed to the rat's skull. Another tube, attached to a fixture on the pedestal, led to a reservoir of liquid food. A special pump was arranged to deliver preset amounts of liquid food from the reservoir, through the tube system, and into the rat's stomach. This technique had an advantage over Kohn's in that rats could move about rather freely while attached to the food delivery system, and they could still eat food in the normal way by mouth. Also, they could remain attached to the food system for days or weeks at a time.

With a technique for direct gastric injection of food at hand, Epstein and Teitelbaum then asked a very interesting question: Could rats be trained to feed themselves and regulate hunger when the only way in which they could receive food was through the gastric tube? Here is what they did. After gastric tubes had been inserted into the stomachs of four rats, the rats were placed in a Skinner box and things were arranged so that a lever press delivered a small quantity of liquid food into a food cup. This food was to be eaten in the normal way by mouth. After this preliminary training, the system incorporating the gastric tube was attached to the pedestal on the rats' heads, and from that time on, lever presses caused a small amount (2.5 cubic centimeters) of food to be pumped directly into the rats' stomachs.

The results of the experiment are straightforward and striking. In general, the rats maintained perfect control over their body weight; they pressed the lever just as often as necessary each day, for periods of

13 to 44 days, to obtain a proper quantity of food. This was true even when the experimenters cut the amount of food delivered with each self-injection by half, when they doubled the amount, when they diluted the food with water, and when they increased the number of lever presses required to produce one injection of food to as many as 36. In each case, the rats simply adjusted the frequency of their lever presses to compensate for the changes in amount that each lever press produced. Further, to show that the rats were regulating their intake solely on the basis of some factor associated with the stomach and were not somehow tasting or smelling the food (perhaps through regurgitation), quinine hydrochloride, a bitter substance indeed, was added to the liquid food. Those rats who lever-pressed for injections of this adulterated food directly into their stomachs continued to work for food as they always had, while a control group of four rats that were fed the same substance by mouth decreased their daily food intake by an average of 57 percent. Clearly, hunger drive can be reduced and regulated very accurately in the absence of any stimulation of the senses of taste, smell, or other "mouth factors."

Although the experiments at which we have just looked show that hunger, as a representative drive, can be reduced on the basis of stomach factors alone, they do not show that hunger reduction of this sort can reinforce the learning of a *new* response. The Epstein and Teitelbaum experiment comes close; rats did learn rapidly to *transfer* from lever pressing for food eaten by mouth to lever pressing for food injected directly into the stomach. But it is nevertheless true that the rats had acquired this response initially with food eaten in the normal way as the reinforcing event. Evidence is available, however, which shows that drive reduction on the basis of stomach factors alone is an event which can be used to reinforce the acquisition of a response that an organism has never had the opportunity to learn. This evidence is provided by an experiment of Miller and Kessen (1952).

Miller and Kessen fitted rats with stomach fistulas in the same way that Kohn (1951) did, deprived them of food, and trained them to go to a goal box at the end of one arm of a T maze. For half the rats, choice of the right arm was arbitrarily determined as the correct response (with the left arm incorrect); for the other half, the reverse conditions prevailed. The first of two trials each day was a "free-choice" trial. That is, the rats were free to go to either the correct or the incorrect sides of the T. The second trial, given about four hours later, was "forced." That is, the rats found the door closed to the side they had chosen on the first trial, and there was no alternative but to go to the other side. This procedure assured that the rats would have equal experience with the things that happened in both end boxes. The critical measures of learning, of course, were those obtained on the free-choice trials.

Five rats in one group (the mouth–no-delay group) found a dish which contained 13 cubic centimeters of milk that they could drink by mouth in the correct end box, and 13 cubic centimeters of an isotonic saline solution that they could drink the same way in the incorrect end box. Six rats in a second group (the stomach-injection group) received a direct stomach injection of 13 cubic centimeters of milk for a correct choice and an injection of 13 cubic centimeters of saline solution for an incorrect choice. Six rats in a third group (the mouth–delay group) also received 13 cubic centimeters of milk or saline solution by mouth for correct and incorrect choices, but the rewards were not presented to the rats until after they had been in the goal boxes for 7 minutes and 35 seconds—the time that was required to make stomach injections for the stomach-injection group. This delay group was run as a control to counter the possible argument that, in Miller and Kessen's terms, "The effect of reward begins with the first sip when milk is taken by mouth, but only after a considerable volume of milk has been injected directly into the stomach."

The results of the experiment are shown in Figures 3.4 and 3.5. All reinforcement conditions eventually led the rats to choose the correct arm of the T on 100 percent of the free-choice trials. The rats that received milk by mouth learned fastest, but after 35 to 40 free-choice trials, the rats rewarded with stomach injections of milk had also learned. Figure 3.4 shows, however, that rats receiving milk by direct stomach injection did not increase their running speed to the correct arm, while rats receiving milk by mouth did. This result suggests that drinking milk by mouth may produce an increase in a nonlearning, motivational factor (due, perhaps, to some kind of mouth factor associated with taste) which does not appear when milk is injected directly into the stomach. However, the important result of the experiment is that rats could learn which was the correct arm of the T on the basis of stomach injections alone, though they may not have become as highly motivated to get there as rats receiving milk by mouth.

Taken as a whole, the experimental work which we have described in this section demonstrates in convincing fashion that food injected directly into the stomach can not only reduce hunger drive long before there is any opportunity for an actual physiological need to be reduced, but can also be used to reinforce the learning of a new response. It should not be forgotten, however, that the experiments also show that food taken by mouth functions generally as a much more effective reinforcer than food injected directly into the stomach. So it would be dangerous to conclude that stomach factors alone are responsible for reinforcement based on a substance like food.

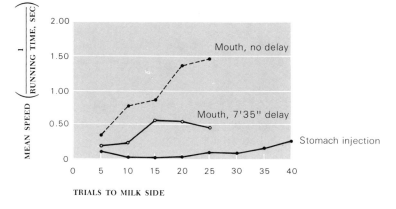

FIG. 3.4 Mean speed of running as a function of different methods of giving a milk reinforcer. Milk taken by mouth produces a progressive increase in speed across trials, but milk injected directly into the stomach does not. (N. E. Miller & Kessen, 1952.)

The search for the relative contributions of mouth and stomach factors to the reinforcement process, assuming the validity of the drive-reduction approach, is a continuing task. Why does food injected directly into the stomach reduce hunger drive long before the physiological changes associated with digestion have time to take place? To what extent is the central nervous system involved in the process, which it must certainly be? These questions, and many others like them, are clearly of interest to the physiologist as well as to the psychologist. And there is

FIG. 3.5 Percent correct responses as a function of different methods of giving a milk reinforcer. In each case, learning occurs, but it takes somewhat longer for this to happen if milk is injected directly into the stomach than if it is given by mouth. (N. E. Miller & Kessen, 1952.)

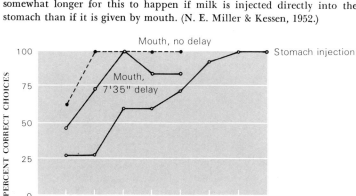

little doubt that the answers to such questions are going to be complicated (Teitelbaum & Epstein, 1962; Mook, 1963; Teitelbaum & Cytawa, 1965). In a very real sense, the answers involve the ultimate determination of all the factors that regulate an organism's intake of substances like food and water.

A PSYCHOPHYSICAL APPROACH TO REINFORCEMENT THROUGH DRIVE REDUCTION. If, as Miller says, drives can be thought of as strong stimuli that impel action, and if reduction in the intensity of such stimuli can reinforce behavior, how much must a drive be reduced in intensity before a measurable reinforcement effect can be obtained? Further, is it true that we would have to have a greater reduction in the intensity of a very strong drive, as compared with a weak drive, in order to produce equivalent reinforcing effects?

These questions, of course, are borrowed from psychophysics. For example, the psychophysicist asks how intense a light must be before the light can just barely be seen; this physical intensity is called an *absolute threshold*. Similarly, the psychophysicist asks how much two lights must differ in physical intensity before the *difference* between the lights is barely detectable; a difference of this sort is called a *just noticeable difference*, or *difference threshold*. The psychophysicist also asks how the size of a difference threshold changes when it is determined at different points along a dimension of stimulus intensity. In general, the magnitude of the difference threshold becomes larger as the physical intensities of stimuli increase. According to Weber's Law, however, if difference thresholds are determined for a number of standard intensities, then the *ratios* of the difference thresholds to their respective standard intensities will all be the same. Thus, Weber's Law says that $\Delta I/I$ is a constant, where I stands for the intensity of any standard stimulus and ΔI stands for the difference threshold determined for that particular standard stimulus. Weber's Law holds pretty well for the middle ranges of intensity for a wide variety of stimuli, although it tends to break down at extreme intensities—those that are very high or very low.

Campbell (1955, 1956, 1958) reasoned that if a drive-reduction approach to reinforcement has merit, it ought to be possible to ask some psychophysical sorts of questions about reductions in the intensity of drive stimuli and their corresponding ability to reinforce a response. Since, as we have seen, the experimenter has many problems in controlling precisely the things that produce and, in particular, reduce drive stimuli like those associated with hunger, Campbell chose to use another type of drive-producing stimulus. In one experiment (Campbell, 1955), he exposed rats to intense noise, and in another (Campbell, 1956), he used electric shock. The chief advantage of using externally applied stimuli such as these is that the experimenter has very precise control over their onset, offset, and intensity. Consequently, he can easily vary drive strength and the amount by which drive is reduced.

Let us look at Campbell's shock experiment in some detail. The apparatus was a simple cage with a floor made from metal rods through which electric current could be passed. The floor was pivoted in the middle so that it would tilt slightly as the rats Campbell used for subjects went from one side to the other. When a rat was on one side of the floor, it received a "standard" shock of one intensity. When, and if, it moved to the other side of the floor, it received a "comparison" shock of a lower intensity. A clock measured the amount of time that the rat spent on the lower-shock side of the cage. The standard intensities that were used were 55, 72, 95, 165, 287, and 500 volts passed through a resistor that limited the current flow through the rat. For each standard intensity, several (at least three) comparison intensities were chosen; each comparison intensity was progressively less intense than its standard. Separate groups of six rats each were run for each combination of standard and comparison intensity. This was done so that the behavior measured under one set of conditions would not be affected by earlier experience with another set

FIG. **3.6**   The curves show, for each of several standard intensities (filled circles), the percent preference for the side of the tilt cage with the lower shock as a function of the intensity of the lower shock (open circles). Campbell assumed that had each standard intensity been compared with itself, the rats would have spent equal amounts of time on each side of the cage, so "preference" for each standard was set arbitrarily at 50 percent. (Campbell, 1956.)

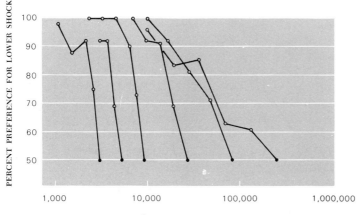

of conditions. The procedure was simple. A rat was placed in the tilt cage and a standard and comparison shock were turned on for eight minutes. Then, for the last four minutes of the eight-minute session, the percentage of time that the rat spent on the side of the cage with the lower-intensity comparison shock was determined. Median percentages for the groups of rats run under each condition are shown in Figure 3.6, which also includes points at 50 percent for the hypothetical state of affairs that would occur, presumably, when the standard and comparison shocks were of the same intensity.

From the data shown in Figure 3.6 Campbell then calculated, for each standard intensity, the reduction in intensity that would lead the rat to spend 75 percent of its time on the side of the grid floor with the less intense shock. Campbell assumed that if a rat did this, it was demonstrating a reliable preference for this side as compared with the other. Then Campbell assumed that the difference in intensity between the standard and comparison shock at the point of 75 percent preference constituted a reduction in shock intensity which was "just noticeably reinforcing" for the response of going to and staying on the side of the cage with the weaker shock. The reductions in shock intensity that were required to produce a just noticeably reinforcing effect for each standard intensity are shown in Figure 3.7.

Figure 3.7 indicates that as the intensity I of the standard shock increased, there had to be a much larger decrease in intensity $(-\Delta I)$ before the decrease was sufficient to produce just noticeable reinforcement. For example, when I was about 100,000 units, there had to be a decrease in intensity of about 70,000 units for just noticeable reinforcement

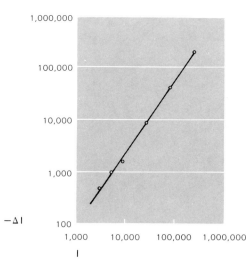

FIG. **3.7** Reinforcement difference limens $(-\Delta I)$ as a function of the log intensity of the standard shock I. Each reinforcement difference limen was determined by calculating the amount of shock reduction required to produce 75 percent preference for the lower-shock side of the cage. Both axes are plotted in E^2 units. (Campbell, 1956.)

to occur.[4] When *I* was about 10,000 units, however, a decrease of only 1,100 or 1,200 units was required.

Figure 3.8 shows Campbell's plot of a type of Weber function for his data. As you can see, the *ratio* between $-\Delta I$ and *I* is roughly constant at 0.2 for intensities to about 100 volts. At higher intensities, the ratio is no longer constant and begins to increase rather rapidly. "Failures" in Weber's Law of exactly this sort are quite common in psychophysics. In all respects, Campbell's data are directly analogous to those that are obtained when the same sorts of functional relationships are determined for the responses of humans to the intensity of a wide variety of stimuli.

In general, Campbell has demonstrated that the concept of "just noticeable reinforcement" achieved by reductions in the intensity of a strong drive-producing stimulus like electric shock has notable merit. As such, his work in this connection adds to the viability of an approach to reinforcement that stresses the drive-reduction concept. We should note, however, that his data can be incorporated into some other theoretical approaches—in particular, into any theory which emphasizes the *stimulus* properties of reinforcing events. We shall be looking at a bit of this kind of thinking shortly, and you can also check Kimble (1961) if you want to find out more about the problem.

INCENTIVES AND REINFORCEMENT

Though drive-reduction theory can clearly hold its own in accounting for many conditions of reinforcement, it is by no means the only approach

[4] For reasons that we need not go into, Campbell assumed that the proper way to specify the physical intensity of the shock was in terms of the power (E^2) dissipated through the rat, not the voltage (E) delivered to the grid floor of the cage. Figure 3.8 gives both units of intensity, however, so that they can be compared.

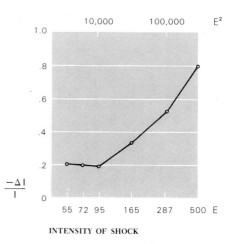

FIG. **3.8** A Weber function for reinforcement difference limens. The ratio between a reinforcement difference limen and the standard from which it was determined is fairly constant for low standard intensities of shock, but the ratio begins to increase markedly as the intensity of the standard increases. (Campbell, 1956.)

that has received theoretical and experimental attention. The germ of another approach that is quite different is contained in a portion of a talk given by F. D. Sheffield at Brown University and since published (Sheffield, 1966). Sheffield had this to say: "If one dangles a carrot in front of a rabbit it does not relax the rabbit; on the contrary, it arouses him to action. [If] the carrot is on the wrong side of a wire screen, the action may involve considerable struggling." Sheffield then went on to develop the proposition that reinforcing stimuli operate as they do because they tend to act as *incentives,* that is they are events that *increase* or *induce* drives. A proposition that emphasizes the drive-*producing* properties of reinforcing events is, of course, in complete contrast to the drive-reduction approach, which emphasizes the notion that reinforcing events are those which tend to reduce or eliminate the tensions associated with basic drives like hunger or thirst. An example from the experimental literature readily illustrates what Sheffield was talking about and demonstrates the contrast between an incentive and a drive-reduction approach to the problem of reinforcement.

Sheffield, Wulff, and Backer (1951) asked this question about the reinforcing effects of sexual behavior in rats: Would male rats learn an instrumental response when, as a reinforcing event, they were permitted to copulate with another rat, but not to ejaculate? This question distinguishes between the incentive properties of sexual stimulation (and the consummatory activity of intromission and copulatory movement that such stimulation elicits) and drive reduction that would occur through ejaculation. First, 24 male rats were pretested in a circular box 30 inches in diameter, to see if they would copulate with a female in heat. Of the 24, 8 copulated with the female, but the investigators removed the female before actual ejaculation occurred. Of the remaining males, 6 showed "sustained pursuit" of the female, but never actually copulated. The 10 male rats who neither copulated nor showed interest were not used in the rest of the experiment.

All rats were trained to run a 32-inch runway which opened into the circular goal box in which they had been pretested. Half the rats who had copulated during the pretest (the experimental group) found a female in heat in the goal box and were permitted to copulate. However, the female was removed before ejaculation occurred. The other half of the copulators (the control group) found a male "companion" rat in the goal box; the male "companion" was removed after two minutes or after two attempts had been made to copulate (male rats will, on occasion, show copulatory activity with other male rats). Of the remaining 6 rats who had not copulated, but who had shown "interest" during the pretest (the noncopulator group), half were run to a male and half to a female in heat. A total of 28 trials, 2 per day, were run in the alley, and measures

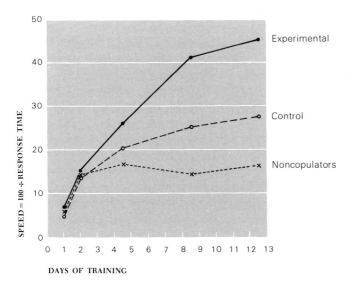

FIG. **3.9** Reinforcing effects of different types of sexual experience. Experimental animals found a female in ·the goal box, control animals found a male, while noncopulators found a male or female, but never attempted to copulate. While copulation was permitted for all animals, no animal was ever allowed to ejaculate (Sheffield, Wulff, & Backer, 1951.)

of running speed were taken over these trials. The results of the experiment are shown in Figure 3.9.

The figure indicates that the speed of running increased for all groups, but that the rats in the experimental group eventually ran fastest. Note also that the rats in the control group ran faster than the rats in the noncopulator group. The investigators attribute this result to the fact that the control rats had copulated during the pretest and attempted to copulate during the learning task even though they found a male rat in the goal box. That is, they exhibited some of the consummatory behavior normally aroused by sexual stimulation, even though this behavior was aimed in rather misdirected fashion at male rats. The rats in the noncopulator group, on the other hand, never exhibited any of the behavior normally elicited by sexual stimulation. This was true even though some of them were run to a female in heat in the goal box. Taken as a whole, the results of the experiment show clearly that female rats are excellent reinforcing stimuli for male rats, and that they function as such in the absence of anything that could reasonably be called a reduction in primary sex drive on the part of the male.

SENSORY STIMULATION AND REINFORCEMENT. We have just seen that the stimulation associated with sex can function as an independent variable to produce the effects characteristic of reinforcement. Since this is true, we might ask if the same thing holds for other kinds of sensory stimuli, and more generally, if the basic defining property of a reinforcer is that it *stimulates* an organism in some special way (Troland, 1928; Young, 1961; Pfaffmann, 1960, 1964, 1965).

There are several sources of evidence that are relevant to this point of view. Some of the best evidence comes from research that has been done on the sense of taste. Oakley and Pfaffmann (1962) showed, for example, that normal rats given an opportunity to drink either a water or a sucrose solution would demonstrate a marked preference for the sucrose. This was true, at least, up to the point where a very concentrated solution of sucrose was used; under these conditions, the preference for sucrose tended to break down because disruption of normal osmotic and other internal gut factors occurred. Oakley and Pfaffmann then showed that essentially all the preference for sucrose disappeared when the portion of the thalamus that monitors the sense of taste was destroyed. Thus, this experiment established the basic point that the sensitivity of the rat to sweet tastes could be controlled by carefully placed lesions in the central nervous system. The next step was to see if a similar procedure could eliminate the well-known reinforcing properties that sweet tastes possess (Guttman, 1953; Hutt, 1954; Hulse, Snyder, & Bacon, 1960). Pfaffmann (1964), on the basis of some unpublished data obtained by Oakley, reported that it could indeed. Rats were trained in a Skinner box to press a lever for drops of solutions that differed in sweetness; both sucrose and saccharin solutions were used.[5] Lever presses that were spaced at least 20 seconds apart, on the average, produced reinforcing stimuli. The rats were free to press the lever during the intervening periods of time, but such presses did not produce reinforcing stimuli. This arrangement, a *variable-interval* schedule of reinforcement (see Chapters 2 and 5), assured that rats who pressed at a high rate would receive the same number of reinforcers as rats who pressed at a lower rate. Thus any drive or need reduction that might have been produced by a given concentration of sucrose, say, was held constant for all rats who were reinforced with that solution. To further control for possible drive-reducing effects of the reinforcing solutions, the rats were satiated for both food and water when they were tested.

After response rates had been measured for a number of concentrations of the saccharin and sucrose solutions, the portion of the thala-

[5] Saccharin is a particularly interesting substance to the reinforcement theorist because it has essentially no nutritive value, though it tastes very sweet even in extremely low concentrations.

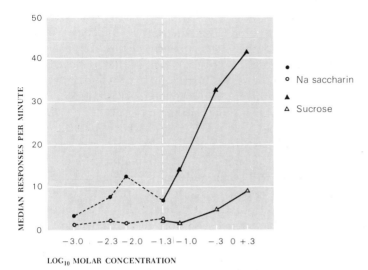

FIG. **3.10** Rates of lever pressing as a function of concentration of sodium saccharin and of sucrose. The filled circles represent data from normal rats, while the open circles represent data from taste-desensitized rats. (Pfaffmann, 1964, data from B. Oakley.)

mus that mediates taste sensitivity was destroyed by passing a small electric current through electrodes inserted into the thalamus. The rats were allowed to recover from this operation, and then they were retested in the Skinner box. The results of the experiment are shown in Figure 3.10, where the data for saccharin reinforcement appear to the left of the figure and the data for sucrose reinforcement to the right.

As you can see from the top line of the figure, response rate before taste desensitization increased dramatically with increases in sweetness of both solutions. The highest concentration of saccharin produced a slight drop in rate, perhaps because of some aversive quality of this substance at relatively high concentrations (high concentrations taste bitter to humans). The striking feature of the data, however, is the enormous decrease in rate after the rats had been deprived of taste sensitivity. This is shown by the line at the bottom of the figure. Remember that because of the schedule of reinforcement which was used, and because the rats did press the lever at least occasionally, just as much of each solution was obtained after taste desensitization as before. But the apparent "eagerness" of the rats for the substances decreased markedly; both the saccharin and sucrose solutions appeared to have lost most of their properties as incentives.

While stimuli that trigger the sense of taste clearly reinforce, taste is intimately connected with other factors which are also known to be important, or at least to be involved, in the reinforcement process (recall our discussion of mouth versus stomach factors, for example). There are other kinds of stimuli, however, which are far removed from any obvious need or drive process, yet possess the characteristics of reinforcers. Light, a visual stimulus, is a case in point (Kish, 1955). There are now many experiments which show that the onset of a dim light will reinforce a response such as a lever press in rats (Lockard, 1963; Kiernan, 1964). However, while there is little question that light can serve as a reinforcing stimulus, we still do not have a clear picture of the specific conditions under which this will occur, and the things that one can do to change the effectiveness of light as a reinforcer. Premack and Collier (1962), for example, varied the amount of time (12, 24, or 48 hours) that rats spent in total darkness between test sessions in a Skinner box. They found that the longer the interval between test sessions, the greater the number of times the rats would press a lever that turned on a dim light. These results would normally lead to the conclusion that rats respond to light deprivation much as they respond to food or water deprivation. Premack and Collier also found, quite in contrast to any possible explanation based on light deprivation, that if rats were maintained under the normal illumination of the laboratory rat colony, they pressed much *less* frequently than if they were maintained in the dark. However, they *still* pressed the lever more frequently as the interval of time between sessions increased. These facts are characteristic of the terrible inconsistencies that emerge from experiments in which the effects of light as a reinforcer have been studied. Yet the basic fact remains: The onset of a dim light does reinforce the behavior of rats.

While much remains to be learned about the properties of dim light as a reinforcer, other kinds of visual or sensory stimulation have been shown to be quite powerful reinforcers. For example, Butler (1953) showed that if monkeys were placed in an enclosed box and required to push at either a yellow or a blue card (one of which was arbitrarily designated "correct"), they would rapidly learn to push the correct card when reinforcement for this response consisted simply of an opportunity to look out of the box at surroundings in the room. Further, the frequency with which monkeys did this was shown to depend upon what the monkey got to see (Butler, 1954). The best incentive was the sight of another monkey, but the sight of an electric train in operation worked, too. In the same vein, Montgomery (1954) showed that rats would learn to go to one arm of a Y-shaped maze when they were reinforced, once they got to the correct goal box, by giving them access to another maze which they could explore for a period of time. When the "reinforcing" maze was shifted to the other arm of the Y maze, the rats reversed their preference, indicating that their choice behavior was indeed controlled by the opportunity to explore an unfamiliar stimulus situation.

BRAIN STIMULATION AND REINFORCEMENT.   Another important discovery that can be placed, albeit indirectly, under the heading of reinforcement by stimulation is that direct electrical stimulation of the brain can reinforce behavior. This phenomenon, first reported by Olds and Milner (1954) was demonstrated in the following way. Fine wire electrodes were implanted in portions of the limbic system of the rat's brain; the limbic system involves some of the basal, lower structures of the brain, including portions of the thalamus and hypothalamus. Then the rats were placed in a Skinner box, and lever presses were reinforced with a brief half-second pulse of 30–90 microampere current delivered through the electrodes. The behavior that resulted was dramatic: after rats pressed once, they began to press at a very high rate and continued to do so in some cases until physical exhaustion set in (Olds, 1958).

Since the original discovery of the phenomenon, further work has demonstrated a great many reinforcement-like effects of brain stimulation. As the voltage of the stimulating current is increased, for example, the rate at which a rat will press a lever will, within limits, also increase (Reynolds, 1958). This effect is reminiscent, at least, of the effects that we saw would occur when the amount of an ingested reward was varied. It is also possible to obtain negative as well as positive reinforcing effects through brain stimulation. Delgado, Roberts, and Miller (1954) showed that for certain electrode placements, cats would perform a wheel-turning response in order to *avoid* electrical stimulation of the brain, and Bower and Miller (1958), using a T maze to test for learning, found loci in the medial forebrain bundle where the onset of the stimulus was reinforcing, but if stimulation then continued, the stimulation became aversive and its *offset* was reinforcing.

While there is considerable evidence which shows that electrical stimulation of the brain produces effects characteristic of reinforcement, there is also evidence which suggests that it produces effects quite unlike those found with other types of reinforcers. For one thing, the course of experimental extinction for a response reinforced by brain stimulation is quite different from that obtained following reinforcement with substances like food. For a lever-pressing response learned with a food reinforcer, for example, extinction is generally a relatively prolonged affair, often involving hundreds of responses before an animal stops pressing altogether. Following reinforcement with brain stimulation, however, extinction is very rapid—so rapid, in fact, that an animal may make only two or three responses before stopping (Olds, 1958; Deutsch, 1963; Deutsch & Howarth, 1963). This happens even though the animal has been emitting a great many responses at a very high rate just before "extinction" begins. It is much as if the removal of brain stimulation turns off a motivational system that is basically independent of the reinforcing effects which brain stimulation also produces. As a matter of fact, Deutsch and Howarth suggest that this may be precisely the case. Further discussion of the effects of brain stimulation upon behavior would quickly carry us beyond the scope of this book, but the phenomenon of rapid extinction is quite representative of the problems that need to be solved before we shall have full understanding of the effects of brain stimulation upon behavior.

CONSUMMATORY RESPONSES AND REINFORCEMENT. Stimuli that function well as incentives, like those associated with taste and sex, have another property which has been identified by some as of potential importance in the reinforcement process. Such stimuli generally produce a characteristic pattern of highly stereotyped behavior: licking or drinking in the case of a taste stimulus (assuming the taste is palatable) and intromission and copulatory movements in the case of sex, for example. Perhaps the critical defining feature of events that reinforce is that they reliably elicit prepotent *consummatory responses.*

If you will recall the Sheffield, Wulff, and Backer (1951) experiment, you will remember that rats in the control group who ran to male lures ran faster than rats in the noncopulator group, even though some of the latter actually ran to females in heat. In accounting for their data, Sheffield and his associates stressed the fact that rats in the control group exhibited at least *some* of the consummatory behavior aroused normally by sexual stimulation, while rats in the noncopulator group never did. In other words, the aspect of the goal animal that was most consistently correlated with its incentive value was not its sex at all. Instead, the most consistent indicator of incentive value was the degree to which the goal animal, whether it was male or female, elicited the consummatory responses normally triggered by sexual stimulation.

In other work, Sheffield, Roby, and Campbell (1954) showed that rats would run faster in a straight runway the greater the vigor of the consummatory response elicited by liquid rewards of different kinds. They trained hungry rats to run an alley using reinforcing solutions of water, saccharin, dextrose, or dextrose plus saccharin. The amount of fluid that the rats drank in a four-minute period in the goal box was taken as an index of the vigor of the consummatory response of drinking. The data show a remarkable correlation between the vigor of the consummatory response and the speed with which the rats ran the alley at the end of a 42-trial training period. Fast running was consistently associated with vigorous drinking, slow running with lackadaisical drinking. The experimental data also provide a telling point regarding the drive-reduction approach to reinforcement. Though dextrose is a sugar, and thus need-reducing for hungry rats, it was no better than saccharin as a reinforcer when the two solutions were equated for vigor of drinking by determining the concentrations of dextrose and saccharin that had to be used to produce equal fluid intake during the four-minute drinking period in the goal box.

As Sheffield and his associates point out, their experiment tends to rule out a drive or need-reduction theory as adequate to account for their data, but it does not rule out the notion that sweetness, rather than vigor of the consummatory response, was the critical feature determining the effectiveness of the reward in the goal box. This is true because as the sweetness of the solutions that were used increased, the vigor of the consummatory response that each solution elicited also increased, and we cannot be sure which of these two variables was in fact producing the observed differences in running speed in the alley. Since Snyder and Hulse (1961), for example, failed to find any differences in running speed in an alley, even though they could produce large differences in vigor of drinking by varying the amount of water that rats got with each lick from a drinking tube, it appears that the truly critical variable in the Sheffield, Roby, and Campbell experiment may have been the sweetness of the various reinforcing solutions. At least the Snyder and Hulse data tend to limit the generality of Sheffield's basic consummatory-response approach to reinforcement. Perhaps the safest thing that can be said about the role of consummatory responses in the reinforcement process is that they are not absolutely necessary for reinforcement to take place, but may often be a characteristic signal of an effective set of reinforcement operations.

THE FRACTIONAL GOAL RESPONSE. Before we leave the general topics of reinforcement and incentives, we must introduce a hypothetical construct that is of theoretical importance in connection not only with incentives, but also with a good many other processes of learning that we shall be discussing later in the book. The construct in question is the *fractional goal response*, r_g (Hull, 1930, 1931; Spence, 1956, 1960). It is a particularly useful tool whenever the theoretician must account for the way events of one kind or another are mediated or bridged by an organism.

Suppose, to take a very simple example, a hungry rat enters a goal box after running through a maze and finds a goal stimulus, an S_G, of a piece of food. Since the rat is hungry, it is quite likely that the goal stimulus will elicit, perhaps reflexively, a characteristic overt goal response, R_G. The overt goal response would include behavior we have talked about under the general heading of consummatory responses; in the case of food, for example, it might consist of seizing, chewing, and swallowing the food.

Now R_G occurs directly as a function of the appearance of S_G, but there are other stimuli that could, through classical conditioning, become associated with R_G. One such class of stimuli would be those of the goal box itself, since these are present as the rat finds and eats the food. To the extent that stimuli in other parts of the maze are similar to those of the goal box, they too could become associated with the goal response. The same thing would be true of drive stimuli arising from the rat's particular state of deprivation (Guthrie called these maintaining stimuli, if you will remember). Drive stimuli are particularly important because they are present not only when the rat sees, seizes, and eats the food in the goal box, but also as the rat responds throughout *every* part of the maze. In other words, since the drive stimulus is conditioned to the overt goal response, and since the drive stimulus is always present, it ought to come to elicit the goal response throughout the entire sequence of responses that the rat must make to get through the maze.

Of course, until the rat gets to the goal box, it cannot seize and eat a piece of food it does not have. But it could make anticipatory responses that are *fractional* components of the full-blown goal response. These *fractional goal responses,* r_g, might be chewing movements, salivation, or any other similar sort of response that would not interfere with the rat's main task of getting from one end of the maze to the other. Further, since they are conceived to have the properties of responses, the r_g's, would produce their own proprioceptive stimuli. Such proprioceptive stimuli, in turn, would provide the rat as it runs through the maze with a kind of symbolic representation of the goal object, a *fractional goal stimulus* or s_g, arising from the fractional goal response. And finally, because r_g's produce s_g's throughout the entire maze, the s_g's themselves should eventually become part of the general stimulus complex to which responses occurring at different points throughout the maze are conditioned. In effect, the r_g-s_g mechanism provides a means by which the rat, through conditioning, can come to "think ahead" and to anticipate whatever waits at future choice points and at the goal.

SPENCE'S INCENTIVE MOTIVATION, K, AND THE r_g-s_g MECHANISM. We shall meet the r_g-s_g mechanism in many guises later on, but as an example appropriate to our discussion of incentives, let us see how one learning theorist, Spence (1956, 1960), has used it in his treatment of positive reinforcers. For Spence, instrumental learning is an *S-R* contiguity affair in which reinforcement is postulated as unnecessary for learning; the strength of an instrumental response, H, is simply a function of the number of times a stimulus is paired with a response. In his theory, Spence assigns an incentive or motivation-producing role to events that have the operational characteristics of positive reinforcers. He does this by introducing an intervening variable K, or *incentive motivation,* the strength of which is presumed to depend directly on the strength of the classically conditioned fractional goal response r_g. The total motivation present during the learning of some simple instrumental response, like running an alley, is then presumed to be a direct function of two things: the magnitude of K and the magnitude of generalized motivation, D, produced by other operations such as food or water deprivation. The excitatory potential, E, of running (measured by the usual indices of response strength, such as running speed) will be a function of the strength of both H and the total motivation present on any learning trial. Spence puts this relationship into the form $E = H \times (D + K)$.

The magnitude of K is presumed to depend directly on the strength of the fractional goal response, so any experimental operation that increases the strength of r_g should also increase the magnitude of K. Since r_g is a classically conditioned response, one simple way to do this would be to increase the number of trials on which conditioning of r_g can take place. In simple terms, this could mean nothing more than increasing the number of times that S_G evokes R_G in the presence of goal box, drive, or other stimuli that are to acquire the ability to evoke r_g. That is, we simply increase the number of times that a hungry rat runs to a goal box at the end of a maze, sees food there, and gets to eat it. Another way to vary the strength of r_g would be to vary the frequency, duration, or vigor of the consummatory behavior comprising R_G. For example, rewards consisting of large as compared with small amounts of food take longer to eat, require more bites, and so on. Therefore, over a number of learning trials, a large amount of reinforcement should produce an r_g more strongly conditioned to goal box and other stimuli in the learning situation. This, in turn, should produce correspondingly greater incentive motivation, and faster running in the alley.

It is very important to recognize that as Spence uses the r_g-s_g mechanism, and as others use it, it is nothing more nor less than a hypothetical construct (Chapter 1). It is a kind of conceptual model, tied to independent and dependent variables, that has been assigned some properties which make it useful as a theoretical tool in accounting for certain kinds of learning phenomena. It is easy to lose sight of this fact, since terms like "fractional goal response" could lead one to think that the validity of the concept might depend upon actual measurement of "real" fractional goal responses in the laboratory. In fact, at least one successful attempt has been made to measure fractional goal responses (Miller, 1935). But if it were impossible to find a fractional goal response and to measure it in the laboratory, this would in no way invalidate the concept, nor would it destroy its utility as a theoretical tool. As a matter of fact, the only reason that the fractional goal response is so labeled is because Hull (1930, 1931), who first developed it as a construct, wanted to emphasize an approach to learning where everything was to be explained in peripheralistic terms like stimulus and response.

SOME PERSPECTIVE

Psychology generally, and the psychology of learning particularly, has been marked by the exotic variety of its theories—of which you have had a taste in this chapter—and by bitter argument among the proponents of one theory as opposed to another. Not too many years ago, a psychologist interested in learning was identified by his adherence to one theoretical school or another, and these schools were "opposed" to one another from top to bottom. Theoreticians (and experimentalists) spent much time in fruitless argument with one another, either by damning the logic of an opposing theory or by attempting to demolish it through the performance of "crucial" experiments.

Such theoretical argument has not entirely disappeared today, for the good reason that hardly any of the basic issues have been settled to everyone's satisfaction. However, there is absolutely no question that one basic lesson has been learned: The strong emphasis upon large-scale theories of learning (such as Hull's) and the devoted allegiance to one theory as opposed to another have proved barren and have largely disappeared. Currently, psychologists in learning are more likely to quarrel about methods of approach and about fruitful areas for research than about universal theories. Since we now recognize that there is no theory of learning currently available which can handle all the facts of learning, there is little talk about the exclusive and ultimate correctness of one or another theory.

One of the things likely to arouse an argument among psychologists is the question of the relative merits of trying, on the one hand, to use rigorously quantitative deductions or elegant mathematical models to derive limited hypotheses about highly specialized problems, or on the other hand, trying to sketch in a rather intuitive fashion a qualitative description of fundamental problems which are of general interest. Thus, one group of psychologists may be interested in rigorously deriving a mathematical theory of the effects of delay and amount of reinforcement upon the behavior of a rat in a runway, and another group may be interested in trying to find the main elements in the relationship between associative learning and problem solving in intelligent human adults. There is really little to argue about between such groups, except the relative merits of the problems they have chosen to work on, since the problems themselves will only at some future time come to a common ground.

What is to be made, then, of our discussion of theories such as those of Guthrie, Tolman, and Hull? Perhaps the most important point is that each represents an important *historical* point of view out of which has grown our current approach to theoretical matters in the psychology of learning. Although it is easy to be critical of Hull, for example, we must not forget that he was perhaps the first to introduce learning psychologists to the merits of quantitative theory. Also, Hull fixed for many years the basic problems and concepts of learning theory; a large number of these—such as the distinction between learning and performance—are still of great importance.

Today, the psychology of learning seems to have passed from an era of the grand, broad theory into an era of the microtheory. The lesson of Hull, Tolman, and Guthrie is that behavior is much too complicated, and far too little is yet known and understood about it, to make the development of general theories of learning a fruitful undertaking at this time. Instead, the modern theorist attacks a rather specific bit of behavior, collects a lot of data about it, teases it apart, and then attempts to put it back together in the form of some necessarily limited theoretical structure. Nowhere is this approach more clearly demonstrated, for example, than in the case of statistical learning theory, where the typical end product is a mathematical model describing the behavior of organisms in some rather simple, limited situation.

The same principle has been at work—perhaps in extreme form— in the hands of Skinner. As long ago as the 1930s, Skinner (1938) doubted the ultimate usefulness of a broad, highly mathematical, deductive theory such as Hull was then in the process of building. He advocated an approach to the theoretical structure of the psychology of learning which had then, and seems to have now, the characteristic of little systematic point of view at all—beyond some simple distinctions like that between respondent and operant behavior. Instead, Skinner has insisted, psychology should busy itself with an industrious collection of facts, and a general theory of behavior can then be built from these facts by a process of induction. Facts, in the hands of Skinner and those who espouse his point of view, have continued to accumulate for almost 30 years, but the job of putting them together has yet to be undertaken in any serious fashion. Perhaps it is still too soon. In any event, we owe much to the Skinnerian point of view and to the things it has produced. Much of the general shape of the psychology of learning, particularly in terms of tool and technique, stems from Skinner's thinking—as we have seen in this and earlier chapters, and as we shall continue to see later on.

If psychologists have become eclectic about matters of general theories of learning, they have done the same thing about theoretical descriptions of the reinforcement process. In this chapter, we have looked at some ramifications of two general approaches to a strong definition of reinforcement—drive reduction and drive induction or incentive (among others we could have added). There was a time when each approach had its own armed camp behind it; today psychologists have blunted their weapons. The reasons for this are similar to those that have led to the demise of general theories of learning. One of the most important is that *both* approaches to reinforcement have something useful to say and are partly right (you should be able to conclude this for yourself from our discussion of the experimental data); and neither can handle all the things that are known about the process psychologists label with the term reinforcement. Furthermore, there is a growing doubt that the process of reinforcement can be legitimately separated from the process of motivation. As we have hinted here, and as we shall continue to see later, much of what gets placed under the heading of reinforcement could be placed with equal facility under the heading of motivation—the two are probably closely connected if, indeed, they should be distinguished at all. In such matters, only time—and data—can tell.

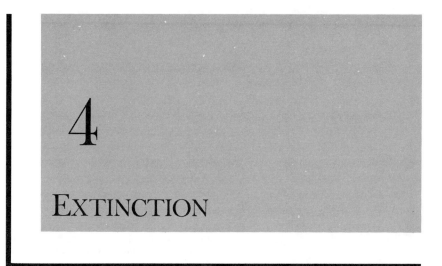

4

EXTINCTION

When learned acts are no longer reinforced, they usually diminish in strength. It is said, for example, that babies learn to cry sometimes so that they will get extra attention. If this happens, parents are generally advised to avoid picking up the baby so that it will stop crying for attention. It is the rare parent who can last out the process, no doubt, but we can think of many such everyday examples which indicate that people have some good commonsense notions about the effects of withdrawal of reinforcement.

Psychologists apply the term *extinction* to the operation of removing reinforcement following the occurrence of some response that has been reinforced in the past. The general effect of this operation is to reduce the strength of the response, but the variables which affect the process are numerous, and the manner in which they interact is often quite complicated indeed. In this chapter we shall look at the way in which extinction is modified by certain basic variables, and we shall examine some attempts that have been made to account for the extinction process in theoretical terms.

THE DEFINITION OF EXTINCTION

In the simplest examples of learning, a response is reinforced every time it occurs. Thus, in simple reward learning, each time the rat presses the lever in the Skinner box, the rat receives a pellet of food. After the rat learns the correlation between food and pressing the lever, it will continue to press the lever at a reasonably steady rate so long as it remains hungry. If reinforcement is discontinued, the rat will continue to respond

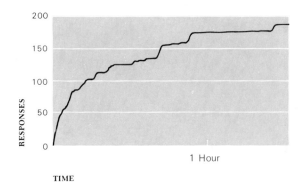

FIG. **4.1** An extinction curve for lever pressing in a Skinner box. The cumulative number of responses appears on the ordinate. The rate of responding is high at the beginning, but then declines and becomes more irregular. Long periods of time pass without responding, until finally the animal stops responding almost completely. (Skinner, 1938, data from F. S. Keller & A. Kerr.)

for a while, but it does so at a gradually diminishing rate and with increasing irregularity. Figure 4.1 shows the process of extinction taking place. From the figure it is clear that the rate of responding is high at the beginning of extinction (right after reinforcement has been stopped), and that it gradually decreases, so that by the end of the first hour without reinforcement, the rat is going long periods of time without giving a response. It is also clear that the rate of responding is quite irregular during extinction (compared with the highly regular rate under reinforcement shown in Figure 2.1, for example). The rat may press the lever rapidly for a few minutes and then stop pressing it altogether for a long period of time.

In the same way, a response that has been classically conditioned gradually diminishes in strength if reinforcement, the unconditioned stimulus in this case, is removed. Thus, in Pavlov's experiment that we looked at in the first chapter, if the tuning fork is sounded a number of times without being paired with the food powder, the salivary response to the sound of the tuning fork gradually decreases and finally disappears.

RESISTANCE TO EXTINCTION. It is apparent from the examples we have just looked at that reinforcement creates a kind of reservoir of responses that can be emitted by an organism after reinforcement is withdrawn. Skinner (1938) has called this reservoir of behavior the *reflex reserve*. A more commonly used term is *resistance to extinction*. Responses vary in resistance to extinction to the extent that an organism will continue to produce them after primary reinforcement has been withdrawn.

In practice there are a number of ways in which resistance to extinction is measured, and we shall be looking at experiments which will furnish good examples of each method. Generally, the indices that are used to measure behavior during extinction are the same that are used to measure behavior during acquisition: indices which reflect the strength of the response. If you will recall, these include measures such as the probability that a response will occur, the latency and amplitude of the response, the speed or duration of the response, and so on. In addition to watching changes in these measures as extinction proceeds, the psychologist may also adopt some form of *extinction criterion*. When this criterion is met, he will conclude quite arbitrarily that extinction is complete. For example, it could be decided arbitrarily ahead of time that extinction is complete when an animal in a Skinner box fails to make a response for the duration of some preset period of time. Thus, we might adopt a two-minute nonresponse criterion for extinction. This means, simply enough, that we would consider extinction to be complete when the animal reaches the point where it fails to emit a response for two minutes. As a numerical index of resistance to extinction in this case, we might simply count the number of nonreinforced responses the animal made until it met the nonresponse criterion. The larger this number, of course, the greater the resistance to extinction.

SOME BASIC VARIABLES

NUMBER OF REINFORCEMENTS AND EXTINCTION

Resistance to extinction depends, to some extent, upon the number of reinforcements given an organism before extinction begins. Figure 4.2 shows some classic data that were obtained from rats in the Skinner box by Perin (1942) and Williams (1938). The figure demonstrates that if a small number of reinforcements is given, a few lever-pressing responses are emitted in extinction before animals cease responding altogether. As the number of reinforced responses increases, the number of responses in extinction also increases, although resistance to extinction appears to approach a limit rather quickly. Maximal resistance to extinction is obtained with relatively few reinforcements, and after a certain point, one can go on giving reinforcements without adding appreciably to the number of responses an organism will give when reinforcement stops (Skinner, 1938).

As a matter of fact, however, evidence now exists that the function relating number of reinforcements to resistance to extinction may be nonmonotonic under some conditions. This means that as number of reinforcements increases during training, subsequent resistance to extinction

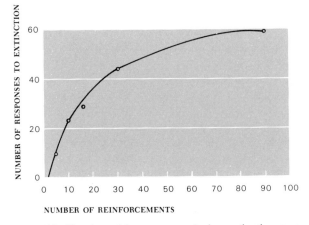

FIG. **4.2** Number of lever presses during extinction as a function of the number of reinforcements administered during training. (Redrawn from Perin, 1942; data from Perin, 1942, and S. B. Williams, 1938.)

first increases and then *decreases*. The evidence for this effect is by no means consistent, however, and we are still not certain about the exact conditions under which the effect will occur. North and Stimmel (1960) found that rats would run faster during extinction in a straight runway if they had received 45 reinforced trials during acquisition than if they had received 90 or 135 trials. Ison (1962), and Siegel and Wagner (1963), who also used runways, report the same general effect. Hill and Spear (1963), however, found that resistance to extinction continued to increase as number of reinforcements increased to as many as 128 trials; and Bacon (1962), in an experiment we have already looked at in Chapter 2, got the same results for numbers of reinforcements that varied from 10 to 300.

D'Amato, Schiff, and Jagoda (1962) did an experiment in the Skinner box in which two training procedures were used. Under one condition, simple reward training was given, so that all lever presses were reinforced. Under another condition, however, discrimination training (Chapter 1) was used, so that reinforcement was available during a 45-second period in which a light was on in the box, but was not available during intervening 33- to 65-second periods in which the discriminative cue of the light was off. Within each condition, rats were permitted to make 50 reinforced lever presses per day until the total number of reinforcements for different groups reached 200, 400, 800, or 1,600. Then the rats were extinguished over five daily 10-minute periods. The results show that following simple *reward* training, the number of nonreinforced lever presses emitted during extinction increased regularly with the number of prior reinforcements. Following *discrimination* training, however, resistance to extinction increased to the point where 800 reinforcements had been given, then fell sharply. The group of rats that got 1,600 reinforcements with the discrimination training procedure gave fewer responses than any of the other groups run under that condition. D'Amato and his coexperimenters concluded that discrimination training coupled with a very large number of reinforcements may be one of the critical sets of conditions that can be used to get a nonmonotonic relation between number of reinforcements and resistance to extinction (see also Murillo & Capaldi, 1961). This cannot be the complete answer, however, in view of the results of experiments such as that of North and Stimmel (1960), which did not include discrimination training as part of the experimental procedure.

Another approach to the problem comes from some thinking of Theios and Brelsford (1964). These experimenters suggested that the non-monotonic relation between number of reinforced acquisition trials and resistance to extinction might be tied to some sort of incentive phenomenon associated with reinforcement conditions in the goal box. They noted that, because of the very definition of the problem, the number of acquisition trials an experimenter chooses to use also determines the number of rewards he provides in the goal box. What would happen, they asked, if the effects of number of rewards were separated from the effects of number of runs in the alley? To answer this question, three groups of rats were run in a straight runway. The rats in one group (the 10-10 group) ran 10 acquisition trials and received 10 rewards, one on each trial. A reward consisted of 0.7 gram of food. Similarly, the rats in another group (the 60-60 group) ran 60 trials and received 60 rewards. The rats in a third group (the 10-60 group) were placed *directly in the goal box* and permitted to eat the 0.7-gram reward for 50 trials, then *ran the alley* for 10 more rewarded trials.

As you can see, this experimental design sets things so that rats in the 10-60 group received just as many *rewards* as rats in the 60-60 group, but just as many *runs* as rats in the 10-10 group. After acquisition, all three groups were extinguished for a total of at least 80 trials. The running times obtained during extinction showed that the 60-60 group was much slower at the end of 80 trials than the 10-10 group; that is, the data showed clearly that resistance to extinction decreased as the number of reinforced runs increased with the apparatus and experimental technique that the investigators used. However, the 10-60 group ran *slowest of all*—in spite of the fact that the rats in this group had *run* the alley no more frequently than the rats in the 10-10 group.

On the basis of their data, Theios and Brelsford suggest that the nonmonotonic relation between number of reinforced acquisition trials and resistance to extinction may be obtained not because rats receive so many *runs* down the alley, but because they receive so many *rewards* in the process. They note, too, that experiments which have failed to obtain the nonmonotonic relation have generally used relatively small rewards, while experiments that have obtained it very clearly (e.g., Ison, 1962) have incorporated relatively large rewards such as the 0.7-gram reward Theios and Brelsford used. Perhaps giving many rewards is functionally similar to giving large rewards, both procedures tending to decrease resistance to extinction. In this connection, as we have seen, Spence (1956) has suggested that the magnitude of K, incentive motivation, increases as a function of both number and amount of reinforcement, and Hulse (1958) and Wagner (1961) have shown that resistance to extinction decreases as amount of reinforcement increases, so there is both theoretical and empirical precedent for these assumptions.

The condition of our knowledge concerning the relation between number of reinforcements and resistance to extinction is another good example of the murky state of affairs with which psychologists often have to contend. It should be emphasized, however, that in spite of the conflicting data we have examined, the relation between number of reinforcements and resistance to extinction shown in Figure 4.2 is probably much better than a first approximation to the data that can be obtained most consistently in cases of simple reward learning.

TIME AND EFFORT IN EXTINCTION

Two variables of considerable importance in their effects upon extinction are (1) the distribution of responses in time and (2) the effort required to make responses during extinction. These are linked together at this point not only because they are of interest in their own right, but also because they bear jointly on a particular theory of extinction that we shall discuss later. Let us look at each in turn.

DISTRIBUTION OF RESPONSES IN TIME. In Chapter 1 we noted that psychologists find it useful to distinguish between free-responding situations, where the organism determines when responses occur, and controlled-responding situations, where the experimenter determines when responses occur. It is simple, of course, to use a controlled-responding technique with a simple apparatus such as a straight runway; in fact, a runway essentially requires a controlled-responding procedure. The same sort of thing could also be done in the Skinner box, however, by quickly removing the lever after a response occurs and then reinserting it at some later time so that another response can be made. The important point in either case is that the experimenter has precise control over the rate with which individual responses can occur; he can vary the interval of time between successive responses quite easily.

Interest in the effects on behavior of different intervals of time between responses began, like many other things, with Pavlov. Pavlov (1927) reported that a classically conditioned response extinguishes more rapidly when trials occur close together than when they are spread apart. More recently, experiments have been performed to see if this is also true of instrumental conditioning.

First of all, if we look at the data that are available concerning the effect of different intertrial intervals upon instrumental behavior during *reinforcement,* we find a highly ambiguous state of affairs. While Hovland (1936) found that massing trials together in time impaired performance appreciably, the great weight of the evidence shows that learning proceeds at just about the same rate regardless of the interval of time that elapses between successive responses (e.g., Wilson, Weiss, & Amsel, 1955; Lewis & Cotton, 1959). Second, if we look at the effect of intertrial interval upon resistance to extinction, we find an almost equally ambiguous state of affairs. When significant effects are found (e.g., Lewis & Cotton, 1959), they generally indicate that resistance to extinction is greater if trials are spaced close together in time than if they are spaced farther apart. Exceptions to this rule are not hard to find, however; Gagne (1941) and Hill and Spear (1962) report that spaced trials during extinction produce greater resistance to extinction than massed trials.

Teichner (1952) and Cole and Abraham (1962), among others, point out one factor that may help to unravel things a bit—at least so far as the extinction data are concerned. Teichner, for example, suggests that extinction is faster under massed conditions (his data showed this to be true), but that this is a relatively small effect easily obscured by other conditions. Of much greater importance, Teichner feels, is the relation between the intertrial interval used during training and that used during extinction. The greatest resistance to extinction is found when the training and extinction intervals are the same; if they are different, resistance to extinction will be reduced. As we shall see in Chapter 6, response strength tends to decrease when an organism is conditioned to respond to one set of stimulus conditions and is then shifted to another set (a phenomenon known as stimulus generalization), so there is good reason to believe that something akin to stimulus generalization could be at work when intertrial intervals change as part of the switch from conditioning to extinction.

In this connection, Cole and Abraham's experiment is of some interest, since they attempted to minimize the effects of a change in intertrial interval by exposing each of their subjects, during training in a Y maze, to a sample of the intertrial intervals that were to be used during extinction. Thus, while rats were learning to find food in a goal box at the end of one arm of the Y, trials were separated by either 20 seconds or 24 hours, with the two intervals used in random fashion so that there were from one to five trials per day. *All* rats in the experiment learned according to this procedure. Then, during extinction, subgroups of rats were run with a 20-second, 5-minute, or 24-hour intertrial interval. The results show that, in general, the group which was extinguished with the 24-hour intertrial interval persisted longer in making correct responses and ran faster for more trials than the groups which were extinguished with the two shorter intertrial intervals. However, all groups appeared to approach much the same level at the end of extinction.

EFFORT AND EXTINCTION. A well-known experiment by Mowrer and Jones (1943) provides evidence suggesting that the effort which must be expended in making a response during extinction affects the resistance to extinction of that response. These investigators trained rats to press a lever for food in a Skinner box. During training, the lever was counterweighted by different amounts so that rats learned to press the bar when it required 5 grams to produce reinforcement, when it required 42.5 grams, and when it required 80 grams. At the end of training, the rats were divided into three groups, and each group was extinguished with a different counterweight attached to the lever. The results showed that resistance to extinction decreased as more and more force was required to press the lever during extinction. Similar results were obtained by Capehart, Viney, and Hulicka (1958) in an experiment in which *all* rats received equal amounts of training on *all* the lever weights that were to be used during extinction (5 grams, 40 grams, and 70 grams). Under these conditions, a group extinguished with a 5-gram lever emitted a mean of 146 presses during the course of two extinction sessions, while groups extinguished with 40-gram and 70-gram levers gave means of 98 and 45 responses, respectively.

Offhand, it would seem on the basis of these data that resistance to extinction is a neat, straightforward, decreasing function of the amount of effort that an animal has to expend to produce responses during extinction. But, as you may well have anticipated, things are not quite that simple. For one thing, if reinforcement is made contingent upon pressing heavy levers during conditioning, the rat may learn not only the response of "pressing the lever," but also, in a sense, the response of "pressing the lever *hard*." And this might well be a *different* response from that which a rat learns when it must press a lighter lever to obtain reinforcement (Logan, 1956, 1960). If such were the case, we might expect that a rat trained on a 50-gram lever and then extinguished on a 100-gram lever would make just as many *attempted* depressions of the lever as a rat both

trained and extinguished on a 100-gram lever. However—and this is the
crux of the matter—these presses would not have sufficient force in all
cases to be recorded as complete responses, and it might appear in the
recorded data that the rat was extinguished when, in fact, it was still
worrying the lever at a great rate. What is needed is an experiment in
which both complete and incomplete presses are recorded during extinction. Neither Mowrer and Jones (1943) nor Capehart et al. (1958) obtained these data. Stanley and Aamodt (1954) did.

In their experiment, Stanley and Aamodt conditioned two groups
of rats in a Skinner box to press a lever that required 50 grams of effort
for one group, and 100 grams of effort for another. Then the two groups
were split, and half the rats in each were extinguished with a 50-gram
lever, half with a 100-gram lever. During extinction, a response was called
complete if the rat pressed the lever far enough, and with enough force,
so that reinforcement would have been produced during conditioning.
Responses were called incomplete if the rat pressed the lever a certain
preset minimum amount, but did not press it through the distance or
with the force that had been required to produce reinforcement during
conditioning. Extinction was carried out in two 10-minute sessions in the
apparatus, one session per day. The results of the experiment for the two
days of extinction combined are shown in Table 4.1.

TABLE 4.1   **Median Lever Presses during Extinction**
(Stanley & Aamodt, 1954)

GROUP *	COMPLETE R's	INCOMPLETE R's	TOTAL R's
50–50	79.0	10.0	89.0
100–50	88.0	5.0	93.0
50–100	44.5	35.5	74.0
100–100	49.0	14.5	62.0

* The first number in the designation for each group
stands for the force, in grams, required to press the lever
during conditioning; the second number is the force
required during extinction.

If we look, first of all, at the column labeled complete R's (usually the sole data reported), it appears that the groups extinguished with
the 100-gram lever show far less resistance to extinction than the groups
extinguished with the 50-gram lever. We would expect this observation
on the basis of other experiments. But the data in the column labeled
incomplete R's show that this conclusion must be hedged extensively. Rats
which were trained on the 50-gram lever and extinguished on the 100-

gram lever, for example, made a very large number of responses that did not meet the force criterion for extinction, but that in all likelihood would have been sufficient much of the time to produce reinforcement during conditioning. The column labeled total *R*'s, which shows median scores based on the combined scores for complete and incomplete *R*'s, indicates that heavy levers do tend to reduce resistance to extinction overall (though none of the differences are statistically significant—owing, most likely, to the fact that only three rats were run in group 50–50 and four rats in the other groups). Nevertheless, it is clear that including incomplete with complete responses during extinction attenuates the effects reported in experiments such as that of Mowrer and Jones to a considerable degree. As part of the conditioning process, rats apparently do learn to press the lever with a certain force characteristic of the force required to produce reinforcement, and the effects of this procedure carry over to extinction to modify performance there (see also Herrick, 1964).

A final experiment pretty much lays to rest the notion that resistance to extinction always decreases as a function of the effort required to make responses during extinction. Lawrence and Festinger (1961, Exp. 14) trained rats to run a runway for food, 60 trials in all. For one group, the runway was tilted so that the rats had to run a 25-degree incline to get to the goal box. For another group, the incline was set at 50 degrees. After the rats were conditioned with the effortfulness of the running response varied in this manner, they were extinguished by running them until they made four 90-second runs, not necessarily consecutive. *During extinction they ran up the same incline they ran during conditioning.* The results show that at the end of training, the rats which ran the 50-degree incline took an average of 2.0 seconds to reach the goal box, while those which ran the 25-degree incline took an average of 1.8 seconds. This difference is in the direction we would expect, but it is not appreciable. During extinction, the rats conditioned on the 50-degree incline ran consistently and reliably *faster* (on each of three five-trial days of extinction) than the rats conditioned on the 25-degree incline, and they took *more trials* before reaching the extinction criterion of four 90-second trials. In other words, this experiment demonstrates in conclusive fashion that the greater the effort required during extinction, the *greater* the resistance to extinction. Of course, Lawrence and Festinger ran their experiment with a controlled-trial procedure, and they used a runway rather than a Skinner box. But it is clear from their data that increased effort does not always reduce resistance to extinction; sometimes it may actually increase resistance to extinction.

SPONTANEOUS RECOVERY AND DISINHIBITION.   Pavlov, in his studies of conditioned salivation, discovered two phenomena that he thought to be of considerable theoretical importance. They are called *spontaneous recovery* and *disinhibition*. Again, they are interesting phenomena not only in their own right, but also because they bear on certain theoretical treatments of extinction that we shall come to later. In both spontaneous recovery and disinhibition, the major effect is a recovery of some of the strength of the conditioned response after a certain amount of extinction has taken place. This leads, in turn, to the notion that extinction generates an active inhibition of the conditioned response and that this inhibition can be removed to some extent under certain conditions.

An example from Pavlov's laboratory will illustrate the basic principle of *spontaneous recovery*. Pavlov (1927) produced a conditioned salivary response by allowing a dog first to *see* some meat powder and then to eat it. After the dog had learned to salivate at the sight of the meat powder, Pavlov extinguished the response by no longer putting the meat powder into the animal's mouth. It took only a few trials of this sort to extinguish the conditioned response. The animal was then removed from the experimental room for approximately two hours. When the dog was brought back and allowed to look at the meat powder again, the conditioned response returned. True, the amount of saliva flow was not so great this time as it had been before the extinction process began, but there was no doubt that the conditioned response had recovered to a considerable extent—actually about one-sixth of the original amount under the conditions that Pavlov used.

Another experiment (Ellson, 1938) shows the occurrence of spontaneous recovery in an instrumentally conditioned response. Four groups of rats were conditioned to press a lever in a Skinner box. Following the conditioning procedure, all animals were permitted to operate the lever without reinforcement until they had failed to respond for a period of 5 minutes. One group of rats was then removed from the box and allowed to rest for 5 minutes. These rats were then placed in the box again, and additional unreinforced responses counted. The second group of rats resumed extinction after a pause of 25 minutes, the third after 65 minutes, and the fourth after 185 minutes. All animals showed an immediate tendency to press the lever when replaced in the box, even though all of them had failed to press the lever for a period of five minutes prior to their removal from the box. Figure 4.3 shows that the amount of recovery, or the number of responses emitted after rest, is an increasing function of the length of time of the rest period. Like most effects associated with the learning process, however, this function seems to have its limit, so that an extremely long rest period yields no more spontaneous recovery than a moderately long one. In this experiment, the amount of recovery reached its limit at about one-fifth the original strength of the response.

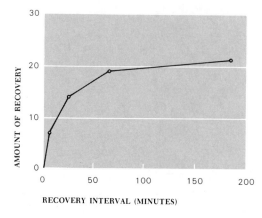

FIG. **4.3** Number of lever presses in a second extinction period following various intervals of rest. In this experiment, most spontaneous recovery occurs within an hour after original extinction. (Data from Ellson, 1938.)

Spontaneous recovery is a genuine and stable part of the extinction process. We may, for example, try to stop the family dog from begging at the dining-room table by ignoring it when it does so, and we may find that by the end of the meal the dog has retired to the living room. Nevertheless, the next evening it will probably beg as before. Since spontaneous recovery is incomplete, however, the dog will not be so persistent this time and will stop sooner. If we repeat the extinction process for a few days, and if we are *consistent* about doing so (which is not easy), the response will eventually stop occurring.

Our second phenomenon, that of *disinhibition,* stems from Pavlov's theory of extinction, and he placed great stress upon the importance of this effect. In his original demonstration of disinhibition, Pavlov established a conditioned salivary response to the sight of meat powder. Once it was well established, he extinguished it by showing the meat to the dog without letting the animal eat it. When the conditioned response was completely extinguished, Pavlov paired a new stimulus with the original stimulus. The new stimulus was not one that could elicit the conditioned response itself, but when it was paired with the old stimulus, it did. Thus, the salivary response extinguished to the sight of food reappeared, or was *disinhibited,* when the old CS was paired with a stimulus that was novel to the animal.

THEORIES OF EXTINCTION

Animals stop responding when they are no longer reinforced. So simple a fact would hardly seem to demand very subtle theoretical explanation, yet extinction has been one of the aspects of behavior to which the psychologist has directed some of his most intricate and complicated theorizing. Actually, of course, a theory of extinction is fundamental to any theory of behavior, for the fact that organisms stop performing un-reinforced acts is just as important as the fact that they learn reinforced acts in the first place. Unimaginable chaos would exist in the world if learned responses did not extinguish when the environment failed to provide reinforcement for them.

In the following sections we shall study some of the more important theories of extinction. In each case we shall see what a particular theory has to say about the extinction process, and we shall see whether the theory thrives or wilts under the harsh light of laboratory testing.

RESPONSE-PRODUCED INHIBITION THEORY

The response-produced inhibition theory is, in a certain historical sense, the major classical theory of extinction. Like "classical" theories in many other fields, however, it has been pretty thoroughly demolished by critics —among them that ultimate critic, experimental data. Some of the rubble has been used to build new theories, and some of the empirical bits and pieces still hold and deserve their place in psychology today. For these reasons, and because the theory provides a good case history of the fate of psychological theories, we shall examine it in some detail. The most complete statement of the response-produced inhibition theory comes from Hull (1943), though he took the basic concept of inhibition from Pavlov and borrowed ideas from other sources as well.

REACTIVE INHIBITION. Hull started with the assumption that whenever an organism makes a response it also generates some inhibition with respect to that response. This means that, all other things being equal, once a response takes place, it is somewhat less likely to occur in the immediate future. Such inhibition may be thought of as analogous to fatigue in that it makes the next response more difficult to produce. And like fatigue, reactive inhibition disappears after a period of rest. If there is not enough rest between responses, however, the inhibition accumulates from response to response.

Hull (1943) advanced the hypothesis that the amount of inhibition which results from a series of responses is a positively accelerated function of the amount of physical work the response requires. In other words, as the response requires more effort, the inhibition accumulates at an increasing rate. Later, Hull (1951) revised the substance of this assumption to the effect that for responses involving large amounts of work (relative to the ability of the organism involved), the inhibition generated is not much greater than that for smaller amounts of work. In other words, he said that the function which relates responding to work is S-shaped. In both cases, he specified that rest reduces the inhibition generated by each response in a way that is best described by a simple negative exponential function. Eventually, with enough rest, the response will completely recover its strength.

In Hull's theory, reactive inhibition will accumulate whether the response is reinforced or not. If the response is reinforced, the positive effects of reinforcement must overcome the negative effects of reactive inhibition. This leads to the logical conclusion that in a long series of massed trials, response strength might eventually begin to decline and to reach zero *even though responses were always reinforced.* There is some evidence which suggests that under certain conditions this may occur (Calvin et al., 1956; Kendrick, 1958), and the effect has been called *inhibition of reinforcement.* But, as Prokasy (1960) points out, the evidence is by no means clear-cut, and it is probably safest to accept with considerable reservation the notion that decrements in response strength can be obtained during the continued reinforcement of a response. There is an enormous number of experiments in the learning literature where literally thousands and thousands of responses have been obtained at very high rates without any significant or appreciable drop in the rate of emission (e.g., Ferster & Skinner, 1957).

The most important aspect of the response-produced inhibition theory, however, concerns its statement about what goes on during extinction. When responses are no longer reinforced, reactive inhibition is thought to increase without the counteracting effects of positive reinforcement. The result is that the organism eventually ceases to respond. Since reactive inhibition decreases with time, however, we should predict spontaneous recovery after a period of rest. Remember, too, that Pavlov showed spontaneous recovery to be only about one-sixth the original response strength, and at best, we might expect only 50 percent recovery. Since spontaneous recovery is incomplete, Hull postulated a second factor, *conditioned inhibition,* to account for the permanent effects of extinction.

CONDITIONED INHIBITION. Hull regarded reactive inhibition as a negative motivational state. Presumably, animals are motivated to avoid reactive inhibition much as they are motivated to avoid an electric shock. If we accept the drive-reduction theory of reinforcement, it is easy to see how escape from, or avoidance of, reactive inhibition would constitute reinforcement. Thus, when an organism ceases to respond, its fatigue state, or reactive inhibition, is reduced. But this, in keeping with the drive-reduction point of view, is precisely the operation that is required for reinforcement to occur. Reduction of reactive inhibition supposedly reinforces the organism for doing nothing, and the state of affairs which results and produces failure to respond is called conditioned inhibition.

HOW REACTIVE AND CONDITIONED INHIBITION WORK IN EXTINCTION. The theory of extinction based on reactive and conditioned inhibition seems complicated, but its essentials are simple. Extinction is the result of an active inhibition of a learned response. This inhibition is composed of two parts—reactive inhibition, which is temporary and disappears with rest; and conditioned inhibition, which is permanent and does not. Thus, spontaneous recovery of an extinguished conditioned response is predicted from the assumption that reactive inhibition disappears with rest. In the process, however, conditioned inhibition is produced, so that complete recovery of the extinguished response does not occur.

Hull's two-factor theory of extinction (as it has been called) has been applied to a variety of problems in behavior—for example, to the fact that rats generally prefer not to repeat the same response on successive trials in a maze (Heathers, 1940; Zeaman & House, 1951; but see Prachtl, 1953; Rothkopf & Zeaman, 1952). To take another instance, the theory has also been applied to the pronounced effects of massed as compared with spaced practice in the learning of complicated human motor skills, such as learning to type. Despite the fact that the theory has been applied in the past to a wide variety of phenomena, we now are pretty certain that it contains a number of serious defects, and therefore we should look at some criticisms of it. Since attempts to test Hull's theory have led to some valuable new information about behavior, the next part of this chapter will serve as more than just a critical analysis of the response-produced inhibition theory of extinction.

TIME AND EFFORT IN RELATION TO RESPONSE-PRODUCED INHIBITION. In an earlier section in the chapter, we examined the effects upon resistance to extinction of the duration of the interval of time between responses and the amount of effort that an organism had to make to produce responses. In both cases, if you will recall, one of the best ways to characterize the data was to consider the effects of changing the experimental conditions of time and effort as training was terminated and extinction begun. If a change occurred, resistance to extinction was less than if it did not. The data were rather ambiguous and inconsistent when we looked at the effects of the interval of time that was used during extinction per se, for example. Some studies showed resistance to extinction to be greatest during massed-extinction trials, some showed it to be greatest if spaced-extinction trials were used, and so on.

The response-produced inhibition theory of extinction says that in the process of extinguishing a response, resistance to extinction will be less if massed trials as compared with spaced trials are used and if more effort as compared with less effort is required. This follows directly from the fact that resistance to extinction is supposed to decrease as a function of the buildup of reactive inhibition on the one hand and the correlated buildup of conditioned inhibition on the other. Massed trials and effortful responses are precisely those things which should produce the greatest rate of increase in reactive and conditioned inhibition, so resistance to extinction should be least under these conditions. Yet as we have seen, the data from animal experiments involving fairly simple responses are essentially, if not completely, at odds with this deduction. Since time and effort are two of the simplest sorts of variables that we can introduce into extinction to test the theory, and since the theory does not do a very good job of predicting the data that appear when we do so, the response-produced inhibition account of extinction is already in serious trouble.

LATENT EXTINCTION AND EXTINCTION WITHOUT RESPONDING. The most important single idea in the response-produced inhibition theory is that decrement in responding is the result of a sort of negative feedback from responding itself. Thus, the more effort a given response requires, the greater the difficulty in producing additional responses. Yet to begin with, there is evidence from the classical conditioning literature that a decrement in responding can occur even when no overt response causes it. For example, there is the phenomenon of "subzero" extinction reported by Pavlov (1927). Pavlov showed that if we extinguish a classically conditioned response to the point at which it completely disappears and then *continue* to present the conditional stimulus, these additional trials weaken the response even further (shown by tests for spontaneous recovery). This means that presenting the conditional stimulus alone was effective in producing further reduction of response strength—it was not necessary for the animal to give the conditioned response at all. Thus response-produced inhibition could not have occurred.

Some of the most telling data concerning the response-produced inhibition theory come from experiments in which an animal, following training, is exposed directly to a stimulus situation (such as a goal box) in which reward was formerly available but from which it has now been removed. In the process, things are set so that the animal *does not perform the complete learned response at all*. Instead of running the runway to get to the goal box, the animal is placed directly into the empty goal box by the experimenter. Then, after a number of direct placements of this sort, conventional extinction trials begin, and the animal runs once more. The effect of the direct-placement procedure upon resistance to extinction of running is checked by comparing the performance of animals subjected to this procedure with the performance of other animals placed the same number of times in some "neutral" location (such as a carrying cage or a box not associated with reinforcement). The response-produced inhibition theory of extinction has to predict that direct placements in an empty goal box will have essentially no effect upon the sub-sequent resistance to extinction of running. This would be true because reactive inhibition of running cannot build up unless an animal actually runs. Yet there is now an overwhelming abundance of evidence which shows that direct, nonreinforced exposure to a place formerly associated with reinforcement produces latent effects that carry over to reduce the resistance to extinction of a conditioned response. The phenomenon is termed *latent extinction.*

The first example of latent extinction comes from an experiment of Seward and Levy (1949). They trained rats to run a runway to secure food in a goal box. After conditioning, one group of rats was placed directly in the goal box when it was empty of food, so that they saw that reinforcement was no longer there. A second group of rats did not have the benefit of this preview. The next day, all the rats were given a series of extinction trials. The group that had been able to see beforehand that food was no longer available extinguished approximately twice as quickly as the other group of rats. It was evident that the running response had been reduced in strength by the sight of the empty goal box, and there-fore some extinction took place without the actual occurrence of the running response.

In other experiments, latent extinction has been demonstrated for the rate at which errors reappear during extinction in a T maze (Deese, 1951), and for resistance to extinction in the Skinner box (Hur-witz, 1955). A number of other studies have also demonstrated the phe-nomenon in its basic form (Moltz, 1955; Dyal, 1964; Clifford, 1964). The Dyal experiment is particularly interesting, since it demonstrated that latent extinction would occur if the interval between placements was 60 seconds or 1 hour, but not if the interval was 24 hours. An observation of this sort indicates that the depression in response strength produced by latent extinction will recover spontaneously provided that the interval between placements in the empty goal box is long enough. This suggests, in turn, that the phenomenon of spontaneous recovery is not necessarily due to the buildup of reactive inhibition through overt responding and its subsequent reduction through rest.

Clifford's (1964) experiment also deserves special mention, not only because it demonstrated latent extinction so neatly, but also because it looked at the phenomenon as a function of the number of reinforced training trials rats received before the latent-extinction procedure began. And as things turned out, the results lend some further insight into the effects of number of reinforcements upon resistance to extinction. Clifford ran separate groups of rats down a runway for 24, 48, 84, 132, or 192 re-inforced trials. Then he split each group and placed half the animals in the empty goal box for 12 trials and the other half in a "neutral" carrying

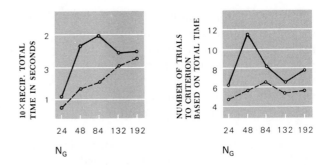

FIG. **4.4** The effect of number of reinforcements (N_G) on resistance to extinction following 12 direct placements into the goal box (dashed curve) or into a neutral cage (solid curve). Both running speeds and trials to an extinction criterion show that the latent-extinction procedure of direct placements into the goal box markedly speeded later regular extinction. (Clifford, 1964.)

cage for 12 trials. Following this procedure, all rats ran the runway for 22 regular extinction trials. Figure 4.4 shows some of the extinction data—those based upon the speed with which rats ran the alley during extinction, and those based upon the number of trials to an extinction criterion determined, in Clifford's terms, by noting each rat's slowest speed on the last 21 extinction trials and selecting the fastest speed in the list.

The data indicate a striking effect of the latent-extinction procedure. First, if we ignore the number of reinforced training trials that were used, resistance to extinction was less for those animals placed directly into the goal box than for those placed in the carrying cage. Note too, however, and add to our previous discussion of the relation between number of training trials and resistance to extinction, that resistance to extinction was a nonmonotonic function of the number of reinforced trials following placement in the carrying cage, but that it increased regularly following placement in the goal box.

LATENT EXTINCTION UNDER CURARE. While placing rats in empty goal boxes during the latent-extinction procedure certainly makes it impossible for them to go through the entire response sequence of running from start box to goal box, it could be argued—although on rather shaky grounds, perhaps—that animals might emit in the goal box at least some components of the response conditioned originally. If this were the case, these components of the full-blown response ought to extinguish and so reduce proportionally the overall strength of the conditioned response when it is subjected to conventional extinction later. We could administer the *coup de grâce* to this objection, and inflict further serious damage upon the response-produced inhibition theory of extinction, if it were possible to prevent literally *any* kind of overt skeletal movement during the latent extinction procedure. And it is quite possible to do so.

When a form of curare, d-tubocurarine chloride, is administered to animals, it produces a flaccid paralysis in which all the skeletal musculature is rendered immobile. A curarized animal must, for example, be given artificial respiration in order to keep it alive. At the same time, curare does not appear to have any effect on sensory mechanisms; while the curarized animal cannot move its skeletal musculature, it apparently can see, hear, and feel in a perfectly normal way. Can latent extinction be demonstrated when the latent-extinction procedure is carried out on a curarized animal? It certainly can.

Black (1958) placed dogs in a harness and trained them to avoid a shock. In order to avoid the shock, a dog had to turn its head and press one or the other of two panels; one panel was located directly to the left of the dog's head and the other was located directly to the right. The discriminative cue for the avoidance response was a tone, and the interval between the onset of the tone and the onset of the shock (applied to one of the dog's feet) was five seconds. If the dog turned its head and pushed one of the panels within this five-second interval, shock was omitted; if the dog failed to do this, the shock came on and both tone and shock continued until the dog made the head-turning response and escaped the shock.

A group of dogs was trained with this simple avoidance-learning procedure until each of the dogs made 15 successive avoidance responses, 10 on one day and 5 on the next. Then half the dogs were curarized and given 50 presentations of the tone alone while they were unable to move —the latent-extinction procedure. The other half were given 50 regular extinction trials, with tone but no shock, and then were curarized and allowed to recover in the apparatus. This group served as a control for the effects of curarization per se.

Two days later, all dogs were placed in the apparatus in the *normal, noncurarized state* and given regular extinction trials. The tone was turned on until the head-turning response occurred or until five seconds elapsed, but shock was omitted. Regular extinction trials occurred at the rate of 100 per day until the dogs failed to make the head-turning response for 10 consecutive trials or until a total of 400 extinction trials had been run. The results of regular extinction are dramatic. The dogs that had been subjected to the latent-extinction procedure under curare responded for a median of 41 trials before meeting the extinction criterion, while the control dogs that had received only regular extinction trials responded for a median of 450 trials (50 on the day they were subsequently curarized and allowed to recover in the apparatus, plus 400 during the following regular extinction sessions). In short, Black's experiment demonstrated a very powerful latent-extinction effect even though his dogs were unable to make any kind of overt muscular movement during the latent-extinction procedure.

THE THEORY BEHIND THE PHENOMENON OF LATENT EXTINCTION. Before we turn to a general evaluation of the response-produced inhibition theory of extinction, let us take a look at one way in which the phenomenon of latent extinction, a very interesting effect in its own right, can be handled in theoretical terms. First of all, there is little question that whatever goes on to produce latent extinction must occur *during* the time that animals spend in the stimulus situation associated with reinforcement when they are placed directly there. One way of looking at this is to assume that changes take place in the strength of the classically conditioned r_g-s_g mechanism described in the last chapter (Moltz, 1957; Spence, 1960; Clifford, 1964). If you will recall, the strength of the fractional-goal response is presumed to depend upon such things as the number of reinforcements, the size of each reinforcement, and so on. Furthermore, the elicitation of fractional-goal response by cues in the learning situation is supposed to add to the general level of *motivation* that is conditioned in the learning situation—specifically, in Spence's terms, to incentive motivation, K.

Now when a rat is placed directly in a goal box that formerly contained reinforcement, the cues of the goal box elicit the fractional-goal response. But since reinforcement is not there, the strength of the fractional-goal response should decrease according to the general rules that hold for the extinction of any response. This, in turn, should reduce the strength of incentive motivation. The extent of the reduction will depend upon a number of things, such as the number of times the animal is exposed to the empty goal box and the length of the period the animal is confined there on each occasion—in general, that is, upon any experimental operation which will reduce, through extinction, the tendency for goal-box cues to elicit fractional-goal responses. Of course, for control animals placed in some neutral location in which reward has never occurred, there are no cues associated with reinforcement, and so there is nothing to elicit the fractional-goal response and produce its extinction. According to this reasoning, then, the latent-extinction procedure produces relatively fast extinction of running because it reduces that part of the motivational base for running which is conditioned to cues specific to the place where original learning occurs.[1]

[1] An alternative way of looking at latent extinction is to assume that direct placements in a goal box extinguish some of the conditioned reward value of the goal-box cues. Since there is precedent for accounting for the principle of conditioned reinforcement

You may wonder how a theoretical account based on the r_g-s_g mechanism could explain the data Black obtained from curarized dogs. That is, how could a curarized dog emit even fractional components of some conditioned response, since it cannot make any skeletal movements at all? And how, therefore, could these fractional responses occur and extinguish so as to produce a latent-extinction effect? The best way to approach these questions is to remember that fractional-goal responses and fractional-goal stimuli are *hypothetical constructs* to which the theorist attaches certain properties to suit his theoretical ends. Though he talks in terms of stimulus, response, and motivation (as Spence does, for example), the theorist does not necessarily require that these things be "real" or directly measurable for them to have meaning within his theory. He simply uses the terms to label a theoretical model that can be used to describe certain classes of behavioral events. He picks particular terms for no better reason, perhaps, than that they are compatible with the language used in the rest of some more general theoretical structure. So, though Black himself did not do this, we could think of a fractional-goal response in Black's experiment as a kind of covert "response" buried somewhere in the central nervous system, perhaps. Then we could still apply the r_g-s_g mechanism *as a model* to account for the latent-extinction data Black obtained. In these terms, extinction of the "central fractional response" could be assumed to occur even in a curarized dog, and the latent-extinction effect could be deduced here just as we have deduced it for rats in runways and goal boxes.

THE FATE OF THE RESPONSE-PRODUCED INHIBITION THEORY.   Putting all the evidence together—evidence concerning the distribution of trials, the effects of effort on response strength, and so forth—we may conclude that responding does, sometimes, have an inhibitory effect upon the future tendency to respond. The evidence even here is far from consistent, however. Furthermore, if we look at behavior during extinction per se, it is readily apparent that the theory does not fare very well when put to experimental test. In the light of phenomena such as latent extinction, there appears to be little question that the response-produced inhibition theory of extinction faces a formidable task if it is to extricate itself from the serious trouble in which the data place it. For the present, the task does not seem worth attempting—if it can in fact be accomplished at all.

The root of the matter is that the concept of conditioned inhibition is weak. As originally stated in Hull's theory of learning, it leads to

in terms of r_g-s_g, or some highly similar mechanism (e.g., Hull, 1952), the basic rationale behind an approach to latent extinction in terms of conditioned reinforcement would be the same, essentially, as that we have just outlined. For still another alternative, see Mowrer (1960).

contradictory properties or to predictions that data simply do not support. We have seen that extinction can occur when conditioned inhibition based upon response-produced inhibition should be very weak. Therefore, it would seem that the notion of conditioned inhibition is superfluous. This leaves us with the idea that there may be a temporary, fatiguelike decrement in response strength produced by continued responding. This inhibition may have something to do with the organism ceasing to respond *temporarily*, but it cannot have much to do with the *permanent* effects of the extinction process. It is clear that even if we do accept the general proposition of response-produced inhibition, we still need some concept that will help explain the permanent effects of extinction, and the notion of conditioned inhibition does not seem to be a good one.

COMPETITION THEORY

A second theory of extinction is that put forward by Guthrie (1935, 1952) and by Estes (1950, 1959). In its most general form, it is called a *competition* or *interference* theory. In a word, the theory attributes extinction of a particular response to the acquisition of competing response tendencies. Thus, when an animal stops responding in a particular situation, it may be because it has formed an association between "not responding" and the stimuli present in the situation. In some cases the animal will learn responses that are alternative to those conditioned during original learning, while in other cases it will learn to do nothing. In both instances, the important thing is that the animal learns behavior that *competes* or *interferes* with the behavior acquired during initial training.

Guthrie, following the above reasoning, says that there are three ways in which responses may be eliminated. The first method is to introduce the conditional stimulus subliminally, so that it is too weak to be detected by the organism and to produce a response, and then to increase its strength gradually. This is what we do when we train a horse to saddle by first putting on only a light blanket and then gradually working up to full gear. The blanket, by itself, is not a sufficient stimulus to set off bucking, and the horse is not disturbed by the gradual addition of heavier loads. An experiment by Kimble and Kendall (1953) shows that this method of "toleration" works quite well in creating a simple avoidance habit in rats. A second method is to repeat the conditional stimulus until the original response is exhausted and the organism is too fatigued to give the original response (though it may, perhaps, be able to give other responses). This is the bronco-busting technique. The third method is to present the conditional stimulus when it is mechanically impossible for the organism to respond in the way that it was formerly conditioned to respond.

The chief feature of these methods is that they tend to create a situation where, at the time the conditional stimulus is presented, there is a very low probability that the old response will occur and, therefore, a correspondingly high probability that other new responses will occur. This sets the stage for the association, by simple contiguity, of the new responses with the old conditional stimulus. As always, resistance to extinction will be a function of many things, but it will vary chiefly with the extent to which the conditions of the environment assure that new behavior can attach itself to and be triggered by the old conditional stimulus. The basic idea, then, is that a response extinguishes as it is displaced by other incompatible or alternative responses.

Guthrie left his analysis of the extinction process pretty much at this level. Estes, however, has gone quite a bit farther and, among other things, his approach has the merit of considerable logical elegance. For one thing, conditioning and extinction become simply different aspects of the same thing—they are both learning by a process of contiguous association of elements of particular responses with elements of stimulus complexes. Furthermore, as Estes (1955, 1959) points out, spontaneous recovery under this theory is not a special phenomenon of inhibition. Rather, it is a function of the fact that the elements of a stimulus compound which are conditioned (or extinguished) on one trial may not be present on the next. These elements, which may be both internal or external to the organism, *fluctuate* from trial to trial, so the tendency to respond "spontaneously" can change between trials (see also Homme, 1956).

It is perhaps not surprising that competition theory in its bare form has difficulties that are similar in magnitude, if not in kind, to those we have seen within the theory of response-produced inhibition. For one thing, a simple, bare competition theory must be sufficiently weighted so that it teeters more than a little bit if it is to handle the kinds of phenomena we looked at under the headings of latent extinction and extinction without responding. Furthermore, there are few simple one-to-one relationships between the properties of conditioning and extinction—for example, a maximal rate of responding can sometimes (but not always) be obtained in a Skinner box with a single reinforcement, while extinction after one reinforcement may require as many as 150 responses before the rate of responding returns to the unconditioned, or operant, level (Skinner, 1938). And in classical conditioning, extinction is usually more rapid than the original conditioning.

These, however, are relatively minor objections. Though there are some who might disagree, they do not seem nearly so serious as those that can be raised about the theory of extinction based upon response-produced inhibition. Perhaps the most serious objection to the competition theory is not a logical one. That is, there is good reason to believe that extinction reflects many factors other than loss of habit per se. One such factor is that extinction appears to provide a source of motivation—frustration-produced motivation in particular. If we take the general logic of competition theory and add a dash of frustration, we have a very potent mixture to use as a tool in handling a number of the phenomena of extinction—as we shall now see.

FRUSTRATION AND REINFORCEMENT

There are obviously many ways in which we can frustrate an organism and so, perhaps, arrive at a definition of a frustrating state of affairs. We could, for example, train a rat to run a simple runway with food as a reward, and then introduce frustration by placing a barricade in the runway so that the rat could not get into the goal box (Lambert & Solomon, 1952). In this case, there would be two essential ingredients involved in the production of frustration: *initial training* with a food reward so that the rat, in effect, has a chance to learn that the response of running the alley leads to a fine-tasting morsel in the goal box, and subsequent *blocking* of the response so that the rat can no longer get into the goal box and obtain the reward. This is not the only way in which frustration can be produced, of course, and a technique that is of particular interest to us at the moment is the following: Let the rat continue to run into the goal box after initial training trials which were rewarded with food, but now remove the food. In this case, running trials continue, but frustration is produced by blocking the behavior most critically involved in obtaining reinforcement—the eating response itself. The eating response is blocked, obviously, in the sense that it cannot occur when there is no food to eat. What we now have is frustration produced by the *nonreinforcement* of a previously reinforced response, and as you can see, we also have the experimental operations that we use to extinguish a response.

Many experimenters have observed that when an instrumental response is extinguished, animals tend to become emotionally excited, as if they were frustrated by the withdrawal of reinforcement. Skinner (1938), for example, has noted this in rats undergoing extinction and has proposed that it contributes to the comparative irregularity of extinction curves. Other investigators have assumed that extinction gives rise to a frustration drive and that this accounts for some of the effects we find in a study of extinction. Theoretical and experimental descriptions of the things that happen when frustration due to nonreinforcement occurs have been developed extensively by Spence (1956, 1960) and Amsel (1958, 1962). Much of what is known comes from experiments in which frustration has been introduced during the *conditioning* of a response, but this information has been used to generate ideas and experiments aimed directly at the extinction process per se.

In one of the very first experiments on the problem, Amsel and
Roussel (1952) ran a single group of rats down a straight runway that
consisted of a start box, an alley (alley 1), a goal box (goal box 1), a
second alley (alley 2), and a second goal box (goal box 2). After some preliminary training, the rats were run for 84 trials, 3 trials per day, with
food available in both goal boxes. At the end of these trials, running
times had reached a low asymptote in both runways. Then the rats were
run for 36 more trials with food available in goal box 1 on a random
half of the trials, and no food available in goal box 1 on the other half
of the trials. Food was always available in goal box 2. The experimenters
report their results by comparing the running times in runway 2 for those
trials where the rats had just eaten food in goal box 1 and those trials
where they had not. The data appear in Figure 4.5. As you can see, the
rats ran down runway 2 at just about the same speed they always had on
those trials in which they had just been rewarded in goal box 1. However,
on those trials in which they found no food in goal box 1, they ran
significantly *faster* down runway 2.

Amsel and Roussel interpret their data by assuming first of all
that during the initial 84 training trials, the rats were building a strong
tendency to approach and eat food in both goal boxes. Then they assumed

FIG. **4.5**   The effect of frustration on running. At the left, running times during preliminary training are shown. At the right, running times in the second
alley following reward (solid line) or nonreward (dashed line) in the first goal
box are shown. Frustration from nonreward clearly reduces running time.
(Amsel & Roussel, 1952.)

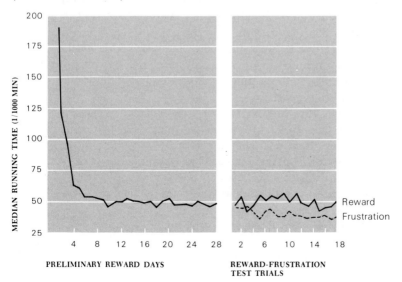

that once this tendency was strongly established, *frustration* was introduced by removing food in goal box 1 on some trials, and that the effects of frustration showed up on those trials as an increase in running speed in runway 2. In other words, they assumed that frustration induced by nonreinforcement of a previously reinforced response has drive or *motivational* properties that channel into running down runway 2. Their data, of course, support their interpretation. Other data (Wagner, 1963) also support the idea that frustration has drive properties.

Bower (1962) carried things a step farther. He assumed that if frustration could be produced by introducing *zero* reward following a series of rewards of a consistent amount, then some frustration, albeit less, might be produced by simply *reducing* suddenly the amount of reward that rats were accustomed to obtain. Bower's observations on this problem were extensive, and we shall only look at part of them. His apparatus was patterned after Amsel and Roussel's in that it contained a start box, two runways, and two goal boxes. It also contained a third runway, into which the rat ran after leaving goal box 2, and a third goal box; but it is the data obtained from the first and second runways that are of interest to us at the moment. Rats were trained initially for 198 trials, 6 trials per day, to run alleys 1, 2, and 3, with 8 food pellets present in goal boxes 1 and 2 and 1 pellet in goal box 3. Then test trials began, 6 per day. On 3 of the test trials each day, the rats received the same reward combination (8 pellets in goal box 1 and 8 pellets in goal box 2) that was used during initial training. On the remaining 3 trials, other combinations were used, so that over 36 test days, the rats ran alley 2 after receiving 16, 12, 8, 6, 4, 2, or 0 pellets in goal box 1. The running speeds in alley 2, as a function of the number of pellets just received in goal box 1, are shown in Figure 4.6. Note that the data are reported in terms of the *difference* in speed between trials on which the rat received the standard 8-pellet reward and trials on which one of the test magnitudes was used. The 8-pellet condition thus serves as a base line with which the other conditions can be compared.

The data show the biggest "frustration effect"—that is, the biggest net increase in speed in alley 2—when the number of pellets in goal box 1 was reduced on test trials from the standard 8 pellets to zero pellets. Bower reports that the increase in speed of 34 points under the zero-pellet condition corresponds to an increase in speed of about 26 percent relative to the 8-pellet base line. The other conditions arrange themselves nicely; in general, rats ran faster and faster in alley 2 as the number of pellets they received in goal box 1 approached zero. You should also note that the rats actually *slowed down* relative to their base-line performance if they received a reward in goal box 1 that was *bigger* than the 8-pellet reward they were used to getting there.

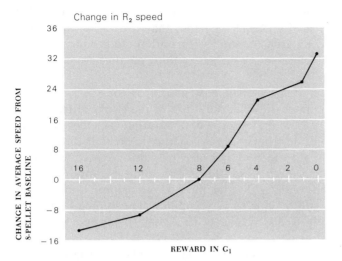

FIG. 4.6 Changes in running speed in the second alley following test rewards greater and less than the regular eight-pellet reward. If the reward was less than eight pellets, the rats ran faster than usual, while if the reward was greater than eight pellets, they ran slower. (Bower, 1962.)

Offhand, you might think that the results reported by Amsel and Roussel and by Bower might simply reflect changes in drive level when a rat runs alley 2 after receiving something as compared with nothing in goal box 1. For example, Bower's 16-pellet condition might have produced slower speeds in alley 2 than the 8-pellet condition simply because the rat was less hungry after eating 16 pellets and therefore less motivated to run alley 2. For the same reason, a rat might run alley 2 faster after receiving zero pellets in goal box 1 than after receiving 8 pellets there. But there is considerable evidence which suggests that the frustration effect is not due to simple changes in hunger drive. For one thing, Bower observed that rats tended to run faster and faster in alley 2 over the three test trials on any given day. This is hardly the sort of behavior that one would expect to find if there was any appreciable drop in hunger drive during the course of a trial or of a day's testing (see also Wagner, 1959). Taken as a whole, the data clearly indicate that the frustration effect is due to something correlated with the contrast between what rats have found in goal box 1 when they have been trained initially and what they find there when the experimenter imposes test trials involving other magnitudes of reinforcement.

Keep in mind, then, the fact that there is good evidence that withdrawal of reinforcement is an operation which can be shown to produce emotional effects characteristic of those we would associate with a frustrating state of affairs. Remember, too, that frustration appears to have the properties of a drive or motive—frustration can produce increases in the vigor with which responses such as running an alley are performed.

THE r_f-s_f MECHANISM AND THE COMPETITION THEORY OF EXTINCTION. Now that we have some basic demonstrations of the effects of frustration before us, let us see how the concept of frustration—together with the principles of competition theory—can fit together to account theoretically for the phenomenon of extinction. In order to do this, we need to develop the concept of the r_f-s_f *mechanism;* this is easy to do, because the *model* for the concept is the same as that for the r_g-s_g mechanism, a mechanism with which you should by now be very familiar. The approach we want to discuss specifically is due primarily to Amsel (1958) and to Spence (1960).

If an animal is first reinforced on a number of trials in some simple learning situation like a straight runway, and if we then remove the reinforcer on some subsequent trial, we have, as we have seen, performed the necessary operations to produce a *primary frustration response,* R_f. If we wanted to see some aspect of R_f in action, we would look for overt signs of emotional activity which, in the rat, might consist of such things as urination, defecation, biting parts of the apparatus, and so on. Now it is assumed that, like the primary goal response R_g and its fractional component r_g, there can be a fractional component of the full-blown frustration response. Let us call this fractional component r_f. As primary frustration occurs over a series of nonreinforced trials, r_f, like r_g, is assumed to occur earlier and earlier in the chain of responses leading to the place where primary frustration takes place. That is, r_f can become *anticipatory* so that the rat, in a manner of speaking, begins to "act frustrated" before it actually arrives at the place where reinforcement has been removed and primary frustration occurs. Just as the elicitation of r_g is presumed to add to general drive level (in the form of incentive motivation in Spence's system), the elicitation of r_f is also presumed to add to general drive level.

Now, to reach the crux of things, the r_f response is presumed to yield its own response-produced stimuli, s_f. And the s_f stimuli, in turn, elicit overt responses in the learning situation. Some of these responses to s_f may be quite compatible with the original conditioned response of running to the goal box. But others will appear for the first time, and many of these will be *incompatible* with running. What the r_f-s_f mechanism yields in the end, then, is a source of incompatible responses that are both *triggered* and *motivated uniquely* by the frustration that nonreinforcement produces.

By now you may be able to anticipate the next and final step. Given that frustration produces incompatible responses, all we have to do is add the now-familiar propositions associated with learning by contiguity. As incompatible responses which are stimulated and motivated by frustration occur, they become attached through simple contiguity to the stimuli that have been eliciting the original learned response. In so doing, they interfere or compete with that response and produce its extinction. The process begins in the goal box, of course, but as non-reinforced trials continue, interfering responses produced by frustration should occur earlier and earlier in the chain of behavior leading from start box to goal box. Thus, the sequence of behavior that was conditioned originally will eventually disappear.

SOME APPLICATIONS OF THE FRUSTRATION-COMPETITION THEORY. A theory is no better, of course, than its success in accounting for data, so let us examine several experiments in which the frustration-competition theory can be applied and see how well it fares.[2] Adelman and Maatsch (1955) studied the effect upon resistance to extinction of the type of response elicited by frustration during extinction. They trained rats in a short straight runway and then extinguished different groups under one of three conditions. One group was given regular extinction in that it was simply confined in the empty goal box for a set period of time following a run down the alley. A second group was encouraged to make a response compatible with running as a function of the elicitation of frustration in the empty goal box: the goal-box lid was raised, and the rat was coaxed into jumping from the goal box onto a small ledge at the edge of the goal box (it is not hard to get a rat to do this). A third group was encouraged to make a response quite incompatible with running down the alley and into the goal box: the goal-box door that was normally closed to prevent retracing once the rat reached the goal box was opened on extinction trials, and the rat was permitted to "recoil" from the empty goal box and to make the incompatible response of running all the way back to the start box.

The results of the experiment are quite striking. The rats in the group that could respond to frustration by running into the goal box and jumping directly out of the frustrating situation did not slow their running speeds at all during extinction. The rats in the group that was permitted to retrace extinguished quite rapidly, while the rats in the

[2] In some cases we shall apply the frustration-competition theory as an alternative to the theoretical interpretation given by the creators of the experiments themselves. It is, of course, not uncommon—though perhaps it is unfortunate—that more than one approach can be used to explain data in theoretical terms.

group that was simply confined in the empty goal box extinguished at an intermediate rate. In short, the experiment clearly demonstrates that the *nature* of the response elicited by frustration can have a marked effect upon the rate at which the response conditioned originally will extinguish. The greater the incompatibility of the response to frustration with the response that the rat has learned initially, the faster extinction proceeds. And this, of course, is an observation that would be predicted directly by the frustration-competition theory.

In a second experiment (Stanley and Rowe, 1954), rats were trained in a runway to run for food and were then extinguished. During extinction, the duration of confinement in the empty goal box on each trial was varied: One group of rats was confined for 10 seconds, another for 30 seconds, and a third for 60 seconds. Our theory would predict that the longer the confinement period in the empty goal box, the greater the opportunity for the elicitation of frustration and incompatible responses, and the faster extinction should occur. This is exactly what happened. The longer the duration of confinement on each extinction trial, the faster the running response extinguished.

Finally, Kirkpatrick, Pavlik, and Reynolds (1964) varied the size of the goal box into which rats ran during extinction. They used a small goal box which was 12 inches long, 3 inches wide, and 4 inches deep, and a large goal box which was 12 by 14 by 6. Again, the theory would predict that the greater the size of the goal box, the more physical room there would be for rats to make responses to frustration during extinction that would be incompatible with running. Thus a large goal box might lead to a greater variety and frequency of incompatible responses than a small one, and thereby lead to greater interference with the running response. Again, the data support the theory: animals extinguished with the large goal box slowed their running speeds much more rapidly than animals extinguished with the small goal box.

All in all, the frustration-competition theory fares pretty well when put to these sorts of experimental test. Actually, the area in which it has received perhaps the greatest experimental attention has to do with the effects of *patterns* of reinforcement on behavior, a topic which we will treat at considerable length in the next chapter. So be prepared to meet the theory again.

THE CURRENT STATUS OF THEORIES OF EXTINCTION

Following our general practice, we have looked at a small number of theories of extinction in considerable detail. We have done so, of course, at the expense of a number of other theories that psychologists have also developed to account for the things which go on during extinction. While we could mention other theories in passing, we could hardly do them justice. If you are interested, you can, of course, go directly to books such as that of Kimble (1961) to find out about them.

In this chapter we have seen both the strengths and weaknesses of an account of the basic phenomena of extinction in terms of response inhibition, and in terms of the concepts of competition among responses and of frustration. It is very important to recognize that no single one of these approaches can handle all the things we know about the basic extinction process. For example, Pavlov (1927) did a very successful job of accounting for extinction following *classical* conditioning in terms of inhibition, yet we have seen that at least one form of an inhibition theory runs into serious trouble when it is applied to extinction following *instrumental* conditioning. By the same token, competition theory and frustration from nonreinforcement can, together, do a commendable job of handling extinction following instrumental conditioning, but these principles must be stretched more than a little bit when applied to classical conditioning. If we have classically conditioned an eye blink, for example, does extinction really produce another response that *competes* and *interferes* with the eye blink, and if so, what is the nature of this response? And how, if such be the case at all, does frustration enter the picture? There may very well be answers to these questions (it is probably not legitimate to speak of frustration, for example, when we extinguish an eye blink by removing the UCS of a noxious air puff), but we do not have all of them yet.

There is another important question about the matter of extinguishing an old response by learning a new incompatible activity. It is not clearly established that learning the new response necessarily results in truly "unlearning" the old one. What does happen to the "old" behavior? The theories of Guthrie and Estes, even when supplemented by frustration from nonreinforcement, do not clearly specify the answer to this question. As we go about measuring behavior, we record a decrease in the strength of the old response during extinction, but this occurs presumably because there are so many other new responses occurring and interfering with the old response. So we are left with this basic question: Does extinction actually *eliminate* the old response, does it simply supplant the old response with other responses, or does it do both? And again, we do not have a final general answer to the question.

But no matter which theory of extinction we may choose as a working guide to a study of behavior following the removal of reinforcement, it is important not to lose sight of the basic phenomenon we label with the term extinction: Organisms stop doing things when they are no longer reinforced for doing them. We know much about the process. Much remains to be learned. But by now, these should be familiar comments to you.

5

PATTERNS OF REINFORCEMENT

From all the things we have discussed in this book, it should be amply clear that behavior is maintained at high strength by reinforcement, and that behavior declines in strength if it is not reinforced. Perhaps you have also remarked to yourself that we have done more than a little bit of oversimplification with respect to conditions of reinforcement and nonreinforcement. But as we have noted before, there are good reasons for this, and we have simplified deliberately. It is much easier to develop some of the basic ideas about learning if we choose situations in which a response is always reinforced or situations in which reinforcement fails consistently to occur. But simplicity has its price. It is quite doubtful if there are many instances in the real world where a particular bit of behavior is *always* reinforced under *precisely* the same conditions, or for that matter, where removal of reinforcement is utterly final and complete. The environment in which animals and people live is just not that consistent.

In this chapter we are going to complicate things a bit and look at what happens when conditions of reinforcement *change* from response to response—that is, where conditions of reinforcement vary according to some *pattern*. There are, in fact, many ways in which patterning of reinforcement can occur. One way of establishing a pattern of reinforcement is to reinforce some, but not all, of the responses an organism makes. As you can see, this is a type of pattern that is, in a sense, intermediate between continuous reinforcement of all responses and continuous nonreinforcement of all responses (extinction). Psychologists have attached the general label *partial reinforcement* to this type of pattern, but they also speak of *schedules of reinforcement* to describe specific ways in which reinforcement and nonreinforcement can be intermixed. We shall examine some of these schedules in the next section.

A second method of establishing a pattern of reinforcement is to vary the *amount of reinforcement* that is given from response to response. Thus, we could reinforce some responses with a large amount of reinforcement, some with an intermediate amount, and some with a small amount, and we could intermix these according to any particular pattern we might want to use. Still a third method of developing a pattern of reinforcement is to change the *delay of reinforcement* from response to response. Some responses could be reinforced with no delay, some with long delays, and so forth. It is not hard to think of ways in which some of the basic reinforcement variables can be used in a pattern of reinforcement, and perhaps you can add to this list yourself. The important point is that in the real world, the consequences of behavior vary. We are rewarded—and punished, for that matter—according to an intricate set of rules that are sometimes under our control and sometimes not. And these rules often involve not just one pattern of events, but many, many different patterns that are twined and intertwined in an enormously complex fashion.

In the interests of simplicity we shall look in detail at just two patterns of reinforcement: *partial reinforcement* and *variable amounts of reinforcement*. In their effects upon behavior, these are representative of other patterns of reinforcement in many respects.[1]

PARTIAL REINFORCEMENT

In Chapter 1 we made a precise distinction between a study of behavior in a free-responding situation as compared with a controlled-responding situation. Nowhere is this distinction more important to keep in mind than it is in connection with a study of partial reinforcement. In a controlled-responding situation, if you will recall, the experimenter administers discrete trials one by one, and generally measures something about an organism's behavior *within* a particular trial (such as response latency or speed) to assess the effects of an experimental procedure. In the case of partial reinforcement, these facts commit the experimenter to define a particular pattern of reinforcement and nonreinforcement in terms of the relative *number* of such trials that shall occur. Typically, this is done by establishing the *percentage* of trials that will be reinforced out of some total number of trials that will be run. Thus, if 75 percent reinforcement is to be used, and 100 trials are to be run, 75 trials will be reinforced and 25 will not. The common procedure is to distribute reinforced

[1] If you are interested in reading further about patterns of reinforcement, consult books such as Logan (1960).

among nonreinforced trials in some random fashion, although other sorts of patterns can be used (like reinforcing 50 percent of the trials by systematically rewarding every other response) .

In a free-responding situation, such as that of a Skinner box, the organism is free to respond and to distribute its responses in time as it chooses. Here, as in a controlled-responding situation, we can count responses and reinforce some particular percentage or ratio of the responses the organism makes, but we can also use *time itself* as an independent variable to establish a pattern of reinforcement. Let us turn now to free-responding techniques and to the topic of schedules of reinforcement to see how these things are done.

SCHEDULES OF REINFORCEMENT

There are two basic ways in which we can correlate a pattern of reinforcement and nonreinforcement with behavior in a free-responding situation. In the first case, we can set things so that a certain *period of time* must elapse after one reinforcement has been obtained before the next one can be obtained. In the Skinner box, for example, we could arbitrarily decide that at least five minutes must elapse after a lever press has produced one reinforcement before another lever press will produce a second reinforcement. The organism is free to respond as often as it chooses in the interim, but only those responses that are spaced at least five minutes apart produce reinforcement.

The other basic way in which we can develop a pattern based on reinforcement and nonreinforcement is to vary the *number of responses* that an organism must make to produce successive reinforcements. In this case, we might decide to reinforce every tenth response, withholding reinforcement on the intervening nine responses. Here, it is up to the organism to determine how quickly the required number of responses is made —it does not matter whether it takes five minutes or one. When we use either of these two methods, we can alter the schedule of reinforcement so that it is either haphazard or highly systematic. We might set things, for example, so that successive reinforcements are obtained for five responses, then ten responses, then two responses, and so on. Or we can reinforce systematically—as in our initial example above—by rewarding every tenth response. Since these different methods of scheduling reinforcement and nonreinforcement produce rather different effects upon behavior, let us look at them in greater detail.

FIXED-INTERVAL REINFORCEMENT. Fixed-interval, or periodic, reinforcement occurs on a fixed time schedule. Only those responses which occur at intervals greater than some fixed interval of time are reinforced. This kind of schedule has a particular and systematic effect on previously learned behavior. When an animal becomes accustomed to a fixed-interval schedule of reinforcement for, say, pressing a lever, its behavior becomes stable. In general, the animal will emit a constant number of responses per reinforcement. If, for example, the animal gives an average of 20 responses for each reinforcement and it is being reinforced for responses spaced at least one minute apart, its overall average rate of responding will be 20 responses per minute. If, however, the animal is reinforced once every two minutes, the same 20 responses will be spread out over this period, so that the animal's average rate of responding will be only 10 per minute. The general rule—though there are exceptions—is that the rate of responding is inversely proportional to the interval between reinforcements (Skinner, 1938, 1950).

Basically, of course, a fixed-interval schedule presents an organism with a *timing* problem. The optimum way to behave on this type of schedule is to make one response just after the preset interval elapses, but organisms cannot time the length of an interval that accurately (unless they can use external aids like clocks). What can be learned readily, however, is that responses early in the interval are never reinforced immediately; and from what you know about delay of reinforcement, you would predict correctly that such responses would come to occur very rarely. As the interval of time runs its course, however, delays of reinforcement become much shorter, and it becomes correspondingly more probable that the fixed interval has elapsed and that any given response will be the one that produces reinforcement. Consequently, the organism tends to "pile up" its responses toward the end of the interval and is usually responding at a high rate as the end of the interval is reached. If you look at a cumulative record of an animal's behavior on a fixed-interval schedule (Ferster & Skinner, 1957), you will see that the occurrence of none, or few, responses at the beginning of an interval, together with a great many responses at the end of the interval, produce a kind of *scalloped* appearance to the record as the animal works along from reinforcement to reinforcement. The scalloping becomes more pronounced as the fixed interval that is used becomes longer.

VARIABLE-INTERVAL REINFORCEMENT.   Instead of administering reinforcement at fixed intervals, we can change things so that reinforcement becomes available at *variable* intervals of time. Thus, after an animal has learned a particular response, we might then make reinforcement available after one minute, then after thirty seconds, then after three minutes, and so on.[2] Under these conditions, it is not possible for the

[2] There are, of course, many ways we could determine variability among intervals in a variable-interval schedule. One way to do this is to select a number of different intervals of time, say 1, 7, 5, 3, and 9 minutes, and to pick randomly from this list to

animal to learn to time the interval at all accurately; reinforcement is, in a sense, likely to occur at any time longer than the shortest interval that is used in the schedule. Consequently, an animal tends to respond at an extremely stable rate on a variable-interval schedule.

FIXED-RATIO REINFORCEMENT. In fixed-ratio reinforcement, the reinforcement is contingent upon the occurrence of a fixed number of responses. Here, as you might expect, the effects on performance are dramatically different from those of fixed-interval reinforcement. First of all, reinforcement on a ratio schedule places a premium on rapid responding, for the higher the rate of responding, the higher the rate of reinforcement. A peculiarity of performance on a particular fixed ratio, however, is that the animal tends to pause for a while (sometimes for several minutes or more) just after it has obtained a reinforcement; then it responds at a rapid, fairly constant rate until the next reinforcement is obtained. This so-called *postreinforcement pause* tends to become longer as larger fixed ratios are used. If we exclude the period of the postreinforcement pause, however, the general rule is that the rate of responding on a fixed ratio becomes higher as the size of the ratio increases.

VARIABLE-RATIO REINFORCEMENT. Within the domain of ratio schedules, the variable-ratio case is perhaps the most interesting because it is probably most characteristic of the conditions under which natural behavior occurs—at least those conditions where patterns of reinforcement involve nothing but reinforcement and nonreinforcement. Variable-ratio reinforcement is analogous to variable-interval reinforcement, but with a variable-ratio schedule, of course, different numbers of responses are required to produce successive reinforcements. If we reinforce a well-learned habit on a variable-ratio schedule, postreinforcement pauses do not become a dominant part of performance, and extraordinarily high rates of responding can be generated.

OTHER SCHEDULES OF REINFORCEMENT. We have described only a few of the many possible schedules of reinforcement that can be generated, though we have carefully examined those that are most basic. It is possible, for example, to use combinations of different schedules, perhaps arranging them in sequence so that the animal responds on one schedule for a while, then must respond on another. We can, if we wish, pair stimuli with the schedules so that one kind of stimulus is on when one schedule is in effect, and another kind of stimulus is on when another

---

determine the interval of time between any two successive reinforcements. The variable-interval schedule is then labeled in terms of the *average* interval of time between reinforcements—5 minutes in this case.

schedule is in effect (a so-called *multiple schedule*). Or we can reinforce only when responses occur at a rate faster or slower than some arbitrary rate we decide upon in advance (differential reinforcement, respectively, of high and low rates of responding). Of course, each sort of schedule generates its own unique pattern of behavior. In general, the variety of schedules of reinforcement that can be studied is limited only by the complexity of the experimenter's programming equipment and his ingenuity in making use of it. If you want to look at a good catalogue of many kinds of schedules of reinforcement—and the sort of behavior that each generates—consult Ferster and Skinner (1957).[3]

VARIABLE AMOUNTS OF REINFORCEMENT

A second class of patterns of reinforcement can be developed if we reinforce successive responses of some kind with different amounts of reinforcement. As a rat runs a runway, for example, we might reinforce the first run with 5 food pellets, the second with 15 food pellets, the third with 10 food pellets, and so on. In this case, the rat is *always* reinforced in the sense that it always gets something to eat when it arrives at the goal box. However, the amount of food that is used as a reward changes from trial to trial.

It is quite likely that a pattern of reinforcement based on variable amounts of reinforcement describes the things that go on in the environment of most organisms more realistically than a pattern of reinforcement based on a combination of simple reinforcement and nonreinforcement. If you stop and think for a moment, it is hard to imagine many examples where the environment pays off with something of exactly the same magnitude or with nothing at all each time that a response occurs. Instead, a bit of behavior is more apt to be reinforced from time to time with one of a *number* of different amounts or kinds of reinforcement. Thus, an employer rewards an employee from time to time with a raise in salary, a smile and a hearty handshake, a simple pat on the back, or perhaps just a quick nod. Similarly, an animal on the hunt for food is rewarded sometimes with a large kill that may supply food for several days, sometimes with a mere morsel, and sometimes with nothing at all—though the latter must not happen too often if the animal is to survive.

As you can imagine, the general concept of a pattern of reinforcement based on variable amounts of reinforcement can lead potentially to

---

[3] A convenient set of labels for schedules of reinforcement has been developed (Ferster & Skinner, 1957). Thus, FR 5 is a label for a fixed-ratio schedule in which five responses are required to produce one reinforcement. Similarly, a VI 3 schedule is a variable-interval schedule in which reinforcement is available, on the average, once every three minutes.

a very large and complex collection of specific ways in which responses could be reinforced with different amounts of reinforcement. For simplicity's sake, and also for the reason that the concept of variable amounts of reinforcement has not yet received as much experimental attention as the concept of schedules of reinforcement, let us look at just one way of developing a pattern of reinforcement based on different amounts of reinforcement.

MEAN AMOUNT OF REINFORCEMENT.   One way to choose a pattern of different amounts is to begin by picking a certain *mean* or *average* amount of reinforcement that an organism will receive per response over a large number of responses. We might decide, for example, that we are going to run a rat down an alley for 100 trials, and that we want to reinforce each trial with 10 pellets of food, *on the average*. Having set our mean amount of reinforcement, there are many ways in which we could actually reward the rat from trial to trial, developing a pattern of reinforcement but still keeping within the restriction that the mean amount must equal 10 pellets per trial by the time we have given 100 trials.

To keep things simple, let us give the rat one of just two possible amounts of reinforcement on each trial. We can satisfy our mean-amount requirement by giving the rat 5 pellets on half the trials and 15 pellets on the other half, perhaps intermixing the two amounts in some random fashion. We could also do the same thing by giving 9 pellets on half the trials and 11 pellets on the other half, by giving 18 pellets and 2 pellets, and so on. In each case, by the time we have completed all our training trials, the rat will have gotten a mean amount of 10 pellets per trial. In each case, too, the size of the *difference* between the two numbers of pellets changes. Thus, the rat is exposed to much greater changes in magnitude from trial to trial in the case of 18 pellets versus 2 pellets than it is in the case of 11 pellets versus 9 pellets. In a sense, the pattern of reinforcement from trial to trial wobbles over a much greater range of amounts in the former case than in the latter.

If you have this clearly in mind, let us carry things a stealthy step farther. Suppose we give the rat 10 pellets on half of the trials and 10 pellets, the same amount, on the other half of the trials. This, obviously, is consistent *continuous* reinforcement with exactly the same amount from trial to trial—the kind of "pattern" with which we have dealt throughout most of this book. But now suppose that we give the rat 20 pellets on a random half of the trials and 0 pellets (that is, nothing at all) on the other half. This, of course, is random 50 percent *partial* reinforcement! In each case, remember, we have continued our restriction that the mean amount of reinforcement per response be 10 pellets, but what we have done is to derive continuous and partial reinforcement as *special cases* of a pattern of reinforcement in which amounts of reinforcement vary over trials. Continuous reinforcement, generally speaking, is the limiting case where there is *no* change in amount, and partial reinforcement is the limiting case where there is *maximum* change in amount.

Of course, to generalize a bit, we do not have to restrict ourselves to the use of just two amounts of reinforcement, as we have done in the examples above. We could pick a certain mean amount and then select half a dozen different amounts to give to the rat from trial to trial. We could make each amount occur with a different frequency over a group of trials. In general, there is an infinite number of patterns that could be developed with different amounts of reinforcement, just as there is an infinite number of possible schedules of reinforcement and nonreinforcement.

To what extent do patterns of reinforcement of the type we have discussed have common effects upon behavior? Let us turn to this problem now as we look at some of the things that have been learned about the matter in the laboratory.

THE EFFECTS OF PATTERNS OF REINFORCEMENT ON LEARNING AND EXTINCTION

PATTERNS OF REINFORCEMENT AND LEARNING

PARTIAL REINFORCEMENT. If we tried to train a rat to press a lever in a Skinner box by reinforcing it once for every 10 responses, we would have a long wait before the animal would learn to press the lever and begin to perform consistently. This would be true because the strengthening effects of one reinforcement upon behavior would be pitted against the weakening effects of nine nonreinforcements. Of course, once the response was learned, a rat reinforced on FR 10 would respond at a much faster rate than another rat reinforced continuously. But the course of acquisition would be much slower in the former case than in the latter. As a practical matter, rats that are to be placed on schedules of reinforcement in free-responding situations are generally "shaped" toward the final schedule. Thus, we begin by reinforcing quite frequently, gradually decreasing the frequency of reinforcement as the rat's behavior develops.

Much the same effect holds for controlled-responding situations. A running response in a straight alley, for example, tends to develop at a much slower rate when partial as compared with continuous reinforcement is used. In controlled-responding situations, too, the strength of a partially reinforced response at the time learning is complete tends to be no greater—and is often less—than the strength of a response that has been continuously reinforced. This is just as true, perhaps more so, of a classically conditioned response as it is of an instrumentally conditioned one (Kimble, 1961). There are exceptions: A few experiments (e.g., Weinstock, 1958; Goodrich, 1959) show that rats reinforced less than 100 percent of the time in runways run faster by the end of training than rats reinforced continuously. But these do appear to be exceptions, and we are not yet sure about the specific things that produce this particular result. In short, the tendency for anything less than 100 percent reinforcement to slow the development of learning is so prepotent an effect that it can be taken as a general rule (Jenkins & Stanley, 1950; Lewis, 1960).

VARIABLE AMOUNTS OF REINFORCEMENT. If a pattern of reinforcement is used in which amounts of reinforcement vary over trials, organisms tend to behave during the learning of a response as if they were responding to some sort of *average* of the amounts involved in the pattern. Response strength does not develop in the manner we would expect if the organism were responding alone to either the largest or the smallest amount in the pattern. Instead, the organism behaves as if it were being reinforced by an amount somewhere between these two extremes. As a matter of fact, if a specific mean amount is established in advance, a number of patterns of different amounts of reinforcement can be used over training trials, and the rate of development of response strength will be about the same in each case. In many cases an organism behaves as if it were being reinforced by a single amount of reinforcement: the mean amount (Logan, Beier, & Ellis, 1955; Yamaguchi, 1961; Hulse & Firestone, 1964).

Yamaguchi's experiment demonstrates this point nicely. He ran hungry rats in a straight runway for 40 acquisition trials and then for 30 extinction trials. During acquisition, one group was rewarded with 9 units of wet mash on a random half of the trials and 1 unit on the other half (1 unit of wet mash weighed .05 gram). A second group received 8 units and 2 units. A third group received 5 and 5 (continuous reinforcement), while a fourth received 10 and zero units (partial reinforcement). Note that the mean amount of reinforcement per response in each case was 5 units—the amount that the continuously reinforced group received.

The results of the experiment are shown in Figure 5.1. If you look at the left half, which shows the acquisition data, you will see that all groups learned at just about the same rate. The group given 9 units and 1 unit ran somewhat faster than the others, but Yamaguchi's statistical analyses show that this difference is due to chance variability in the data. Thus, in Yamaguchi's experiment, as long as the mean amount of reinforcement is constant, the course of learning is essentially independent of the range of amounts that occur over successive responses.

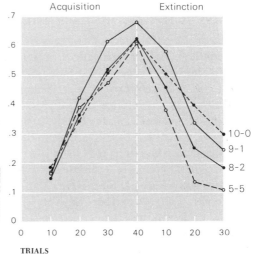

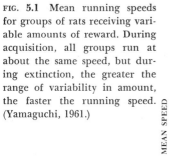

FIG. 5.1 Mean running speeds for groups of rats receiving variable amounts of reward. During acquisition, all groups run at about the same speed, but during extinction, the greater the range of variability in amount, the faster the running speed. (Yamaguchi, 1961.)

The kind of result that Yamaguchi reports is by no means limited to rats and runways. Identical effects have been reported for rats in a free-responding situation (Hulse & Firestone, 1964), and highly similar effects have been reported when human beings learn to trace a path with a pointer through a kind of stylus maze (Bevan & Adamson, 1960).

It would be a mistake, however, to think that organisms will *always* behave as if they were responding fairly precisely to some arithmetic mean derived from two equally likely amounts of reinforcement. Logan (1960) feels, for example, that if a high mean amount is used, performance will be better if there is a relatively small difference between the two absolute amounts actually used in the experiment. Thus, if rats run a runway to a mean amount of 20 pellets of food, they ought to run faster on the average if the absolute amounts are 18 pellets and 22 pellets than if the absolute amounts are 30 pellets and 10 pellets. Logan presents some data which suggest, at least, that this may be the case, and he notes that there are potentially many other things which can determine the way organisms will respond to variable amounts of reinforcement. He has also done some work which shows that things become proportionately more complicated if organisms are allowed to *choose* between alternatives leading to different conditions of variable reinforcement (Logan, 1965). Here is a very interesting set of ideas and of research, but it is clear that a great deal needs to be done before we will fully understand how organisms respond in situations where they are faced with rewards that change from response to response.

PATTERNS OF REINFORCEMENT AND EXTINCTION

The most dramatic effect of patterns of reinforcement is upon resistance to extinction. All patterns affect resistance to extinction somewhat differently, but it is a general rule that a pattern which involves some change in the nature of reinforcement conditions from response to response will produce greater resistance to extinction than a condition where all responses are reinforced immediately, 100 percent of the time, in just the same way. Since this is just as true for a pattern based on reinforcement and nonreinforcement as it is for a pattern based on variable amounts of reinforcement (Jenkins & Stanley, 1950; Lewis, 1960; Logan, Beier, & Kincaid, 1956; Hulse & Firestone, 1964), we shall discuss the effects of the two general types of pattern together.

Earlier in this chapter we saw that the number of times a particular activity had been reinforced determined, within broad limits, how many times the activity would be performed in the absence of reinforcement. The maximal resistance to extinction after 100 percent reinforcement is not great. No matter how many times we reinforce lever pressing in the rat, for example, it is unlikely that the animal will respond much more than 200 times or so during the course of extinction. Thus, habits established and maintained with 100 percent reinforcement are not very resistant to extinction.

Results obtained by many, many investigators from behavior conditioned both instrumentally and classically show that a pattern of partial reinforcement greatly increases resistance to extinction. Skinner (1938) and Humphreys (1939) demonstrated this in some of the earliest experiments on the problem, and since that time, literally hundreds of experiments have repeated these results with a wide variety of subjects, apparatuses, and experimental procedures.

The large effects of a pattern of reinforcement and nonreinforcement on resistance to extinction can be seen in Figures 5.2 and 5.3. Figure 5.2 shows the course of extinction following instrumental conditioning with continuous reinforcement and with aperiodic (variable-interval) reinforcement (Jenkins, McFann, & Clayton, 1950). When a VI schedule is used, 200 reinforcements during training produce about five times as many responses during extinction as when continuous reinforcement is used. The upper curve in Figure 5.3 shows resistance to extinction following 560 reinforcements on different FR schedules, including continuous reinforcement (Boren, 1961). The number of individual responses emitted in the first three, of a total of five, one-hour extinction sessions increases rapidly as the size of the fixed ratio increases.

Resistance to extinction following conditioning with a pattern of variable amounts of reinforcement increases as the range, or variability,

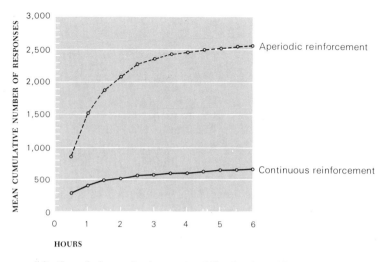

FIG. **5.2** Cumulative extinction curves following intermittent and continuous reinforcement. For the intermittent-reinforcement condition, the animals were placed on a variable-interval schedule. The animals in both groups received 200 reinforcements before extinction began. (W. O. Jenkins, McFann, & Clayton, 1950.)

of the amounts increases. This is shown quite clearly in Yamaguchi's (1961) data, which appear in the right half of Figure 5.1. Greatest resistance to extinction was obtained following training with 10 units on half the trials and zero units on the other half (partial reinforcement), and resistance to extinction was least if all trials had been reinforced with the mean amount of 5 units (continuous reinforcement). The important point, however, is that intermediate resistance to extinction was obtained when the range in amounts given from trial to trial lay between the extremes of continuous and partial reinforcement; the 9-1 and 8-2 groups

FIG. **5.3** Number of extinction responses as a function of the size of the fixed ratio of reinforcement. The solid curve gives the total number of individual lever presses the animals made during extinction. The lower curve shows the same data plotted in terms of response units, one response unit representing the number of responses that had been required to produce one reinforcement during training. (Boren, 1961.)

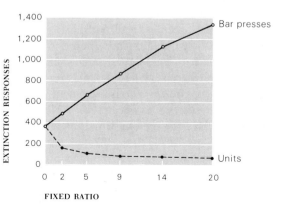

arrange themselves neatly between the 5-5 group and the 10-0 group. These data, together with other virtually identical observations (Logan, Beier, & Kincaid, 1956; Hulse & Firestone, 1964), clearly suggest that, so far as resistance to extinction is concerned, partial and continuous reinforcement are but special cases on a continuum of patterns of different amounts of reinforcement.

There is apparently no limit to the extent to which a pattern of reinforcement, particularly a pattern based upon a schedule of reinforcement and nonreinforcement, can increase resistance to extinction. Even in the laboratory it is possible to produce habits that will resist the shattering effects of thousands of unreinforced responses. As a matter of fact, Skinner (1950) suggests that if conditions are proper, it is possible to produce an extinction curve with no curvature at all; in other words, the organism goes on responding without reinforcement ad infinitum. Incidentally, Skinner remarks, such a result is a telling blow against a theory of extinction built upon the supposed accumulation of response-produced inhibition.

The effect of patterns of reinforcement upon resistance to extinction is of the greatest theoretical, practical, and adaptive significance. For one thing, we have a key to the understanding of why behavior in natural settings is likely to be so persistent: most behavior is probably not reinforced for all tries, and when reinforcement does come, it tends to come in amounts which vary from try to try. It is fortunate that organisms have evolved to respond the way they appear to do to patterns of reinforcement, since the real world seems to be arranged so that reinforcement is inconsistent, often unpredictable, even capricious.

THEORETICAL INTERPRETATIONS OF THE EFFECTS OF PATTERNS OF REINFORCEMENT

We have seen that the importance of patterns of reinforcement is twofold. First of all, at least in the case of schedules of reinforcement based on reinforcement and nonreinforcement, momentary characteristics of response strength depend upon the particular schedule of reinforcement under which an organism performs. Thus, we have postreinforcement pauses with FR schedules, and scalloping with FI schedules. Second, we saw that patterns of reinforcement have the very prepotent effect of increasing resistance to extinction. This is perhaps the most fundamental point; at least, it is the one which has received by far the most theoretical attention.

Given the fact that patterns of reinforcement based on variables other than reinforcement and nonreinforcement are relative newcomers to the experimental study of learning, it is not surprising that the head scratching of most psychologists has been aimed at the extinction phenomena associated with partial reinforcement. This is not to say that other patterns of reinforcement have not received their share of theoretical scrutiny, and eventually it is probably going to be the case that a theory which accounts for behavior under one pattern will also account for behavior under another with only minor modifications. But right now, we must use the theoretical tools which are at our immediate disposal, and these are all best designed to pry into the secrets associated with partial reinforcement. So let us turn our attention to the theoretical analysis of the *partial-reinforcement effect:* the fact that partial reinforcement produces greater resistance to extinction than continuous 100 percent reinforcement.

Broadly speaking, there have emerged two general approaches to the problem (Lawrence, 1958). One says that the partial-reinforcement effect occurs because of things the organism learns about the *sequence* of reinforcements and nonreinforcements as conditioning trials progress. This way of looking at things emphasizes the importance of *inter*trial events, the things that happen from one trial to the second, to the next, and so on. The second approach places emphasis on how organisms learn to respond specifically to the reinforced trial as distinct from the nonreinforced trial. This way of looking at things is concerned not so much with the effects over a number of trials of the sequence or pattern of reinforcement and nonreinforcement, but with what organisms learn to do *within particular trials,* especially those that are not reinforced. That is, the second approach emphasizes *intra*trial events.

Within this bipartite framework, there are many variations on a variety of themes, and we would only cloud the basic issue if we were to discuss them all. So, as has been our custom, we shall be selective and look at just a few.

INTERTRIAL PHENOMENA AND THE PARTIAL-REINFORCEMENT EFFECT

EXPECTANCY.   The expectancy approach says that organisms come to expect, or predict, over a series of trials, that reinforcement is associated in a particular sort of way with responding. Thus, a rat reinforced 100 percent of the time for pressing a lever comes to expect food after each response. If an animal is reinforced only part of the time during training, however, it will not expect a reinforcement on every occasion, so that when reinforcement stops altogether, the animal is likely to be more persistent. This explanation has great commonsense appeal, and it would almost certainly satisfy your grandmother.

The concept of expectancy does not satisfy many psychologists, however, and it has been roundly and justifiably criticized on several grounds. Some critics have claimed that it is an anthropomorphic notion.

Others have pointed out that the definition of expectancy is vague and ambiguous. Certainly, the criticism of anthropomorphism is justified. Human learners are capable of expectancy—as a form of implicit or explicit verbal behavior. We can tell ourselves when we ought to expect something to happen, and we do so frequently, but it is highly doubtful that organisms lower than man are capable of expectancy in this sense.

The most serious criticism of the notion of expectancy is that it is, in its bare form, an *ad hoc* explanation. It would be acceptable if it were defined in some operational way, such as demanding that an organism be able to respond to a conditional cue before the unconditioned stimulus appears. If this is all that one means by expectancy, there is no quarrel. But nothing much has been explained, either. The basic problem with an expectancy approach to the partial-reinforcement effect is not that the notion of expectancy explains too little. Rather, the bare notion of expectancy explains too much too easily.

DISCRIMINATION. Another simple idea used to account for the partial-reinforcement effect says that under partial reinforcement it is less easy for the organism to discriminate between conditions of reinforcement and those of extinction than it is under continuous reinforcement. This implies that the major determiner of the rate (and probably the limit) of responding during extinction is the extent to which the overall stimulus situation during extinction is the same as that during original reinforced training. In partial reinforcement, there are occasions when responses go unreinforced; organisms have a chance over a number of conditioning trials to learn to respond in a stimulus situation which sometimes contains reinforcement and sometimes does not. Consequently, when extinction begins it is difficult for the organism to tell when original training ends and extinction begins. Of course, for a continuously reinforced organism this is not the case at all. The change from the reinforcement conditions of acquisition to those of extinction is marked, abrupt, and therefore easy to discriminate. So the organism should be able to detect the failure of reinforcement easily and stop responding quickly.

At this point you may be thinking that the discrimination notion is quite similar to a general concept of expectancy. The difference is that the discrimination hypothesis is stated in such a way as to preclude our attributing symbolic human processes to rats or other lower organisms as they generate extinction curves. Another difference is that we know a great deal about the process of discrimination (as we shall see in the next chapter), and if we are to use the notion of discrimination to account for the partial-reinforcement effect, this means that we ought to be able to apply some of the rules about discrimination to that effect. In other words, a discrimination hypothesis—in contrast to that of expectancy—

commits us to explain the partial-reinforcement effect with some principles that are not part and parcel of the effect itself. If a prediction based on discrimination fails to find support in the laboratory, it is not so easy to wiggle around the data with *ad hoc* explanations.

Let us look at a bit of data to see the discrimination hypothesis at work. Tyler, Wortz, and Bitterman (1953) ran rats down a runway. When the rats got to the end, they had to jump a short distance into a goal box, leaping through a window covered with an easily movable card. The purpose of the card was to keep the rats from seeing what was in the goal box until they got there. Two groups of rats were run. One group was reinforced on a random 50 percent of 120 training trials and then extinguished. A second group was also reinforced on 50 percent of 120 training trials and extinguished, but things were set so that *every other* trial was reinforced during acquisition. Thus, in contrast to the rats of the first group, it was possible for the rats of the second group to learn something about the regular serial nature of the pattern of reinforcement. Whether rats could learn to discriminate a pattern of single alternation of reinforcement and nonreinforcement of this sort was, of course, an experimental question, but as things turned out, they could indeed. By the end of training, the rats in the single-alternation group had learned to run quickly on a trial that was to be reinforced, and quite slowly on a trial that was not to be reinforced. The rats in the random group, on the other hand, ran at just about the same speed on all training trials; there was no particular set sequence of reinforcement and nonreinforcement that they could learn to detect.

Perhaps you can already predict the extinction results: The rats in the single-alternation group extinguished faster than the rats in the random group. According to the discrimination hypothesis, the rats in the former group had learned a good deal about the pattern with which reinforcements came during training, and it was relatively easy for them to discriminate the change in the pattern when extinction began. Not so for the rats in the random group; there was no consistent pattern of reinforcement and nonreinforcement during training which could help them discriminate the change from training to extinction, so they maintained their performance for a longer time.

There are other experiments aimed at testing the discrimination hypothesis (e.g., Longnecker, Krauskopf, & Bitterman, 1952; Bitterman, Fedderson, & Tyler, 1953), and all support it. But all of them, and the discrimination hypothesis too, must be modified in the light of some more recent data.

DISCRIMINATION AND BLOCKS OF CONTINUOUS AND PARTIAL REIN-FORCEMENT. Jenkins (1962) and Theios (1962), working independently, asked a very simple question about the effects of partial reinforcement on extinction. What would happen, they wondered, if during the course of training, animals were partially reinforced for a while, but were then continuously reinforced for a number of trials just before extinction began? Would the effects of the early partial-reinforcement procedure weather the effects of the subsequent continuously reinforced trials in such a way that the partial-reinforcement effect would still appear? Or would the animals behave during extinction as if they had been continuously reinforced throughout training? A bare discrimination theory would predict that they would behave as if they had always been continuously reinforced. This would be true because on the trials prior to extinction, the pattern of continuous reinforcement then in effect ought to make it easy for the animals to discriminate the change to the consistent non-reinforcement characteristic of extinction. But that is not the way things worked out.

Theios, with rats in a runway, and Jenkins, with pigeons in a Skinner box, found that subjects who were first partially reinforced for a block of trials, then continuously reinforced for a block of trials, behaved during extinction very much as if they had not been continuously reinforced at all. In Theios's experiment, for example, all rats first received 30 preliminary training trials in a runway. One group of rats then received 70 trials reinforced at random 40 percent of the time, followed by 70 additional continuously reinforced trials. A control group received 140 continuously reinforced trials. The group which had the mixture of partial followed by continuous reinforcement was far more resistant to extinction than the group which had continuous reinforcement throughout training. Its resistance to extinction was almost, but not quite, as great as that of another control group which, following preliminary training, had received nothing but partial reinforcement.

To top things off, Sutherland, Mackintosh, and Wolfe (1965) did an experiment in which rats did not receive any preliminary training with continuous reinforcement at all before the experiment proper began (Theios, if you will recall, used 30 such preliminary trials). Under their conditions, Sutherland et al. found that resistance to extinction in a group given a block of partially reinforced trials followed by a block of continuously reinforced trials was essentially identical to that of a group given nothing but partial reinforcement throughout training. To summarize in Theios's words, it is quite clear that the partial-reinforcement effect can be sustained through a block of continuously reinforced training trials.

Though the data at which we have just looked are quite damaging to the discrimination theory as we have introduced it, there is no reason why the discrimination theory could not be appropriately modified to account for the new information. All we would have to do is to postulate that organisms, once exposed to a pattern of partial reinforcement, can carry with them through a series of continuously reinforced trials some kind of *permanent trace* of their experience with the pattern of partial reinforcement. When extinction begins, the first nonreinforced trial or two reintroduces the conditions characteristic of partial reinforcement, and the organism begins to behave once again as it ought to according to the rules associated with that pattern.

All this is admittedly more than a trifle *ad hoc;* we are doing a bit of wiggling with our theory. But what we are saying, basically, is that a rat, a pigeon, or a person ought to be able to *remember* its experience with partial reinforcement, and that subsequent experience with continuous reinforcement ought not to interfere very much with that "memory." When viewed from the vantage point of common experience, this does not seem to be too rash a working assumption, though like all such assumptions, it must withstand the rigors of experimental test before we can accept it.

RESPONSE UNITS.   Another approach to the partial-reinforcement effect is particularly well suited to the data that come from free-responding situations. As a matter of fact, it is not easily applied to other kinds of experimental situations at all, but it deserves at least brief mention because it is elegantly simple and because it is of some historical interest. This is the *response-unit hypothesis* of Mowrer and Jones (1945).

For most purposes, we define the unit of response as that which will produce reinforcement. Thus in the Skinner box, a response is often defined as a lever press capable of operating the device that delivers the reinforcer. It does not make any difference how the animal presses the lever so long as it is pressed hard enough. By the same token, we might argue that in a partial-reinforcement situation in a Skinner box—at least, one where reinforcement is delivered on a ratio of some kind—the unit of response is defined by the *number* of lever presses necessary to activate the reinforcement device. If we did this, we would consider all the nonreinforced lever presses between reinforced ones to be part of the activity necessary for reinforcement, and we would count them as just one response. For example, if we were to use an FR 10 schedule of reinforcement, in which we reinforce every tenth lever press, we would count 10 lever presses as *one response unit.* We might then suppose that organisms can learn to chunk their behavior, perhaps discriminating or learning something about the number of responses that constitute a chunk.

When applied to extinction behavior, the response-unit hypothesis predicts equal resistance to extinction for all ratios of reinforcement—so long as extinction performance is examined in terms of the appropriately sized response unit, and each unit has been reinforced the same number of times during training. Thus, an FR 10 schedule might give many more *individual* lever presses than an FR 20 schedule during extinction, but both should give the same number of response units. In order that there be an equal number of response units in this particular example, an animal trained on FR 20 would have to emit twice as many individual lever presses during extinction as an animal trained on FR 10.

Unfortunately, though the response-unit hypothesis has great intuitive appeal, the data do not support the hypothesis very well. Mowrer and Jones themselves found that as the fixed ratio increased, the number of response units emitted during extinction did not remain the same, but decreased. You can see this for yourself in the lower curve of Figure 5.3, where Boren (1961) has plotted his data in terms of response units. Boren reports, too, that when he inspected the individual extinction records of his rats, there was no indication of the chunking of responses that might be expected if the animals had been "counting" their responses somehow and responding on the basis of some sort of response unit. Perhaps, though no one has apparently thought it useful to do so, the response-unit hypothesis could be applied to human behavior, because people, after all, can really count the number of times they do something. But the hypothesis does not appear to stand up very well when applied to lower organisms, nor has it found any application in experimental situations other than those involving free responding.

INTRATRIAL PHENOMENA AND THE PARTIAL-REINFORCEMENT EFFECT

Let us turn now from an approach to the partial-reinforcement effect which emphasizes intertrial events, like learning to discriminate something about the overall pattern with which reinforcement and nonreinforcement occur, to an approach which emphasizes the fact that organisms learn how to respond in certain ways *within* a reinforced or nonreinforced trial. The general point to be made here is that training with partial reinforcement provides an opportunity—through the nonreinforced trial—for an organism to learn how to cope with and to maintain its behavior in the absence of reinforcement. Continuous reinforcement does not do this, since by definition continuous reinforcement does not include nonreinforced trials. So when extinction begins, the partially reinforced organism is better equipped than the continuously reinforced organism to resist the effects of a complete withdrawal of all reward.

While all theories of the intratrial type look within individual trials in search of an explanation for the partial-reinforcement effect, they differ in terms of what they find going on there. For example, Weinstock (1954) says that nonreinforced training trials tend to elicit responses which are incompatible with the response that the experimenter wants to condition with partial reinforcement. But as training proceeds and the organism is exposed to more and more nonreinforced trials, the incompatible responses tend to *habituate,* that is, they tend to extinguish (because they are not reinforced) and to disappear from the organism's repertoire of behavior. When extinction begins, the organism continues to respond for a relatively great many trials because, compared with an organism that has been continuously reinforced, there is less extraneous incompatible behavior to interfere with the response the experimenter has conditioned during training.

Hulse and Stanley (1956) take a somewhat different tack. They say that the nonreinforced trial furnishes an organism with an opportunity to learn an *alternative response* to the cues associated with nonreinforcement. Thus, a partially reinforced organism learns to make a response and perform the appropriate goal activity on a reinforced trial, but on a nonreinforced trial, it learns to make the response and then do something else upon discovering that there is no reward. During extinction, again, the partially reinforced organism is better equipped by its training experience to cope with nonreinforcement. It tends, when faced with nonreinforcement, to make the alternative response it has learned to make under such conditions during the course of acquisition.

As you can see, the theories of Weinstock and of Hulse and Stanley are quite different, though both stress the notion that rats and people learn how to deal with the specific effects of nonreinforcement in consistent ways. Weinstock says, speaking very loosely, that organisms learn to be rather complacent when faced with nonreinforcement, while Hulse and Stanley say that they go busily about some other task upon discovering that reward is not available. Let us turn now, however, to a somewhat more complete development of a theory based upon our old friend, the concept of frustration.

FRUSTRATION AND THE PARTIAL-REINFORCEMENT EFFECT. In Chapter 3 we developed the concept of incentive motivation from the fractional anticipatory goal response and the r_g-s_g mechanism, and in Chapter 4 we looked at a parallel concept, the fractional anticipatory frustration response and the r_f-s_f mechanism, to show how this played a role in a theoretical account of the general phenomenon of extinction. If we combine these two mechanisms, we have a tool that we can use to account for the partial-reinforcement effect (Amsel, 1958).

Once a rat has been run in a runway to food, say, for a few trials, incentive motivation will have developed to some extent; that is, r_g-s_g will have grown in strength, and the cues of the runway will be eliciting for the rat the rather exciting prospect of a morsel of food in the goal box.

If we now remove the food for a few trials, we have set the stage for the parallel development of $r_f\text{-}s_f$, since nonreinforcement now will produce a frustrating state of affairs and this, too, can become anticipatory so that it is elicited by cues in the runway. As training continues, and we continue to mix reinforced and nonreinforced trials together, the rat faces a dilemma and is, in fact, in quite a state of conflict. On the one hand, the cues of the runway promise an ultimate payoff of food, but on the other hand, the same cues also promise the upsetting frustration of an empty goal box. Nevertheless, the rat continues to run—unless we provide altogether too few rewards—since reinforcement is available at least some of the time.

The important point, however, is that the rat has been conditioned to make the running response to *one* identical set of runway cues that signals *two* distinct goal events and their associated properties: the "excitement" of reinforcement (mediated by the $r_g\text{-}s_g$ mechanism) and the "frustration" of nonreinforcement (mediated by the $r_f\text{-}s_f$ mechanism). In effect, while the $r_f\text{-}s_f$ mechanism typically mediates and elicits behavior that is incompatible with running, as we have seen earlier, partial-reinforcement trains the rat to run in the presence of such frustration-produced cues. While all this is true of a partially reinforced rat, it is not true of a continuously reinforced rat. The latter is conditioned to make the running response to cues that signal just one sort of goal event—reinforcement.

Perhaps you have already anticipated the next step. If we now extinguish the running response, the partially reinforced rat runs for a relatively long time because it has been *conditioned* during training to maintain its behavior in the face of cues that signal the frustration associated with nonreinforcement. The continuously reinforced rat, of course, has not had the benefit of this unpleasant but educating experience. When extinction begins following continuous reinforcement, frustration occurs for the first time, produces incompatible responses, and leads to relatively rapid extinction.

On the face of things, this theoretical system does not sound enormously different from that of, say, Weinstock; we are simply postulating another sort of thing which subjects can learn about on nonreinforced trials that will stand them in good stead during extinction. The frustration approach does add one important element, however, which—as things have turned out—gives it some rather unique advantages among intratrial explanations of the partial-reinforcement effect. Frustration is assumed to have the properties of a *motive* that, in a partial-reinforcement situation, can add to the vigor with which a response is performed (recall the fact that in the Amsel and Roussel experiment, rats ran relatively faster in the second runway if they had just been frustrated in the first goal box). Let us look at some experiments which show the usefulness of this extra feature.

AMOUNT OF REINFORCEMENT AND THE PARTIAL-REINFORCEMENT EF-FECT.   What happens to the size of the partial-reinforcement effect when a response is conditioned initially with different amounts of reinforcement? Hulse (1958) and later Wagner (1961) and Hulse and Bacon (1962) sought an answer to this question. Hulse trained rats to run a runway, reinforcing one group on 46 percent of the training trials, and another group on 100 percent of the training trials. Within each group, half the animals were rewarded with a piece of food that weighed 0.08 gram, and half were rewarded with a piece of food that weighed 1.0 gram. At the end of training, the continuously reinforced groups ran faster than the partially reinforced groups, and large rewards produced faster running speeds than small rewards. But the extinction data are of primary concern; they are shown in Figure 5.4.

Look first at the extinction performance of the groups that had received a *large* reward during training. The partially reinforced group was much more resistant to extinction than the continuously reinforced group. Now look at the data for the groups that received a *small* reward.

FIG. 5.4 Running speeds during extinction as a joint function of percentage of reinforcement and amount of reinforcement. The rats had been reinforced 100 or 46 percent of the time with either a 1.0-gram (Lg) or an 0.08-gram (Sm) food reward. The reference point includes data from the last training trial and the first extinction trial. (Hulse, 1958.)

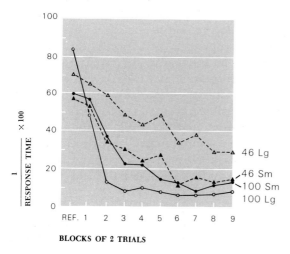

Here, there is still some indication that the partially reinforced group was more resistant to extinction than the continuously reinforced group, but as you can see, the difference in running speed is quite small. In other words, the partial-reinforcement effect is much greater when large as compared with small rewards are used during the conditioning of a response.

Though Hulse has taken more of an intertrial approach in accounting for these data (Hulse, 1962), the frustration approach to the partial-reinforcement effect can handle the data quite well (Wagner, 1961). When large rewards are used during training, a much stronger conditioned anticipatory goal response, r_g, results than if small rewards are used. This, in the case of partial reinforcement, should produce a relatively strong conditioned anticipatory frustration response, r_f, and the drive properties of r_f should channel into running. All this follows from our previous discussion, and from Bower's (1962) experiment where, if you will recall, he found the size of the frustration effect to increase as the amount of reduction in reinforcement became larger. When extinction begins, partial reinforcement should produce faster running than continuous reinforcement because partial reinforcement trains the rat to keep running in the face of cues that signal frustration, but continuous reinforcement does not. This accounts for the bare partial-reinforcement effect, as we have seen before.

Now for the following reasons, the *magnitude* of the partial-reinforcement effect should increase with increases in amount of reinforcement. First of all, with *partial* reinforcement, large as compared with small rewards should produce greater frustration, greater frustration drive, and hence faster running speeds during extinction. Following *continuous* reinforcement, similarly, large rewards should produce greater frustration during extinction. But what happens as a result of this frustration? It cannot channel directly into running because there has been no opportunity for the rat to learn to cope with frustration in this way during training. Instead—and this is the interesting and critical point—the larger the reward, the greater the frustration that is elicited as extinction begins. This, in turn, assures that large as compared with small rewards will produce more vigorous incompatible responses, and lead to a relatively quick collapse of the running response. In other words, our thinking has led us to predict that with continuous reinforcement, large rewards should produce *less* resistance to extinction than small rewards; and if you go back and check Figure 5.4, you will see that this is exactly what happened in Hulse's experiment.

FRUSTRATION AND BLOCKS OF REINFORCEMENT AND NONREINFORCE-MENT. Let us return very briefly to the fact that the partial-reinforcement effect can be sustained through a block of continuously reinforced trials (Theios, 1962) and see how the frustration theory would apply there. If you will recall, we spoke rather loosely of the rat being able to "remember" something about its experience with partial reinforcement, and we said that perhaps this "memory" could carry through a period of continuous reinforcement and still work to produce a partial-reinforcement effect during extinction. The concept of conditioned frustration furnishes a vehicle that is quite a bit more specific and concrete than the notion of a rat being able to "remember" something.

The key word here is *conditioned;* conditioned frustration has the properties of a permanent habit. During initial training with partial reinforcement, conditioned frustration develops as a result of nonreinforcement. During subsequent training with continuous reinforcement, the motivation associated with conditioned frustration extinguishes to some extent. Thus, while the rat runs in the presence of cues that have acquired the ability to elicit conditioned frustration, the reinforcer for conditioned frustration—primary frustration from nonreinforcement—has been removed. What does not extinguish, however, is the tendency for the rat to make compatible as opposed to incompatible responses to frustration cues when they do appear. This stays with the rat through the period of continuous reinforcement, and when extinction finally does begin, the rat with a history of partial reinforcement has a greater tendency to run to frustration cues than the rat without such a history. So the partial-reinforcement effect is indeed sustained through a block of continuously reinforced trials.

THE PRESENT STATUS OF THEORY

We have looked at a rather large number of theories concerning the partial-reinforcement effect, perhaps a larger number than the general approach of this book warrants. It is unfortunately true, however, that we have simply mirrored the current state of affairs with respect to what psychologists think about the effects of patterns of reinforcement upon resistance to extinction. Someone has said that in the absence of fact there will be theory, and nowhere does this seem a more appropriate comment than in connection with the partial-reinforcement effect. In all likelihood, what will eventually emerge will be a general theory that will combine features of a number of less comprehensive theories, some of which are already available so that we have been able to see what they have to say, and some of which remain to be developed. Already, it seems clear that important things go on both between and within trials which, as we understand things now, help to account for the effects of patterns of reinforcement upon resistance to extinction. Which of these will still be of value to the theoretician in the future remains to be seen.

It is important that, in spite of theoretical controversy, you do not lose sight of the great wealth of things that are known about the effects of patterns of reinforcement upon behavior. While it may be true that absence of fact leads to abundance of theory, this is not to say that facts themselves cannot be of extraordinary value. It is useful to know, for example, that while partial reinforcement can increase resistance to extinction, the effect can be made considerably larger by combining large amounts of reinforcement with a pattern of reward. And patterns of reinforcement find their place not only in the laboratory, but also in other domains where, for example, they have led to highly reliable performance of very complicated tasks by chimpanzees under the weightless conditions of space.

It is important, too, to recognize the signal importance of the concept of patterns of reinforcement to the psychologist when he must account for the extraordinary persistence which behavior often exhibits. While there are many things which will lead to a highly persistent habit—such as strong motivation, for example—patterns of reinforcement are one of the most powerful set of tools that can be used to create and maintain such a habit.

PROBABILITY LEARNING

Before we move on, we must look at a topic that has received considerable attention over the past decade and has attracted ever-increasing interest on the part of psychologists. This problem has to do with the way in which organisms behave under conditions where irregular patterns of reinforcement can have an effect upon decisions. Stated another more general way, we can conceive of this as a problem in the *probabilistic* nature of events that influence human and animal behavior.

Brunswik (1956) for many years insisted that the major variables in psychology were to be considered as only probabilistic, not certain, in nature. For instance, a cue for visual depth, or size, of retinal image does not always yield unequivocally correct information. Objects that loom large in our visual field are *probably* objects close to us in space, but it is not necessarily the case that this be so. So it is with reinforcements; they occur in a probabilistic way (and in different amounts, and so forth, as we have seen), seldom in an all-or-nothing way. With this general view in mind, Brunswik (1939) reported an experiment on rats in a T maze in which most of the time reinforcements occurred on the right side, but sometimes occurred on the left. Under these conditions, rats came to distribute their choices according to the probability of reinforcement. Thus, if the right side was reinforced 75 percent of the time, and the left side only 25 percent of the time, the rats would choose to go to the right side 75 percent of the time and to the left 25 percent of the time. In other words, they tended to distribute their choices according to the *probability* that a particular choice would pay off with reward.

Of great current interest in the theory of behavior is what determines the likelihood of an organism making a particular choice, given the probability, but not the certainty, of a particular event taking place. While—as with many things in psychology—a good part of the background for this problem has come from work with animals, most experimental work has been directed toward choice behavior in human beings. In a typical experimental situation, a subject is presented with a panel which has two lights and a button. By pressing the button, he predicts whether the second light will come on after the first one does. If he thinks the light will come on, he presses the button; if not, he does nothing (or perhaps presses a second button so that the experimenter will know when he has made a choice). The experimenter, of course, has arranged things ahead of time so that the second light comes on after the first according to some set pattern, or with some particular probability. In a manner analogous to Brunswik's rats in a T maze, human beings apparently learn to make predictions according to the probability that the to-be-predicted event will occur.

You can see this effect in Figure 5.5, which reports some data from an experiment of Grant, Hake, and Hornseth (1951). They arranged things so that the second light would come on at random for different groups 100, 75, 50, 25, and 0 percent of the time. All groups started out by predicting at a chance level; that is, they all guessed that the second light would come on about 50 percent of the time. As training progressed, however, the groups diverged, and the subjects in each group eventually wound up predicting that the second light would come on just about as often as it did, in fact, come on. In other words, the subjects' frequency of prediction tended to match the frequency of occurrence of the light. Put still another way, the probability that a subject would *predict* that the light would flash by pressing the button matched the probability that the light would indeed flash, and for this reason, the phenomenon has been labeled *probability matching*.

The phenomenon of probability matching is a curious thing, for to probability-match in a situation of this sort is not the optimal strategy. This is true because, given a situation in which the frequency of two events is not equal, the best strategy is always to bet on the more frequently occurring event—assuming, of course, that there is no additional information to help the guesswork along. Thus, while probability matching is the general rule which seems to describe the way in which subjects will behave in a situation of the kind we have described, there are other things that can be done to change the way in which subjects will respond

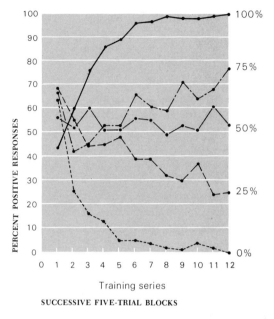

FIG. **5.5** Percent frequency of predictions that a second light would follow a first as a function of the percent frequency that the second light actually did follow the first. At the end of training, there is a close correspondence between frequency of occurrence and frequency of prediction. (Grant, Hake, & Hornseth, 1951.)

(Hake, 1955; Estes, 1964b). For example, if we reward correct guesses, punish incorrect guesses, or perhaps use a combination of the two, subjects show much more of an inclination to adopt an optimal strategy. They no longer probability-match; instead, they are much more likely to predict that the rewarded alternative will occur (Edwards, 1956; Estes, 1964b). Furthermore, we can lead subjects to probability-match or not by the type of instructions that we give when an experiment begins. As Estes points out, subjects tend to "overshoot" the matching probability if they are told ahead of time that they are dealing with a random series of events, or if they are told, in fact, that guessing correctly over a series of trials is a desirable thing to do.

Probability matching is a phenomenon that seems to be unique to human behavior, and—curiously enough—to the behavior of much lower organisms like cockroaches (Longo, 1964) and fish (Behrend & Bitterman, 1961). As Warren (1965) points out in his summary of the literature, turtles, pigeons, rats, and monkeys—animals occupying a place on the phylogenetic scale intermediate between that of cockroach and man—do not probability-match. Instead, they adopt something more closely approximating an optimal strategy, picking the alternative that is more likely to produce reinforcement over a number of trials. Why should this be the case? It is difficult to give a reasonable answer in the case of the poor lowly cockroach, but there is little question that people use all sorts of mediating behavior, including language, when they are faced with a situation in which decisions of the type we have been describing must be made. People seem to be highly sensitive, as they make one decision, to the outcomes of a string of decisions they have just made (Peterson & Ulehla, 1965).

For example, if someone has picked an alternative several times in a row—and been wrong each time—he is apt to be dead certain that if he picks the same alternative again, he will be right this time. This, of course, is the "gambler's fallacy." Whether or not a prediction will be correct on any given occasion is in all likelihood entirely independent of what has just happened on immediately preceding occasions, but people seem to have that happy (sometimes unhappy!) capacity to convince themselves that they can "beat the system" and predict events at a better-than-chance level. As Hake (1955) points out very cogently, the phenomenon of probability matching in human beings is the *result* of a potentially enormous number of things that may be going on—both overtly and covertly—as people make decisions. It does not necessarily describe, per se, what people are actually doing.

By far the largest impact of phenomena like that of probability matching has been upon the development of theory in psychology. Statistical learning theory, from which you are able to sample in this book, stems in large part from a consideration of the things that happen in situations where events occur, or are presumed to occur, in some probabilistic sort of way. The same is true of a host of other theories and models aimed at a description of many facets of human behavior: choice behavior, decision theory, game theory, and so on. Most, if not all, of such theorizing is couched in highly mathematical terms that place it beyond the confines of this book, but there is a wealth of material available if you are interested in finding out about such matters (see, for example, Luce, Bush, & Galanter, 1963).

6

GENERALIZATION AND DISCRIMINATION

One of the major functions of the learning process—if not the most important of all—is to assure that the right response occurs at the right time. This generally means that, *on signal,* an organism performs a response which is already a part of its basic behavior. Most animals, at least, seldom if ever find it necessary to learn highly skilled acts; much of the behavior (considered purely as response) of animals is unlearned. Animals must frequently learn, however, under precisely what conditions it is appropriate to do something—they must learn what sorts of cues set the stage for doing one thing as compared with another. To be sure, we sometimes require our laboratory rats to perform skilled acts, such as picking up a marble, turning around twice, and dropping the marble down a chute, but this is hardly the sort of thing we would expect a rat to undertake in its normal environment. More typically, we approximate what rats do normally by, for example, running them in mazes and alleyways. Under these conditions, we can study how rats learn to detect one pattern of cues as compared with another, and how they attach appropriate responses to the cues in question. Some psychologists maintain that, in this simple sense, all learning is little more than a process of discrimination.

Much of innate behavior, particularly in lower organisms, is highly discriminative; some instinctive act is likely to be emitted only in the presence of a rather precisely defined (unconditioned) stimulus. This has always been more or less understood, but in recent years we have greatly extended our knowledge of the precision with which particular stimuli set patterns of innate action. For example, in the case of the three-spined stickleback fish, a very crude model of a female will elicit the innate pattern of mating behavior in the male, providing the model is painted red on its underneath surface (Tinbergen, 1951). Here, the critical feature of the stimulus seems to be its red color.

While it is patently clear that telling the difference between one pattern of cues and another is of tremendous importance for the proper behavior of organisms, it is equally clear that there are occasions where it is best to respond to two cue patterns as if they were more or less the same. Thus, a given cue pattern—considered purely as an array of light intensities or sound waves striking a receptor—never reaches the organism in *exactly* the same form on any two given occasions. This can be true for no more complicated reason than the fact that an organism is almost certain to orient its body toward some object in its environment in different ways at different times. In the limit, the cues to which a response is to be attached through learning are never truly identical, though, of course, they are apt to be quite highly similar. Here, then, is another important problem: What happens when an organism is asked to respond to two or more cues that, while different, are nevertheless similar in some particular way? How similar must the cues be before the organism responds to them as if they were identical? What happens to behavior as we progressively reduce the similarity among them? Before we turn to a discussion of the process of discrimination per se, then, let us look at the phenomenon of *generalization,* the label which psychologists have attached to the things that go on when these problems are subjected to experimental attack.

GENERALIZATION

While investigating the conditioned salivary response in dogs, Pavlov discovered that the conditioned response was not limited to the stimulus to which it was originally conditioned. It would spread to other related stimuli. Experiments from Pavlov's laboratory (Pavlov, 1927) established the fact that if tactile stimulation of a small area of the dog's skin is used as a conditional stimulus, stimulation of other areas of the skin will also elicit the conditioned response, though the effect diminishes with the distance along the skin from the original conditional stimulus. This important effect is what is now known as *stimulus generalization.*[1]

The two important points about stimulus generalization are that (1) the effectiveness of a conditioning operation is not limited to the stimulus originally used in conditioning, and (2) the ability of a stimulus to elicit a conditioned response decreases as the stimulus becomes less similar to the one used during original conditioning. There is little argument about the first point: as an empirical fact, two different stimuli

[1] "Irradiation" and "induction" are some of the other terms that have been used to describe stimulus generalization.

can—under the proper conditions—elicit the same response, albeit at different strengths, perhaps. There is less agreement about the second point, however, particularly when it comes to deciding how concepts like "related" or "similar" should be defined. Here, as we shall see, psychologists have talked in terms of some simple physically defined dimension, such as distance along the skin or perhaps the wavelength or intensity of a light, and they have also talked in terms of some psychophysically determined *scale* of similarity. Let us elaborate both points by turning to some things that have emerged from the laboratory.

GENERALIZATION WITH CLASSICALLY CONDITIONED RESPONSES. The experiments from Pavlov's laboratory are, of course, experiments on generalization with classically conditioned responses. Let us, however, look at some experiments that have used other classically conditioned responses and have more carefully controlled the quantitative relations among stimuli.

In one experiment, the investigators conditioned the galvanic skin response [2] in man (elicited by electric shock) to a vibrator applied near the shoulders (Bass & Hull, 1934). The strength of the conditioned response was then tested with various stimuli placed at increasing distances from the original conditional stimulus. The results of this experiment are shown in Figure 6.1. The conditioned GSR was greatest in amplitude when it was nearest the original conditional stimulus and diminished in amplitude as the test stimuli increased in distance along the skin from the original conditioning site.

---

[2] The galvanic skin response (GSR) is associated with the electrical activity of the sweat gland cells when they are excited. These glands are largely innervated by the sympathetic branch of the autonomic nervous system; hence this response is often termed an "emotional" one.

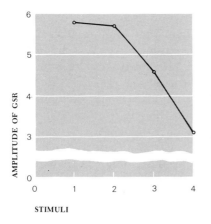

FIG. **6.1** Generalization of a conditional galvanic skin response (GSR) to different stimuli. Stimulus 1 is the conditional stimulus used during training. All stimuli used for testing differed from the conditional stimulus only in location. (Data from Bass & Hull, 1934.)

In another experiment involving classical conditioning and the GSR, Hovland (1937a) looked for generalization among different pitches of sound. His experiment is particularly interesting because, instead of using tones arrayed along a dimension of raw frequencies, he did some preliminary psychophysical work to select the stimuli to be used in his experiment. In particular, he picked four frequencies of sound—153, 468, 1,000, and 1,967 cycles per second—such that neighboring pairs of tones were separated from each other by 25 j.n.d.'s (just noticeable differences). Thus, when the tones were equated for loudness, the 153-cycle tone was as different from the 468-cycle tone as the 468-cyle tone was different from the 1,000-cycle in terms of the number of discriminably different steps in pitch between them. What Hovland did with this procedure, in effect, was to translate a physical scale based on simple frequencies of sound into a psychological scale where his stimuli were about equally spaced in terms of their apparent pitch.

After selecting his stimuli in this manner, Hovland conditioned the GSR to the 153-cycle tone for half his subjects and to the 1,967-cycle tone for the other half. Shock was used as the unconditioned stimulus. Then he tested for generalization by presenting the tones during extinction. Testing was carried out in such a way that the data from the two groups could be pooled, and the results of the experiment are shown in Figure 6.2. As you can see, Hovland obtained a progressively greater decrease in the amplitude of the GSR the farther test tones were removed in similarity from the original CS. In another experiment (Hovland, 1937b), a very similar set of results was obtained for tones arranged along a dimension of loudness.

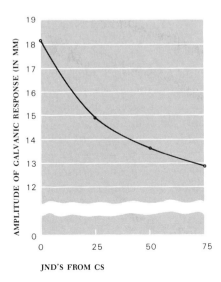

FIG. 6.2 Generalization of the galvanic skin response (GSR) for tones differing in frequency. In preliminary work, four tones were determined that differed from each other by 25 j.n.d.'s in pitch, and conditioning was carried out for different subjects using the highest or the lowest tone as the conditional stimulus. The data show that on test trials, the amplitude of the GSR decreased as the test tones became progressively less similar to the original CS. (Data from Hovland, 1937a.)

Although we have looked at just two, there are in fact a great many experiments that have demonstrated the basic phenomenon of stimulus generalization with classical conditioning procedures (Kimble, 1961). In most cases, functions similar to the ones we have seen—though differing in general shape, perhaps—have been obtained, and psychologists have attached the label *generalization gradient* to examples of such functions. Generalization gradients are by no means limited to the realm of classical conditioning, so let us now have a look at some that were obtained with instrumental conditioning.

GENERALIZATION WITH INSTRUMENTALLY CONDITIONED RESPONSES. Generalization in classical conditioning is a relatively straightforward matter, since in classical conditioning some stimulus is always used to elicit the conditioned response, and we have very precise control over the properties of that stimulus and what we do with it in the conditioning situation. In simple instrumental conditioning, however, we do not ordinarily attach a response by direct experimental means to some specific stimulus. In fact, as we saw in Chapter 1, we are hard-pressed (perhaps impossibly so) to identify the precise stimulus which comes to control the behavior we study. We can, of course, arrange things so that we are more sure of stimulus control by using the technique of simple discrimination training that we also discussed in Chapter 1, and we shall look at experimental work in which this was done in a moment (meeting, incidentally, a few surprises). Right now, however, let us look at some experiments in which no *direct* attempt was made to assure that the stimulus dimension along which generalization was tested had control over behavior.

In one study (Grice & Saltz, 1950) rats were trained to run down an alley and obtain food by pushing back a small door. The door was embedded in the stimulus to which the rats were trained; it consisted of a white circle on a black background. The rats were trained to run to a stimulus of a certain size, say 79 square centimeters, and then were tested with circles of different sizes, say 50 square centimeters. The test consisted of finding out how many times the rats would run during extinction to each of several test stimuli.

The results of the experiment are shown in Figure 6.3. As you can see, well-defined gradients of generalization were obtained. The more remote (in terms of spatial size) the test stimulus from the training stimulus, the fewer the responses during extinction. Thus, it is clear that if a reinforcement is associated with a particular stimulus during instrumental training, some of the response strength generated by that association "spills over" to stimuli related to, but not the same as, the stimulus originally conditioned.

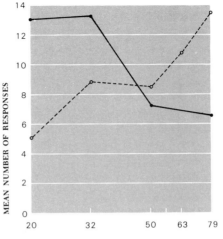

FIG. **6.3** Generalization gradients for an instrumental response. The two curves show the mean number of responses during extinction to various test stimuli. The solid curve shows generalization after training on the 20-square-millimeter stimulus, and the dotted curve shows the same thing on the 79-square-millimeter stimulus. (Grice & Saltz, 1950.)

In another experiment, Guttman and Kalish (1956) tested pigeons for generalization along a continuum of wavelengths of light—that is, along a dimension of hue or color. They did this by training pigeons in a Skinner box to peck at a key upon which was projected a CS light of a particular wavelength. Different pigeons were trained initially to peck under CS wavelengths ranging from 530 to 600 millimicrons. After some preliminary training, pecks were reinforced on a VI 1-minute schedule during 60-second periods in which the light was on the key. Successive light-on periods were separated by 10-second "time out" periods in which the key and the entire environment of the pigeon were completely dark (pigeons will not respond under such conditions). Tests for generalization were made under extinction conditions where the pigeon was permitted to peck for 30-second periods on each of 11 test wavelengths spread about the original CS. The data from the experiment are shown in the upper part of Figure 6.4.

Once again, well-defined generalization gradients were obtained. A regular gradient appears about both sides of each of the CS wavelengths used during initial training, and while there is a considerable difference in the total number of responses emitted during the generation of the several gradients, there is no marked difference in their overall shape.

In developing their experiment, Guttman and Kalish reasoned that the shape of the generalization gradient might be a function not so much of the physical dimension of wavelength per se as of a psychological dimension associated with wavelength (reasoning analogous to Hovland's). In particular, they thought that the shape of their generalization gradients might be related to *discriminability functions* for color, two of which are plotted in the lower part of Figure 6.4 (one for human

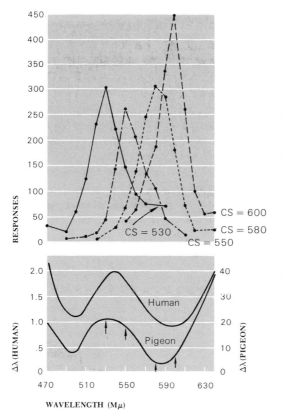

FIG. **6.4** The upper panel shows the generalization gradients that were obtained for each of several training stimuli that differed in wavelength. There is a progressive decrease in response strength as test stimuli become farther removed in wavelength from the original training stimulus. The lower panel shows, for humans and for pigeons, how much change in wavelength ($\Delta\lambda$) is required to produce a discriminable change in hue at different points along the spectrum. (Guttman & Kalish, 1956.)

vision and one for pigeon vision). If their reasoning was correct, the generalization gradient should be quite broad and flat for a CS picked at a high point on the discriminability function—that is, a point, say in the middle of the greens, where a relatively large change in wavelength must be made before an observer can tell that a change has occurred. Correspondingly, of course, the gradient should be steep at a low point on the discriminability function—a point like that around 590 millimicrons, where there is a *transition* from one broad range of hues to another and a relatively small change in wavelength can be detected. Of course, as we have already seen, the shapes of the generalization gradients did not change as a function of the CS wavelength, so Guttman and Kalish concluded that hue generalization, in the pigeon at least, was not related in any systematic way to the ability of the bird to detect simple differences in hue, per se.

WHAT UNDERLIES THE GENERALIZATION GRADIENT? The empirical phenomenon of the generalization gradient is a fact with which no one argues. As we have noted before, however, there is considerable argument about what sorts of things lie behind that fact. Lashley and Wade (1946) have maintained, for example, that generalization gradients occur only in the absence of an opportunity for the organism to learn to discriminate among the stimuli which are used to produce the gradient. In other words, they say that if animals are not allowed to *compare* stimuli in some fashion, they find it difficult to discriminate among closely related stimuli. Thus, generalization does not represent a spillover of the influence of habit (as Hull, for example, would have it) so much as it does the failure to discriminate the relevance of some sensory dimension.

There is considerable evidence to support, in broad terms, the point of view taken by Lashley and Wade. First of all, simple discrimination training (Chapter 1) can have marked effects upon generalization gradients. Jenkins and Harrison (1960), for example, ran an experiment in which they tested for generalization of pitch in the pigeon. Pigeons were run in a Skinner box under one of two conditions. In one, training to a CS of a 1,000 cycle per second tone was carried out in a manner essentially identical to that of Guttman and Kalish: periods of reinforced responding in the presence of the CS, separated by short "blackouts." In a second condition, the birds were reinforced for pecks in the presence of the CS, but they were also exposed to a number of other intervening periods in which the CS was absent. During these periods, the pigeons were free to peck, but *pecking was not reinforced*. This, if you will recall our discussion in Chapter 1, is simple discrimination training, and it normally leads—as it did for Jenkins and Harrison—to a state of affairs

FIG. **6.5** Generalization gradients for three pigeons following training in which the training tone of 1,000 cycles per second (S^D) was not used as a discriminative cue. The gradients are flat, indicating that all pigeons generalized completely to all test tones—including no tone at all. (Jenkins & Harrison, 1961.)

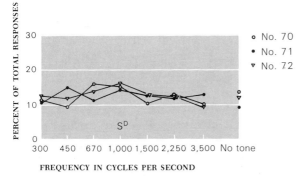

FREQUENCY IN CYCLES PER SECOND

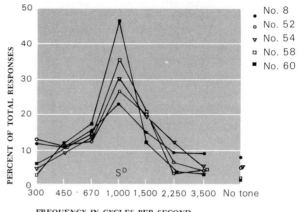

FIG. **6.6** Generalization gradients for five pigeons following training in which the training tone of 1,000 cycles per second (S^D) was used as a discriminative cue. Here, typical generalization gradients were obtained that show the familiar falloff in response strength as test tones become progressively less similar to the training tone. Responding to no tone at all (S^Δ) was quite low. (H. M. Jenkins & Harrison, 1960.)

where the pigeon reserves most of its pecks for the periods of time that the discriminative cue of the tone is on. When the pigeons in both groups were tested subsequently under extinction for the strength of their responding to tones arranged about the 1,000-cycle CS, they produced the generalization gradients shown in Figures 6.5 and 6.6.

The nature of the "gradients" is interesting indeed. Following training in which the 1,000-cycle tone was *not* used as a discriminative cue, there is essentially no "gradient" at all—the pigeons demonstrated about the same response strength to each of the test stimuli and—curiously enough—to no tone at all. However, when the 1,000-cycle tone was used as a discriminative cue, marked differences in response strength to the test stimuli appeared, and gradients much like those of Guttman and Kalish were obtained. These results represent striking confirmation of the Lashley-Wade point of view. When discrimination training was not used, the birds showed *complete* generalization—they responded to one tone in just about the same way they responded to any other (including silence!). In effect, sound—from the pigeons' point of view at least—was not a relevant stimulus at all. Discrimination training, however, seems to have brought the pigeons' behavior under control of auditory stimuli. In common terms, this procedure singled out sound as an important stimulus dimension, one that was "attention-getting" and relevant to the pigeons' task in the experiment. So, when faced with a series of different tones in the test for generalization, the pigeons demonstrated they could, in effect, tell the difference between the original training tone and the new different ones.

Why, you may ask, were Guttman and Kalish able to obtain gradients under experimental conditions where Jenkins and Harrison were not? There are many possible answers to this question, but one of the most reasonable is that pigeons are basically much more of a "visual" animal than they are "auditory"—in the sense that they probably depend more upon the sense of sight than the sense of hearing to find their way around in the world. Consequently, a visual stimulus may, without any special training, be much more of a salient attention-getting stimulus than a sound—it may be higher on an "attending hierarchy" (Baron, 1965). Psychologists are coming to be increasingly concerned about problems of this sort, and concepts like "attention" (Reynolds, 1961) and "attending hierarchy," together with the question of the process by which various kinds of stimulus dimensions acquire control over behavior, are beginning to receive a good deal of experimental attention in connection with the phenomenon of generalization (Mostofsky, 1965).

GENERAL LAWS FOR GENERALIZATION GRADIENTS.   Much of the original impetus for the study of generalization was provided by the hope that experimental work would reveal some kind of general mathematical law that could be used to describe the "shape" of generalization gradients for a wide variety of response and stimulus dimensions. Psychologists have worried, often for theoretical reasons, about whether gradients should be "concave upward" or "concave downward," and whether the ultimate gradient would be relatively "flat" or "steep" along some stimulus dimension. An enormous amount of work has been done in the laboratory on this and related problems (Mednick & Freedman, 1960; Kimble, 1961; Mostofsky, 1965), and while we may be progressing toward some general rules about stimulus generalization and the "shape" of the generalization gradient, there is still considerable ground to cover before we reach any kind of final answer.

There are many good reasons why an exact mathematical law of stimulus generalization has not yet been found. Some of these are purely mechanical. For example, even for the case of the galvanic skin response, there are many ways in which the response can be measured—as electrical resistance, as current flow, as electrical potential, and if a-c circuits are used, as other quantities. Unfortunately, there is no rational choice for the basic measurement that should be used. This precludes a fundamental mathematical law of stimulus generalization for even so restricted a case as the classically conditioned GSR; and of course, things do not become any simpler for instrumentally conditioned responses, where we often do not have as precise control over the sequence of stimulus and response events. If you will check, you will find that instrumental conditioning experiments such as that of Guttman and Kalish have used the rate, relative frequency, or perhaps the probability with which responses occur during extinction tests as an index of generalization. Yet again, there is no rational consideration which suggests that any of these related indices is to be preferred to others that might also be used. Also, the "shape" of generalization gradients can be changed in any number of ways by doing things like using different levels of motivation (Jenkins, Pascal, & Walker, 1958) or varying the way in which extinction tests for generalization are introduced into an experiment (Honig, Thomas, & Guttman, 1959)—things which do not, at a simple straightforward level, appear to have any intrinsic connection with generalization per se.

Just as there are problems in choosing the proper sort of response index to use in tests for generalization, so are there problems when it comes to choosing the proper way to define a rational stimulus dimension along which generalization presumably occurs (Blough, 1965). In Hovland's experiment, we saw one attempt to do this—the use of a scale of just noticeable differences between adjacent test frequencies of sound. But in the experiment of Guttman and Kalish, we saw that there was little correspondence between generalization and a very similar sort of psychophysical function, a discriminability function for wavelengths of light. The upshot of such work seems to be that a meaningful stimulus dimension for generalization is hard to come by so long as we stick to simple physical dimensions or to rather simple kinds of psychophysical functions to describe our stimuli.

Shepard (1957, 1958, 1965, etc.) has argued, however, that if we are willing to accept a measure such as probability of response as an index of generalization (recognizing the problems inherent in this assumption), then it ought to be possible to develop stimulus dimensions for generalization by means of scaling techniques rather more sophisticated than those used to generate the simple scales described above. To this end, Shepard has used *multidimensional scaling* to define points that are equally distant from each other in "psychological space" and has shown how generalization gradients can be deduced from mathematical models based on such scales. Thus in physical terms, stimuli like pure tones may be specified in one dimension, frequency. But in "psychological space," two or more dimensions may be required to specify relations among pure tones. For example, as Shepard (1965) reminds us, Blackwell and Schlosberg (1943) found that there was greater generalization between two tones if they were an octave apart than if they were just less than an octave apart. So, psychologically, the similarity between two tones may be determined by two things: their frequency and whether or not they stand together as an octave.

Any further discussion of Shepard's work would carry us quickly into an elegant mathematical world and beyond the scope of this book, but basically he and others like Torgerson (1965) are attempting to find new ways of describing how stimuli are *similar* to each other. On the reasonable assumption that generalization gradients are closely bound to the process by which organisms perceive the similarity among stimuli, this kind of work should have some important contributions to make to the discovery of a general law or set of rules describing the generalization process. Time will tell.

EXTINCTION ALSO GENERALIZES.   We have seen that the effects of reinforcement generalize to stimuli other than those specifically used in training. As might be expected, the effects of extinction also generalize in this way. Let us illustrate this with an example from classical conditioning (Hovland, 1937a). Suppose we condition a galvanic skin response in human subjects by pairing an electric shock with a tone of a certain frequency. After conditioning, we shall, of course, find that another frequency will elicit the response. Suppose we next *extinguish* the response to the *second* tone. If we then go back and test with the first tone, we shall find that extinction of the response to the second tone will reduce the tendency to respond to the first. Thus, the effects of extinction generalize as do the effects of reinforcement. Furthermore, the phenomenon is not limited to classical conditioning, since the same thing can be shown for instrumentally conditioned responses (Kling, 1952; Honig, 1961).

The generalization of the effects of both reinforcement and extinction are extremely important in the theory of discriminative learning, and a large portion of this chapter, as well as later chapters, will be devoted to the application of the principles of stimulus generalization to an understanding of discriminative learning and of related questions in the psychology of learning.

DISCRIMINATIVE LEARNING

Organisms come to *discriminate* among stimuli when they are trained to respond differentially to them. In an empirical operational sense, then, discrimination is the opposite of generalization, and we can look upon discriminative learning in a general way as the process of breaking down generalizations.

There are many ways to set up laboratory studies of the process by which organisms come to discriminate among stimuli. You are already familiar with one: simple discrimination training in a Skinner box, where the organism is reinforced for making some response in the presence of one stimulus (S^D) and not reinforced when the response occurs in the presence of another stimulus (S^Δ). Under these conditions, as we noted in Chapter 1, the organism comes to reserve most of its responding to the S^D period and responds very little during the S^Δ period. The process by which this occurs is gradual. Initially, as S^D and S^Δ periods are alternated, an animal will continue responding in the presence of both cues, but gradually, the opposing effects of reinforcement and extinction that are associated with the two cues take hold, and the animal tends to respond only when it is appropriate to do so—during S^D, when reinforcement is available.

Another procedure for the study of discriminative learning involves the use of the Lashley jumping stand. An example of this device is shown in Figure 6.7. In studies of discriminative learning using the jumping stand, rats are trained to jump from a platform about 8 inches from the stand to one of two doors in the stand. Light pieces of cardboard are placed over the doors, and these carry the stimuli. The problem illustrated in Figure 6.7 requires the rat to discriminate between vertical and horizontal stripes. If the rat makes the correct choice, the door falls, and the rat eats food placed inside the stand. If it makes the wrong choice,

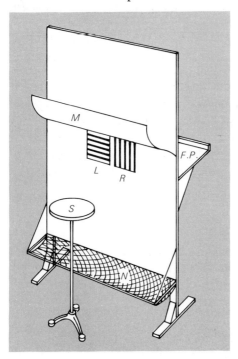

FIG. **6.7** The Lashley jumping stand. The rat jumps from the stand to one door or the other. If the choice is correct, the stimulus card gives way; if the choice is wrong, the rat falls to the net below. (Lashley, 1930.)

the door does not move and the rat falls to the net below. Thus, typically, the Lashley jumping stand makes use of punishment.

In other types of discriminative studies, single choice-point mazes and runways have been used (recall, for example, the double runway in Grice's study of the role of conditioned reinforcement in learning with delays of reinforcements). Regardless of the type of experimental apparatus that is used, however, the fundamental rule remains the same: Subjects are required to respond in different ways to a cue that is associated with reinforcement as compared with a cue that is not (or is associated with some unpleasant stimulus) .

The way in which animals learn such discriminations appears simple enough—with increasing frequency, the correct alternative is chosen or, in simple discrimination training with a free operant, behavior tends to appear only in the presence of S^D. It would be a mistake to think, however, that animals are able to make "perfect" discriminations in that they always come to do precisely what they are supposed to do. This is particularly clear in the case of simple discrimination training in the Skinner box, where it is often extremely difficult to get an animal to make *all* its responses to S^D, inhibiting all behavior in the presence of S^Δ. Generally, a *criterion* for learning the discrimination will be adopted; the experimenter may arbitrarily decide that the discrimination has been learned when the animal emits 90 percent of its responses to S^D and only 10 percent to S^Δ. Obviously, criteria for the learning of a discrimination may also be used in other kinds of situations in which discrimination learning is studied. With the Lashley jumping stand, for instance, the experimenter may term the problem learned when, over a series of trials, the animal is correct 90 percent of the time.

Despite the outward simplicity of discriminative learning, the events that go on in the organism must be very complicated indeed. Let us look at some of the attempts that have been made to deal with this problem theoretically and experimentally.

THEORIES OF DISCRIMINATIVE LEARNING

Most theories of discriminative learning fall into two classes. One of these places great emphasis upon gradients of stimulus generalization and upon the gradual accumulation of habit strength and inhibitory tendencies to correct and incorrect stimuli. The other class stresses the importance of the active problem-solving character of discrimination and the all-or-nothing characteristic of hypotheses that organisms might use in learning to discriminate.

Unfortunately, no single theorist of either class has dealt with all the problems in discrimination learning. This has undoubtedly been due, in part, to the fact that no single theory can do an adequate job of handling all the problems in discrimination learning, a fact with which you have had plenty of opportunity to become familiar in a number of other contexts. So, in discussing theoretical matters in connection with discriminative learning, we must draw upon the work and thinking of a number of people, recognizing that for the present there is no single completely satisfactory account of the process by which organisms learn to discriminate.

THE ALGEBRAIC SUMMATION AND CONTINUITY THEORY

The theory of discriminative learning that makes the greatest use of the concepts of stimulus generalization and of the gradual accumulation of habit strength comes primarily from the work of Spence (1936, 1937a, 1940, 1952), though most of his fundamental notions are close to those of Hull (1943, 1952). Let us look at some of the principles these theorists have emphasized.

First of all, Spence and Hull have insisted that gradients of stimulus generalization interact algebraically. Suppose that an animal is trained on a discriminative problem by the reinforcement of a response to one stimulus and the extinction of the response to a second stimulus. The effects of reinforcement will generalize to all other related stimuli, and so will the effects of extinction—facts which we have looked at earlier in this chapter. According to this view, the strength of the tendency to respond to a stimulus is obtained by subtracting the strength of generalization of extinction from the strength of generalization of reinforcement for that stimulus. The following equation expresses the notion:

$$R_a = R - I$$

R_a is the *net* strength of response after the inhibition from extinction is subtracted.

This hypothesis is illustrated in Figure 6.8. Here, the solid curve represents the generalization of conditioning, R; the lightly dashed curve, the generalization of extinction, I; and the heavily dashed curve, the net response strength, R_a, after I has been subtracted from R for every stimulus. The exact form of the generalization curve, as well as the values of its constants, is of course unknown (and open to all the questions that can be leveled at an attempt to specify the shape of a generalization gradient). But despite this limitation, the idea of algebraic interaction leads to some important conclusions.

SPENCE'S ANALYSIS OF TRANSPOSITION. One of the most interesting by-products of the algebraic summation notion is the way in which it can be used to account for a special phenomenon in discriminative learning known as *transposition*. Transposition is the apparent ability of

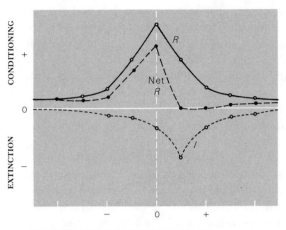

DEVIATIONS FROM STIMULUS REINFORCED

FIG. **6.8** The algebraic summation notion of discrimination learning. Net response strength is the result of the subtraction of the effects of generalized extinction from those of generalized reinforcement. (Suggested from Hull, 1952.)

organisms to make *relational* discriminations. We can best illustrate what these are by an example.

Köhler (1915) once trained chickens to respond (with food as reinforcement) to the darker of two gray surfaces. The chickens were never reinforced when they responded to the lighter surface. When this discrimination was well established, the animals were presented with a new choice between the *original* reinforced gray and one *darker still.* When faced with this new problem, the interesting thing was that the chickens chose the darker of these two grays, even though they had always been reinforced for choosing the other one. In other words, argued Köhler, the animals had learned the *relationship* "darker than" rather than the specific association of a particular stimulus with reinforcement.

This result presents a problem for a theory of learning, such as that of Spence or Hull, which says that animals learn by attaching responses to specific absolute stimuli; for here is a case in which reinforcement apparently has no effect (or even a negative effect) on choice of the particular gray surface that was paired with reinforcement initially. It turns out, however, that this example of transposition can be explained by the principle of stimulus generalization. Let us see how Spence goes about the matter.

Spence (1937a, 1937b) uses an illustration based on a study of the discrimination of visual size in chimpanzees. He trained animals to discriminate between two squares, 256 square centimeters and 160 square centimeters in size. The response to 256 was reinforced and the response to 160 was extinguished. Then, after the discrimination between stimuli 256 and 160 was well established, the values of the stimuli were shifted to 256 and 409. The animals then chose 409—a stimulus which had never been reinforced.

The theoretical analysis of this problem is presented in Figure 6.9. The extinction to stimulus 160 generalized to 256 to some extent, and the conditioning to stimulus 256 generalized somewhat to 409. To arrive at the comparative value of response strength after discrimination of 256 and 409, we subtract the amount of generalized extinction from the amount of generalized conditioning. As shown in Figure 6.9, when the net response strength is obtained by this procedure, it is greater for 409 than for 256. Thus we would predict that, on the average, animals would choose to respond to 409 instead of to 256. This is a prediction of the transposition effect.

It is important to recognize that the curves in Figure 6.8, as contrasted with those in Figure 6.9, do *not* yield the transposition effect. In Figure 6.8, the highest net response strength occurs to the stimulus reinforced originally. From a comparison of this figure with Figure 6.9, you can infer that the prediction of whether or not transposition will occur

FIG. **6.9** How the algebraic summation notion accounts for an example of transportation. The net response strength is greatest not at the stimulus size specifically reinforced (256), but at the larger ones (409, etc.). (After Spence, 1937a.)

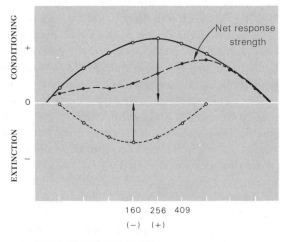

STIMULUS SIZE (LOG SCALE)

depends upon the shape, relative location, and slope of the generalization curves. This latitude offered by the selection of arbitrary values (presumably to be determined experimentally) for curves of generalization is, theoretically, both an advantage and a weakness. It is a weakness in that the theory can provide no rational way of stating exactly the quantitative aspects of its assumptions—a weakness which, as we have seen, besets all attempts to specify general rules for generalization gradients. It is an advantage in that it suggests that transposition will occur only sometimes. The *gestalt* notions from which the transposition problem originally comes imply that transposition will always occur. The theory based on generalization gradients suggests that the occurrence of transposition depends upon how we affect the generalization gradients by training, amount of reinforcement, and so on.

The obvious way to *prevent* transposition is to make the positive and negative stimuli very different from each other. A demonstration of what this would do can be seen by moving the curves in Figure 6.9 apart. In general, experimenters have found that when they move the stimuli far apart along some stimulus dimension, there tends to be a failure of transposition. Thus Kendler (1950) and Ehrenfreund (1952) found that as they systematically increased the difference between stimuli, the percentage of responses showing transposition decreased—results that would be expected from generalization gradients.

Another simple prediction provided by the analysis shown in Figure 6.9 has to do with the way in which discrimination training will affect the point of maximum response strength on a generalization gradient. In particular, you can see from Figure 6.9 that the algebraic summation theory predicts a maximum beyond 409 at a point that is displaced from the original S+ in a direction away from S−. Hanson (1959) has shown that just such a displacement or "peak shift" in the post-discrimination gradient occurs. He trained pigeons to respond to a 550-millimicron wavelength of light as S+ and, for different groups, to S− stimuli that ranged from 555 to 590 millimicrons. Responses to S+ were reinforced, but those to S− were never reinforced.[3] When the pigeons were tested for generalization after this discrimination training, they all produced generalization gradients with their maxima at a point displaced from S+ in a direction opposite that of S−, just as the algebraic summation theory requires. Furthermore, Terrace (1964) has shown that the "peak shift" does not occur if special training procedures are used

---

[3] Note that this is a *different* sort of discrimination training from that used by Jenkins and Harrison (1960), who taught their pigeons to respond in the presence of a tone and to stop responding in the *total absence* of the tone. Hanson taught his pigeons to respond to one of two stimuli that were *both* picked from the same stimulus dimension—wavelength of light.

so that the pigeons are exposed to the S— stimulus but are induced never to respond to it. Since the pigeons never experience nonreinforcement of responses to S—, a gradient of extinction around S— never gets a chance to develop, presumably, and the shift in the generalization gradient called for by the algebraic summation theory does not appear.

A number of experimenters have studied the problem of transposition in children (e.g., Kuenne, 1946). It has been argued that as children pass from preverbal to verbal stages of development, their solution of the transposition problem shifts from one based upon generalization gradients to one more like adult formation of mediated "relationship" concepts (Stevenson, Iscoe, & McConnell, 1955; Hebert & Krantz, 1965). The evidence is by no means conclusive on this point, but again, it would be quite surprising if verbal organisms attacked a transposition problem in just the same way as nonverbal organisms. Language is an obvious tool to use in mediating the solution of such problems—for those organisms that possess the tool.

OTHER USES OF THE ALGEBRAIC SUMMATION PRINCIPLE IN GENERALIZATION. The basic notion used in the prediction of transposition from generalization gradients, namely, the algebraic summation of generalized habit tendencies, has many other applications. It has been generally assumed by those working in the psychology of learning that stimulus generalization is a basic component in the ability of organisms to *transfer* what they have learned in one situation to another similar one. The relationship between stimulus generalization and more general problems in the transfer of training across learning tasks involves many difficulties, however, and we must postpone a discussion of some of these. Part of our difficulty, of course, is our inability to specify the exact form of generalization gradients. Perhaps some progress is being made; Lawrence (1955), for example, pointed out certain important restrictions that must be incorporated into generalization gradients if they are to account for the existing data on discriminative learning. Lawrence suggests that only certain types of gradients that are *concave downward* will do. But—as our earlier discussion of the problems inherent in specifying general rules for generalization gradients indicates—this can be little more than a bare beginning to a general solution of the problem.

THE NONCONTINUITY THEORY

The theory of discriminative learning at which we have just looked places great emphasis upon the gradual accumulation of habit strength and upon the algebraic summation of gradients of generalization based on reinforcement and extinction. In general, this theory has been contrasted with one which emphasizes the problem-solving behavior of organisms in discriminative learning. This is generally called a *non-continuity* theory, because it implies that learning a discrimination is not a continuous accumulation of positive and negative habit strength, or the like. The essential idea is that animals try out hypotheses about the discrimination problem they are required to solve, testing one hypothesis and then another until they hit upon the correct solution. Let us see how this might work.

A rat is trained to jump to one or another window in the Lashley jumping stand. The problem for the rat is to learn to jump to the white window and to avoid the black one. When faced initially with a choice between black and white, the white window might by chance be on the right side. If the rat jumps successfully to the white window, it might learn either that white is correct or that the right side is correct. Let us suppose that it learns right to be correct. The rat will then work on this hypothesis until it is either punished or extinguished. The rat might then adopt some other hypothesis, based upon a chance contingency of reinforcement and some aspect of the environment. This would continue until the rat happened on the correct hypothesis and kept at it long enough to convince the experimenter that the rat had solved the problem.

In other words, instead of gradually learning a single habit through the accumulation of the effects of reinforcement and nonreinforcement, the rat would have adopted a number of different strategies, learning (and unlearning) a whole series of habits analogous to those that human beings would call hypotheses.

This notion, that animals adopt a succession of strategies or hypotheses in solving problems, has been advanced by many investigators, most notably Krechevsky (1932) and Lashley (1938, 1942; Lashley & Wade, 1946). The noncontinuity theory has never been entirely expressed by one author, and many more points than the simple one about hypotheses have been made. Lashley, for example, in nearly all his publications emphasizes the momentary attentional set the animal may have in perceiving a portion of the stimulus field set in front of it by the experimenter.

The theorists who have supported the noncontinuity viewpoint have tended to look at experimental problems that arise out of intuition. The continuity theorists, on the other hand, have tended to develop experimental hypotheses in more rigorous fashion, choosing them from formal (and sometimes mathematical) principles. In the light of this difference in approach, it is not always possible to compare the continuity and noncontinuity theories line for line, as it were; but let us look at some of the experimental problems designed for this purpose and see what the outcome has been.

COMPARISON OF THE CONTINUITY AND NONCONTINUITY THEORIES

THE EFFECTS OF CHANGING THE PROBLEM. Some of the best evidence on the comparative adequacy of the continuity and noncontinuity theories has come from experiments in which a problem is altered partway through the training program. One way to do this is to *reverse the discriminative cues* early in training while an animal is still responding at a chance level. Here is how this could be done. Suppose that we start to train a rat to discriminate between white and black cards. We reinforce choices of the black card and extinguish choices of the white one. Then after a few trials, we reverse the cues, so that the white card is now associated with reinforcement and the black card with nonreinforcement. What effect will this have on the speed with which the animal learns the problem? If the animal has been following a wrong hypothesis (a position hypothesis, say) during the initial phase of training, we should expect no effect if we reverse the cues, since the animal has not yet begun to associate black and white cues with the presence or absence of reinforcement. If, however, each trial adds a small increment both of habit strength to the positive stimulus and of inhibition to the negative stimulus, as the continuity theory would suggest, then reversing the cues ought to lead to negative transfer or interference—thus to relatively slow learning. Note that this reasoning holds only for early trials where the animal is responding at a chance level, that is, during the *presolution period* where, presumably, noncontinuity rats have not had a chance to stumble upon and to identify a hypothesis as correct.

There are a number of experiments which have used the technique of reversing cues during the presolution period, and the overwhelming majority show that reversing cues *does* retard learning (Ehrenfreund, 1948; Mackintosh, 1965). It is clear, then, that the results of discrimination experiments in which cues are reversed early in learning favor the continuity view.

The continuity theory does not fare so well, however, if we reverse cues during a later stage in the learning process. Suppose we train animals on a discrimination problem until they have learned the problem well. Then suppose we give them a large number of additional training trials on the problem; that is, we *overtrain* or permit the animals to *overlearn* the problem. While noncontinuity theory might not have any specific prediction to make about behavior if we now reverse cues, continuity theory would have a very specific prediction to make—namely, that it ought to be progressively more difficult for the animals to reverse their behavior as the number of overtraining trials increases. This would be true because overtraining should add additional habit strength to the correct solution to the original problem (though perhaps not an overwhelming amount, given what we know about the relation between number of reinforcements and habit strength). Consequently, it ought to be more difficult for the animals to drop (extinguish) their original behavior and to respond appropriately to the reversed cues.

But in a number of experiments, at least, this does not seem to be the case at all. The data indicate that overtraining in fact *speeds up* the process of learning the reversal (Reid, 1953; Pubols, 1956; Sperling, 1965a, 1965b). The reason why this happens is not yet clear, and there are many experiments where the effect has not been obtained (e.g., D'Amato & Schiff, 1965), but the phenomenon—termed the *overlearning reversal effect*—is sufficiently reliable to be worrisome to a continuity theorist. This much is clear: The effect is most clearly obtained if large rewards are used and if the experiment involves the reversal of a position discrimination (going right versus left in a T maze, for example) as compared with the reversal of a discrimination based on exteroceptive cues (responding to white versus black, for example). Also, the effect is quite reminiscent of a phenomenon that we looked at in Chapter 4: Resistance to extinction of a simple response like running an alley increases and *then decreases* as a function of number of reinforcements.

In addition to the experiments on the reversal of cues, there are some in which cues are modified rather than reversed during the presolution period and still others in which more than one kind of cue is used. Let us look at some of these experiments.

One that seems to favor the noncontinuity view is an experiment by Lashley (1942). Lashley first trained some rats to discriminate between large and small circles (the large circle was reinforced). Then Lashley continued the training, but this time he substituted a large triangle for the large circle. Thus, the animals now discriminated between a large triangle and a small circle. Yet these animals failed to make the distinction in shape, for when they were tested with the large triangle and the large circle they showed no preference. Furthermore, they showed a preference for a large circle over a small triangle. The results of this experiment suggest that the rats did not learn the incidental cue (shape), but only the cue on which they had originally been trained (size).

On the other hand, there are experiments which suggest that rats *do* learn such incidental cues. For example, Bitterman and Coate (1950) showed that if a spatial cue is made incidental to the learning of a brightness discrimination, the spatial cue is learned also. Similar results were obtained by Hughes and North (1959). It is obvious that this question is by no means settled, though some experiments we shall look at later will suggest a way of making sense out of the finding that incidental cues are sometimes learned and sometimes not.

SUCCESSIVE VERSUS SIMULTANEOUS DISCRIMINATION. Another comparison of theoretical importance in discriminative training is that between simultaneously and successively presented cues. (It is not always clear which theory is on which side, however. Compare Grice, 1949, with Spence, 1952.) The problem is especially important to the matter of relational versus absolute discrimination. If animals respond to relationships between stimuli in learning how to discriminate, then successive presentation of stimuli should make the problem more difficult than simultaneous presentation. If, however, animals respond simply to the positive reinforcement of one stimulus and to the extinction of the other, it should not make much difference, all other things being equal, whether the stimuli are presented together or not.

One experimental test of this problem is that of Grice (1949). It is difficult to compare the learning which occurs to simultaneously presented stimuli and that which occurs to successively presented stimuli, because in the latter there are no errors, since the animals have no choice to make. Grice, however, estimated the errors in successively presented stimuli by counting as errors all runs to the positive stimulus with latencies greater than the median latency and all runs to the negative stimulus with latencies less than the median. With this estimate, there was no difference in the learning curves for the two conditions. Thus, Grice concluded, it is not necessary for animals to compare stimuli in order to learn a discrimination.

Other kinds of experiments, however, indicate that simultaneous versus successive training can produce very different effects upon discriminative learning—effects which seem more compatible with the noncontinuity view than with the continuity view. In particular, these experiments have looked at the effect of the two training procedures upon our old friend, the phenomenon of transposition.

Baker and Lawrence (1951) trained two groups of rats to discriminate between circles of different sizes. A 6½ centimeter circle was positive and a 9 centimeter circle was negative. The rats were trained to run through a door in a discrimination apparatus to the stimuli which were mounted on the far wall of an end box. The rats responded to the stimuli by pushing with their noses against a small window located in the center of each circle. If they chose the positive stimulus, they could reach a pellet of food in a cup behind the stimulus; if they chose the negative stimulus, they found the window locked so that they could not push it open. The two groups differed in just one respect: one group (the simultaneous group) found both the positive and negative stimuli side by side on a given trial, while the second group (the successive group) found just one of the stimuli present on any particular trial. Following training to a criterion of 18 correct choices out of 20 trials, a test for transposition was made by running both groups to a positive 4 centimeter circle and a negative 6½ centimeter circle. The results on the transposition test showed that the simultaneous group responded correctly 78 percent of the time, while the successive group responded correctly 43 percent of the time—that is, at just about a chance level.

Other experiments (e.g., Honig, 1962; Riley, Goggin, & Wright, 1963) have shown the same thing that Baker and Lawrence did. In other words, a simultaneous-training procedure produces a clear-cut transposition effect, while a successive-training procedure does not. Since the transposition effect is a phenomenon of crucial interest to those concerned with a distinction between the continuity and noncontinuity approaches, it appears that a comparison of simultaneous- versus successive-training procedures in terms of their effect upon this phenomenon supports the noncontinuity point of view. Apparently, the opportunity to compare stimuli simultaneously is a distinct help in the learning of relations among stimuli.

DISCRIMINATION AMONG STIMULI IMPLYING RELATIONSHIPS. Since the noncontinuity view stresses the notion that animals actively attend to and compare stimuli in the process of learning a discrimination, what would happen if an experiment were done in which the discriminative stimuli actually consisted of *relations* among stimuli? Let us look at a classic experiment on this problem, that of Lawrence and DeRivera (1954), which was arranged to test predictions that the continuity and noncontinuity theories would make about transposition.

Lawrence and DeRivera used a Lashley jumping stand for their experiment, and an array of stimuli were chosen and used as follows. Stimulus cards were prepared that consisted of two brightnesses. The bottom half of each card was always a middle gray, a brightness of 4 on a scale ranging from 1 (bright) to 7 (dark). The top half of each card consisted of a gray selected from one of the other scale values. Thus, card 1/4 had the top half brighter than the bottom half, while card 7/4 had the top half darker than the bottom half. During initial training, identical cards were placed over *both* windows of the apparatus. If the top half of the cards was lighter than the bottom half, the rats had to jump to the right to obtain a food reward; if the top half was darker, a jump to the left produced a reward. In effect, the rats could approach the discrimination problem in one of two ways. They could respond to a *relationship:* top lighter than bottom—jump right; top darker than bottom—jump left; or they could respond to the *absolute brightness* of the top half of the cards (since the bottom was always the same brightness): top bright (value 1, 2, or 3)—jump right; top dark (values 5, 6, or 7)—jump left. After initial training, the experimenters tried to find out which strategy the rats were, in fact, using by subjecting them to a series of transposition tests. In general, this was done by changing the brightness of the *bottom* half of the cards to values other than the single one used during training.

Think, for a moment, of the stimulus card 3/1, one of the cards used during the transposition tests. If the rats had learned to respond during training to the absolute brightness of the top part of the card, a rat faced with a 3/1 card during transposition should jump to the right, since both the 3 stimulus and the 1 stimulus were rewarded during initial training for this response. If, however, the rats had learned to respond on the basis of the *relation* between the top and bottom brightness, a rat faced with a 3/1 card should jump to the left, since initial training set things so that jumps to the left were rewarded when the top of the card was darker than the bottom.

Lawrence and DeRivera used a great many combinations of this sort and found that about 80 percent of the responses during transposition fitted a relational interpretation of what the rats had learned during initial training, and only 20 percent fitted an absolute interpretation. Once again it appears that rats will learn to respond in a relational way— providing we set things so that the task which the animal faces is one that clearly implies a relationship.

AN EVALUATION OF THE CONTINUITY AND NONCONTINUITY THEORIES. It should be evident to you by now that experimental data on discriminative learning have far outrun theory. Certainly, the absolute, continuity theory is correct in asserting that animals can be trained to have positive responses to certain stimuli without comparing these stimuli with others on the same sensory continuum. In the process of training, even though animals give no signs of having grasped the discrimination, experience at the task has effects which can be detected by transfer tests—by changing the problem, for example. On the other hand, there are abundant data to show that animals do not simply react to stimuli, any stimuli, that come within range; they are selective in what they attend to. Furthermore, there is good evidence that animals test "hypotheses" about the nature of a problem, and that they can behave in a relational manner if we present them with a problem which, in a more or less obvious way, leads them to respond relationally.

Clearly we have at hand a great abundance of information about discriminative learning which sometimes jibes with one theory or another and sometimes does not. At the same time, we need more and better data before we shall be able to understand the phenomena associated with discriminative learning and to develop appropriate theories to handle that data. There is no question that both the continuity and noncontinuity theories have something worthwhile to say, but it is equally certain that neither speaks overwhelmingly louder than the other. From the vantage point of the moment, it looks very much as if we are headed toward a melding of theories that are currently available. And, of course, we always have the prospect of new information and new systematic approaches that can do a better job than those at hand.

THE DEVELOPMENT OF DISCRIMINATIVE CAPACITY

An important problem which has received much experimental and theoretical attention is that of the development of the capacity for discrimination. This has been looked at in two ways. In the first place, there has been much experimental work on the acquisition of the distinctiveness of cues in discrimination learning, and secondly, there has been an experimental program to study the gradual improvement in discrimination that comes from learning how to discriminate. Both problem areas have led us to consider the prospect of *mediational* factors, or something closely akin to them, in the process of learning how to discriminate.

THE ACQUIRED DISTINCTIVENESS OF CUES

Much of the theoretical analysis of discriminative learning has incorporated the assumption that responses are always learned to particular cues—that learning is a simple matter of stimulus-response bonds. Nearly all theorists agree, however, that at best this is an oversimplification (though it may provide a useful *model* for the study of behavior), and there has been much work showing that discriminative learning involves some mediated or central associations. Some of the best of this work has been on the acquired distinctiveness of cues.

Lawrence (1949, 1950, 1963) has established that when organisms learn to discriminate among cues, they can transfer this discrimination to new situations in which entirely different instrumental responses are required. Thus, the distinction between cues is not correlated exclusively with the responses used in discrimination learning, and therefore discrimination learning cannot be simply a matter of stimulus-response bonds. So, in addition to considering the factors of positive and negative stimulus generalization in any complicated learning problem, we must also consider the extent to which particular cues acquire distinctiveness for organisms as the learning process proceeds. Let us amplify this point by looking at one of Lawrence's experiments.

Lawrence (1949) first trained rats to make a simultaneous discrimination. One group of animals was trained to step across a short gap to one compartment of a two-compartment box on the basis of the brightness (black or white) of the two compartments—with black, say, being a correct choice rewarded with food. Incorrect choices were punished by dropping the floor of the apparatus and letting the rats fall a short distance to a platform. A second group had to choose between compartments with rough or smooth floors, while a third had to discriminate between a large or a small compartment.

After they had learned to do this, the animals were shifted to another problem involving a different response, a *successive* discrimination in which they had to learn to go right or left in a T maze. In the T maze, the animals were exposed to two sets of cues. One set, say black versus white, was *relevant*—the rats had to turn to the right if the maze was black on a given trial, to the left if the maze was white. Correct responses were rewarded with food, incorrect responses punished as before. Another set, say rough floor versus smooth floor, was *irrelevant* —besides the difference in brightness, the T maze had a rough floor on some trials, a smooth floor on others, but these cues were not correlated in any consistent fashion with the brightness cues the rats had to use to learn the new discrimination. The critical variable in the experiment was the relation between the relevant and irrelevant cues in the T-maze problem and the set of cues that had been used in the simultaneous-discrimination problem.[4]

Now think for a moment of rats who, for example, learned the T-maze problem with black versus white the relevant cue and rough versus smooth the irrelevant cue. Some of these animals had learned the simultaneous discrimination on the basis of black versus white. Lawrence ventured the guess that these animals would learn the T-maze problem relatively rapidly—on the assumption that black versus white had acquired some special distinctiveness by virtue of being used in the simultaneous discrimination that would transfer to the successive discrimination and help learning there. Other animals, however, had learned the simultaneous discrimination on the basis of rough versus smooth cues. If these cues had acquired some special distinctiveness, and if the rats used them in the T-maze problem, they would be responding not to the relevant cues, but, in fact, to the irrelevant ones. Consequently, interference ought to occur, and the rate at which the rats learned the successive discrimination would be relatively slow. The third group of animals trained initially on wide versus narrow should be neither helped nor hurt on the successive discrimination, since that particular stimulus dimension was not used in the T maze. So the rate at which they ought to learn should lie somewhere between the rates of the other two groups.

In general, the data supported Lawrence's reasoning, particularly for those conditions where the stimulus dimension used on the first prob-

[4] Lawrence's experimental design was considerably more complete than this, but we shall simplify things a bit by talking about only part of it.

lem was the relevant one on the second. These animals learned the T-maze discrimination relatively quickly—more quickly, say, than the animals who had had no prior experience with the relevant stimulus dimension. Clearly, then, animals seem to *learn* something about a stimulus dimension when acquiring one response in one experimental situation that will transfer to another experimental situation and facilitate learning of another response there. Again, the animal cannot be transferring on the basis of some simple stimulus-response bond because, while the stimulus dimension is the same in the two learning situations, the responses are different. Instead, there must be some kind of central coding process (Lawrence, 1963), a kind of general abstraction having to do with the distinctiveness of "brightness-as-a-cue" that, once learned in one situation, can function to mediate and speed up learning in a new situation.

An important outcome of this work has been to point toward the solution of some of the issues in the continuity-noncontinuity controversy. Lawrence and his associates (Lawrence & Mason, 1955; Goodwin & Lawrence, 1955) have suggested that in complicated discrimination problems, organisms learn several habits simultaneously. First of all, they can learn to attend to a particular kind of stimulus dimension (brightness, for example), and secondly, they can learn an actual discrimination (a *particular* brightness is reinforced). Suppose, however, that there are other cues present, such as the height of a hurdle over which an animal must jump. If the experimenter changes the problem so that the height of the hurdle is now the cue, the animal need not necessarily unlearn the brightness discrimination. All that is necessary is that attention towards brightness be extinguished. If this is so, the animal can learn the new discrimination without disturbing much of what it has learned about the old one.

REVERSAL AND NONREVERSAL SHIFTS.   Another closely related problem has to do with the relative effects of *reversal* and *nonreversal* shifts upon discriminative learning (Kendler & Kendler, 1962). The two are diagrammed in Figure 6.10. Subjects first learn a discrimination in which two stimulus dimensions are used, only one of which is relevant. In Figure 6.10, the stimuli vary in both size and brightness, but size is the relevant cue; large objects are positive (correct) and small objects are negative (incorrect). Now the subjects are shifted to another discrimination involving the same stimulus dimensions. In the case of a *reversal* shift, the *same* stimulus dimension is still relevant, but the subject must reverse his choice behavior; small objects are now positive and large objects negative. In the case of a *nonreversal* shift, the previously *irrelevant* stimulus dimension becomes *relevant,* and a correspondingly

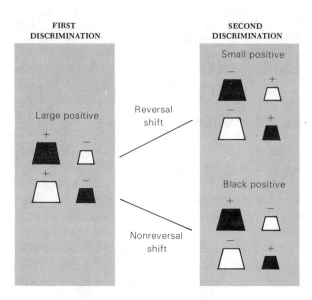

FIG. **6.10** Reversal and nonreversal shifts. In each case, subjects first learn the discrimination on the left, where *size* is the relevant dimension and *brightness* is the irrelevant dimension. In the case of a reversal shift, subjects then learn a second discrimination in which size is still relevant, but *small* is now the positive cue. In the case of a nonreversal shift, the previously irrelevant dimension becomes relevant, so that subjects must now respond on the basis of *brightness*. (After Kendler & Kendler, 1962.)

different type of overt choice behavior must be used. Thus brightness becomes the relevant stimulus dimension; black is positive and white negative.

Now here is the critical question: Which should be learned faster, a reversal shift or a nonreversal shift? Following some of our thinking in connection with the overlearning reversal effect (p. 191), we might expect that a nonreversal shift would be learned faster than a reversal shift, since at the time the shift occurs, there is a relatively strong habit for reversal-shift subjects to continue responding to the cue that was correct but is now incorrect. If we think in terms akin to those of Lawrence, however, we might predict just the opposite. If subjects had coded on the first problem something about size in general as a relevant cue, they would still attend to the relevant dimension when the shift occurs and all they would have to do is reverse their overt choice responses. With the nonreversal shift, however, they would have to learn not only to make the appropriate choice behavior, but also to make it on the basis of a *newly* relevant stimulus dimension.

The experimental data on this problem are interesting. It turns out that if college students or children over the age of approximately five years are used as subjects, reversal shifts are easier to learn than nonreversal shifts (Kendler & D'Amato, 1955; Kendler & Kendler, 1962). However, preschool children (Kendler, Kendler & Wells, 1960) and nonverbal organisms like rats (Kelleher, 1956) learn a nonreversal shift faster than a reversal shift. As a matter of fact, there is a consistent relationship between the age of children and the extent to which they will choose to respond in a reversal as compared with a nonreversal way; Figure 6.11 shows that there is an increasing tendency for children to select a reversal shift as they become older.

How are these data to be explained? Clearly, there is little to be gained, once again, by sticking to an approach couched in terms of simple stimulus-response bonds, since this does not do a very adequate job of accounting for all the data (though it might explain the behavior of rats and preschool children). Kendler and Kendler favor a *mediating response* notion—an external cue sets off an *implicit* nonovert response which, in turn, has its own cue properties that become attached to the final set of overt choice responses. The mediating response acts as a sort of generalized go-between, a *label,* linking a number of different (though related) stimulus inputs and response outputs. What Kendler and Kendler have in mind for a mediating response is, of course, verbal behavior or something closely akin to it. In effect, children learn to *label* a relevant dimension on a reversal shift, for example, with a general implicit verbal tag (e.g., *size* is relevant), and they learn to use such mediating labels to help make the switch from one discrimination problem to its reverse. Moreover, children's facility with verbal labels ought to increase with age, and they ought to respond increasingly often on the basis of these mediating responses. That they clearly appear to do so is shown by the data in Figure 6.11. Nonverbal organisms do not have

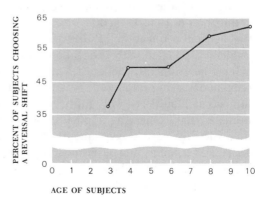

FIG. 6.11 When children are given an opportunity to respond in a reversal as compared with a nonreversal way, the tendency to pick the reversal shift increases with age. Somewhere between the ages of six and eight, the reversal mode of response becomes preferred. (Kendler & Kendler, 1962.)

PERCENT OF SUBJECTS CHOOSING A REVERSAL SHIFT

AGE OF SUBJECTS

this helping hand available, of course, so they tend to respond on re-versal and nonreversal shifts much as if they *were* making simple direct associations between stimuli and responses.

OBSERVING RESPONSES.   Some psychologists have approached the sorts of problems we have been discussing through the concept of an *observing* or *orienting* response (Wyckoff, 1952; Reid, 1953; Spence, 1960). An observing response can be defined as any response that results in exposure to a discriminative stimulus (Stollnitz, 1965). What is meant by this is that an organism must make the "response" of attending to the stimulus, to say nothing of the relevant stimulus, in any kind of discrimination problem before it can go on to produce the specific choice behavior that will lead, say, to reinforcement. If it does not attend to the stimulus—does not "observe" the stimulus—it obviously does not have the information it needs to solve the problem. The property of observing responses that makes them of interest to us in connection with things like reversal and nonreversal shifts is that they are presumed to vary in the *probability* with which they occur initially, and in the facility with which they are learned and with which they extinguish.

For example, Stollnitz (1965) tells us that monkeys tend to look where they put their fingers. If we pick a discrimination problem in which a monkey must actually touch the relevant cue—a pattern in the center of a card, for example—and push it in order to move the card aside and obtain a reward, the probability that the monkey will observe the cue ought to be very high. If, however, we require the monkey to touch a point some distance away from the cue, the probability ought to be correspondingly lower—at first, at least—that the monkey will observe the cue. In fact, this seems to be the case; monkeys have a relatively diffi-cult time solving certain kinds of discrimination problems if there is any appreciable separation between the locus of a cue that must be used to solve the problem and the locus of the spot where the monkey must put its finger to indicate its choice. The distance does not have to be large—on the order of $\frac{1}{2}$ to $\frac{3}{4}$ inch.

The application of the concept of observing responses to the problems associated with reversal and nonreversal shifts, say, is not hard to imagine. Subjects who must learn a reversal shift have been trained to make observing responses toward stimuli which are relevant when the shift occurs. Subjects who must learn a nonreversal shift have been trained to make observing responses toward stimuli which are not relevant when the shift occurs; consequently they must both extinguish their old observing responses and learn new ones. Thus, we would expect that a reversal shift ought to be easier to learn than a nonreversal shift—a pre-diction that seems to hold pretty well for at least some organisms. Much the same kind of reasoning could, of course, be applied to phenomena such as the overlearning reversal effect that we discussed earlier.

AN OVERVIEW.   The concept of the observing response may seem like the result of an attempt, perhaps an overly tenacious attempt, to express in terms of simple stimulus and response something that is basically little more than the concept of attention. There is certainly some justification in looking at things this way. In fact, besides the comments that Lawrence has had to make about the matter, there are others such as Sutherland (1959), Zeaman and House (1963), and Mackintosh (1965) who have expressly stated that the concept of *selective attention* and a study of the things which determine how organisms come to attend to one set of cues as compared with another lies at the root of many problems associated with the development of the capacity to discriminate. And no doubt you have noticed that we have more than occasionally used the term in this and other chapters.

In any event, it is patently clear that organisms learn to do more than one thing when faced with a discrimination problem. The central point is that at the very least, they learn many things about how to handle and deal with the stimuli among which they must discriminate— in addition to learning how to tell the experimenter through some arbitrary choice response that they have solved a problem. We do not know yet whether this process is best expressed in terms of selective attention, mediating behavior, or observing responses. Perhaps each functions at certain times, with certain types of discrimination problems, for certain species. Perhaps all boil down to essentially the same thing in the final analysis; there is certainly a simmer in this direction. The most important development is the abandonment of the notion of simple stimulus-response bonds as the mechanism by which organisms acquire their capacity to discriminate. Discriminative learning is much too complicated to be explained in these terms.

DISCRIMINATION LEARNING SETS

One of the major characteristics of the examples of discriminative learning at which we have looked so far is that learning is a fairly gradual process taking place over a number of trials. This is the case even where animals show that they can transfer something which they have learned about stimuli in one situation to the stimuli of another situation. Another class of experiments shows, however, that it is possible to produce a kind of behavior on a discrimination problem in which there does not appear to be much learning at all, because the animal solves the problem immediately. In such an experiment, for example, two stimuli are presented to a monkey; one of the stimuli, say, is a red cylinder and the other is a blue pyramid. Under one of these objects is hidden a peanut. When the two stimuli are exposed to a monkey, it carefully examines each and chooses to look under one. If, by chance, it looks under the wrong one, on the very next trial it looks under the other one and will continue to do so with almost no errors on subsequent trials. The discrimination is perfect, and it is only a matter of chance whether the monkey discovers the reward on the first or on the second trial.

Immediate and perfect discrimination of this sort does not, of course, happen automatically. It comes from a history of learning to make such discriminations. As animals solve a *number* of successive discrimination problems of the same type, they show an orderly and gradual improvement in their ability to solve any given problem, until finally they can produce an essentially immediate solution. An improvement in ability of this sort has been called by Harlow, who was the first to study the phenomenon in detail, the formation of a *learning set*.

Let us look at one of Harlow's experiments (Harlow, 1949) to see in a bit of detail how a learning set develops. Eight monkeys were trained in a special apparatus to pick one of two stimulus objects that were exposed on a tray side by side; a reward was found under one object that the experimenter designated correct, while nothing was found under the other. After the monkeys spent some time on one problem, they were shifted to another, then a third, and so on until they had worked on 344 successive problems. The stimuli varied from problem to problem in terms of their shape, color, height, etc., but in all cases, the monkeys' basic task was simply to learn which of the two different objects of the moment hid the reward. On each of the first 32 problems, the monkeys were given 50 practice trials. On each of the remainder of the problems, the monkeys received 6 to 11 practice trials. The results of the experiment are shown in Figure 6.12, which indicates the percent of correct responses that the monkeys made on the *first 6* practice trials for successive blocks of the total number of discrimination problems.

The figure shows that on early (preliminary) problems, there was *gradual* improvement over the first 6 trials. The improvement continued over the remaining 44 practice trials that were used on each of these problems, though this is not shown in the figure. By the time the monkeys were working on problems 101 to 200, however, they were correct about 85 percent of the time after just 1 trial (remember that the nature of each problem set things so that they could perform no better than chance on the first trial). And on the last block of 56 problems, they were correct on the second trial 95 percent of the time, maintaining their accurate performance from this point on. In other words, the monkeys eventually "learned how to learn" discrimination problems so

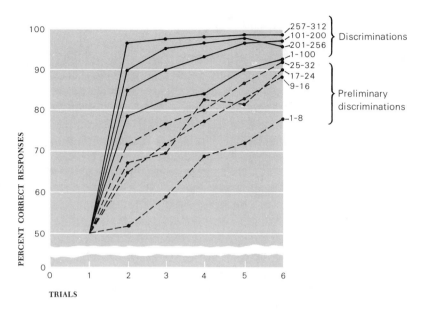

FIG. **6.12** The development of a discrimination learning set. Early discriminations require a large number of trials to master, but later ones are learned in
essentially one trial. (Harlow, 1949.)

efficiently that their performance on any given discrimination problem
was essentially perfect from the outset.

On the basis of these results, we might imagine—with Harlow
(1959)—that there ought to be some particular number of practice trials
to use with each successive problem that would produce maximally efficient development of a learning set. We might not have to use so many
trials on each problem that animals would learn to discriminate perfectly,
but offhand we might guess that the number required might have to be
large enough to produce a good deal of learning on one discrimination
before moving to the next. Over quite a broad range of practice trials
per problem, this does not seem to be the case at all (Miles, 1965). Levine,
Levinson, and Harlow (1959), for example, ran an experiment in which
two groups of monkeys were given 2,304 successive discrimination problems to learn. One group received 12 practice trials on each problem,
while the other group received only 3. The experimenters then plotted
their data by first calculating the percent of correct responses on trial 2
for the 12-trial group. Then they calculated the percent of correct responses on the second trial of every fourth problem for the 3-trial group.
In this way, the development of learning sets could be compared between
the two groups at points where each had equal numbers of practice
trials (but, of course, different numbers of problems). The data are

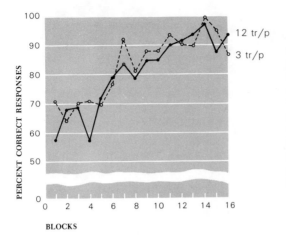

FIG. **6.13** The development of a discrimination learning set with 3 trials per problem and with 12 trials per problem. The data are the percentage of correct responses on the comparable second trials within successive blocks of 144 trials. Clearly, the functions do not differ. (Levine, Levinson, & Harlow, 1959.)

shown in Figure 6.13, which as you can see, indicates that both groups developed learning sets at just about the same rate.

Levine et al. go on to summarize similar data from a number of other experiments, and these, together with other data discussed by Miles (1965) clearly show that the development of a learning set does not depend critically on the number of practice trials which are assigned to each discrimination problem. Rather, over the range of 3 to 12 trials per problem, at least, it does not matter how many practice trials are used. However, 2 trials per problem does not produce a learning set, and there is some suggestion that if as many as 50 trials per problem are used, the efficiency with which a learning set develops is reduced. Thus, the basic rule of thumb seems to be—over quite a broad range— that the development of a learning set is a function simply of how many practice trials are given over the sum total of all discrimination problems, not how these practice trials are distributed among each successive discrimination problem. This is not to say that the number of discrimination *problems* which are used is not an important variable in the development of a learning set; obviously, the greater the number of problems, the better the learning-set formation.

TYPES OF LEARNING SETS. The type of learning set at which we have been looking so far is one which involves a simple discrimination between two stimulus objects, one of which is "correct" and the other of which is "incorrect." Learning-set formation is by no means limited to rather simple *object-quality* discriminations of this sort. For example, monkeys can easily learn a *discrimination reversal* learning set. Harlow (1950) trained his animals on a series of 112 problems, each problem consisting of 7, 9, or 11 trials of simple discrimination training between two objects followed by 8 trials in which the stimulus that was formerly incorrect was now correct. The monkeys gradually learned over a series of problems to reverse their choice at the appropriate time in each problem; by the time they had been exposed to the full set of problems, the sudden discovery of no reward for picking an object produced an immediate shift to the other object on almost all occasions. This observation should remind you of our earlier discussion of reversal learning, but keep in mind that here the animals had experience with a great many reversals, while in the work we looked at earlier, our main interest was in the things that happened the first time an animal met a discrimination reversal.

Another kind of learning set is called a *response-shift* learning set. Here, the monkey is faced with the usual object-quality discrimination on trial 1 of a problem, selects one of the stimulus objects, and finds a reward no matter which object gets picked. On the *second* trial within a problem, however, the monkey must shift its choice to the other object of the pair in order to obtain a reward. An experiment by Brown and McDowell (1963) showed that monkeys could learn this kind of problem very well. Note that a response-shift learning set is quite similar to a discrimination-reversal learning set, except that with the former the animal must use its first choice, per se, as a cue to what to do, while with the latter, the monkey uses the *outcome* (sudden nonreward of a choice) of its first response as a cue to shift its behavior.

There are many other kinds of learning sets that have been developed and studied. From these has come an interest in the general range of hypotheses and strategies that monkeys can be required to use in order to solve discrimination problems or which they might, in fact, adopt themselves as they tackle a problem. And from this interest has come a number of models (e.g., Levine, 1959, 1965; Restle, 1957, 1958), often couched in mathematical terms, that describe the "hypothesizing behavior" of animals in discrimination situations in which learning sets develop. The basis for these models is quite reminiscent of the Kreschevsky (1932) noncontinuity approach to discriminative learning, but a description of them is beyond the scope of this book. They are well worth pursuing, however, if you want to find out more about them.

THE THEORETICAL SIGNIFICANCE OF LEARNING SETS.   How are we to place the phenomenon of learning sets within a theoretical framework based on, say, continuity as compared with noncontinuity learning? It is difficult to do so. Riopelle (1953) has shown that transfer from problem to problem based upon stimulus generalization of cues associated with successful solution becomes less and less as additional problems are solved. In other words, animals learn that they cannot rely on stimulus generalization from one problem to the next to lead them to rapid solution of successive problems. This means that stimulus generalization of the sort we discussed earlier either becomes completely suppressed or radically altered in character.

Warren (1954) points out that test-wise monkeys approach each recombination of stimuli as a *new* problem, however many times the specific stimuli required in the discrimination have been differentially rewarded. Thus, even if one of the stimuli had been much more frequently rewarded than the other in the past, the animal would not tend to choose this stimulus more often. Warren suggests that this means that the analysis of discriminative learning according to the excitatory and inhibitory strengths built up to particular stimuli as the result of reinforcement and extinction does not apply to animals which have learned many problems. Furthermore, the *non*reward of a stimulus choice can function just as well as the reward of a stimulus choice in establishing a learning set.

Harlow and Hicks (1957) presented monkeys with a *single* stimulus object which, for different monkeys, was either rewarded or not rewarded when moved aside. Then the monkeys were presented with a *pair* of objects for 5 trials, one of which was the object to which they had just been exposed. If the object was not rewarded when presented by itself on the first trial, it was not rewarded on the remaining trials when it was paired with another object, so the monkey had to learn to shift its choice on the basis of the initial nonreward in order to be correct on the remaining trials. Similarly, if the object was rewarded on the first trial, it was rewarded on the remaining trials when paired with another stimulus, and here the monkey had to learn to stick with the original object. Reward and nonreward operated in a perfectly comparable manner: both first-trial conditions produced essentially equivalent learning-set formation. If we add to this the fact that monkeys, at least, can acquire a learning set by simply *watching* other monkeys perform in a discrimination situation (Darby & Riopelle, 1959), we would be properly hesitant to fit the phenomenon of learning sets into any kind of classic theoretical account of discriminative learning.

Harlow (1950, 1959) has approached the theoretical analysis of learning sets in terms of *error factors*. His basic assumption is that the process of forming a learning set is essentially the problem of eliminating or suppressing response tendencies that lead to mistakes or errors. He lists four such error factors: position preference, stimulus perseveration, differential cue, and response shift. An animal may have a built-in tendency to respond consistently to the left, say, of two stimulus objects (position preference), and it may also tend to continue picking an object that it has just picked (stimulus perseveration). By the same token, an animal will spontaneously shift on occasion from one object to another even though it has been picking the first, and correct, one consistently for a great many trials (response shift)—a factor which Harlow attributes to the monkey's tendency to explore. Also, an animal can be fooled early in learning a two-object discrimination by the fact that the things which determine a correct choice are ambiguous at the outset of a problem (differential cue). From the animal's point of view, picking a particular object *could* be correct because the object is on the left, say, or because the object is red. The animal might begin responding initially on the basis of the position cue rather than the color cue, a factor that could produce errors if this happened to be the incorrect approach.

According to Harlow, then, learning is *not* basically a process of building response strength for a correct choice; it is basically a process of reducing the strength of incorrect ones. Kimble (1961, p. 391), in comparing the Kreschevsky noncontinuity approach with that of Harlow, says that if Kreschevsky's point of view represents a one-trial learning theory, then Harlow's represents a no-trial learning theory. This is an interesting idea—an idea that would, for example, not unfairly describe some of the things that go on in the classrooms of many elementary schools. Often the teacher's problem is not one of getting across to the pupil the idea that something is correct—to the contrary, it is often the problem of getting the pupil to understand what is incorrect.

Regardless of theory, the phenomenon of learning sets is a very good example of one way in which organisms develop their discriminative capacity. Given extensive experience with discrimination problems as a *class* of events that occur in the world, organisms are no longer limited to the simple notion that red objects or square objects are associated with reinforcement; they learn that one of two stimulus objects will be reinforced, that the object reinforced last time will not be reinforced this time, that a shift in behavior is appropriate now but not later, and so on. Learning of this sort is truly the solution of a problem at a level far above the simple. As such, it fits with and must be closely related to the facts that cues and relations among them acquire distinctiveness for organisms, and that organisms attend to particular aspects of their world —transferring what they have learned in one place to something they must learn in another.

7

LEARNING AND THE CONCEPTS OF EMOTION AND MOTIVATION

Most psychologists make a distinction between the things we learn—our habits—and the things which prompt us to use these habits—our motives. In general terms, we can think of motives and emotions as things which provide the impetus behind behavior, that is, we can think of them as *needs* or *drives.* To constructs of this sort, which emphasize the energy behind behavior, many psychologists would add as a closely related construct the concept of *goals,* things which provide *direction* to motivated behavior. Earlier in this book, you were warned that the distinction between reinforcement and motivation would be a difficult one to maintain, particularly when the incentive characteristics of reinforcing stimuli are emphasized. In this chapter you will be able to sense some of the problems that the psychologist might encounter were he to insist on a rigid separation of the two. Nevertheless, we shall find it useful to make at least a loose distinction between operations which energize behavior—whether we call them motives, drives, or emotions—and operations which tend to focus energized behavior in some particular direction, toward some goal or incentive.

At the outset we must, as usual, admit to having culled a few topics for discussion from an enormous number that would appropriately fit into a chapter such as this one. Nowhere is the overabundance of material a greater problem than in the case of the concepts at hand, since motivation and emotion pervade all psychology, to say nothing of the psychology of learning, and have received an enormous amount of theoretical and experimental attention in their own right. Here we shall attempt to be rigid in limiting discussion to points where there is a clear relation between motivation, emotion, and *learning.* We shall see how motivation and emotion affect the learning process, and conversely, we shall see how learning processes can play a role in the acquisition of new motives and emotions.

THE PROBLEM OF DEFINING MOTIVES.   If we limit ourselves to the relatively simple world of animals for a moment, we can think of motivation as having two fundamental components, a need state and a goal—or some appropriate change in external stimulation—which tends to reduce or eliminate that need. Some needs tend to be periodic or cyclic in character, in which case they usually depend upon changes in the internal physiological or neurological balance of the organism. Hunger and thirst are such cyclic needs. Not all needs are governed by internal changes, however, since some exist at a more or less constant level, awaiting only the occurrence of the appropriate external stimulus to set off the appropriate behavior. The avoidance of pain is such a need, and in all animals there are many other such needs, needs we often characterize as instincts.

When a need is aroused, either by internal changes or an appropriate external stimulus, the result is usually that the animal performs some behavior designed to reduce or eliminate the need. Thus, when an animal finds its leg in the jaws of a trap, it struggles to free itself; or when it is thirsty, it finds its way to a familiar watering place. A good many, though not all, of these patterns of behavior are learned. Furthermore, animals learn to anticipate need states before they actually occur, and to act accordingly. Thus, animals learn to *avoid* traps, and they sometimes find their way to food or water when they are not hungry or thirsty—or at any rate, they seem to learn to stay in the vicinity of food and water supplies.

Obviously, though the animal world is complex enough, we find that things are much more complicated when we look at the realm of human behavior. People are motivated in a rich variety of ways, most of which do not have much of anything at all to do with basic physiological needs or drives (though there are certainly places in the world where this statement would be justifiably debatable). Instead, most adult human behavior is based upon *learned* motivation; people acquire much of their motivation through experience, with the "need" for money, for fame, for a new car, and so forth, being cases in point. There is an enormous literature which represents the attempts of psychologists to study, describe, and classify human motives of this sort, and there is a corresponding variety of emphasis and of definition of the concepts of motivation and emotion. It would be beyond the scope of this book to go into this material in detail, and we shall not do so. Nor shall we offer a rigorous definition of the concepts of emotion and motivation—beyond definitions that you may be able to abstract for yourself from our selection of the topics and the experiments we shall discuss.

It will be useful, however, to look briefly at some things having to do with the way in which psychologists *use* concepts like that of motivation when they go into the laboratory to perform experiments. Kimble (1961), following Spence (1948), distinguishes two general approaches here. Both take note of the fact that motivation is, after all, a *concept* which depends for its meaning upon operational definitions. Thus, on the one hand, we can define a motivational state of affairs by exposing an organism to a particular set of antecedent conditions involving something that we do to the organism or to its environment and then measuring some resulting change in the organism's behavior. In the case of hunger motivation, for example, we might deprive rats of food for a fixed period of time, prefeed groups of them with different amounts of food, then measure how fast the groups would press a lever for food in a Skinner box. If we were to define hunger motivation by different amounts of prefeeding in this way, we would get the results shown in Figure 7.1, which indicates that the greater the amount of food prefed, the slower the rate of responding.

The second way to do something with a motivational variable, say Spence and Kimble, is to measure one aspect of an organism's behavior and see how this aspect co-varies or is *correlated* with a second aspect of the organism's behavior. Thus, if we stick with rats for a moment, we could deprive different groups of rats for various periods of time and then see how fast they would eat a given quantity of food when it was

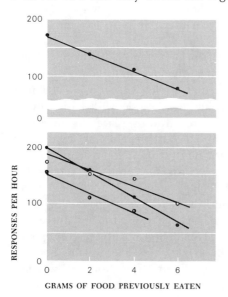

FIG. **7.1** Rate of responding under partial reinforcement as a function of amount of food just eaten. The lower curves are based upon averages of data from four rats each. The upper curve is an average of the lower curves. (Skinner, 1938.)

RESPONSES PER HOUR

GRAMS OF FOOD PREVIOUSLY EATEN

made available to them. Then we could reintroduce the various conditions of food deprivation and see how fast the rats would press a lever for food rewards. Finally, we would see if rate of lever pressing were correlated with speed of eating, guessing that the faster the rats ate the food (i.e., the "hungrier" they were), the faster they would press. Note that this way of looking at things is by no means necessarily independent of the first; in fact, we used deprivation time as the operation to establish differential rates of eating. The important difference lies in the nature of the thing we finally choose to use as an independent variable—in the first case we use some antecedent condition defined apart from the organism, while in the second we use some aspect of the organism's behavior itself.

The correlational approach to motivation has found its greatest application, perhaps, in the study of motivation in human learning. Here, one common procedure is to obtain scores on some kind of self-report inventory, a test such as the Manifest Anxiety Scale (Taylor, 1956), and to see how scores on the test correlate with some other kind of behavior, such as performance on a learning task of some kind. The assumption behind the Manifest Anxiety Scale (which consists of items such as "I am sometimes troubled by what others think of me," to which true or false answers are given), and others like it, is that the items composing the scale tap an emotional responsiveness which is related to drive or motivational level. Those individuals scoring high on the inventory are said to be anxious, and their anxiety state is assumed to act as a generalized motivator of behavior. Thus, though our example of the Manifest Anxiety Scale runs into trouble when applied to more complex types of human behavior, there appears to be fairly good evidence that classically conditioned responses occur more readily among people scoring high on the test than among those scoring low (Taylor, 1951; Spence, 1958).

MOTIVATION AND LEARNING JOINTLY DETERMINE PERFORMANCE. At this point it would be well to recall something we have mentioned in other places, not only in connection with the concept of motivation, but also in connection with concepts such as the amount of reinforcement (Chapter 3). The factors which influence behavior are divided by contemporary psychologists into two classes, associative and nonassociative. Both factors are responsible for the overt performance of any instrumental act. If an animal performs a particular act, it is highly probable that this is because (1) it has learned to do so and (2) it is motivated to do so. If motivation directed toward the particular goal or incentive associated with the act is low, the probability of occurrence of the act will be correspondingly low. Likewise, if the habit strength for this particular act is low, the probability of occurrence of the act will be low, even though the appropriate motivation may be present. In short, the response strength of any habit at any given moment will be a function of how well the habit has been learned (determined, say, by how much the habit has been practiced) as well as by the strength of motivation present at the time—on the assumption, of course, that we have held other factors such as amount of reinforcement or delay of reinforcement at some constant value.

It is important to recognize that the foregoing says nothing at all about the way in which motivation might *modify* learning—that is, whether what is learned under high as compared with low motivation is quantitatively or qualitatively different. Is a habit that has been learned under high motivation different from one that has been learned under low motivation, or does level of motivation simply determine the momentary strength with which a given response will be displayed? If high motivation affects the learning process in a way which is different from that of low motivation, what is the nature of the difference? Let us turn now to questions such as these and see what psychologists have learned about them.

THE EFFECT OF MOTIVATION UPON LEARNING

If we are to assess the effects of motivation upon learning, we are faced at the outset with the problem of finding some way of disentangling the effects of motivation upon momentary performance from those it may have upon actual habit strength. As you can see, rats who run down an alley under high hunger drive may run faster than those under low hunger drive, but we do not know from this information alone whether we are dealing with two different amounts of learning or habit strength, or with the same amount of learning energized at different levels by our two degrees of hunger. The solution to this problem involves, in general, conditioning animals under one set of motivational levels and then changing something about the task or the motivational conditions under which the animals are run. If the original motivational conditions are creating permanent differences in habit strength—as opposed to momentary differences in the strength with which a given habit is displayed in performance—then we would expect some relatively long-lasting effects of our original conditions to appear when we *transfer* to the new set of conditions. This approach is based, of course, on the reasonable assumption that learned habits are basically stable things, while simple performance of a given habit is a fleeting state of affairs which quickly changes, adjusting almost immediately to the conditions of the moment.

In practice, psychologists have used a number of different kinds of *transfer experiments* in assessing the effects of motivation upon learning. One of the most common procedures is to condition animals under a number of different motivational conditions, and then to *extinguish* them under some common level of motivation. Here, the assumption is that if different levels of motivation produce different effects upon amount of learning, resistance to extinction in the various groups should be different (even though all animals are extinguished under the same motivation), because resistance to extinction should reflect the effects of the original conditions of learning. Another similar procedure is to condition under one set of motivational conditions and then to *shift to another set,* watching behavior as practice continues for residual effects of the old set of motivational conditions upon the new. A third, less common, procedure is to condition under one set of motivational conditions, to allow a period of time to pass during which the effects of the original conditioning are presumably "forgotten" in part, and then to *recondition* under another set of motivational conditions. Here, we look for residual effects of the original set of motivational conditions upon the course of reconditioning. With each of these procedures, some form of a *factorial design* is often used (Kimble, 1961; Cofer & Appley, 1964). The basic format and strategy of such a design is shown in Table 7.1.

TABLE 7.1   **A Sample Design for Comparing the Effects of Motivation upon Learning and Performance**

(The tabled scores are hypothetical running speeds during extinction)

		EXTINCTION (HOURS OF HUNGER)		ROW MEANS
		2	24	
TRAINING (HOURS OF HUNGER)	2	0.6	4.4	2.5
	24	1.0	4.0	2.5
COLUMN MEANS		0.8	4.2	

As Table 7.1 indicates, we might condition two groups of rats, say, to run an alley, each under a different level of motivation. We have picked 2 hours and 24 hours of food deprivation as examples. Then we split the two groups and test each half for resistance to extinction under one of the two levels of hunger used during conditioning. For example, half the group conditioned under 24-hour hunger drive is tested under

24-hour hunger drive, while the other half is shifted and tested under the 2-hour hunger drive. For scores, we use some measure of resistance to extinction, such as running speed averaged over some suitable block of extinction trials.

An experiment incorporating this design can tell us a number of things. First of all, we can ignore drive level during conditioning (since it is counterbalanced among the groups) and combine scores so as to look at the effects of drive level *during extinction* upon resistance to extinction. This is done by combining scores in each column (we have simply averaged them). As you can see in our hypothetical example, rats extinguished under 2-hour hunger drive ran, on the average, 0.8 feet per second during extinction, while rats extinguished under 24-hour hunger drive ran 4.2 feet per second during extinction. Similarly, and this is of primary interest for the topic at hand, we can combine scores in each row and look at the effects of drive level *during conditioning* upon resistance to extinction. If we do this, we see that rats conditioned under 2-hour hunger drive ran 2.5 feet per second, on the average, during extinction, while rats conditioned under 24-hour hunger drive ran at just the same rate during extinction—2.5 feet per second on the average.

We would conclude from these data, then, that drive level during extinction had a marked effect upon resistance to extinction, but drive level during conditioning did not. That is, motivational level affected performance of the moment, but did not produce any permanent differences in amount learned or in habit strength that would weather the transfer from training conditions to extinction conditions.

EXPERIMENTS COMPARING EFFECTS OF LEVEL OF MOTIVATION UPON LEARNING. Let us look now at some experiments that have used the experimental strategies just outlined to assess the influence of motivation upon learning. A great many have been done. Kimble (1961), for example, lists some twenty-odd, and a large number of others have been carried out since his list was compiled. The picture that emerges from this literature is by no means a clear one. If we look, first of all, at experiments which have used different levels of motivation during conditioning and a common level during extinction, we find negative results most often. Resistance to extinction in the Skinner box, at least, does not vary with the motivational level used during training (Kendler, 1945).

If a factorial design is used, so that changes in drive level are counterbalanced as we transfer from training to extinction, there are some experiments which indicate a different state of affairs. Barry (1958), for example, trained two groups of rats to run an alley under high and low hunger drive. Then he split each group, extinguishing half under high motivation and half under low. There are two aspects of his results which are of interest. First, resistance to extinction was a function of the drive level prevailing during extinction: high motivation during extinction produced greater resistance to extinction than low motivation during extinction. This is a common finding (Cofer & Appley, 1964). Second, resistance to extinction was also a function of the drive level used *during training;* that is, there was a residual effect of the motivational conditions prevailing during the original learning of the response. For example, rats trained under high motivation and extinguished under low were more resistant to extinction than rats who were both trained and extinguished under low motivation. Apparently conditioning under high as compared with low drive in Barry's experiment produced some permanent differences in amount learned which were retained into and through the extinction period.

If we test for the effects of motivation upon learning by shifting drive levels during the conditioning process, we find some experiments suggesting that level of motivation does affect amount of learning. Deese and Carpenter (1951) discovered, for example, that animals trained in a runway under high motivation and then switched to low motivation performed better as training continued than animals always run under low motivation. Theios (1963) got much the same results. However, Deese and Carpenter also found that animals trained under low motivation and then switched to high motivation performed just about as well as those trained under high motivation all along. Surprisingly enough, even in so complicated a habit as that involved in learning a 10-unit maze, animals trained under low motivation do as well as animals trained under high motivation when tested under high motivation (Hillman, Hunter, & Kimble, 1953).

Finally, if we look for the effects of motivation upon learning by looking at reconditioning after a period of a month or so has elapsed since original learning, we find that level of motivation during original learning carries over to affect the rate at which reconditioning proceeds. Brush, Goodrich, Teghtsoonian, and Eisman (1963) trained groups of rats to run an alley under high or low hunger drive. Then, they let the rats rest for four weeks, shifting the high-drive animals to the low-drive condition in the process. When reconditioning began, the animals who were shifted from high drive to low ran faster initially than animals who were run under low drive during both original conditioning and reconditioning. However, the relearning curves for the two groups came quickly together as reconditioning trials progressed.

So if we take a general look, there seems to be some evidence which, on its face, suggests that level of motivation will affect habit strength or the amount learned. There are many experiments, however, (perhaps a majority) which show negative results, and the effect is by no means a striking, powerful, or common one (Kimble, 1961). There are at least two other factors which may be involved in the problem, and a glance at them may help to untangle things a bit and point the way toward a more complete understanding of the situation.

First of all, it appears that different motivational levels have different characteristic stimulus patterns associated with them. In the case of relatively "simple" motives like hunger or thirst, we could think of these as different sets of internal stimuli arising from various degrees of stomach distension and other physiological factors. If we switch from one level of motivation to another, according to this line of reasoning, we are simultaneously changing the pattern of stimulation under which our experimental animals behave. And from our discussion of the last chapter, you should be able to guess what we would expect when we do this. On the basis of stimulus generalization, there ought to be some decrease in response strength as we go from the stimulus pattern associated with the drive level used during conditioning to another stimulus pattern associated with a new drive level during extinction (or to any other test situation, for that matter, where we shift drive levels).

Hatton (1965) obtained some data which clearly suggest that something like stimulus generalization of this sort can take place. He conditioned rats in a Skinner box under one level of thirst motivation. Then, just before the animals were extinguished in later sessions, different levels of drive were introduced by preloading the animals with 4 or 2 percent of their body weight of water, or with a constant volume of 2, 4 or 6 percent salt solution. Another group was given a "sham" preload so that their thirst motivation would be the same as that used during original learning. These procedures produced different levels of thirst (as measured by how much water the animals would drink during a subsequent test) which ranged from lowest (at 4 percent of body weight of water) through the original training level (sham preload) to highest (at a preload of 6 percent salt solution). Some of the extinction results, namely how many lever presses the animals made during extinction, are shown in Figure 7.2.

As you can see, the greatest number of lever presses was made at a thirst level very close to the one in effect when the animals received their initial training in the Skinner box. Thirst levels which were lower *or higher* than the one used originally produced fewer responses, indicating that a change in the stimulus pattern associated with a particular level of thirst could, in and of itself, produce the decrease in performance we would expect on the basis of simple stimulus generalization. So Hatton's data should be kept in mind in interpreting the results of experiments in which drive levels are changed in an attempt to assess the effects of motivation upon learning. The residual effects of an original set of

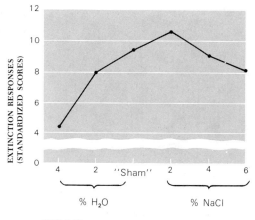

FIG. **7.2** Resistance to extinction as a function of the type of preload given just prior to extinction. Each score represents the ratio of a mean to its standard error. Details of the preload conditions are given in the text, but in general, drive level increases from left to right on the abscissa. Resistance to extinction is greatest for a drive level just above that used during training. (Redrawn from Hatton, 1965.)

motivational conditions—as tested during extinction or by a simple shift in drive level as in the Deese and Carpenter experiment—may be due in part to habit or learning factors, but they may also be due in part to the fact that a change in drive level necessarily involves a change in the stimulus situation under which an organism behaves.

The second factor which is almost certainly relevant here is that animals trained under different levels of motivation may, in fact, learn to do different things, things that our method of measuring their behavior may not detect. An experiment by Cotton (1953) illustrates this point very well. He trained a group of rats to run a runway, then tested the group at different times under 0, 6, 16, or 22 hours of food deprivation. In analyzing the behavior of the animals in the runway, however, Cotton went a step farther than the usual procedure of looking at overall running times or speeds. He broke trials into two classes: those in which the animals ran directly to the goal box, and those in which the animals made some sort of competing response, a response (such as stopping to sniff in a corner or retracing) which interfered with direct progress into the goal box. Looking at the data this way produced the results shown in Figure 7.3, where you can see that on trials involving no competing responses, running times did not vary with deprivation time at all, while on trials in which there were competing responses, overall running times decreased as deprivation increased. Viewed another way, the data indicate that rats do not *run* more slowly under low as compared with high motivation; instead they are more apt to *engage in extraneous activity,* the hand on the running-time clock moving all the while. Campbell and Kraeling (1954) have made the same point. They observed that rats run under low as compared with high motivation were less apt to be oriented toward the start-box door as a trial was about to begin.

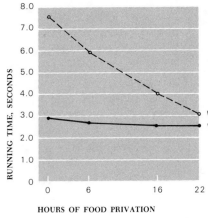

FIG. **7.3** Running time in an alley as a function of hours of food deprivation. The upper curve shows running times on trials in which competing responses were made, while the lower curve shows running times on trials where competing responses did not occur. (Cotton, 1953.)

With competing responses
Without competing responses

The upshot of all this work is that motivation affects learning in the limited sense that there must be enough of it to get an organism to behave—to expose itself to the problem it must learn and to the reinforcing or other events which ensue. Beyond this, however, it looks as if the associative mechanisms of instrumental learning are largely independent of level of motivation. Where there are apparent effects of motivation upon learning, one must look very carefully for factors (like stimulus generalization correlated with the shifts in drive level associated with a particular testing method) that could just as easily account for the data or be at least partly responsible for producing it. Then too, the fact that different levels of motivation may well lead to *qualitatively different* responses must be considered. Here, the strength of a motive apparently does not affect the way in which some single habit is learned, but rather it determines which of a *number* of different responses available to an organism will be performed and so learned.

THE EFFECT OF LEARNING ON MOTIVATION: ACQUIRED DRIVES AND EMOTIONS

In this section, we shall reverse the basic question of the last one and ask how organisms come to acquire new motives through a learning process. For a long time many psychologists took the view that there were but a handful of unlearned motives, most of which, if not all, were tied to biological needs. If one takes this view, of course, it is difficult to describe all the elaborate motives of adult human behavior unless great emphasis is placed upon the development of learned motives. All the complicated motives not directly and obviously connected with biological motives have been considered by some in the past to be derived from biological needs by a process of learning.

Although today most psychologists grant an important role to learned motives, the prevailing opinion seems to be that the view stated above is too simple. We are less sure that all *unlearned* motives are exhausted by a simple catalogue of biological needs. Yet, as we examine the behavior of animals and men in nature, it is difficult to untangle motives that seem to be learned from those that are not. It is possible that all motives, even those rooted directly in biological needs, are modified by learning and that there are some important motives which are simply the result of associative learning. So, whatever the original source of "pure" motivation, there is little question that learning plays an important part in the elaboration of motives. It will be our task now to see what psychologists have found out about this important matter.

It is convenient to start by looking at the way in which *emotions* aroused by unpleasant or noxious stimulation can become learned. Then, we shall see how such emotions can serve as acquired motives for learning new responses. We do this in part to fulfill a promise of an earlier chapter that we would examine learning based on aversive as compared with appetitive reinforcement operations, and in part because, curiously enough, it is a great deal easier to demonstrate learned motivation if we use an unpleasant negative reinforcer like electric shock than if we use a positive reinforcer like food or water—a matter to which we shall return in due course.

CLASSICAL CONDITIONING OF EMOTIONS

The neurophysiological and behavioral correlates of emotion are enormously complex and involve mechanisms of both the central and peripheral nervous systems (Stellar, 1954; Morgan, 1965). One feature of emotional activity which is of interest to us in particular at the moment, however, is that it seems to depend in large measure upon activity of the autonomic nervous system—the part of the peripheral nervous system controlling the actions of the heart, glands, and smooth muscles. Generally speaking, the operation of the autonomic nervous system is not voluntary, and many of the elements of emotional expression autonomically controlled are automatic and reflex-like in character. Changes in heart rate, sweating, blushing, etc., are all things that occur more or less automatically, given the presence of some emotion-producing stimulus.

The involuntary characteristic of elements of emotional expression is important, because it suggests that the conditioning of these responses is classical rather than instrumental. In Chapter 1 we saw that classically conditioned responses are elicited directly by stimuli, and that this is not the case in instrumental conditioning. We also noted that there is very little evidence (though the possibility of new discoveries always lurks) that responses under the control of the autonomic nervous system can be conditioned instrumentally. Perhaps it is not surprising, then, that early attempts to condition emotions took advantage of their reflex-like properties and used Pavlovian techniques. Let us look at a classic example of such an attempt.

THE WATSON AND RAYNOR STUDY.   One of the best known of such studies is by Watson and Raynor (1920). These investigators were interested in the development of fears in infants, and they made a long series of observations of a number of infants. One baby boy, who was about a year old at the time, was the subject of their conditioning study. Previously, they had discovered that a number of stimuli which one might ordinarily think would arouse fear were not fear-producing for this youngster. White rats, dogs, masks, burning newspapers—none of these produced fear, but one stimulus that did produce a startle reaction followed by crying and other signs of emotional activity was a loud sound. Consequently, they decided to use the loud sound as an unconditioned stimulus for emotional activity.

In the actual conditioning procedure, they paired the sight of a white rat (previously not fear-producing) with the occurrence of the sound. A very few pairings were sufficient to elicit a full-scale emotional response simply by presenting the white rat alone. An interesting development is that this conditioned fear generalized to other animals and to other furry objects, such as a wad of cotton.

This was a rather clear and dramatic demonstration of the possibilities of conditioned emotions, as well as a demonstration of the importance of such principles as stimulus generalization in the extension of the conditioned reaction. Watson and Raynor thought that this experiment could serve as a model for the way in which the complex and irrational fears of daily life might arise. They placed much emphasis upon the importance of emotional reactions in the child's personality development—emphasis which few present-day psychologists would find altogether appropriate. Nevertheless, the Watson and Raynor experiment stands as one of the very first examples of the conditioning of an emotion.

THE IMPORTANCE OF EMOTIONAL CONDITIONING.   Such examples of conditioned emotional responses, simple though they may be, are extremely important in the theory of learning, particularly as the theory applies to situations in which emotional disturbances have occurred. The essential point of such work is that emotional activity is conditioned by Pavlovian principles. Since the emotional reaction is aroused originally by an unconditioned stimulus, there is no need to control it through reward. It is behavior that is, by and large, beyond voluntary control. Few of us can directly elicit emotional activity in ourselves in the same sense that we can open doors and recite the pledge to the flag. A few people can "voluntarily" cry, and so forth, but there is every reason to believe that this is an indirect kind of control afforded by some sort of mediated behavior. Thus, actors and actresses probably learn initially to cry on demand by thinking of some situation likely to arouse the sort of emotion associated with crying; crying is indirectly aroused by the presence of some internal (perhaps conditional) stimulus.

So the conditioning of emotional reactions seems to be largely a process of association. Organisms learn to become emotional in new situations simply because these situations occur when they are emotional for other reasons. Earlier, however, we hinted that emotions could have the properties of motives or drives like hunger and thirst. Clearly, people can learn to stay away or to escape from situations that arouse strong unpleasant emotional feelings. Where, then, does this aspect of emotional reactivity fit in? Certainly not in the transference of emotional reactions themselves from an unconditioned to a conditional stimulus, since this merely involves the association of the response elicited by both these stimuli. If the emotional reaction itself is motivating, however, then *reduction* of it ought to serve as reinforcement for instrumental activity —on the assumption, of course, that drive reduction is a tenable reinforcement process. Let us see how this line of reasoning fares in the laboratory.

FEAR AS A LEARNED DRIVE

Miller (1948, 1951) presents us with the classical example of fear as a learned drive. A rat is introduced into an apparatus like that illustrated in Figure 7.4. There are two compartments in the apparatus, a white one with an electrically wired grid as the floor and a black one with a smooth solid floor. There is a door between the two compartments; the rat can open this door either by pressing a lever at the side of the white compartment or by turning a wheel at the end of the white compartment. First of all, the rat is shocked in the white compartment and allowed to escape through the door into the black compartment. This procedure pairs the cues of the white compartment with the painful shock stimulus and presumably conditions a learned fear reaction. It also teaches the rat that a run to the black compartment leads to safety. In order to see if conditioned fear of this sort has drive properties, however, it is necessary to find out whether the rat will learn a *new* response to escape from the white compartment *without further electric shocks*. If such a response can be learned, it would have to be learned not on the basis of the pain produced by the shock as a motivator, but on the basis of the conditioned fear as a motivator. Miller showed that rats could learn to turn the wheel when the reinforcement consisted of a reduction in fear correlated with escape into the black compartment. Figure 7.5 shows that

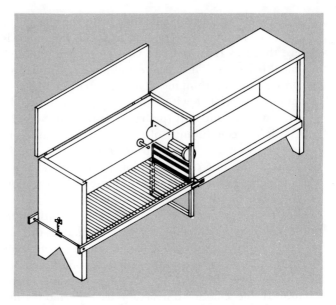

FIG. 7.4   Apparatus for demonstration of fear as a learned drive. One compartment is white and one is black. The door between the compartments can be opened either by pressing a lever or by turning a wheel. The rat learns to escape one or the other compartment by the association of electric-shock-produced pain and the stimuli from that compartment. (N. E. Miller, 1948.)

each time the rat is placed in the white compartment, it takes less time to get around to turning the wheel.

Another demonstration of fear as an acquired drive is based on the notion that drives facilitate the vigor or "energy" behind some kinds of response, and that if fear is a drive, it ought to do this too. Brown, Kalish, and Farber (1951) tested this hypothesis in the following way. They placed animals in a stabilimeter—a cage resting on a movable platform rigged so that the extent of movement of the platform could be measured and recorded on a moving strip of paper. Animals in an experimental group were placed in the cage and given a number of conditioning trials in which a CS of a light and a buzzer was followed three seconds later by an electric shock delivered to the floor of the cage. On occasional test trials, a novel stimulus—the sound of a popgun—was introduced in place of the shock, and the amplitude of the startle response produced by the popgun was measured by means of the recording device on the stabilimeter. A control group received the same number of CS and shock presentations, but sometimes the CS preceded the shock and sometimes the shock preceded the CS—a procedure designed to prevent the CS from

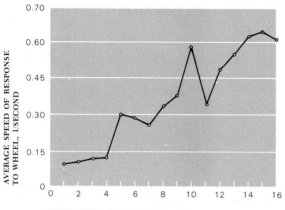

FIG. **7.5** Learning to turn the wheel with escape from the conditioned fear of the shock compartment as the motive. The rat is shocked in the white compartment from which it can escape by an open door. On subsequent nonshock trials, the rat must learn to turn the wheel, which now opens the door, in order to escape from the white compartment. (N. E. Miller, 1948.)

acquiring the ability to elicit learned fear. The results of the experiment are shown in Figure 7.6, where you can see that the magnitude of the startle response increased quickly and dramatically as the CS acquired fear-producing properties, while the magnitude of the startle response remained essentially constant under the control procedure. Other experiments have used the basic principle behind the Brown et al. experiment —inserting a test or "probe" stimulus at various intervals after the onset

FIG. **7.6** Magnitude of the startle response to the sound of a popgun. For the experimental group, the pop occurred in the presence of a fear-producing stimulus. For the control group, the pop occurred in the presence of a stimulus which had not acquired fear-producing properties. The pop clearly produced a much larger startle response when it was paired with fear than when it was not. (J. S. Brown, Kalish, & Farber, 1951.)

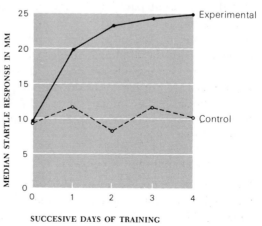

of a CS, and watching the effects of this upon the elicitation of some sort of startle or reflex-like response. These have indicated that conditioned fear in such situations occurs somewhere betwen 0.5 to 5 seconds after the onset of the CS (Spence & Runquist, 1958; Champion, 1964).

Still another application of fear as a learned drive falls under the heading (perhaps an unfortunate one because of the general nature of the terms) of a *conditioned emotional response* (CER). The phenomenon to which this label has been attached is that a neutral stimulus which has acquired the ability to elicit conditioned fear can function to *suppress* ongoing behavior under certain conditions. Typical conditions (Estes & Skinner, 1941; Brady & Hunt, 1955; Kimble, 1961) in which this occurs involve, first of all, training a rat in a Skinner box to work for food on some sort of variable-interval schedule. After this response is well established, a neutral stimulus is turned on and followed three minutes later with a brief electric shock. The shock is *not* contingent in any fashion upon bar pressing; it occurs independently of anything the animal is doing at the time. Initially, the neutral stimulus has no effect upon the lever-pressing behavior, but as successive presentations of neutral stimulus and shock occur, the animal begins to reduce the rate at which it presses the lever during the period of time that the neutral stimulus is on. Eventually, if the strength of the shock is strong enough, for example, the animal may stop its lever-pressing behavior altogether during the "danger" period, resuming rapid lever pressing as soon as the shock occurs.

Fear as a learned drive, then, can have a number of effects. Of primary importance, it can lead to the learning of new responses: those which will get an organism away from the cues that have come to arouse fear. We have seen too, however, that conditioned fear can operate simply both to facilitate *and* to suppress responses which occur in its presence, and this apparent paradox deserves a further word or two. The key to the problem, as Kimble (1961) reminds us, is that conditioned fear can produce one or the other of these effects depending upon how it is associated with the response. An electric shock given to animals *outside* a place where the animals are used to drinking facilitates drinking when the animals are put back into the drinking situation (Amsel & Maltzman, 1950). Shocking the animals *in the drinking situation itself,* however, leads to interference and suppression of drinking (Amsel & Cole, 1953; Leaf & Muller, 1965).

AVOIDANCE LEARNING

Before we move on, we must also see how conditioned fear functions in the kind of learning situation we identified in Chapter 1 as *avoidance learning.* Here, the basic question goes a bit beyond the general point that fear can motivate the learning of responses which get organisms away from situations in which strong, unpleasant things have happened in the past. Instead, our question becomes this: How do organisms learn to *anticipate* that something horrendous is about to happen and to do something about it, namely, to prevent exposing themselves to it at all? In Chapter 1, we described how avoidance learning could occur in a shuttle-box; dogs could learn to leap across a barrier when a signal came on, doing so before the onset of a shock programmed to occur a few seconds after the signal appeared. Let us review a bit by looking at an example of avoidance learning in another situation.

A dog is trained to stand perfectly still in an experimental apparatus which permits the careful recording of the movements of all its legs. One of its rear legs rests upon an electrode that completes a circuit through the dog, so that it can be shocked through this leg. If the dog lifts its paw, of course, the shock is terminated. In the conditioning procedure, a buzzer sounds about two seconds before a brief shock is applied to the dog's leg. Soon after the conditioning procedure has begun, there are obvious signs of emotional distress elicited by the buzzer and a good deal of struggling, struggling that may occasionally lead to "accidental" lifting of the paw at the right time in a manner which might make us think we were dealing with a classically conditioned response. But by and large, the dog takes a good number of shocks. After a bit, however, the dog begins to lift its paw when the buzzer comes on, holding it up until the buzzer goes off, and so avoiding the shock in consistent fashion. Clearly, this is an example of instrumental learning.

The experiment could be turned into an example of classical conditioning, however, by strapping the electrode to the dog's leg so that it could not escape or avoid the shock by flexing its leg. Since shocks do directly *elicit* leg flexion reflexes, we could obtain classical conditioning; but there would be a number of differences in results between this and the avoidance-learning procedure. At a gross level, there would be a difference in the frequency with which leg flexion would be a specific part of all that was being learned in the two situations. Thus, in an experiment of Brogden, Lipman, and Culler (1938), a buzzer was sounded a number of times, each time just before the guinea pigs that were used as subjects were shocked in a revolving cage. Half the animals could avoid the shock if they ran when the buzzer sounded; half could not, and took the shock no matter what they did (classical conditioning). The results of the experiment are shown in Figure 7.7. As you see, the animals that could avoid the shock by running learned to do so very well, while those that could not avoid it did not learn the running response very well at all.

These results do *not* mean that classical conditioning in general produces poorer learning than instrumental conditioning, though there are some more recent experiments in which this appears to be the case, at least for human eyelid conditioning (Moore & Gormezano, 1961; Gormezano, Moore, & Deaux, 1962). There is little reason to doubt that, at the very least, the guinea pigs subjected to the classical procedure had a very well established conditioned emotional reaction. The results do mean that in this situation running was not being singled out in the classical conditioning group as the particular response to be reinforced; sometimes, as a matter of fact, running was probably punished—on those occasions when the guinea pigs already happened to be running at the moment the shock was turned on (Sheffield, 1948; Kimble, Mann, & Dufort, 1955).

THE PARADOX OF AVOIDANCE CONDITIONING. From what source does avoidance learning of the type demonstrated in the Brogden et al. experiment come? For some time there seemed to be a paradox associated with experiments of this sort and with others demonstrating avoidance conditioning. When an animal *escapes* a noxious stimulus such as shock, this constitutes a rewarding state of affairs. But why should *avoidance*

FIG. **7.7** A comparison of classical and instrumental conditioning of a response. The solid line (open circles) shows the frequency of conditioned responses to a buzzer when the animals are shocked for not running, but can avoid if they run. The broken line (filled circles) shows the frequency of conditioned responses when the buzzer is always followed by shock regardless of what the animals do. (From Brogden, Lipman, & Culler, 1938.)

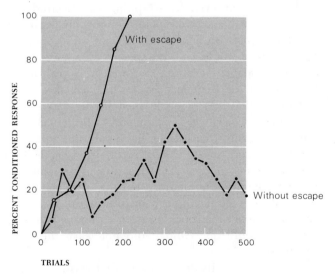

TRIALS

of the noxious stimulus be rewarding? How can a stimulus not experienced by the animal be said to be a source of reinforcement?

Common sense would say, of course, that the animal comes to anticipate the shock, and that this is why it responds to a warning signal such as a buzzer. The learning theorist is not likely to be satisfied with this answer, however, since he will want to know how and why the anticipation develops. A number of theorists have tackled the problem, and one of the most widely accepted accounts is that of Mowrer (1947, 1960). Let us see what he has to say about the matter.

MOWRER'S THEORY OF AVOIDANCE CONDITIONING.   In an early form of his theory, Mowrer (1947) says that an animal in an avoidance-learning situation first learns to give a classically conditioned emotional response to the discriminative cue—the tone or buzzer—that precedes the shock or other noxious stimulus. This, of course, is a matter of pure involuntary association; it does not depend on the animal's selecting some response that is drive-reducing, for example. As we saw earlier in this chapter, however, emotional disturbance or conditioned *fear* correlated with a formerly neutral stimulus has itself the properties of a drive or motivational state. If the animal performs an instrumental response that reduces the emotional disturbance, this is a reinforcing state of affairs, and in subsequent situations the animal will again choose this response. Thus, if flexing the leg (or jumping a hurdle) to escape shock also serves to reduce slightly the emotional responsiveness to the discriminative cue, it will be a response preferred by the animal. In a nutshell, then, Mowrer's theory says that the animal avoids the shock not just in order to avoid it, but to escape from the emotional state now conditioned to the buzzer.

In this form of his theory, Mowrer considered the development of avoidance learning as a two-stage process, and the term *two-factor theory* was applied to his approach. Learning to avoid an unpleasant shock consisted first of all in acquiring a *classically* conditioned emotional response to the buzzer or tone (the first factor), and secondly in acquiring some *instrumentally* conditioned response, reinforced by fear-drive reduction, that would get the organism away from the fear-producing buzzer or tone (the second factor).

In the later form of his theory, Mowrer (1960) drops the instrumental conditioning factor and places primary emphasis on the classical conditioning of emotions. Thus, conditioned fear to the buzzer or tone is retained in the theory; in Mowrer's terms the onset of such a stimulus comes to mark the beginning of a danger period. But now Mowrer adds another kind of classically conditioned emotion to the situation: conditioned *relief* that comes to occur when the buzzer goes *off*, marking the *end* of the danger period. In effect, the organism learns in an avoidance situation to get away from fear-producing situations and to get to places or to things that, through classical conditioning again, trigger another kind of emotion—*relief* from fear.[1]

One problem in Mowrer's newer theory, recognized both by him and by others (e.g., N. E. Miller, 1963—who offers a solution to the problem) is that it provides no explanation of why an organism elects to make one sort of response out of the very large number available *at the time learning begins*—before emotions have had a chance to become conditioned to cues in the situation. But the theory is an interesting and important account of how conditioned emotional responses can come to play a role in avoidance learning, and the theory accounts for and has generated a great deal of research. Let us look at a bit of that now.

Mowrer and Lamoreaux (1942) altered the typical avoidance situation slightly. They arranged things so that a warning cue of a buzzer did not always sound continuously until the shock came on. Instead, performance of an instrumental response not only avoided the shock, but also *terminated the buzzer.* Avoidance learning under these conditions was more rapid than under conditions where performance of the avoidance response did not terminate the buzzer. Thus, if it is possible for the animal to *escape* the conditional stimulus (that is, to control directly the emotional effects of *both* fear and relief associated, respectively, with the onset and offset of the buzzer) learning to avoid a shock is easier than if the avoidance response merely prevents the occurrence of the shock—doing nothing to the danger signal of the buzzer.

This point is also made in neat fashion by an experiment of Bower, Starr, and Lazarovitz (1965). They trained rats in a shuttle box to avoid a shock under one of three conditions. In the first (group G-100), an avoidance response immediately terminated the tone that was used as a warning stimulus. For a second group (group G-0), the avoidance response prevented the shock, but the tone continued for 8 seconds after the response occurred. For a third group (group G-L), a *light* came on for 15 seconds when the avoidance response occurred, but the *tone* continued for 8 seconds. The results of the experiment are shown in

[1] It is beyond the scope of this book to go into Mowrer's newer theory in detail. Suffice it to say that Mowrer considers all learning to be based upon the classical conditioning model. Different types of learning are distinguished, essentially, in terms of different reinforcement operations and the emotions that are conditioned to cues, both internal and external, which are paired with them. Thus, there are two basic kinds of reinforcement operation: that based on an increment in stimulation (like shock onset) and that based on a decrement in stimulation (like shock offset or hunger reduction). Corresponding to these, different sorts of emotions can be classically conditioned to cues in the learning situation. Hence, *fear* is conditioned to the onset of a danger signal and *relief* to its offset, *disappointment* to the offset of a safety signal and *hope* to its onset Mowrer, 1960, p. 213).

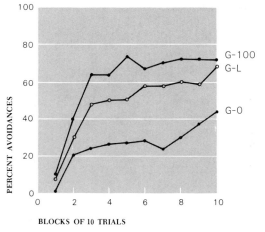

FIG. **7.8** The development of an avoidance response under various conditions of change in the warning stimulus of a tone. For group 100, the tone ends immediately following a response. For group 0, the tone ends 8 seconds after the response, while for group L, a light comes on for 15 seconds after the response while the tone persists for 8 seconds. (Bower, Starr, & Lazarovitz, 1965.)

Figure 7.8, where you can see that the rats in groups G-100 and G-L learned at just about the same rate (the differences between the groups are not statistically significant), while learning was much slower for the rats in group G-0. Thus, the light as a *safety* signal (marking the point at which the rats could begin to feel *relief,* in Mowrer's terms) facilitated learning considerably. This was true even though the original danger signal of the tone was *still on* after the avoidance response occurred for the rats in the G-L group.

EXTINCTION OF AVOIDANCE LEARNING.   Like other kinds of learned behavior, avoidance responses extinguish. But the process, viewed from both an empirical and a theoretical vantage point, is an exceptionally interesting one that has many implications for a general theory of learning. At the simplest level, we would expect avoidance learning to be more resistant to extinction than simple escape learning. This would be true because during conditioning, according to the avoidance-learning paradigm, the organism is exposed to what is essentially a partial-reinforcement situation. The animal takes the shock on those occasions where it fails to respond in time to the warning signal, but the shock is omitted on those trials in which successful avoidances occur. With escape learning, on the other hand, the shock occurs no matter what the organism does. Sheffield and Temmer (1950) showed that this way of looking at things is essentially correct; avoidance learning produced greater resistance to extinction than escape learning.

Solomon and his associates (Solomon, Kamin, & Wynne, 1953; Solomon & Wynne, 1954) have looked at the extinction of avoidance behavior from another point of view. In particular they have asked what happens to conditioned emotion in an avoidance situation under conditions where the intensity of the shock that an animal must avoid is

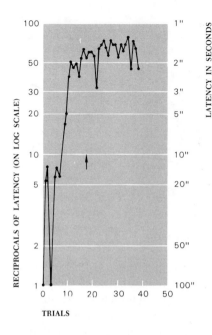

FIG. **7.9** Traumatic avoidance learning. Here, a typical dog takes the strong shock for a few trials, but then begins to avoid the shock by responding to the warning stimulus within 10 seconds. Once an avoidance response occurred, this dog never again took a shock. Note, too, that response latencies continue to decrease for a few trials after the first successful avoidance. (Solomon & Wynne, 1953.)

extraordinarily intense. Solomon and Wynne (1953) trained dogs in a shuttle-box apparatus to avoid a shock that was just subtetanizing; had the shock been stronger, the animals would have been thrown into muscular tetany so that they would have been unable to move. An interval of 10 seconds was used between a CS and the onset of the shock, and the dogs could avoid the shock by leaping from one side of the box to the other within this 10-second interval. Figure 7.9 shows the behavior of a typical dog in this situation.

Two features of the data are particularly interesting. First of all, the animal goes along for a few trials making simple escapes, but then a single successful avoidance occurs, and *never again does the animal fail to avoid the shock.* Secondly, the latencies with which the animal makes successful avoidances *continue to decrease* even though the animal is no longer being shocked. What is more, Solomon, Kamin, and Wynne found that the avoidance response under these conditions would persist for *hundreds* of trials—it was essentially nonextinguishable unless special "therapeutic" procedures were used, like introducing a glass barrier into which the dogs crashed as they attempted to leap from one side to the other. Furthermore, these results are not restricted to dogs. Turner and Solomon (1962) trained human subjects to avoid a traumatically strong shock by, for example, requiring that they move a lever on a box placed in front of them back and forth from one side to the other (an apparatus designed to be analogous to the shuttle box used with the dogs). Resistance to extinction under this, and a number of other conditions, was extremely great; of those who learned the avoidance response, only 9 of 36 extinguished at all. Most subjects continued to respond for 200 trials or so, at which point the experimenters ended the experiment since there was little indication that extinction was ever going to occur.

How are these things to be explained, particularly the extraordinary persistence of the avoidance behavior after shock had been removed completely from the situation? One explanation, suggest Solomon and Wynne, lies in the fact that the animals perform the avoidance response very rapidly, so rapidly in fact that there is not enough time for the conditioned fear established during the first few escape trials to appear in full-blown form. This would have to happen, of course, for conditioned fear to extinguish. Therefore, they argue, conditioned fear is *conserved* by extremely rapid avoidance responding. Since this responding does not allow anxiety to develop to a very large extent, the animal may occasionally lose interest in responding rapidly (note the occasional long-latency responses in Figure 7.9). If, however, the animal does make a long-latency response, this provides enough time for the full-blown emotional response to appear, and the animal immediately returns to responding with short latencies—again conserving conditioned anxiety by protecting it from extinction.

Of course, although this kind of reasoning suggests that extinction of avoidance ought to be a very protracted affair, it does predict that extinction ought to occur *sometime,* a prediction that runs counter to the results Solomon and his associates obtained. To handle this fact, Solomon and Wynne introduce a second concept, that of *partial irreversibility,* which says in a nutshell that anxiety conditioned under the traumatic procedures used in these experiments is simply so strong that it will *never* extinguish completely (without the use of "therapeutic" procedures, at least).

These things provide a grim prospect for those concerned with the role of trauma in human personality development! But the implications of the results are important. They suggest at the very least that many of the mechanisms of neurotic behavior are learned responses used by the individual to reduce in part some learned fear or anxiety. And they suggest, too, that severe human anxiety may be very difficult to deal with when it is brought to the attention of the therapist. But in order to solve problems, one must have a clear picture of the problem that is there to be solved, and Solomon's work—to the extent that it can be generalized to the clinic—is very important in this respect.

CONDITIONED APPETITIVE DRIVES: SOME PROBLEMS

Conditioned fear, about which we have just had a great deal to say and which we shall meet again, is fairly easy to produce. As a matter of fact, it is sufficiently simple and reliable that it can be used in a laboratory demonstration in elementary psychology. Learned drives based on primary drives like hunger, however, are very difficult to demonstrate. Myers and Miller (1954), for example, trained rats in an apparatus like that shown in Figure 7.4. Different groups of rats, all run under 23-hour hunger drive, received 0, 10, 30, or 70 training trials. On each trial, the rats could get from the white compartment to the black one, which contained a pellet of food, by pressing the door between the two compartments with their noses. Then the rats were satiated with food and required to press a lever to get from the white to the black compartment. All the rats were about equally skillful in learning to do this, thus providing little evidence of the development of a conditioned hunger drive which could motivate the learning of the new response of lever pressing. As you can see, this was a failure to get a hunger drive conditioned to the cues of the white compartment under precisely the same conditions where it had been simplicity itself to establish a conditioned fear drive in Miller's (1948) experiment. The fact that the rats stumbled upon and learned to press the lever at all is attributed by Myers and Miller to an "exploratory" drive or to curiosity.

Thus, there seems to be a real difference in the ease with which conditioned appetitive drives and conditioned aversive drives are produced. In fact, there is not yet an unequivocal demonstration of a conditioned appetitive drive in the literature. Both Miller (1951) and Mowrer (1960), among others, have argued that this may have to do with the relative abruptness of onset of the primary drive. Aversive drives can be readily and almost instantaneously aroused by noxious stimuli (like electric shock), so it is relatively easy to pair a particular stimulus condition with the arousal (and reduction) of the drive. Appetitive drives develop slowly—it takes time to become hungry. Therefore, hunger as a drive cannot be neatly paired with a particular stimulus—at least in terms of aligning the onset of the two sharply. Furthermore, the reduction of hunger (by eating) is probably a more gradual and complicated affair, as our discussion in Chapter 3 clearly suggests.

INCENTIVES AND THE AROUSAL OF CONDITIONED APPETITIVE DRIVES. In Chapter 3 we devoted a good deal of discussion to the concept of incentives, and we said then that there is much merit in looking at reinforcing stimuli as drive-*arousing* stimuli. We noted that Spence's (1956) concept of incentive motivation, K, was based on the r_g-s_g mechanism and the pairing, according to the paradigm of classical conditioning, of cues in the learning situation with consummatory responses. And we saw, too, that Sheffield (1966) had much the same idea in mind when he spoke of conditioned "excitement" triggered by the conditioned arousal of the consummatory response. Both these positions could be taken to imply that cues associated with reinforcing stimuli (viewed as incentives) acquire the property of producing motivation, and this, in turn, could lead to the guess that such cues ought to be usable to motivate and produce learning of a *new* response. As we have seen, there is scanty evidence that this is in fact the case (Myers & Miller, 1954).

At the same time, there is good evidence that a cue which has presumably acquired the functional properties of a conditioned appetitive drive can *energize ongoing behavior* and act as a motivator in this sense. Marx and Murphy (1961), for example, paired the sound of a buzzer with feeding in a goal box for one group of rats, but did not pair it with feeding for a second group. Then both groups were trained to run an alley. Finally, both groups were extinguished with the buzzer sounding *in the start box* at the beginning of certain extinction trials. The results show that the group which had the buzzer paired with feeding ran significantly faster on test trials than the group for which this was not the case. Clearly, the buzzer was acting as a conditioned motivator—in the sense that it energized behavior. In short, there is considerable evidence, much of it reviewed by Cofer and Appley (1964), which indicates that a cue associated with positive reinforcement can energize a response which the organism has already learned; but there is little, if any, evidence that such a cue can function as a counterpart to conditioned fear and lead to the learning of new behavior.

Be careful! We do not mean to imply by what we have just said that cues which have the presumed ability to arouse incentive motivation can not lead to new learning if they are used operationally as *reinforcers*. Viewed from this standpoint, of course, such cues are nothing more than conditioned reinforcers, and as we have seen, there is a good deal of evidence that new responses can be acquired on the basis of conditioned reinforcement. But from the reinforcement point of view, the proper operation is to present the cue *after* the new response occurs, while the cue must be presented *before* the new response occurs if we are to demonstrate that it has motivating properties. Clearly we are dealing here with a knotty problem which hinges, basically, around the interesting and perplexing question of how a cue can simultaneously have the properties of both a motivator and a reinforcer. The problem has bothered psychologists for some time (Hull, 1943; McGuigan, 1956; Mowrer, 1960), and it is doubtful, unfortunately, if we have seen the end of it.

PUNISHMENT

In general, a response is punished when some painful stimulation or the threat of such stimulation is made contingent upon the response. If I punish my dog by cuffing it for chewing up the newspaper, in effect I have made the cuffing contingent upon chewing newspapers. Usually, punishment is administered to ongoing behavior in order to stop it, though as we shall see, things do not always work this way. Thus punishment, like reward, is a technique for one organism to control the behavior of another.

In Chapter 1, we noted that punishment training involved learning to *withhold* a response upon which some noxious or negative reinforcer was contingent. Mowrer (1960) has called this kind of situation *passive avoidance training,* in part to emphasize that the organism must, in effect, learn *not* to do something, and in part to distinguish it from *active avoidance conditioning* where, as we have seen, the organism must learn to do something in order to prevent the occurrence of some unpleasant event. Solomon (1964) points out some of the intricacies that can be involved in setting up punishing situations if we go beyond the simple sort of operational definition of punishment which we have used so far. We can punish responses that have been established originally on the basis of some appetitive reward (like pressing a bar for food); we can punish consummatory responses (like eating and drinking) that are, relatively speaking, "built into" the organism; we can punish responses that have been themselves established on the basis of noxious stimulation (like escape and active avoidance responses); and we can punish so-called instinctive acts—patterns or sequences of behavior that are largely unlearned. We cannot discuss all these in this section, though we shall look at some of them; but it is important to recognize—as Solomon emphasizes with great vigor—that the effects of these various punishing operations upon behavior can be markedly different.

CLASSICAL WORK ON PUNISHMENT

For many years, experimental and theoretical work on punishment was dominated by the views of the late E. L. Thorndike. For most of his professional life he was an educational psychologist, and consequently his concern with the problem of punishment was influenced by the formal demands of the classroom. In a word, he was concerned with the influence of verbal praise and reproof upon behavior. Since his views and experiments were very influential, let us look briefly at them.

THORNDIKE'S VIEWS AND EXPERIMENTS. In his earliest writing, Thorndike simply adopted the commonsense view that punishment would reduce the tendency to repeat behavior which it immediately followed (weakened connections, as Thorndike put it). Later, however, Thorndike (1932a) examined the problem more thoroughly and came to another conclusion. He decided that punishment really has no inherently weakening effect upon behavior. Let us see how Thorndike arrived at this rather surprising position.

Thorndike performed a number of experiments on punishment with both animal and human subjects. As his experiments on human subjects are better known, let us review one of these. Thorndike (1932b) asked subjects who were not familiar with Spanish to guess the correct English equivalent to a Spanish word. He gave a series of such words in the form of a multiple-choice test. If the subject chose the correct word, the experimenter informed the subject by saying "right"; if the word was incorrect, the experimenter said "wrong." It was possible to discover the influence of "right" or "wrong" by finding out, on further testing, if the subjects gave the punished or rewarded responses with a frequency greater or lesser than must be expected by chance. Since there were five alternatives for each item, the frequency of repetition by chance would be 20 percent. This was the base line against which Thorndike measured the effect of saying "right" or "wrong." As things turned out, "right" did not increase the tendency to repeat the initially given response. The consequence "wrong," however, rather than being weakening, seemed to Thorndike to have a slight strengthening effect.

Many experiments by Thorndike (1935) led him to the same conclusion. Other investigators made serious criticisms of him, however. First of all, they argued, the use of "chance" as a base line against which to measure the effects of reward and punishment is not proper; it is extremely unlikely that responses given by subjects in such tests are at the chance level. Rather, responses go in "runs," or sequences, to which the one-in-five chance expectancy would not apply. Stephens (1934), for example, used an empirically determined probability of repetition by including items to which the experimenter gave no reward or punishment. The frequency of repetition without any consequences turned out to be 36 percent instead of the 20 percent assumed by Thorndike. Measuring from this base, punishment did have a slight weakening effect—and given the mildness of the punishment and the low motivation for repetition, we should probably not expect a large effect.

Thorndike argued that wherever punishment appears to weaken a response, it is an *indirect* effect. This happens because punishment tends to produce variability of behavior. In maze learning, for example, punishment of an error may lead the learner to make the correct response accidentally, and because the correct response is strengthened by reward, say, the punished response does not tend to recur. It has never been

precisely clear what Thorndike meant by the indirect weakening of punished responses (see the controversy, Postman, 1947; Stone, 1948), but it
would probably run something like this: Punishment may or may not
weaken a response, but it clearly cannot be the mirror image of the action
of reward. This is true at least in the sense that if a response is rewarded,
it is apparent to the organism in a typical test that repetition of *this*
response will be rewarding; but if a response is punished, it is not clear
to the organism which of the other available responses will be rewarded.
In effect, punishment does an exemplary job of telling the organism
what not to do, but it carries no information by itself which tells an
organism what particular alternative course of behavior should be followed. Thus behavior after punishment tends to be more variable; the
prediction, for example, of the exact response to be made by the organism
will be more difficult. This is the most general statement we can make
within the confines of Thorndike's thinking. In the kinds of experimental
situation with which Thorndike tended to work, the punishment was
a mild one, and perhaps its main function was to provide information. If
this is so, reproof for making a particular response does not supply as
much information as praise, for it does not tell the subject which response
is correct.

Many of the important conditions of punishment are ignored in
the Thorndikian experiments. The magnitude and quality of unpleasant
effects are ignored, and perhaps more important, the effects of restricting
the available responses are ignored. In Thorndike's experiments, the
learner may be content to satisfy himself (and the experimenter) by
making responses other than the ones punished. He is seldom interested
in defending his original response as the "right" one, and he will readily
abandon it when he knows it is "wrong." So the effect of punishment is
to produce variability of behavior, as Thorndike suggested.

What happens, however, when the *only* response that is appropriate for a particular motivational state of affairs is punished? The youngster who is punished for taking cookies from the cupboard may know no
other way to satisfy a craving for sweets. No matter how many raps on
the knuckles (or elsewhere) the youngster may receive, the cookies lose
none of their attraction, and he is not likely to find another way of
getting cookies. This leads us to some of the very fundamental questions
about punishment, questions which force us into the controlled world of
the animal laboratory to find answers to them. Let us look at a couple
of the classical experiments on punishment in free-responding situations.

THE EXPERIMENTS OF SKINNER AND ESTES.   Skinner (1938) studied
the effect of punishment upon the lever-pressing response in the Skinner
box. In his experiment, the punishment was a sharp slap on the paws

from the lever itself. To measure the effects of punishment, Skinner obtained extinction curves for four rats following training with a fixed-interval schedule of reinforcement. Two rats were slapped at the beginning of the extinction period and two were not. The result was that the rats slapped at the beginning of extinction showed a much lower rate of responding during extinction. As a matter of fact, the punishment seemed to *suppress* the response entirely for a period of time. The curious thing, however, is that by the time extinction was complete, the slapped rats had caught up, in terms of total number of responses emitted, with the rats which were not slapped. These results can be clearly seen in Figure 7.10.

Skinner interpreted the data to mean that punishment has only a temporary effect upon behavior—an unfortunate interpretation, as later research has shown. Nevertheless, Skinner thought that punishment does not affect the total number of responses which the animal will eventually emit during extinction; it only affects the *rate* at which some total will be emitted. Early in extinction the punished animals show a lower rate of responding; their response rate is suppressed. But eventually, the suppression disappears and the rates accelerate so that in the end the punished animals give just as many responses altogether as the unpunished animals.

Estes (1944) followed Skinner's work with an intensive investigation of the factors affecting punishment of an isolated instrumental response—again, lever pressing in the rat. In these experiments, he substituted an electric shock for Skinner's slap. The shock was delivered through the lever, so that rats used to receiving food as the result of lever pressing sometimes received the shock instead.

FIG. **7.10** Some classical effects of punishment upon resistance to extinction. The initial effect of punishment is to reduce the rate of responding. In this experiment, however, there is recovery, and eventually the total number of responses is about the same for the punished and control animals. (Skinner, 1938.)

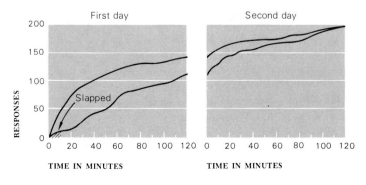

Estes' first conclusion was much like Skinner's. The effect of punishment is primarily upon the rate of responding rather than upon the total overall tendency to emit a particular response. Estes did find, however, that if the punishment were intense enough or lasted long enough, there was a slight permanent depression in the total number of responses the animals would emit. Nevertheless, punishment was never able to eliminate the extinction curve completely—rats always came back to respond after punishment, even though they were never again reinforced. It is interesting that when Estes punished his rats only now and then, instead of for every response, the depression of the rate of responding was not nearly so severe, *but it lasted longer.* Thus the results of partial punishment are quite like the results of partial reinforcement, a fact which, incidentally, is now very well established (Azrin, 1956; Azrin, Holz, & Hake, 1963).

THE SUPPRESSION OF BEHAVIOR BY PUNISHMENT

The most characteristic feature of a punishment operation, as the experiments of Skinner and Estes clearly suggest, is to reduce at least temporarily the strength of the response that is being punished. There are many exceptions to this rule, however, and we shall look at some of them later. Right now let us see what has been done to pin down the conditions under which behavior is reduced in strength by punishment. As it turns out, this is a particular characteristic of instrumental responses that are established by *positive reinforcement* before punishment begins.

SOME PARAMETERS OF PUNISHMENT. One of the first things that comes to mind is the question of how punishment varies in effectiveness as its intensity changes. A good deal is known about this subject. Appel (1963), for example, trained rats to press a lever in a Skinner box using food as a reward on a variable-interval schedule. After the rats had stabilized on this schedule, electric shocks were delivered through the bar and grid floor immediately after each lever press (food continued to be available on the variable-interval schedule). The animals were tested at a number of different shock intensities, beginning with the lowest and ending with the highest in the series. Punishment continued at a particular shock level until behavior stabilized; then punishment was stopped for five days so that the course of recovery from a particular intensity could be studied before moving on to the next intensity. Appel's results are shown in Figure 7.11.

As you can see, there is little indication of a decrease in rate—that is, suppression of the lever-pressing response—at low intensities, but there is essentially complete suppression of behavior at the higher inten-

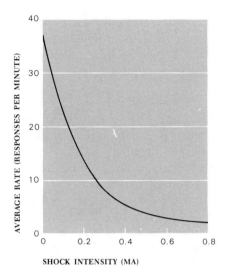

FIG. 7.11 The suppression of lever pressing by a punishing shock stimulus. When each response is punished, the rate of response decreases, the decrease becoming greater as shocks grow stronger. With the range of shock intensities used in this experiment, all animals returned to their unpunished rate of responding when shock was removed. The curve was fitted to data from several animals. (Redrawn from Appel, 1963.)

sities. Appel also reports no indication of recovery from suppression at any shock level as long as shock was being administered for each response. Other experimenters, however, have found that animals—pigeons, in this case—will show response suppression as a punishment session begins, but will then gradually recover, increasing their rate of responding back to their original prepunishment rate in spite of continuing shocks. Azrin (1960) demonstrated this, at least for relatively low intensities of shock, and the best guess is that here the animals were adapting to the shock stimulus (Solomon, 1964; Church, 1963). As you might expect, however, recovery of this sort was limited to low intensities of shock; Azrin was able to find intensities sufficiently high to produce complete permanent suppression. These observations are not by any means limited to free-responding stiuations; Karsh (1962) was able to show a consistent decrease in running speed in a straight alley as a function of the intensity of a punishing shock in the goal box.

What happens when punishment is removed in instrumental learning situations like those we have just examined? Appel found that all his animals recovered from suppression completely, returning to their prepunishment rates. Azrin found something a little different. When punishment stopped, his pigeons responded initially at a *faster* rate than that at which they responded before punishment began. Eventually, they settled back down to a rate characteristic of the schedule of food reinforcement which was used, but their immediate reaction to the removal of punishment was to go faster than they ever had before. In short, under the conditions of these experiments (and many others like them), punishment has dramatic and powerful effects—it can eliminate behavior completely if it is strong enough—so long as it is being administered; but there is very little indication in the literature that punishment of an instrumental response based upon a positive reinforcer has permanent effects that will suppress behavior much beyond the punishment period itself.

PUNISHMENT OF CONSUMMATORY RESPONSES.   While punishment of instrumental responses based on positive rewards has effects which are limited primarily to the punishment situation itself, such is patently not the case for other kinds of behavior. In particular, punishment of consummatory behavior, responses like eating, drinking, or sexual activity, has devastating effects that can last indefinitely. Masserman and Pechtel (1953), for example, presented a toy snake to a spider monkey while the monkey was eating. The monkey never ate again and, in fact, starved to death. Solomon (1964), in summarizing some of this literature, notes similar if not quite so dramatic suppression of sexual behavior and of feeding behavior in other species. We cannot help but agree with Solomon that this is a curious state of affairs; offhand it would seem that responses which are so intimately tied to the well-being of the members of a species, and to the species as a whole, would be highly resistant to the effects of punishment. Perhaps the fact that this is not the case should emphasize the need for caution in making general statements about punishment.

THE EFFECTS OF CONTINGENT VERSUS NONCONTINGENT PUNISHMENT. In an earlier portion of this chapter we discussed briefly the concept of the *conditioned emotional response* (CER). If you will recall, we said that a CER was established by pairing a punishing stimulus with some neutral stimulus, like a light, but doing this in such a way that the punishing stimulus occurred independently of anything that the organism was doing at the time. And if you will also recall, we noted that the appearance of the light tended to *suppress* ongoing behavior once the light had acquired the ability to produce a CER. The critical difference between the CER procedure and the punishment procedures we have just been discussing, of course, is the fact that punishment is *contingent* upon some particular response in the latter, but is *not contingent* upon some particular response in the case of the CER.

What are the differential effects of contingent as compared with noncontingent punishment? It is important to recognize that both procedures produce prime effects which are more similar than dissimilar: Both suppress behavior in the presence of a stimulus that has been paired with punishment. Hunt and Brady (1955), for example, trained two groups of rats to press a lever for food in a Skinner box. After stable performance was reached, a neutral cue was turned on for three minutes. For animals in a punishment group, each response that occurred during the three-minute interval was followed with a brief electric shock. For animals in a CER group, no responses were punished during the three-minute interval, but a brief unavoidable shock occurred just as the neutral stimulus went off. The results showed that both groups of animals reduced their rate of responding during the presence of the neutral cue; both groups, in fact, eventually stopped responding altogether while the cue was on. However, Hunt and Brady also found that it took longer for the effects of the CER procedure to extinguish than it did for the effects of the contingent procedure. When shock was removed from the situation, animals in the CER group showed suppression in the presence of the neutral cue for a longer period of time than did animals in the punishment group. Furthermore, animals in the CER group tended to do things during the presence of the neutral cue that were different from the things that animals in the punishment group did. In the case of the former, a common pattern of behavior was to crouch, freeze, urinate, and defecate, while for the punishment group, the common pattern was to tickle and tease (but not press) the lever until the neutral stimulus went off.

Some work of Hoffman and Fleshler (1965) indicates that if procedures which are a bit different from those of Hunt and Brady are used, noncontingent punishment tends to produce greater response suppression than contingent punishment. These investigators modified the general Hunt and Brady procedure in two ways. First of all, they started their experiment with a 1.0 milliampere punishing stimulus (Hunt and Brady had used a 1.5 milliampere shock). Secondly, they used a procedure in which an animal in the CER group received the *same number* of shocks as an animal in the contingent group. They did this by *yoking* the two animals together insofar as the presentation of shock was concerned. Thus, two pigeons were run simultaneously, each in their own Skinner box. During punishment periods, a neutral cue of a tone was turned on in both boxes. Each time that one pigeon pecked in the presence of the neutral cue, both it *and* the pigeon in the other box were shocked. With this procedure, as you can see, one pigeon was punished for pecking, while the other pigeon was punished regardless of what it happened to be doing.

Under these conditions, Hoffman and Fleshler found that the noncontingent procedure produced much greater suppression than the contingent CER procedure; often, animals in the former group stopped responding altogether. If shock level was increased from 1.0 to 2.0 milliamperes, however, Hoffman and Fleshler found—just as Hunt and Brady did—that both procedures would produce about the same degree of suppression of responding in the presence of the neutral cue, and the results of both experiments agree in showing that it takes relatively longer for the suppression produced by the CER procedure to extinguish.

One thing which emerges, if we set these two experiments side by side, is that *intensity* of punishment is an important parameter in situations where contingent and noncontingent punishment are compared. Apparently, a given intensity of shock tends to suppress behavior more if it is contingent upon a response than if it is not contingent upon a response. In this connection, Annau and Kamin (1961) point to a minimal intensity of shock that apparently works to suppress behavior when contingent upon a response but does not seem to suppress behavior when it was used according to the CER procedure.

What is the best way to summarize the effects of contingent as compared with noncontingent punishment upon behavior? One thing which certainly seems to be true is that contingent punishment tends to have its effects upon a much more restricted segment of an organism's behavior—in particular, the segment that is being punished. The noncontingent procedure, on the other hand, tends eventually to knock out a large part of all the behavior that occurs in the punishment situation—particularly if the intensity of the punishing event is high. In effect, and speaking a bit loosely, the animal subjected to contingent punishment has a relatively easy time figuring out what it is in the situation that must not be done, while for the animal subjected to the noncontingent procedure, it is impossible that this can ever become quite clear. The latter may continue lever pressing or pecking more than the contingent-punishment animal (providing the punishment is not too intense), but in general, a much greater cross section of the animal's behavior will be punished in the long run—in fact, anything the animal happens to be doing at the time the unavoidable shock comes on. Such an animal is left, traumatized, to "take" the shock and to handle its conditioned "situational anxiety" as best it can. In the case of the rats of Hunt and Brady, stereotyped freezing, crouching, and other forms of generalized emotional behavior became predominant. Given these things, it is perhaps not surprising, too, that it would take the animal exposed to noncontingent punishment a relatively long time to "get over" the effects of punishment during an extinction session.

THE USE OF THE SUPPRESSION PERIOD AND ITS CORRELATED EFFECTS. It is fairly clear that the use of punishment does not completely eliminate a response conditioned with a positive reward (though there are some exceptions to this rule, as we have seen). Punishment may momentarily weaken a response, but most typically it does little to eliminate such behavior altogether. This conclusion seems to be in accord with the clinical and anthropological evidence about aggressive behavior punished by parents or by some agent of society. The tendency toward aggression is not removed until it can be brought to free expression, and thus special psychotherapeutic techniques are often used for the express purpose of allowing aggression to occur in displaced (therapeutic) situations.

It is possible, however, to use the temporary period of suppression produced by punishment—and its correlated emotional effects—to teach an organism a new method of getting at the same goal object. An experiment by Whiting and Mowrer (1943) suggests that this may be a valuable technique in the control of behavior. These investigators studied ways of getting rats to abandon old, preferred adjustments in favor of new ones. They used three groups of rats. All three were taught to run a simple maze, and after this habit had been acquired, the experimenters extinguished it in one group of rats by omitting the food reinforcer. They continued to reinforce the habit for the second group, but placed a barrier in the path leading to the goal box and food. In the case of the third group, they punished the running response with an electric shock. The situation was then changed so that all three groups could find the way to the goal by an alternative route. The animals that had been punished on the original habit showed the fewest errors in reaching the goal by the alternative pathway. They also showed less regression to the original habit after the alternative habit had been learned. Thus, it appears that teaching an alternative response during the perod of suppression induced by punishment can work as an effective means of redirecting behavior.

Some further evidence on this point comes from an experiment of Azrin, Hake, Holz, and Hutchinson (1965). In part of their work, these investigators trained pigeons to peck at a key, reinforcing pecks with food on an FR 25 schedule. After pecking was well established, responses were punished with a brief electric shock. However, a single response on another key eliminated the punishment on the first until the pigeon obtained the next scheduled reward. Thus, the pigeon's optimal strategy here was to make a single peck on the "escape" key, run off 25 now-unpunished pecks on the "food" key, and return to the "escape" key for another peck after the reward was obtained. And this is exactly what the pigeons did. Azrin et al. conclude that their experiment provides evidence for motivation to escape from a punishing situation, since the most likely reason why the birds would switch to the second key would be to get away from the noxious effects of punishment on the first. Here, then, is further evidence that punishment can be used to redirect behavior, particularly the kind of behavior which gets the organism away from punishment.

SOME NONSUPPRESSIVE FUNCTIONS OF PUNISHMENT

In the last section, we examined some of the ways that punishment works to knock out rewarded behavior, and we saw that the use of a punishing stimulus does a pretty good job of doing this—at least temporarily, and sometimes more permanently—in a number of different situations. Now, let us turn things around a bit and look at some situations in which a punishing stimulus not only does not suppress behavior but can actually be used to facilitate learning, on the one hand, and to maintain behavior on the other. Along the way we shall meet some rather strange paradoxes which, at the very least, suggest that we have a great deal to learn before we shall have much more than a rudimentary understanding of the effects of punishment upon behavior.

THE USE OF PUNISHMENT AS A CUE. What happens if, instead of following a usually rewarded response with an electric shock, we use the electric shock to signal that if a response is made, a reward can be obtained? In other words, what happens if we *reverse* the usual temporal relation between a "punishing" stimulus and reinforced behavior, using the "punishing" stimulus as a discriminative cue? Will behavior be suppressed under these conditions? Solomon (1964) thinks not, and there is considerable evidence to support his point of view. The key here is to think of a punishing event not so much in terms of its unpleasantness, but in terms of its properties as a *stimulus,* a cue which ought to function like any other cue.

An experiment of Holz and Azrin (1961) demonstrates that an electric shock can function in exactly the same way as a buzzer or a light in simple discrimination learning. These experimenters trained pigeons to peck at a key on a VI 2 minute schedule of food reinforcement. When the response was running along at a steady rate, they added an electric shock to the situation so that each response on the key produced the shock. The intensity of the shock was adjusted so that the rate of key pecking was reduced by about half. When this condition was well established, extinction periods were introduced in which pecks produced neither food nor shock. This procedure—periods of reinforcement in the presence of a cue (shock) interspersed with periods of no reinforcement in the absence of the cue—is precisely that used to establish the cue as a discriminative stimulus. Under these conditions, we would expect shock to come to signal that food was available, and we would look for the pigeon to reserve most of its responding for the period in which the shock was delivered following each response. This is exactly what happened. Figure 7.12 shows the cumulative response data from one of the tests the experimenters used, a test in which all food reinforcement was withdrawn (extinction) and behavior was examined both in the presence of the punishment cue and in its absence. As you can see, the pigeon responded hardly at all during the period of no punishment, but responded quite rapidly *when each response was followed by shock.* Clearly, punishment had been established as a cue which set the occasion for responding for a positive reinforcer.

FIG. **7.12** An example of a nonsuppressive function of punishment. Here, during previous training, a shock had been paired as a discriminative cue with food so that when shocks followed pecks, shocks signaled that food was available. When no shock was present, food was not available. The extinction data shown here indicate that the pigeon responded rapidly when pecks were followed by shocks, but responded hardly at all when shock was absent. (Holz & Azrin, 1961.)

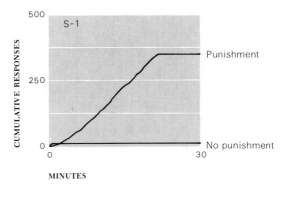

In a long series of experiments, Muenzinger (1934, etc.) demonstrated another aspect of punishment as a cue for learning.[2] In one of his experiments, he ran rats in a discrimination box, rewarding them with food if they made a correct response, and punishing them with shock if they made an error. Not surprisingly, perhaps, he found that the group run under these conditions made about one-third as many errors as a group that received food alone for a correct response. But here comes a surprise. Muenzinger was also able to demonstrate that shocking an animal after a *correct* response leading to food produced learning that was almost as rapid as shocking the animals for incorrect responses (both conditions, of course, leading to faster learning than if no punishment at all were used).

How are we to account for this rather astonishing result? Muenzinger felt that the function of shock for correct responses was to slow down the animal and, in effect, make the animal do a little more deliberating before making a choice. Wischner (Wischner, 1947; Wischner, Fowler, & Kushnick, 1963) emphasized the fact that Muenzinger used a correction procedure in discrimination training and was unable to show such dramatic effects of punishment for correct responses if a noncorrection procedure were used. It is quite possible that such procedural factors may be involved in the phenomenon; but on the basis of the things we have been looking at in this section, another approach suggests itself. This is simply that shock in these experiments is paired with food (albeit after some delay) and as such can come to function as a discriminative cue—signaling to the rat just after it has made its choice that it has indeed

[2] Muenzinger's work, and other work related to it, has been reviewed by Church (1963) in an excellent article which you should look at if you are interested in finding out more about this problem.

made the correct one. The key here, once again, may be to look at the *information* that shock gives the rat about its choice behavior and to de-emphasize any presumed emotional consequences of punishment. After all, a bit of punishment may be a trifle upsetting at the moment, but can this be more than a fleeting state of affairs, if at the same time it signals certainty that a highly valued reward lies just ahead?

ANOTHER PARADOX: PUNISHMENT OF RESPONSES ESTABLISHED BY PUN-ISHMENT. Think, for a moment, of the conventional avoidance-learning experiment. A dog is trained to jump a hurdle in response to a discriminative cue, and if the leap occurs within a prescribed time interval, punishment (electric shock, etc.) is avoided. As we have seen, this sort of behavior is readily established and quickly becomes quite stable. Now let us perform an experimental operation which would lead us to expect suppression of behavior, that is, let us punish the animal for making the avoidance response. A simple way to do this would be to electrify the formerly safe grid floor so that the animal now jumps into shock. We could combine this with an extinction procedure, so that if the animal fails to leap and stays in the start compartment, shocks no longer occur there. Under these conditions—on the basis of what we have seen to be the case for responses based on positive rewards—we would expect the dog to quickly suppress its jumping behavior and to stop jumping much sooner than another dog, say, that was not punished. But things simply do not work that way—there is now a great deal of evidence which shows that punishment administered under these conditions *increases* the tendency to respond far beyond what we find if punishment is not used.

Solomon and his associates (e.g., Solomon, Kamin, & Wynne, 1953) reported in their experiments on traumatic avoidance learning that dogs would jump *faster* and *more vigorously* into the shock than they would under conventional extinction procedures, and Church (1963), in his review of the literature, cites a host of experiments showing essentially the same thing.

Furthermore, the phenomenon is not limited to avoidance learning. Brown, Martin, and Mitchell (1964) trained rats to run an alley in order to *escape* shock. The rats were dropped onto an electrified grid in the start box and had to run the entire length of the electrified alley before reaching safety in the goal box. After this response was well learned, the animals were extinguished under one of three conditions. For one group, regular extinction was used—after a few trials during which shock intensity was gradually reduced, all shock was turned off in the apparatus. For a second "short-shock" group, shock was left on in the final 2-foot segment of the alley just before the goal box, but was turned off elsewhere. For a third "long-shock" group, the entire 6-foot length of

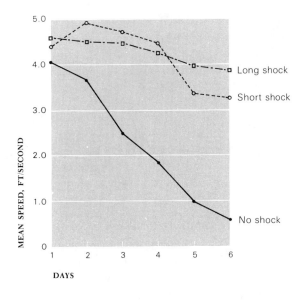

FIG. **7.13**   Resistance to extinction of an escape response as a function of punishment conditions during extinction. In the long-shock condition, the entire alley was electrified, while in the short-shock condition, the last 2 feet of the alley were electrified. In the no-shock condition, shock was absent throughout the apparatus. Resistance to extinction of running was least when the alley contained no shock, while it was greatest when the animals ran into shock. (J. S. Brown, Martin, & Mitchell, 1964.)

the alley was electrified, but shock was absent in the start and goal boxes. You can see the extinction results in Figure 7.13.

In terms of running speed in the last 2 feet of the alley, the group that extinguished *first* was the group which *received no shock at all.* The other two groups, which were both punished for making the former escape response, showed much greater resistance to extinction and were in fact running about 3.5 feet per second after six days of extinction (60 extinction trials). Here was truly "masochistic" behavior on the part of the rats, since all they had to do to avoid shock entirely was to sit still in the start box!

How are we to account for a paradoxical effect of this sort? As you might expect, there are many ways of looking at the problem, and each, in all likelihood, will have to be modified as more information becomes available. We could, however, recall once again that punishing events like electric shocks are stimuli, and like all stimuli, they can become associated with particular responses. Thus, an animal that has learned to run when an electric shock comes on might tend to run under *any* conditions where the shock appears—failing to discriminate, perhaps, that from the experimenter's point of view shock is being used in two ways. In the Brown et al. experiment the rats were conditioned to *run* to the onset of shock during training, and when they stumbled into shock during extinction they simply did what they had learned to do when hit by that stimulus: They ran—fast.

This kind of thinking leads to the proposition that the paradoxical effect of punishment might be *limited* to situations in which the noxious stimulus used to establish the response is the same as the one used subsequently to punish the response. If the punishing stimuli were different, it might be easier for the animal to discriminate the change from one set of conditions to the other. There is a bit of evidence which suggests that this might be the case. Carlsmith (cited in Church, 1963 and Solomon, 1964) found "masochistic" behavior in an avoidance-learning situation when shock was used to both train and punish the avoidance response, but not when shock was used to establish the response while an equally noxious loud noise was used to punish it. Here, presumably, the animals could tell the difference between the two punishing events, and they behaved in what would seem to be a much more appropriate fashion.

A COMMENT ABOUT THEORIES OF PUNISHMENT

It should be evident from the variegated effects of punishment upon behavior that a theory which will be able to handle all we know is not going to be simple. It is relatively easy to account for the general suppressive effects of punishment upon a response; a theory emphasizing the development of fear classically conditioned to cues associated with the punishing event could do the job. Here, given a few trials for conditioned fear to develop, we would guess that the organism would simply learn to make some response—albeit one that we do not generally specify —which would get it away from the fear-producing cues. And what we have as a consequence, of course, is essentially the same kind of two-process analysis that we applied to active avoidance learning (Solomon, 1964). It is difficult, however, to make this kind of approach work when it comes to some of the paradoxical effects of punishment upon behavior, such as the things which happen when we punish a response that has been established by punishment. As we saw, it might make better sense to look at that particular kind of situation in terms of whether or not the organism can discriminate differences between the conditions of original training and the conditions of subsequent punishment.

Of course, there is no particular reason—other than a commendable wish for parsimony—which compels us to insist that a single theoretical system must account for all the phenomena associated with punishment. As a matter of fact, we would no doubt be very wise to abandon a search for parsimony at this stage of the game and look for microtheories that can handle a few facts at a time. While this is a statement that can be leveled at many facets of the psychology of learning—and we have so taken aim on a number of occasions—it seems particularly appropriate for the topic at hand.

One final comment seems in order. It should be clear from all we have said in this section that punishment can have rather dramatic effects in quashing behavior. At the same time, however, we have seen that punishment can be equally useful in helping along the learning process—particularly when it is used as an information-carrying cue and when it is combined with reward for some other kind of behavior. Some of the earlier classical work on punishment (that of Skinner, for example) placed primary emphasis on only one side of a coin that has two sides—and an edge as well. From this literature, one can gain the strong impression that punishment is a maladaptive, ineffective, and wasteful technique to use in the establishment and guidance of behavior. Such is patently not the case, and we should welcome further research aimed at an area of the psychology of learning that has not received all the attention it deserves.

A FINAL WORD

This has been a long chapter, and it could have been a good deal longer. Following our opening warning, however, we have not included many things that could have been quite legitimately included in a chapter on motivation and emotion—topics such as conflict, experimental neurosis, the effect of stress upon learned behavior, and more generally, a study of the facts and broad theories of motivation and their application to psychology. These things, while they are unquestionably important to behavior theory, are best treated in other places, and there are now a number of excellent books which deal specifically with the topic of motivation. To name a few, we can mention Hall (1961), Brown (1961), Young (1961), Cofer and Appley (1964), and Atkinson (1964). If you are interested in the specific thinking and research of individuals working in the area of motivation, you can also look at Haber (1966) and at the yearly issues of the *Nebraska Symposium on Motivation*. All these will lead you to other excellent material.

What we *have* attempted to do in this chapter is to develop a place for motivation and emotion within the psychology of learning, looking specifically at how these things enter into the learning process itself, on the one hand, and how learning produces new motives and emotions on the other.

In Chapter 8 we turn to new things—new in one especially important way. We now add *verbal behavior* to our learning mix, and we shall be seeing what psychologists have learned about the way in which this extraordinarily important class of behavior enters into the psychology of learning. It should not surprise you that for the most part we shall be leaving behind our good friends the rat, the pigeon, the dog, and the monkey, turning to an organism with which we all have a good deal of personal familiarity: man. You will discover, however, that the ideas we have developed with lower animals will be weaving their way through much of what is to come.

8

THE EXPERIMENTAL ANALYSIS OF VERBAL LEARNING

In the next few chapters we shall examine learning processes in human beings. Of the various problems in the study of human learning, none is more important than verbal learning. In the study of verbal learning we examine the way in which people acquire linguistic relations. There is nothing either more characteristically human or more psychologically significant than language, so the study of verbal learning is part of many psychological investigations. In one way or another, the study of thinking or the development of human abilities entails the study of verbal learning.

Verbal learning provides a very large area to explore, and here we shall have to limit ourselves to the study of those aspects of the subject that have been investigated experimentally in the psychological laboratory. We shall, for example, have little to say on the question of how children develop the use of language. In many ways, however, experimentally determined information about how adult human beings learn to use the elements of language does bear on the question of how children learn to talk. That information, taken together with some of the facts and theories about elementary aspects of learning (reviewed in the earlier chapters) does provide us with some theories about how people learn to talk and learn the basic structure of the languages they speak. In due course we shall refer to these theories.

The present chapter, however, is devoted almost entirely to the experimental study of verbal learning in adults. The experimental techniques and findings that we shall discuss not only have importance for the study of verbal behavior, but also provide a significant part of the theoretical basis for educational psychology and other applied fields. Consequently, despite the limited context in which we shall find these techniques and results, they have wide use and general importance in the study of human behavior.

EXPERIMENTAL TECHNIQUES IN VERBAL LEARNING

The basic elements of human languages are sounds made by action of the vocal apparatus. Therefore, some considerable part of the study of verbal learning should be concerned with the perceptual-motor learning in ear-vocal coordination. When we are concerned with adult verbal learning, however, we seldom deal with the perceptual-motor aspects of the learning of language. Nevertheless, in order to understand some of the fundamental aspects of speech and language and how these are important in verbal learning, we must take a few paragraphs to describe human speech.

The kinds of sounds that can be made by the human vocal apparatus are amazingly varied—consider the imitations of animal and natural sounds that a person can make with his mouth. Yet the sound elements of a given language are surprisingly few, discrete, and separate. The structure of human language is made possible by the fact that the continuously variable sounds which human beings can make are chopped up into distinctive segments, each different from the next. We assimilate a wide range of physically different sounds to the same linguistic element. Many Americans, for example, say the word *water* with the consonant in the middle sounding more like *d* than *t*. Nevertheless, we all understand that middle consonant to be *t;* we assimilate it to one linguistic element, the phoneme /t/.

All languages reduce the almost endless variety of possible speech sounds made by speakers of those languages to a relatively few phonemes—usually less than fifty. These phonemes correspond to the letters (or, as they are called technically, graphemes) of written language. There are twenty-six characters in written English. No matter how each character is written, how indistinct our writing, each letter is interpreted to be one of these twenty-six, not something in between or something additional to the set of twenty-six.

Therefore, one of the fundamental characteristics of the material people learn when they learn about language is that all of it is compounded from a small number of basic elements. Part of the problem of understanding verbal learning is in seeing how we learn to combine these elements, and another part is in seeing how we group these elements into larger elements such as the words and sentences of languages.

We do not think of the separate letters and phonemes of languages as being meaningful in themselves. Meaning is certainly the most important characteristic of language and, therefore, of verbal learning.

Meaning comes into language when the separate basic elements are combined into units which obey the grammatical rules of the language and which refer to things outside of the language. English words are meaningful, though sometimes these words are composed of more basic meaningful units called morphemes. The word *writer* consists of two morphemes: *write,* signifying the action, and *-er,* signifying the agent performing the action.

Adult speakers of a language treat words and sometimes morphemes as integrated and more or less distinct units. We dot not have to learn that the phrase "Give me a glass of water" includes the sequence of letters *ss of wa;* we need only learn the separate words that compose the phrase. From those words, with a little effort, we can reconstruct any sequence of letters in the phrase we wish. How we combine these elements into words provides one problem in verbal learning, and how we learn the meaning of the words as well as the meaning of the grammar behind the phrase provides another problem.

The experimental techniques and problems we shall outline in the next few pages are all, in one way or another, directed toward obtaining information about how we combine the elements of language into larger units and how we use these larger units in our ordinary verbal processes. The purpose of this section is to examine these techniques and problems critically in some detail.

Materials in the Study of Verbal Learning

One of the important characteristics of much experimental work on human verbal learning is that the material given subjects to learn is not meaningful. That is to say, it does not consist of the ordinary words and phrases of language. Rather, subjects are given sequences of letters or other verbal materials which do not make sense. The purpose in so doing is to rid the experiments of the problem of meaning in so far as possible. The object is to study the way people learn how to combine elements into the ordinary structures of language. The earliest of these studies of the learning of meaningless material concerned acquisition of three-letter nonsense syllables.

NONSENSE SYLLABLES

The inventor of the nonsense syllable for studies of human verbal learning was H. Ebbinghaus, who in 1885 published the first experimental study of human memory. Ebbinghaus devised his nonsense syllables for the purposes of that study. He wanted to examine learning and retention of "new ideas"; he could not use ordinary (German) words, he argued, because there were already too many associations between these words and other words. Learning and retention in the laboratory would be contaminated by these previously learned associations. Therefore, Ebbinghaus formed new, meaningless words out of all the possible consonant-vowel-consonant (CVC) combinations which did not form real German words. These nonsense syllables, he argued, were devoid of associations and meaning, and various combinations of them would have to be learned without aid from associations already established by speakers of German.

Therefore, nonsense syllables were supposed to be devoid of meaning and to be uniformly difficult. They could be learned in any order or combination, and one order or combination would be about as difficult or easy as the next. That made it possible to perform the experiments Ebbinghaus did. For example, he compared the effects of a test for retention 24 hours after learning compared with a test 48 hours after learning for two different sets of nonsense syllables of equivalent difficulty.

In fact, however, the subsequent history of experimentation with nonsense syllables showed that Ebbinghaus expected too much of them. They are not devoid of meaning, and they are most certainly not uniform in difficulty. Therefore, much experimental work was subsequently devoted to finding out how meaningful they are and just how they do differ from ordinary words in meaning and difficulty. These attempts led to systematic efforts to measure the important characteristics for learning of *all* kinds of verbal material. These efforts provide us with calibration of many aspects of language, all of which are important for verbal material. At the same time, from these investigations it became clear that it is not easy, or even possible, to draw a clear line between material that can be characterized as "nonsense" and that which can be called "meaningful." Indeed, the whole study of the range of verbal materials from arbitrary three-letter combinations to real words in real sentences gives us a great deal of information about what the structure of real language is like and how that structure is important in verbal learning.

Some appreciation of the kinds of calibration that are possible can be achieved by considering some of the ways in which nonsense syllables can differ from one another and from ordinary words. One of these is in *meaningfulness*. For reasons that will be more apparent later, experimental students of verbal learning have considered meaningfulness to be revealed by the sheer number of associations that any given nonsense syllable (or real word, for that matter) is likely to elicit in an individual. Consider the difference between XYH and LYP. Both are nonsense syllables, but the second elicits more associations than does the first; therefore, it is more meaningful.

Nonsense syllables also differ in the specific associations they elicit. Consider the different responses that are likely to be made to the pair LYP and SOK, both highly meaningful nonsense syllables. A third way in which nonsense syllables can differ from one another is in the frequency with which the separate letters go together in the language at large. The sequence of letters XYH, for example, is a very rare one in ordinary English, while the sequence WEL, itself not a word, occurs as a part of many English words.

These differences between nonsense syllables are like similar differences between real words, so it is not very efficient to describe the calibration of nonsense syllables as something distinct from the calibration of verbal materials generally, even though many of the older accounts of verbal learning tend to do so. If we do understand that nonsense syllables differ enormously from one another, we are ready to move on to a general account of the calibration of verbal materials.

THE CALIBRATION OF VERBAL MATERIALS

MEANINGFULNESS.   The earliest attempt to calibrate the meaningfulness or association value of CVC nonsense syllables is in a study by Glaze (1928). Glaze simply exposed a large number of nonsense syllables to subjects one at a time and asked these subjects to indicate whether or not that syllable produced an association for them. Glaze's procedure was quite casual, and he used only 15 subjects. Perhaps as a testimony to the importance of the measurement of meaningfulness or association value is the fact that despite the methodological defects of Glaze's study, his measurements have proved to be reliable and important predictors of various measures of learning. The percentage of subjects reporting an association for any given nonsense syllable predicts how easily that nonsense syllable may be combined with other syllables in learning. We shall deal with the studies of learning at length later; suffice it to say now that, in general, it takes many more trials or repetitions for the typical subject to learn a list of nonsense syllables which Glaze's subjects reported as producing few or no associations than a list which they said produced many associations.

Since association value or meaningfulness has been an important predictor of learning, there have been several attempts since Glaze to provide more adequate calibration. One of the most extensive of these is a study by Archer (1960).

Archer examined the meaningfulness of all possible three-letter combinations of the CVC type in the Roman alphabet. As Glaze did, Archer asked his subjects simply to indicate whether or not a particular syllable was meaningful. The subjects were told to ask themselves the following questions: "Is it a word? Does it sound like a word? Does it remind me of a word? Can I use it in a sentence?" If the answer was yes to these questions, the subjects were supposed to indicate an association for that syllable.

Table 8.1 shows the meaningfulness, according to Archer's subjects, of some selected syllables. In Archer's study there were 510 CVC

TABLE **8.1**   **Association Value or Meaningfulness for Selected CVC Trigrams**
The numbers are the per cent of subjects indicating that a given syllable is meaningful to them. (Data from Archer, 1960)

TRIGRAM	% S's	TRIGRAM	% S's	TRIGRAM	% S's
XYF	3	DUJ	13	BUP	34
YEQ	4	BIW	15	LOZ	40
MYV	5	RUV	16	VOX	46
QEJ	6	TIW	18	QIN	50
NIJ	7	QED	20	MYR	58
WUQ	8	HOJ	22	BEK	66
GEX	9	BIQ	24	VIK	74
PYB	10	SIW	26	NEV	80
ZOF	11	DYT	28	DAT	90
NYV	12	TAZ	32	TEX	100

combinations that were the same as those used by Glaze and other early investigators. Over the entire range of meaningfulness, the values found by these earlier investigators correlated about .8 with Archer's values. That is a reasonably high correlation, but for a more restricted range of meaningfulness the correlations are considerably lower. Therefore, while the differences between very high and very low meaningfulness are important, differences between small degrees of meaningfulness probably are not.

A very closely related technique in establishing meaningfulness for a given verbal item is to ask people to give as many associations as possible to it in a fixed period of time. In most studies of this type, a word or nonsense syllable is given to a group of subjects, and these people are asked to list all the words associated with the stimulus item that they can in a one-minute period. Two examples are calibrations of two-syllable nonsense or real words by Noble (1952) and of three-letter nonsense syllables by Mandler (1955). Table 8.2 shows the number of associations given by Noble's subjects to some selected items in one minute.

These measures of meaningfulness predict rate of learning. For example, Figure 8.1 shows the number of items correctly recalled in an experiment in which students were asked to study, for either one minute or two minutes, some CVC syllables which differed in meaningfulness. You can see in this figure that there is a large variation in the number of

TABLE **8.2** List of Disyllables and the Meaningfulness Values for Them. The meaningfulness value is defined as the average number of associations given to each disyllable in one minute. (Data from Noble, 1952)

DISYLLABLE	*M* VALUE	DISYLLABLE	*M* VALUE
GOJEY	0.99	BODICE	2.80
NEGLAN	1.04	JITNEY	3.51
BELAP	1.22	PALLET	3.62
XYLEM	1.24	ORDEAL	3.91
QUIPSON	1.26	YEOMAN	4.60
BODKIN	1.39	KENNEL	5.52
ATTAR	1.71	INCOME	6.24
MAELSTROM	1.84	ZEBRA	7.12
ROMPIN	1.90	JELLY	7.70
JETSAM	2.54	ARMY	9.43

syllables correctly remembered as a function of association value (McGeoch, 1930).

SPECIFIC ASSOCIATIONS.   Another kind of information concerns the specific associations which occur to verbal items. For example, most people, when asked to say what the word *table* makes them think of, will say *chair*. Since a great deal of verbal learning consists of forming new associative relationships, the specific responses that a particular word will elicit at the beginning of learning are important. In later chapters we

FIG. **8.1** The mean number of correct responses during learning as a function of the meaningfulness (Glaze association value) of the items learned. (Underwood & Schulz, 1960; data from McGeoch, 1930.)

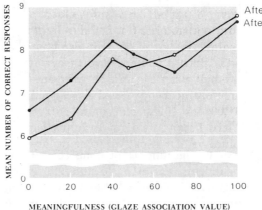

MEANINGFULNESS (GLAZE ASSOCIATION VALUE)

shall examine this problem of forming new associative relations in greater detail. For now, we need only note that there has been a large number of studies designed to find out just what responses do occur to specific words or nonsense items.

Among these studies are the norms for 100 ordinary English words collected by Russell and Jenkins (1954) and the less extensive information available on CVC nonsense syllables (for example, Mandler, 1955).

FREQUENCY.   Another important characteristic of specific verbal items is their sheer frequency in the experience of the average person. Again, it is possible to establish normative information which tells us how often the average person is likely to have seen or heard any particular verbal item. One of the most useful and extensive works of this sort is a count of the relative frequency of occurrence of ordinary English words. The count (Thorndike & Lorge, 1944) is based upon a large number of different kinds of printed sources, such as popular magazines, high school textbooks, etc. The total count lists 30,000 words in the English language, and it is based upon about twenty million words of text. These 30,000 words occur in frequency anywhere from once per million words to thousands of times per million. The distribution is a logarithmic one; that is to say, there are relatively few words that are common in the language and a large number of words that occur infrequently.

Frequency is a predictor of rate of verbal learning. One example of this predication can be seen in Figure 8.2, which shows the number of

FIG. 8.2   The mean number of words recalled in free recall as a function of the relative frequency (Thorndike-Lorge) of the words presented. (Data from Hall, 1954.)

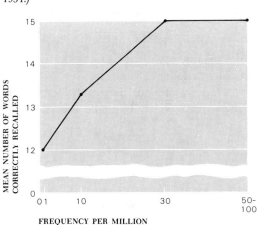

FREQUENCY PER MILLION

words out of twenty presented to subjects that could be correctly recalled after one presentation. The lists varied in frequency by the Thorndike-Lorge word count, and it is apparent that a larger number of frequent words are correctly recalled than infrequent words. Since, from the very beginning of association theory, sheer frequency of occurrence has been considered an important—perhaps the most important—condition for the establishment of associations, frequency norms or word counts have been basic to theoretical studies of verbal learning.

SEQUENTIAL DEPENDENCIES. Another aspect of verbal material that is important in learning is the sequential dependencies which exist between the items in ordinary language. It is very clear that in ordinary discourse, one word depends upon the others that are present, and the statistical frequency with which this kind of dependency occurs has been often investigated. It is one way of studying the internal organization of language.

Sequential dependencies occur at several levels of linguistic analysis. Take, as an example, the occurrence of letters in written English. Everyone who has read Poe's *The Gold Bug* knows that letters in English do not occur with equal frequency. The letter *e* appears more frequently than any other letter; consequently, if we were to guess at a missing letter in a passage of ordinary English, our best guess, all other things equal, would be *e*. Likewise, the occurrence of any given letter is influenced by what has gone before and what follows. Thus, *e* is more likely to be preceded by *g* in ordinary English than by *y*.

As we read or listen to someone, we use our knowledge of the statistical structure of the language to fill in what we miss and to predict what is coming next. When we read someone's poor handwriting, we can guess the obscure letters from the sequential dependencies that exist among letters in ordinary English. We make use of the fact that ordinary language is highly redundant.

The analysis of statistical structure in language is part of what is known as information theory or uncertainty analysis. Information theory has some very important methodological and theoretical consequences for the study of learning, and throughout the remainder of this book we shall have occasion to draw upon the analyses and ideas derived from it.

In order to make a complete analysis of the sequential dependencies within a language, it is necessary that we have a finite and, in general, rather small set of elements. The letters which make up printed English do quite well in this respect, so that we can study the sequential structure of letters in printed English rather easily. With only a little more difficulty, we can study the sequential structure of the phonemes of oral

English. In practice, there are many ways in which such sequential structure can be investigated (see Garner, 1962). We may, for example, investigate the predictability of letters, in continuous discourse from the other letters.

For the study of verbal learning, one method of investigating sequential structure has been particularly important. It is embodied in a count of the relative frequency of occurrence of various three-letter combinations in English. Underwood and Schulz (1960) counted the frequency with which every possible combination of three letters (trigrams) occurred per 15,000 words of printed English. Table 8.3 presents some selected values from this count. A common trigram, such as THE,

TABLE **8.3**   **The Frequency with Which Certain Trigrams Occurred in 15,000 Words of Running English Text**
(Data from Underwood & Schulz, 1960)

TRIGRAM	FREQUENCY	TRIGRAM	FREQUENCY
ABB	5	GST	1
ACK	31	IBB	1
ALE	14	IVE	114
BAG	3	LLY	47
BBE	5	MPO	10
BLE	70	NAL	33
DAP	1	NCE	77
DUC	21	ONE	126
EDS	7	SCL	1
ERS	115	THE	1,201
GHT	104	ZZL	3

will occur as often as 1,200 times in 15,000 words, while a rare trigram, such as TFI, may occur only once.

These trigram frequencies also predict the rate of verbal learning. Figure 8.3 shows the number of correct responses in 20 trials in a paired-associate task (see p. 291) in which the responses the subjects had to learn were trigrams of different frequencies. The number of correct responses increases with the increase in frequency of the trigram. This result comes from a large study by Underwood and Schulz (1960), but these investigators also show that trigram frequency is not as good a predictor of learning as a measure which indicates the subject's ability to pronounce these three-letter combinations. Pronounceability predicts better because trigrams do not take into account the syllable structure of the language. We know that the flow of language can easily be divided into syllables. While the criteria for deciding on syllable boundaries are not perfectly

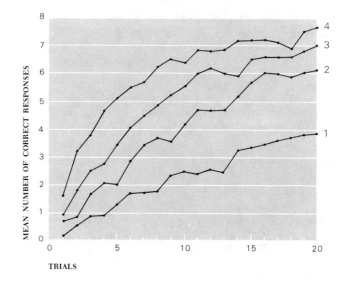

FIG. **8.3** The mean number of correct responses in paired-associate learning as a function of meaningfulness of the response terms, from low (1) to high (4). (Underwood & Schulz, 1960.)

reliable, the syllable is a real part of the structure of the language. For example, the sequence NDS, merely considered as a sequence of letters, has a fairly high frequency of occurrence, but it is not a highly pronounceable sequence. The perfectly pronounceable sequence TIP has a relatively low frequency of occurrence. Therefore, to be really an effective predictor of learning, sequential dependencies among letters have to take into account the syllable boundaries of ordinary speech.

Letters, syllables, and other more or less phonetic units of language are organized into meaningful units called morphemes and words. These morphemes and words reflect the sequential organization of letters. For example, a position in the middle of an English word is more predictable, given the other letters in the word, than the positions at the ends of the word (Garner, 1962).

Not only do words consist of sequentially predictable combinations of letters; they are also arranged in predictable sequences. If you see the word *the,* you might expect *people* or *reasons* or *car* to follow it, but not the words *for* or *communicate* or *electrify.* Furthermore, among the sequences that we might think of as grammatically possible, some are more probable than others. For purposes of the psychological investigation of the influence of sequential dependencies among words, various investigators have produced sequences of words which reflect different degrees of sequential structure. These sequences are called approximations to English (or to French) .

Approximations to English may be constructed in the following way. A particular approximation to English is defined by the number of preceding words which determine the selection of any given word. If we select words from the dictionary at random, we do not allow any preceding words to determine our selection—it is completely random. Such a selection would generate a zero-order approximation to English. An example of a zero-order sequency might be "pack byway phosphor kettle hypermetrical gloat." A first-order approximation to English results when words are selected according to their relative frequency in English usage. A first-order list of words would consist, by and large, of words that commonly occur in the language. In practice, a first-order approximation could be made simply by scrambling the words in ordinary English sentences. Obviously, such a list of words would contain more words like *the* and *before* than it would words like *hypermetrical*.

We could construct second-order approximations to English by giving a word to an individual and asking him to use that word in a sentence. We would then take from his sentence the word which *follows* the given word and give that to another person to make up a sentence. Then, by continuing the procedure for a large number of words and putting the words following the given word together in a list, we would have a list in which each word is statistically dependent upon the word which precedes it—in a word, a second-order approximation to English. An example of a second-order approximation is the sequence "was he went to the newspaper is and deep and." For higher-order approximations, an individual is given a sequence of words to use in a sentence. For the next individual, the first word in the sequence is dropped and the new word given by the preceding subject is added. If the sequence consists of four words, it results in a fifth-order approximation to English.

G. A. Miller and Selfridge (1950) developed the first orders of approximation to English. Other investigators have developed similar samples for English (Sharp, 1958; Moray & Taylor, 1958; Deese, 1961). Lists for other languages have been developed also (Taylor & Moray, 1960) . A sample set of approximations to English is reproduced in Table 8.4. You can see that the higher-order approximations appear to make a vague kind of sense—a sort of stream of consciousness sense. That is so because they preserve the dependencies of ordinary speech without having anything in particular to say.

Figure 8.4 summarizes some of the data gathered by Miller and Selfridge on the effects of orders of approximation to English on immediate recall. The curve shows the percent of words correctly recalled at each order of approximation after a sample of subjects had listened to

TABLE 8.4   Some Sample Approximations to English
Each list is 50 words in length.

---

zero-order approximation

OUTFLOW FESTOON SHEAVES CANNOT LUMINOUS VELVET TRACTION DETESTABLE MUSLIN INTERPOLATION CENTAUR AMAZINGLY VICINITY WOBBLE PRECLUDE MISCHANCE RECIPROCAL BANDBOX FRITTER BEAMING DIFFICULTY UNWILLING COOKBOOK BUFFER PLENARY TROUT VULTURE BARK STROKE NECKWEAR UNATTENDED BREACH WORTHLESS HELPMATE BLOT ARROW EXIST BLINKER CAPE PLOTTER EARNEST PRETTY PLAYFULNESS GREW GOSH PERICLES IDENTIFICATION SUBSTANTIALLY OCCUPANCY FORTITUDE

---

first-order approximation

THE THEN IS LAST LAKE THERE WHETHER INSURANCE BE THE IS INTO CLOSED WENT SIGHT HAD ORDER IN DUST COULD WHAT TERMS FRIENDS BOY A GOVERNMENT NIGHT OUR STUDYING SINCE DEEDS IT CAME A FIRE WHEN BALL SWIM AT WE WILL SHE WHEN THE OF IS TO CLOSED BE CAR

---

second-order approximation

IS THIS IS THERE THEY WENT TO GO BACK HOME TO SEE THE DOG IS A BOY GOES THE PICTURE WAS IS GOING TO GO TO CLASS IS THAT IS THAT IS THAT WHICH ONE DAY IS THIS COURSE OF MICE ARE THEY SKY FOR HER FRIEND OF MARYLAND WILL

---

third-order approximation

ARE SOMETIMES PROBLEMS OVERCOME ARE THE COLTS ARE A GROUP CAN DO ONLY WHAT IS THEY BOY MOUNTED HIS HORSE WAS A BOY JOE AND SAM CAME TOO WHICH IS THE GLEE WAS NOT THERE BUT I THOUGHT HE WOULD NOT BE HOME IN THE DRAWER STICKS IN DAMP WEATHER

---

fourth-order approximation

BELL WAS RINGING TOO LOUD THE NOISE DISTURBED THE MEN BECAUSE THEY HAVE NO LAWS IS NOT THE CORRECT METHOD TO DO THIS HE HAD LAST WORKED TUESDAY BUT NOT WEDNESDAY BECAUSE I HAD A NICKEL BUT THAT IS NOT RIGHT IN THE FIRST DIVISION SPLIT INTO TWO PIECES AND

---

fifth-order approximation

GREAT PEOPLE ARE HUMBLE BECAUSE THEY HAVE NO ELECTRICITY BUT WE MADE IT IS TOO AND ALWAYS WILL BE IN HIS ROOM BY HIMSELF SO HE HAD A COLD BUT WENT AFTER THE BALL AFTER DINNER WAS TOO LATE LAST TIME SO DON'T MISS WHAT IS BEING SAID ABOUT ME

---

sixth-order approximation

HOMES FOR PEOPLE ARE A NECESSITY CAN YOU DO THE JOB IF YOU ARE CAPABLE IS THE PHRASE SAID WHEN YOU WRITE ENCLOSE THREE DOLLARS BEFORE YOU REMIT THE BOOK READ THE RULES TWICE THEN BEGIN THE PROCEDURE AGAIN HE SAID SLOWLY SO ALL THE WORDS COULD BE LISTED IN

---

eighth-order approximation

AN AUTOMOBILE WHEN THE VALVES GET STICKY NEEDS THE PROPER TREATMENT IS OUT OF THE SCOPE OF OUR IMAGINATION COME OUR NIGHTMARES WHICH ARE OFTEN REALITY CONFUSED CAN INDICATE A LIVING INSECURITY FOR WE WILL BASE HIS SALARY ON OTHER FACTORS IF WE FIND IT TO BE IMPORTANT WE SAID

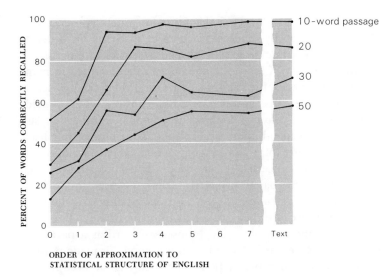

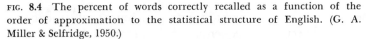

ORDER OF APPROXIMATION TO
STATISTICAL STRUCTURE OF ENGLISH

FIG. 8.4 The percent of words correctly recalled as a function of the order of approximation to the statistical structure of English. (G. A. Miller & Selfridge, 1950.)

these words from a tape recording. Notice that after the fifth-order approximation, there is little improvement in recall. Indeed, some later studies (Coleman, 1963) emphasize the existence of a slight decline in recall after about the fourth-order approximation.

In general, however, the organization introduced into verbal material by arranging words in statistically likely sequences is reflected in superior recall; the causes for such a relation will be discussed later in this chapter.

GRAMMATICAL STRUCTURE.   The statistical approximations to English are neither grammatical nor particularly ungrammatical. As we increase the order of approximation to a language, we do not necessarily make extended sequences of these words more grammatical. That is to say, the sequences which result from higher-order approximations to English are no more likely to be generated by the grammatical rules of the language than are the lower-order approximations.

The fact is that the grammar of natural languages is not purely associationistic. There are certain elementary forms in grammar which determine how words are used. We can easily recognize these forms in our mother tongue, even though pure nonsense may be put into the forms. "Gelax frimmaged a leble." That can readily be identified as a simple declarative sentence. It is not at all difficult to identify the subject, the verb, and the object of the sentence. Such nonsense sentences are frequently used by modern teachers of grammar in order to instruct children in the basic grammatical characteristics of English.

Since the grammar of a given language can be described in many ways, it is not easy to specify the relation between grammatical structure and verbal learning. There are, however, two basic notions which provide the most commonly used ways of looking at grammar.[1] Somewhat surprisingly, both of these depend upon assumptions about how people learn the grammatical structure of their language. One of these notions is relevant to our present concerns; it can be described as asserting that people learn equivalences based primarily upon position in ordinary sentences. Thus, the words *concert, meal,* and *baby* belong to the same class of words, nouns, because they can all fit into the frame, "The ——— was good." The identification of a new (nonsense) word as a particular part of speech in a sentence, as in "The barup was good," is made possible by the fact that "barup" occupies a position which can be occupied by other nouns.

The ability to produce and to recognize grammatical structures is not based on the detection of sequential probabilities; it is based upon the occurrence of elements in sentences which signal the grammatical structure. Words like *the* and *of,* suffixes like *ness* and *ing,* all serve as grammatical signals, and when they occupy particular positions in sentences, they serve to identify the grammatical structure of those sentences and all the parts of the sentences.

The occurrence of such grammatical signals would make sentences easier to learn and remember if they provided some kind of structure on which the rest of the parts of the sentences could be said to depend. The effect of grammatical signals on learning is demonstrated in an experiment by W. Epstein (1961). If you look at the two sentences under Category I in Table 8.5, you will see that the essential grammatical features of ordinary English are retained, even though nonsense material is substituted for nouns, verbs, etc. Category II presents the same nonsense material without the suffixes which identify grammatical position. Category III has no grammatical structure, and Category IV includes grammatical elements, but these are arranged contrary to the structure of English.

These sentences were briefly exposed, one at a time, to subjects, who were asked to write them down from memory. The numbers in Table 8.5 are the number of exposures (trials) required, on the average, for the subjects to recall the sentences perfectly. Notice that of all the

---

[1] A good source for discussion of modern grammars is H. A. Gleason, Jr., *An Introduction to Descriptive Linguistics,* rev. ed., New York: Holt, 1961.

TABLE 8.5 **Types of Nonsense Sentences Used in Experiments on Grammatical Structure and Learning. The number of trials to learn is the average for each pair of sentences of a different type.**
(After W. Epstein, 1961)

CATEGORY	SENTENCE	TRIALS
I	A VAPY KOUBS DESAKED THE CITAR MOLENTLY UM GLOX NERFS.	
	THE YIGS WUR VIRMLY RIXING HUM IN JEGEST MIV.	5.77
II	A VAP KOUB DESAK THE CITAR MOLENT UM GLOX NERF.	
	THE YIG WUR VUM RIX HUM IN JEG MIV.	7.56
III	KOUBS VAPY THE UM GLOX CITAR NERFS A MOLENTLY.	
	YIGS RIXING WUR MIV HUM VUMLY THE IN JEGEST.	8.15
IV	A VAPY KOUBED DESAKS THE CITAR MOLENTS UM GLOX NERFLY.	
	THE YIGLY WUR VUMS RIXEST HUM IN JEGING MIV.	6.90
V	CRUEL TABLES SANG FALLING CIRCLES TO EMPTY PENCILS LAZY	
	PAPER STUMBLED TO SHALLOW TREES LOUDLY FROM DAYS.	3.50

nonsense sentences, the one containing the grammatical structure of English was easiest to learn. The only sentence easier to learn was the sentence employing normal English syntax and common English words. Despite the fact that the same nonsense sequences occurred in all the nonsense sentences, those nonsense sequences embedded in sentences with normal English syntax were easier to learn. Therefore, it is clear that grammatical structure helps the retention of individual words in ordinary sentences.

OTHER PREDICTORS OF LEARNING. It should be clear by now that there are many ways in which learning can be predicted from the structure of the verbal materials presented to subjects for learning. In addition to those we have already described, there are such conditions as category clustering (Bousfield, 1953), associative clustering, and many others. We shall discuss some of these later, and we shall discuss the clustering phenomenon at length. Furthermore, various relations in meaning—that is to say, the relations between words and natural and social events—are important in the prediction of verbal learning. The various kinds of measures we have described thus far, however, give a fairly comprehensive idea of the ways in which the learning of verbal material can be predicted from the internal organization of the material. A discussion of some of the other predictors will be deferred for a more appropriate place. A good portion of the remainder of this chapter is devoted to the interpretation of the kinds of correlations between the structure of verbal material and learning that we have been discussing.

Procedures in the Study of Learning

We have examined the structure of materials for verbal learning. In this section, we shall examine some of the procedures for presenting these materials to people. Again, we shall try to review the empirical evidence concerning various procedures without, at this point, offering too much in the way of an interpretation of the processes evoked by the different procedures.

The simplest way of testing the effects of presenting verbal material, free from special constraints introduced by the testing situation, is provided by a recall test administered immediately after the presentation of the material. Such a test is ordinarily called immediate free recall, and we shall consider the consequences of a test of immediate free recall first.

IMMEDIATE FREE RECALL

The immediate free-recall test examines what someone has learned from a single exposure of verbal material. We simply ask people to tell us all they remember of what they have seen or heard. We do not ask them to recall it in any particular order or any particular way. Even so, as we shall see, people impose their own constraints upon the way in which they recall, and such constraint reveals some important aspects of the process of verbal learning and recall.

UNSTRUCTURED MATERIAL. The recall of unstructured or unrelated material can best be illustrated with an experiment on the recall of ordinary English words. Figure 8.5 is taken from a study of one of the most important characteristics of free recall: the probability of recall of individual items as a function of their position in the list presented to the subject. The material in this experiment (Murdock, 1962) consisted of unrelated English words with high frequency of usage. They were presented one at a time, and after the presentation of the complete list, the subjects were asked to recall as many words as they could in any order they wished.

The lists were alike except that they varied in number of items from 10 to 40. The results given in Figure 8.5 show a characteristic bow shape to all the curves. The items most likely to be recalled were those at the ends of the lists, and the probability of recall of the last three items did not vary much for lists of different length. The middle items of all lists were least likely to be recalled, so that there was a greater probability of recall of the first few items than the items in the middle. Notice, however, that the middle and beginning positions varied somewhat with the

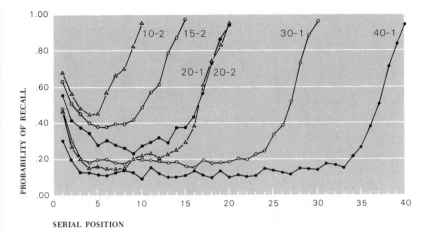

FIG. 8.5 The probability of recall in free recall as a function of serial position of items in the original list. (Murdock, 1962.)

length of the list. There was, for example, a somewhat smaller probability of recall of the initial item for a 40-item list than for a 10-item list.

These curves, called serial-position curves, are correlated with another feature of immediate free recall: the order in which people recall the individual items. Several experiments (Deese & Kaufman, 1957; Bousfield, Cohen, & Silva, 1956) show that the probability of recall of individual items and their order of occurrence in recall is positively correlated. From this result, and the curves in Figure 8.5, it becomes apparent that the most frequently recalled items are those that occur first in recall and last in presentation. The beginning items in presentation will, on the average, occur next in recall, and the middle items will appear in recall last. Thus, recall seems to be in order of strength; the strongest items are recalled first and the weak middle items are recalled last.

It is possible, however, to change this relation between the order of recall and the probability of recall. One way to change it is to introduce structure into the experimental material, as we shall see. Another way is simply to instruct people. Suppose, for example, that we compare the effects of asking people to recall unstructured material in any order they wish with the effects of instructing them to recall the items in the order of presentation. The curves in Figure 8.6 (Deese, 1957) tell the story.

In the experiment from which these curves were taken, subjects were presented with lists consisting of 20 unrelated English words. After some practice lists, an experimental list was given. Subjects were allowed to recall the items from this list in any order, and these instructions were

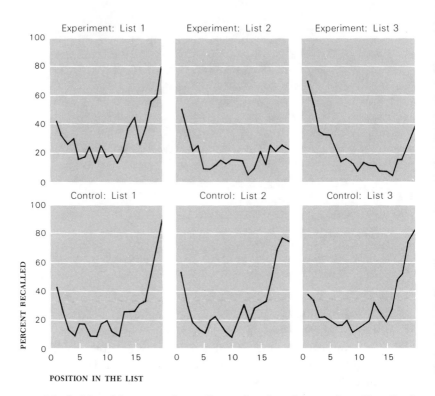

FIG. **8.6** Serial-position curves in recall as a function of instructions. Exp. list 1 is for instructions for free recall; exp. list 2 for instructions for serial recall after presentation; exp. list 3 for instructions for serial recall before presentation. The control lists are all for instructions for free recall. (Deese, 1957.)

given both before and after the presentation of the list. The instructions were repeated because, in this·experiment, it was necessary in the other conditions to give instructions for recall after presentation of the list, and there was a need to keep conditions constant. The results of recall of this list are to be seen in the first of the three curves in Figure 8.6. You can see that it is very like the curves in Figure 8.5. Next, the same subjects were given another list with no further instructions (so that they were set for free recall). Afterwards, however, they were told to recall the list in the order of presentation. The results are in the second curve in Figure 8.6. The major effect was to reduce drastically the correct recall of the items at the end of the list. These were lost while the other items were being re-called. The final curve in Figure 8.6 shows what happens when the in-structions for recall in order of presentation are given both before and after presentation. In this case, the subjects were set for ordered recall when they heard the list. Therefore, they were able to increase the recall at the beginning of the list, but the end of the list is still depressed compared with the first curve. The last curve looks very much like the curve that is obtained by the method of serial anticipation (see page 282), and we shall have something to say about the processes at work in this case later on.

The main point for our present purposes, however, is that there was a change in the total number of items recalled under the three conditions. When the lists could be recalled in any order, the subjects recalled about 6.7 items on the average; when they were recalled in serial order after instructions for free recall, subjects recalled about 3.7 items; and when given complete instructions for serial recall, subjects recalled about 4.2 items. Therefore, forcing the subjects to recall in serial order rather than in order of strength reduces the total amount recalled. This is a very general result, as we shall see; any time people are forced to recall in something other than an order of strength or availability of items, there is a drop in recall. It is probable that such a drop occurs even when organized material is recalled, though in this case the drop will be masked by the increased recall due to organization.

If you go back to Figure 8.5, you can see that there is an increase in total recall as lists are increased in length. The proportion of presented items actually recalled declines with an increase in list length, but the absolute amount of recall increases. There are two studies relevant to the processes in this increase.

One study (Murdock, 1960) shows that the number of words beyond the memory span in free recall is determined by the total length of time in presentation, rather than by the number of items. This result requires a word of explanation, because, for one reason, we have not yet defined the immediate-memory span, a measure of considerable importance in the study of human ability.

The immediate-memory span is defined as the number of items an individual can produce with complete accuracy after one presentation. For unrelated materials and for subjects of the sort typically used in verbal learning experiments (college students), the span is on the order of 7 or 8 items. This means that the typical subject can recall up to 7 or 8 unrelated common words in a single hearing. As we shall see later, this is a bit of an oversimplification, but it will do for present purposes.

Beyond the immediate-memory span, as the number of items in a list of unrelated items is increased, there will be an absolute increase in number recalled and a decrease in the proportion of the presented items recalled. Murdock shows that the critical condition which determines how many items are recalled is the total time in presentation. If you present a 40-item list and a 20-item list at the same rate (say, one word every two seconds) the recall will be greater for the 40-item list. If, however, we double the length of time between items in the presentation of the 20-item list, the recall for the two lists will be the same, since the total presentation time will be the same. Total presentation time is the same as the product of the number of items and the rate of presentation, so a simple equation will express the total number of items correctly recalled. It is

$$N = k \,(\text{length} \times \text{rate}) + M$$

N is the number of items recalled, k is a constant which will vary from individual to individual and from kind of material to kind of material, and M is the memory span.

It is not altogether certain why length of list and rate trade in the way they do, but one likely guess is that during the slower presentations, subjects can rehearse to themselves items that were presented earlier (Deese, 1960). If that is so, there ought to be an increase in the frequency with which words *early* in the list are recalled, and no difference for items at the end of the list as length increases or presentation time increases. If you look back to Figure 8.5, it is apparent that such is the case—for an increase in list length, at least.

STRUCTURED MATERIAL. We have already examined some data about the effects of structured material on immediate free recall—as when we looked, for example, at recall as a function of approximation to English. At this point, however, we need to make a more detailed study of the problem. For one thing, we need to consider a variety of ways of introducing structure into verbal material.

One way of providing structure is by means of free associations. In an experiment by Deese (1959a), 18 different lists of words were presented to subjects for free recall. There were 15 words in each list, and the lists differed in the degree to which their words were related by free association. Some lists consisted of words which were very likely to be associated with one another (for example, BLUE, SKY, BIRD, BUTTERFLY, MOTH, etc.), while other lists consisted of words that were totally unrelated.

The number of words recalled for the different lists can be seen in Figure 8.7. As the average interword association increased, the frequency of correct recall went up. Not illustrated in the figure but also found in the experiment was the fact that as the lists became more highly organized, the number of extraneous intrusions (incorrect words) in recall decreased. Furthermore, what intrusions did occur in the more highly organized lists tended to be the same from subject to subject. That was so because words which are themselves highly interassociated tend to elicit the same words from outside the list (Deese, 1959b); therefore, the "mistakes" in recall for the highly organized lists tended to be the same with

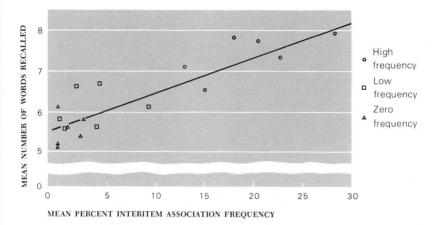

FIG. 8.7 The mean number of words recalled in free recall as a function of the interitem associative frequency of the lists presented. These lists were all either high-, low-, or zero-frequency associates to particular stimulus words. (Deese, 1959a.)

all subjects. One simple interpretation of these results is to say that recall is enhanced to the extent that subjects free-associate during recall. While there are some difficulties with this interpretation (Cofer, 1961), it is a plausible one.

A related effect is that of clustering in recall. Here the emphasis is not so much upon changes in the amount of material recalled as it is upon changes in the order of recall as organization is introduced into the list. Clustering can be based upon free association, or it can be based upon the conceptual categories into which some words seem naturally to fall. In order to demonstrate associative clustering, subjects are given lists of words to recall in which associated pairs occur (for example, TABLE-CHAIR, BLACK-WHITE, MAN-WOMAN, HAMMER-NAIL, etc.). The pairs, however, are separated, and the list is presented as a scrambled, unrelated set of words. The subjects are allowed to recall freely, and the result is that they tend to recall the associated words together in pairs (J. J. Jenkins & Russell, 1952; J. J. Jenkins, Mink, & Russell, 1958). Furthermore, the pairs occur together in recall in proportion to their frequency of occurrence as natural free associates. Therefore, once again, it appears as though free association enters into recall; this time in the form of reorganizing the order in which items are recalled.

Category clustering is best exemplified in a series of studies by Bousfield and his associates (Bousfield, 1953; Bousfield, Cohen, & Whitmarsh, 1958, etc.). In these studies subjects were presented with lists of words for free recall. The words fell into two or more conceptual categories: they might be, for example, all names of animals, chemical elements, vegetables, and occupations. In most of Bousfield's experiments, the lists were 64 items long and consisted of four categories of 16 items each. As in associative clustering, the items were presented in scrambled order, so that a word from one category was likely to be followed by a word from another. In recall, subjects tended to bring the words of a class together. The tendency varied according to the extent to which the words formed well-defined categories.

Bousfield points out that one of the principal determiners of whether any particular item in a free-recall test is recalled is what the subject's previous experience with that word has been. If it is a word that has occurred often in the past, it is more likely to be recalled than if it is new. In addition, argues Bousfield, there is a "relatedness increment." Words which are related to one another facilitate one another in recall, not directly but by arousing a supraordinate concept. Once the supraordinate concept is aroused, subjects are able to recall the individual items that belong to the conceptual category defined by the supraordinate. The important point which Bousfield makes is that clustering doesn't have to be direct; it can be mediated. That is to say, the grouping together in recall of related terms is not necessarily because they arouse one another, as in association, but because the occurrence of one word arouses a general concept to which the others belong.

Several questions come out of this interpretation of category clustering. For one thing, if this is the correct interpretation, recall should have many intrusions—intrusions which are relevant to the categories. Furthermore, clustering should be stronger when the individual words are more likely to elicit a general category name and, in turn, when a general category name is likely to elicit the particular items occurring on a list.

The latter question can be tested in the laboratory, because category norms exist. In them are found the various frequencies with which subjects tend to give examples of the classes. Thus, for example, the norms tell us that people are much more likely to say "horse" when asked for an example of an animal than "giraffe." The experiment by Bousfield, Cohen, and Whitmarsh (1958) shows us that the category norms predict the results of clustering experiments. That is to say, words cluster together more readily when they are frequently given instances of category items than when they are not. Such a result favors the interpretation of category clustering as the result of mediation by a supraordinate concept or category name. There is, however, a difficulty, for common instances of a category also tend to elicit one another by simple free association more frequently than do uncommon category instances. Therefore it is possible that some, if not most, of the grouping together of words in recall which defines clustering is the result of simple free association. That interpretation is further supported by a comparison of exhaustive and nonexhaustive categories.

In such a comparison (Cohen, 1963a), a clustering experiment was performed with categories of two types, exhaustive and nonexhaustive. The exhaustive categories consisted of sets like FRESHMAN-SOPHOMORE-JUNIOR-SENIOR, or NORTH-EAST-SOUTH-WEST. Nonexhaustive categories consisted of four words drawn from much larger categories, such as BEAR-HORSE-DOG-LION. As in the earlier experiments, words from several categories were mixed together and presented in a list to be recalled. Also, as in the earlier experiments, clustering occurred; subjects tended to group related words together in recall. But words from exhaustive categories were both more likely to be recalled and better clustered than the words from nonexhaustive categories. If a subject recalled three out of four words from an exhaustive category, he was very likely to recall the fourth. But if he recalled three out of the four words presented from a nonexhaustive category, he was likely to forget the fourth word.

The main result, however, is that these differences paralleled a difference in free associations. That is to say, words from exhaustive categories are much more likely to elicit one another as free associations than words from nonexhaustive categories. In fact, this seems to be about the only psychological way in which one can define the difference between these kinds of categories. Exhaustive categories are simply more internally organized than equal-sized collections from nonexhaustive categories. Incidentally, words from exhaustive categories are no more likely to elicit a category name than words from the nonexhaustive categories, so the greater degree of clustering associated with the exhaustive categories appears to be dependent upon the readiness of these words to elicit one another in recall.

One final feature of this study deserves comment. No matter how the categories are arranged, subjects tend to recall about the same number of categories (Cohen, 1963a; 1963b). If total presentation time is controlled, 20 *categories* are about as well recalled as 20 unrelated words, even though each category consists of four words. Such a result implies that subjects can recall a constant amount of material, but that the organization within the categories enables subjects to recover more individual items from free association and similar processes in the case of the categorized lists.

CHUNKING.   In making such an interpretation, Cohen drew upon an extremely influential notion in the study of recall: the notion of chunking (Miller, 1956). This concept implies that people have fixed capacities for memorizing. The fixed memory span is a measure of that capacity upon one exposure to verbal material; after a single exposure, the average college student can recall about seven "chunks" of information.

Why is it, then, that people can produce many more individual words in recall, say, for higher orders of approximation to English than for lower orders? Miller argues that it is because people recode information into chunks. A sentence is not just a string of words. It is a sequence that is organized by a few grammatical rules and held together by some relations in meaning and association. In order to remember a sentence, we may need only to remember a few key words and the general form (the phrase structure) of the sentence. From these we can reconstruct the entire sentence. Mnemonic devices provide other means for introducing organization into material and hence increasing the number of words per chunk. If the memory span is limited to seven chunks, then whenever we recall more than seven words after a single hearing, it is because there is enough internal predictability or structure within the collection of words to enable us to reconstruct some of them from those we actually remember.

There are many facts about immediate recall that fit with this view. Take, for example, the comparison of recall of zero-order approximations with recall of English and first-order approximations. If you go back and look at Figure 8.4, you will discover that the largest difference between any adjacent orders in recall is between zero and first. Zero-order approximations consist of lists of words selected at random from the dictionary, and first-order lists consist of words selected according to their frequency of use in ordinary speech but listed in a random mixed-up order. There are two major differences between zero and first-order lists. Zero-order lists consist, by and large, of very exotic and rare words (most entries in dictionaries are rare words), whereas first-order lists consist of mundane everyday words. Also, it is very unusual to see words repeated in any zero-order list; they would only be repeated to the extent that, by chance, you would hit the same item in random search through the dictionary. First-order lists, on the other hand, have many repetitions within lists of common words such as *the* and *and*.

In one study of the recall of first- and zero-order approximations (Deese, 1961), when subjects were presented with lists 50 items long, they could remember an average of 7.9 words from zero-order lists and an average of 12.7 words from first-order lists. This is a difference of 4.8 words. The difference can be understood when we consider what happened when the recall protocols were scored against the wrong list. There were 10 different first-order and 10 different zero-order lists. Therefore, it was possible to score a given subject's recall not only by comparing it with the list he heard but by comparing it with another list selected at random. For the zero-order lists, practically no words are the same from list to list, so if a recall record is scored against the wrong list the result is that no words are "correct." That is not true for first-order lists, however. If we score the recall of a first-order list against another first-order list selected at random, there will be an appreciable number of the same words in both the recall and the list; even by such a misscoring there will be quite a few "correct" words in recall. In fact, in this study there was an average of 4.6 words "correct" for misscoring of the recall of first-order lists. These were nearly all common words such as *the*. The number correct by this misscoring procedure is almost precisely the difference in recall between the zero and first orders of approximation. Therefore, it leads to a simple interpretation of the difference in recall between first and zero orders as a kind of guessing. Subjects do not need to remember the specific common words they have heard in a first-order approximation. All they need know is that there are a certain number of *the*'s, *and*'s, and *but*'s in the list presented to them; therefore, these should be added to the list of words in recall. In fact, one or two subjects always go about systematically listing these common words at the beginning of their recall lists.

In a word, the correctness of recall can be increasing simply by guessing words which, from the structure of the lists, the subject knows ought to be there. When the effort of this guessing or reconstruction is eliminated, the number of unrelated words in first-order lists correctly recalled is just about what it is in zero-order lists, which come close to measuring the memory span without chunking.

In a closely related experiment (Tulving & Patkau, 1962), some attempt was made to discover how subjects recalled more of higher orders of approximation by chunking material into longer units. There is no foolproof way of discovering just what the chunks are in the recall of sequentially dependent (higher-order) lists, but Tulving and Patkau, drawing upon the work of Postman and Adams (1960), used the number of words correctly recalled *in an unbroken sequence* as a measure of the size of a chunk. When the unbroken sequence is adopted as the unit rather than the single word, there is very little change in the *number* of chunks recalled as order of approximation is increased. For zero-, second-, fourth-, and sixth-order approximations, and real English textual material, subjects recalled from five to six chunks for each order. What did change was the number of words in a sequence. At zero order the chunk was one word, but in higher orders it consisted of several words. If you have to remember the three words *monsoon sheaves glitter,* you must remember each one; but if you have to remember the three words *many people have,* one word can arouse the others. Therefore, it seems to be very likely that whatever advantage is introduced in recall by statistical structure is the result of *prior* experience with that material. In a word, the advantage of structure is the result of transfer of training.

REPEATED TRIALS AND FREE RECALL. One experiment on repeated trials in free recall compares three conditions (Waugh, 1961). In all these conditions, lists of unrelated words were flashed on a screen before the subjects. After each exposure, the subjects recalled as many words as they could. In one condition subjects were supposed to recall in serial order, and in the other two conditions they were allowed to recall the lists in any order they saw fit. For one of the free-recall conditions, however, the order of words in the lists was varied from exposure to exposure, while in the other condition it was kept constant from trial to trial.

Figure 8.8 shows the mean number of words correctly recalled regardless of position under all three conditions. Notice that the curve under serial instructions is a straight line; that is to say, the same number of words is added to the recall score by each additional exposure. For free recall there is curvature; subjects did better on the first few trials under free recall, but by the sixth trial, they were doing better under serial instructions. Therefore, there is some initial advantage in free recall for the first few trials, but that advantage is lost as learning progresses.

These results, together with others (Waugh, 1962), led the experimenter to the view that people learn the same number of new items each time a list is recalled. The decreasing addition to recall for the later trials in free recall is an artifact of list length—of the fact that there are a finite and, in general, rather small number of items to be learned. In short, Waugh argues, the learning curve for the recall of unrelated verbal items

FIG. **8.8** The mean number of words recalled as a function of trials for free recall (with words either varied or in constant order from trial to trial) and for serial recall. (Waugh, 1961.)

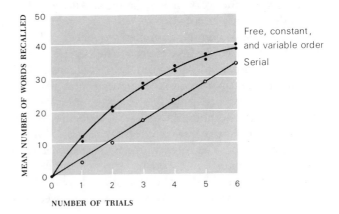

can be considered a kind of a cumulation of memory spans. Each repetition allows the subject to add a constant number of new words. No provision is made in this view for forgetting between trials or for the possibility that a given word may be gradually strengthened by repeated exposures, so perhaps the analysis made by Waugh is too simple.

What about the curvature in the increase in recall with repeated exposures and free-recall instructions? Is it possible that serial ordering provides a certain structure to the material which prevents forgetting or interference in later exposures? When recalling in no particular order, a person may not be able to remember whether something has been left out or not. Consider what would happen if the instructor checked the roll simply by reading names at random out of the roll book. He would have a hard time remembering whether he had read a certain name or not. But going down the roll in alphabetic or some other systematic order makes it very difficult to skip someone's name.

One other comparison will help explain the process in the cumulative effects provided by repeated exposures: a comparison between the effects of repeated exposure on free recall and the effects of repeated exposure on the ability to arrange the items in serial order. In two experiments (Horowitz, 1961; Carterette, 1963), the free recall of some consonant nonsense syllables was compared with the ordering of these same items. In ordinary serial recall, the subject must not only remember the order of the items but he must remember the specific composition of the items as well. In the ordering technique used by Horowitz and Carterette, the memory for order is divorced from the memory for specific items. On each trial the subject is presented with the list of items. He is then given a randomly arranged deck of cards with one item printed on each card and is told to arrange the items in the order he saw them during presentation. On the next trial, he is presented with the list in the same order and given the deck of cards, well shuffled, from which he tries once again to reconstruct the order in which he saw the items. The procedure continues until the subject can correctly order all the items.

In these experiments, free recall and ordering were compared for two different lists. One list consisted of nonsense syllables composed of only 4 different letters. Since there were 12 syllables with 3 letters each, there was a lot of duplicate use of letters. For example, two sample items were XSF and SFX. The other list consisted also of 12 syllables, but this time there were 12 different consonants used, so there was considerably less duplication necessary for the 36 letters. The free recall for these lists can be seen in Figure 8.9, taken from Carterette's study (the results were identical in Horowitz's study). Notice that, as in Waugh's experiment, the learning curve for free recall is not straight. Also notice that, while the list with many duplications starts out with superior recall, it doesn't show much improvement, so the list with few duplications produces superior performance after 10 or so trials. The superiority early in practice for the list with many duplications is because guessing results in greater accuracy when there are only 4 possible letters to choose from. Perhaps because there is a great deal of interference or confusion between the highly duplicated syllables, however, learning for this list is slower. For ordering, the curves are more or less straight (Figure 8.10). Also, there is a consistent superiority in rate of improvement for the list containing items with few duplications. These items are much more discriminable, and this factor seems to be particularly important in the serial ordering task, in which subjects must discriminate among the items in order to place them correctly.

STRUCTURE AND REPEATED TRIALS. Finally, another study of the cumulative effects of practice in free recall makes one important and very general point. It is that the ease of free recall of any material is not determined by the characteristics of the individual items *as such* so much as it is by the characteristics of the entire *set* of items presented for free recall. The same word in two different lists could conceivably produce vastly different effects, because that word could have very different relations to other items in one list than it would in the other. We have just seen that

FIG. **8.9** The mean number of words recalled in free recall of lists high in similarity (many duplications) compared with those recalled from lists low in similarity (few duplications). (Data from Carterette, 1963.)

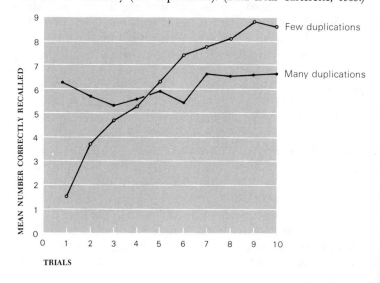

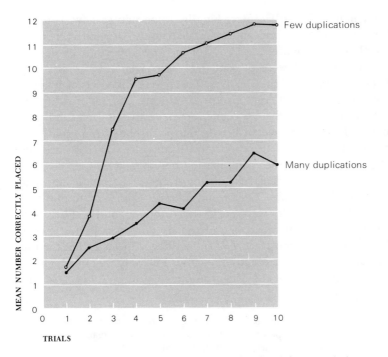

FIG. **8.10** The mean number of words correctly placed in an ordering task for lists high in similarity (many duplications) compared with those low in similarity (few duplications). (Data from Carterette, 1963.)

the duplication of letters in nonsense syllables determines the rate of learning of those syllables, not because one set of letters is inherently different from another but because the two sets of letters have very different internal structures.

This general point is made in a book by Garner (1962), and it is illustrated in an experiment by Whitman and Garner (1962). The point of the experiment is to show that the form of the internal relations among items to be learned is just as important as the amount of relation between the items. In other words, the study shows that it isn't sufficient to say that some material is more structured or organized than other material; we must describe the nature of the organization in order to know how rapidly or slowly that material will be learned.

The items in this experiment consisted of all possible combinations of a set of abstract forms. These forms can be seen in Figure 8.11; here you can see that there are three different kinds of shapes: squares, triangles, and circles. The shapes have a break on one side and no break at all on the other side; there are two dots with some figures, one with others, and none with still others. Finally, some figures have two lines through them, some have one, and some have none. Altogether, there was a total of 81 possible figures ($3 \times 3 \times 3 \times 3$). The important point, however, is that not all 81 were presented to any given subject for recall; each subject saw only 9 of these figures. There were three sets of 9 figures, each presented to three different groups of subjects. One set of figures was completely uncorrelated: there was one representative of each condition—one figure with one dot, one with two, one with none; one square, one triangle, one circle, etc. A little reflection will convince you that since there were only 9 figures in all, each combination had to be a unique one. That is to say, if the two dots occurred with the triangle, they could not occur with the circle or the square. The second subset was selected to that three of the six pairs of variables were perfectly correlated, and a third subset of figures was selected in which one of the six pairs was perfectly correlated. The other important feature of these three subjects is that the total amount of organization was exactly the same. The only way in which they differed was in the form of the organization; in subsets 2 and 3, some of

FIG. **8.11** Three lists of stimuli used in free-recall experiment. These vary in internal organization (redundancy). (Whitman & Garner, 1962.)

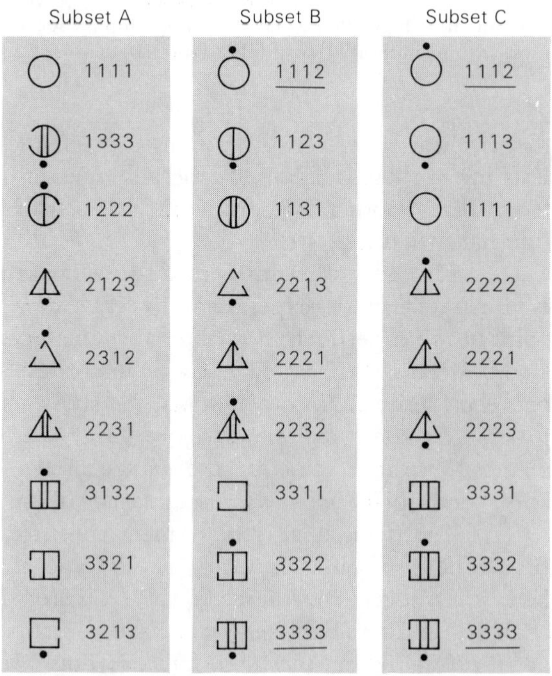

Subset A	Subset B	Subset C
1111	1112	1112
1333	1123	1113
1222	1131	1111
2123	2213	2222
2312	2221	2221
2231	2232	2223
3132	3311	3331
3321	3322	3332
3213	3333	3333

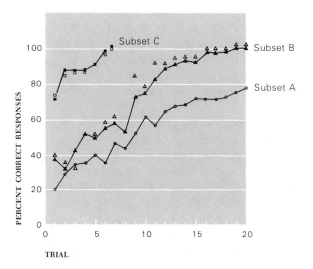

FIG. **8.12** Percent correct responses for free recall of the three sets of stimuli presented in Figure 8.11. (Whitman & Garner, 1962.)

the organization was present in direct, simple correlations between pairs of variables.

The percentage of correct responses in successive free recalls of each set can be seen in Figure 8.12. It is clear that the subset with no direct correlations was learned only with great difficulty. These results, then, show that if the set of stimuli is organized in a particular way (remember, all sets were equally well organized), it is easy for the subjects to reconstruct the subset and thus remember the items with a minimum of difficulty. In general, organization is easy to perceive and remember when it is based on direct associations or correlations between the elements of the set. If the relations are indirect or in the form of complicated interactions between members of the set, they are difficult to perceive, and as a result, subjects are apt to treat the set as if it consisted of randomly arranged unrelated items.

SERIAL LEARNING

So far, we have examined verbal learning when it occurs with a minimum of special constraint—the case of free recall. Learning, however, may be constrained in various ways, such as by forcing—not merely requesting—learning in serial order.

The earliest experimental studies of verbal learning were experiments on serial learning. Ebbinghaus (1885) used what has come to be called the method of complete presentation; that is to say, he spread the complete material out before himself (he always used himself as an experimental subject) before he began to learn. He would read each word once at the stroke of a metronome and try to make an association with the next item, so that when given any one item, he could *anticipate* what the next one would be. Thus, he learned by serial anticipation.

SERIAL ANTICIPATION.   Most studies of verbal learning make use of the technique of anticipatory prompting. One word is exposed at a time in a particular variety of teaching machine called a memory drum (see Figure 8.13). In serial-anticipation learning, when the subject sees that word he is supposed to anticipate the next one. The memory drum controls the time of exposure so that the subject can have either a short or long time in which to try and anticipate the next item before it appears. Sometimes a blank space is interposed between each item. A complete presentation of the list of items constitutes one trial, and usually there is an extra space between the last item of the trial and the repetition of the first one on the next trial.

In the method of serial anticipation, each item serves as a stimulus for the recall of the next. For example, the first item in a list might be the nonsense syllable syj. When the list begins on each trial, the stimulus for this syllable is provided by the extra blank space, and with the blank space the subject is supposed to try to anticipate this first syllable. The next syllable might be LOZ; syj then serves as a stimulus for the anticipation of LOZ. LOZ will serve as a stimulus, then, for the next item, say NEP, and so on through the list. If nonsense syllables are used, the subjects are

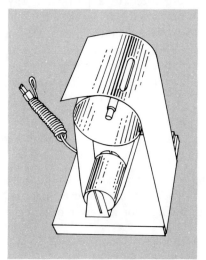

FIG. **8.13** A memory drum. The items are printed on the paper behind the shield. The drum does not move continuously but moves each item into place and then waits a brief time before moving the next one into place. (Courtesy of Ralph Gerbrands.)

usually required to spell the items, but if ordinary English words are used, the subject need only pronounce them.

Table 8.6 shows the results for one subject of an experiment on rote serial learning by the method of anticipation. The columns give the 12 items (nonsense syllables) in the list; the rows represent successive trials. The zeros indicate either a failure to anticipate an item or an error, and the pluses represent correct anticipations. In some experiments we may want to record the actual errors made by subjects when they anticipate incorrectly.

The first time through the list, of course, the subject cannot anticipate any of the responses. Notice that on the second trial, this subject guessed at the first syllable and got it right. On the third trial, he correctly anticipated the first syllable, the second syllable, and the last syllable. On the nineteenth and twentieth trials, he anticipated all the syllables correctly; most experimental studies carry subjects to a criterion of two correct trials in a row.

THE SERIAL-POSITION EFFECT.   This table also illustrates the most striking, stable, and thoroughly studied characteristic of rote serial learning: the serial-position effect. The serial-position effect can be seen in Figure 8.14, which shows the total number of correct responses made by this subject at each position in the list. While the curve is limited to data from only one subject, there are countless experiments in the literature

FIG. 8.14   The serial-position curve for the data on serial anticipation in Table 8.6.

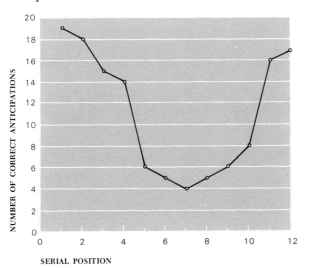

SERIAL POSITION

TABLE 8.6 The Subject's Record Sheet from a Serial-learning Experiment

TRIAL	CEX	MOQ	RUY	GAF	LIQ	KOC	QUZ	DEJ	TAH	WOG	FIK	VUS	NUMBER CORRECT
1	0	0	0	0	0	0	0	0	0	0	0	0	0
2	+	0	0	0	0	0	0	0	0	0	+	+	3
3	+	+	0	0	0	0	0	0	0	0	0	+	3
4	+	+	0	+	0	0	0	0	0	0	+	0	4
5	+	+	0	+	0	0	0	0	0	0	0	+	4
6	+	+	+	+	0	0	0	0	0	0	+	0	5
7	+	+	+	0	0	0	0	0	0	0	+	+	5
8	+	+	+	0	0	0	0	0	0	0	+	+	5
9	+	+	+	+	0	0	0	0	0	0	+	+	6
10	+	+	+	+	0	0	0	+	0	+	+	+	8
11	+	+	+	+	0	0	0	0	0	0	0	+	5
12	+	+	+	+	0	0	0	+	0	+	+	+	8
13	+	+	+	+	0	0	0	0	0	+	+	+	8
14	+	+	+	+	+	0	0	0	+	0	+	+	8
15	+	+	+	0	+	0	0	0	+	0	+	+	7
16	+	+	+	+	+	+	+	0	+	0	+	+	10
17	+	+	+	+	0	+	+	0	+	0	+	+	10
18	+	+	+	+	+	+	0	+	+	+	+	+	11
19	+	+	+	+	+	+	+	+	+	+	+	+	12
20	+	+	+	+	+	+	+	+	+	+	+	+	12
NUMBER CORRECT	19	18	15	14	6	5	4	5	6	8	16	17	

which reveal essentially the same curve (see Hovland, 1938, for example). The easiest part of a list learned by serial anticipation is the beginning, the end is next easiest, and the middle is the hardest. Also, the curve is slightly asymmetrical. The serial-position curve is the same in form for meaningful material as for nonsense syllables (McCrary & Hunter, 1953; Deese & Kaufman, 1957).

The curve in Figure 8.14 is a total serial-position curve for all trials during learning. It is possible to obtain such a curve from a single trial by adding together the correct responses on that trial from a number of subjects. If this is done for the second trial (the trial immediately after one complete presentation of the list), we would have a condition analogous to that in testing free recall after one presentation of the material. Figure 8.15 compares an idealized curve of serial position for free recall with one for serial anticipation. These curves are roughly the reverse of one another; for serial anticipation the greatest recall is at the beginning of the list, while for free recall the greatest recall is at the end. We have already seen that *instructions* for recall in serial order, without forcing serial anticipation, produce the same kind of curve as serial anticipation. This is strong evidence for the fact that serial anticipation is actually the process subjects use in serial recall.

One experiment shows how changes in the structure of the material presented for *free recall* changes the serial-position curve from that characteristic of free recall to that characteristic of serial anticipation. In this experiment (Deese & Kaufman, 1957), the serial-position curves for the free recall of various orders of approximation to English were studied. These curves can be seen in Figure 8.16. Notice that for the zero- and first-order approximations, the serial-position curve is like the one for free recall generally—that is to say, the greatest recall is at the end of the

FIG. **8.15**   Idealized serial-position curves for serial recall and for free recall.

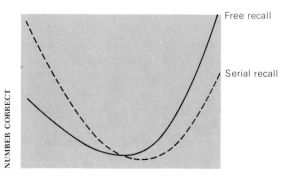

SERIAL POSITION

FIG. **8.16** Serial-position curves for free recall of lists of various orders of approximation to English. (Deese & Kaufman, 1957.)

list; for seventh-order approximation, however, the greatest recall is at the beginning of the list, as in serial anticipation. This difference is accompanied by a shift in the order in which words are emitted in recall. For the zero-order and first-order approximations (in which, you will remember, there is no connection between adjacent items), the serial-position curve looks like that for ordinary free recall, and the subjects did what subjects usually do in free recall—they recalled the last few items first, the first few items next, and the middle items last of all. For the higher order of approximations, the lists were recalled nearly always in the order in which they were presented.

Therefore, simply introducing some association between adjacent items seems to force subjects into the habits induced by English syntax; that is to say, they recall from beginning to end, more or less in order. The result is a serial-position curve which looks more like one obtained from serial anticipation than from free recall. We have already seen that serial recall tends to reduce the number of items recalled; consequently, the advantage that comes from the structure of the higher order of approximations is slightly offset by disadvantage in serial recall. In any event this comparison provides further evidence that what the serial-recall people do (even when they are not specifically instructed for serial recall) is very much like the process in serial anticipation.

THE STIMULUS IN SERIAL ANTICIPATION. One of the major questions that has occupied the attention of people in studies of serial learning is whether or not the stimulus for the recall of any item is the immediately preceding item and nothing else. That would seem to be a logical position to take, since in the method itself, each item is supposed to be anticipated on the basis of the stimulus provided by the preceding one. Some experimental studies of the effective stimulus in serial anticipation make the picture more complicated, however.

If each item in a serial list is the stimulus for the recall of the next, it can be said that the subject learns a series of discrete associations of the form A–B, B–C, C–D, etc. An experiment (Primoff, 1938) showed, however, that when the arrangement A–B, B–C, C–D is compared with the normal arrangement in serial learning, A–B–C–D, there is a difference in rate of learning. Doubling the presentation of items as in this arrangement slows down learning. Another investigator (R. K. Young, 1959) also noticed that when lists of words are arranged by pairs, learning is slower. Thus there seems to be something more to serial learning than each item providing a stimulus for the anticipation of the next one.

One possibility is that people learn to identify absolute positions or orders within a list of items. This was the point of view taken by Ebenholtz (1963), and he was able to present some experimental evidence which indirectly supported the position that people learn not just sequences of associations, but positions in a list. In one of his experiments, he showed that people transferred more readily from one serial list to another when the second list had a few items at identical positions as in the first list. Learning of this kind of second list was much faster than learning of a second list that had the same items from the first list placed at other positions. In this experiment, sequences couldn't have helped, because most of the items were new on the second lists; the subjects had to learn new sequences. Yet there was more positive transfer from first to second list if a few items from the first list occupied identical positions in the second.

Another aspect of what is learned in serial learning can be seen in an experiment (Horowitz, Lippman, Norman, & McConkie, 1964) which is the result of a "cluster" hypothesis about the effective stimulus in learning (Horowitz & Izawa, 1963). The idea here is that the effective stimulus for the anticipation of any given item in serial anticipation is not simply the immediately preceding item but some cluster or group of items preceding the item to be anticipated. Item E is a response to the preceding cluster A–B–C–D, not just to D. If this is so, one would expect ordinary serial anticipation to produce faster learning than the procedure which doubles each item (A–B, B–C, C–D, etc.).

In any event, it is fairly certain that the immediately preceding item does not provide the only effective stimulus for anticipation of the next item. The item's absolute position within a list also has an influence, and probably the sequence of several preceding items does too.

THE ANALYSIS OF SERIAL LEARNING. What of the serial-position effect itself? What causes it? That is one of the questions to which various investigators have addressed themselves for a long time. One of the best known of the older theories attributed the shape of the serial-position curve to the influence of *inhibitory* tendencies during learning. Learning of the items in the middle of the list was suppressed, it was said, as the result of inhibition produced by strong associations between the items at the two ends of the list. In fact, it has been known for some time that *remote associations* do develop as the result of serial learning. An item becomes associated not only with the item that immediately follows it but with other items at remote positions. That fact can be substantiated by giving a free-association test immediately after practice by serial anticipation. If you give the items used in the serial task as stimuli, subjects will respond in free association with other items as a function of their degree of remoteness from the item used as a stimulus (McGeoch, 1936).

Remote associations exist, but it is not clear how they are directly responsible for the serial position and other effects in serial learning. There have been several rather formal and abstract theories which have tried to incorporate the existence of remote associations into a theory of serial learning. Their argument usually embodies the proposition that there are a greater number of remote associations spanning the middle of the list than the ends of the list, and hence that the items in the middle are more inhibited or interfered with by the other items. No one of the various versions of this notion, however, has managed to explain all the facts of serial learning in a satisfactory way.

Current views of serial learning have been less concerned with remote associations, possibly because it has been possible to demonstrate the role of other factors in producing the serial-position effect. One experiment (Glanzer & Peters, 1962) has been aimed at an analysis of several factors in serial learning. The experimenters point out that there are three features which define the serial-position effect. These features all depend upon the existence of a gap in the repeated presentation of a list by serial anticipation. The gap is marked, first of all, by the fact that there is an initial item or position—the list must begin somewhere (and, of course, it also has a final position so marked). Secondly, the period between the end of the list and the beginning of a repetition is marked by the appearance of a gap, during which the subject is not required to anticipate. Finally, there is an associative break. Every item in the list is both a stimulus and a response, except for the first. The subject is not required to form an association between the first and last item. In several experiments, Glanzer and Peters tried to separate these factors.

In one experiment, they set the beginning-and-end feature against the other features. That is to say, they kept a gap between the first and last items, but on the first trial, subjects began with an item in the middle of the list instead of with the first item. This scarcely made any difference at all; the unusual serial-position effect appeared. In another experiment, these investigators varied the duration of the gap between the first and last items from zero to 16 seconds. This produced a considerable variation in the serial-position curve; and the longer the gap between the beginning and the end, the more marked was the variation. This and some other results convinced the investigators that the primary factor in the production of the serial-position effect was the location of a gap in the series.

Another experiment shows that the form of the serial-position curve, which has two components, is partly a matter of confusion within the middle of the list and partly something else. In this experiment (Deese & Kresse, 1952), subjects were given an ordinary list to learn by serial anticipation, but instead of the usual technique of pacing the subjects, they were allowed as much time to anticipate each item as they wanted. The subjects were urged to guess, but if they couldn't guess, the next item was exposed. Thus, there were two kinds of errors possible: an overt error (usually another item from the same list), and failure to respond. The results of the experiment are in Figure 8.17. Notice that the total errors are very much like an ordinary serial-position curve—the first and last positions are easiest, with the whole curve skewed or tilted to the right. The lower curve shows that this tilting is the result of the failures to respond. The erroneous guesses are almost precisely symmetrically distributed about the middle. But as the subject moves through the list, his tendency to fail even to guess increases until about the middle of the list and then stays about the same until the end. Therefore, it appears as though internal confusion is responsible for the peaking of errors in the middle, while something else is responsible for the tilting of the curve—perhaps the firmer anchor provided by the certain and unambiguous beginning of the list.

Finally, we can look at an experiment which produced a serial-position curve even though there was no serial learning. Jensen (1962) shows that the essential characteristics of the serial-position curve arise when there is neither serial anticipation nor temporal order in the presentation of the items. In one of Jensen's experiments, subjects looked at a *row* of nine geometric designs and then tried to reconstruct these designs from memory. The errors of reproduction produced a regular serial-posi-

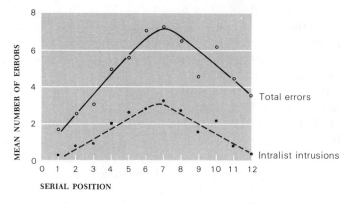

FIG. **8.17** Serial position curves for total errors compared with errors due to intralist intrusions. (Deese & Kresse, 1952.)

tion curve, identical in all its essential features to that produced by serial anticipation.

Do these studies add up to a clear picture of the causes of the large differences in rate of learning at different locations in a series of items? Certainly the Jensen experiment serves to relate these differences in rate of learning to some well-known effects in the study of perception and judgment. The ends of a list of items in serial-anticipation learning are like the perceptual anchors which define the beginning and ends of perceived series—such as the row of designs in Jensen's experiment. The ends of the series are perceptually unique and, therefore, marked for individual storage in memory.

If that is so, it ought to be possible to mark, by various means, other positions within a list as perceptually unique and thus to cause them to be individually stored in memory. It has been known for a long time that a unique item in an otherwise homogeneous series of items will be learned more rapidly. If, for example, a number is buried in the middle of a series of nonsense syllables, the number will be correctly anticipated on earlier trials than will the syllables around it. This effect—known as the "von Restorff effect" (von Restorff, 1933), has been the subject of much study, and the results of that study tend to confirm the idea that perceptual uniqueness is reflected in learning. For example, it is not certain that the von Restorff effect is purely the result of "isolation" of the unique item (Green, 1958), for the recall of other items changes also when a unique item is introduced into the middle of a series. In other words, introducing a unique item restructures the entire list to some degree.

A further study of the von Restorff effect shows that isolation simply causes the isolated item to be *emitted* more, without necessarily being emitted with greater frequency in the correct position (Saltz &

Newman, 1959). Therefore, the uniqueness serves to mark the item, but not necessarily to mark where it is located in the series. While the ends of the list provide more or less stable positions, uniqueness in the middle of a series may not.

Putting all these facts together, we can say that the first and last positions in a series have an advantage of being located in highly discriminable or isolated positions. The uniqueness of the first position provides better learning than the uniqueness of the last position because there is less uncertainty about where it is located. That subjects do have a considerable amount of uncertainty about the location of the last item, while knowing that the item *is* the last one, is shown by an inspection of individual records of rote serial learning. It very frequently happens that through the middle of a list on some particular trial, a subject will erroneously anticipate the last item repeatedly, finally getting it right when he reaches the end of the list. In a word, the subject gives evidence that he knows a particular item to be the last one but he is not sure exactly where the end of the series is.

The serial-position effect, then, can be described as the combined result of isolation of the end items, intralist confusion within the middle, and a general imbalance in learning in favor of the beginning of the list. In large part, that imbalance may simply be a matter of the uncertainty of location of the terminal position of a list or series of items.

Such an account of serial learning is sketchy and unsatisfactory. For so simple a problem, the serial-position effect has been surprisingly resistant to a thorough and workable theory. Yet if it is related to perceptual anchoring and other phenomena, it is an effect of considerable general importance. While some highly quantitative and rigorous theories about the effect have been attempted (R. C. Atkinson, 1957), nothing much more concrete can be said about the underlying causes than what is said above.

PAIRED-ASSOCIATE LEARNING

Except for the arrangement of elements in serial order, the patterning of verbal items that has been most thoroughly studied is that of paired-associate learning. The paired-associate arrangement has been important for several reasons. For one, it is commonly viewed as representative of the things people do when they learn verbal materials under ordinary conditions. Consider, for example, the learning of a vocabulary of foreign words by traditional methods. The essential feature is a pairing between English words and the words in the foreign language so that when a foreign word is presented, its English equivalent readily comes to mind.

The paired-associate technique has also been important for theoretical reasons: it is the model example of the associative process. One item of a pair serves as the stimulus for the response which is learned. In much of the contemporary psychological theory, learning is thought of as the process of acquiring new responses to stimuli. The stimuli are sometimes events in the external world and sometimes ideas or internal events which prompt us to respond in a particular way. Forgetting, transfer of training, problem solving, and concept learning have all been viewed as special cases of the associative process. Therefore, the study of discrete associations, as in paired-associate learning, has had some important theoretical consequences.

The traditional paired-associate method is rather like the familiar flash-card technique. The subject learns a set of paired items by anticipation. A stimulus item is presented, and then that item is presented together with the response it is supposed to elicit. The next time the stimulus is presented alone, the subject is supposed to anticipate the response before the stimulus and its response are presented together. The presentation of the stimulus-response pair provides immediate knowledge of results, and it has sometimes been described as a reinforcement in verbal learning.

An alternative method is to present the entire set of pairs and then ask for recall of the responses by presenting the stimuli one at a time. Surprisingly enough, so far as rate of learning is concerned, it doesn't seem to make much difference which way practice is accomplished (Battig, 1961; Lockhead, 1962). This result is surprising, because the method of complete presentation does not provide for knowledge of results or reinforcement until the entire series has been studied. Many developers of teaching programs have assumed that immediate knowledge of results is beneficial to learning, yet for paired-associate learning that does not necessarily seem to be the case. In either case, practice is usually continued to some criterion, usually two correct trials in a row.

WHAT IS LEARNED IN PAIRED-ASSOCIATE LEARNING?   One of the questions people have asked about paired-associate learning is whether or not the stimulus items are learned as responses, as well as those items which are supposed to be the responses. In other words, would people be able to give the stimuli associated with responses after a certain amount of practice by the paired-associate method?

The answer seems to be quite clear. People do learn the reverse relationships; subjects can recall the stimulus when presented with the response, though reversed learning is usually not quite so efficient as learning in the usual direction. This is equivalent to saying that in, for example, the learning of English equivalents to foreign words, people also learn to give the foreign words when presented with the English words.

The learning in the reversed direction is not quite so strong as the learning in the forward direction, however. Such a result is in accord with most learning theory (as well as with the older association theory from which modern learning theory stems). According to a strictly associationistic view of the learning process, we do not learn pairs in association, we learn to get from one term to the other by a process of one term leading to or, as the older theorists said, suggesting the other. According to this view, it is more or less an accident that sometimes people learn reverse associations—learn to give a stimulus when presented with the response.

Another view, only occasionally championed, is that associations are symmetrical. When we are presented with pairs, according to this view, we simply learn the paired relationship; it is only an accident of the usual method of practice that we are commonly able to recall better in one direction than the other. While this theory has never been widely accepted, it has been the subject of several recent papers (Asch & Ebenholtz, 1962; Horowitz, Brown & Weissbluth, 1964). The main point of these experiments has been to compare associations in the forward and backward directions by means of tests of transfer of training. That is to say, subjects first learn a series of paired associates; then they learn some task such that if they had learned the original paired associates in the backward direction, they will show transfer, either positive or negative (Harcum, 1953; Murdock, 1956).

A more direct technique of assessing the relative strengths of forward and backward associations is reported in an experiment by Horowitz, Brown, and Weissbluth (1964). This experiment did not make use of the traditional paired presentation of items. Rather, the subjects had to learn a structure of associations—one which would enable a test of the possible symmetry of associations. The basic structure is illustrated in Figure 8.18. Each letter stands for an item (in one experiment the items were nonsense syllables, and in another they were English words). The sequences that the subjects had to learn are given by the arrows. When presented with item A, the subjects had to learn to respond with C; but they also had to learn to respond with C when presented with item B.

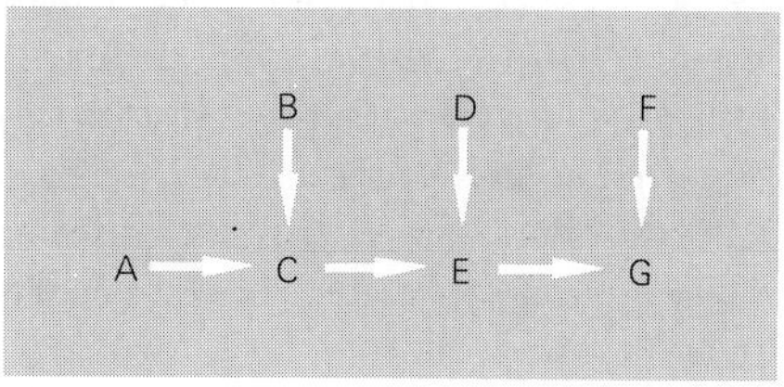

FIG. 8.18 The arrangement of items in the experiment by Horowitz, Brown, & Weissbluth (1964).

Furthermore, C was a stimulus for E, which was also a response for D, etc. Notice that C, E, and G are the only responses—the only items which subjects had to overtly guess. E and C are stimuli also, and they are stimuli as often as are A, B, D, and F.

After the subjects had received a certain amount of practice, they were tested in a free-association test. Of course C, E, and G were the most frequent responses subjects gave in the free-association test when they were presented with the items in the learning task. That was so because these were the items which the subjects had overtly practiced as responses. But what was more important, when C was a stimulus, it would elicit E no more often than E as a stimulus would elicit C—despite the fact that during practice, C was always the stimulus and E the response. Thus, the equal practice on the responses wiped out all directionality imposed by the fact that E was never a stimulus specifically for C. Even though the sequence in practice had always been C—E (E was the stimulus for G), E could elicit C in the free-association test about as well as C could elicit E. This experiment provides very strong evidence for the view that associations are, in themselves, merely pair structures. The apparent directionality is merely the result of the specific technique of anticipation during practice; in ordinary practice, one term is made more "available" than another, but that is because it has been practiced as an overt response while the other has not. When the sheer amount of overt responding has been equalized, the association appears to be perfectly symmetrical.

TWO PROCESSES IN PAIRED-ASSOCIATE LEARNING. This result seems to separate the process of paired-associate learning into two aspects: (1) the making of responses available and (2) the learning of the relations between the terms in the association. Such a separation is very much like a distinction between sheer frequency of responses (as in first-order approximations) and contingent frequencies or paired relations (as in second-order approximations).

In fact, however, this distinction first occurred in another problem: the separation of the process of paired-associate learning into two stages (Underwood, Runquist, & Schulz, 1959). The authors of this experiment viewed paired-associate learning as a combination of two tasks. First of all, the subject has to learn to produce the set of responses that are to be paired with the stimuli. In this stage, he may not learn that each response is to be paired with a particular stimulus; he simply learns what the responses are. If the responses are strange or unfamiliar (as are nonsense syllables), he may have to learn to "integrate" the parts of the items to be learned; he may have to learn that a particular nonsense syllable is QBZ and not QDZ.

Underwood, Runquist, and Schulz first demonstrated the functional importance of the distinction by showing that these two aspects of paired-associate learning are differently affected by variations in degree of similarity among responses. If responses are very similar to one another, the responses, as such, should be easier to acquire than if they are very different. Because of a greater degree of similarity, however, there should be more confusion among them when they are paired with individual stimuli. These authors showed that paired-associate learning was speeded by teaching subjects the particular responses (without pairing the responses with stimuli), and that such learning was especially helpful when the responses were very similar to one another. However, more interference occurred among these responses when they had to be paired with stimuli in the paired-associate phase.

Even when there is no pretraining of the responses, it is possible to separate paired-associate learning into two phases: (1) the response-learning phase and (2) the associative phases, in which stimuli are paired with responses. These two phases can be marked out distinctly in paired-associate learning by defining the first phase as the trials between the initial presentation of an item and the first trial on which the subject gives that item as a response (whether or not the response is paired correctly), and by defining the second stage as the interval from that trial to the first trial on which the pairing does correctly occur. Notice that the phases are defined by individual items. The response-learning phase may be very long for one item and short for another.

A series of experiments by Underwood and Schulz (1960) helps establish the functional importance of this distinction between the phases of paired-associate learning. While a particular response may be very readily available (and hence easy to learn in the first phase), that same response may be extremely difficult to associate with some particular stimulus. In fact, these experiments by Underwood and Schulz show that such variables as association value and frequency are mainly important in the response-learning phase.

Another technique (Horowitz, 1962; Horowitz & Larsen, 1963) allows the associative phase to be studied without the influence of response learning. In this technique, there are no responses to learn. The subject is exposed to the stimulus-response pairs and is then supplied with a form board which has all the stimuli printed on it and a packet of cards containing the responses. He simply matches the responses to the stimuli. After one matching, the pairs are exposed again, and the subject is given a second trial of matching. Horowitz (1962) demonstrated that if the responses are highly similar to one another, such matching is more difficult than if they are not, a result which is like that obtained by Underwood, Runquist, and Schulz.

OTHER ARRANGEMENTS.   Paired-associate and serial arrangements provide only two examples of the various kinds of structural patterns that can be employed in the study of learning. Other techniques are usually aimed at some special problem, such as the role of syntax in learning.

Consider an experiment by Glanzer (1962) which investigated the learning of triplets rather than pairs of items. This was done in order to compare learning items within a grammatical frame appropriate to English with learning the same items in a frame not appropriate to English. For example, compare the two triplets BIP—STRANGE—VEC and VOJ—AND—KEX. The first of these has a content word embedded between the two nonsense syllables, while the second contains the grammatical element AND between the two syllables. In an earlier experiment, Glanzer had discovered that in ordinary paired-associate learning, nonsense syllables paired with content words were easier to learn than nonsense syllables paired with such purely grammatical words as AND, LIKE, OF, etc. But in the triplet arrangement, when content words were placed between the nonsense syllables, there were fewer correct responses than when grammatical words were so placed. The reason is that triplets with content words have no apparent grammatical structure or syntax. The function or grammatical word placed between the two nonsense syllables begins to look like an English phrase (JACK—AND—JILL, VOJ—AND—KEX). Therefore the three elements are related to one another more easily, and learning is more rapid.

CONDITIONS OF PRESENTATION

In this chapter we have examined the influence of the nature of verbal material and various patterns of presentation upon learning. But we have not yet considered the various ways in which people can practice these verbal materials. The kind of practice is determined by the method of presenting material and by the strategy or attack people are induced to use on the material. In this section, we shall briefly consider some of these factors.

Temporal Factors in Presentation

When we considered the effect of length of list upon immediate free recall, we observed that, so far as the effect upon number of items correctly recalled was concerned, there was a kind of trading between time and number of items. We could increase the number of words correctly recalled either by increasing the number of items or by increasing the time allotted to each item. It is clear from such a result that time per item, or the distribution of practice time among the items to be learned, is an important variable in learning. Furthermore, a long history of experimental studies has taught us that not only is the amount of time per item important, but the distribution of total time between active practice and rest has a large influence. This problem, the distribution of practice, has been most important in perceptual-motor learning (see page 457), but the question has received attention in the study of verbal learning as well.

Therefore, there is a wide range of temporal arrangements in practice, most of which can be studied experimentally by pacing the presentation of the material to experimental subjects. Perhaps the most elementary of the problems that arise in the study of various temporal arrangements is how time is distributed among the repetitions or trials.

TIME AND TRIALS

If we have a certain amount of time to give to the practice of some verbal material, we can arrange that time in various ways. We can devote the whole period to one repetition of the set of material, or we can make each repetition as short as possible and have a large number of repetitions.

Two experiments establish the fact that for laboratory tasks, the effect of presentation time (generally, time per trial, X trials) is a constant. That is to say, it doesn't matter whether the total time in practice is divided into many brief repetitions of the material or whether it is concentrated in a few repetitions with a lot of time allowed for each.

One experiment (Bugelski, 1962) studied the effect of various arrangements of time in paired-associate learning. The stimuli were exposed on each trial for a constant interval (2 seconds), and the stimuli and responses were exposed together for an additional period of time that varied from 2 to 15 seconds. There was a constant time interval of 2 seconds between each syllable and between each trial or repetition of the entire list of stimulus-response pairs.

The results of this experiment are in Table 8.7. Notice that the group which had a total of 6 seconds per item per trial (2 seconds before the stimulus, and 2 seconds for the stimulus alone, and 2 seconds for the stimulus-response pair) took more than three times the number of trials to learn the list than did the group with a total of 19 seconds per item per trial. Notice further, however, that when time per trial is multiplied by the number of trials required to reach criterion, the *total exposure time* to reach criterion comes out to be roughly a constant. It took a total of 61.2 seconds per item for the presentation time of 6 seconds per item per trial and a total of 62.2 seconds for the 19 seconds per item per trial (though the latter condition took, on the average, only 3.3 trials to reach criterion).

TABLE **8.7** Mean Trials and Total Times to Learn Lists as a Function of the
Presentation Time of Pairs of Items
(Bugelski, 1962)

PRESENTATION TIME	TRIALS		TOTAL EXPOSURE TIME (SEC.)	
	MEANS	S.D.	MEANS	S.D.
6 seconds	10.2	4.1	61.2	24.3
8 seconds	8.8	3.8	70.1	30.4
10 seconds	5.8	1.9	57.9	19.0
12 seconds	4.7	2.5	56.1	29.6
19 seconds	3.3	1.2	62.2	22.2

The same constancy of total time holds when subjects are allowed to pace themselves (Bugelski & Rickwood, 1963). Total learning time does not materially vary when subjects are allowed to control their own exposure time for the individual items. If subjects go through the list rapidly, it takes more trials than if they go through slowly, but the total time to reach criterion is a constant.

DISTRIBUTION OF PRACTICE

A related problem is presented by the question of the distribution of practice. Here distribution refers to the way in which active practice is distributed around rest periods or periods of no practice. It has been commonly supposed, as the result of a long history of experimental comparisons, that interspersing brief rest periods throughout practice facilitates learning. Such an effect can readily be demonstrated with tasks that demand some motor coordination as the major feature of performance, and it has long been supposed that the same result must hold for verbal learning.

But a series of experiments makes the relation between performance in verbal learning and the distribution of practice much less certain than it was once thought to be. These experiments come from a systematic attack on the problem by one investigator (Underwood, 1961), who carried out a thorough analysis of the problem.

Earlier experimental evidence had suggested that short periods of rest were beneficial to learning. It was thought, for example, that for the learning of almost any task, imposing a rest of 10 seconds between the trials of practice would produce more rapid progress to a criterion. Beyond rather short intervals, the total amount of rest did not seem to be very critical, but a very few seconds of rest seemed to have a pronounced beneficial effect. As we have already noted, the experiments which resulted in this generalization were, by and large, experiments in which the essential task to be learned depended upon motor coordination or perceptual-motor relations. Very few experiments were concerned with the learning of patterns of relations among verbal items—the kind of activity, as we have seen, that is the defining characteristic of verbal learning.

Underwood's results show, however, that several matters are critical to the occurrence of any effect due to distribution of practice. Therefore, the generalization about the superiority of distributed practice cannot be applied in any simple way to verbal learning.

The most important characteristic upon which the distribution-of-practice effect for verbal learning seems to depend, according to Underwood, is the amount of potential interference between items during the response phase of learning. If the responses are highly similar to one another, there will be a beneficial effect from imposing brief rest intervals between trials. Therefore, for paired-associate lists in which the responses are composed of nonsense syllables compounded from a few letters, some brief rest intervals between successive trials will improve performance during learning. According to Underwood's analysis, the beneficial effects of distributed practice are a result of what happens during the response acquisition phase; they do not depend upon the way in which subjects learn to connect responses with particular stimuli during the associative phase.

The exact form of the effect of distribution depends upon an interaction between the internal structure of the material to be learned (the degree of response similarity) and the magnitude of the time interval allowed for rest. The effects, however, are quite small and of relatively little importance when measured against the influence of other variables in learning. In general, the greater the degree of internal organization within the material to be learned, the less the influence of distribution as a variable affecting learning. It should be noted at this point, however, that we shall have to return to the question of the distribution of practice during learning when we come to consider the question of forgetting.

Strategies of Practice and Incidental Learning

One of the most difficult problems in the study of verbal learning is the task of describing just exactly what people do when they practice some particular verbal material. Why is it that practice seems to be effective at some times and not others? We have already seen that the structural relations among materials must account for much of the variation we ordinarily think of in connection with the varying degrees of difficulty we experience in learning different things. Some things require more practice per unit-material because the material is unstructured; we cannot bring to bear our previous experience to help us in practice at the moment. Yet differences in material do not account for or describe all the variations in the difficulty of learning. Some of them are associated with the way in which we practice.

It is very difficult to describe, in any precise way, the kinds of differences that make practice on one occasion different from practice on another. In a casual way, we may say that we didn't learn something because we didn't pay attention. Such a statement is very difficult to evaluate, however, because we do not know exactly what psychological activities go into "paying attention." One series of experiments—experiments on incidental learning—describes some of the conditions that go into what we may loosely call paying attention. These experiments help to characterize the nature of activities during practice.

INCIDENTAL LEARNING

We learn some things without trying. The writer has never deliberately tried to learn the names of students in a large lecture course, but simply as the result of experience with some of these students he has (incidentally) learned their names. We can characterize all practice as being somewhere on a continuum between intensive intentional practice and casual incidental practice. Experiments on incidental learning are intended to find out what conditions make the difference between intentional and incidental practice.

While we concentrate on the study of incidental learning, our interest, of course, is in intentional learning. Comparisons between incidental learning and intentional learning are mainly aimed at finding out what we do when we learn intentionally. One of the main questions we would want to consider is whether or not the intent to learn is itself the cause of the difference. Postman (1964) came to the conclusion, after a thorough study of the problem, that intent per se has no relevance for learning. What differences emerge as the result of intent to practice are the result of specific activities during practice. Some of these specific activities have been uncovered by experimental investigations of incidental learning.

EXPERIMENTAL DESIGN IN INCIDENTAL-LEARNING STUDIES. There are several experimental methods for comparing incidental and intentional learning. One of these compares exposure of materials without specific instructions to learn with exposure and instructions to learn. The comparison is based upon a test for retention at some later time. Another technique is to give people something to learn, but while they are learning that material, expose them to other materials which they are not specifically instructed to learn. A test of retention compares performance with that of people instructed to learn *all* materials.

In the first instance, performance on recall without specific instructions to learn is compared with performance after instructions to learn. In the second instance, performance after instructions to learn just one aspect of the material exposed is compared with performance after instructions to learn all aspects of the materials. There are advantages and disadvantages to both methods of studying incidental learning. The second kind of approach is subject to possible interference from the cover task—the task that subjects learn under incidental instructions. The first kind of study suffers from the fact that the motivation of subjects under the two conditions is necessarily different. Actually, what we know about the effects of instruction to learn depend upon experimental analysis, first using one kind of design and then the other.

In virtually every experimental comparison that has been made, instructions to learn are favorable to learning. That is hardly a surprising result. What is more important is that different conditions of incidental learning produce different degrees of learning.

RESULTS IN INCIDENTAL-LEARNING STUDIES. Probably the most important difference between incidental and intentional learning is the requirement placed upon the subject by instructions to learn to respond to each element in a task differentially. For verbal material, this usually means that the subject must make some implicit or overt verbal representation of each item, a condition which helps set that item apart from all the other items. When, under incidental conditions, subjects are forced by the nature of the task to respond differentially to each item, the differences in results between incidental and intentional practice are drastically reduced (Mechanic, 1962). This finding is important enough to warrant a detailed account of the experiment.

Mechanic's study is also noteworthy because it shows us that incentive—which perhaps most people would think of as the most important condition determining the difference between incidental and intentional practice—is relatively ineffective in producing a difference. In this experiment, subjects saw sets of three-letter nonsense syllables. The conditions of exposure were such that some subjects were required to learn half of these but not the other half. The syllables were presented in pairs; the first member of the pair was to be learned by subjects under incidental conditions, while the other member of the pair was not. Also, as a cover task, the subjects rated both members of the pair for phonetic similarity. This task required the subjects to pronounce both syllables as best they could and, furthermore, to compare the syllables with one another—in other words, to respond to *all* syllables differentially, not just to those to be learned. In another condition, the rating for pronunciation was replaced by another cover task, one which would not require the subjects to try to pronounce each item. In this task, the subjects were to cancel certain letters in each syllable, while learning only the first syllable in a pair.

The results showed that the items for which specific instructions to learn had been given were better remembered, a fact which indicated that the incidental versus intentional instructions had been followed. The difference between the items learned intentionally and those learned incidentally markedly declined, however, when the subjects were required to pronounce the items and not just cancel letters in them. The simple act of comparing the pronounceability of syllables and actually pronouncing them enormously reduced the difference between incidental and intentional practice. Therefore, one of the things that happens when people learn intentionally is that they respond differentially to the items to be learned. Probably, as the result of a lifetime experience at learning, adults—particularly college students—know just how to respond differentially to verbal materials in a way to make learning very efficient.

In summary, intentional learning accomplishes its results by imposing different activities during practice; there is nothing special about the intent itself. It aids only to the extent that it causes people to impose modes of responding on material to be learned that they do not use for verbal material they do not intend to remember.

The details of the ways in which such differential responding works are surprisingly consistent with the above general statement. For example, by this interpretation of how intent accomplishes its purpose, incidental learning should produce not only far less learning of the correct responses, but also less learning of errors. An experimental investigation shows this proposition to be correct (Postman & Adams, 1957).

Perhaps the adage "try harder" should be replaced by "try again, but try in a different way." Ineffective practice, no matter how hard the effort, is like casual incidental practice. This is not to deny that motivation has a role in human learning, but it may not be the simple, obvious one. Sometimes the kinds of activities that make for effective practice are hard, and therefore an increase in motivation may produce more effective practice. But practice is not necessarily made more effective by an increase in motivation.

PART VERSUS WHOLE PRACTICE

There are a number of other possible questions about strategies in learning. One of the most thoroughly examined from an experimental point of view is the difference between learning verbal material by parts compared with learning the same material by whole. The question of whole versus part learning is one that has been attacked both for practical and theoretical reasons. While the topic has been comparatively neglected in recent years, it deserves mention here in order to illustrate the necessity of asking the right kind of questions in experimental investigation in order to obtain interpretable results.

First of all, let us consider the kinds of comparisons that are important in studying the differences between learning by parts and learning by wholes. If verbal material is learned as a whole, it means that the entire task is practiced at least once before any part of it is repeated. If the material is learned by parts, it generally means that the task is divided into two or more parts and each part is brought to some criterion before the parts are combined. In a part-progressive method, many parts may be combined by stages. For example, a set of materials may be divided into four parts; each part is practiced to criterion separately, and then the quarters are combined into halves and finally the halves into a whole. The efficiency of the processes in the various methods may be compared by measuring the total time required to bring all material to a criterion under the different conditions. Therefore, in comparing the whole with some version of the part method, the time (or trials) taken to learn the whole by the whole method is compared with the time taken to learn each part separately added to the time taken to learn to combine the parts into a whole.

The results of a number of comparisons between part and whole practice, measured in time to criterion to learn the whole, are disappointingly ambiguous.[2] Such ambiguity should not be surprising, however, for we have already learned that the major determiner of the speed of learning is the kind of structural relations existing within the sets of materials to be learned. Also, as Garner (1962) reminds us, the learning of verbal material depends on the relations between the internal structure of material and the relations that material has to verbal items outside of the set to be learned.

In one experiment, Garner and Whitman (1965) compared the speed of learning for various combinations of items which comprised either a complete set of possible items (given the elements used in the task) or various portions of the complete set. They also studied the combination of portions into the whole, so they examined the part-whole problem.

First of all, it should be pointed out, Garner and Whitman reversed the logic of the part-whole experiment in one of their comparisons. That is to say, they investigated the transfer from being able to recall the whole set correctly to being able to recall a portion. Intuition would say that this ought to be very easy, for after all, when one learns the whole one must also learn the parts. Yet for the method of free recall, Garner and Whitman were able to show that there was virtually no

[2] McGeoch and Irion (1952) provide a thorough review of the experimental literature, most of which is now quite old.

transfer from the learning of the whole list to the learning of an easy subset. It took people who had learned the whole list just about as long to learn an easy subset as it took people to learn the easy subset who had never seen any part of the material. There was, however, transfer from learning an easy subset to learning the whole set.

What do such results mean? They indicate the importance of organization in the material to the learning process. Consider what would happen if you were asked to learn by serial anticipation one of the two following lists: (1) NORTH, MAN, RED, SPRING, WOMAN, EAST, AUTUMN, YELLOW, SUMMER, BOY, BLUE, WEST, WINTER, GIRL, GREEN, SOUTH; (2) NORTH, EAST, SOUTH, WEST, SPRING, SUMMER, AUTUMN, WINTER, RED, YELLOW, GREEN, BLUE, MAN, WOMAN, BOY, GIRL. Intuitively, it is fairly easy to see that the first list would be much harder to learn, and experimental comparisons of the learning of such lists in different arrangements (the items, of course, are the same in the two lists) show that there is a large difference in speed of learning as a function of the structural arrangement within such lists (Weingartner, 1963; G.R. Miller, 1963).

Suppose one were to divide such lists into two halves by splitting them in the middle. The two halves of the first arrangement would be relatively difficult to learn. Furthermore, these halves would be difficult to combine, because there is no inherent organization which tells you, even approximately, which kinds of words belong where. The second list would be much easier to learn by parts, and would produce almost no problem at all to combine, once the parts were well learned. There would be possible confusion about where, within a set of four, a given word belongs (Weingartner, 1963), but there would be little or no confusion between the halves of the list.

Therefore, the part-whole problem resolves itself into the study of the internal arrangements of material to be learned. Whether or not it is sensible to split some task up into two or more parts depends upon whether or not the interrelations within the task are such that the splitting makes the task structurally simpler or more difficult.

9

THEORETICAL PROBLEMS IN VERBAL LEARNING

While it is important to know about the range of conditions that control the main characteristics of verbal learning, it is even more important to know about the processes that are behind these characteristics. Here we shall examine some of the theories about the processes, concentrating particularly on the theoretical work which deals with processes described in later chapters. Unfortunately, theories sometimes contradict one another, and experimental evidence does not always manage to resolve the contradiction. Even so, however, we learn something, both from the contradictions themselves and from the data that arise in an attempt to settle them. We may learn that we have been asking the wrong questions. Or we may find new ways of looking at the data of verbal learning which have practical and theoretical consequences.

THE EFFECTS OF REPETITION

One of the first questions that people ask about the process of learning concerns the effects of practice. Practice results in improvement (sometimes), but the question of how improvement is accomplished is surprisingly difficult to answer. In fact, most of the experimental evidence on practice is aimed at the simpler question of finding out in what way the improvement takes place.

The usual manner in which questions about practice are asked is to inquire about the effects of repetition. What does repetition do? The most common assumption is that each time we repeat a verbal item, we gradually "strengthen" its connections with the other items in the set of material being learned. It turns out, however, that the problem of discovering what repetition does is more complicated than we might at first imagine.

For one thing, we have the difficulty of making clear what we mean by "strengthen." William James, in his famous chapter on habit, stated that repeated practice gradually deepens the physical impression of a habit on the nervous system. Practice creates a well-traveled path in the nervous system, so that neural discharge can more easily follow one pathway than another.

Such a notion is extremely naïve and serves as much as anything else to remind us of the ignorance about neurophysiology that prevailed in James's day. In the end, however, more recent and more sophisticated views often come down to saying the same thing about practice; each repetition produces a little bit of change which is added to the change produced by the previous repetition. The implication is that the effects of repetition on any learned act are cumulative from one occasion to the next.

This kind of idea is very old; it is part and parcel of the classical theory of association. At the beginning of the nineteenth century, Thomas Brown stated as one of the "laws" of association the gradual strengthening that results from practice. When experimental investigations of learning began, they too emphasized the gradual course of improvement which attends practice.

Gradual improvement also appears to be revealed in the learning curve. If you ask someone to learn a set of paired associates, and if you chart the number of items correctly anticipated on each trial, you will find that the curve shows a general, albeit somewhat irregular, improvement. If you average the results from ten or so subjects, the curve will be fairly smooth and regular. Such curves of smooth, slow, and regular improvement were, for a long time, regarded as more accurate reflections of how learning took place than the irregular, up-and-down progress that shows in the learning curve of any particular individual. These average curves, it was said, were free from the influence of extraneous variables and chance irregularities which made the learning curve for an individual erratic.

Despite the wide acceptance of the notion of gradual and cumulative improvement during learning, criticism has not been wanting. After all, learning curves may be artificially smooth; the process, at the bottom, could be quite irregular. Indeed, perhaps learning is never gradual and cumulative; the notion that learning instead happens suddenly and all at once is one which keeps coming up in a variety of problems. It occurs in some theories about conditioning and elementary processes in learning, and as we shall see, it also occurs in the study of verbal learning.

The viewpoint that learning is never gradual but happens all at once is referred to, usually, as the all-or-none theory. The idea is that, on any one trial, learning either occurs completely for a particular item or doesn't occur at all. If learning occurs completely for that item, further practice will have no effect whatever, and if learning doesn't occur, that particular trial was worthless so far as that item was concerned. By this view, repetition only *seems* to produce gradual improvement because different items are learned on different trials. Such a viewpoint is quite consonant with the idea, stated in the last chapter, of learning as the cumulation of memory spans. It is also easy to see how such a point of view could be related to a theory of conditioning by sampling of stimulus populations (see p. 72).

In order to find out which of these views of the learning process is correct, one needs to construct an experimental situation in which the gradual-improvement hypothesis would predict an outcome different from that predicted by the all-or-none hypothesis. There have been several such experiments, and in this section we shall examine two of these.

Changing Materials and the All-or-None Hypothesis

One of the experimental tests of the question as to whether learning is gradual or sudden is provided by the method of changing materials. As it has been applied to the study of verbal learning, the method depends upon replacing items practiced but not learned by new items during the course of practice. This kind of test first arose in some experiments by Rock (Rock, 1957; Rock & Heimer, 1959).

THE NATURE OF THE TEST. In these experiments subjects learn lists of paired associates. On any one trial, the items that are not correctly anticipated are replaced by new items. The next trial, then, includes the items the subject remembered on the previous trial plus some new items that he has never seen before; of course, on each trial the total number of items remains the same. Again, after this trial, the items which the subject did not correctly anticipate are replaced. This replacement procedure goes on until he can correctly anticipate the entire list; on each trial a few new items are added, and these are the items he must learn. The list the subject finally learns may be very different from the list with which he started.

The critical test between the all-or-none hypothesis and the view which says that learning of each item is a process of gradual strengthening of associations comes from a comparison of the learning of such an ever-changing list with the learning of a list that remains the same throughout practice. Intuitive judgment would say that the changing list would take more trials—because, after all, the subjects must start from the beginning with the new items. If, in fact, there is no difference in the number of trials to criterion between such a changing list and a constant list, we could infer that the repeated exposure of unlearned items is of no value; there is no cumulative effect from these repeated exposures. An item is learned on the trial on which it is first correctly anticipated, in all-or-nothing fashion, and all the exposures of that item before that test have no effect.

The test, however, is a deceptively simple one. Let us examine Rock's experiment in detail. He begins with the proposition that repetition appears to be essential in verbal learning only because a limited number of items can be learned on any one trial (the limited memory span). Each trial allows us to learn a few new items, and after a number of trials that will depend upon the number of items and their inter-relations, we shall have finally learned them all. If it were true that associations are formed by a process of gradual strengthening, each repetition would add a little bit to the strength of association, and learning would not just depend upon the total number of items we have to learn but upon the number of times we had previously seen each item.

THE EXPERIMENTAL EVIDENCE. With such an analysis in mind, Rock (1957) tested some subjects on the learning of paired-associate lists to the criterion of one errorless trial. In one of his experiments, the list consisted of letters of the alphabet paired, arbitrarily, with some numbers from 1 to 50. Therefore, all the subjects had to learn was a series of arbitrary combinations, such as B-23, J-7, M-38, etc. Letters and numbers are highly overlearned, so there was very little to the response-learning phase in this experiment; most of the learning consisted in learning the right combination of these very familiar elements.

There were just two groups of subjects in the experiment. For one group, on each trial, the unlearned items were removed and replaced by totally new arbitrary combinations; the other group of subjects practiced the same items to criterion.

Rock's data very clearly showed that there was practically no difference at all in the number of trials it took to reach criterion under the two conditions. Therefore, on the surface such a result would seem to be rather convincing evidence that individual associations are learned on one trial, and that all the repeated presentations of those associations before that trial have absolutely no influence on the course of learning.

Rock's experiments were quite simple and the conclusions strong; furthermore, his conclusions had important implications, both theoretical and practical (regarding the problems of programed instruction). It isn't surprising, therefore, that the inferences Rock drew from his experiments were immediately challenged by a number of other investigators (Underwood, Rehula, & Keppel, 1962; Postman, 1962b; Battig, 1962; J. P. Williams, 1962; Wollen, 1962). Most of these challenges came down, in the end, to the assertion that Rock's conclusions were unwarranted.

POSSIBLE ARTIFACTS IN THE EXPERIMENTAL DESIGN. The most obvious possibility for an artifact in Rock's method was in item selection. That is to say, the method of replacing items for the experimental group might result in some advantage for that group. Such would be the case if it were the easiest items that subjects manage to learn first. The hard items are those unlearned and replaced by other items. If, in fact, these unlearned items are harder than average, then just by chance they will be replaced by easier items. The subjects who learn an unchanging list have to learn easy and hard items alike; the experimental subjects end up learning only easy items. If that were so, Rock's result of no difference between the two conditions would occur because there were two approximately equal factors at work which tended to cancel one another out. One factor would be that of gradual strengthening, which would operate in favor of the control subjects, and the other factor, which would operate in favor of the experimental subjects, would be selection of the easier items by the process of replacement.

It hardly seems possible at first glance that arbitrary combinations of letters and numbers could vary that much in difficulty. Yet once it is clear that the unlearned items were replaced individually and uniquely for each subject, such variation seems almost inevitable. To most male subjects, for example, any one of the items B-17, B-36, or B-52 would be easy to remember (feminine readers who don't know why are urged to ask male acquaintances).

Furthermore, analysis of the experimental results (Underwood, Rehula, & Keppel, 1962; Postman, 1962b) shows that most of the item-selection effect is the result of learning during the response phase, even though such a phase is of minimal influence with very familiar items. The critical matter seems to be that when hard items are replaced by other items known to be even more difficult, the learning of the changing list takes a greater number of trials (Postman, 1962b).

Therefore, Rock's simple experiments do not seem to lead to the conclusions he drew. This fact, however, does not mean that the evidence is in favor of the case of gradual strengthening rather than all-or-none learning. It does mean that the experimental situation employed by Rock is inadequate to test the difference between gradual strengthening and the all-or-none hypothesis. In theory, it ought to be possible to conduct an experiment in which all items are of equivalent difficulty, but in practice such an experiment is almost impossible to manage. That is because item difficulty is (as the above example suggests) unique to certain kinds of subjects and often unique to particular individuals. There is no way to find out how difficult a particular item is for a given individual without having such an assessment influence the test of learning.

It appears to be unlikely, then, that the method of changing materials can provide a crucial test of these two hypotheses about the process of associative learning. No one disputes the experimental results, and they provide an empirical fact of some importance: namely, subjects learn some items first, and it is likely that they do this by a deliberate strategy of learning which leads them to concentrate on the items that are easiest.

Repeated Measurement and the All-or-None Hypothesis

There are other methods for testing the possible implications of the notion that learning is an all-or-none process. One is based upon the commonplace observation that once a subject gets an item right, he nearly always gets it right on succeeding tests. If the all-or-none hypothesis is accepted as strictly true, then once a subject gets a particular pair correct in paired-associate learning, he should never miss it on succeeding tests (unless some provision is made for forgetting). Furthermore, an item that was not right on any one trial has only a *chance* possibility of being right on a repeated measure of recall. These possible outcomes lead to another test of the all-or-none hypothesis, a test based upon the repeated measurement of the effects of learning.

THE NATURE OF THE TEST. The experiments on repeated measurement grow out of a theoretical analysis by Estes (1960)—an analysis that is quite sophisticated. The experimental situation, like Rock's, is simple, however. It can be illustrated by an example.

In one experiment (Estes, Hopkins, & Crothers, 1960), subjects learned a list of paired associates consisting of 8 items. The stimuli were nonsense syllables, and the responses were numbers from 1 to 8, randomly paired with the syllables. Since there were just 8 items (and the subjects knew the set of numbers), on the first trial the subjects would have a $\frac{1}{8}$ (.125) probability of getting any given item right. Results show that a single paired presentation of the items raises the probability to about $\frac{1}{2}$. This result could develop in several ways. It could happen if, for approximately half the subjects, the probability of getting a particular item correct were 1.00, and for the other subjects, the probability were $\frac{1}{8}$ (or close to zero). That would average out to a little better than $\frac{1}{2}$, considering all the subjects. The same result could occur if the "strength" of a particular association had been raised to an average of $\frac{1}{2}$ for all subjects (with some subject-to-subject and item-to-item variability in strength).

To distinguish between these two possibilities, a repeated testing is necessary. The subjects are first exposed to the pairs, so that there is an opportunity to learn. A test of retention is provided by presenting the nonsense syllables with the requirement that the subjects guess the numbers associated with them. Following this test a second test, exactly like it, is administered. If the single exposure of the pairs raises strength to an average of $\frac{1}{2}$, with some random fluctuation from subject to subject, it shouldn't matter on the second test whether a particular subject got a particular item right or not on the first test. Some of the subjects who knew an item on the first test would miss that item on retesting, and some of the subjects who missed that item on the first test should correctly guess it on the second. In a word, there should be some fluctuation around the average probability of $\frac{1}{2}$, just as there is supposed to be fluctuation around the smooth learning curve which is said to represent the smooth and regular course of learning free from random accidents of testing a single individual.

If learning is all-or-nothing, however, a repeated testing should reveal exactly the same pattern of items by subject recall. That is to say, subjects who failed a particular item on the first test should fail it on the repeated test, and those who remembered it correctly on the first recall should get it right on a repeated test.

THE EXPERIMENTAL RESULTS.   Some data on such a repeated testing can be seen in Table 9.1. Notice that the pattern of results very closely follows what one would expect from the all-or-none principle. Very few people miss an item they got correct on the first test, and very few

TABLE 9.1   Results of Two Simple Free-recall Experiments Showing Near-zero Correct Responses on a Second Test for Cases Which Did Not Have a Correct Response on a First Task
(Estes, 1960)

NO. OF CASES	FIRST RECALL	SECOND RECALL
280	39% correct	75% correct 25% incorrect
	61% incorrect	00.5% correct 99.5% incorrect
816	28% correct	54% correct 46% incorrect
	72% incorrect	2% correct 98% incorrect

people get an item right that they missed on the first exposure. A number of similar comparisons, some of them slightly more complicated, convinced Estes, Hopkins, and Crothers (1960) that any such analysis would show the pattern of results to be expected from the all-or-none principle. It is true that the results were not perfect, but perhaps that fact could be taken care of by the known experimental facts concerning short-term memory.

How is this experiment to be interpreted? It is probably a very puzzling experiment to someone not caught up in the associationistic tradition of learning theory. Why would one ever expect a person to make a mistake on a repeated test immediately after the first? In fact, while the outcome of the experiment seems to agree with common sense, it does not agree with any rigorous deduction made by a viewpoint which says that learning consists of the gradual strengthening of associations.

How sound is this and other experiments like it? They seem to provide evidence that people learn in some all-or-none fashion, usually on a single exposure. Interpretations of the learning process would be vastly simpler if the all-or-none hypothesis could be accepted without question, for it leads to a certain mathematical simplification in predicting the quantitative results of experiments.

CRITICISMS OF THE EXPERIMENT. Nevertheless, severe criticisms can be leveled both against the repeated-recall experiments and against the all-or-none hypothesis. Underwood and Keppel (1962) argue that essentially the same artifact of item selection (and subject selection) which was important in interpreting the changing-lists experiments turns up in the repeated-recall experiments. Furthermore, these authors raise some general questions about the inferences to be drawn concerning the assumed all-or-none process. Underwood and Keppel seize on the fact that results like those in Table 9.1 are not perfectly in accord with the theory. The theory says that *all* items correct on test 1 must be correct on test 2. While a very high proportion of those correct on the first test are correct on the second, they are not all correct. Therefore there is, as the supporters of the all-or-none hypothesis are willing to admit, evidence for some forgetting between recall tests. While such forgetting is not large, it does reflect the fact that the theory neglects one aspect of learning. And as we shall see when we examine the study of short-term memory, it is potentially a very important aspect.

Finally, Underwood and Keppel bring up the matter of overlearning. It is a well-established fact that further practice, after a criterion of perfect performance has been reached, does have an effect on the retention of verbal material. It makes that material more resistant to forgetting, a result that was established in Ebbinghaus's pioneering investigations.

All-or-none theory seems quite unprepared to handle this important effect. Even after an association has been brought to the point where it will always occur in an immediate retest, further practice on that response will make it more likely to turn up in a *delayed* test of retention. Such a result implies the further strengthening of an association by practice beyond the point of perfect performance during learning. Therefore, even when a response has a probability of 1.0 of occurring on some particular occasion, that response can be further strengthened by additional practice.

What is more, an additional experiment (Eimas & Zeaman, 1963) shows that if other measures of association are used, there is evidence for a gradual change even when the probability of response seems to follow an all-or-none principle. Eimas and Zeaman were able to show that there were decreases in reaction time in giving correct items on successive trials *after* the first test on which correct recall occurred, just as there should be if responses were gradually being made stronger. Such a result points up two features in the repeated-recall experiment. First of all, it shows that while getting something right or wrong seems to follow an all-or-none principle (as it should, by definition), there are still systematic changes in behavior; responses are given more rapidly as repetitions increase in number. Furthermore, these changes occur even though there are no additional presentations of the associated pairs. In other words, simply recalling, in the absence of anything but the stimulus for recall, seems to change the strength of an association.

These criticisms have not prevented the extension of the mathematical and logical development of all-or-none theory (Bower, 1961; Crothers, 1962). Bower, for example, manages to derive a large number of predictions about paired-associate learning by the assumption of an all-or-none process plus random guessing before the all-or-none learning occurs. What is more, those who are unhappy with the basic assumptions of all-or-none theory have not been as rigorous about their own views. For example, what do we mean by the term "strength"? We have used it simply to mean some general psychological changes which are indexed or reflected by observed changes in behavior. By and large, those who have criticized the all-or-none view have been content to say that these changes, however abrupt and irregular they may be, are not completely and accurately characterized by the phrase all-or-none.

PRESENT STATUS OF THE PROBLEM.   Underwood and Keppel (1962), in the concluding paragraph of a general critique of the all-or-none view, point out that verbal learning and verbal behavior may not be the appropriate place to test fundamental equations in a mathematical theory of behavior. We do know enough qualitatively about verbal behavior to know that simple outcomes are often the result of complicated processes. We know, for example (though unfortunately little empirical research has been directed to the question), that human subjects bring different strategies to learning situations. It is not uncommon to find a subject in paired-associate learning who will concentrate on one pair at a time, ignoring the others until he gets that one right. Other subjects may not have such well-articulated or easily reconstructed strategies of learning. Furthermore, as we have seen in the last chapter, the major task confronting a human being learning verbal materials is to learn the structural relations within the material. In one repeated-recall experiment, a subject persisted in holding to the hypothesis that there was some systematic relation between the consonant nonsense syllables used as stimuli and the order of the numbers 1 through 8. Such a hypothesis actually slowed his learning. It would be wrong to apply Bower's assumptions as a literal interpretation of the processes of learning in that subject, and yet such a subject (or others like him) may well be included in the data which Bower uses to test his theory.

If utility, practical or theoretical, can be found for the kinds of distributions and learning curves generated by the mathematical development of assumptions behind the all-or-none process (and similar theories of free recall; see G. A. Miller & McGill, 1952), then these theories justify themselves. It may not be fruitful, however, to take the assumptions of the theories as a literal account of the processes behind the molar facts of learning.

It seems a bit weak and untidy to suggest that the learning of associations (or other structural relations among verbal items) is sometimes sudden and sometimes the result of a cumulation from trial to trial, but this seems to be the safest conclusion at the moment. The fact is that repeated presentation of material is about the only technique available to us to provide the conditions of learning. In this and subsequent chapters, we shall see that our experiences in learning consist of the combination and recombination of basic linguistic elements. We sometimes forget, and we sometimes find it difficult to learn new relations because old relations interfere with the learning of the new. The one way we have for combating the influence of forgetting is repetition. The best available evidence we have seems to show that the effect of such repetition in producing resistance to forgetting and interference is cumulative from repetition to repetition.

MEDIATION

The all-or-none controversy arose within the traditional associative view of the learning process. Another important problem that stems from this same context is the problem of mediation. Mediation, however, has considerably more generality, for it concerns theories about the kinds of relations people learn when they learn to associate one thing with another.

Nearly every theorist who has dealt with the problem of association has assumed that, at bottom, the process is one of contiguity. If two elements, A and B, become associated with each other, it is because they are experienced close together in time. Contiguity in time has been offered as the basic cause of association since Aristotle's day. Yet, as nearly everyone who has ever written on the topic of association has pointed out, one idea sometimes seems to lead to another without any contiguity evident between the two ideas in previous experience. If one is to hold to contiguity as a basic principle of associative learning, one needs some way of describing these apparently noncontiguous associations. Such a description is provided by the concept of mediation.

The principle of mediation asserts that associations sometimes come about between two elements, A and B, because they are both associated with a third element, C. The third term serves to bridge the gap between the two noncontiguous terms. Such a notion has been extremely important in most theories of learning; it has been used to derive problem solving, concept learning, and a whole group of relatively complicated processes. Furthermore, experimental tests of mediation have shown that people can profit, sometimes in remarkable ways, during the learning of new elements by mediated connections these elements may have with some old associations.

In this section, we shall examine the experimental evidence on the process of mediation itself. We shall defer, for the most part, the theoretical applications of the notion of mediation to more appropriate places in later chapters. The essential problem in the study of mediation is the determination of the ways in which intervening terms can bridge the gap between two items. We shall see later that the problem is considerably more general than that of finding the missing link between two ideas, but the simplest illustrations of mediation are within this limit. Therefore, we shall illustrate the basic types or paradigms of mediation by considering the ways in which a single term can mediate between two others.

Mediation Paradigms

THREE BASIC TYPES OF MEDIATION

The ways in which a single term can mediate between two others reduces to three main types (J. J. Jenkins, 1963). These types are presented schematically in Table 9.2. In order to understand the table, you can think of each type as illustrated by a hypothetical experiment in transfer of training. The subject of such an experiment would learn the relationship in the first line of each column and then learn the relationship in the second, and the effect of this learning would be tested by seeing how rapidly the subject could learn the relationship in the third line. It would be compared with a control condition in which the subject learned some item unrelated to the first two phases.

MEDIATION BY CHAINING. The first and best known paradigm of mediation is illustrated in the first column of Table 9.2. This type is the

TABLE **9.2** **Principal Types of Mediation Paradigms**

STAGE	CHAINING	STIMULUS EQUIVALENCE	RESPONSE EQUIVALENCE
Learn:	A—B	A—B	B—A
Then learn:	B—C	C—B	B—C
Test for:	A—C	A—C	A—C

chaining paradigm. It is called chaining because the mediating term serves as an intervening link between the two terms which are to be associated.

In a hypothetical experiment, we first teach a subject to associate A and B. The training is by the paired-associate method; the subject learns to give B when he is presented with the stimulus A. Then the subject learns to give a new response, C, when he is presented with B as a stimulus. Finally, he is tested for the association A—C. If he readily gives C as the association with A, mediation has occurred; A has elicited B implicitly, and B then serves as a stimulus for the production of the overt response C. Notice that once we admit the implicit response B to have stimulus properties, the whole chaining paradigm reduces to a direct stimulus-response sequence, even though one of the terms is implicit rather than overt.

MEDIATION BY STIMULUS EQUIVALENCE. The stimulus equivalence paradigm is illustrated in the second column of Table 9.2. The term stimulus equivalence arises because the mediation serves to make two stimuli equivalent to one another.

During the first stage of a hypothetical experiment illustrating stimulus equivalence, the subject is taught that A should elicit B. Then in the second stage, he is taught that C should also elicit B. Mediation through stimulus equivalence occurs in the third stage if there is some facilitation of the learning of A to C or C to A. The two stimuli, A and C, have been made equivalent to one another by eliciting a response (B) in common.

While the stimulus equivalence paradigm cannot be derived from a stimulus-response analysis quite so easily, it can be done. One way to achieve it is simply to say that some stimulating aftereffect of A is still present when the subject is making the B response. Thus there is some slight tendency for B to be a potential stimulus for A. Likewise, there is some slight tendency for C to be elicited by B. Therefore, indirectly A and C come to be contiguous through the mediation of the B term. On the test, in the third stage of the learning of A–C, there should be some facilitation. Because mediation is indirect, stimulus-response analysis would lead us to expect only a slight degree of facilitation, certainly less than we should expect from the chaining paradigm.

MEDIATION BY RESPONSE EQUIVALENCE. The third kind of mediation, response equivalence, is illustrated in the third column of Table 9.2. In the first stage, B is the stimulus for A. In the second stage, B is the stimulus for C. According to stimulus-response analysis, when B is being trained to elicit C during the second stage, the subject has a tendency to make the implicit response A. Consequently, there is some tendency for A and C to be contiguous, and during the third stage we would expect facilitation of the learning of an A–C or a C–A connection. Again, as in the case of stimulus equivalence, the amount of facilitation expected during the third and final phase would not be very great—certainly less than that expected in the chaining paradigm, although perhaps a little more than that expected in the stimulus equivalence paradigm.

A COMPARISON OF THE PARADIGMS. If you consider all the possible combinations of two terms taken in groups of three, you can see that there are a total of eight different combinations of letters to form the three paradigms. Actually, the paradigms are incomplete as we have described the situation, for there is also a possible reverse-chaining paradigm. By stimulus-response analysis we would expect reversal of stimulus or response equivalence paradigms to be the same as the paradigms in the forward direction, but reverse chaining is something else again. Stimulus-response analysis would lead us to think that there would be little help in learning the third list from reverse chaining, because things go in the wrong direction.

One large experiment by Horton and Kjeldergaard (1961) compares all the eight possible arrangements within the three paradigms (including the reverse-chaining arrangement). All the subjects in this experiment learned three lists of paired associates, and each list corresponded to one of the stages in the paradigms in Table 9.2. The lists consisted of eight items, which were short but relatively rare words such as BANAL, KRONE, UMBER, etc. Practice was by the method of anticipation. In the third stage, half of the list to be learned consisted of items which reflected the paradigm, and half consisted of items that were controls. For example, for the chaining paradigm, the subjects might be required to learn the association BANAL—KRONE and then the association KRONE—UMBER, and finally they would be tested on the association BANAL—UMBER. The final list would contain three other items the learning of which could be helped by chaining and four control items, for which there would be no transfer from the previous two stages.

The net effect of this large and carefully designed experiment was that all the paradigms showed positive transfer in the third stage. In fact, each one of the eight possible arrangements, except the reverse-chaining arrangement, showed a statistical advantage over the control items. In absolute value, even the reverse-chaining arrangement was above the control, though it was not significantly so. There was, in brief, ample evidence of transfer to the final list as the result of the relations between the three stages.

The surprising result, however, was that the paradigms did not differ among themselves. One paradigm produced just about as much positive transfer as another, and no statistically reliable difference could be found in any comparison among the paradigms. Chaining did not produce more transfer than stimulus or response equivalence, nor was there any difference between the two equivalence paradigms.

What are we to make of the failure to find differences among the various paradigms? Is the analysis which leads us to expect differences in error, or is there something wrong with the experiments? Unfortunately, it is very difficult to tell. Despite the care with which the experiments were done, they are open to some general experimental errors which plague transfer designs (see Cofer & Musgrave, 1963, p. 253). The lack of a difference between the paradigms could result from many factors, some of them quite irrelevant to the question of differences in mediation.

FURTHER ANALYSIS OF MEDIATION

Before we consider some of the possible interpretations of the mediation effect, it would be well to examine two other kinds of experiments. One of these is a remarkable series of studies which makes use of a four-stage chaining paradigm, and the other is an experiment which illustrates the importance of a mediation process in perceptual identification.

THE FOUR-STAGE MEDIATION EXPERIMENTS. In an experiment by Russell and Storms (1955) the intervening links in the chain were inferred rather than actually taught to the subjects in the course of the experiment. The subjects learned two lists, one an original training list and the other a test list. There was a stimulus-response chain presumed to exist between these two lists, but the steps in the chain were inferred from the norms of free association.

In the original training, subjects learned to respond with English words to nonsense syllables. For example, the subjects had to learn to produce the word STEM when they saw the syllable CEF. Now, the word "stem" is a stimulus which, by free-association norms, frequently elicits the response "flower." "Flower" in turn frequently elicits the response "smell." In the second list, the subjects had to learn to produce the response SMELL when they saw the original stimulus CEF. That learning could be helped by the chain CEF—STEM—FLOWER—SMELL. For a control comparison, the subjects learned a word in the second list that was unrelated to the response in the first list. For example, instead of learning CEF—FLOWER in the second list, they might learn CEF—SOLDIER. The actual lists learned by subjects, together with the intervening steps in the chain inferred from free-association norms, are presented in Table 9.3.

TABLE **9.3**   **Nonsense Syllables, Associative Chains, and Control Words Used in Forming Paired Associates in a Mediation Experiment**
(Russell & Storms, 1955)

NONSENSE SYLLABLE	FIRST CHAINED WORD	SECOND CHAINED WORD	FINAL CHAINED WORD	CONTROL WORD
CEF	STEM	FLOWER	SMELL	JOY
DAX	MEMORY	MIND	MATTER	AFRAID
YOV	SOLDIER	ARMY	NAVY	CHEESE
WUB	WISH	WANT	NEED	TABLE
GEX	JUSTICE	PEACE	WAR	HOUSE
JID	THIEF	STEAL	TAKE	SLEEP
ZIL	OCEAN	WATER	DRINK	DOCTOR
LAJ	COMMAND	ORDER	DISORDER	CABBAGE
MYV	FRUIT	APPLE	RED	HAND

The results of this experiment are in Table 9.4. The first row shows the comparison between the number of correct anticipations on the

TABLE **9.4**   **Results of the Chained Mediation Experiment**
(Russell & Storms, 1955)

EXPERIMENT	INITIAL CORRECT RESPONSES		TOTAL CORRECT RESPONSES (MEAN OF CHAINED MINUS UNCHAINED)
	CHAINED	UNCHAINED	
Main	67	48	+3.74
Control	30	30	−0.50

learning of the second list for the chained and unchained items. The second row gives the number of correct anticipations for a group of subjects who learned only unrelated items. The table makes a strong case for the proposition that the intervening chained steps inferred from free-association norms help in learning the connection between the nonsense syllables and the second-list words related to the responses on the first list. The associations that subjects brought with them to the experiment provided for mediation which made the paired associates learned on the first list transfer to the learning of those on the second.

This experiment has been repeated several times (Cofer & Yarczower, 1957; McGehee & Schulz, 1961) with essentially the same results. In one of these repetitions (McGehee & Schulz, 1961) some additional experimental comparisons reinforced the inference which leads us to assert that the mediation was through the intervening chained links. For example, one possibility tested in this experiment was that the positive transfer observed in the chained items of the second list resulted from a general increase in the availability of related associations—not just from the specific chains revealed by the association norms. The tests were negative; the inference that specific stimulus-response chains were responsible for the facilitation of the learning was supported. One of the tests consisted of the reversal of the test and training lists. This would make the specific associations work backwards, but the amount of response availability should be the same. The results showed less facilitation for reversal, so the notion of specific chains seemed to be the correct one.

Some additional experiments which studied all possible four-stage paradigms were reported by J. J. Jenkins (1963). These, however, show a disappointing absence of any effect which could be ascribed to mediation. Training for the intermediate steps rather than inferences from norms was used in these experiments, so they are not quite the same as the Russell and Storms experiment. In any event, the inability to find mediation in four-stage experimental paradigms is puzzling.

Jenkins reviewed a large and sometimes contradictory literature on the subject of mediation and came to the conclusion that the tendency to mediate in individual subjects is itself something that must be aroused. He argued that this tendency is controlled by such familiar conditions as reinforcement, order of training, etc. Presumably the act of mediating can be itself reinforced. Therefore, in any experimental test, the extent to which individual subjects will mediate should depend upon their previous habits and the extent to which the conditions of the experiment arouse mediation. Jenkins's thorough analysis leaves us with the conclusion that we ought not to think of mediation as an automatic and immediate process but as something that depends upon cognition and direction. We shall return to this possibility shortly.

THE VERBAL-LOOP HYPOTHESIS.   One situation in which mediation appears to be important is in the identification of complex perceptual organization. An experiment on perceptual identification led Glanzer and Clark (1962) to the verbal-loop hypothesis, a notion which points up the importance of mediation in perception.

In this experiment subjects looked briefly at rows of figures like those in Figure 9.1. Immediately after they had seen the figures, they were required to reproduce what they had seen. They studied a very large number of such rows, of which those in Figure 9.1 are only a sample. The numbers at the right-hand side of Figure 9.1, which show the percent accuracy of reproduction for each row, indicate that the rows vary enormously in the extent to which they are reproducible. Glanzer and Clark argue that this variation is determined by the information in the array (and, as we know from Chapter 8, most likely by the possible set of patterns from which any row can be drawn). In addition, however, a separate experiment shows that reproducibility is determined by verbal mediating activities aroused in the subjects by the forms.

In this experiment, the authors drew a random sample of 65 of the possible rows. They presented these, one row at a time, to people and asked for a short verbal description of each row. This procedure

FIG. **9.1**   A sample of the stimulus arrays presented by Glanzer and Clark (1962).

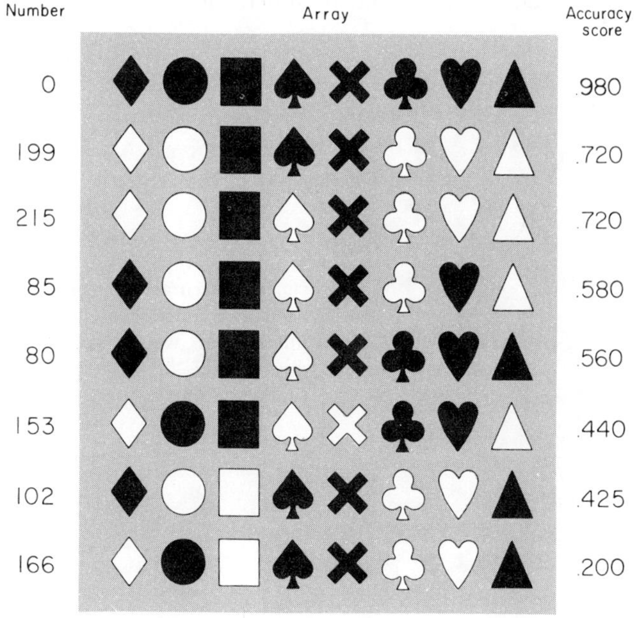

Number	Array	Accuracy score
0		.980
199		.720
215		.720
85		.580
80		.560
153		.440
102		.425
166		.200

provided information about the verbal activity aroused by the forms and allowed for a test of some inferences of the verbal-loop hypothesis. The hypothesis states that the visual information presented by the array is translated by subjects into a series of words. This verbalization is retained until the time for reproduction is required. Therefore, the accuracy of reproduction ought to be determined by the difficulty of retaining the verbal translation of the perceived figures.

An analysis showed that the accuracy of reproduction was very highly correlated with the mean number of words the subjects required in order to describe any given array of forms. The authors simply counted the number of words the subjects used in describing the row of figures. Figure 9.2 shows that the greater the number of words required to describe the rows, and hence the greater the number of words which must be held to the time of reproduction, the less the accuracy of reproduction. This relation provides evidence in support of the verbal-loop hypothesis.

The experiment constitutes a straightforward demonstration of the influence of verbal behavior on the identification of perceived elements. The verbal loop, of course, refers to the fact that the verbal translation enables the subject to reproduce what he saw earlier. Such storage is mediation. The original term is the presented perception, the intervening term is the linguistic association aroused by the form, and the final response is the reproduction of the form. Therefore, here is another instance of the role of mediation in the control of behavior.

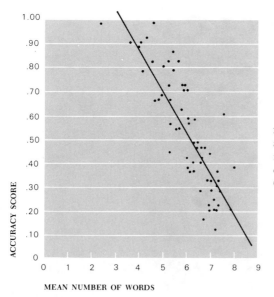

FIG. 9.2 Accuracy scores for each array as a function of the mean number of words needed to describe the array. (Glanzer & Clark, 1962.)

Interpretations of Mediation

We have already examined one interpretation of the way in which mediation works, for it is implicit in the descriptions we have given of the mediation paradigms. These descriptions assumed that mediation works by stimulus-response units. Stimulus equivalence and response equivalence are not easy to state in a stimulus-response analysis, but some very ingenious arguments, borrowed mostly from conditioning theory, make it possible to do so. One of the most important and influential of these arguments is the attempt by Cofer and Foley (1942) to make a beginning to the study of the meaningful organization in language by the propositions derived from an elementary theory of behavior. There are, however, alternative ways of describing mediation, and we should consider some of these.

MEDIATION AS THE RESULT OF CONCEPTUAL STRUCTURES

Mandler (1963) argues that if reinforcement and other such conditions control the tendency to mediate, as Jenkins claims, then the problem becomes one of knowing whether subjects in an experiment can learn the theory of mediation as a concept. If they can, then in a sense it is possible for them to outguess the experimenter. They can learn to profit in learning a final task by invoking some rule which relates the earlier task to the final task. The rule of chaining or that of stimulus equivalence are possible examples. The task for the subject is to discover the rules whereby the experimenter made up the lists.

The stimulus-response point of view, however, would argue that subjects simply learn relations without necessarily learning the generality that would be implied by a deliberate evocation of a rule. That is to say, subjects are supposed to learn to connect elements to elements—A to B—because they are contiguous. Furthermore, they are thought to learn these in order, so that it is easier for subjects to think of B when given A than to think of A when given B.

Mandler seeks some alternative to this view. He shows, by way of example, that the various paradigms could be interpreted as propositions in logic. If that is the case, the chaining paradigm would read:

$$\text{If A, then B}$$
$$\text{and} \quad \text{if B, then C}$$
$$\text{then} \quad \text{if A, then C.}$$

If this interpretation is correct, subjects simply learn the terms in a series of propositions which can be cast in logical form. There are a number of specific ways in which such propositions can make equivalent logical statements. For example, the chaining paradigm may be stated in this form: If A includes B and B includes C, then A includes C. Or in an even more familiar form: If C is B and all B is A, then C is A. Mandler points out that of the eight possible arrangements in a three-stage mediation paradigm, all but two make logically possible propositions, though some are logically stronger than others. The stimulus equivalence paradigm, for example, does not make a logically necessary conclusion (as does the chaining paradigm), but it does make a logically possible conclusion. The only unlogical propositions are the reverse-chaining paradigms, and the data of Horton and Kjeldergaard suggest that these may produce the weakest mediation.

In his analysis of mediation paradigms as logical propositions, Mandler cites an experiment (Mandler & Cowan, 1962) which we would not ordinarily think of as a mediation experiment but which shows a pattern of results remarkably like mediation. The basic elements were CVC nonsense syllables. On any given trial the subjects were presented with six pairs of such syllables made up of all possible combinations of three different elements. Each pair was presented on one side of a card. Some cards contained a check mark on the reverse side and others did not. The task for the subjects was to learn to predict which cards had the check mark simply by looking at the pairs of nonsense syllables. The assignment of check marks followed the paradigms. For the chaining paradigm, the cards containing the syllable pairs A–B, B–C, and A–C would have check marks; the cards containing B–A, C–B, and C–A would not contain check marks. For the stimulus equivalence paradigm, the cards containing A–B, C–B, and A–C would have check marks; the remaining cards would be without check marks.

The results of the experiment showed large differences in the rapidity with which the various structures were learned. The chaining or transitivity paradigms were learned much faster than the others. Therefore, Mandler suggests, instead of looking for contiguity as the basis of mediation we may wish to consider logical relations as the basis. Mandler does not assert that the associative-contiguity view of mediation is incorrect; he merely points out that there are other possible structures which subjects could call upon in mediation.

MEDIATION BY SUPERORDINATION

In the previous chapter (see page 271), we examined something called category clustering. In the study of category clustering, subjects are presented with long lists of words which are naturally grouped into several different classes. Examples of the different classes, however, are presented in random order. The clustering effect occurs when, in recalling the lists, subjects tend to recall words of the same class in adjacent positions. Bousfield (1953), who studied clustering because it provides an organizing

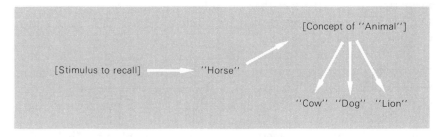

FIG. **9.3** Illustrates Bousfield's account of the process in the recall of categorized data that give rise to clustering.

principle for memory, came to the conclusion that it was the result of mediation through superordinate concepts.

Figure 9.3 illustrates Bousfield's concept of clustering through superordination. When a word occurs to a subject in recall, Bousfield asserts, that word activates a general concept (perhaps the name of a class, such as, in the illustration, the concept "mammal"). The general concept in turn arouses other words which belong to the same class. The general concept need not be a specific word or a particular class name; Bousfield implies only that there is some superordinate structure which is activated by a class instance and that this structure arouses other class members. It is a form of mediation, and Bousfield describes it not by the language of association theory but by the language of the structure of classes. He borrows heavily, in his description, from the neurophysiological construct of "cell assemblies" described by Hebb.

The notion of mediation through superordinate concepts seems to work quite well for the description of category clustering, though, in his later work on the clustering effect, Bousfield abandons the idea in favor of purely associative mediation (Bousfield, 1961). Some recent experiments by Cofer and his associates (Cofer, 1965) show, in fact, that some results of studies in clustering appear to demand both the kind of categorical mediation described in Figure 9.3 and the kind of mediation which is described by associative chaining. So, once more, we are faced with the possibility that several kinds of mediation are possible.

GRAMMAR AND MEDIATION

What is common to the various concepts of mediation? Such a question requires that we examine the notion of mediation stripped of the particular principles by which it is supposed to be accomplished. When we do that we become aware that the concept of mediation always entails the learning of something other than direct relations between the elements to be learned. You will recall that Jenkins's interpretation of mediation stressed the fact that the subjects seem to learn to mediate—they learn the rules by which lists are constructed. It is this "rule" which constitutes the something other.

It would be a mistake, however, to say in a literal way that subjects explicitly learn rules when they learn to mediate. What we mean is that subjects come to behave as if they understood the rule, whether or not they can explain it in words. Such a statement may seem to make mediation mysterious, but it can at least be made familiar by reminding you that it is part of the most basic experience people have in learning how to use language. It is the way in which most people learn the grammar of their native languages.

GRAMMAR AS CONCEPT. In some ways the most remarkable aspect of our verbal behavior is the learning of grammar. Most of us, because we have been subjected to a long history of deliberate schooling in the formal rules of our mother tongue, know some of the "formal grammar" of that language. To a more or less satisfactory degree, we can describe what we do when we create sentences. Most of us are aware of the fact that adjectives usually precede nouns in English. Such a statement implies that we can identify a class of words called adjectives and another class of words called nouns, and that we know something of the relation between these. We may even know the grammar of French and be aware of the fact that in French, adjectives usually follow the noun they modify.

Yet we would be able to speak English even if we had never heard of the term adjective or had never learned to identify the class of words that term describes. Speakers of French would be able to do the same. The most illiterate French peasant, who hasn't the faintest notion how to describe the grammar of his language, speaks grammatical French. It may not be the French of the French Academy, but it is nonetheless grammatical. The acid test which tells us that his speech is grammatical is that his friends and neighbors understand him. They would not be able to do so if his speech did not conform to some generally understood rules.

Our verbal behavior, then, is in a sense mediated by grammatical rules. Or in any event, it is mediated by some structures which can be cast into the form of grammatical rules. We are not explicitly aware of the mediation in verbal behavior, but its presence can be detected by the kinds of transfer tests used in mediation studies and by comparison of the verbal learning of structured and unstructured material. We shall have more to say about such conceptual mediation in Chapter 12 on concept formation, but for now we can illustrate the role of mediation in grammatical learning.

EXPERIMENTS ON THE LEARNING OF GRAMMAR. For practical reasons we might wish to compare the learning of ordinary English materials which exhibit various kinds of grammatical structures, but for theoretical purposes we profit more from a study of special experimental grammars. At this point, we shall examine two such investigations.

In one experiment (G. A. Miller, 1958), subjects practiced recalling strings of letters consisting of various combinations of four letters of the alphabet: G, N, S, and X. These strings (artificial sentences) are illustrated in Table 9.5. Notice that the strings are divided into two

TABLE 9.5 **Lists of Structured (Redundant) and Random Strings Used in Experiment on Grammar**
(G. A. Miller, 1958)

STRUCTURED (REDUNDANT)		RANDOM	
L_1	L_2	R_1	R_2
SSXG	NNSG	GNSX	NXGS
NNXSG	NNSXG	NSGXN	GNXSG
SXSXG	SXXSG	XGSSN	SXNGG
SSXNSG	NNXSXG	SXNNGN	GGSNXG
SXXXSG	NNXXSG	XGSXXS	NSGNGX
NNSXNSG	NNXXSXG	GSXXGNS	NGSXXNS °
SXSXNSG	NNXXXSG	NSXXGSG	NGXXGGN
SXXXSXG	SSXNSXG	SGXGGNN	SXGXGNS
SXXXXSG	SSXNXSG	XXGNSGG	XGSNGXG

classes, "redundant" and "random." The random strings are just that; they are sequences of the four letters arrived at haphazardly. The redundant strings were arrived at by the application of a certain special kind of rules called finite-state rules. One of the rules embodied in these redundant strings, for example, is that N in the initial position can never be followed by S. Notice, further, that N is never followed by X in these strings. Another rule is that a string never begins with G or X; still another rule is that the strings always end with G.

Subjects were presented with nine strings, all either redundant or random, and then asked to recall all nine. This procedure was repeated for the same nine strings either until they were learned or for 10 trials. The results are in Figure 9.4. As you see, there is a very large difference between the learning of redundant and random strings. Furthermore, the second set of curves in the figure shows that subjects generally learn to know whether they are dealing with redundant or random strings. Subjects who had a random list on the first task did not do so well with a structured list on the second task as those who had studied a structured

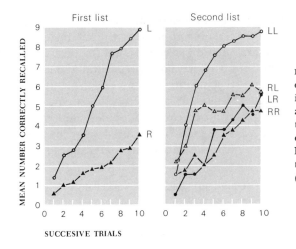

FIG. **9.4** The mean number of letters correctly recalled in free recall of random (*R*) and redundant (*L*) lists of letters. Notice that on the second list, those exposed to *L* lists at first performed better than those exposed to *R* lists. (G. A. Miller, 1958.)

list on the first trial. Evidently people learn how to deal efficiently with structure in the lists.

Another experiment by Saporta, Blumenthal, and Reiff (1963) shows that an even more striking difference in performance can be produced by converting finite-state rules into phrase-structure rules. Phrase-structure rules are much more like the rules of the grammars of natural languages. A phrase-structure grammar differs from a finite-state grammar in that the rules are not derived from the transition from one element or state to another. Thus we would not describe a rule in phrase-structure grammar by saying that N, in the initial position, cannot be followed by S. We would say that a complete string can be divided into two or more phrases and that each phrase must obey some rule. For example, we could say that the initial phrase can be either N, GN, or NN, but never G alone and never NS. In fact, a given phrase-structure grammar could produce exactly the same strings (or sentences) as a finite-state grammar, but there is a difference in the way in which the rules for making up strings are phrased. Phrase-structure grammars are more general, however; finite-state grammars are limited to artificial languages, while phrase-structure rules can apply to both natural and artificial languages.

Table 9.6 shows the material used in this experiment. Notice that the strings for the finite-state, phrase-structure, and random conditions are precisely the same. The difference is only in the spacing introduced between letters. In the finite-state condition, there is a space between each letter. In the phrase-structure condition, there is a space between phrases, so that the initial phrase is always GN or N, and the second phrase is always X, S, XN, or XGN. In the random condition, spaces are haphazard and obey no simple rule.

TABLE **9.6**   **Materials Used in Experiment on Learning of Grammatical Structure**
Notice that the lists are exactly the same except for spacing between letters. (Saporta, Blumenthal, & Reiff, 1963)

FINITE STATE	PHRASE STRUCTURE	RANDOM
N X S	N X S	N X S
N S X N	N S XN	N S XN
N X N S	N XN S	N XN S
G N S X	GN S X	G N SX
N X N X N	N XN XN	N X NXN
G N X N G N	GN XN GN	GNX N GN
N X N X G N	N XN XGN	N XN XGN
N X G N X	N XGN X	NX GN X
G N X G N X	GN XGN X	G NX GNS
G N X G N X G N	GN XGN XGN	GNXGN XG N

Subjects practiced recalling nine finite-state sentences, or nine phrase-structure sentences, or nine random sentences for ten trials. The results are illustrated in Figure 9.5. Notice that there is a small difference between finite-state and random sentences; the random spacing perhaps misled subjects to expect some phrase structure when there was none. There was, however, a great advantage for the phrase-structure sentences.

Both of these experiments show that subjects profit from rules which are available to them in the material, even though no explicit mention is made of the rules or their existence in the material. Are such results to be ascribed to mediation? We would certainly think that the subjects organized what they learned as they learned it, that they entertained various hypotheses about the arrangement of items, and that there must have been some concordance between these hypotheses and the rules from which the material was derived. Therefore, it is reasonable to infer that subjects engaged in some other activity than just learning the associations between one element and the next. Such activity is not directly described by stating the possible associations between items; it is only described by the rules which generated the material. We are justified in assuming that some activity mediated the learning, or at least the improvement in learning, for the subjects who were faced with structured material.

We reach the conclusion, then, that the kinds of processes which can serve as mediating activities are many and varied. Mediation may be through chained associative links, or it may be through grammatical or logical rule. Mediation not only may serve to make performance more efficient, but as we shall see in succeeding chapters, it can, under the

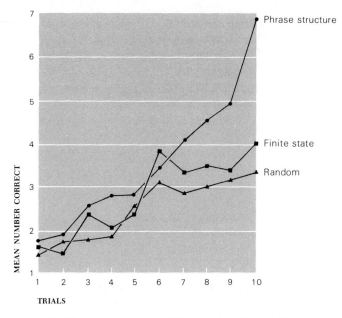

FIG. **9.5** The mean number of items correct in recalling strings of letters which were either random, organized according to a finite-state grammar, or grouped by phrase structure. (Saporta, Blumenthal, & Reiff, 1963.)

right conditions, make learning inefficient. That will happen when the subject is misled or confused about the structure of the material he is to learn.

In some instances the mediation employed by people during learning may be explicitly stated by them. In other cases they will be unable to articulate in any proper way the rules which are behind the material they learn. Furthermore, people may apply a principle of mediation which is different from and not describable by the rules which generated the material they learn. In any case, it is clear that mediating activities are important to learning and intellectual processes generally; we shall have many occasions to call upon the principle of mediation.

MATHEMATICAL THEORIES OF VERBAL LEARNING

We have already examined some of the issues in mathematical theories of learning. In this chapter, for example, we have discussed the all-or-none issue, and that issue has turned in large measure on mathematical arguments. In fact, almost every problem of importance in the study of learning has been touched by mathematical theorizing. We cannot examine the full range of mathematical theories of learning, but in this section we shall illustrate some of the ideas that have gone into mathematical thinking about learning. We shall eliminate nearly all the technical aspects of the mathematics, but our discussion should provide some insight into the general outcomes of mathematical theories and the role they have played in the development of theories of verbal learning.

Learning Curves

While nearly all aspects of verbal learning have been studied by the methods of mathematics, some have been more intensively studied than others. Consider the learning curve. Learning curves result when we plot, in a graph, some measure of performance on a task as a function of time or trials at practice. Such graphs very often exhibit smooth regular curves, curves which suggest simple mathematical relations between the measure of performance and time at practice. It is not surprising to find that most of the earlier efforts in the mathematical analysis of the learning process were directed toward the problem of finding some equation or equations which would describe the learning curve.

Learning curves for individual subjects are sometimes (though not always) rather haphazard and irregular, so it is altogether natural that a great deal of the mathematical theorizing in learning has been from a probabilistic point of view. Probabilistic theories assume that processes are, at bottom, random or statistical in nature. When a large number of observations, each of which may be subject to some random influences, is averaged, the general result is a smooth and regular process. It is a fact that even when individual learning curves are irregular, the average curves for a number of subjects are smooth and regular.

A learning curve can be described by a mathematical equation in two ways. One can simply look at the curve (or study it in some more rigorous way) and decide that such a curve can be fitted by some particular equation. There may be no attempt to find out what the equation means; it is simply a convenient and more or less accurate way of summarizing the relation between performance and practice. Such an empirical mathematical fit is to be seen in Figure 9.6. The individual points are the observations that come from an experiment; the connected line is a curve that is described by the equation which seems to fit the data.

The other, and more powerful, way to describe the data of learning by means of a mathematical equation is to derive the equation from some assumptions about the processes at work in learning. The theory arises in the assumptions and in the derivations which can be made from them. Very frequently a mathematical theory is quite general; it may not only describe the learning curve, it may describe a number of other facts

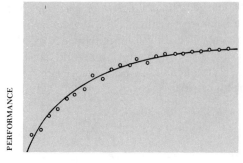

PERFORMANCE

TRIALS

FIG. **9.6** The fit of a theoretical equation to performance data during learning. The circles reflect the actual performance.

about learning. In the next section we shall examine some of the assumptions behind a particular mathematical theory of learning, one which derives a learning curve and some other relations as well.

Thurstone's Mathematical Theory of Learning

Thurstone's (1930a) theory is one of the earliest of the attempts to write a quantitative, rational theory of learning by means of mathematical assumptions. It has one important feature in common with the more recent theories: it is statistical in nature. For that reason, some of the steps Thurstone employs in reasoning to his conclusions are to be found in later efforts. In a word, the theory is of more than historical interest.

THE GENERAL THEORY

Thurstone begins by pointing out that we can conveniently categorize all actions performed in practicing some tasks as either correct or in error. That is not true for all skills (for example, consider learning to play golf), but it is a very useful way of beginning the analysis of verbal learning. In verbal learning a response is either right or wrong; therefore, we can define the proportion of the total actions which lead to success as

$$p = \frac{s}{s+e} \tag{1}$$

In the equation, p is the proportion of successful acts, s the number of successful acts, and e the number of errors. We may also write

$$q = \frac{e}{s+e} \tag{2}$$

where q is the proportion of errors in the total performance. And, of course, $q = (1 - p)$.

As learning increases, e tends to decrease. Eventually, when perfect performance is reached, $p = 1.0$. By using the two definitions in

Equations (1) and (2), Thurstone is able to write an equation for rate of improvement in performance from the following argument.

At any given moment during the learning process, there is a probability p that the learner will perform a correct response, and there is another probability q, or $(1 - p)$, that he will perform an incorrect response. If he performs an incorrect response, there is another probability k that the incorrect act will be eliminated on the next trial. There is, of course, the probability $(1 - k)$ that the incorrect response will be repeated. Therefore, we may write

$$kq = \text{probability that an incorrect act will be performed and eliminated from future performance} \qquad (3)$$

and

$$(1 - k)q = \text{probability that an incorrect act will be performed and then repeated on the next trial} \qquad (4)$$

Thurstone points out that a good learner is one who profits by his mistakes and a poor learner is one who does not. In that sense, the difference between good and poor learners can be characterized by the parameter k. If a given person makes an error twice, on the average, before eliminating it, $k = 0.50$. If he makes a mistake four times before eliminating it, $k = 0.25$. In general, the less a person profits by his errors, the smaller k is. If a subject makes each error only once before eliminating it, $k = 1.0$; and if he anticipates and eliminates some errors before they occur (if he, in other words, learns rationally), $k > 1.0$. It is such sensible interpretations of the parameters that make theoretical equations more useful and understandable than empirical equations.

From these considerations, it is clear that the rate of elimination of errors with practice is proportional to kq. Therefore, it is possible to write the following differential equation:

$$\frac{de}{dt} = -kq \qquad (5)$$

A differential equation expresses the rate of change in some quantity; in this case, the rate of change in errors (de) with change in trials or practice (dt) is the quantity expressed. The equation says that errors are reduced (hence the minus sign) at a rate proportional to their frequency and proportional to the magnitude of k. Because errors occur more frequently early in learning, the rate of error reduction will be greater earlier in learning. Learners characterized by large values of k will show faster rates of error reduction than learners characterized by small values of k.

It follows from Equation (5) that the rate of change in errors may also be expressed as

$$\frac{de}{dt} = \frac{-ke}{s+e} \tag{6}$$

since $q = e/s + e$

Finally, Thurstone argues, correct responses have some effect favoring their reoccurrence. Therefore, a similar series of equations could be written expressing the rate of change in successful acts with trials (ds/dt). This consideration leads Thurstone, after integration of the two differential equations, to write as his fundamental equation

$$se = m \tag{7}$$

Equation (7) says that the product of the total number of errors and effective number of successes is a constant, m. That constant m reflects, in turn, the difficulty of the task. The value of m is large for difficult tasks and small for easy ones; therefore, learning will be rapid for easy tasks and slow for difficult ones.

RESULTS OF THE THEORY

From these considerations Thurstone is able to write a number of equations, all of which fit various aspects of data in human verbal learning. Perhaps the most interesting consequence of his work is a general equation which expresses the relationship between length of a task and amount of time at practice.

We hardly need a theory to tell us that the more material we have to learn, the longer it takes us. The exact nature of the relation between time to learn (or trials) and amount of material is rather surprising, however. In fact, while it is true that it takes us longer to learn more material, it does not take us proportionately longer. A monograph by Lyon (1917) summarizes most of the available evidence on this point.

Figure 9.7 shows some data from one of Lyon's experiments in which he taught himself lists of nonsense syllables of various lengths. It was truly a heroic experiment. As you can see from the figure, one of Lyon's lists had 200 nonsense syllables! Notice that when Lyon practiced at the rate of one repetition a day, learning a list of 200 items scarcely took more time per item than learning a list of 100 syllables. With small numbers of syllables, the addition of a few more syllables makes a large difference in the time it takes to learn, while for a large number, the addition of the same number scarcely makes any difference at all.

This rather surprising result can be derived from Thurstone's general theory (Thurstone, 1930a). He arrives at an equation from his original differential equations which tells us that time per item should increase with the square root of the number of items beyond the immediate memory span. Such an equation fits the data presented in Figure 9.7 quite well, and in fact it will fit almost all the data that have ever

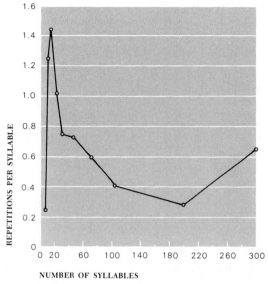

FIG. **9.7** The number of repetitions per syllable required to learn lists of nonsense syllables of varying lengths by the once-per-day method. (Data from Lyon, 1917.)

been reported on this problem. From a mathematical point of view the equation is especially interesting because it requires only one parameter or constant in order to make an excellent fit. We can independently estimate the memory span, so the whole curve can be recovered by just knowing one point on it. This is a very unusual situation for data so extensive.

Statistical Learning Theory

Though Thurstone's theory is essentially a statistical one, it does not make use of the full range of possibilities in a statistical or probabilistic analysis of learning data. Some other more recent statistical theories (Estes, 1958; Bush & Mosteller, 1955) have introduced mathematically more sophisticated and advanced statistical treatment.

We have already examined some of the work on recent statistical theories of learning. Recall, for example, the discussion of the all-or-none issue at the outset of this chapter. Many of the arguments in that issue came out of the equations derived from statistical learning theory. In fact, we can illustrate both the basic method and some of the outcomes of current statistical theory by returning to the all-or-none problem as an example.

A SIMPLE LINEAR MODEL

You will recall that one of the methods for examining the question of all-or-none learning versus gradual incremental learning was to present a list of items followed by two tests for recall. The basic experiment can be diagrammed as

$$P \qquad T_1 \qquad T_2$$

where P stands for the original presentation, T_1 for the first test of recall, and T_2 for the second test which follows immediately.

Let us assume that the probability of a correct response at the outset is zero; this assumption means that guessing would lead to negligible correct responding. If such is the case, the probabilities of various combinations of correct responses on T_1 and T_2 can be predicted from a very simple model (Estes, 1961), which is a linear model. The model is described as a linear one because the basic equation required is linear.

The various combinations of probabilities of correct responses on T_1 and T_2 are presented in Table 9.7, together with some expressions from the theory which should predict these probabilities. For example,

TABLE **9.7** **Various Combinations of Probabilities of Correct Responses on T_1 and T_2 Together with Some Expressions from the Theory That Will Predict These Probabilities**
(Estes, 1961)

TRIALS	PROBABILITIES	SIMPLE LINEAR MODEL
Correct both T_1 and T_2	0.238	θ^2
Correct T_1, incorrect T_2	0.147	$\theta(1-\theta)$
Incorrect T_1, correct T_2	0.017	$(1-\theta)\theta$
Incorrect both T_1 and T_2	0.598	$(1-\theta)^2$

the probability of correct responses on both T_1 and T_2 is indicated by p_{11}. That value is the probability of a recall on T_1 being followed by correct recall on T_2. The probability of a correct recall on T_1 being followed by an *incorrect* recall on T_2 is given by p_{10}. These various p's were obtained from an experiment which measured the *proportion* of items correct on T_1 and T_2.

The basic equation which is used to predict these various outcomes is

$$p_{n+1} = (1-\theta)p_n + \theta \tag{8}$$

The equation is really quite simple. It says that the probability of a correct response p on trial $n+1$ is proportional to the probability on trial n, p_n. The factor of proportionality is $(1-\theta)$, and we can say that p_n is operated upon by $(1-\theta)$ in order to obtain p_{n+1}.

Even that equation, however, is simplified by our assumption that the probability of correct response at the outset of trial 1 is zero. With that assumption, the probability of correct responding on T_1 is simply θ. The whole expression $(1 - \theta)p_n$ in Equation (8) disappears, because p_n is zero. No further presentation intervenes between T_1 and T_2, so the operation represented in the equation does not occur; the joint probability of recall on both T_1 and T_2 is simply θ^2 or $\theta \times \theta$.

Table 9.7 clearly shows that the data obtained from the experiment do not square with these assumptions. For example, if we take the value of p_{11} as 0.238 (the first row in Table 9.7), then the value of p_{01} should be 0.250. The value of θ is approximately 0.49 (the square root of 0.238), and in order to obtain p_{01} we find the quantity $(1 - \theta)\theta$, which is approximately 0.250. Notice, however, that the experimentally obtained value for p_{01} is 0.017, which is far from 0.250.

The basic trouble seems to be with the application of a simple linear model. The simple linear model appears to work quite well in some situations, including certain studies of conditioning and instrumental learning, but it does not work well here.

OTHER STATISTICAL MODELS

Bower (1961) and other investigators have been able to show that essentially the same plan of analysis, but with fewer restrictive assumptions than in the simple linear model, suffices to predict many features of verbal learning. For example, Figure 9.8 shows the fit derived from some principles very similar to those expressed in Equation (8). In this case the data are the number of errors on successive trials in verbal paired-associate learning, where a test trial followed each presentation. The figure shows that the fit between the empirically arrived-at data and the theoretical curve is strikingly good.

Here we have an apparent contradiction. An equation like Equation (8) works very well in some situations, but it must be altered somewhat in order to fit other kinds of data. Such a situation is not at all unusual in mathematical development of theories. Sometimes an equa-

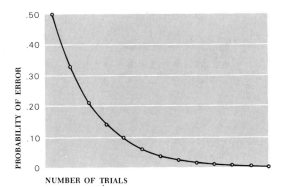

FIG. **9.8** The fit of an equation for a learning curve to actual data. The points are data; the line represents the fit of the equation to these data. (After Bower, 1961.)

tion may generate something that is approximately true for a general process but that must be modified in order to fit certain other details. In fact, the basic principle behind Equation (8) has occurred in a variety of quantitative theories of learning, though sometimes it has been stated in very different ways and without the mathematics of probability.

It should be noted that Bower (1961) attempts to correct some of the deficiencies of the linear model and to substitute a more general expression of the same kind. He is able to show that on certain critical issues there is a divergence between the simple version of the model, which fails to fit data like those in Table 9.7, and his own version of the model, which fits such data quite well.

Evaluation of Mathematical Theories of Learning

The number of specific facts in the study of verbal learning is very large, and it would take a very general theory indeed to be able to generate many of them from theoretical equations. Mathematical theories of learning are quite specialized, and we cannot treat the topic exhaustively. For a convenient summary, the interested student may consult the collection of original papers reprinted by Luce, Bush, and Galanter, *Readings in Mathematical Psychology* (1963a). Not all mathematical theories of learning are primarily statistical in nature (some of the older ones, in particular, are not), but the fact that the data of verbal learning lend themselves so readily to the classification of correct and incorrect responses makes the binomial treatment, in terms of p and q, very attractive.

What do mathematical theories of learning accomplish? They can be said to achieve three things. First of all, such theories provide a coherent and precise description of experimental data. Secondly, the logical and orderly presentation sometimes reveals implications that would ordinarily be overlooked. Finally, it is sometimes argued, mathematical theories of learning lead to very general theories about the nature of behavior, theories which transcend ordinary experimental data.

Undoubtedly all these things are, to some degree, true. Furthermore, it is possible that some of the principles derived from rigorous quantitative theories may have some greater generality. They may, for example, serve as a bridge between neurophysiology and psychology or between psychology and economic theory. Some of the older nonstatistical quantitative theories, such as that of Hull (1943), were couched in a semiphysiological way, and for a long time it was assumed that the processes described by the mathematical constants of the theory would also have some physiological meaning. Many versions of statistical learning theory have implications for decision processes and, by extension, for econometric theory.

The elegance and rigor of modern mathematical theories should not, however, blind us to certain defects. One defect is in the kinds of problems the theorists have chosen to examine. To a very considerable extent they have reviewed existing data, and have scarcely ever examined the possibilities in collecting data which depart from existing techniques and ideas. In this respect, the concern over the all-or-none issue is an exception. It is not an exception in another respect, however. The problems mathematical theories choose are often very restricted and minute in conception and implication.

Therefore, mathematical theories of learning are likely to strike many psychologists as sterile and of limited interest. Very often the mathematical theorists deal with matters of no significance to the basic problems of human learning and the use of language. But though there is a certain truth in these criticisms, the question has another side. The rigorous logic which mathematical argument requires of us sometimes shows us that our larger, intuitive notions are equally empty and sterile. It is easy enough to think about "significant" problems when one is required only to deal with the generalities and the unspecified. Furthermore, we often find that when we rigorously derive some conclusion by mathematical steps, our original intuitions are in error.

In short, the application of mathematical analysis to the problems of verbal behavior is rewarding—and sometimes rewarding in a way we do not anticipate. Furthermore, there is a growing realization on the part of many people who study language and verbal behavior—linguists and anthropologists as well as experimental psychologists—that the tools of statistical theory are suited to the solution of many problems. Therefore, there is some chance in the future for a general mathematical theory of verbal behavior, one which will encompass aspects of linguistics and communication theory as well as learning theory.

10

TRANSFER OF TRAINING

How is the way in which we acquire some new skill determined by what we have learned in the past? This question defines the problem of transfer of training. The question is not unique to the study of transfer, however, for many of the topics we have considered thus far concern relationships between things learned at different times. In this chapter, we shall not be so much concerned with relations between a particular task and past experience in general as we shall be with the specific relations between two or more tasks. In brief, here we shall examine the general principles governing the effects of specific previous experience upon the acquisition of some particular skill.

Almost all educational and training programs are built upon the basic premise that human beings have the ability to transfer what they have learned in one situation to another. This assumption is fundamental to the American faith in the importance and practicality of formal education. It is not surprising, therefore, to find that the topic of transfer of training has been one of the central problems for educational psychologists and educational theorists.

Even though transfer of training has broad implications, we shall have to limit this chapter to the special issues that arise when we evaluate the relations between tasks. The number of such relations is limited only by the number of ways in which we can describe the things that human beings learn. Some tasks are mainly characterized by the fact that they depend upon motor skill or dexterity. Other tasks demand only that we be able to perceive patterns of relations within complicated stimuli. Still others are primarily linguistic or demand the application of logical analysis. It will make our job easier if we adopt some general way of characterizing various tasks so that we can discuss the relations between them in terms of general principles instead of being limited to a description of specific relations. Such a broad characterization will be very useful, though it will run the danger of overstating the generality of empirical laws and principles. At various times we shall have to introduce a note of caution into the generalization of the various principles that are arrived at by empirical study. This is because such generalizations are limited by the degree of accuracy in the application to particular tasks of our description of possible relations between tasks.

One task can consist in large part of components of skills learned at earlier times. For example, the ability to multiply two- and three-digit numbers obviously depends not only upon an understanding of the principle of addition but upon the ordinary rote-memory skills of addition. Two tasks can also be related to one another by some underlying common principles: the rules we learn to use in doing one thing may be extended with little or no additional experience to perform some other task. Finally, two tasks may be related through components or general principles that are similar though not identical. To make matters confusing, the relations between tasks may lead to both positive and negative transfer. The components of some skill learned earlier may have a detrimental, as well as a beneficial, effect upon performance of another task. It is obvious, for example, that we often incorrectly extrapolate or generalize principles to some new case to which they do not apply.

The theoretical analysis of transfer of training has been concerned largely with these possible relations between tasks. In addition, there are many purely empirical studies of transfer, studies in which the influence of some particular task upon another task—irrespective of how the relation between them can be described—is the object of investigation. These studies are, for the most part, applied studies of educational and training programs.

Before we can begin to describe the available information about transfer, we need to know something about how transfer is studied. All the issues we shall examine depend upon adequate experimental designs and appropriate measures of transfer. Therefore, our first problem is to look at the general nature of transfer studies.

THE EVALUATION OF TRANSFER

The fundamental solution to the study of transfer lies in the use of an appropriate experimental design, so that the right comparisons can be made. If we make the correct comparisons, however, we still have the problem of evaluating the amount of transfer, so a secondary problem in the study of transfer is measurement. These two problems are considered in this section.

Experimental Designs in Transfer

SIMPLE DESIGNS

There are two basic types of designs for transfer studies. One of these evaluates the effect of a prior task on the acquisition of a second task, and the other evaluates the effect of an interpolated task upon further practice or retention of an initial task. The second type of design is particularly appropriate to the study of forgetting, and as a result we shall have more occasions to deal with it in the next chapter than in this one.

THE PROACTIVE DESIGN. The proactive design is the simplest arrangement for the study of transfer. It requires two groups of subjects, one of which practices a preliminary task either for some specific period of time or to some specified criterion and is then tested on acquisition of a second task. The other group of subjects learns only the second task. Transfer is said to take place if there is a statistically significant difference between the two groups in performance of the second task. The transfer is positive if the group exposed to the prior task does better than the other group, and negative if its performance is worse.

The basic conditions are summarized as follows:

Experimental Group
Practices task A .... Tested on task B

Control Group
Rests .... Tested on task B

One variation in the proactive design provides for a test of retention of task B after it has been acquired. This particular variation is critically important to the experimental analysis of forgetting.

THE RETROACTIVE DESIGN. The other commonly used plan for the study of transfer can be summarized in this way:

Experimental Group
Practices task A ...... Practices task B ...... Tested on task A

Control Group
Practices task A .... Rests .... Tested on task A

The critical comparison in this case is on the final test for A. Any difference between the two groups of subjects is attributed to the influence of the interpolated practice on task B. For readily apparent reasons, this design is sometimes called the fore-and-after method. It has the advantage that initial practice on task A can serve to equate two groups of subjects in performance on that task. Also, it sometimes happens that transfer is not to the initial stage of practice on a task but to some later stage, so it is useful to get the preliminary practice on task A out of the way before the other task is introduced.

ADDITIONAL COMPARISONS AND THE NATURE OF CONTROL

ADDITIONAL COMPARISONS. It takes at least two groups of subjects to perform a transfer experiment. There are many occasions, however, in which a larger number of comparisons should be made. In order to see how task B is related to task A—that is to say, whether it is similar, contains elements identical to A, or employs a principle common to A—we should have some variations in A suitable for comparison. In that case we should want to compare each of a number of variations in task A with a control or rest condition. Furthermore, we may want to compare the amount of transfer from A to B with the effects of an equivalent amount of direct practice on B. For example, we may wish to know not only whether the study of Latin transfers to the acquisition of formal English grammar but how such transfer compares with the effect of direct practice in English grammar. Therefore, a more complicated experiment might be summarized as follows:

Group 1: Practices task B .... Tested on task B
Group 2: Practices task A_1 .... Tested on task B
Group 3: Practices task A_2 .... Tested on task B
Group 4: Practices task A_3 .... Tested on task B
Group 5: Rests .... Tested on task B

It is surprising to find that there are circumstances in which transfer from one task to another is greater than direct practice on the task to be tested. We shall later examine some of the circumstances surrounding this unusual case.

THE NATURE OF THE CONTROL. What we mean by "rest" for the control condition deserves some comment. In an ideal experimental study of transfer, the subjects under the control condition would be held in some kind of suspended animation or absolute inactivity until the time for the test on task B. In practice, it is impossible to keep a control group of subjects completely inactive while the experimental group learns task A. So the comparison is always between some practice on task A and some activity totally unrelated to task B. The problem is a more serious one with the retroactive design than with the proactive design, for while the experimental subjects are learning the interpolated task, the control subjects may rehearse the original task. This is not a matter for concern in studies of animal behavior, since we can assume that, under proper conditions, animal subjects will not be doing something appropriate to the test task under rest conditions. But human beings do rehearse or engage in other activities that might have an influence upon the final test. Consequently, in most transfer experiments, control subjects are not allowed to be passive. Rather, they are given some task to perform in the "rest" condition which keeps them occupied but which is totally unrelated to the eventual test task.

Every so often, transfer studies are deliberately relative. That is to say, they compare the transfer value of two preliminary tasks instead of a preliminary task and a control condition. While such comparisons are useful for some purposes, they do not enable us to distinguish between positive and negative transfer. Suppose, for example, that performance on task B is better after practice on task A_1 than after practice on A_2. That might be because there is less *negative* transfer from A_1 to B than from A_2 to B, or it might be because there is more *positive* transfer from A_1 to B.

There are, of course, many variations in experimental designs, and in addition, there is a whole class of "mixed designs." In these, the same subjects are given many or all of the conditions in a transfer experiment within one task. A list of paired associates, for example, may include some A_1 pairs and some A_2 pairs, and there may be some B pairs on the final task that have no counterparts in the first or A task.

The Measurement of Transfer

Since the particular measures used in studies of learning have only an arbitrary value when we are considering the problem of transfer, most studies prefer to express transfer as a percentage. Murdock (1957) has evaluated a number of the formulas which have been proposed from time to time for doing this, and he has come to some conclusions about what these various formulas emphasize. A brief review of Murdock's evaluation will be useful to our understanding of the problem of transfer.

COMPARISONS WITH CONTROL AND MAXIMUM POSSIBLE TRANSFER

COMPARISONS WITH CONTROL. It is possible to express amount of transfer between two tasks relative to the performance of the control subjects. Such an expression would emphasize the extent to which transfer is greater than zero. Percentage of transfer by such a measure would be expressed as follows:

$$\text{Percentage of transfer} = \frac{E - C}{C} \times 100$$

E refers to the performance of the experimental group on task B, and C refers to the performance of the control group on task B. If the experimental subjects perform no better than the control subjects, transfer is zero. One difficulty with the measure is that, depending on the measure of actual performance, the experimental group could be infinitely better than the control. It is not uncommon, by such a measure, to arrive at transfer scores of 300 or 400 percent. Furthermore, with negative transfer, this formula produces a different result. Here the maximum value of negative transfer is −100 percent.

COMPARISONS WITH MAXIMUM POSSIBLE.   Another way to evaluate transfer is to compare the obtained transfer with the maximum possible value. The maximum possible value is the very best score on test B which theoretically could be obtained. The formula is expressed as follows:

$$\text{Percentage of transfer} = \frac{E - C}{T - C} \times 100$$

As before, E refers to a measure of performance on task B for the experimental subjects, and C refers to a similar measure for the control subjects. T expresses the maximum possible score on task B. Like the preceding one, this formula gives rise to difficulties. The maximum positive transfer is 100 percent, but the maximum negative transfer is minus infinity. Furthermore, for some tasks there is no theoretical best score.

A BALANCED MEASURE.   Murdock suggests a measure which is symmetric about zero. That is to say, it can range from a value of 100 percent positive transfer to a value of 100 percent negative transfer. The formula is

$$\text{Percentage of transfer} = \frac{E - C}{E + C} \times 100$$

It expresses the ratio of the difference between the experimental and control scores to the sum of these scores. While it is symmetrically distributed about zero, it has the disadvantage of being rather insensitive. Only when the control subjects achieve a very poor score on test B and the experimental subjects do extremely well would there be a very large value for the percentage of transfer. The transfer score of 100 percent would be achieved only when the control subjects scored zero (positive transfer) or when the experimental subjects scored zero (negative transfer). Despite this difficulty, it is probably the most satisfactory purely empirical measure of transfer. Table 10.1 lists some sample data and possible transfer scores for all three formulas.

TABLE **10.1** **Percentage of Transfer for Some Sample Scores as Determined by Each of the Three Formulas for Scores in Terms of Number of Correct Responses**
(Murdock, 1957)

NO. OF CORRECT RESPONSES			FORMULAS		
E	C	T	1	2	3
20	0	20	$+ \infty$	$+100\%$	$+100\%$
15	5	20	$+200\%$	$+ 67\%$	$+ 50\%$
10	5	20	$+100\%$	$+ 33\%$	$+ 33\%$
5	5	20	0%	0%	0%
5	10	20	$- 50\%$	$- 50\%$	$- 33\%$
5	15	20	$- 67\%$	-200%	$- 50\%$
0	20	20	-100%	$- \infty$	-100%

We need to note that if the measure of performance itself is a negative one, all three formulas need to be altered. The last one, for example, becomes

$$\text{Percentage of transfer} = \frac{C - E}{E + C} \times 100$$

Examples of negative measures of performance are errors and trials to criterion. Both of these decrease as skill increases.

ANALYTIC EVALUATION OF TRANSFER

We should not think that all problems in evaluating transfer of training can be solved by the application of a simple percentage measure of the influence of one task upon the performance of another. Frequently, we wish information of a more analytic sort. All learning curves must be described by at least two parameters. That is to say, equations for all learning curves require at least two constants and sometimes more. The two necessary parameters are (1) the origin or performance level at the beginning of practice (which, to oversimplify, we can think of as ability without specific practice), and (2) the rate of change in performance or the slope of the curve. It is quite possible that practice on one task may transfer to the initial level of performance on another without at all affecting the slope or rate of improvement on the second task. If this were the case, a simple percentage transfer measure based on averaging correct performance over a number of trials would hide the differential effect. Consequently, in some situations at least, we need a more elaborate analysis of the transfer than would be provided by a simple percentage formula.

That a more elaborate analysis is not something merely of theoretical significance is illustrated by a study of transfer in perceptual-motor learning (Hammerton, 1963). This study examined the influence of training in a mock-up or simulated task upon performance in the real task. The situation was something like learning to handle a dummy airplane before learning to control a real one.

The investigator found large negative transfer on initial performance of the second task as the result of practice on the first or simulated task. The negative transfer was of short duration, however; and after some practice on the second task, there was a large positive transfer. Practice on the simulated task resulted in a saving of about 70 percent in the amount of practice on the final task required to bring performance to a specified criterion. Thus, in this example, there was negative transfer to the origin of the learning curve on the final task and positive transfer to the rate of improvement on the final task.

THE THEORY OF TRANSFER

We have pointed out that the possible relations between tasks can be described in three ways. Tasks can have components in common, the principles underlying them can be identical, or they can have components or general principles which are similar though not identical. A great deal of the theory of transfer of training simply concerns the problem of finding rules that will predict what combinations of conditions relating tasks in these ways will produce what amounts of transfer.

Transfer theory, however, did not have its beginning in an abstract analysis of human skills; it began with very practical educational questions. Educational theories dealing with transfer of training, among other things, are older than the experimental study of human learning. Aside from its intrinsic value, there would be no point to the formal institution of education if there were no such thing as transfer. We assume that a large part, if not most, of what children learn in schools will be useful to them in the great variety of conditions they face outside the schoolroom. Because transfer of training has always occupied a central position in educational theory, it is not surprising that the earliest educational problems which were studied experimentally included transfer.

In the pre-experimental period, educational views of transfer were dominated by the notion of formal discipline. This idea, simply put, stated that sheer mental exercise was beneficial to mental functions. It took no account whatever of possible relations between tasks. The classical preparatory curriculum embodied this notion. The hapless student worked at Greek, rhetoric, geometry, and Latin, not so much for their intrinsic merit but because of the belief that these exercised and sharpened the mind. Learning to conjugate in Latin, it was sometimes alleged, made for a keen wit in a lawyer. Training in logic made a physician's diagnosis more certain.

The idea of formal discipline is, of course, quite vague. It depended, in part, on a supposed analogy with the alleged effects of physical exercise on muscular development and in part on the view that mental processes are basically all of one kind, so that practice on one function necessarily entails improvement in others.

Even when the idea of formal discipline came under critical scrutiny, many educational psychologists took the view that it was possible to improve specific mental functions by generalized practice. In this view, the prolonged practice of rote-memory exercises should improve memory generally, and it would be possible to produce rigorous thinking by the repetitious solution of syllogistic propositions. These assertions, however, did not escape the skeptical attention of the early experimentalists, and consequently, many of the pioneering studies of transfer of training concern just such questions as the possible improvement of memory in general by means of specific exercises in memorizing.

The most influential of the early experimentally minded educational psychologists was E. L. Thorndike. He devoted some attention to practical educational problems. For example, he examined the transfer value of Latin to aspects of the use of English (Thorndike, 1923). More important, however, he was responsible for the first theory of transfer of training that dealt with the possible relations between tasks. His was a theory of "identical elements." The theory grew out of some experiments by Thorndike and Woodworth (1901) in which they gave subjects practice estimating the areas of various geometrical figures such as triangles and rectangles. The experimenters measured the transfer from estimating the areas of certain forms to estimating the area of other forms. These experiments led Thorndike to the view that there would be positive transfer in learning to the extent that one ability required components acquired in some other skill. In his view, the transfer was quite specific, and it would not occur unless at least part of the final task consisted of things specifically learned in the first task.

These early experiments led other investigators to examine similar problems. Some psychologists preferred to describe transfer as the result of the learning of general principles which were common to both the original and the final tasks. The description of transfer as the result of generalized principles has always appealed to those psychologists who have not liked the idea that people learn sequences of elementary responses. They point out that it is not merely that a child learns to apply what he knows about specific sums to the multiplication of *n*-digit numbers; instead, he generalizes the arithmetic rules of addition to multiplication.

Both ways of stating the case are reasonable if we choose the right examples, but the controversy that developed in educational theory often was not. In fact, one can describe particular cases of transfer in either way, though clearly one description is more appropriate to some tasks than the other. There are, however, some more general ways of describing the nature of transfer, ways which do not depend upon a view of transfer either as the result of identical elements or as the result of the application of general principles. Or, to put it another way, these principles would apply no matter what our views of the processes underlying learning and transfer. The usual version of these principles grows out of stimulus-response theory, and, for convenience as much as anything else, we shall describe them in terms of stimulus and response.

The Stimulus-Response Analysis of Transfer

The stimulus-response description of transfer is important because of the generality of stimulus and response analysis. Any task can be characterized by its stimulus components and the responses, both overt and implicit, made to those stimuli. The relationships between two tasks can usually be very well described by stating how the stimuli in the two tasks resemble one another and by characterizing the relations between the things people do and think when faced with each of the tasks.

RELATIONS AMONG STIMULI

If we train an organism to respond to a particular stimulus and then test that organism by presenting a different stimulus, we have an example of a possible transfer situation. The two tasks differ only in the stimuli to which the organism is expected to respond. You will recognize this situation as the procedure for testing stimulus generalization (see page 171), and indeed, stimulus generalization can be regarded as a special case of transfer, just as it can also be regarded as providing one of the basic principles by which transfer in a number of situations operates. The application of the principle of stimulus generalization to transfer, then, defines the case of studying variations in stimuli between tasks while the responses required in the task are the same.

STIMULUS VARIATION WITH RESPONSES HELD CONSTANT. The essential characteristic of stimulus generalization requires that we test the strength of some conditioned response to stimuli other than the stimulus used during training. The basic principle is that the more similar the test

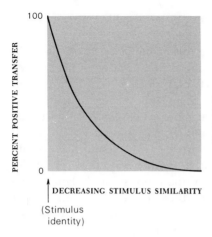

FIG. **10.1** The percent transfer of training between two tasks when the responses are identical and the stimuli are varied from identical to completely dissimilar.

stimuli are to the training stimulus, the greater the response elicited by the test stimuli. From such a principle, we should guess that the amount of positive transfer would gradually decline as we changed stimuli in a second task from what they had been on an original task. Such a theoretical relation is illustrated in Figure 10.1. One axis shows the amount of positive transfer varying from 100 percent to zero, and the other axis shows stimulus similarity. Notice that 100 percent transfer would occur only when the stimulus is exactly the same as the one used in original learning. The symmetrical formula suggested by Murdock would yield such a result.

Does this relationship in fact hold? In one well-known experiment (Yum, 1931), subjects learned paired associates consisting of nonsense syllables as responses and either nonsense syllables or geometric forms as stimuli. In one condition in which geometric forms were the stimuli, the subjects learned to pair each of 12 forms with a different syllable. Then, 24 hours later, these subjects were presented with stimuli and asked to recall the syllable associated with each stimulus. In some conditions the stimuli used during original training were presented, and in other conditions the stimuli were changed. Some of the changed stimuli closely resembled the originals, while others resembled them only slightly. The results are presented in Table 10.2. It is apparent that recall depended upon the similarity of the test stimulus to that presented during learning. Therefore, it does not seem too much amiss to apply the notion of stimulus generalization to the analysis of transfer.

While this experiment provides a reasonable parallel to experiments on stimulus generalization in conditioning or instrumental learning, the experimental design is not altogether satisfactory. For one thing, it is not certain that the subject failed to respond to the altered forms

TABLE 10.2   **Recall of Previously Learned Responses to Stimuli That Are Altered between Training and Test Trial**
(Data from Yum, 1931)

STIMULI	PERCENT RECALLED	PERCENT OF RECALL TO IDENTICAL STIMULI
Identical	84.6	100
Highly similar	64.5	76
Similar	49.2	58
Less similar	45.3	53
Least similar	36.3	43

because they could not recall the correct responses. Possibly they did so because they were not quite certain whether or not they ought to respond. A better experiment would be one in which learning, rather than recall, of the altered material is tested. Several experiments which do exactly this agree in showing that degree of transfer does decrease as one decreases the resemblance between training and test stimuli.

One of these experiments deserves detailed mention because (1) the stimuli in the experiment were words rather than abstract visual forms, and (2) the experiment was well designed. The experiment (Staner, 1956) used three degrees of stimulus similarity. Similarity in this study was determined by judgments about the meaningful similarity among the adjectives used as stimuli. An example of a highly similar pair is DIRTY-UNCLEAN; a pair having medium similarity is LAZY-IDLE, and a pair of low similarity is SPIRAL-IMPURE. The responses were a set of adjectives totally unrelated to the stimuli or to one another. The results showed a sharp gradient of transfer from one list to the other depending upon the similarity between the adjectives used as stimuli. For the first trial of anticipation on the second list, the mean correct responses for the three degrees of similarity were 3.42, 2.33, and 1.00.

CHANGING RESPONSES AND HOLDING STIMULI CONSTANT.   What happens if responses are changed from one list to the next while stimuli are held the same? There is an old principle in psychology which says that this situation should produce negative transfer. The principle implies that a second task containing the same stimuli but requiring totally unrelated responses should produce negative transfer. It should be more difficult to learn such a second task than if the previous task had not been learned at all.

There is, as we shall see, a sense in which this principle is correct, but it does not always work so simply in experiments. In actual experiments, changing responses while holding the stimuli constant does not always result in negative transfer when measured against an absolute (rest) control. In fact, measured by Murdock's symmetric formula, such a situation more often than not produces net positive transfer. That is because there are some general features of transfer which make the simple experimental comparison with an absolute control not appropriate for detecting the influence of intertask similarity upon transfer. There are some "general" factors of improvement—such as learning how to do paired associate learning efficiently—which result in positive transfer, even when the conditions of similarity should produce negative transfer. The obtained positive transfer is *net;* we suspect that there really is a detrimental influence of altering responses but that it is overwhelmed by the positive transfer which comes from the general conditions of transfer. In fact, the only condition that consistently produces net negative transfer is one in which the same responses are used in paired-associate learning but are rearranged. In this kind of experiment, the subjects learn new pairings of old responses on the second list, and this condition nearly always produces large amounts of negative transfer. In principle, however, it is like learning new responses to old stimuli.

An experiment by Postman (1962c) allows us to see how response relations in transfer do produce negative transfer. This experiment compared the degree of transfer under three conditions, only two of which are important to us. In these conditions, (1) new, unrelated responses were paired with previously used stimuli in paired-associate learning, and (2) the responses to different stimuli were interchanged in the second list. Because of general factors in transfer, the control was not complete rest, but the learning of two paired-associate lists which were completely unrelated to one another. It is standard practice to designate the stimulus and response conditions in paired-associate learning by letters. In all three conditions (the two experimental and the one control), the first list can be designated by A-B. The condition of learning new responses to old stimuli becomes, then, A-B, A-C; the condition of rearranging the responses becomes A-B, A-B$_r$, and the condition of totally unrelated lists is described as A-B, C-D. The materials for both stimulus and response members in this study were unrelated English adjectives.

The results of the experiment can be seen in Figure 10.2. As measured against the A-B, C-D control, both experimental conditions showed considerable negative transfer. The amount of negative transfer when new responses were learned (A-B, A-C) varied with the amount of practice on the original list, but in a curious way. With relatively low amounts of practice, negative transfer was low, and then it increased with more practice. With very extensive practice on the original pairs, however, the amount of negative transfer decreased again. Evidently, as the subjects became more familiar with the responses in the original list,

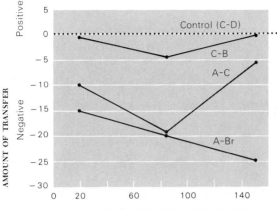

FIG. 10.2   Negative transfer as a function of the relations between two lists and the number of reinforcements. Notice that the largest negative transfer occurs
when two items are scrambled. (Postman, 1962c.)

it became easier for them to discriminate the differences between the
responses in the second list and those in the first and thus avoid a certain
amount of confusion. The rearranged responses, however, produced more
and more negative transfer as practice on the original list was increased.
This result occurs because the more thoroughly the original pairs are
learned, the more difficult it is to re-sort them into their new pairs,
and it becomes even more difficult when these responses are very
familiar.

       This experiment shows rather conclusively, then, that negative
transfer does result when new responses have to be learned or old ones
rearranged. As in most of the earlier experiments, the greatest amount of
negative transfer comes from the rearrangement of the original responses.
It is always harder to learn such rearranged pairs than to learn paired
associates with no previous practice at paired-associate learning. Negative
transfer is at a maximum for the condition of rearrangement because all
the factors, such as task differentiation, which contribute some positive
transfer and thus tend to reduce the net negative transfer do not occur
in such an experiment.

       What about response similarity? In verbal learning the responses,
like the stimuli, are usually words. Words can be more or less similar to
one another. Generally, it has been asserted that if responses are very
similar to one another, positive transfer will occur, but as responses become more and more unrelated, negative transfer develops. This possibility is best seen in the transfer surface.

THE TRANSFER SURFACE

We have seen that stimuli can vary in their resemblance to one another, as can responses. The relationships in similarity determine the amount and direction of transfer, and we need only, at this point, put all the possible relationships together to have a complete picture of transfer and intertask similarity. When we do that, the transfer surface, or more properly, the transfer solid results.

THE TRANSFER DIAGRAM. The transfer surface is a diagram which requires three dimensions. One dimension describes the degree of similarity between the stimuli in two tasks, another describes the degree of similarity between responses for these same tasks, and the third dimension describes the direction and amount of transfer. Such a diagram, derived from one originally presented by Osgood (1949), is shown in Figure 10.3.

The curves between each of the pairs of axes show how amount and direction of transfer varies as a function of either stimulus or response similarity. The curves, put together, describe a peculiarly curved surface. The part of the surface in the lower right-hand corner is that combination of conditions which produces the greatest negative transfer. That is defined by the case in which the stimuli for two tasks are identical but the responses are completely unrelated. On the other hand, maximum positive transfer is found when both stimuli and responses are identical for the two tasks. From this result, we can see that further practice on the same task is only a special and limiting case of positive transfer, as logically it should be. On the opposite or far side of the

FIG. 10.3 The hypothetical stimulus-response transfer surface. (After Osgood, 1949.)

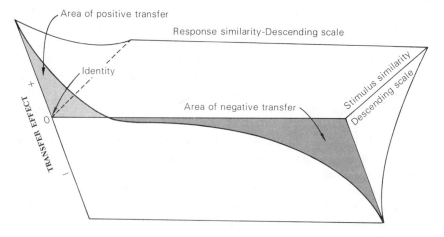

diagram, where the similarity between stimuli for the tasks is at a minimum, transfer, either positive or negative, is very weak. No transfer should
occur at all when the two tasks are unrelated in both stimuli and responses. We should not expect learning how to swim to have much transfer to learning how to take shorthand.

We have already seen that positive transfer varies with the
similarity of stimuli when the responses between two tasks are identical
and that learning new responses (or rearranged pairs) to old stimuli
produces negative transfer. We need, therefore, only to examine the cases
in between.

EXPERIMENTAL STUDIES OF THE TRANSFER SURFACE.   Several studies
(Bugelski & Cadwallader, 1956; Dallett, 1962, and Wimer, 1964) have
examined a fair sample of all the possible relations within the transfer
surface. As we might expect, these experiments are rather large and complicated. One of them (Wimer, 1964), for example, combined five degrees
of stimulus similarity between tasks with five conditions of response
similarity. This makes twenty-five different conditions in all which had
to be compared within one experiment. Furthermore, because there are
differences in the degree of learning of the original task among the
experimental groups in these studies (almost necessarily, given the large
number of conditions), the results have to be adjusted statistically. Therefore, it is not surprising that all the details of the results of these experiments agree neither with one another nor with all the implications of the
diagram. In general, however, the broad outcomes of these three experiments are in agreement both with one another and with the diagram
as it is presented in Figure 10.3. All three experiments show decreasing
amounts of positive transfer when responses are held the same and
stimulus similarity varied. The one anomalous case occurs in Wimer's
experiment, in which opposite or antonymous words as both stimuli and
responses in the second task produce positive transfer. This may well be
the case because there is opportunity for mediation (see page 314) between the lists which have opposites for stimuli and responses. If you are
to respond with "hot" to a particular stimulus on one list, mediation will
enable you to respond with "cold" to its opposite.

The experiments agree in showing that *unrelated* responses between the two lists produced negative transfer, though Bugelski and
Cadwallader (1956) also showed that negative transfer occurred when
responses were similar. This result is the most difficult and unusual one
to explain within the model of transfer suggested by the diagram.

These three experiments, taken together, show us that we can
take the transfer surface as an approximately accurate schematic picture
of the effects of stimulus and response variation between tasks. Transfer,

even in a situation as simple as paired-associate learning, is complicated, however, and many things enter in to contaminate a pure stimulus-response analysis. You will recall that, in paired-associate learning, when people learn to give the response terms to the appropriate stimuli, they are also able to give the stimulus term when presented with the response, even though such reversed learning is not ordinarily tested. Such reversed relationships make the actual transfer situation more complicated than this diagram would imply, so perhaps it is surprising that it works as well as it does.

Other Analyses of Relations Between Tasks

The stimulus-response analysis is a powerful one, and for tasks in which it is peculiarly appropriate, such as paired-associate learning (or its school-room equivalent in, for example, the learning of vocabulary for a foreign language), the results summarized in Figure 10.3 are very useful. Not all tasks, however, so easily lend themselves to a stimulus-response analysis. We can see some of the characteristics of tasks that do and those that do not lend themselves to such an analysis by examining some cases.

Consider, for example, the practical problem of moving from one typewriter keyboard to another. Once we have learned to type on a specific typewriter, there is enormous positive transfer from one instrument to the next. This is as it should be, and it is altogether reasonable to apply stimulus-response analysis to the case. Notice that while the *net* transfer in this case is certainly the general outcome, there is potential for some negative transfer. The few specific keys which may be different for two typewriters provide such an instance. The difficulty most typists experience when they first face an electric typewriter provides another. A whole set of nonspecific responses (such as resting the fingers on the keys while not actually typing) produce some components of negative transfer in going from a manual to an electric machine. In all cases, however, the net transfer is overwhelmingly positive.

But what about the relationships between the study of physics and that of chemistry? The application of stimulus-response analysis to this case seems to miss the point. It can be done, but the results are clumsy and not particularly convincing. The tasks of learning both physics and chemistry can better be characterized as learning networks of relationships among concepts and learning how to solve problems by the application of general rules. We may indeed agree that there is positive transfer between these two tasks, both by way of common elements and by means of general principles. It should also not be forgotten, however, that specific components of negative transfer are possible in these kinds of situations. Some of the particular concepts and ways of solving problems in physics are incorrect from the point of view of what the chemist expects his students to learn. Students may innocently extrapolate some principle from one field to the other when it is inappropriate or inaccurate to do so.

In order to have some conceptual apparatus to discuss these more general cases of transfer, we need a kind of task analysis which does not depend on specifying stimulus and response components. In this section, we shall discuss some of the characteristics of such an analysis.

TASK COMMONALITY

The most basic concept we need is that of task commonality. We can say that two tasks can positively transfer to one another to the extent that there is some commonality between the outcomes required by the tasks. It does not make any difference whether that commonality is the result of shared responses in paired-associate learning or the result of the mathematical techniques common to two scientific disciplines. Transfer is only possible when two tasks require something in common in order to meet some satisfactory standard of performance. Therefore, if there is nothing in common between the requirements of two tasks, positive transfer is not possible. If two tasks are identical in their requirements, perfect transfer is possible. Notice that the latter statement does not imply that the two tasks need be identical; only their requirements (the responses to be performed) have to be identical—or capable, in turn, of being generated from common rules.

Figure 10.4 shows the relation between the amount of commonality in outcome and the possible percent transfer between two tasks. All possible transfer is limited to the crosshatched area. In fact, transfer will seldom achieve the maximum possible value. As a general rule, people

FIG. 10.4 Maximum possible transfer is limited by task commonality. The crosshatched area is the area of possible transfer. The theoretical limit of obtained transfer may be something like the dashed line.

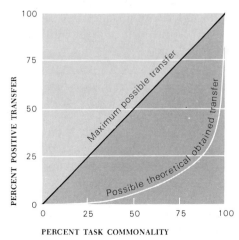

PERCENT TASK COMMONALITY

learning a new task bring something less than the best possible selection of previous experience to bear.

If there is in fact zero commonality between the requirements of a task, but the individual, because of previous experience, brings elements from previous tasks to bear, there will be negative transfer. Therefore it is theoretically possible, at least, for negative transfer to occur when there is no relation between tasks whatever. Such an outcome is contrary to the transfer surface; and for at least one class of tasks—paired associates—we know the transfer surface to be approximately correct. Negative transfer, however, is not the simple mirror image of positive transfer.

We cannot draw a diagram like that in Figure 10.4 for negative transfer, because the misapplication of previous experience to a given task is, in theory, unlimited. That becomes obvious when we realize that the set of conditions which *do not* satisfy effective performance on any given task is infinite. In theory, people can go on forever trying out the wrong habits in the attempt to learn some new skill. In reality, of course, negative transfer is never that severe. Furthermore, the extent to which people do apply previous habits to some new task depends upon the perceived degree of similarity between the tasks. This accounts for the importance of stimulus similarity in the results of experiments on negative transfer. People do not apply previous habits willy-nilly. Sometimes they do not because there are only a limited number of habits which are aroused by the circumstances of a particular task, and sometimes they do not because, in testing various hypotheses, they very quickly exhaust what are perceived to be the reasonable possibilities. The important point, however, is that the limit on negative transfer is not set by the commonality between the requirements of tasks; it is set by the conditions which induce human beings to try to give up the application of old habits. Low similarity, punishment of particular attempts, and simple extinction are among the elementary conditions which can reduce or prevent negative transfer.

Experimental Studies of Intertask Relations

PREDIFFERENTIATION

There have been many situations to which the analysis of intertask relations has been applied. One of these to which the simple, stimulus-response analysis of relations has often been applied is the problem of predifferentiation. Tasks in which many responses are to be associated in pairs with many different stimuli have, as a first requirement, the need for the stimuli to be clearly discriminable. Two stimuli cannot be associated with different responses if they cannot be easily told apart.

Predifferentiation refers to tasks which serve to differentiate among stimuli before the stimuli are to be associated with particular responses in the final tasks.

The more experience a subject has with stimuli to be used, say, in paired-associate learning, the easier it is for him to tell them apart and thus learn to associate them with the correct responses. This proposition, or something very like it, was first put forward by E. J. Gibson (1940). She meant to imply that if we make the stimuli discriminable without specific practice on the associative aspects of the task, we could produce transfer from the discrimination task to the association task.

The application of such an analysis of stimulus-response learning to problems in verbal learning is not without difficulties, however. The clearest example of predifferentiation among stimuli occurs in a simple motor task. In one experiment (Gagné & Baker, 1950), the investigators gave subjects the task of moving a switch when a particular light appeared. There were several different lights located in various positions, and each light signaled a different switch. The problem for the subject was to learn which light was controlled by which switch, so that he could react swiftly and accurately.

In the experiment, some of the subjects were given preliminary practice, not in moving the switches, but merely in assigning letters of the alphabet to the lights. This practice in associating the lights with particular letter names had a large positive transfer to the problem of learning to turn the right switch when a particular light appeared. Those subjects who had no predifferentiation made about 7 mistakes in their first 20 trials, while those with some training made only about 3 errors in the first 20 trials.

One simple interpretation of the results of this experiment asserts that stimulus predifferentiation reduces the amount of stimulus generalization between the various lights, so that in the final task, when these lights are to be associated with the different switches, there is less likely to be confusion about which stimulus is paired with what switch. Such an interpretation of stimulus predifferentiation is appealing, and there are enough data described by it to show that the idea has considerable merit. Many different kinds of training can establish distinctiveness of stimuli, and furthermore, there are probably many different ways in which this acquired distinctiveness of cues—as it has sometimes been called—can be produced (Arnoult, 1957). It is a mistake to assume, however, that any kind of pretraining which produces distinctiveness among stimuli will result in positive transfer to a paired-associate task with verbal materials. Several studies (Battig, Williams, & Williams, 1962; Battig & Brackett, 1963) show that it is not possible to obtain consistent transfer from a verbal-discrimination task to paired-associate learning. In fact, negative transfer to paired-associate learning can easily be produced by deliberate mispairing of items in the verbal discrimination task. Therefore, in many tasks, stimulus predifferentiation will be masked by conditions which create negative transfer.

DIRECTION IN PROBLEM SOLVING

One of the most fruitful applications of the analysis of similarity relations in transfer of training can be made to the investigation of certain effects in problem solving. Problem solving occurs when an individual must find, through discovery, the way to accomplish some end. The solution of a problem may be arrived at by the extrapolation of some previously learned principles, by trial and error, or by the rational analysis of the nature of the problem. Very often all three methods may, at various times, be used by a single person in his attempt to solve some problem.

It is obvious, therefore, that transfer is an essential aspect of problem solving in human behavior, since both the extrapolation of some previously acquired principles and the rational analysis of the nature of some problem must depend upon previous experience. Undoubtedly, the dominance of particular responses in a particular situation—what has been called the habit-family hierarchy—depends also upon transfer from previous learning. Therefore, there is ample room for the application of the study of transfer to problem solving.

Curiously enough, the most extensive and best-known applications of the principles of transfer to problem solving have been to situations which produce negative transfer—to conditions in which previous experience reduces the probability of correct solution of a problem or delays solution of that problem. Negative transfer in problem solving generally goes by the name of fixation. Fixation on some nonadaptive behavior during problem solving produces negative transfer.

FIXATION BY HABITUAL MODES OF SOLUTION. A well-known set of observations by Luchins (1942) demonstrates the influence of habitual solutions upon the efficiency of problem solving. Luchins studied the solution of some problems which are familiar as a kind of item on some intelligence tests. Here is an example: Given a 3-quart jar, a 21-quart jar, and a 127-quart jar, how would one measure out exactly 100 quarts in the smallest number of moves? One solution is to subtract 21 quarts from 127 quarts, which makes 106 quarts, and then to subtract 3 quarts twice. The first six problems which Luchins gave to his subjects were all like this one; an efficient solution required the use of all three jars. After these problems, however, others were introduced which could be more efficiently solved with only two of the measures, though they could also be solved by using all three.

The majority of the subjects tested by Luchins continued to use all three measures in the later problems, despite the inefficiency of the solutions. When the subjects were asked to write "Don't be blind" on their papers immediately after the sixth problem, a smaller, though still considerable, number of subjects persisted in the more awkward method.

Many other studies show the same pattern of results—the continuation of a previously established method for doing things when it is no longer necessary or efficient. For example, this kind of persistence occurs in the solution of anagram problems (Maltzman & Morrisett, 1953; Maltzman, Eisman, Brooks, & Smith, 1956). In this case, the influence of previous experience upon the solution of anagrams occurred through instructions to the subjects as well as by previous experience at solving anagrams. Some subjects received preliminary practice with anagrams that could only be solved by unscrambling them to words which had something to do with food or eating. For example, the sequence OCNBA unscrambles to BACON. In the test series, these subjects were faced with some words that could be solved either by these food solutions or by other words. The subjects who had been given previous experience with the food anagrams (even without specific instructions) much more often found the food solution than did subjects with pretraining on words from no special semantic class.

FIXATION BY FUNCTIONAL VALUE OF MATERIALS.   Some of the best-known examples of negative transfer from previous experience come from some studies by Duncker (1945). Duncker argued that the perceptual conditions of some problems arouse processes which prevent people from seeing the "obvious" solution. The solution to the problem is delayed or made more difficult because the stimuli from the conditions of the problem arouse the wrong associative or intellectual processes.

The point is illustrated by one of the simple experiments Duncker performed. He gave students a variety of little tasks to perform. One of these was as follows: The subjects were required to mount three small candles on a door (ostensibly for experiments on vision). The materials the subjects needed for solution were scattered in confusion on a table and mixed in with a number of other objects. The crucial items were tacks, matches, the candles, and some cardboard boxes similar to small matchboxes. The solution required the subjects to tack the boxes to the door and then to light the matches to melt wax on the boxes in order to hold the candles upright. The problem was presented to two different groups of subjects in two ways. The difference was small but of critical importance. In one condition, the boxes were filled with experimental materials—tacks were in one box, candles in another, and matches in a third. In the other conditions, the tacks, candles, and matches were loose on the table, and the boxes were empty.

These conditions apparently made a surprising difference (see Table 10.3). Subjects who were presented the problem with the boxes empty all solved it, while only about half the subjects were successful when the boxes were filled. Because the number of subjects was very small, these results can only be taken as a demonstration. But they parallel similar results achieved by Duncker with other problems, and most of the important observations he made have been systematically repeated with positive results (Adamson, 1952). Therefore, we can accept the results of Duncker's experiments.

TABLE 10.3 **Data from One of the Problems Studied by Duncker Showing the Functional Fixity Effect**

CONDITION	NO. OF S's	NO. SOLVING	MEAN NO. PRESOLUTIONS
Fixed	7	7 (100%)	1.3
Unfixed	7	3 (42.9%)	2.3

These experiments demonstrate the extent to which previous experience may lead to negative transfer as the result of the arousal of inappropriate responses. One interpretation of Duncker's observations emphasizes the possible mediating responses that the two versions of the problem described above might arouse. When the boxes are filled, they are more likely to elicit a mediating response such as "container" or "box." When the boxes are empty the mediating responses are less likely to center on the boxlike characteristics of the boxes. Perhaps other mediating responses, such as "stand" or "platform," are more likely to occur. While this account emphasizes the verbal character of the mediating activity which leads to the results of the experiment, it is possible that some of the mediation is nonverbal and has to do with perceptual organization.

The direct influence of previous verbal habits in a situation like problem solving is indicated by some observations of Judson and Cofer (1956). In this study, subjects were given a number of groups of four words and told to indicate the one word which did not belong to the set. Suppose, for example, that ADD, SUBTRACT, MULTIPLY, and PERCENT are given. This item is easy. It is obvious that PERCENT is the word that does not belong, since it is the one word that does not indicate an arithmetic operation. Suppose, however, that the words were ADD, SUBTRACT, MULTIPLY, and INCREASE. Here the answer is not so clear-cut. To be sure, the same arithmetic operations are present, and INCREASE is not an arithmetic operation. But ADD, MULTIPLY, and INCREASE all belong to a class of words indicating increasing magnitude, while SUBTRACT belongs to a class of words indicating decreasing magnitude. Perhaps SUBTRACT is the word that doesn't belong.

Judson and Cofer administered many such ambiguous items to students. The object was to find out which ambiguous words the student would reject. One of the things that turned out to be important was the order of the words. SUBTRACT, INCREASE, MULTIPLY, and ADD would more likely lead to INCREASE being rejected, whereas MULTIPLY, INCREASE, ADD, and SUBTRACT would more likely lead to SUBTRACT as the rejected word. Therefore, whatever scheme the subject develops which leads him to reject one as opposed to another of the words is very sensitive to the word that comes first.

More important for our present purposes, however, is the fact that subjects were likely to accept ambiguous words which conformed to their well-established verbal habits. For example, in problems like PRAYER, TEMPLE, CATHEDRAL, and SKYSCRAPER, subjects with strong religious interests were more likely to accept the word PRAYER and reject SKYSCRAPER than were those with little religious interest.

NEGATIVE TRANSFER IN FORMAL LEARNING.　One final example (Entwisle & Huggins, 1964) shows the potential for negative transfer between two closely related aspects of a technical subject. The topic examined in this study was the learning of circuit theory by freshmen students in electrical engineering. The authors of the study pointed out that there is a strong possibility of negative transfer in this subject matter because circuit theory involves dual statements of closely related principles. For example, a given circuit can be solved with voltage taken as the unknown or with current taken as the unknown. The rules and procedures for one method of solution are very similar but not identical to the rules and procedures for the other. Therefore, there is room for the incorrect extrapolation of one method to conditions appropriate for the other.

The experimental subjects in this study spent some time studying voltage solutions to circuits and then an equivalent time studying the corresponding current principles. The control group spent the same time studying the voltage solutions, but instead of going on to the corresponding current principles, they studied irrelevant material concerning computer programming. Both groups were tested immediately afterward on the voltage principles. The experiment, therefore, was an example of a retroactive design. The results showed readily detectable negative transfer on the voltage solutions. Furthermore, analysis of the performance on the intervening current solutions showed that the students were poorer than they ought to have been at this task. Therefore, there was probably proactive negative transfer as well as retroactive transfer.

SPECIAL PROBLEMS IN POSITIVE TRANSFER

Learning How to Learn

One of the things we do which results in positive transfer is *learn how to learn*. Every laboratory investigator of verbal learning knows that experimental subjects improve in their ability to learn lists of verbal items by rote as they go from list to list. Such improvement may even assert itself despite considerable opportunity for between-list negative transfer. Several features of learning how to learn, as it can be seen in laboratory experiments, deserve our attention.

LEARNING HOW TO LEARN IN ROTE LEARNING

The results of one study designed specifically to explore the effects of learning to learn can be seen in Figure 10.5. The task used in this study depended upon a modified paired-associate technique. The subjects learned ten successive paired-associate tasks. Notice that the greatest improvement in performance from task to task occurred between the first few tasks. By the time subjects had learned seven or eight of these tasks, there was little further improvement. Evidently, subjects take relatively little time to learn almost all there is to learn about how to practice in such a simple situation as paired-associate learning.

Duncan (1960) used these tasks to examine some of the details of the process of learning to learn. One of the most important results that came out of his analysis is seen in the difference between subjects who learn rapidly and those who learn slowly. Figure 10.6 shows a comparison between fast and slow learners for the first and the last task in the series. Slow learners were those who performed in the lowest one-fourth of the entire collection of subjects, and fast learners were those who were in the top quarter.

Notice that the difference between fast and slow learners is large and striking on the first task. The learning curve for the fast learners is

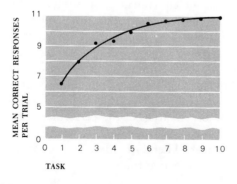

FIG. **10.5** The mean number of correct responses per trial as a function of practice on successive tasks. (Duncan, 1960.)

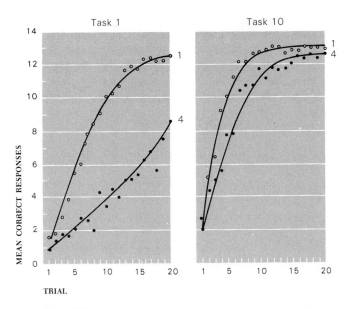

FIG. 10.6 Difference between first task and tenth task performance for the upper quartile of learners (1) and the lower quartile
of learners (4). Notice that the difference is greater for the first
task. (Duncan, 1960.)

negatively accelerated; most of the improvement for these subjects comes
in the first few trials. The curve for the slow learners is positively accelerated. These subjects do very badly on the first few trials of the first task,
and they begin to improve, on the average, only after a number of trials.

The learning curves for both fast and slow learners on the tenth
task are negatively accelerated. Furthermore, there is only a small difference between the subjects in the bottom quarter and those in the top
quarter. One of the things learning to learn does, then, is to reduce the
between-subject differences in performance. Subjects come to be more
alike as the result of experience in learning related tasks. If we generalize
this result, one of the things we would expect is that the differences between people on most tasks is in part to be explained by the differences in
how much people have learned about how to go about learning those
tasks. When people have had an equivalent amount of experience at
learning tasks of a given type, they are likely to be more homogeneous in
their performance on learning a new task of that type.

In another analysis of learning to learn, Duncan (1964) compared the difference in learning to learn two different types of tasks. One
of these was a simple paired-associate task, and the other was a task which
required some choice and variability in the behavior of the subjects. The

task which required more complicated and varied behavior showed a greater improvement in successive examples. Some tasks make more demands on our ability to learn how to perform them, and there will be more transfer between successive examples of such tasks than between tasks which require little experience in order to go about practicing them efficiently.

Learning to learn is a very general phenomenon, not limited to laboratory experiments. However, the components that improve from task to task are often quite specific to a given class of tasks. It may be, for example, that people learn to do better at successive paired-associate tasks because they learn to mediate. Or the major improvement may be simply a matter of adapting the excessive reaction that most people have to the pacing which is part of laboratory experiments in verbal learning. In either case, the change is usually quite specific to the paired-associate task, and it may even be specific to the paired-associate task in the laboratory. There is no general disciplinary value in rote learning, no matter how onerous it may be.

LEARNING SETS

One case in which an extensive analysis of learning to learn has had some general theoretical importance is provided by the learning-set phenomenon. We have already examined this case in Chapter 6, and we need only place it in the present context in this chapter.

We saw, in the discussion of discrimination learning, that as organisms are given successive problems in discriminating between pairs of stimuli, their ability to solve the individual problems improves. Thus it may take a monkey many trials to learn that a raisin is to be found under a red box instead of a blue cylinder, when such a choice is the very first discrimination problem it has faced. But after a number of discrimination tests with different objects, the monkey needs only to make one choice in order to show complete preference for the rewarded stimulus.

Analysis of the learning-set phenomenon showed that it is in part the result of the reduction of stimulus generalization between successive problems. Therefore, at least part of the improvement from task to task is the result of reduction in negative transfer. In addition, however, the monkeys which are tested in learning-set problems also learn something new as they are faced with the successive tasks. They learn the technique of testing stimulus objects irrespective of what they have been rewarded for on previous problems. They learn, as it were, the habit of making a choice and then checking to see if that choice is correct.

The development of a learning set, then, can be described as the emergence of a higher-order habit, one which is composed of the single component of behavior that is consistently reinforced in the individual problems. The only aspect of behavior that is consistently reinforced from problem to problem is the habit of making a choice and changing that choice when the initial one is incorrect. The tendency to choose, say, any blue object because a blue object was reinforced in the previous problem will be reinforced only part of the time. Most of the time such a tendency will fail to be reinforced. The learning-set situation consistently reinforces only the habit of keeping with the initial choice if it is correct and reversing the choice if it is wrong. It is because the animal solves a kind of superproblem that emerges from the whole collection of discrimination problems that the phenomenon is called learning set.

Do learning sets occur outside the discrimination-learning situation? There is a close relation between the problem of learning abstract concepts and the higher-order habit which emerges out of the learning-set situation. Furthermore, many examples of learning how to learn depend upon the building up of such higher-order habits. Indeed, the abstraction of common elements or principles from many related tasks defines the problem of transfer of training, and in the learning-set phenomenon we see such abstraction very clearly at work in a simple situation.

TEACHING HOW TO LEARN

We have seen that there is a general improvement in ability to learn which comes from practice at a particular kind of learning. What is more, when a specific skill is analyzed, as with the learning-set problem, the particular common elements which lead to transfer can be discovered. There is more to the matter than that, however. We may well ask, Do specific kinds of instruction speed or improve learning how to learn? Such is surely the general assumption behind remedial programs of education.

One study (Woodrow, 1927) showed that specific instruction in how to memorize poetry, prose, and factual material resulted in greater improvement in later tests of memorization than an equivalent amount of undirected practice. Woodrow stressed many of the techniques that are standard in teaching students how to learn. He used active recitation, attention to meaning, techniques for maintaining continuous alertness, etc. The study, however, was not analytical, and we cannot really tell which of the factors were important in producing the improvement in ability to memorize. The general point, however, is that specific training in some of the techniques of learning does have beneficial effect over and above that which comes simply from practice alone.

Positive Transfer in School Learning

The literature of educational psychology is full of studies of transfer of training in various aspects of school learning and special training programs. Many of these studies have been directed to the question of the possible transfer between the various subjects in the formal academic curriculum—from mathematics, say, to the various sciences, or from formal logic to reasoning in general. Other studies have examined the value of particular training programs for specific skills. Is one program, for example, better than another in producing the skills necessary to fly a jet airplane? While these kinds of transfer studies are extremely important in an educational or applied context, they usually do not provide much information about the psychological processes behind the general phenomena of transfer.

Other applied studies take as their point of departure unique psychological factors important to some particular skill. Students of the learning of foreign languages, for example, have been concerned about the transfer from learning by ear to learning by eye, particularly in the acquisition of new words (Pimsleur & Bonkowski, 1961). Other studies have examined the transfer of oral (and aural) verbal skills to those of reading (Levin, Watson, & Feldman, 1964). These psychological problems are not, however, general ones in the psychology of learning but specific to particular skills or groups of skills. Therefore, we shall not give them much attention here.

Still other studies have used the techniques developed in the analysis of the learning process in order to understand some of the particular problems that arise in school learning. One study (Wallach, 1963), for example, concerned itself with the ease of perceptual recognition of nonsense words which were either high in statistical approximation to English or low (see page 262). The study showed that there was much greater transfer to the perceptual recognition task for good spellers than for poor spellers among grade school children. This difference probably reflects the greater phonetic generalization and understanding of sequential relations among letters possessed by good spellers. The author of the study reached the conclusion that good spellers are not just good at spelling many particular words; they can guess more accurately about how to spell strange words than can poor spellers. The study also suggested that nonsense words of high-order approximation to English could be useful in teaching children whatever general principles about English spelling can be learned.

Much of the current research on positive transfer in formal education is concerned with the problems which arise in programmed instruction. In programmed instruction a deliberate effort is made to arrange the things an individual must learn in some sequence so that errors are minimized and retention and transfer maximized. One of the great advantages of programmed instruction (aside from its low reliance on a teacher) is that it allows a detailed analytic study of various aspects of practical educational programs. We may take some specific concept to be taught and devise a number of separate statements (items) designed to teach that concept. These items may be rearranged and rewritten in a number of ways, and we may study the influence on performance of (1) the differences between specific items, (2) the differences between whole sets of items, and (3) the differences between different orders of items. All of these affect learning, retention, and transfer.

In one study (Levin & Baker, 1963), for example, the investigators examined the effects of scrambling or randomly rearranging the logical sequence for items designed to teach grade school children certain elementary concepts in geometry. The problem is an important one, because a logical sequence for some set of items is not always the one which is practical or appropriate to use. In this case, it turned out that the complete scrambling of the items made no difference in measures of retention and transfer. That was the case here because each frame or item provided only an instance or exemplification of a concept ("angle," for example) to be learned. The problem was to teach the children the various properties of geometric figures. When a program is designed to teach relationships between concepts (the relationship between angles in a right triangle, for example), the order of items would be much more important.

These various studies in applied educational psychology are important, though they usually do not contribute much that is new to our understanding of the basic psychological questions in transfer. Transfer theory itself, on the other hand, may be useful in applied settings. It is, in point of fact, rather disappointing to find that in recent years there have been relatively few concerted efforts to apply the details of the theory of transfer of training to practical problems. One reason, perhaps, that application has lagged in recent years is because transfer theory has been so completely dominated by the stimulus-response analysis discussed earlier in this chapter. That analysis is important, but it is of limited generality. It is of approximate validity when applied to tasks which can be modeled after paired-associate learning, and as we shall see later, it is of considerable use in application to certain problems in the learning of perceptual-motor skills. But it is only superficially useful in application to more general problems in training and education.

Perhaps, as more general theories, such as that of Ahlstrom (1961) receive increased attention, it may be possible to make more use of the precise relationships implied by theories of transfer and studied in the laboratory. Certainly at one time the theory of transfer stood at the very center of educational psychology, and it would seem that the time is ripe for it to return to its former eminence.

11

RETENTION AND FORGETTING

There are two ways of looking at the problems of learning. For one, we can examine the way in which behavior changes as the result of experience. Ordinarily that means we measure the improvement in performance which results from practice. But we can also take a fixed level of performance and see how that performance is retained over some period of time without practice. The latter case defines the problem of retention, and it is the one to be considered in this chapter. Both approaches, of course, are simply different views of the same problem. If there were no retention, there could be no learning, since improvement with practice depends upon the cumulation of the effects of practice over periods of time during which there is no practice. Looking at the problem this way would lead one to think that the factors underlying retention are the same as those underlying learning, and conversely, that the factors underlying forgetting are the same as those which tend to retard the learning process. If this is so, why the special study of retention?

The answer is that such study allows us to examine changes in behavior uncontaminated by further practice or exposure to the materials being learned. When we have determined to what extent and in what manner something is retained, we have a method for telling how mental processes reorganize material already learned without additional exposure to the material. It should be said, however, that it is not always easy to make sure our study of retention is uncontaminated by further practice— a fact that we shall have to refer to throughout this chapter.

Before we begin to examine the information available, we need to define the two words *retention* and *forgetting*. Retention refers to the extent to which material originally learned is still retained, and forgetting refers to the portion lost. Therefore,

$$\text{Amount forgotten} = \text{amount learned} - \text{amount retained}$$

Amount retained is always measured directly, and amount forgotten is inferred from our knowledge of the differences between the amount learned and the amount retained. It is very important, therefore, when we discuss forgetting to be certain that we know how much was learned originally.

There are several different ways we might organize the information available on human retention and forgetting. One division of the subject matter considers separately studies of the simple measurement of retention and studies of deliberate, experimentally produced forgetting. Another division considers separately short-term and long-term retention. Ordinarily, when we talk about retention, we mean events which take place over some considerable period of time. We think of our retention of material from a specific course over the summer vacation. In addition, however, the experimental psychologist is concerned about short-term memory. In the study of short-term retention, the ability of people to remember a very few items (sometimes only a single item) over a few seconds is the object of measurement.

In this chapter we shall consider both short-term and long-term memory as well as studies of experimentally produced forgetting. As we shall see, the last topic is closely related to the subject of the preceding chapter, "Transfer of Training."

METHODOLOGICAL PROBLEMS IN THE STUDY OF RETENTION

The study of retention is full of difficulties. There are traps everywhere for the experimentalist, particularly if he wishes to know something about forgetting. Therefore, before we introduce the available information about the study of retention, we need to spend some time exploring the methodological problems. Many of these problems arise not only in the study of retention but in the study of transfer of training and other topics in the psychology of learning.

The Problem of Retention

The problem of retention can be stated quite easily. It is that whatever influences the course of learning may, at some later time, be reflected in the course of retention. It may be reflected directly as the result of what went on during learning, or as the result of some delayed effect. Figure

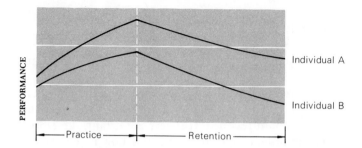

FIG. 11.1 The hypothetical performance curves during practice and retention for individuals whose performance differed during learning.

11.1 illustrates one aspect of the problem. Here we see two imaginary learning curves followed by two forgetting curves (the dotted portion). We could imagine these to be the learning and forgetting curves for two different individuals, A and B, who have practiced the same material.

It is evident that individual A learns more rapidly than B, so that at the end of practice he is the better performer. When retention is measured at the indicated point, he is still superior, and his forgetting has been less rapid than B's during this period. The problem is that we don't know whether he has forgotten less because he was the faster learner (and hence learned more during the fixed period of time) or because he simply forgets more slowly (independent of the fact that he learns rapidly).

The figure illustrates the basic problem in retention experiments. There are always two-stage experiments. During the first stage some learning must occur, and during the second stage retention is measured. In order to interpret any differences in forgetting due to experimental conditions introduced *during* the retention interval, we must assume that the amount of learning for two individuals or two groups of individuals is exactly the same. Otherwise, the differences in forgetting could be attributed either to the experimental conditions introduced during the retention interval or to differences in original learning.

A BASE LINE FOR THE MEASUREMENT OF RETENTION

Before we consider the problem of measuring retention after different degrees of learning, however, we need to settle the problem of finding a base line from which to measure retention. This is the essential problem of the two-stage experiment. There have been several suggestions for the analysis of such experiments (Anderson, 1963; Underwood, 1964).

Suppose we wish to measure retention of some material 24 hours after the original learning, which consisted of six practice trials. We need, first of all, some measure of how much was learned during those six trials. We cannot use the last trial during learning as an estimation of how much was learned, because people learn something on that last trial which requires an additional trial to measure. As a base line for retention, therefore, we must either use a recall test given immediately after the last trial or the performance of a control group which goes on to practice for one additional trial. Even a recall trial without further exposure of the material provides some opportunity for further learning or further changes in performance, so we are really reduced to the necessity of employing a control group which goes on to practice for one more trial than the group which yields the retention measure. The amount of forgetting is the difference between the performance of the control group on the immediate seventh trial and the performance of the retention group on a trial administered 24 hours later.

A separate control group is wasteful, and it would be more efficient to have some way of estimating what performance on an immediately given seventh trial would be without a control group. Underwood (1964) provides us with a method for making such an estimation. He is able to show what the performance on an immediately succeeding trial would be like without ever giving such a trial to actual experimental subjects. The method he uses depends on a relationship between the number of times items have been correctly given (say, in paired-associate learning) and the percentage of times those items would be expected to be correct on an immediately succeeding trial. It is possible to calculate this percentage from the data from the previous trials.

Figure 11.2 shows the predicted percentage of correct responses on a sixth trial as a function of the number of correct responses on trials 1 through 5. In the experiment from which this figure was taken, there were actually a total of 204 correct responses on trials 1 through 5. Of these, 8.8 percent (the first point in Figure 11.2) became correct for the *first time* on the sixth trial; these were items which subjects did not correctly anticipate on trials 1 through 5 but did correctly anticipate on

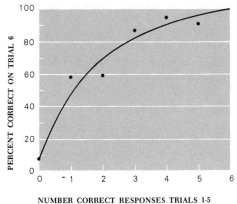

FIG. 11.2 Percent responses correct on the sixth trial in a learning experiment as a function of the number of correct responses on trials 1 through 5. The figure shows that if the response was correct on all five occasions, it was nearly always correct on trial 6. If, however, it had been correct only once during five trials, it would be correct on trial 6 only about 60 percent of the time. (Underwood, 1964.)

trial 6. A total of 11 items were given correctly on all five trials, and 90.9 percent of these were also correct on the sixth.

From these data it is possible to project to a hypothetical seventh trial. That is accomplished by extending the smooth line in Figure 11.2 to the hypothetical seventh trial. By so doing we estimate that 99 percent of the items which had been correct on all six preceding trials would be correct on the seventh trial. From the same curve we would expect that 9 percent of all those items that had never been correctly anticipated before (the zero point on the axis giving number of correct responses) would be correct. Of those items correctly anticipated once before, from the same curve, we would estimate 49 percent to be correct on the seventh trial. About 70 percent of those anticipated correctly twice before would be expected to be correct. From such data it is possible to reconstruct exactly what the hypothetical seventh trial would be like. If such calculations are checked against an actual seventh trial, they turn out to be very close to the real values.

Anderson (1963) has criticized procedures of this sort because the "smooth curve" from which we estimate the values for the seventh trial is somewhat arbitrary and unspecified mathematically. Yet an empirical check of the procedures shows that it predicts, with high accuracy, the results of an actual seventh trial. We can use such a predicted seventh trial as a base line for the measurement of retention. If, for example, the analysis predicts that half of the items would have been correct on an immediate seventh trial, and if an actual seventh trial given 24 hours later shows that subjects actually correctly anticipated only a fourth of the items, we would say that over the intervening 24 hours these subjects had forgotten half of what they had learned.

THE PROBLEM OF MEASURING FROM DIFFERENT LEVELS

Suppose we do an experiment in which we compare learning and retention for two different kinds of material, material which we expect to be learned at vastly different rates. If we had two groups of subjects practice two different sets of material for a constant number of trials, there would be large differences in performance at the end of practice. It would be difficult to compare the amount of forgetting for the two kinds of materials, since retention would be measured from different base lines.

The obvious solution would be to provide for equal base lines even though the materials are not alike in difficulty. One common way to establish such equality is to have all subjects practice until the same criterion is reached. For example, we may stop each subject in a paired-associate experiment at the point where he can correctly anticipate half of the items and no more. A more usual criterion is to require each subject to practice a set of materials until he can respond correctly on two consecutive trials.

Requiring all subjects to practice to the same criterion does not solve all the difficulties, however. Inevitably it means that subjects receive different amounts of practice. If we are systematically comparing materials which differ in difficulty, the subjects who practice the easier material will always reach criterion after a smaller number of trials. Furthermore, every subject, no matter how many trials he takes to reach criterion, will have repeated some of the items many times (the easiest items will be learned almost immediately), while he will have correctly repeated the harder items only a few times. Therefore, for each subject some of the items will be overpracticed compared with others.

Underwood (1954; 1964) has provided some solutions to this problem, though his solutions are not completely free from defect (Anderson, 1963). Underwood's general method is to provide a complete history of the number of times each item is correctly anticipated for each subject. From this history we determine the probability of each subject's being correct on a postcriterial trial (a hypothetical trial after the last trial of practice). For example, a particular item may have been given correctly a total of three times during practice. We determine the probability of that item being correct on the postcriterial trial from the history of all items which were correct a total of three times. The specific method is very much like the procedure described earlier. Although it does not provide the same base line for each item, Underwood argues that it does provide a "true" base line for each item.

THE PROBLEM OF THE 100 PERCENT CRITERION

You may ask, why not allow subjects to learn everything to a criterion of consistent perfect performance, so that there is no problem of unequal degrees of learning? If everyone can reproduce all the items on the next trial, then there is no need to go through an elaborate computation to make a prediction to a hypothetical next trial. Such a procedure, however, leads to the difficulty of the overlearning effect.

The overlearning effect is simply the name for the effect upon retention of practice continued beyond the point of immediate perfect reproducibility. It has been known since the beginning of research on human memory (Ebbinghaus, 1885; Krueger, 1929) that practice beyond a criterion of perfect reproducibility increases resistance to forgetting. A more recent experiment by Postman (1962a) illustrates the effect.

In Postman's experiment subjects learned lists of 12 two-syllable nouns by serial anticipation. Postman compared three degrees of overlearning: 0 percent, 50 percent, and 100 percent. The 0 percent overlearning was achieved by terminating practice after one perfect recitation of the entire list. For the condition of 50 percent overlearning, practice was continued beyond the point of mastery for half as many trials as it took to reach a criterion of one perfect recitation. For example, if a particular subject took ten trials to reach criterion, he practiced for an additional five trials beyond criterion. For 100 percent overlearning, subjects practiced beyond criterion for the same number of trials that it took them to reach criterion.

Postman measured retention by the method of relearning (see the following section) seven days after original learning. The 50 percent overlearning condition produced a slight increase in retention (measured in a decrease in trials at relearning), but the 100 percent overlearning condition produced a marked superiority in retention. The results were clear enough to illustrate that even moderate amounts of overlearning produce increased resistance to forgetting.

The moral is clear. Simply because two items are both available for recall immediately after learning does not mean that the two items are equally well learned. In fact, there is no simple relation between the probability that a response is correct during learning and its resistance to forgetting. The result is that it is always extremely difficult to compare materials which differ markedly in retention without running the risk of confusion between learning and retention. If we know that there is no simple relation between measures of performance during learning and resistance to forgetting, we cannot assume that any difference in the degree of forgetting is free from differences induced at the time of learning but not detected in performance then.

Therefore, in order to make unequivocal comparisons in amount of forgetting during some period of time, we must be certain that the materials learned in the experiment are either identical or similar in all respects. Thus we can compare retention in two groups of subjects who learn similar or identical materials, even though the retention intervals are different for the two groups. In this way we can determine how much is forgotten after, say, 24 hours compared with one week. When we try to compare differences in forgetting for different kinds of material, however, we may not know whether the differences we find are actually differences in retention loss or differences in the resistance to forgetting produced at the time of original practice. As a practical matter, of course, we may be interested in making such comparisons; but we need to be careful in the inferences we draw from them.

Methods of Measuring Retention

Another question in the study of retention concerns what one measures. There is no single method for measuring the effects of either learning or retention, and the various available measures tap different aspects of learning and retention. Postman and Rau (1957) point out that there are three main results of practice which we wish to measure in retention: (1) the differentiation of the learned items from others of the same kind, (2) the availability of the individual items for reproduction, and (3) the position within the series that each item occupies.

DIRECT MEASURES OF RETENTION

To measure these aspects of retention there are both direct and indirect methods. The direct measures, since they require the subjects to produce the material being tested, are measures of recall, and to a greater or lesser extent they exhibit all three of the results of practice. There are, however, several measures of recall, each of which emphasizes special aspects of the results of learning.

Free recall, for example, places greatest emphasis upon the simple availability of the material, while serial anticipation or some other similar method of aided recall also requires the subjects to learn the position within the series occupied by each item. Aided recall always provides some contextual stimulus to which the subject responds. Thus, in serial anticipation the subject responds to the cue provided by the preceding item, while in paired-associate learning he responds to the cue provided by the stimulus term. So, in addition to availability, these various methods of aided recall usually test for location within a series.

It is not always the case that unaided recall produces poorer performance than aided recall. In the experimental comparison of different measures of retention made by Postman and Rau (1957), free recall always produced superior performance. Furthermore, their subjects were able to reproduce in free recall the original serial order of the materials with a high degree of accuracy, a result which duplicates those in an earlier study (Luh, 1922). Therefore, in some situations subjects are best left to create their own contextual cues for recall if performance is to be accurate. Postman and Rau argue that this is the case because free recall produces less intraserial interference or internal confusion among the items. Such an argument is important to the theory of forgetting, since, as we shall see, one of the best-supported theories of forgetting asserts that retention is impaired when there is interference among the materials learned at different times.

Various kinds of materials demand different methods of recall. For example, in the study of perceptual memory we may ask people to draw or otherwise give their reconstruction of the material which had been exposed to them. Therefore, we are not completely free to choose a method for the study of retention to suit some theoretical requirement.

There is, in addition to the various production methods, the important method of recognition. Recognition is the most sensitive of the direct methods for measuring retention: it may show retention when production methods do not. College students are aware of this fact and notoriously rely on less thorough preparation for objective (multiple-choice) tests than for tests which demand recall. Recognition makes no demands upon availability of items with or without contextual cues. It is, therefore, primarily a measure of the extent to which people differentiate among items presented to them.

The difficulty with recognition as a test of retention is that it is very sensitive to differences in the set of alternatives from which an individual must choose the correct item. The outcome of a recognition test depends upon the incorrect items as well as upon the correct items. Consider an absurd example. Not many college students would check the wrong alternative if asked to identify the third book of the Bible as (*a*) Chevrolet or (*b*) Leviticus. But a fair number of college students would have difficulty choosing among the alternatives (*a*) Deuteronomy and (*b*) Leviticus.

One experimental comparison of recall and recognition illustrates that the major difference between them depends upon the availability of items in recognition. Davis, Sutherland, and Judd (1961) compared recall and recognition tests of retention when the set of alternative responses available to the subjects was controlled. The experiment depended upon the subjects under recall instructions limiting themselves to a well-defined, finite set of alternatives. Such a set is the set of all possible two-digit numbers. Between 10 and 99 there are just 90 numbers. In the recall condition, subjects were given 15 of these 90 possible numbers and then asked to recall the particular ones they were exposed to originally. In the recognition test, subjects were given 15 numbers and then these same 15 embedded in a set of either 30, 60, or 90 two-digit numbers. The subject were required to identify the original 15.

The scores on the number right by recall and recognition cannot be compared directly, but under certain assumptions, they can be compared in terms of the information transmitted in each test. Compared in this way, the information transmitted by each *S* was, on the average, almost identical for recall and recognition when the entire set of 90 numbers was presented. This result was almost exactly like that achieved by Ehrlich, Flores, and Le Ny (1960) in a similar study. The important implication to be drawn from these studies is that when subjects recall from a fixed set, such as the set of two-digit numbers, recall behaves much like recognition. Recognition produces evidence of retention, then, when recall does not, because in a recognition test people make their selection from a smaller set of alternatives than they do in recall. If you are presented with a list of words for free recall, during recall you must, as it were, select the correct words from the set of all possible English words, whereas in a recognition test you only may be asked to identify which of two words had been previously presented to you. The greater availability under a recognition test is because the number of alternative responses is smaller. Failures of recall, as when we cannot recall a person's name and yet identify it when it is spoken, may reflect in large part the very considerable number of alternative responses we must carry around with us in order to recall on cue.

INDIRECT MEASURES OF RETENTION

When most people think of testing for retention, they think of the various direct measures such as recall, reconstruction, or recognition. In psychological experiments, however, some indirect measures of retention are often preferred. These indirect measures all rely on the fact that the rate at which some material is relearned depends upon how it was learned in the first place.

One simple indirect measure is simply to compare the amount of time or number of trials it takes to relearn something compared with the original learning. If, for example, it takes 12 trials to learn a set of nonsense syllables and then 24 hours later takes only 2 trials to relearn the same set, we have indirect evidence for retention of the material over the intervening time, even though there may be no direct evidence in recall. While such evidence can be used if proper controls are exercised, relearning measures do have some problems associated with them. Perhaps the most serious is the fact that people learn how to learn. If you ask the same person to learn two perfectly equivalent sets of nonsense syllables, one after the other, the chances are great that the second set will be learned in very much less time than the first. People learn how to learn nonsense syllables as they learn how to learn all other kinds of materials. Therefore, in making use of relearning measures of retention, it is essential to determine that the improvement in performance on relearning is not in part the result of learning how to learn.

When properly used, relearning is a very sensitive measure of retention. In fact it is the most sensitive measure; it can even, theoretically, show *negative* retention, for it is at least possible that someone may take more trials to relearn something than he took to learn it in the first place. Relearning commonly shows evidence for retention when there is little or no evidence from recall. Many people, when they return to the study of something unused in many years, such as mathematics or a foreign language, have the feeling that they remember practically nothing. Yet it is usually evident that relearning is very rapid. What took six months to learn may be relearned in a few hours.

One way to express the improvement in relearning is by means of a savings score. The savings score is a direct reflection of the amount of time or number of repetitions *saved* in relearning compared with the amount in original learning. It is given by the formula

$$\text{Percent savings} = \frac{N \text{ trials to learn} - N \text{ trials to relearn}}{N \text{ trials to learn}} \times 100$$

Critics have condemned the indiscriminate use of the percent savings measure as a *comparative* measure of retention when materials differ in difficulty. But the measure does provide an acceptable means to compare materials which require the same number of trials or same amount of time to learn in the first place. In other words, it may be used to determine how retention changes with time in the absence of practice.

Bahrick (1964) has argued that no curves of retention except those based upon relearning can be interpreted in any simple way. The fact is that from the earliest studies to the present, the preferred method for showing the changes in retention with time has depended upon the use of the savings score measure.

THE NATURE OF RETENTION

We now turn to studies of the nature of retention, particularly its changing course with time. In addition to the quantitative aspects of retention embodied in studies of its temporal course, we shall examine some of the studies which show the important qualitative changes in retention.

The Course of Retention

METHODS

There is some variation from experiment to experiment in the way in which temporal changes in retention are studied. In a few studies, the same subjects may be repeatedly tested at intervals for retention of the same material. Such a technique yields a very impure measure of retention after the first test, since all subsequent measures are contaminated by the practice resulting from earlier tests.

More satisfactory tests of retention allow only one test after learning. The course of retention with time can be measured either by repeated testing of the same subjects using different materials for each test, or by independent measurements of different subjects at different retention intervals but using the same materials. In the first method, subjects learn one set of materials and then are tested for retention after some interval —for example, 1 hour. They then learn another set of materials which is equivalent to the first and are tested for this material after some other interval—say, 24 hours. It is essential in this kind of experiment that subjects be thoroughly practiced before the measurement of retention begins; otherwise, learning how to learn the particular material used in the experiment will obscure the true course of retention. Even so, as we shall see later, this method leads to very different results than those obtained with independent groups of subjects, a fact that is important to theories of forgetting. This is because how well one remembers one set of materials depends in a critical way upon how much material *of the same kind* one has previously learned. The more of such material that has been learned beforehand, the poorer the retention for any one set. Thus, lists of nonsense syllables learned after other lists have been learned tend to suffer more retention loss than do the earlier lists.

Such cumulative effects are minimized by having different groups of subjects learn the same material. Each group of subjects is then tested after some retention interval, and the data may be combined to produce an average retention curve.

Another method of examining some of the effects in retention does not produce a simple retention curve. This method is the serial-reproduction technique. In an experiment making use of serial reproduction, one subject learns some material. At some later time he recalls that material. His recall is then presented to a second person, who attempts to recall the material with which he was presented after a time interval. That recall is presented to a third person, and so on. The point is to determine just how the material is altered by the successive recalls.

EBBINGHAUS'S STUDY

The classical study of retention is that of H. Ebbinghaus (1885). Ebbinghaus was the first experimental psychologist to attempt a study of the higher mental processes by experimental means. One of his most striking results was to achieve, for the first time, a quantitative picture of the process of forgetting.

Ebbinghaus was the inventor of nonsense syllables, and in his investigations he devised over 600 nonsense syllables. In his study of retention he used himself as subject. He would learn a set of nonsense syllables and then, at some later time, test himself for retention of that set. He was, of course, very adept at learning nonsense syllables, so there was no contamination due to learning how to learn. During the course of his studies he learned over 1,200 lists each containing 13 syllables.

His method of presentation was simply to put the entire list before himself. He would read through the list, in serial order, as many times as would be necessary to recite it perfectly twice in a row. He used as his measure of learning the amount of time it took to reach this criterion; since he read at a constant rate, this measure was essentially the same as a trials-to-criterion measure. He would then go on to learn another list. After a certain lapse of time he would relearn this same set of lists, and from the relearning times he calculated a savings score.

Figure 11.3 shows his retention curve. The most important feature of this curve is its extremely rapid fall. Most of Ebbinghaus's forgetting occurred in the first few hours after original learning. His curve has become accepted as the typical forgetting curve for the good reason that nearly every forgetting curve published in the intervening years has been of the same general shape. As we shall see, one of the unique features of Ebbinghaus's curve is that he seemed to forget too much; but otherwise it is a good representative curve.

Forgetting curves, of course, vary with the kind of material. It is customary to summarize this variation by saying that highly organized material is less resistant to forgetting than material of a low degree of organization, and such summaries are usually accompanied by curves like those in Figure 11.4, which are meant to represent a wide variety of

FIG. **11.3** Retention (in percent saved at learning) as a function of time since practice. Since the curve is nearly straight plotted against log time, most of the forgetting took place at the beginning. (Data from Ebbinghaus, 1885.)

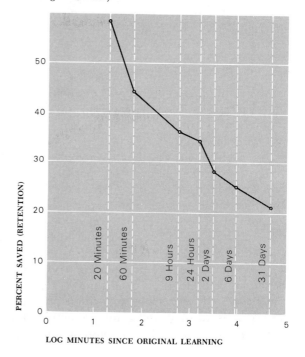

LOG MINUTES SINCE ORIGINAL LEARNING

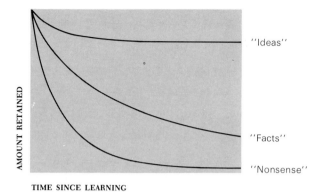

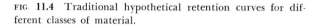

FIG. 11.4 Traditional hypothetical retention curves for different classes of material.

empirical data. However, there has been no systematic study of forgetting curves as a function of organization within a single experiment.

Some investigators have found slight rises in retention after various periods of time. For example, in their comparison of methods of measuring retention, Postman and Rau (1957) found a very slight rise in retention between 24 and 48 hours. Like most other investigators, they found the negative acceleration to be the most prominent feature of forgetting curves; the slight increase in retention is generally very temporary in nature. These rises probably come from a variety of sources, some of them rather obvious, such as rehearsal. When they are studied under carefully controlled conditions, such increases in retention are sometimes of theoretical importance, and we shall discuss them later.

RETENTION AND THE SPEED OF LEARNING

When discussing retention, many psychological textbooks attempt to correct a common misconception about it. Some varieties of folklore hold that someone who learns slowly retains well. The experimental literature, however, shows that those who learn slowly also retain poorly.

A paper by Underwood (1954) examines this result in detail. He analyzed a great deal of data on rote learning, data originally collected for other purposes. These and similar data show that there is nearly a zero correlation between time to learn and amount recalled on a single recall trial. There is, however, a high positive correlation between time to learn and time to relearn. Underwood further studied the problem by finding some items which were anticipated an equal number of times during learning by fast and slow learners. On the average, of course, fast learners anticipate more frequently (are correct more often) than slow learners, but it is possible to find some items in which the anticipations for fast and slow learners are equal. Even for these items, however, retention is better for fast learners.

This result means, in effect, that any given correct anticipation produces more resistance to forgetting for a fast learner than for a slow learner. If this is so, degree of learning is not the same for fast and slow learners. When Underwood adjusted the learning scores by handicapping fast learners, he found no differences in the slopes of the retention curves for fast and slow learners. Thus, the advantage for fast learners in resistance to forgetting is one that is established at the time of learning, not during the retention period itself. Such a result does not mean that fast learners necessarily have an inherent or biologically determined ability to remember things; it simply means that in a given amount of practice, fast learners produce more resistance to forgetting. It is possible that such is the case because they have learned more efficient ways to reorganize or recode the material they learn.

Note that Underwood was not interested in the analysis of individual differences in ability to remember. He was trying to show that in order to assess the effects of experimental conditions introduced during a retention interval, one needs to demonstrate that equal resistance to forgetting was established during learning. His analysis shows that this is very difficult to accomplish, because resistance to forgetting is so thoroughly correlated with speed of learning and ability of learners. As we shall see, it is very possible that the largest part of the effects we associate with differences in forgetting are in fact differences in resistance to forgetting that were established at the time of learning.

Qualitative Changes in Retention

Not all the changes that occur in memory can be described as a decrement in the ability to recall or relearn as time passes. Memory is reorganized and qualitatively altered during the retention interval, and many investigators have argued that such alterations in memory are the result of previous habits, attitudes, and motives of individual learners.

In earlier chapters we examined various effects of organization and redundancy in verbal materials on the establishment of new verbal habits and upon immediate recall. These same conditions of organization are reflected in measures of performance after a retention interval. One of the clearest and most important examples is provided by the phenomenon of clustering, in which the order of emission of items during recall is the important variable.

You will recall that clustering is said to occur in recall when subjects alter the sequence of items presented to them in order to bring them closer together. Unfortunately, there is very little evidence as to how clustering changes over retention intervals. Most studies of clustering with delayed recall measures show that there is usually an increase in the tendency to cluster from one recall to the next (for example, Gonzalez & Cofer, 1959), but we do not know how much such increases are due to the previous recalls. There are several hypotheses which would lead us to expect clustering (and, generally, all measures of internal organization) to increase over a retention interval, but we simply do not have the data available to evaluate such a hypothesis.

In any event, many psychological theories suggest that changes in memory over time would not be limited to simple fading or deterioration of what had once been learned. So far as such theory is concerned, however, the most active study of qualitative changes in memory has concerned memory for visually perceived forms.

PERCEPTUAL MEMORY

Gestalt psychologists have concerned themselves with the way in which people remember abstract visual forms such as circles, squares, and some other forms not so easily characterized. This interest in memory for forms grows out of the gestalt view that fields of organization determine perceptual events and memory for them. The gestalt psychologists have argued that the memory for visual forms is under some internal stress to alter into perceptually simpler and more highly organized forms during a retention interval. Over a period of time, then, the memory for a perceived form should become simpler and "better" than the original form. Unfortunately, one of the difficulties in studies of this notion is that the criteria of simplicity and good form have not always been stated in an unequivocal way. Nevertheless, this idea has led a number of investigators to study changes in the way people remember visual forms they had seen earlier.

In order to study memory for form, it is necessary to have some means of testing retention. Perhaps the simplest technique is to ask people to reproduce, by drawing, forms which they had been exposed to. There are many difficulties with so simple a method, however. How do we know what was perceived and learned in the first place? Did the subject actually perceive the form in the way he reproduced it later, or did the alterations we see in the drawings develop during the retention interval? We cannot altogether solve this problem by asking people to draw at the time of original exposure and at the time of the retention test, for the drawing at retention may then be influenced by the original reproduction as well as by the original perception. Furthermore, how much of the alteration in the reproduced form is determined by changes in memory and how much by sheer inability to draw? Finally, how are the results to be evaluated? How do we describe perceptual changes?

All these problems have been considered by investigators of perceptual memory, and there are a number of alterations of the basic technique of reproduction designed to solve some of the problems. For example, Zangwill (1937) modified the basic reproduction method into a kind of reproduction-plus-recognition test. He allowed subjects to draw figures which they had seen earlier, but then he had these crude drawings redrawn in precise form so that they were like the original figures in skill and finish. He then presented these redrawn reproductions together with the original and asked the subjects to pick the genuine original. He argued that if the memory for the original forms had been systematically changed by internal stresses, the subjects would tend to recognize the reproduction as the original, since it would be closer to the "memory trace." Zangwill found that systematic reproduction errors were not necessarily matched with recognition errors. Therefore, he concluded that there was not good evidence for the kind of internal changes which gestalt theory would lead one to expect.

There have been many other techniques suggested for the evaluation of memory for visually presented forms. Riley (1962) has very carefully considered the experimental evidence that arises from the application of these techniques, and he has concluded that there is no real evidence for the kind of automatic internal changes toward simplicity, symmetry, and "figure goodness" expected by gestalt theory. Instead, there is evidence that memory for form is influenced by verbal labels (see the discussion of the verbal-loop hypothesis, page 321), previous experience, and the process of reproduction itself. Postman (1954) was able to show that first teaching people a code which allowed a partial reconstruction of some forms that were presented later exerted a great influence on the retention of forms. Furthermore, the greater the interval of time between presentation of the forms and the test of retention, the greater the influence of the code—a fact which is very much in keeping with interference theories of forgetting.

BARTLETT'S STUDIES

Qualitative changes in memory were extensively investigated by Sir Frederic Bartlett (1932) in studies which have had wide influence. Like the gestalt psychologists, Bartlett begins with the assumption that there are systematic reorganizations during retention. The memory trace for a perceptual event is not simply a slow fading picture, like a photographic proof; it is something that is actively being changed and reconstructed.

Bartlett's ideas differ from those of the gestalt psychologists in two important respects, however. He has insisted that the processes or reorganization and reconstruction in perceptual memory are essentially the same as those at work in verbal and cognitive memory generally. Furthermore, he has a very different notion of the kinds of changes that go on in memory. He agrees with the gestalt psychologists that the changes in memory with time are most often in the direction of simplification of the memory. His simplification is not the same as that of the gestalt psychologists, however. Bartlett uses the term *schema* to refer to what is remembered. The schema is a highly generalized representation of what was once perceived, though it is distorted by previous experience and attitudes. The schema is the memory trace, but it is not what is produced when we remember. At the time of remembering something, we try to reconstruct, and we reconstruct out of the materials available to us in our general store of information, using the schema as a model. The schema may be altered, incidentally, by this very process of reconstruction, so that our reconstruction may be different the next time.

The schema arises when we first perceive something, Bartlett argues. When we are faced with something unfamiliar, we do not simply receive an impression of it. We reconstruct it in such a way that it is easy to assimilate into our past experience with the world. There is, in Bartlett's terms, an effort after meaning. This meaningful reorganization in perception provides the schematic basis for retention.

Bartlett gives us several quasi-experimental demonstrations of what he is driving at. The best known is illustrated in Figure 11.5. The original drawing in the upper left-hand corner was presented to a person, and he was asked to reproduce the drawing from memory. The result was

FIG. 11.5   A form serially reproduced from memory by different individuals. The form is altered at each reproduction. The influences of labeling as a coding device is seen in the change from a conventional Egyptian symbol for an owl to a picture of a cat. (After Bartlett, 1932.)

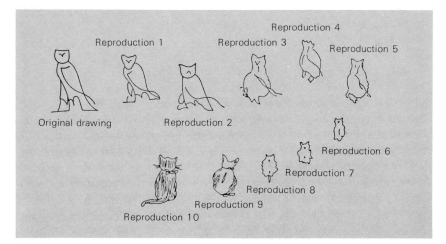

reproduction 1. This reproduction was then presented to another person, who was also asked to reproduce what he had seen from memory. The result was reproduction 2. The process was carried through the entire series exhibited in Figure 11.5, and the form was changed through these successive reproductions from the ancient Egyptian symbol for "owl" to a picture of a pussycat.

Bartlett further argued that the nature and direction of schematization in memory is determined by idiosyncratic personal characteristics. In one of his other demonstrations, he asked people to describe pictures of faces he had presented to them earlier. This task appeared to be particularly susceptible to personal attitudes and motives aroused by some central characteristic of the perception. For example, people tend to describe pictures of faces in terms of the conventional attitudes aroused by the type allegedly represented by the face. A picture of an enlisted man would be described as representing a young, good-humored person, while a picture of an officer would be described as stern, older, etc. Bartlett argued that the attitude aroused by the pictorial schema influenced subsequent memory for and description of the picture.

Unfortunately, in these studies, as in nearly all studies of qualitative changes in retention, there is no way to know for certain if the changes described are actually changes that take place during the retention interval or changes that occur at the time of test for retention. It is possible that what was remembered was what was perceived in the first place. Most commentators have assumed that the reproductions reported by Bartlett reflect changes during the retention interval or changes induced by the reproduction process itself, but the fact is that we do not know what it really was that the subjects learned in the first place. Some investigators have not been concerned with whether schematization occurs during learning or retention (for example, Paul, 1959); but if we are to apply these notions of Bartlett to the problem of forgetting, the distinction is important.

SHORT–TERM MEMORY

Most of us think of memory and its converse, forgetting, as taking place over months and years. Yet one of the most pervasive psychological phenomena of our everyday life is forgetting over very brief intervals of time. How often, for example, do we look up a number in the telephone book only to have forgotten it by the time we turn to dial. Even though we are certain that we know the number when we find it in the book, it is only a matter of seconds before we cannot correctly recall it.

The importance of this phenomenon has not been lost on psychologists. One of the durable and influential psychophysiological theories of memory and learning (Hebb, 1949) takes the forgetting which takes place over seconds as one of the key phenomena to be explained. Hebb argues that the physiological basis of memory is dual in nature. According to his theory, there are two phases in the establishment of the physiological substrate for memory. The first of these phases is dynamic. It consists of a network of activity in a group of nerve cells which recurrently excite one another. This dynamic phase, Hebb asserts, is responsible for a memory trace of very short duration—a memory trace that gradually disappears as activity subsides. Long-term or permanent memory Hebb attributes to structural changes in these nerve networks which are the result of repeated elicitation of the active phase. Many theorists who have worked with the experimental analysis of short-term memory have modeled their theories after Hebb's analysis.

Whether or not such theories are correct, there is certainly, under ordinary circumstances, a considerable decay in the ability to remember something we have been exposed to, a decay which occupies intervals of a few seconds. Some of the important characteristics of this decay are revealed in the experimental analyses of the problem.

Retention of Minimal Verbal Elements

As a convenient point of departure we may use some studies of forgetting over brief periods of time for very small amounts of material. The studies make use of a technique which is more or less continuous with the techniques we have already discussed in earlier chapters. These methods, as Melton (1963) has pointed out, can apply to material beyond the memory span as well as within it. The studies reviewed here, however, are limited to minimal verbal elements—elements well within the memory span for adult persons.

THE BASIC EXPERIMENTS

The basic experimental technique is one invented by Peterson and Peterson (1959). The purpose of these investigators was to measure the forgetting curve for single nonsense syllables over spans of time less than one minute. In their testing situation an experimenter spells for the subject a single three-consonant nonsense syllable. Immediately thereafter, he gives the subject a three-digit number. The subject has already been instructed that when he hears this number, he should begin counting backwards by threes from it. He is to count one number for each beat of a metronome. Then when he is signaled by a small light, he is to recall immediately the original three-letter syllable. This sequence of events is illustrated in Figure 11.6. In the example diagramed in the figure, the delay period is 3 seconds; in the actual experiment, delays, occupied by counting, varied

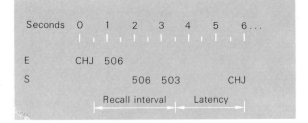

FIG. **11.6** The order of events in a typical short-term memory test. The subject is presented with the syllable CHJ. There is a recall interval (3 seconds, in this case) and a reaction latency, and then the subject gives the response CHJ. (Peterson & Peterson, 1959.)

from 0 to 18 seconds. A number of subjects were repeatedly tested with these various delays, so that the outcome of the experiment was a very reliable determination of the probability of correct recall of the syllables as a function of delay. A syllable was scored as correct only if all three letters were given in the right order.

Figure 11.7 shows the basic results of this experiment. Notice that at a delay of 0 seconds, performance is not perfect; the subjects were correct only about 90 percent of the time. The 10 percent errors were not, of course, failures of memory but failures in perception; the subjects did not hear a few of the letters correctly. Notice, however, that as the recall time is delayed, performance falls off drastically, so that at 18 seconds, less than 10 percent of the syllables are correctly remembered.

An experimental test by Murdock (1961) showed that even though the Peterson and Peterson experiment was titled "Short-term retention of individual verbal items," the material to be recalled really consisted of

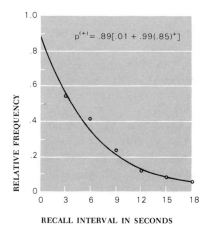

RECALL INTERVAL IN SECONDS

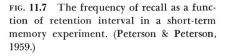

FIG. **11.7** The frequency of recall as a function of retention interval in a short-term memory experiment. (Peterson & Peterson, 1959.)

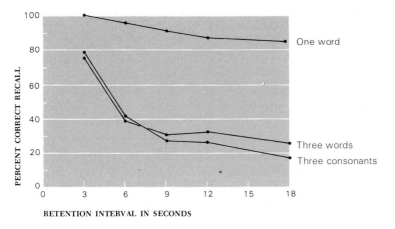

FIG. 11.8 The recall of one word compared with three words and three consonants in a short-term memory experiment. The three words and three consonants are nearly the same in retention. (Data from Murdock, 1961.)

more than one item. Murdock repeated the experimental procedure, but with several additions. Besides testing for recall of three-letter consonant syllables, he tested for the retention of three monosyllabic English words and, in another experiment, for the retention of a single monosyllabic word. Retention of these words was tested under precisely the same conditions.

FIG. 11.9 Theoretical retention curves for different numbers of items in short-term memory. (Melton, 1963.)

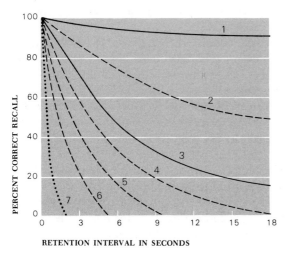

The results of Murdock's experiment are shown in Figure 11.8. If you compare the data from Murdock's test of recall for the three consonants with the curve in Figure 11.7, you will see that he managed to duplicate precisely the results achieved by the Petersons. Even more surprising is the fact that the forgetting curve for the three consonants is almost exactly the same as that for three monosyllabic words. It would appear that each letter in the nonsense syllable acts like a word. Notice that there is very much less forgetting for a single word.

Murdock's experiment leads to the analysis presented in Figure 11.9, which is taken from an experiment by Melton (1963). The curves in this are forgetting curves for one, two, three, four, or five consonants. They were tested under somewhat different conditions, so we would not expect them to be exactly like the data in Figures 11.7 and 11.8. For one thing, these consonants were presented visually. In any event, there is the same pattern of rapid negatively accelerated forgetting, and the extent of the forgetting depends upon the amount of material presented.

OTHER TESTS FOR SHORT-TERM MEMORY OF VERBAL MATERIAL

When we ask what is the cause of the precipitous decline in retention evident in the experiments we have just described, perhaps our first inquiry would be directed to the function of the counting of digits backwards. Obviously, it does one thing that it is intended to do: it prevents subjects from rehearsing the verbal items. When rehearsal is permitted, there is very little retention loss.

However, does the counting actively interfere with retention, or is the decline in retention a matter of the decay of the trace in the nervous system left by the perception of the to-be-remembered material? If there was simply an inevitable decay in the material, one would expect forgetting to go on no matter what happened in the delay interval, provided that rehearsal was effectively presented.

If inevitable decay is the answer, the retention curve should be heavily dependent on time and largely independent of what goes on during the retention interval. One way to approach the question posed here is to vary the rates of presentation and recall. If there is simply decay of a trace without interference from activities intervening between presentation and test for recall, then the shorter the presentation time and the quicker the recall period, the greater should be the number of items remembered.

We have already cited data (Murdock, 1960) in Chapter 8 which showed that the slower the presentation rate, the higher the recall. But the rates in this case were slow enough to allow for rehearsal. What would happen if the rates were never slow enough to allow for rehearsal?

Conrad and Hille (1958) have examined this question. They conducted an experiment in which subjects listened to series of random digits. The subjects would listen to eight of these digits and then attempt to recall them. Eight digits is just about the immediate memory span for adult subjects. Conrad and Hille compared fast and slow rates of delivery of these digits, and they compared conditions of rapid and slow pacing of recall. In addition, they examined recall under unpaced conditions.

Table 11.1 shows the percentage of digits in correct order and also the average delay between presentation and recall of individual digits. Notice that the highest percentage of recall occurs with unpaced recall, but under paced recall, the fast pacing produces better performance. Also, the faster the presentation rate, the better the performance. These and subsequent data (Conrad, 1959; 1960) make a very convincing case for the proposition that it is delay, not interference by the digit counting, which is responsible for the decline in retention.

TABLE 11.1   Percentage of Digits Correctly Recalled and the Mean Delay between Presentation and Recall of Individual Digits
(Conrad & Hille, 1958)

| | PRESENTATION RATE | | | |
| | FAST | | SLOW | |
RECALL RATE	% CORRECT	MEAN DELAY (SEC.)	% CORRECT	MEAN DELAY (SEC.)
Fast	41.00	6.00	39.60	11.75
Slow	35.00	12.25	32.10	17.00
Unpaced	62.30		42.90	

Despite the fact that the counting itself does not seem to be responsible for the decay in retention, some other experiments suggest that the critical condition producing forgetting is interference—interference not from intervening activities but from the attempt to store too many things. These experiments (Lloyd, Reid, & Feallock, 1960; Reid, Lloyd, Brackett, & Hawkins, 1961) make use of a very different technique, in which there is a continuous presentation of material. Every so often, the presentation of material is interrupted, and the subject is asked to recall a certain class of the material he has just heard. The procedure is somewhat reminiscent of the clustering experiments, in that the material presented for recall falls into distinctly separate classes. For example, all the words might be either the names of trees or the names of cities. In that case, whenever the subject hears the word *tree* or *city* he is to recall all the appropriate words. The subject might hear the sequence PINE,

LONDON, PONTIAC, MOSCOW, BOMBAY, HEMLOCK, CITY, WILLOW, TREE, DODGE, CROW, EAGLE, AUTO, BIRD. When the word CITY occurred, he should have responded with LONDON, MOSCOW, and BOMBAY.

This technique enables one to study the effects on immediate memory of average storage load and the reduction in average storage load. The average storage load is simply the number of items the subject is required to remember over a sequence, and the average storage-load reduction is the average number of items the subject is required to recall at any of the various recall points.

The results show that as average storage load increases, the number of errors in immediate recall increases. Errors decrease with increasing average storage-load reduction. The major factor determining performance, then, is the amount of material the subject must store before he can recall the material. The greater the amount of material, the more likely the internal interference among the items being stored.

The critical dependence of this technique upon the recall to the class name as a cue makes the memory process look, in part at least, like a search task. That, in any event, was the view held by Yntema and Trask (1963). As a point of departure, they take some observations by Broadbent (1958). In the course of some studies of attention, Broadbent presented pairs of digits to subjects by leading one digit into one ear and the other into the other ear simultaneously. Subjects can, under such conditions, report ·both digits. In one experiment, subjects were given three pairs of these digits in rapid succession and asked to recall them. Broadbent discovered that subjects usually reported all the digits presented to one ear first, and then all the digits presented to the other ear. In other words, subjects categorized by input channel.

Yntema and Trask used the same technique to present a digit to one ear and a word to the other. However, sometimes the digit would be presented to the right ear and sometimes to the left ear. Various subjects were given different instructions about how they should recall (for example, by grouping simultaneous pairs, etc.). The results showed that recall was not most accurate when subjects grouped by side of head, as would be implied by Broadbent's results; instead, recall was most accurate when subjects grouped by type (digit or word). There is greater recall, then, when the search is organized so as to fit the method of storage of items. One implication of these results is that deficiencies in memory are not always due to the unavailability of items for recall but to inefficiency or inadequacies in memory search.

INTERFERENCE IN SHORT-TERM MEMORY

Much of the data we have just reviewed suggest that confusion among stored items which are not yet "cleared" from memory by recall is respon-

sible for decrements in retention. Some additional data show that interference from items already recalled is an even more important source of
decrement in retention.

These experiments make use of the single-item (or triplet) technique of Peterson and Peterson. Without giving too much thought to
the matter, we might conclude that the task of counting backwards is
the major source of interference in the experiments. In fact, however,
contemporary theories of forgetting would incline us to believe that the
major source of forgetting would be the influence of previous habits on
short-term memory. During the delay interval, previous habits would
intrude and interfere with the retention of the item just presented.

If that is the case, the amount of forgetting in a short-term memory experiment should depend upon the number of recall tests preceding
any particular test. There should be less forgetting, if all other things
are equal, for the first item in a testing session than for the last item.
It was this hypothesis that was examined by Keppel and Underwood
(1962). They studied the amount of forgetting as a function of position
in the test series. The first item in the test series had not been preceded
by any other syllables, while recall of the fifth item had been preceded by
four other items.

The results of the Keppel and Underwood study can be seen in
Figure 11.10. Notice that for a three-consonant item with an 18-second
delay before the test of retention, there is practically no forgetting when
that item is first in the series. After tests have been given on five other
items, however, the probability of a correct recall for the sixth syllable
declines to less than 50 percent after a delay of 18 seconds. These data
clearly show, then, that the cause of the precipitous decline in retention

FIG. 11.10   Retention after 3 seconds compared with retention after 18 seconds as a function of number of previous
retention tests. (Keppel & Underwood, 1962.)

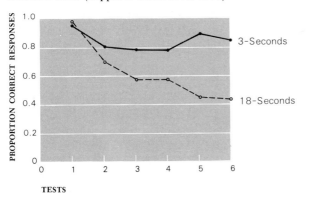

TESTS

reported by Peterson and Peterson as well as by Murdock is the fact that, on the average, items were preceded by many earlier tests.

The complete absence of a difference between recall at a delay of 3 seconds and a delay of 18 seconds (Figure 11.10) makes it very improbable that decline in retention in these experiments is the result of the simple fading of a trace. Interference appears to be the major cause.

PERCEPTUAL TRACE EXPERIMENTS

Two experiments (Sperling, 1960; Averbach & Coriell, 1961) provide evidence for the existence of a very brief perceptual trace which does decay automatically. In Sperling's experiment, subjects were given extremely brief presentations (around 5/100 of a second in duration) of arrays of letters. They looked something like this example:

X M R J
P N K P
L Q B G

Subjects looking at such arrays for so brief a period of time cannot report anything but a fraction of the letters presented. In Sperling's experiment, however, they were instructed to respond by recalling, immediately after presentation, only one of the rows of the array. They did not know which row. After presentation, a signal sounded which told them which row they were to try to remember. They could not concentrate on any one row ahead of time and have any hope of being accurate.

Under these conditions, subjects could recall almost every letter. Theoretically, they should report no greater proportion of any row than of the total array, since they do not know while actually seeing the array which row they are to report. But the fact is that the subjects do enormously better under Sperling's conditions. The only conclusion, Sperling asserted, is that subjects are able to hold a brief memory image of the array for enough time to be able to "read out" any one row from the memory image. They cannot recite the whole correctly because the image fades while they are reciting the first few letters. Also, perhaps recitation of the first few letters interferes with memory for the remaining.

Averbach and Coriell were able to show that they could interfere with such a brief memory trace by presenting a visual stimulus immediately after the array had been presented. These investigators showed arrays of letters in much the same way as Sperling did. But after a very short delay, they flashed a circle around the place where one of the letters had been and asked the subjects to recall that letter. The remarkable thing was that the circle *erased* the memory image for the letter. Apparently the memory image is entirely visual in nature. Another stimulus presented in the same perceptual field a short time afterwards causes the image for the circled item to disappear by washing it out.

These experiments provide evidence for the existence of a pure perceptual memory trace, one which decays very rapidly. The maximum duration for such a trace, these experiments show, is on the order of one second. Therefore, the events studied here define a very short-term memory indeed, and one that does not seem to have anything to do with the decline in the course of retention of verbal material over several seconds.

The Interpretation of Short-Term Memory

All the experimental evidence we have just examined suggests several processes at work in short-term memory. First of all, there seems to be a purely perceptual trace which runs its course in a second or less. It can be preempted or erased by succeeding perceptual events but not, evidently, by stored information. Thus, while this extremely short trace does seem to be free from ordinary interference, it is subject to erasure by new information coming in a sensory channel.

If memory is to be longer than a fleeting second, it must be translated into some more permanent form. For verbal material this probably means transforming a purely perceptual event into a linguistic one, something which involves cognition and probably motor components as well. Even memory so linguistically encoded may have a very brief life. It is not subject to erasure by displacement, but it is subject to interference from previous memories. Thus it is subject to proactive inhibition (see page 400).

The question remains as to whether we must think of memory as a dual process, as proposed by Hebb (1949) or by Broadbent (1954). If decay of a memory over a very brief period of time is to be attributed entirely to interference from other learned acts, we need not consider memory as dual in nature. The evidence would be strong that short-term memory, of the sort defined by the Peterson and Peterson experiment, and long-term memory are based upon the same process. That is the conclusion drawn by Postman (1964) in his careful review of the evidence on short-term memory.

If such interference is the only real cause of the decay in short-term memory (aside from the perceptual trace), there is some problem in the fact that the decay is so complete. Within 30 seconds, a three-letter combination which has a 90 percent probability of being recalled can be driven nearly to zero. In order to create continuity between short-term memory and long-term memory, we must reconcile this with the prolonged retention (over months and years) found in other studies. The problem can be resolved by asserting that memories which decay so

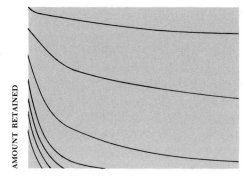

AMOUNT RETAINED

RETENTION INTERVAL

FIG. **11.11** Theoretical retention curves. The figure shows that the length of the retention interval will be determined by the strength of the material at the end of practice.

rapidly are probably very weak. In their original experiment, Peterson and Peterson (1959) showed that short-term forgetting was markedly decreased by overlearning. Even though a single nonsense syllable may be given with a probability of recall of nearly 1.0 immediately after one presentation, that single presentation is not sufficient to make it very resistant to forgetting.

Therefore, there is some continuity between the long-term and short-term retention studies. The difference between the two lies in the vastly greater resistance to forgetting produced at the time of learning in the studies of long-term retention. Theoretically, we might imagine all experiments on either short-term or long-term retention to fall on one of the curves in Figure 11.11. The lowest curve would be representative of short-term retention, while the highest curve would be representative of long-term retention. There is a correlation between the rapidity of forgetting and the origin of the curves (the strength of habits at the time of original learning); the stronger the verbal habits at original learning, the slower the process of forgetting.

A continuity between short-term and long-term memory makes the search for the major causes of forgetting a simpler one than would have been the case if these two aspects of memory had turned out to be completely different processes. We have already seen that the major identified cause of the decrement in short-term memory is interference. We now turn to the detailed study of interference in long-term retention as well as to some other possible causes of forgetting.

THE CAUSES OF FORGETTING

The recurring theme in all the chapters on verbal learning has been that one of the fundamental determinants of the course of learning and retention is the relation between material under study at the moment and material learned at other times. In this section we shall describe some of the ways in which such relations are responsible for the decrement in performance that is ordinarily described as forgetting.

An assumption still made very often by those who have not experimented with the phenomenon is that forgetting is due simply to disuse—that is to say, to the lack of practice. Something once learned seems to fade away without practice, much as a footpath will be overgrown with weeds if no one walks on it. Therefore, the assumption of disuse seems to be a reasonable one.

There are, however, many grounds for dismissing disuse as a serious notion in the study of forgetting. The late J. A. McGeoch once pointed out that disuse does not explain forgetting if disuse implies only the passage of time without practice, for time in itself does not cause anything. Events happen in time; certain conditions change over time, and it is these that provide the explanations. Thus we find that forgetting should be determined by the nature of the events which fill a retention interval.

It is, of course, possible that some of the critical events which determine forgetting are purely physiological in nature. If so, some forgetting has nothing to do with psychological events at all, but itself constitutes a unique psychological fact determined by changes in the nervous system. In that event, there is an important problem in the nature of the relation between the psychological facts of forgetting and the physiological events which cause them. Thus far, we have very little evidence which tells us about that relationship. Nevertheless, we may take it as a strong possibility that the psychological causes of forgetting, discussed below, are superimposed upon a physiological process in which there is a kind of deterioration of the physical substrate of memory.

Experimentally Produced Forgetting

Once we admit that the major psychological determinant of forgetting is the events that intervene between learning and a test of retention, it becomes apparent that the kinds of experimental designs suitable for the study of transfer of training are also suitable for the study of experimentally produced forgetting. For if the retention of one learned act is interfered with by the influence of other things learned, negative transfer is the essential description of forgetting. Because retention, not original learning, is the object of study here, the designs for the study of forgetting are slightly different in detail than the designs for the study of transfer.

EXPERIMENTAL DESIGNS

As we saw in Chapter 10 on transfer, there are two types of designs in the study of transfer. One of these, the proaction design, measures the effect of an older learned act upon the acquisition of a new one. The other, the retroaction design, is limited to retention. It evaluates the effect of an intervening or new learned act upon the retention of an old one. For the purposes of the study of forgetting, the retroaction design would seem to be the appropriate one, since it is concerned with retention. In the retroaction design the condition which produces the negative transfer occurs in between original learning and a test for retention. In fact, however, the retention test can be added to the proaction design, and as it turns out, the proaction design has come to be of perhaps even greater theoretical importance than the retroaction design in the study of forgetting.

Here are the two designs as they apply to the study of retention.

PROACTION

Experimental Group

    Learns task 1 . . . . . . Learns task 2 . . . . . . Retention test for task 2

Control Group

    Rests . . . . Learns task 2 . . . . Retention test for task 2

The difference in the amount of retention of task 2 reflects the influence of the learning of task 1 by the experimental group. Obviously, if proaction is to influence retention of task 2, it must operate somewhere between the learning of task 2 and the test for retention of task 2. That means the major influence of the prior task is through *its* retention after task 2 has been learned, for it is the retained aspects of task 1 that must interfere with the retention of task 2.

RETROACTION

Experimental Group

    Learns task 1 . . . . . Learns task 2 . . . . . Retention test for task 1

Control Group

    Learns task 1 . . . . (Rest) . . . . Retention test for task 1

The retroaction design is the more obvious one, because the interfering condition is actually produced during the retention interval for task 1. More and more, however, the importance of interference from retention of prior experiences is being emphasized as the cause of forgetting, so that the proaction design has come to be the more thoroughly studied in recent years.

Of course, in both designs, experimentally produced forgetting is said to take place when the retention by the control group is better than the retention by the experimental group. In that case, it is customary to say that retroactive inhibition, or proactive inhibition, depending upon the design, has taken place. The term *inhibition* refers to the lowered performance for the experimental group on the test for retention, which shows that some forgetting has been produced experimentally.

THE EXPERIMENTAL ANALYSIS OF RETROACTION AND PROACTION

We may begin the analysis of retroactive and proactive inhibition with two experiments that have been more important in determining the course of research on the causes of forgetting in recent years than any other investigations. These two experiments were designed to determine the nature of the differences between retroaction and proaction, and they are the work of A. W. Melton and his students.

One experiment was intended to compare the relative importance of retroactive and proactive inhibition under analogous conditions. In this study subjects learned lists of nonsense syllables by serial anticipation. While the actual design of the experiment was rather complicated, the basic comparison between proaction and retroaction was straightforward. It depended upon the equating of the time intervals between learning and the test of retention. In terms of the designs presented earlier, the critical comparison was between the retention of task 2 (proaction) and the retention of task 1 (retroaction when they were both subjects to interfering effects (Melton and von Lackum, 1941).

The results of the comparison showed that retroactive inhibition was greater than proactive inhibition. That is to say, the greater amount of forgetting occurred for the list learned prior to the learning of the interfering list. This finding will not violate many prejudices, since, in the proactive experiment, the more recent task is the one for which retention is measured, while in the retroactive experiment, retention for the more distant task is measured.

If, however, a long time interval occurs between original learning and the test for retention, the difference between retroaction and proaction disappears (Underwood, 1948). Again, this is not surprising from a naïve point of view, for the difference in order between the tasks in the two designs will be slight compared with the time difference over a long retention period. What is important, however, is that the reduction in the difference between proaction and retroaction with time is largely the result of recovery from retroactive inhibition. Thus, if one learns a task, learns another, and waits a period of time before testing for retention, the influence of the second task upon retention of the first will be less harmful than if one tests for retention immediately after learning the second task.

This fact has great theoretical significance, as was first suspected from the results of an experiment by Melton and Irwin (1940). In this experiment, the object of interest was the influence of amount of practice in the interpolated or inhibiting task upon the retention of the first task in a retroactive design. As in the study by Melton and von Lackum, the material consisted of lists of nonsense syllables learned by serial anticipation.

The basic results of this experiment are described by the curve in Figure 11.12 labeled "total obtained *RI*." The investigators found total retroactive inhibition to increase rapidly as the amount of practice on an interpolated task increased from zero to a very few trials. The total inhibiting effect on retention of the first task reached a maximum, however, with very little additional practice on the inhibiting task, and there is even the suggestion of a slight decline in total inhibition as practice on the second task continued.

When Melton and Irwin came to present reasons for this relation, they were able to draw upon some additional data. They tabulated the overt errors which occurred during the recall of the first list. Of particular interest were errors which were actually *correct* syllables from the second list. These, then, were failures of recall of the first list which could definitely be traced to competition from items learned during practice on the second list.

When the frequency of these errors was plotted as a function of

FIG. **11.12** Retroactive inhibition as a function of the number of trials of interpolated learning. The dashed lower curve shows the inhibition attributable to overt intrusion at recall. The upper dashed curve shows inhibition attributable to factor *X*. (Melton & Irwin, 1940.)

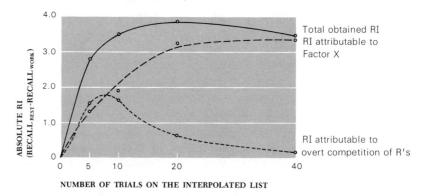

NUMBER OF TRIALS ON THE INTERPOLATED LIST

the number of trials on the interpolated list, the results did not look at all like the curve for the total obtained retroactive inhibition. The frequency of such errors is described by the curve in Figure 11.12 labeled "*RI* attributable to overt competition of *R*'s." The errors are relatively common after a very few trials of practice on the interpolated list, but they decline practically to zero after extended practice on the interpolated list. Melton and Irwin reasoned that this was so because as the interpolated list became better learned, it was more easily differentiated from the original list and therefore less likely to produce intrusions during recall of the original list.

The problem, however, is to account for the fact that retroactive inhibition remains high after overt competitive intrusions have declined to near-zero. How do we account for the sustained high retroaction? As shown in Figure 11.12, Melton and Irwin plotted the difference between retroactive inhibition attributable to overt competition and total retroaction as factor *X*. Notice that factor *X* continues to increase as the result of additional practice on the interpolated task.

What is factor *X*? Melton and Irwin argued that it might represent the *unlearning* of the material from the first list. They pointed out the analogy with experimental extinction of instrumental responses. As a subject learns the second list, items from the first list occasionally intrude. That is to say the subject may mistakenly think of, or even overtly give, an item from the original material he learned. Such responses are incorrect during the learning of the second list, and so they go unreinforced or even punished. Therefore, the tendency to give items from the first list is weakened during the learning of the second list. The more the practice on the second list, the greater the cumulative unlearning of the first list.

If unlearning is analogous to extinction, one would expect spontaneous recovery (see page 121) to occur. Therefore, some of the harmful effects on retention of the first list from learning the second list would disappear if a time interval were allowed for the material from the first list to spontaneously recover. Such an analogy to extinction would account for Underwood's (1948) finding that the amount of retroactive inhibition tends to decline as a time interval is lengthened between the learning of the second list and the test of retention of the first.

However, all such evidence is indirect. In the standard technique of rote learning, it is very difficult to observe what actually happens to other responses as the subject learns the material assigned to him. Several experiments (Briggs, 1954; 1957) utilize a technique which makes it possible to follow what happens to responses appropriate to the first task during the learning of the second. Specially designed recall tasks are inserted during the learning of list 2. These tests show that as the material from the second list is learned, the material from the first list becomes less likely to occur. In a word, the original learned responses appear to be weakened. Furthermore, the material from the first list "spontaneously" recovers if a time interval occurs between practice on the second list and a recall test. Therefore, the analogy to extinction seems to be more than circumstantial.

Such experiments suggest two factors at work in the retroactive inhibition experiment and one in the proactive inhibition experiment. In the retroaction design, learned responses appropriate to the first task are weakened or made unavailable during the learning of the second. In addition, the second task produces learned responses which compete, at the time of the retention test for the first task, with those of the first task. This is particularly the case if the cues differentiating the occurrence of responses from one or another of the tasks are very much alike. There is confusion at the time of recall between the materials from the two tasks.

In the proaction experiment, only competition can be at work. Since the interfering task is learned first, there is no additional learning task interposed before the test for retention that would permit unlearning of the correct responses. Both from the analogy with experimental extinction and from direct experimental evidence, we know that the responses weakened through unlearning recover. Therefore, when equivalent tasks are learned to equivalent degrees, there is very little difference between retroactive and proactive inhibition after a time interval has elapsed prior to the final retention test.

One further experiment provides some direct information about what happens to material from the first task during learning of the second. In this experiment (Barnes & Underwood, 1959) subjects learned lists of paired associates in which nonsense syllables were the stimuli and unrelated two-syllable adjectives were the responses. There were eight pairs in the lists, and each subject learned two lists. In the critical condition of the experiment, the nonsense syllables (stimuli) were identical for the two lists but the responses were different. Therefore, the subjects had to learn two different responses to the same stimuli in rapid succession.

At various points during the learning of the second list, subjects were asked to give, in special recall tests, the items appropriate to *both* the first and the second lists. The essential results of these recall tests can be seen in Figure 11.13, which shows the number of responses correctly recalled and identified with the appropriate stimulus for both lists. It is clear that responses appropriate to the first list decline in strength during the learning of the second. The really important feature of such an effect is that the responses from list 1 seem to become totally unavailable. This result is demonstrated by an experiment much like that of Barnes and

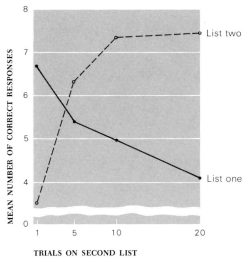

FIG. 11.13 The number of responses correctly recalled as a function of degree of practice on the second list. The more practice on the second list, the fewer responses subjects could recall from the first list. (Barnes & Underwood, 1959.)

TRIALS ON SECOND LIST

Underwood (Goggin, 1963). Goggin did not, however, do what Barnes and Underwood did in the recall tests; she asked subjects to write down all the items they could possibly remember, even though some of them might be wrong or identified with the wrong stimulus. Her results were almost identical with those of Barnes and Underwood. The only conclusion seems to be that during the learning of the second list, the material from the first list becomes unavailable. Therefore, it isn't just that people learn second responses to the same stimuli which are more likely to occur than the first responses. The first responses are actually weakened, so that they become more difficult to recall.

EXTRAEXPERIMENTAL SOURCES OF INTERFERENCE IN FORGETTING

The proaction experiment is important because it suggests that the vast number of things we have previously learned interfere with our retention of something just learned. Furthermore, it is the proaction effect which allows us to account theoretically for some of the uncontrolled forgetting that occurs in experiments on experimentally produced forgetting. In such studies it is not only the experimental group that shows a decrement in retention. Generally the control group shows a loss also; it is only that the loss for the experimental group is greater.

The uncontrolled forgetting that goes on in the control subjects could be the result of interference from previously learned habits—habits acquired outside the experimental laboratory. It is possible that a great deal of, perhaps most, uncontrolled forgetting is the result of interference.

With such an idea in mind, Underwood and Postman (1960) set about to investigate extraexperimental sources of interference in the retention of simple verbal tasks in the laboratory. They investigated the retention of three-letter syllables which had been learned by serial antici- pation in lists of 12 syllables each. During learning, the subjects tried to anticipate, by spelling, each syllable before it was shown to them. Re- tention was tested in exactly the same way. All the lists were learned to a criterion of one perfect repetition of the entire list.

After learning, the subjects were divided into two groups. One group was tested for retention immediately after learning (almost imme- diately—30 seconds later), and the other group was tested for retention one week later. The immediate retention test provided a base line against which the amount of forgetting that took place in a week's time could be measured. Underwood and Postman took the view that such forgetting would be the result of previous habits interfering with retention of the experimental lists.

The critical variable in the study was in the actual lists the sub- jects learned. The lists were constructed in such a way that some of them would be more subject to interference from previously acquired habits than others. Two potential sources of interference came from ordinary sequential relations among letters in spelling and from ordinary linguistic relations among words. Consider the question of letter sequences. Sup- pose one of the items is JQB. This sequence is an extremely unlikely one in ordinary English. If the subjects were required to remember JQB, the more usual sequences of English (A or E following J, etc.) would tend to interfere with the retention of the experimental syllable during the time interval. The amount of such interference would be less when the letters in the syllables to be remembered were already like those of ordinary Eng- lish. Therefore, Underwood and Postman compared the retention of two types of nonsense syllables: those consisting of very probable sequences in English, such as EST, and those which are relatively improbable in English, such as ARP.

The same argument can be applied to words. Common words have many associations which are very strong. Rare words have relatively few associations, argued Underwood and Postman, and these are weaker. Consequently, we would expect lists of very rare three-letter words, once they had been learned, to be retained better than lists of very common words. There would be more interference from previous associations during the retention interval for the common words.

The results of the experiment are disappointing. There was a considerable amount of forgetting during the one-week period for all lists, but no statistically reliable *differential* forgetting among the lists. What did appear in the way of differences was contrary to the original hypothesis. There was, for example, more forgetting for the uncommon words than for the common words. Virtually the only reliable evidence the investigators found for the notion which led to the experiment in the first place lies in the fact that the high-probability nonsense syllables were relearned more rapidly than everything else. While the authors performed a variety of analyses which convinced them that their original hypothesis was still tenable, the whole experiment amounted to a very weak demonstration of the importance of extraexperimental sources of forgetting. As such, it casts doubt on the general importance of interference in ordinary forgetting—for, if anything, one would expect the extensive previous experience with linguistic usage to have produced much bigger effects than it would be possible to achieve with experimentally produced forgetting.

The very small amount of positive evidence for interference in this experiment led Postman (1963) to pose the question, Does interference theory predict too much forgetting? While Postman did not put it quite so strongly, we might say that a certain naïve view of interference theory, particularly as it has been applied to the study of extraexperimental sources of interference, would lead one to wonder why every adult is not reduced to total mutism as the result of the cumulation of massive proactive inhibition. In fact it is possible that we expect too much of interference theory.

Nevertheless, we need to examine a different kind of experiment in order to see that interference can produce considerable changes in memory. Coleman (1962) performed an experiment which employed the method of serial reproduction. He began with the same assumption made by Underwood and Postman, namely, that previous linguistic habits would compete with experimentally taught habits when a test for retention of the experimentally produced habits was called for. As in the earlier experiments, Coleman's study examined both word-sequence interference and letter-sequence interference. Here, however, the resemblance between the study by Underwood and Postman and that by Coleman ends.

In the serial reproduction method, one subject learns something which is then transmitted to another subject. That subject learns and passes on what he has received from the first subject, and so on, through a chain. The object of the experiment is to see how the material transmitted is altered by the memories of the successive subjects. Coleman simply applied this technique to the study of interference. He presented to the first subject a sentence in which the letters (including the space as a letter) were completely scrambled. Thus, the sentence TODAY IS THURSDAY might come out as DDI TUOSYYA TRHSA. The sentences were somewhat longer than this example, since they ranged from 25 to 33 letters.

The first subject examined the scrambled sentence and tried to memorize the sequence of letters, though he was stopped before he could have reached a criterion of 100 percent accuracy. He was then given a packet of cards, each with one letter on it, and was asked to arrange the letters in the order in which he had seen them. His ordering was typed and presented to the next subject, who also attempted to memorize that sequence and then reconstruct it from a packet of cards, and so on through a number of subjects. In an identical experiment, a second group of subjects was tested with words, not letters, scrambled.

Coleman argued that the letter and word sequences of ordinary English would interfere with the bizarre arrangements during the brief period of time the subjects had to remember the sequences before trying to reconstruct them from the packet of cards. The result should be that each subject would construct a sequence *more* like natural English than the one he received.

The major results for the experiment on letter sequences are illustrated in Figure 11.14. Here the "mean trigram occurrence" of sequences of three letters in the reconstructions made by each subject are plotted as a function of the successive reconstructions. The higher the "mean trigram occurrence," the more closely the sequences remembered by the subjects resembled ordinary English and the less they resembled the original scrambled sentences. Notice that there is a large change in the direction of ordinary English for the first two or three reproductions, and not much change thereafter. There was a definite limit to the process of approximating ordinary English through the interference of ordinary linguistic habits. The orderings never did quite reach the sequential characteristics of ordinary English. That was, of course, because the subjects remembered something else than the simple sequences of letters. They remembered that what they had seen was not English but nonsense, so they always reconstructed some degree of nonsense.

Coleman's experiment provides very powerful evidence for the intrusion of strong habits into the memory for weaker ones, through the uncontrolled nature of the original learning in Coleman's experiment does not allow us to estimate the extent to which the experimental habits

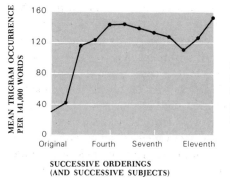

FIG. **11.14** Mean trigram occurrence as a function of number of orderings. The figure shows that later rearrangements yield higher-frequency trigrams. (Coleman, 1962.)

were, in fact, weaker than the linguistic ones. It furnishes, however, a convincing indication of the role of extraexperimental habits in interference—and furthermore, it suggests some limits to the process of interference in retention. Ordinarily we do not remember nonsense; we remember sequences of organized linguistic elements, encoded into chunks. These chunks are themselves frequently overlearned and very resistant to interference. Hence we would expect that interference would not have much influence in breaking up such organized sequences. It is only where there are weak links in the sequence of verbal habits that interference can work.

Interference appears to be an important mechanism in forgetting, though it is limited in its operation by the high degree of organization imposed upon much of what we learn. The limited opportunities for interference outside of the experimental laboratory make us want to search for some additional causes of forgetting.

GENERALIZATION DECREMENTS AS SOURCES OF FORGETTING

Interference is not the only possible source of forgetting. Various others have been suggested from time to time. Among these are the conditions associated with changes in *context* between original learning and a test for retention. Context is provided by the incidental cues in the learning situation. Incidental cues include the general set the subject provides himself; the nonspecific aspects of the task such as, for example, learning from a memory drum rather than flash cards; and the aspects of the task that the subject does not have to learn in order to produce some particular responses.

Irion (1948) points to the important role of set in determining the adequacy of retention. He introduced the concept of set in trying to explain the uncontrolled forgetting which occurs during the rest condition in a proactive or retroactive experiment. He reviewed a number of earlier studies and demonstrated that forgetting occurred almost universally in control conditions. We have already seen that a certain amount of such uncontrolled forgetting can be accounted for by proactive inhibition from earlier, nonlaboratory tasks. But a certain amount, Irion argued, can also be due to a change in set between the conditions of original learning and those that prevail at the time of a test for retention.

When an individual stops practicing a specific task in the experimental laboratory, a number of self-imposed conditions are changed. The person relaxes, turns his head from the memory drum or exposure device, and perhaps begins to talk to the experimenter. When a retention test comes up, he tries to concentrate on the task again, but it is certain that the specific manner in which he does so will be subtly different in a number of ways from what it was during original learning. Irion argued that some of the retention loss we ordinarily observe during control or rest conditions may occur because the subject cannot quite reestablish the exact state under which he learned the material in the first place.

As an experimental test of this notion, Irion proposed that before a test for retention, the subject be given some condition which would help reestablish the conditions prevailing at the time of original learning. In a retroaction experiment, for example, instead of doing nothing during the control condition, subjects might be required to read color names as they appear in the window of a memory drum. There would be nothing to learn, but the conditions would stimulate those of serial-anticipation learning.

In an experiment reported by Irion, the simple task of color naming before the test of retention did improve performance at recall; as a matter of fact, in one experiment he found no retention loss at all under such conditions. Several additional experiments have confirmed Irion's original observations, though others have not (see Adams, 1961). The results seem to depend on whether the new task actually does serve to reorient subjects to the original task or whether the new one produces some subtle interference. In summary, set is probably a small though significant factor in retention.

Another closely related factor in producing retention loss is a change in external context. A very diverse and exhaustive experimental literature on stimulus generalization shows that nearly always, a change in stimulus conditions is accompanied by a decrement in the strength of learned responses. With this as a basic fact, most investigators have assumed that when a time interval elapses between learning and a test for recall, not only does the subject's internal set change but there is likely to be a change in the external conditions. Consider, for example, the student who studies French vocabulary in his room but must recall the French equivalents of English words in the classroom the next morning.

Such decrement from changed stimulus conditions can provide quite a difficult problem for analysis. One direct experimental study shows the influence of contextual stimuli on recall. In this experiment (von Wright, 1959b) subjects learned paired associates in which each pair was presented on a card of a different shape and color. The subjects were later tested for recall with the associates either presented on the same cards or on cards of a uniform gray. The change to the uniform card always led to a decrement in recall, and even a couple of recalls with these uniform cards led to a decrement when the original cards were returned.

Furthermore, individual verbal tasks are held together by a

network of potential stimuli. From the analysis of the "stimulus" in serial-anticipation learning (see page 288), you will recall that the cue which elicits an individual item is not just the preceding item alone but may be an entire context created by a list. That context serves to keep the list intact and preserves it from interference from outside sources. Some of the decrement in retroactive inhibition experiments may be the result of a confusion of contexts.

In one experiment (Deese & Marder, 1957) subjects learned two lists by serial anticipation, one immediately after the other. After various periods of time ranging from 4 minutes to 48 hours, subjects were tested for recall of the first of these lists. Unlike most such experiments, the presentation of items was not paced. Therefore, the subjects could produce many overt errors. This condition made it possible to obtain very reliable estimates of the sources of errors during recall. Figure 11.15 shows how the proportion of errors on recall of the first list were distributed among the two lists. The proportion of within-list errors, which were mistaken anticipations of incorrect items from the same list, decreased as the time since original learning increased, while the proportion of between-list errors increased. The longer the time since learning the two lists, the more confused subjects were about which list items belonged to, though the tendency to remember individual responses did not change much.

Therefore, one of the things that happens during a time interval is that the internal relations among items, relations which serve to maintain context, disappear. These relations may themselves suffer from interference, but one of the consequences is that context is weakened.

FIG. 11.15 Between-list errors increase in frequency and within-list errors decrease as a function of retention interval. (Deese & Marder, 1957.)

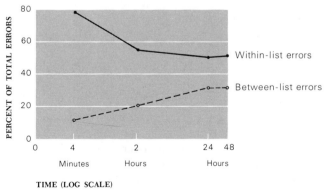

TIME (LOG SCALE)

FORGETTING OUTSIDE THE LABORATORY

The experimental study of forgetting shows that at least two major factors are at work. One of these is interference, of which unlearning is a special case in retroactive inhibition, and the other is generalization decrement arising from a loss of set or change in contextual stimuli.

So far as both of these sources of decrement in forgetting are concerned, the principles of similarity between tasks apply. These were discussed in Chapter 10, "Transfer of Training," and they need not be further described here. When we put these relations together with the facts presented in this chapter, we seem to have a fairly comprehensive picture of the nature of forgetting.

Nevertheless, the extension or generalization of these principles to situations outside the laboratory is not so certain. After all, most of the experimental work has been done within the highly constrained conditions of the laboratory; in the laboratory people learn by rote with highly restricted methods and learn relatively exotic material which is sometimes unique to the experimental laboratory. We may then ask whether these principles do extend to the commonplace phenomena of school learning and even the less controlled and casual experiences of daily life.

Postman (1963), when he raised the question about whether interference theory predicts too much forgetting or not, made some comments which can be applied to the problem of retention under ordinary circumstances. There are, Postman points out, many factors which tend to conserve memories. The most important of these is inherent in the organization of what we learn. We can remember extensive sequences of verbal materials because these materials are internally organized. Furthermore, we assimilate unique experiences into the framework of what we already know so that they become part of a larger organization. Therefore, we should perhaps expect that forgetting in the laboratory is greater than that for things we learn outside the laboratory.

Another important point to be considered in making some generalization from the laboratory to the conditions of ordinary experience is the fact that, by casual standards, laboratory material is usually very highly practiced. In our ordinary experience we seldom learn things by rote memory. We may wish to be able to reconstruct a passage from a history text for purposes of an examination, but we seldom try a verbatim reconstruction of the passage. Therefore, by the standards of the laboratory, practice for what we learn in school is often very limited. We saw, in considering the difference between the experiments on short-term and long-term memory, that the rapidity of a decline in retention depends upon the strength of habits at the end of learning. Therefore, if we *seem* to forget a great deal in daily life, it is probably because we actually did not learn much in the first place.

All this is speculation, but it serves to place the phenomena of the laboratory and our casual experience in some kind of perspective. There are, however, some studies of retention of meaningful material, and these studies tend to reinforce what has just been said. A brief review of some of these studies will help to make the discussion a bit more concrete.

If orders of approximation to English are employed in a retroactive inhibition experiment, the maximum decrement in recall is produced when both interpolated materials and original materials are orders of the same degree of approximation (King & Cofer, 1960). Furthermore, it is possible to produce retroactive inhibition in the unaided recall of ordinary English prose (Slamecka, 1959). The results depend upon a strict scoring of recall. In a series of experiments on the forgetting of ordinary prose, Slamecka showed that the recall of the first passage depends upon the degree of similarity to an interpolated passage and upon the degree of first-passage practice. His experiments show that all the variables known to be important in the retroactive inhibition of more typical laboratory tasks also work with ordinary prose.

Furthermore, von Wright (1959a) was able to show that an interpolated recall of part of a prose passage had a demonstrable interfering effect on the later recall of the remaining portions of the same material. Thus, there is ample evidence that no real discontinuity exists between the materials of the laboratory and the materials which we study in our ordinary experience. We are left with the strong implication that we forget less often than we do not learn in the first place.

IN CONCLUSION

We have seen that the interaction between various things learned at different times is an important determiner of forgetting. We have also seen that, despite the rapid forgetting exhibited by Ebbinghaus and others, most retention is remarkably good. We may well ask whether or not complete forgetting ever occurs. Certainly we can say that the residual effects of something presented in the past can be detected after very long intervals of time and under very improbable circumstances. Burtt (1941) describes an experiment conducted on his son in which he read the boy passages, in Greek, out of Sophocles's *Oedipus Tyrannus*. There were three selections of 20 lines each, and for a period of time Burtt read these selections to the boy every day. All this occurred when the child was less than two years of age. Six years later the boy was required to learn these selections by rote, plus some new ones from the same source. It took the boy an average of 435 repetitions to learn the new selections and only 317 repetitions to learn the old ones. Thus there was a savings of better than 25 percent.

Furthermore, we need to point out that there are other sources of inability to recall which we did not touch upon in this chapter. These include the so-called dynamic factors—the influence of emotional and motivational conditions upon recall. There exists a very large literature devoted to these topics, though not much of that literature stands up to critical scrutiny from an experimental point of view. Forgetting, however, is a subtle phenomenon and there are undoubtedly many features of it that we have not yet begun to explore. We are just beginning to understand the role of organization in memory, both in the retaining and in the altering of things remembered. We need to know how much the mechanisms of interference and generalization decrement interact with organizational features. For example, it is probable that once material is "assimilated," it becomes very resistant to interference, though it may suffer some alteration in the process of assimilation.

In short, our past experience is being continuously altered by new experience and by changes in our interests and attitudes. Thus memory is neither a static thing nor the victim of gradual decay. Our past is reshaped for us by what we do now as much as what we do now is directed by our past.

12

CONCEPT LEARNING

One of the basic facts about human learning is that it is inventive. Human beings discover new rules in nature, make new generalizations, and invent new principles. Furthermore, once a new general principle is discovered, we teach it to one another. A bit of reflection on these aspects of human thinking make it clear that human learning cannot be simply described as the acquisition of new responses. People learn and create higher-order generalizations out of which they can generate or invent responses appropriate to new occasions. Therefore, in order to provide even a moderately complete account of human learning, we need to examine human concepts and how they are learned.

The human ability to invent and utilize concepts is one aspect of linguistic activity. A fundamental human characteristic is the naming of things. We do not, however, give unique names to everything in the world. Most of the objects of our experience are named only generically, not uniquely. The object outside of my window, for example, I designate a tree. I may even know that it is a linden tree. I do not, however, call it "Harold" or "old Brownbark." Unique names I reserve for the relatively few things in my experience which require them. Otherwise, my perceptual and cognitive world is organized into broad conceptual categores, and these categories are the most general and most basic of human concepts. They enable me to group and classify objects on the basis of common characteristics possessed by those objects.[1]

The ability to name things and group them generically is fundamental to human experience. Children, when they first begin to talk,

[1] This view of the nature of concepts reflects a particular theory of human cognitive-linguistic activities. See Deese (1965).

are able to name generically (though they do not always do it quite properly—to the small child all furry animals are "doggies"). Furthermore, human concepts have the peculiar characteristic that we cannot easily analyze them even when we know them. We may find it easy to name instances of a particular concept, but at the same time we may be unable to describe the common characteristics that these instances exemplify. Thus, while I have a well-organized concept of what a tree is, I would be hard put to describe accurately just what it is that makes me call one thing a tree and another a shrub. In another context we have noted that grammatical categories are universal in human speech but that most human speakers are happily unaware of the nature of the grammatical categories that govern their speech.

The fact that we can readily identify instances of a concept without being able to describe the underlying attributes which make any particular object an instance of a concept is revealed, as we shall see in this chapter, in experimental studies of concept learning. These studies also tell us the processes that go on in human thinking during the course of concept attainment or concept learning.

EXPERIMENTAL TECHNIQUES

A discussion of the experimental literature on concept learning requires a brief word about method. The procedures used in concept-learning studies differ in certain critical respects from the procedures we have become familiar with from earlier chapters. Furthermore, we need to say a brief word about the structure of the kinds of concepts that have been most often used in the experimental studies.

Materials

ARTIFICIAL STIMULUS OBJECTS

The basic operation in human concept learning is discrimination. An essential element in concept learning is the ability to differentiate among objects. Furthermore, those objects must have some common characteristics so that they can be grouped together in various ways. Because we wish to be able to specify the ways in which the experimental stimulus objects are formed and how they may be classified logically, we do not use real objects in experiments but instead use artificial stimuli invented for the specific purpose of studying concept learning. Analytically, such stimulus objects may be said to be collections of attributes or dimensions. Each particular stimulus object is a unique union of some attributes.

Attributes are things like size, shape, color, etc. In an experimental study, for example, we may have two sizes of objects, two shapes (round and square), and two colors (red and green). In the "universe" created by these particular values for the attributes of size, shape, and color, there will be a total possible set of eight unique objects. Among them there will be a large red square as well as a small red square.

A typical collection of the kinds of stimuli used in experiments on concept attainment can be seen in Figure 12.1. In this collection, there are three different shapes of objects (circle, square, cross), three different numbers of objects on each card (one, two, three), three different colors (in the original, green, red, black) and three different numbers of borders. That makes 81 stimulus cards in all. These 81 cards define the universe created by these values for these four attributes.

A given concept can be defined in various ways. *Conjunctive* concepts are those in which two or more attributes in common describe a concept. For example, we might decide that all square red stimuli were instances of a particular concept, no matter whether those red squares had one, two, or three borders and no matter how many appeared on a card. Another such concept might be all cards with two round green

FIG. **12.1**   Instances used in a concept-learning task. The forms varied in (1) shape, (2) color, and (3) number of borders. There were three values for each attribute (color was either red, black, or green). (Bruner, Goodnow, & Austin, 1956.)

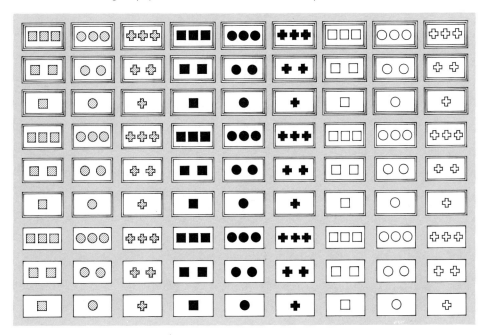

circles. *Disjunctive* concepts are defined by "either-or" values. Thus, a particular disjunctive concept might be two red squares or two black crosses.

Inevitably, in defining concepts, some attributes are going to be relevant and others irrelevant. For example, if all square red stimuli are instances of a particular concept, then shape and color are relevant attributes, while borders and numbers are irrelevant—they have nothing to do with the definition of the concept. At the beginning of a concept-learning experiment, of course, the subject does not know which attributes are relevant and which are irrelevant. It is his task to discover the relevant attributes and the particular values of them that define a given concept.

One more distinction is important in concept learning. Those objects which are examples of a particular concept (all red squares, for example) are called positive instances. All other objects—green circles, for example—are called negative instances, since they are not examples of the concept in question. With these two distinctions—relevant and irrelevant attributes, negative and positive instances—it is possible to understand nearly all the experimental literature on conjunctive concept formation. Relatively little experimental work has been performed with disjunctive concepts, probably because they are both more difficult and rarer in human experience.

NATURAL STIMULUS OBJECTS

While we generally prefer to use stimulus objects for which we can specify the attributes or dimensions, sometimes we find it necessary to use more nearly natural stimuli. These are stimulus objects—either real objects or pictures of them—which are so "complex" as to make it difficult to tease out the attributes which make them what they are. Typically, we may be able to identify the relevant attributes in such a case (we need these in order to define the concepts), but we cannot really identify the irrelevant attributes present. As we shall see, the nature of the irrelevant attributes is important in the rate of concept learning, so this is a matter of some concern. Nevertheless, natural stimuli are necessary for certain problems.

Figure 12.2 shows a set of figures providing instances of more nearly natural concepts. Notice that there are several pictures of heads or faces—one of a man with a mustache, one of a baby, one of a boy, etc. These exemplify a concept of "faceness." In concrete terms it is very hard to specify just what it is about each figure that enables us to group them conceptually. People, of course, have no difficulty with this concept when it is pointed out to them, but analysis of relevant and irrelevant attributes is difficult.

FIG. **12.2** Instances used in a concept-learning task. These instances cannot so easily be decomposed into their attributes. (Heidbreder, 1946.)

Procedures

There are several ways of going about an experimental study of concept attainment. Nearly always, the experimenter delimits the "universe" of objects defining the concept. That is to say, the subject must learn the concept not by exploring among objects at large but by exploring a very small set of stimuli in the laboratory. In real life, of course, we may have to form concepts out of an almost unlimited range of things, but in order to understand the processes of thought in concept attainment, we need to have a very careful control over the universe of events presented to the subject.

In one way or another, a subject must indicate, by picking and choosing among stimuli that he can identify all the stimuli with certain concepts or can identify all instances of some one particular concept. There are two ways in which he can go about such a task: one is a kind of generalization or extension of the method of paired associates, while the other is a more direct method of identification.

IDENTIFICATION METHOD

In this method the subject is generally—though not always—presented with the entire sample of stimuli at once (all the items in Figure 12.1, for example). He is then asked to pick one. The experimenter tells him whether or not it is an instance of the concept the experimenter had in mind. The subject continues picking stimuli as instances of the experimenter's concept until it is obvious that he has formed the concept correctly. Usually a very long string of correct choices is taken as the criterion of concept attainment. Notice that this method requires the subject to learn only one concept.

The exact procedure in the identification method will vary considerably from experiment to experiment. It is not necessary, for example, to expose all the stimuli at once; but exposing them one at a time makes the task very difficult for the subject. In most studies the subject will not be allowed to keep an external record of his choices. If he does, the task is vastly different, and most people adjust their processes in solving the problem accordingly. Commonly, the subject is required to keep all information in his head, and the purpose of using the method of identification is to observe the strategies he employs when he must rely exclusively on the resources of his own mind.

RESPONSE METHOD

In the response method the subject is required to name all stimuli as instances of one or another concept. He does so by actually giving the name of the concept. The concept name (like the stimuli) may be artificial, or it may be a natural one in the language. Usually in the response method, the stimuli are exposed one at a time. The subject guesses at a name, and the experimenter either tells him wrong/right or supplies the correct name. The subject continues through a series of stimuli. Each concept is represented by a new instance either until a criterion is reached or until a fixed number of series have been presented. In this method there are two or more concepts, and the subject must learn the name for each. For example, in Figure 12.2 the subject would be required to give all the objects with faces one particular name and all the buildings another name.

It is clear that this technique is an extension of the standard paired-associate technique. In fact, the two techniques are continuous, and it is possible to regard the paired-associate technique as a special case of the more general response method in concept learning.

Given the similarity, how do we know that the subject has learned a concept and not just memorized by rote? In fact, it is sometimes very difficult to tell. Typically in a concept-learning experiment, the subject will be exposed to new instances of a given concept until the concept is acquired. No instance will be repeated. But that is rather like learning by rote when there is some variation in the nature of the stimulus from trial to trial. It is hard to decide purely on the basis of a performance criterion whether a concept has been learned or whether there has been pure rote memory of discrete associations. The problem is compounded by the fact that it is often difficult or impossible for people who have attained some criterion of performance to tell you exactly what it is they have learned. Nevertheless, we now know rote learning to be complicated, and we know enough about the human tendency to leap to inductive generalizations so that the question tends to be the other way around. That is to say, one current viewpoint asserts that rote learning, for the most part, is not so rote, that it too calls upon processes of hypothesis formation, mediation, and generalization by rule. In any event, the line between rote learning and concept learning is not so clear as we once thought it was.

There are, of course, countless variations in concept-learning experiments, but the outline presented in the past few pages will enable us to follow the main course of the experimental literature without too much mystification. We can now turn to the studies themselves.

PROCESSES IN CONCEPT LEARNING

The Basic Process of Learning

Most of the earlier experiments on the learning of concepts concentrated on the problem of finding out how people come to give a common response or label to stimuli which, while they differ, contain attributes in common. A representative study is that of Hull (1921). Hull studied the way in which students learned to find common elements in complicated stimuli. He presented his subjects with traditional Chinese characters paired with certain names. Chinese characters are compounded of certain basic elements called radicals. The individual radicals may vary in position or size within the character, but whenever one is present, it means that the character has something in common with other characters containing the same radical. The subject's task was to learn to identify each radical and to call the character possessing that radical by the arbitrary name supplied by the experimenter.

Hull viewed the process of concept learning as a more or less mechanical affair which depended upon little more than discrimination and conditioning. The subject, according to this view, would guess or blunder onto the correct response, which would be reinforced. He would then generalize this response to other similar forms. In the long run, the most similar forms would be those containing the same radical. Sometimes, however, the generalization would be wrong, in which case it would be punished or extinguished. Such a view makes the whole process very much like the experiments we examined in Chapter 6 on discrimination learning.

Hull's view was not an unreasonable one. He showed that learning is gradual in concept attainment of this sort. Errors do generalize in a systematic way, as we might expect from a principle of stimulus generalization. Furthermore, sometimes subjects who had obviously learned to pair the correct word with the proper radical element could not identify that radical. They had learned the correct pairs, but they had not acquired a mediated recognition of their accomplishment.

As much as anything else, Hull's work illustrates the continuity between concept learning and the rest of learning. It is undoubtedly true that the kind of variables we examined in discrimination learning are at work in concept learning and in the highest levels of human thinking as well. At the same time, it is a mistake to describe the learning of concepts as nothing more than a kind of passive process of discrimination, because we know that the behavior of human beings depends upon more than this. There is, for example, the matter of hypotheses in concept learning. Even more to the point, there is the matter of strategies. The use of strategies clearly lifts concept learning out of the domain of simple discrimination learning.

Strategies in Concept Learning

Sometimes people arrive at the correct solution in concept-learning experiments by a kind of random selection. Most of the time, however, there is evidence to show that they use organized plans or strategies in solving concepts. The trouble is, of course, that the plans most people form are usually sketchy and only dimly articulated. Thus, it is possible for a person to make use of a particular strategy in concept learning without being aware of the fact. However, by exploring the patterns of guesses that subjects make while concept learning, it is often possible to infer kinds of strategies.

That is what Bruner, Goodnow, and Austin (1956) did in a large investigation of the strategies people use in learning concepts. These investigators displayed the stimuli in Figure 12.1 to subjects and asked them to learn various concepts by making successive choices of stimuli as instances of the concept in question. By observing the choices their subjects made, they were able to detect a number of different strategies at work. Sometimes subjects would stick consistently with one strategy through a series of problems.

The problems Bruner, Goodnow, and Austin used were conjunctive concepts: they were of the "green circles with two borders" sort. For such concepts there are 255 possible arrangements. A first *positive* card eliminates 240 of these, and there is a similar value for all the positive and negative instances thereafter. A computer could keep track of all the alternative possibilities eliminated by any given choice and thus solve the problem in the minimum number of choices. It is quite possible to define a logically best strategy for solving these problems, and such a strategy, in the long run, would produce the quickest solutions. In order to solve a problem logically, however, the subject must remember each card and the combination of values of attributes it contains. Further, he must remember whether or not every stimulus he has seen was an instance of the concept. This is an impossibly difficult task for human memory. It can be accomplished by allowing the subject to keep an external record of his choices and their outcomes, but even then most people feel harassed and confused when they have to keep checking back over their previous choices. A few people—mainly those with some mathematical or logical training—try to keep to such a strategy even without an external record, but the evidence is that it slows down their solutions.

A more reasonable strategy for people with their limited memories is what Bruner, Goodnow, and Austin call conservative focusing. In conservative focusing, the subject concentrates on just one attribute at a time. He tries to find out, for example, whether color makes a difference between instances of the concept or not. He might have the initial hypothesis that all red items are instances of the concept. He would then identify a single red circle with two borders as an instance. If that is a failure, he might change his hypothesis to, say, green as an attribute of the concept. His next choice would then be a single green circle with two borders. If that turns out to be correct, he would then stick with green and vary some other attribute. He might, for example, pick a single green circle with one border. The point is that the subject would stick with one attribute at a time until he had narrowed the choice down to a unique combination of attributes. Notice also that this strategy requires the subject to remember only the previous card. That is the advantage of the strategy for human beings over a logical strategy.

Another possible strategy is focus gambling. In focus gambling, the subject takes a gamble and changes two or more attributes at once. For example, given a positive instance on a single red circle with two borders, the subject may chance it and guess two green circles with two borders. In so doing he would have changed both number and color. If that turns out to be a positive instance, the subject has learned an enormous amount in one strike, for now he knows that all ones and twos and all greens and reds among circles with two borders are instances of the concept. Logically, such correlating of variables ought to be very inefficient, but sometimes it is used by subjects. Subjects tend to resort to it when they are under time pressure or when they are allowed to make only a limited number of choices.

As we might suppose, subjects do better on the average with conservative focusing than with anything else. The superiority of the focusing strategies over the logical strategy becomes greater as a greater burden is placed on memory and the assimilation of information. Subjects often change their strategies, however, as they move from problem to problem. Those who have had many positive examples in earlier problems gradually change to a focus gambling strategy, while those who have had many negative instances shift more toward the conservative single-attribute strategy. So it appears that strategy is partly under the control of the kind of experience subjects have and, as we might expect, of the pattern of reinforcements they receive in the course of solving a number of problems.

Finally, some people adopt a "partist" strategy rather than a "wholist" strategy. These individuals ignore certain attributes and focus all their attention on just a part. This kind of approach is very inefficient, and Bourne (1963) has shown that it is characteristic of the poor rather than the good concept learner. For most people under most circumstances, the best approach is wholistic, conservative focusing. If the subject is allowed to keep a complete record of his choices and if time is unlimited, an intelligent person can carry out a logical strategy. It should be noted, however, that only a small minority of subjects seem willing to use consistently a completely wholistic strategy when problems grow very complicated (through the presence of many attributes).

Information Processing in Concept Learning

A number of questions of experimental importance arise when we consider the subject of information processing in concept learning. It turns out that different choices provide different amounts of information for subjects in solving problems, and the difficulty people have in solving problems depends upon the distribution of information within the problem. There are, therefore, several questions about information processing in concept learning. Perhaps the easiest to examine first would be the question of the different effects of positive and negative instances.

POSITIVE AND NEGATIVE INSTANCES IN CONCEPT LEARNING

One early experiment (Smoke, 1933) showed that subjects learned very little from negative instances. In this experiment, learning that a particular stimulus was not an instance of the concept contributed little toward the eventual solution of the problem. For a time this result was accepted as a general conclusion. A more careful analysis revealed, however, that the amount of information in negative and positive choices was very different in this experiment. The amount of information provided by a negative instance was much less than that given by a positive instance; a negative instance did not logically eliminate as many possibilities as did a positive· instance. The major reason for this state of affairs was that the stimuli were "natural," and therefore the population or universe of potential stimuli was not clearly limited.

Hovland and Weiss (1953), however, performed an experiment in which negative and positive instances transmitted the same information. This experiment came out of an analysis of the problem of concept learning from the standpoint of information theory (Hovland, 1952). Hovland showed that it is possible to design problems in which the amount of information in positive and negative choices can be deliberately varied. It would be possible, for example, to make the amount of information in a negative or a positive instance the same by setting up a problem that could be solved logically by either four positive instances or four negative instances.

Without going into the details of the actual experiment, we can say that Hovland and Weiss found that it was possible for subjects to learn a concept entirely through negative instances. Thus not only is it logically possible; people can do it. Given that there are a fixed number of possibilities, we can learn what something is by learning all the things that it is not. However, even when the information was the same for negative and positive instances, Hovland and Weiss found that their subjects did much better with positive instances.

Freibergs and Tulving (1961) thought that this might be so because people are more accustomed to arriving at concepts through positive instances. In other words, positive instances provided the easier channel for the subjects of Hovland and Weiss because there was positive transfer from ordinary experience. Therefore, Freibergs and Tulving performed an experiment in which they compared negative and positive instances after subjects had had a lot of experience solving problems through negative instances alone. The concepts they gave their subjects were made of geometric forms varying in three attributes. There were four possibilities for each attribute, so there were twelve instances in all. The concept problems were such that each could always be solved either through four positive or four negative instances. Half of the subjects were asked to identify the concept after seeing four positive instances, and half of the subjects were asked to identify the concept after seeing four negative instances. Each group of subjects solved 20 successive problems.

On the initial problem, the subjects who inspected positive instances did much better than those who inspected only negative instances. By the twentieth trial, however, the median performance (in time to solution) for the two groups was almost identical. Freibergs and Tulving interpreted this result to mean that the practice with negative instances managed to provide an equivalent transfer to that from ordinary experience. Thus, people can learn to deal with negative instances about as efficiently as they can with positive instances.

As a practical matter, however, it is true that in the real world most concepts cannot be solved with negative instances alone. That is because the number of things something cannot be is generally much vaster than the number of things it can possibly be. Negative instances are important in certain cases. Medical diagnosis, for example, is often carried out almost exclusively on the basis of negative instances.

RELEVANT AND IRRELEVANT ATTRIBUTES IN CONCEPT LEARNING

We have already pointed out that there is a continuity between ordinary paired-associate learning and concept learning. We can make that continuity quite explicit and extend it to the problem of irrelevant attributes and redundant stimuli in concept learning by drawing upon an analysis made by Garner (1962).

Garner reminds us that in the usual case of paired-associate learning, one response is assigned to each stimulus. By definition, however, concept learning depends on having several stimuli to each response, because the task is for the subject to discover what is common between two or more stimuli. There are, then, more stimuli than responses in the general concept-learning case. If you think about this a bit, it is apparent that the excess of stimuli over responses in the concept-learning situation is achieved by making certain stimulus attributes irrelevant. If the concept is "red circles" the attributes of number, borders, etc., will be irrelevant, and having all values of these will merely serve to increase the stimuli relative to the responses.

Increasing the number of irrelevant stimuli by increasing the number of irrelevant attributes has a markedly deleterious effect upon performance in learning concepts (Archer, Bourne, & Brown, 1955). The more irrelevant attributes there are, the harder it is to discover those attributes that are correlated with the correct response and hence are defining attributes of the concept. This result holds even when the irrelevant stimuli are correlated with one another so that they are redundant

(Bourne & Haygood, 1959), though when relevant attributes are correlated (redundant), performance is improved. The issue is complicated, however, and a thorough appreciation of Garner's discussion of the *form* of stimulus redundancy would lead us to be cautious about any simple conclusions. The results of Bourne and Haygood probably hold, however, where the correlations defining the stimulus redundancy (the correlations between attributes) are readily perceivable.

TRANSFER AND MEDIATION IN CONCEPT LEARNING

Some concepts are easier to learn than others. What is more, that statement is true even when the formal logical structure of concepts does not differ. Therefore, some concepts are easier than others not for logical reasons but for psychological reasons. Some of the differences in ease of learning concepts may be the result of the perceptual organization among the objects used as concept instances. Much of the psychological difference, however, must stem from the effects of previous experience upon the learning of any given concept, rather than the perceptual organization in stimuli. The difficulty of concept learning will often depend upon whether or not the material being learned encourages negative or positive transfer from previous experience. Sometimes such transfer may come automatically from the habits aroused by the material, and sometimes it may come from hypotheses. We have already noted that the greater difficulty in attaining concepts from negative instances is the result of the lesser transfer from previous experience for negative instances. We are simply not accustomed to dealing with negative instances. In this section, we shall examine other relations between concept learning and transfer, including those which seem to be covered by the notion of mediation.

Mediation

Mediating processes, as we learned in Chapter 9, are those events which serve to bridge the gap between the stimulus or problem presented to an individual and the responses he makes. The classical case of mediation is provided by the chained-association paradigm, in which a stimulus A elicits an implicit response, B, which in turn elicits the overt response C. Thus, the stimulus A seems to lead to the unrelated response C. B is the mediator between A and C.

There are many possible mediating processes, not all of them so easily described as associations. The major purpose of all mediational activity is the same, however; it is to provide for some indirect relation between a stimulating situation or problem and behavior. Sometimes the mediating process interferes with the performance of a response, and sometimes it facilitates a particular response. In either case, the mediating activity is based upon previously learned activity and, therefore, is an example of transfer. One important instance of the possible role of mediation in the analysis of concept learning comes from the comparison of reversal and nonreversal shifts in concept learning, particularly in children.

REVERSAL AND NONREVERSAL SHIFTS

In testing for the subject's knowledge of a concept, the experimenter may, at any time, change the concept rules. He may, for example, make green circles instead of green squares the instances of the concept. The subject has no way of finding out that the concept is changed, except through those choices which the experimenter designates as correct. If the shift is to a new value for the same dimensions, it is said to be a reversal shift. If, for example, the concept is changed from green circles to red squares, the shift is a reversal. A nonreversal shift occurs when some of the previously correct instances are still correct. That would occur, for example, if the concept is shifted from green circles to all large circles, irrespective of color.

As H. H. Kendler and D'Amato (1955) point out, studies of discrimination reversal uniformly show that reversal shifts are more difficult than nonreversal shifts for very small children and animals. For adult human beings and school-age children, however, nonreversal shifts are much harder than reversal shifts. Kendler has argued that the answer to the puzzle created by these data is to be found in the concept of mediation. Preverbal children and animals learn by having cues conditioned to the appropriate reactions. Learning is gradual, and because old habits have to be unlearned or extinguished, a reversal shift becomes more difficult the better the original problem is learned. Verbally able human beings, however, can name the stimuli in various ways and adopt hypotheses about what it is they are supposed to learn. These hypotheses may shift from time to time, and as a result, when a new hypothesis turns out to be correct, learning may be sudden. When a given solution is no longer correct, it isn't a matter of extinguishing habits conditioned to the cues provided by the stimuli, but of shifting to a new hypothesis. In a nonreversal shift, some of the instances of the old concept will still be correct. The result is that the subject finds it much more difficult to shift to a new hypothesis than in the case of the reversal shift, in which all the instances of the old concept are now incorrect.

T. S. Kendler and H. H. Kendler (1959) compared the performance on reversal and nonreversal shifts of children of kindergarten age. They discovered that the children who rapidly learned the *initial* problem did better with the reversal shift. The children who made a large number of errors on the initial problem had trouble with the reversal shift. The investigators came to the conclusion that the children who learned concepts only slowly and poorly were learning by discrimination and without the mediation of conceptual hypotheses. These children found a reversal in the problem to be extremely difficult. Children who learned well in the first place did so via mediation. Because they were encouraged by occasional successes to continue old hypotheses following nonreversal shifts, they made fewer errors following reversal shifts than following nonreversal shifts.

DOMINANCE LEVEL

The experiments comparing reversal and nonreversal shifts were based upon expectations arising out of the assumption that mediational processes are at work in the problem solving of adult subjects. These experiments, however, do not tell us very much about the nature of the mediational activity. Some other experiments do show us that among the possible mediational processes, associative ones play an important role. These are experiments on what has come to be known as dominance level.

Dominance level refers to the degree, in ordinary experience, to which a concept instance is dominated by a particular dimension or attribute. Dominance level can be measured by frequency with which particular descriptive adjectives are given in normative data in response to nouns (Underwood & Richardson, 1956a). For example, most people think of snow as white. Relatively few people, on the other hand, think of white in connection with sugar, though sugar is usually as white as snow in our experience. Sugar, however, is dominated by the impression of sweetness.

TABLE 12.1   The Extent to Which WHITE Is Elicited by Various Names
(From Underwood & Richardson, 1956a)

HIGH DOMINANCE FOR WHITE		MEDIUM DOMINANCE FOR WHITE		LOW DOMINANCE FOR WHITE	
MILK	83%	BONE	34%	BASEBALL	11%
CHALK	80%	COLLAR	44%	FANG	10%
SNOW	71%	FROST	34%	PASTE	16%
TEETH	72%	LINT	38%	SUGAR	11%

Underwood and Richardson obtained sense impressions from 153 college students to 213 nouns. They were able to find some nouns which were highly dominated by a particular sense impression and others which were not. Table 12.1 shows some representative high, medium, and low dominance-level values for the names of things which yield the impression *white.*

In an experiment on concept learning, Underwood and Richardson (1956b) presented subjects with lists of 24 nouns. These were constructed so that there were four instances each of six concepts. The subjects were told that there were six concepts in the list, and their object was to find each of the six groups of four words that could be followed by the same response. Of the six concepts, two were high-dominance concepts, two were medium-dominance, and two were low-dominance.

There was, of course, a close correlation between the ease of learning the six concepts and the dominance level. High-dominance-level concepts were learned rapidly with few errors, while low-dominance-level concepts were not always learned in the allotted trials, and if they were learned, they produced many errors.

This experiment, however, perfectly illustrates the possible confusion between rote learning and concept learning. It would be quite feasible for the subjects to learn to respond to the nouns not by grouping them in some conceptual way, but simply by giving the appropriate response by rote association. It is possible in the Underwood and Richardson experiment that some subjects learned some of the concepts by rote and others by a conceptual grouping.

For this reason, Coleman (1964) performed an additional experiment with the same materials. He did not use the paired-associate technique employed by Underwood and Richardson. Instead, he simply presented his subjects with the four nouns making up a concept and asked them to produce an adjective descriptive of all the nouns. He was able to demonstrate that high-dominance-level concepts were solved much more readily than low-dominance-level concepts. Therefore, the readiness with which a stimulus elicits an associative sense description determines the ease with which it may be grouped with other stimuli having the same sense description. The verbal description serves as a mediating link between the otherwise unrelated stimulus objects. The stimuli BONE, MILK, and CHALK are much easier to link together than the stimuli BASEBALL, FANG, and SUGAR.

Further evidence for the fact that when faced with experimental tasks like these, people (1) learn concepts and not rote associations, and (2) use mediating associations to do it, can be obtained from an experiment by Reed (1946). Reed had subjects learn to respond with a nonsense syllable to each member of groups of four nouns. In some cases, the groups could be related to other groups through common instances (the names of foodstuffs, for example), and in other cases they could not. Learning was vastly easier when they could, but even when they could not, there was evidence that subjects grouped the words into concepts. Furthermore, unlike the results in the learning of rote associations, increasing "list length" or the number of groups to be learned had a negligible effect upon the difficulty of learning. Mediating associations are ubiquitous and important in describing the differences in ease of attaining concepts, even when those concepts do not really differ in logical or conceptual structure. We shall return to the role of mediating devices in concept learning shortly.

Transfer

There is an important and fundamental relation between transfer and concept learning. Concept learning is, in its outcome at least, a special case of transfer. People attain concepts because they can recognize similarities or identities in attributes of various stimulus objects. That, in turn, makes it possible for them to learn to identify or name those objects more readily than they could otherwise. Bourne (1966) has pointed out that Harlow (1949), in his famous idea of learning sets, simply described the acquisition of a rule (concept learning) as a kind of transfer from problem to problem or from instance to instance. As Bourne says, learning that takes place in a concept-learning task transcends effects attributable to specific stimulus and response features in any particular task within the series. The important feature of the task in concept learning is learning the rule or concept itself. Nevertheless, as the data on mediation tell us, stimulus relations and response relations which have been previously learned do hinder or facilitate the learning of concepts. Therefore, we can describe the influence of previous experience (transfer) on the kind of transfer evidenced within the concept-learning experiment itself.

VARIETY OF EXPERIENCE AND TRANSFER

One important comparison is that which can be made between transfer from many problems and transfer from equivalent practice on just one problem (Adams, 1954). In one experiment, half of the subjects practiced for 8 trials per problem on 24 different problems. A second group of subjects practiced for a total of 192 trials on a single problem. These two groups of subjects were then compared for performance on a special problem which was designed to evaluate transfer. The result of the comparison was that the subjects trained on the single problem did better. Such a result seems so contrary both to common sense and the kinds of notions that come out of Harlow's analysis of the learning-set phenomenon that another investigation (Callantine & Warren, 1955) challenged it.

This investigation revealed that the larger the number of stimuli presented beforehand, the better the performance on the transfer task. The main difference from the previous experiment was that in this one the subjects were allowed to practice for a sufficient number of trials on each concept in the multiple-concept case so that they could learn something. There are two reasonable conclusions from these experiments: (1) The more different problems an individual experiences, the more general the set of rules he can draw upon for the solution of an additional problem, and (2) in order to profit from multiple-problem transfer, he must practice the earlier problems to some reasonable level of proficiency.

Therefore, experience at concept learning itself transfers to further concept learning. In part that must be so because the subject learns how to test hypotheses, and hypotheses are necessary to the efficient solution of concept problems. However, the transfer must also be the result of features that are not unique to concept learning. These features may be characterized as general experience.

TRANSFER OF GENERAL EXPERIENCE TO CONCEPT LEARNING

Two experiments illustrate the transfer of general previous experience to the solution of specific concepts. These experiments also, incidentally, emphasize the importance of verbal mediation for adult problem-solvers.

Cofer (1960) points out that some of the most important factors in determining specific hypotheses in human problem solving and concept learning are mediating verbal responses. The verbal mediating responses which lead to attempted solutions of a problem or to specific hypotheses about correct alternatives in concept learning may be only indirectly elicited by associations.

The way in which verbal mediating responses can give direction to hypotheses in problem solving is illustrated by an experiment we have already discussed in a previous chapter (see page 362). In this experiment (Judson & Cofer, 1956) subjects were asked to indicate which one of a number of words did not belong (for example, ADD, SUBTRACT, MULTIPLY, INCREASE). The problems were ambiguous, and it was clear from the data that subjects picked concepts and rejected concepts according to their stable verbal habits.

A similar kind of influence of previous verbal habits upon problem solving is illustrated in an experiment by Gelfand (1958). In this experiment there were two phases. One was a concept-learning exercise in which the concepts were based upon geometric figures of different colors, shapes, and sizes. Some of the dimensions were relevant (color, for example), and others were irrelevant. Before the concept-learning phase, however, the subjects served in a separate experimental session devoted to rote serial learning. Here there were three critical conditions. In one, the words the subjects learned named values on the dimensions that were relevant to the concept learned later (though not the specific values used in the concept experiment). Suppose, for example, that one of the concepts was "green triangles." The serial-learning task would then include words like "red" and "square." In another condition, the subjects learned words that described values of irrelevant dimensions in the later concept tasks. In still other conditions, the subjects learned neutral words.

The results of the experiment showed unmistakable influence of the prior verbal habits. Those subjects who had learned relevant words made very few errors in concept learning, particularly when there were many irrelevant dimensions. They chose the dimensions for which they had been primed. The group which had learned irrelevant dimensions in the serial-learning task made more errors than subjects who had studied neutral words. Evidently this group was unconsciously primed to attend to irrelevant dimensions. The experience of these subjects produced negative transfer to the concept-learning situation.

DIFFERENCES AMONG CONCEPTS IN EASE OF LEARNING

One more influence of previous habits upon the general nature of concept learning can be illustrated by an interpretation of a phenomenon known as *hierarchy of dominance* (not to be confused with dominance level of a few pages back). Hierarchy of dominance refers to the order in which concepts of different degrees of abstractness are solved.

The concept instances illustrated in Figure 12.2 were the subject of a series of experiments by Heidbreder (1947). If you look at Figure 12.2, with a little effort you can see that the instances could be conceived as falling into three classes: concrete objects, abstract forms, and numbers. That is to say, some were concrete things such as buildings and faces. Others were abstract forms that could only be described as "circles" or "wavy lines." Still others embodied specific numbers, such as "six things" or "two things," no matter what the "things" were.

TABLE 12.2   **The Mean Number of Series of Examples Required by Subjects before Concepts Are Attained**
(Data from Heidbreder, 1946)

OBJECT CONCEPTS		FORM CONCEPTS		NUMBER CONCEPTS	
NAME	NUMBER	NAME	NUMBER	NAME	NUMBER
SILM (bird)	3.85	FARD (circle)	4.70	MANK (6)	9.35
GLIF (hat)	4.70	QUAN (V form)	7.00	JOFT (3)	9.40
RELK (face)	4.90	PALT (T form)	8.65	PERG (4)	9.00

Heidbreder discovered that there was a regular order in the attainment of these concepts. Some of her results, which group the concepts according to degree of abstractness or dominance hierarchy, are illustrated in Table 12.2. The concrete-object concepts are the easiest to learn, the nonsense forms are intermediate in difficulty, and the abstract numbers are most difficult. Heidbreder explained this result as the influence of a special factor of hierarchy of dominance. That in turn describes the objectlike character of percepts. The concept of "face" is easy to attain, since the instances of it make complete perceptual entities—in a word, faces. Numbers are difficult to attain because the instances of them are embodied in concrete objects rather than being concrete objects themselves. Thus, the concept of "two" might be exemplified by two spoons or two rabbits.

Although we cannot really tell what attributes serve to make up these figures, it is almost certainly true that for the number concepts, the amount of attributes irrelevant to the concept is greater than the amount for the face concept. This is probably generally true when abstract—in Heidbreder's sense—concepts are compared with concrete concepts. Nevertheless, it is not the end of the matter.

A subsequent series of experiments (Dattman & Israel, 1951) did not confirm Heidbreder's specific results. The reason for the discrepancy apparently was that these investigators used a different way of embodying concepts. When the right kind of instances of numbers or abstract figures are used, the order of difficulty in the attainment of concepts virtually disappears. Therefore, not all the difference between concepts in Heidbreder's experiments can be described as owing to the number of irrelevant dimensions associated with type of concept. Rather, the ease of attainment of concepts depends upon the stimuli and the relationships between the stimuli used to exemplify the concepts. Such relationships, in turn, depend upon the previous experience of the individuals in the concept-learning experiments.

An experiment by Baum (1954) shows that the relative ease with which concepts like those in Figure 12.2 are attained depends upon how much interference there is from the similarity among items belonging to *different* concepts. By noting the amount of confusion between guesses, Baum was able to account for all the differences in ease of attaining concepts found by Heidbreder. For example, subjects in Baum's experiment had greatest difficulty attaining the concept of "sixness." They would frequently give the response appropriate to "threeness." There is, then, generalization between the instances of these concepts. You can see from Figure 12.2 how the instances of six could be easily confused with the instances of three, since the stimulus objects embodying the concept of six are often given in two rows of three objects each. Instances of the face concept would, in all likelihood, produce generalization only with some such concept as "hat." Generalization in this case would produce confusion only between instances of the same concept. Since subjects in the experiment learned to attach a nonsense name to the instances, they would tend to attach the same nonsense name to these instances, simply by generalization. It would matter little whether the learning was mediated by a concept of face or one of hat. We could even describe the results without resorting to the mediation of a concept and say that stimulus generalization was at work.

Baum's experiment shows us that concept attainment in which complex stimuli are used as instances of the concept to be learned is influenced by the discriminability among the stimuli. Discriminability is the reverse side of the coin of generalization. It depends only on where generalization occurs. If generalization between instances of a concept is great (and conversely, discriminability is low), learning will be facilitated. If generalization between instances of the same concept is low and generalization is great between instances of different concepts, learning will be slow.

Discriminability of most stimulus objects is determined by what we have learned already. Abstract concepts are not necessarily less discriminable, though Heidbreder's examples of them turned out to be so. Perhaps, however, Heidbreder may be right in one sense. It would seem likely that abstract concepts would, on the average, provide instances which are less discriminable from other concepts. That would be the case if instances of abstract concepts usually contained many irrelevant attributes and, perhaps, only one relevant attribute. Such a state of affairs would be considerably more general than the condition described by Heidbreder. The concept "tree" is neither less abstract nor less concrete than the concept "weed." Yet, I suspect, most children have less difficulty learning the concept of "tree" than that of "weed," simply because trees are more easily discriminated, in their specific instances, from the general class of growing things. Placed in the context of the nature of the dimensions of concepts, we can say that trees have correlated relevant attributes and weeds correlated irrelevant attributes.

THEORIES OF CONCEPT LEARNING

Some aspects of the various theories of concept learning have been embodied in what we have had to say thus far. However, in order to make certain issues clear, we need to consider theories grouped together in a slightly different way. Some theories of concept learning, as we shall see, are little more than extensions of ordinary theories of learning. Others seem to be invented for the specific purpose of describing conditions as they occur in the learning of concepts. Perhaps because of this reason, there is not much outright contradiction between various theories. Depending upon the situation and the aspects of concept learning under consideration, now one and now another theory may seem to be the better one.

There are two phenomena which, if they are not unique to

concept learning, are more important to concept learning than to any-thing else. These are hypothesis formation and strategies. Hypotheses are systematic guesses about or anticipations of the rule or appropriate set of responses for a concept. They may be indicated by an ability to state a rule. Hunt (1962) has distinguished between concept *learning* and concept *attainment* on the basis of the individual subject's ability to state such a rule. If a subject can verbalize a rule, he has learned a con-cept. If, however, he can only sort stimuli correctly, or pair them with the right name without being able to state a rule, he has attained a concept but not learned one.

While such a distinction is important, it obscures the fact that hypotheses are evident in patterns of choices or in sequences of responses, even when subjects cannot state a rule. Krechevsky (1932a and 1932b) first pointed out that rats solved discrimination problems by exhibiting systematic sequences of responses, sequences which seemed to reveal that the rats were testing hypotheses about the relevance of various attributes or dimensions of the stimuli. Levine (1959) showed, by an analysis of the mathematical probability of certain sequences, that one could infer which specific hypothesis was at work as well as how these hypotheses were changed by experience. Animals evidently test hypotheses in discrimina-tion learning, though they certainly cannot articulate those hypotheses.

Despite the distinction made by Hunt, and despite the evidence of systematic choices in the presolution period of animal problem solving, some theories of concept formation neglect hypotheses and their rules. These theories cannot possibly account for the full range of data on the learning of concepts, but they may be correct as far as they go. That is to say, different processes may be at work at different times in concept learning, and it is not necessary that hypotheses be involved at all times. Other theories of concept learning rely almost exclusively on the testing of hypotheses and the continuous operation of logical or quasi-logical strategies. Such theories frequently have no place for associations, or other influences of nonrational habits. We know that associations and other ways of describing habits are at work in concept learning, though once again, in particular instances these may be of trivial enough importance to be neglected. However, data on human concept learning tell us that both aspects (as well as others) will be necessary to a complete account of concept learning.

It turns out that theories of concept learning can be conveniently grouped into three major categories: theories which derive from asso-ciative learning, theories which make use of choice or decision making in the form of hypotheses and strategies, and theories which are based upon simulation of human concept learning by computer programs. The last category, incidentally, can have as its essential base either a notion of associative learning or a notion of choice based upon hypothesis or strategy. Largely because of recent developments in the theory of computer simulation, the latter has been the more common choice. In any event, we shall consider alternative theories under these categories.

Concept Learning from the Standpoint of Traditional Learning

The pioneering work of Hull (1921) is one of the best-known examples of experimental work which stems from the assumption that concept learning is in no essential way different from more elementary kinds of learning, particularly the kind evident in associative rote learning. The methods and results of Hull's study can easily be viewed from the position that nothing is needed to describe concept learning other than the classical laws of association. Responses are attached to stimuli by contiguity. The effects of such association are modified by stimulus generalization, and they are limited by the processes which produce forgetting, etc. Since the principles of association are easily described as a kind of conditioning by contiguity, it is not surprising that some theories have cast concept formation into the same category as conditioning.

Even less surprising is the application of statistical learning theory to concept learning. Statistical learning theory is aimed primarily at a description of conditioning (see page 72), though it has been extended to rote verbal learning (see page 335) and to concept learning. Perhaps the best-known extension of statistical learning theory to concept learning is the result of the work of Bourne and Restle (1959). Without exposing ourselves to the mathematics, we can state the general principles behind the work of these investigators.

Bourne and Restle assume that the relevant cues (greenness and triangleness, if the concept is "green triangle") are conditioned to the appropriate response. The response may be an overt one, if the subject has to learn a special response to be associated with the concept, or it may merely be implicit, if the subject is only to choose among alternatives. The irrelevant cues are adapted by a process of extinction. The rates at which conditioning and extinction take place will be determined by the proportion of relevant cues in the entire set. The probability that a person will respond correctly on any given trial is determined by the number of cues in the conditioned state. The theory generates learning curves for concept learning, and these curves may be tested against empirical data.

A model like that put forward by Bourne and Restle does lead to equations which describe the learning curves in various concept-attainment experiments. Furthermore, the theory "behaves" correctly when such variables as number of irrelevant cues, etc., are introduced into the equations. It does not handle the problem of dealing with the relative saliency or importance of various cues, but that is a matter which could be corrected without changing the principle of the theory. But, of course, so simple an associative theory cannot take account of a vast amount of data. Nor would the authors of the theory regard it as universally valid for concept-learning experiments. Nevertheless, it is possible under some circumstances that the processes in individuals may be like those described by the theory. The gravest deficiency in the theory is its inability—which is shared by most other theories—to delimit in an unambiguous way those situations to which the theory does apply and set them apart from the situations to which it does not.

Some of the deficiencies of a direct stimulus-response view of concept learning can be corrected by the introduction of the notion of mediation. Mediational activity is of two general kinds, so far as its function in concept learning is concerned. It can provide a common response which serves to bring together all the separate instances of a given concept. This common response is usually implicit, and it is mediational in nature and thus serves to bridge the gap between the external stimuli and the overt responses. Also, of course, mediational activity can serve to guide behavior in the choice of hypotheses. The hypothesis is a kind of mediated activity aroused by the problem situation and which, in turn, serves to select the next response or choice.

Any view which regards mediating activities simply as extensions of the learning of the same response to a variety of stimuli is little more than a direct extension of classical association theory. Therefore, it is not surprising that such a view is scarcely distinguishable from classical association theory (H. H. Kendler, 1964). It sees the subject's choices as being determined by the frequency of past associations, stimulus generalization, and the like. The behavior is more complicated in mediation because there must be associative links from the stimulus to the mediating responses and from the mediating responses (via response-produced stimulation) to the overt behavior, but the principle remains unchanged.

Hypotheses and Strategies in Theories of Concept Learning

The major characteristic of associationistic theories of concept learning is that the individual is viewed as being under the control of stimulating events in the environment. The major characteristic of theories which emphasize hypotheses and strategies is that the essential characteristics of problem solution are *not* under the direct control of stimuli in the environment. The individual relies on events internal to himself, events which have had a past history of associative learning, perhaps, but among which there is some choice. Whether or not he elects one particular strategy or hypothesis is determined not only by his past learning but by his interests of the moment and his subjective estimates of the likelihood of success of various alternatives. Therefore, the processes in concept learning cannot be described as purely associative.

We have already examined the major experimental work on the role of hypotheses and strategies in concept learning (Bruner, Goodnow, & Austin, 1956). These investigators did not explicitly state a theory of concept learning, but much of their work implicitly assumed such a theory. It assumed that the decision processes were stable individual characteristics of subjects. Yet there is some generality about these processes from one individual to the next, so that it is possible to state general preferences for hypotheses and strategies. Hence, for example, the conclusion that the various focusing strategies (see page 423) are preferred by most people.

It should be pointed out that hypotheses and strategies need not be deliberate processes in individuals. They can be intuitively arrived at, and an individual may scarcely be aware, in a particular problem-solving situation, that his behavior is governed by some particular hypothesis. Given the rather indefinite nature of such intuitive hypotheses, there is a kind of meeting ground between the associationistic theories and those which emphasize strategies. The mediational theory of Kendler and Kendler (1962) is not clearly and solely an associationistic one. These authors regard mediational activities as permitting the subjects to attend to particular stimuli, relevant dimensions, etc. In so doing, subjects rely on past history, and it is this past history which interests mediation theorists. Nevertheless, the process of orientation implies decision, and it may be quite proper to describe such decisions in the terms employed by Bruner, Goodnow, and Austin.

Thus, there is nothing contradictory nor mutually exclusive about associationistic and hypothesis-testing views of concept learning. Those who regard concept learning primarily as a matter of making decisions do not deny the role of past experience, learning, and transfer. Those who emphasize or study the role of associations agree that at times, or perhaps nearly all the time for adult human beings, behavior in concept-learning tasks is determined by decision processes.

Finally, it should be pointed out that Restle (1962) has developed a mathematical theory of hypothesis testing in concept learning. The fact that his theory grows naturally out of the associationistic theory of Bourne and Restle (1959) illustrates the continuity between the two views of concept learning. He is able to follow the implications, for the distribution of errors and rates of learning, of different strategies in the formation of hypotheses. It should be noted in this respect that the testing and rejecting of hypotheses is an all-or-none matter. This model, therefore, is analogous to the all-or-none models of associative learning (see page 305 rather than the continuous incremental models. One interesting point, however, is that the all-or-none rule applies to the testing of hypotheses about *attributes,* not stimuli as a whole (Bregman & Chambers, 1966).

Simulation Models of Concept Learning

The similarities between the general nature of concept learning and the various ways computers may process information lead naturally to the attempt to simulate human concept-learning processes with computer programs. The earliest efforts along such lines are to be found in the work of Hovland (1952) and Hovland and Hunt (1960). A more complete account of the issues in computer simulation of concept learning can be found in a book by Hunt (1962). The Hovland-Hunt models have generally been called information-processing models of concept learning.

Hunt's information-processing model shows three phases: perception, definition of positive instances, and development of a "decision tree." Perception, despite its general importance, is the least developed aspect of the theory. The model does not treat the problem of perception in concept learning in any great detail; it simply assumes that stimuli can be described as values on dimensions, in much the way we described the general problem in the first section of this chapter.

A critical matter to the model, however, is the development and description of a method for discovering concepts. Hunt characterizes this activity as the selection of positive instances. In developing a simulation program, Hunt built into the model a "positive focusing" strategy for selecting instances. Such a selection was made on psychological grounds.

Selecting positive instances, however, does not define the concept based upon them. Therefore, in the model some procedure must be included which serves to define concepts. This procedure Hunt calls developing a decision tree. A decision tree can be roughly characterized as a plan for or description of sequences of decisions. For example, a subject may first ask "Is the concept a triangle or a square?" He may then ask "Is it red or green, etc.?" He will move on through all possible choices until a decision is reached. A real subject may not go all the way through the tree, but may "jump" to a conclusion. Of course, he could have started with color, in which case the decision tree would have been different.

Thus a decision tree, incorporated into a kind of strategy, can provide a description of the sequence of actions of a hypothetical individual solving a problem. Such a description for a conditional focusing strategy is given in Figure 12.3. This description is one that would be appropriate for a machine, but it could also be roughly or even precisely like the sequence of actions an individual engages in. There are various

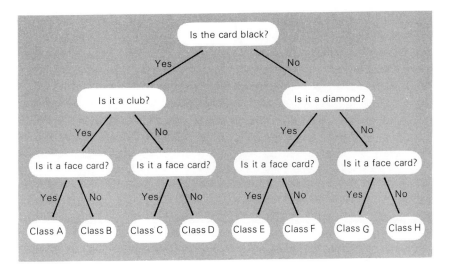

FIG. 12.3 A concept tree. Each of the classes at the bottom can be identified by a sequence of guesses and yes-no answers. (Hunt, 1962.)

ways in which the results of an individual solving problems and a computer program solving problems can be compared. If the results are similar, people who are interested in simulation models assert, there is evidence that human beings operate on the principle described by the program. In any event, if human beings behaved in all particulars like the program, there would be no way to distinguish between human action and machine action, so any distinction would be trivial.

While simulation models of concept learning have led to some interesting results, there is no convincing evidence that the processes described by the program are like the behavior of human beings in any real way. That is so even when the program incorporates some features, as does Hunt's, that have arisen out of empirical research on human concept learning. In fact, such computer simulation theory may have as its major function the sharpening of our definitions of the important variables at work in the empirical study of concept learning. We must have a very precise notion of the concept of "strategy" if we are to design a computer program embodying a particular strategy.

In conclusion, we can say that the theoretical study of human concept learning profits from a genuine eclecticism. Concept learning is complicated. It depends upon memory, associations, associative structures, and knowledge of and ability to apply particular strategies and hypotheses. In a sense, all the features of human behavior discussed here—and many more—enter into and determine the outcome of human efforts at problem solving, concept learning, and thinking in general.

13

PROBLEMS IN THE ACQUISITION OF SKILL

Nearly everything we have discussed about human learning thus far has concerned the acquisition and use of verbal material. The emphasis is not disproportionate, since verbal learning and the system of language which results from it are of the greatest importance in human affairs. Not only does the entire human social structure depend upon language for its existence and the form of its existence, but the very fact of human thought itself seems to be inextricably tied to language. It is neither surprising nor inappropriate that we devote most of our attention in the study of human learning to the topic of verbal learning.

In treating the various problems of verbal learning, however, we have said little about skill. We ordinarily think of skills and skilled performance in connection with muscular movements, perceptual discriminations, and the kinds of human activities which do not depend upon language. Language itself, of course, depends upon skill. The very act of talking is about as complicated a motor skill as any human being ever performs, and the perception of speech as well as of the elements of written language depends upon perception and perceptual learning (E. J. Gibson, et al., 1962). Furthermore, skilled acts always call upon conceptual activities to some extent, and these conceptual activities are nearly always encoded in some linguistic form.

Many of the basic analyses which come out of the study of verbal learning itself also apply to the learning of skills. Skilled acts transfer to one another. They obey all the ordinary principles of learning and forgetting. In fact, the stimulus-response analysis of transfer may be far more appropriate to motor skills than to most of the problems in verbal learning. Therefore, while we have not yet devoted a chapter or a section explicitly to the topic of the learning of skill, we have been concerned throughout with problems in the learning of skill.

There are, however, some important aspects to the learning of skill that we have not examined. These are aspects which either are best studied in the context of perceptual-motor performance or uniquely arise in that context. It is the purpose of this chapter to consider these problems in order to provide a more integrated account of the learning of individual human skills.

CHANGES IN SKILL WITH PRACTICE

In Chapter 9 we examined certain mathematical theories of learning which describe changes in performance with practice or learning curves. These analyses, for the most part, assumed that the changes in performance measures which took place across trials were changes in the proficiency with which a single skill was performed. The skill might be the ability to recall individual nonsense syllables by rote or the ability to find the correct path through a maze. To the extent that these analyses depend upon the assumption that changes are merely the perfection of a single ability or underlying skill, they are inappropriate to most perceptual-motor performance. In fact, practice on skills usually results in a change in the actual abilities that are called upon in the course of performance. Early in practice one set of abilities may be dominant, while later in practice other abilities may be more important. This possibility provides us with one of the basic problems in the analysis of the learning of skills. Furthermore, we need to give some orderly account of how smoothly or regularly such abilities change as practice proceeds. That provides another problem. The second problem logically depends upon the first, but in the history of experimental psychology, the problem of the regularity of changes in ability was the first to be investigated, so we shall examine it first.

Levels of Proficiency and the Hierarchy of Skills

PLATEAUS

One approach to the problem of showing how skills change qualitatively as proficiency becomes greater comes from one of the earliest studies of the learning process, a study of the learning of telegraphic code (Bryan & Harter, 1897; 1899). Bryan and Harter charted the improvement in sending and receiving (American) Morse code as a function of the amount of practice. Some informal observations of the way in which novice telegraphers learned their skill convinced Bryan and Harter that the general picture of improvement, measured in number of letters sent or

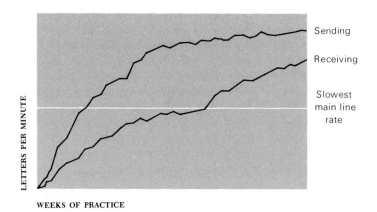

FIG. **13.1** Learning curves for sending and receiving telegraphic code. (After Bryan & Harter, 1897.)

received per minute, would produce results like those pictured in Figure 13.1. The two curves in this figure are not particularly extraordinary except in one respect. They both seem to show a "plateau" or level place where little or no improvement takes place. The plateau in the curve for receiving is a little more obvious than that in the one for sending.

In the actual experimental studies performed by Bryan and Harter, such apparent plateaus appeared. From what students told them about the learning of other skills, these investigators thought that plateaus in the learning curves for various skills were of widespread occurrence and of general importance. What is more, Bryan and Harter thought that the occurrence of plateaus could be explained by a notion which they described as the hierarchy of habits.

HIERARCHY OF HABITS

In a hierarchy of habits, the learning of one aspect of a skill depends upon the degree of mastery achieved in some lower aspect of the same skill. Consider, for example, the situation in the learning of telegraphic code as it was studied by Bryan and Harter. First of all, the learner must come to recognize the individual code signals which stand for the letters of the alphabet (or, even at a more primitive stage, to differentiate the "dot" from the "dash"). The learning of the individual code items takes a long time. But, reasoned Bryan and Harter, the learner must reach a fairly automatic level of recognition of the individual letters before he can tackle the next stage, which is the recognition of entire words as units. Finally, they argued, he can begin to respond to entire phrases and sentences as units. The plateaus occur during the periods after which some lower-order skills have been mastered approximately to their limit but the next-order skills have not yet begun to assert themselves. Bryan and Harter thought that sending (as compared with receiving) telegraphic code should be less likely to produce plateaus because the first stage is longer and more likely to merge with the second than in the case of receiving.

All this makes a very appealing story and seems to be in accord with the extensive data Bryan and Harter gathered concerning the learning of telegraphic code. However, even more exhaustive analyses do not bear out the views presented by these investigators (Keller, 1958). First of all, more extensive and better controlled studies of the learning of telegraphy show not a trace of a plateau. Keller argued that the Bryan and Harter plateau in the receiving curve was an artifact of some switched conditions in the middle of their experiment. In fact, Bryan and Harter expected a plateau before they began their experiment. The curve in Figure 13.1 isn't taken from any actual performance data but is a reconstruction of what telegraphers interviewed by Bryan and Harter thought that a learning curve for telegraphy should look like. The conclusion to be reached from the large amount of evidence reviewed by Keller is that plateaus do not ever seem to occur in the learning of telegraphic code.

Furthermore, Keller's analysis shows us that the notion of hierarchy of habits, while superficially appealing, neglects many important features of the process of learning telegraphic code. It is wrong to describe the learning of telegraphy as a hierarchy of habits and to assume that the transitions between members of the hierarchy are responsible for plateaus.

Plateaus may occur in certain skills. Book (1925) shows us some in objective records of people learning to typewrite, and many writers on the learning of particular skills assume them to be present in the skills they describe. But it is certainly wrong to conclude that there is some simple relation between changes in level of proficiency, as in the learning curve, and qualitative changes in the structure of a skill. There may or there may not be, depending entirely on the peculiarities of the particular case. To be sure, the structure of skills does change with practice, so that the skill being learned at one stage is not the same skill as that being learned at a higher level of proficiency in the next stage. An accurate account of how skills change qualitatively with practice, however, requires a more elaborate analysis than that implied by the supposed relation between plateaus and the hierarchy of habits.

The Structure of Abilities and the Learning of Skills

One way to approach the problem of how skills change qualitatively with practice is through the study of abilities. We can study abilities by examining individual differences between people in performance. We study the structure of abilities by examining the patterns of correlations between performances on different tasks or skills. The study of abilities and the structure of abilities can be applied to the analysis of the learning of skills. By examining a matrix consisting of the correlations betwen performance on different skills, it is possible to determine what latent struc-

TABLE 13.1 Some Important Factors Which Occur in Various Perceptual-motor Tasks
(After Fleishman, 1962)

FACTOR	DESCRIPTION	SOME TASKS
Control precision	Highly controlled adjustments of large muscles	Rudder control, lathe
Multilimb coordination	Coordinating the movements of more than one limb	Shifting gears
Response orientation	Fast visual discrimination with appropriate movement	Any task demanding the rapid choice of a response
Reaction time	Speed of response to stimulus	Any simple response to a single stimulus
Arm movement speed	Rapidity of gross arm movement	Hitting two plates about 6 inches apart alternately
Rate control	Following a moving target	Controlling the movement of a steel ball by tilting a board
Manual dexterity	Skilled rapid arm movements	Wrapping packages
Finger dexterity	Controlling tiny objects with the fingers	Repairing watches
Arm-hand steadiness	Moving an object slowly and steadily	Threading a needle
Wrist-finger speed	Tapping rapidly with pencil	Filling in a circle with dots
Aiming	Hitting small circles accurately with a pencil	Making check marks

ture lies behind the correlations, and it is possible to interpret this latent structure as the structure of ability. The technique for doing so is an application of the study of matrices known as factor analysis. In factor analysis, various primary abilities determining performance on various skills can be identified, and the relative contribution of these primary abilities to performance on the skills at different stages of practice can be determined.

THE STRUCTURE OF SOME PERCEPTUAL-MOTOR SKILLS

Fleishman (Fleishman & Hempel, 1954; Fleishman, 1962) has presented fairly comprehensive factor-analytic studies of the abilities responsible for performance on various skilled tasks as those tasks are practiced and show gradual "improvement" in some criterion measure. The basic approach in these studies is to consider how two or more measures of performance by the same individual co-vary. By comparing or correlating performance on successive trials of the same task and performance on the same trials on different tasks, it is possible to achieve a picture of the underlying pattern of abilities and how they change with practice.

A factor structure of the abilities responsible for a broad range of perceptual-motor skills is given in Table 13.1. The abilities presented in this table are responsible for performance in skills which demand well-coordinated muscular movements. A practical example of such a skill would be the operation of a machine lathe. Not all the factors responsible for such perceptual-motor skills are mentioned in the table, but most of the major ones are. Other major factors would be involved in physical skills demanding gross muscular movements (as in certain athletic skills, for example). All these factors are present at some stage of proficiency in performance of coordinated skills, but they change in importance with the stage.

CHANGE IN FACTOR STRUCTURE WITH PRACTICE

One example (Fleishman & Hempel, 1954) provides some specific evidence for change in the ability structure of tasks as practice continues. In this study, a large sample of laboratory subjects practiced for an extended period of time on a task which made use of complicated perceptual-motor reactions. In addition, the same subjects took an entire battery of tests designed to measure the kind of basic factors represented in Table 13.1. Scores on the practice task were correlated, at various stages of proficiency, with the battery of reference tests, and these correlations were put through a factor analysis. The result is illustrated in Figure 13.2.

The results in the figure make it quite evident that the same task, at different stages of practice, draws on different abilities to different degrees. The figure shows the proportion of the total variance in per-

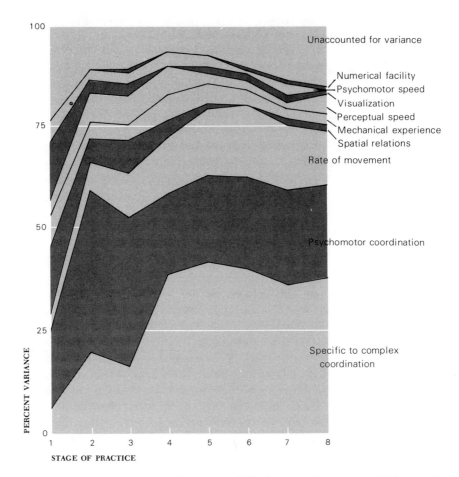

FIG. **13.2**   The factorial composition of a skill changes with practice. (Fleishman & Hempel, 1954.)

formance on the task (variance between individuals), which can be accounted for by the loadings on the underlying factors at various stages. Early in practice, the factor of psychomotor coordination is very important to performance. That factor becomes less important later in practice when rate of movement—which was initially of negligible importance—comes to be dominant. Early in practice, to put it another way, more of the differences between individuals in proficiency on the complex coordination task are accounted for by a factor of psychomotor coordination than by anything else. Later in practice, differences in rate of movement between subjects accounted for more of the individual differences in proficiency.

Fleishman (1962) makes one further point, though it is less evident in the analysis of abilities presented in Figure 13.2 than in some other studies. For most skills, there is an increase in the proportion of variance between individuals specific to a given task as practice continues in that task. The specific variance in Figure 13.2 is the variance labeled "specific to complex coordination." Specific variance is that portion of performance which cannot be described in terms of some general abilities and is, therefore, accounted for by an ability unique to the task in question. You will notice that Figure 13.2 shows a large increase with practice in the variance specific to complex coordination, though the increase here is smaller than it would be for some other tasks. That increase, however, makes a point of some considerable general interest.

The differences between people in proficiency at some task become increasingly determined by the habits and modes of working picked up in the course of practice on that skill. Therefore, performance on the task becomes less predictable from performance on other tasks and hence more nearly unique. Most tests of general ability predict the extent of differences between individuals in skill at some task better at earlier stages of practice than at later stages of practice. The increasing uniqueness of task performance provides the reason for the better prediction in cases where individuals have had little experience at a task.

A little reflection on the matter shows us that such a result is what we ought to expect. It is conceivable, for example, that by very hard work a person with very low mechanical aptitude could become a passably good machine lathe operator. It would be obvious in the early stages of practicing on the requisite skills that such an individual is inept. But if he works at it harder and longer than a person with a high level of mechanical aptitude would need to, he can overcome some of his handicap. The net result is that it would be harder to tell the difference late in practice than early in practice between him and an individual with high aptitude for the task.

TRIAL-TO-TRIAL CORRELATIONS IN PERFORMANCE

While we are considering the general question of individual differences in learning and performance, there is one more topic of general importance that we should examine. It is the matter of trial-to-trial correlations in performance on a particular task. In examining such correlations, we compare the distributions of performance on each trial with every other trial for a group of subjects. Such a comparison can be exhibited in a matrix of correlations.

Jones (1962) points out that there is a remarkable degree of uniformity in the matrices which can be formed by considering the correlations between all combinations of trials. Such matrices are nearly always of the superdiagonal variety. This means that the largest intercorrelations, in general, are between adjacent rows or columns, where the rows and columns represent successive trials at a task. Furthermore, the size of the correlations regularly increases from the first to the last trials.

TABLE 13.2 **The Intertrial Correlations for the Two-hand Coordination Task** (Jones, 1962)

TRIAL	1	2	3	4	5	6	7	8
1		.79	.77	.74	.73	.71	.71	.70
2			.87	.87	.84	.82	.82	.82
3				.91	.89	.87	.85	.86
4					.91	.88°	.86	.88
5						.89	.90	.90
6							.93	.93
7								.94

Table 13.2 presents such a matrix. The intercorrelations in this table are for performance on a kind of perceptual-motor task called the two-hand coordination task, which is rather like running a machine lathe. Trial-to-trial intercorrelations for other tasks, such as those in rote verbal learning, will in general be lower than those in Table 13.2; the overall pattern, however, will be the same. The correlations will be lowest in the upper right-hand corner and largest in the lower right-hand corner.

Jones argues that such matrices show this general form because learning of skills is essentially a process of simplification. Extraneous aspects of performance drop out as practice continues, so that later in practice only those components actually necessary to performance on the task are present. Presumably such a view would be in fair agreement with Fleishman's point about the increase in variance on factors unique to particular tasks. Later trials become purer for a single factor and correlate more highly with one another. Earlier trials sometimes yield performance that correlates more highly with external tests than with performance on other trials of the same task. This may well be the case in rote verbal learning, in which the trial-to-trial intercorrelations early in practice may be smaller than the correlations of those trials with external measures of verbal ability or specific associations.

There are, then, general patterns to the changes in qualitative aspects of performance from trial to trial. Such changes can be seen as changes in the abilities underlying performance at any given stage, though this simply means that the performance itself—not the abilities—changes. These changes may occur in smooth and overlapping fashion or they may be relatively discrete. Furthermore, they may or may not be hierarchical in nature. They will be hierarchical only if performance on some later component of the task depends upon performance reaching a certain level at an earlier stage. There is no evidence that such is generally the case, however.

Task Analysis and the Limits of Learning

TASK ANALYSIS

A quite different though related approach to the problem of describing the changes in the structure of skills as practice continues is provided by various methods of task analysis. The most detailed and theoretically oriented of such analyses have been made by Fitts (1962; 1964). He describes performance during the learning of perceptual-motor skills as passing through three stages. These stages are overlapping and not distinct, but, rather like the changes in proportion of variance in the factor-analytic studies, they represent shifts in emphasis during the learning process. The phases are described as cognition, fixation, and automation.

Cognitive processes are heavily involved in the early stages of performance on motor skills. In these stages pencil and paper tests will often predict performance on some skill with very satisfactory validity. That is because the perceptual-cognitive features tapped by such tests are important while an individual is getting oriented to some task. As he gets the "feel" of some situation—driving an automobile, for example—the importance of cognitive features drops out and the various aspects of perceptual-motor coordination become more important. It is during the cognitive phase that transfer of training is of greatest importance. As a practical matter, performance at this stage can often be helped by training films and demonstrations which do not actually require performance on the part of the learner.

In the next or fixation phase, the correct patterns of motor action are refined and fixated. This is the longest and most difficult of the phases. Fitts reminds us that laboratory studies of perceptual-motor learning seldom get beyond this phase. It is the phase which is usually described in the factor-analytic studies of the shifting patterns of ability in perceptual-motor learning.

Fitts calls the final stage the automation phase. This stage is characterized by rapid, automatic performance. Errors are at a minimum, and if there is any improvement in performance detectable in ordinary testing, it is in such things as quicker reaction times, etc. The skill becomes not only well integrated but resistant to the effects of stress and interference from other activities that may be performed concurrently. The novice automobile driver has to concentrate, but the expert can carry on a conversation or listen to something absorbing on the radio while driving.

In addition to changing structure with practice, most tasks can be broken down into various subroutines, and these subroutines can be learned more or less independently. Usually, without special guidance, people try to learn the various subroutines of a task more or less concurrently. We say "more or less concurrently" because actually the attention given to the various subroutines will be on some time-shared basis. Now the learner attends to one feature and then later to another. In special training programs, however, the various subroutines may be practiced separately. Swimmers, for example, perfect kicking as one routine, stroking as another, and breathing as a third. Actual performance of the integrated act requires some time-sharing direction, but certain levels of skill on the various subroutines may be perfected separately. Because the subroutines are not totally independent and must be integrated, some practice time is then necessary to learn how to put them together.

THE LIMITS OF LEARNING

We have one further important point to discuss concerning the analysis of improvement in skills. We have already seen that plateaus are not necessarily to be expected in perceptual-motor learning. Neither are asymptotic limits to learning, according to analyses made by Crossman (1959) and Fitts (1962; 1964). Fitts presents a number of learning curves all of which chart improvement during extended periods of practice, and these curves make it evident that some improvement is going on even after months and in some cases years of practice. Crossman presents us with similar curves and also with a mathematical derivation of a learning curve (under some special circumstances) that has the property of long-continued improvement.

It may be a peculiar characteristic of motor skills that they are almost infinitely improvable, though the amount of improvement which will occur late in practice is in general very slight. One example that Fitts (1962) presents is derived from some data produced by Snoddy (1926) on mirror drawing. Mirror drawing is a fascinating—and to the subject, frustrating—task. It requires a person to trace a complicated pattern (frequently the outline of a five-pointed star) by watching the movements of his hand in a mirror. The subject is not allowed to see his hand move directly. You can get some idea of the difficulty of the task by trying to write your name (about as overlearned a skill as you possess) so that you can read it normally as you write it by watching your hand in a mirror.

Figure 13.3 shows Snoddy's data, in which the reciprocal of a measure of performance (based upon both time and errors) is plotted

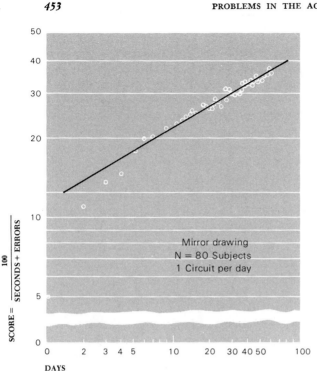

FIG. **13.3** Fitts's replotting of Snoddy's data on the learning of mirror drawing. (Fitts, 1962.)

against days of practice. Notice that both variables are plotted by logarithmic scales. It is clear that there is some improvement on this ostensibly elementary task after more than two months of practice. Both Crossman (1959) and Fitts (1964) bring together other examples, taken from a variety of experimental and actual work situations, which show that there is some measurable improvement in performance with further practice after even years of previous practice. When a task is highly skilled, however, it takes a relatively enormous amount of practice to produce a tiny improvement. All the examples shown by Fitts are linear when plotted on logarithmic scales.

Therefore, the continuous practice which professional athletes and musicians engage in, ostensibly in order to maintain their level of proficiency, probably results in some additional level of skill. Commentators on such skills invariably point out that it rare for peak performance to be reached short of years of intensive and usually daily practice. When performance does level off or deteriorate, it is the result of the operation of physiological aging processes. Thus, for perceptual-motor skills, the attainment of an asymptote or limit of skill with long-continued practice is more an exception than the rule.

THE CONDITIONS OF LEARNING

We have examined some of the structural changes that go on in the practice of perceptual-motor skills, but we have treated these more or less without reference to the conditions of practice under which they occur. Practice at perceptual-motor skills can occur under a wide variety of circumstances, some of them favorable to learning and some of them detrimental. Before we can consider our review of the problems of the learning of skill reasonably complete, we must survey the more important of these conditions.

Feedback

There seems to be universal agreement among those who study the learning of skills that the most fundamental condition determining performance during learning is feedback (Bilodeau & Bilodeau, 1961). Feedback refers to any consequences or results of performance that are perceived by the learner. It may be in the form of direct perception of the adequacy of performance, or it may be in the form of verbal information about the adequacy of performance. In general, then, feedback occurs either as the sensory consequence of motor action or as knowledge of results supplied by a teacher, an experimenter, or an automatic teaching device.

Feedback, either in the form of sensory consequence or knowledge of results, can have two functions: (1) It informs the learner about his responses and thus permits him to correct these in some way on the next trial, and (2) it may provide reinforcement. Furthermore, feedback can in theory affect either learning or performance or both. In one sense feedback is essential for learning, since it defines the direction in which performance is to be changed in the future. Learning is not simply a change in behavior; it is a change in some particular direction or a change which brings performance closer to some (perhaps arbitrary) criterion. It is not possible to teach something to someone without showing him in some way what it is he is to learn. Conversely, you cannot find out what he has learned without telling him what it is you want him to do to show evidence of his learning.

KNOWLEDGE OF RESULTS AS REINFORCEMENT

A great deal of the older literature on feedback concerns knowledge of results as a possible source of reinforcement or reward. Thorndike (1933) argued that knowledge of results has rewarding properties and produces incentive to further activity. He tried to show, in a series of experiments, that the reward or reinforcement value of knowledge of results is automatic and mechanical. His experiments concerned the "spread of effect." The effect consists in showing that knowledge of results (usually saying "right" or "wrong" to a person immediately after he makes a response) spreads in a more or less blind fashion to the immediately adjacent responses in time. In fact, Thorndike thought that he had demonstrated a temporal gradient of effect or reinforcement away from some particular reinforced response. If Thorndike's experiments had held up under critical scrutiny, they would indeed have provided strong evidence for the role of reinforcement in knowledge of results and for the possibility that such reinforcement was automatic and mechanical. However, a large number of experimental investigations (see Sheffield & Jenkins, 1952) show rather conclusively that Thorndike's results depended upon some subtle but powerful artifacts. Therefore, the issue of the "automatic stamping-in effect" of knowledge of results turns out to be of little contemporary relevance.

It is very possible, and indeed in many circumstances, likely that knowledge of results has reinforcing effects. The literature on verbal conditioning (Krasner, 1958; Spielberger, 1965) testifies to the fact. However, as Bilodeau and Bilodeau (1961) point out, no one has ever demonstrated much of a differential incentive effect upon the learning or performance of perceptual-motor skills for various kinds of knowledge of results. Therefore, while we may accept the reinforcement-incentive action of knowledge of results, we have little to go on in any concrete way that helps us understand how its role is to be differentiated from that of information in the learning of skills.

Certainly, the distinction between the informative and incentive aspects of feedback is not without importance. Despite the fact that some twenty years of research on the problem have failed to separate the informative aspects of feedback from the reward aspects, discussion of the matter goes on. Perhaps the resolution of the matter will come when someone devises a useful way of scaling the incentive value of various conditions of feedback.

LEARNING AND PERFORMANCE

The issue of the comparative role of feedback in learning and performance can be resolved in a fairly clear way. One experimental study can serve as an example of a good many others which lead to the same general conclusion (see Bilodeau & Bilodeau, 1961, for an account of the experimental literature).

The experiment in question (Smode, 1958) required subjects to track or monitor a visual display. In essence, they had to turn a knob or handle in order to keep a needle which moved around a dial centered at zero. In its abstract essentials such a task is similar to trailing a moving target with a gun or with some other sighting device. Subjects in this experiment worked under two conditions. In one they were told after every trial how much of the time they had been on target (how successful they had been in keeping the needle at zero). In the other condition the subjects were given this information in addition to that supplied by a clear clicking sound which occurred whenever the needle departed from zero.

All the subjects practiced for 11 trials, some under one condition and some under the other. At the twelfth trial, the subjects switched conditions. Those who had had the information supplied by the clicks no longer did so, and those who had practiced without the click now heard it. The results were clear and obvious: performance switched immediately. The group which had heard the clicks on the first 11 trials got no residual benefit from this experience when the clicks were no longer available, and the subjects who had practiced without the clicks immediately did as well as those who had practiced with them. Thus, knowledge of results does not directly affect rate of acquisition. It affects performance directly and influences acquisition only to the extent that acquisition is dependent upon performance.

DELAY OF FEEDBACK

Delay of reinforcement has a considerable effect upon the performance of simple instrumental conditioned responses. It is not surprising that a number of investigators have asked if the same is true of the relation between delay of feedback and performance of skilled perceptual-motor activity. Common sense would suggest that the same relation would not be found. Symbolic processes in man should enable him to bridge anything but a very long delay between the occurrence of some response and the information which was the consequence of the response. Certainly, we would not expect a few seconds and perhaps even a few minutes to make much difference in perceptual-motor performance.

It turns out that common sense is mostly right. The results depend, though, on what happens between a response or sequence of actions in a perceptual-motor skill and the consequences which follow. One early experiment (Lorge & Thorndike, 1935) investigated the problem. Subjects threw balls at a target they could not see. Some subjects were told how close they were to the target immediately after the throw; other subjects were not given knowledge of results until various periods of time after making a throw. In general, as is to be expected, there was little or no difference due to the interval of time between knowledge of results and the response. If, however, the interval between throwing the ball and obtaining information about a particular throw was filled with another throw, gain in accuracy was severely impaired. Such a result shows that if the delay is filled with another attempt at the same response, interference can result.

One large-scale study (Bilodeau & Bilodeau, 1958) shows that even very long delays may have little influence on the accuracy and gain in accuracy of perceptual-motor performance. This experiment concerned delay of information in a task which consisted essentially of moving an indicator to the desired position. The improvement in performance was closer and closer approximation to a particular position. In this experiment, both the time between intervening trials and delay of information were varied. For example, twenty-four hours might intervene between two responses in one case, one hour in another. The information about the first response could come any time in the interresponse interval.

It turned out that the critical variable which determined how fast subjects learned was the intertrial interval (see the section which follows). Even when there was a delay of an entire week between making a response and being given knowledge about that response, there was no evidence for impairment (though under such long intertrial intervals, performance was so variable that it was hard to tell whether the delay of information itself had an effect or not). In any event, this experiment confirms the notion that what causes a deterioration in performance with delay of information is the interference of further practice at the same activity.

The Distribution of Practice

We have just alluded to the effects of intertrial interval. It turns out that one of the most important variables influencing performance during perceptual-motor learning is the distribution of a fixed amount of practice through time. The variations in distribution usually take the form of differences in intertrial interval.

In verbal learning, the effects of intertrial distribution are small and often contradictory (see Chapter 8). In perceptual-motor learning, on the other hand, the influence of distribution of practice is constant and often of great importance. Furthermore, since the effects of massing practice seem to recover with rest, the question of the relation between fatigue and work enters into theories of distribution of practice.

A number of experiments investigate, for a wide variety of tasks, the question as to whether it is better to practice with as little interruption for rest as possible or whether rests should be frequent. For most of the tasks that have been studied, and apparently for all tasks that are primarily perceptual-motor in nature, some rest is better than none at all. For some tasks the advantage from rest periods is of great importance.

EXPERIMENTAL RESULTS

Two older experiments illustrate the basic effects. In one of these (Lorge, 1930), the effects of continuous practice for 20 trials were compared with the effects of practice in which a rest period of one minute or a rest period of one day intervened between each trial. The tasks used in this experiment were mirror drawing, mirror writing, and a kind of code substitution task. For all three tasks, both cases of distribution produced superior performance. Figure 13.4 illustrates the results found with mirror drawing. Notice that the difference between the group that rested for one minute between each trial and the group that rested for one day is small compared with the difference between no rest and one minute of rest.

It is reasonable to suppose that the relative effectiveness of distributed practice would depend upon the absolute and relative length of the work and rest periods. There are a number of experiments that explore this problem. One of them which varies rest periods while holding work periods constant is by Kientzle (1946). The task studied in this experiment was learning to print random sequences of letters upside down. The measure of performance was the number of letters printed upside down correctly in a trial one minute in duration. The results can be seen in Figure 13.5. They show that short rest periods resulted in great improvement in performance compared with no rest, but not much further advantage is gained by longer rests.

FIG. **13.4** The effect of distribution of practice on learning mirror drawing. (After Lorge, 1930.)

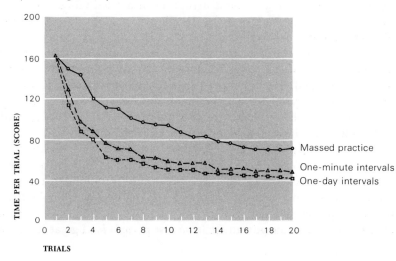

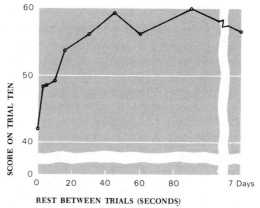

FIG. **13.5** The effect of time between trials on performance when
subjects were learning how to print
upside down. Rest intervals beyond
45 seconds do not appreciably increase performance. (Data from
Kientzle, 1946.)

These results are typical. Even when the work cycles are longer, relatively short rest periods are nearly maximally effective in producing recovery from any harmful effects of continuous work. But in fact, the optimal cycling will depend upon the duration of the work too. The longer the work period, the longer the period of rest for maximal recovery.

THEORIES OF DISTRIBUTION OF PRACTICE

It is not surprising that theories of distributed practice imply the accumulation of something like fatigue. It is perhaps surprising to discover, however, that the theory of distributed practice which held attention for the longest time came originally from a consideration of experimental extinction (Hull, 1943). The basic idea behind this theory was that a certain inhibition to further work or activity (of the specific sort demanded by a particular task) developed as the result of practice at that activity, and was a function of the difficulty of the activity. A certain portion of this inhibition became conditioned to the stimuli associated with the task. According to the theory, rest allowed recovery from the work-produced inhibition, but not from the conditioned inhibition. This aspect of the theory was originally developed to account for the lack of complete spontaneous recovery in extinction, but it was soon applied to the problem of distributed practice in perceptual-motor performance.

Unfortunately, the theory entailed several logical contradictions, contradictions which have not yet been satisfactorily resolved (Jensen, 1961). In addition, the experimental literature on perceptual-motor performance in general does not reveal residual deleterious effects of massed practice, as might be expected from the theory (Bilodeau & Bilodeau, 1961). In accordance with the theory, however, is the fact that the importance of distributing practice varies with the difficulty of the task. An extremely simple task does not show any, or at any rate much, improvement from having practice on it distributed (Bilodeau & Bilodeau, 1958).

There is recovery from completely massed practice when a time interval precedes a test. This recovery produces the phenomenon of reminiscence in perceptual-motor learning, and reminiscence as the result of dissipation through rest of the effects of massing has proved to be of some theoretical interest. Technically, reminiscence is defined as the improvement in performance that results when an individual practices continuously at a task, rests, and then returns to the task. When proper allowances are made for warm-up, etc., performance immediately after a rest period shows a transient improvement.

The phenomenon of reminiscence has some theoretical importance because it transfers bilaterally, and such transfer rules out the inhibition or ʼfatigue associated with practice of a task as being located in the muscles or response elements involved in performance of the task.

In experiments on bilateral transfer of reminiscence (Irion & Gustafson, 1952) subjects practiced following a moving target with a stylus (pursuit rotor) for five minutes. After practice, one group of subjects immediately practiced for five more minutes with the other hand, while subjects in a second group rested for five minutes before practicing with the other hand. It turned out that the group which rested was better with the nonpreferred hand than the group that transferred immediately. Thus the detrimental effects of massed practice transferred from one hand to the other; these effects were not limited in location to the muscles responsible for performance in original practice. Furthermore, Adams (1955) shows with the same task that merely watching someone else practice has a decremental effect on later performance. Therefore it seems fairly certain that the inhibition, fatigue, or however the decrement is to be characterized, may not necessarily be localized within the response-producing mechanisms. Inhibition certainly does not depend upon the maximal activation of those events.

In short, while we can attribute the decrement which occurs when practice is massed rather than distributed to some inhibition which largely or even completely dissipates with rest, we cannot say very much about the more general properties of that inhibition. It is probably only in part the direct result of active participation in a task. There is good reason to believe that there is a strong sensory component in such inhibition. Such sensory inhibition is usually characterized as stimulus satiation (Glanzer, 1953). Most probably, the inhibitory phenomena associated with perceptual-motor performance are unrelated to interference effects of the sort observable in verbal learning, though this is by no means certain. It is very difficult to produce anything like interference in perceptual-motor performance comparable to, say, proactive or retroactive inhibition in rote verbal learning (Barch & Lewis, 1954). What is certain is that no problem in the investigation of perceptual-motor performance warrants more attention at present than that of work-produced decrement. We can hope that a general solution to this problem will provide us with detailed knowledge about the distribution of practice and its consequences.

Other Conditions of Practice

Of course, other conditions of practice determine performance in learning various perceptual-motor skills. Most of these conditions, however, are unique to particular tasks, abilities, or related groups of abilities and tasks. Only a few are sufficiently general to have relevance to a wide range of tasks. Among these more general effects is the phenomenon known as psychological refractory phase. The concept of the psychological refractory phase arises from certain work on perceptual-motor skills performed in British psychological laboratories (see Welford, 1960). Psychological refractory phase refers to the fact that immediately after a response has occurred or some information has been processed, there is an inability to produce a second response or process additional information. The refractory phase is very brief, of course, and would not under any circumstances exceed a few seconds.

The typical demonstration of the psychological refractory phase occurs in a reaction-time experiment. Subjects are required to react to two stimuli which occur very close together in time. If the second stimulus occurs only a few seconds after the first, the reaction time to it will be lengthened. The interpretation of the phenomenon is that the first stimulus is still being processed when the second comes along. Reaction to it must be delayed until the central processes which produce the first reaction have finished. This implies that the individual is capable of re-acting to only one event at a time, a state of affairs which has important implications for the study of attention, perception, and communication (Broadbent, 1958). Knowledge about new stimulus inputs must be delayed while earlier inputs are being acted upon. If an input occurs too soon after another one, it is stored in short-term memory until the individual is ready to react to it.

Psychological refractory phase is important in the learning of skills because a given task may overload the individual with information. Per-formance on early trials may then be degraded until the individual can learn to handle the multistimulus input more or less automatically. When all stimuli can be processed automatically, time is no longer required for a separate decision process about each, and the individual can react to all of them.

The way in which people can learn to handle complex stimulus inputs is illustrated in the choice-reaction experiment. In this kind of experiment, the individual is faced with a number of stimuli—for example, lights on a display panel. He must make a different response to each of the lights. There may be very little to learn: the subject may only be required to touch a particular light when it comes on. In such experiments, it turns out, the reaction time is proportional to the logarithm of the number of stimuli (Hyman, 1953). That result is important because it apparently shows that reaction time is determined by the information available in the display. However, if subjects are practiced for a long time on displays which contain a number of stimuli, they evidently learn to react to any number of stimuli. It doesn't matter how many stimuli there are to react to; the reaction time is the same (Mowbray & Rhoades, 1959). Apparently the longer reaction times early in practice when there are more stimuli are caused by decision processes about where stimuli are located. When the tendency to react to a particular stimulus becomes completely automatic, there is no decision; the information can be processed just about as rapidly as the sensory information can be registered and the response made. In highly skilled performance, most reactions are automatic, and decision may be only occasionally called upon. It is this automaticity of reaction that enables us to perform familiar reactions, such as driving an automobile easily and automatically. We are only aware of the need for rapid decision when we are in a strange and stressful situation (such as driving in heavy traffic in a strange city).

Another characteristic phenomenon of nearly all perceptual-motor tasks (as well as certain highly structured verbal tasks) is warm-up. If an interval without practice intervenes between trials, the initial performance following the rest interval will suffer some slight decrement (Ammons, 1950). At first glance we might suppose that this decrement is to be identified as forgetting. If so, however, it is a peculiar kind of forgetting. Experimental results show that it is (1) a positive function of pre-rest practice, (2) a negative function of the duration of the rest, and (3) nonspecific. That is to say, activity, not merely practice on the particular skill in question, will suffice for warm-up. Rather than being identified with forgetting, warm-up is usually identified with the various work-decrement phenomena. Suffice it to say while warm-up itself is not well understood, it is a general and probably quite important aspect of perceptual-motor learning and performance (Bilodeau & Bilodeau, 1961).

RETENTION OF PERCEPTUAL–MOTOR SKILLS

Warm-up decrement aside, studies of retention of perceptual-motor skills have not yielded much on analytic investigation. In fact, the experimental literature is not even sufficiently analytic to provide a clear-cut distinction between warm-up decrement and forgetting. Presumably, forgetting is specific to the components of the skill that have been practiced, while warm-up decrement is a more general effect which can be overcome by activity only vaguely related to the task under study. The distinction is blurred in many situations, however. Nevertheless, there are some data of consequence on retention of perceptual-motor skills. Furthermore, the study of perceptual-motor forgetting has seen the application of some novel and important analytic techniques which may prove to be of considerable general importance in the study of forgetting.

Forgetting and Perceptual-Motor Skills

EXPERIMENTAL STUDIES

For many skills, if not most, the mere passage of time is not sufficient to produce a retention loss. Certainly, tasks which depend primarily on factors of psychomotor coordination and similar conditions show little decrement over long periods of time. Various tracking tasks provide such cases. For example, Jahnke and Duncan (1956) studied the retention of the pursuit-rotor tracking task over intervals of time ranging from ten minutes to four weeks. These investigators found no evidence whatever for a retention loss. As a matter of fact, they found more evidence of the retention interval serving to distribute practice than anything else. Under some retention intervals there was an actual improvement in performance.

In a task more complicated than the pursuit rotor, Lewis and Lowe (1956) were able to show very slight retention losses over a period of three months. Adams (1964) and Bilodeau and Bilodeau (1961), in their reviews of the matter, describe these and other studies which reveal practically no decrement in ability to perform at perceptual-motor tasks after long intervals of no practice. Apparently, limited retention decrement is nearly universal. William James, in one of his characteristically aphoristic statements, reminded us that we learn to ice-skate in the summer and bicycle in the winter. He was, of course, commenting both upon the advantages of distributed practice and the seemingly extraordinary resistance to forgetting that characterizes most perceptual-motor tasks.

THEORIES OF RETENTION IN PERCEPTUAL-MOTOR TASKS

It is one matter simply to present these data on the comparatively high resistance of perceptual-motor skills to forgetting and another to attempt some serious explanation of them. Such explanations, however, could have important implications far beyond the matter of describing the learning and performance of perceptual-motor skills. They would, incidentally, help distinguish between those perceptual-motor tasks or aspects of perceptual-motor tasks which are very resistant to forgetting and those which are not.

The most obvious explanation for high retention, of course, is overlearning. In nearly every instance in which the retention of some perceptual-motor task has been studied, a great deal of practice has been necessary in order to bring the skill to a sufficient level to measure retention losses. It is well known in the study of verbal learning that retention is a positive function of practice, and that if some set of items is overlearned, these items will be extraordinarily resistant to the effects of forgetting.

It is a very superficial explanation, however, simply to say that perceptual-motor skills are usually overlearned. For one thing, we have seen that these skills are complicated in their structure. The specific components being practiced early in learning are not the same as those being practiced late in learning. It is true to a considerably lesser extent than in verbal learning that practice of a perceptual-motor task consists of repetition of what was done before. Instead, practice of these kinds of tasks involves the improvement of first one and then another aspect of a skill. In fact, given the complex structure of perceptual-motor skills, we might expect that they would have very low resistance to forgetting. What is being practiced at the end is not what was practiced at the beginning, so overlearning in perceptual-motor practice may be more apparent than real.

Perhaps a very different approach will provide better answers both to the question of why perceptual-motor skills are so well retained and to the question of why it takes so long to bring them to some acceptable level of performance. That approach is suggested by the notions of Bartlett (1948) and Welford (1951). The essential idea of these theorists can be put quite simply. It is that what is learned in a perceptual-motor task is not a series of movements or sensorimotor coordinations, but rather some schematic plans for performing things in a certain way. The individual, by this view, does not acquire many finely graded, specific muscular movements; he acquires a kind of program for instructing his muscles, when the need arises, how to do things.

In such a notion, there would be two major components to the learning of any skill. One would consist of forming the schema or the plan for performance, and the other would provide for the execution of the plan by a process of trying out first one possibility and then another. These two aspects would correspond, roughly, to the first two stages in the analysis of perceptual-motor learning made by Fitts (1962). If that is the case, it is not the plan that creates the difficulty in learning perceptual-motor skills, but the problem of finding the right motor representation of it. Once it is found, however, the difficulties created by possible decrements in performance—save for warm-up losses—vanish. There is very little to forget, for compared with the pattern of interrelations within even a small series of nonsense syllables to be committed to memory, the plans for execution of a complicated motor skill are relatively simple.

For the same reason, then, that the content of ordinary verbal discourse is relatively resistant to forgetting, perceptual-motor skills will be. Such a conclusion leads to the strong implication that the ordinary techniques for producing forgetting in the laboratory—proactive and retroactive inhibition—would be of little avail in perceptual-motor tasks. As we saw a few pages back (Barch & Lewis, 1954), such is actually the case.

Structural Changes in Retention

Forgetting should occur in perceptual-motor tasks, then, only to the extent that the schematic representation of the task is difficult to remember. There are examples in which such is the case. It turns out that the simplest of positioning responses may well be forgotten, and precisely for the reason that the schematic representation of the correct response is extraordinarily vague (Bilodeau, Sulzer, & Levy, 1962). Therefore, some forgetting takes place. What is more, the specific experimental situation allows for a structural analysis of the process of forgetting.

Bilodeau and his various collaborators show that many skills can be subjected to a particular analysis of what can be forgotten. Consider the case in which there is only a single response to be performed on each trial. Such a case directly fits the positioning-response example, and in a more extended analysis, more complicated cases could be handled.

There is more to the learning and retention of a positioning response than just that response, however. First the response occurs—a knob is turned through a certain angle or a lever is moved a certain distance. Then comes the knowledge of results. The subject is, told, "You moved it too far," or "You moved it 45 degrees; you're supposed to move it 90 degrees." The subject may have to retain both the response and the knowledge of results. Furthermore, after receiving knowledge of results, the subject may want to correct his response, if only in imagination. Now the situation is really complicated. He remembers an original response, the knowledge of results, and the amount of correction he thinks he should apply to make the response conform to the standard. The knowledge of results is usually encoded verbally, but the memory for the responses is another schematic form, probably in the form of a kinesthetic image. There is ample opportunity for several things and their interrelations to be forgotten.

Suppose, in a positioning response, the subject is allowed to keep his hand on the lever during the retention interval. Such retention intervals, of course, would have to be very short, but one could compare the results with those achieved when the subjects removed their hands during the retention interval. The results achieved by Bilodeau, Sulzer, and Levy in their experimental studies show very clearly that subjects can much more easily *remember their own previous responses* when they keep their hands on the lever. Evidently it is easier to keep a schematic representation of the response.

Bilodeau and Levy (1964) extend these observations to show how a particular kind of analysis very sensitively detects retention losses in simple skills of the sort exemplified by the positioning response. They start with the fact that, for any sample of subjects, there will be a distribution of response scores on any one trial. There will also be a distribution of response scores when the same subjects are asked to recall their own performance at some later time. The usual analysis of retention would compare the mean values of the response distributions for various retention intervals. Bilodeau and Levy, however, point out that one can, with as much logic, compare the variances of these distributions and compute the correlations between them. When this is done, it is clear that even if the means do not change, the variances and the correlations do. Thus, even if average performance doesn't change, subjects may become more variable. Bilodeau and Levy showed that the variances of the retention distribution increase over retention intervals ranging from three minutes to six weeks. Subjects become more variable in trying to remember their own responses. What is more, the correlation between the original responses and the responses at some later time decreases very abruptly over a matter of minutes. So even if the correlation between the original responses and retention of them a few minutes after the original performance is .95, it may fall to .20 in a matter of hours. The correlation remains high, incidentally, if the subjects are allowed to keep their hands on the lever during the retention interval.

In a subsequent study (Bilodeau, Jones, & Levy, 1964), a similar analysis is extended to the problem of multiple recalls. The extension gives rise to interesting possibilities in the structural analysis of the process of retention. The events to be remembered on a single trial can be decomposed into the response made, the knowledge of results, and an alternative response. These investigators ask, What is the effect on future recalling of earlier recalling? If the original response provides a standard to which each successive recall is referred, the intervening recall trials will not themselves be important determiners of performance. If, however, the original response is corrected or changed in some way by each recall, the later reproductions will be determined by those that intervene.

Bilodeau, Jones, and Levy (1964) provide us with a method of analysis that enables us to distinguish between these possibilities. They studied four reproductions or recall trials of a simple positioning response. These measurements were obtained under two different conditions (which do not concern us), and the results of the study are presented in two matrices (Table 13.3). The numbers in these matrices are correlations

TABLE 13.3 **Interresponse Correlations for the Repeated Recall of a Simple Positioning Response**
(Bilodeau, Jones, & Levy, 1964)

CONDITION A

MEASURE	R_1	R_2	R_3	R_4
ORIGINAL	.75	.44	.56	.17
R_1		.73	.71	.22
R_2			.69	.08
R_3				.32

CONDITION B

MEASURE	R_1	R_2	R_3	R_4
ORIGINAL	.61	.59	.41	.54
R_1		.72	.61	.44
R_2			.58	.48
R_3				.38

between trials. They are, therefore, the same kind of matrices as that in Table 13.2. But if you compare the pattern of values within these matrices with the values in Table 13.2, you will notice that they differ in one important respect. The matrix in Table 13.2 showed the largest correlations on the diagonal *increasing* in value from left to right. Both matrices in Table 13.3 show the largest correlations on the diagonal, but they *decrease* in value from left to right. The largest correlations in this table are between the original response and the first reproduction. The smallest correlations are between the final reproduction and the original response. The correlation between the final reproduction and the next to the last is also small.

In earlier studies, Bilodeau and Levy showed that the variances of recall or reproduction scores increased with retention interval. They also increase as a function of number of reproductions of the original response without further knowledge of results. In both cases, there is a kind of deterioration in the memory for the original material. That deterioration is a function either of time or of successive recalls without knowledge of results.

Furthermore, the form of the matrices in Table 13.3 shows us that the deterioration in memory is a kind of random degradation of the information about the original response. Changes are random and irregular from individual to individual. If people were trying to reproduce the *previous* reproduction rather than the original response, the form of the matrices in Table 13.3 would have been exactly like the form in Table 13.2. Therefore, Bilodeau, Jones, and Levy conclude that people reproduce (or attempt to reproduce) the original response, not the last reproduction of it. They do so with less and less success, however. Their lack of success is not the result of systematic distortions in memory introduced by the intervening reproductions, but the result of random memory changes. These are apparently completely unsystematic in the case of such simple positioning responses.

Bilodeau, Jones, and Levy show that a very different pattern holds for retention of knowledge of results. There is a definite trend, in this case, for the neighboring attempts at recall to correlate more highly with each other than with attempts which are further separated. That may be the case because memory for knowledge of results is verbally encoded. When we try to remember verbal material, we may tend to remember our previous reproduction of it rather than the original material. That was certainly the assumption made by Bartlett (1932) in his analysis of schematic memory. Bartlett's analysis would not apply to the nonverbal positioning response, but it might well apply to the verbally encoded knowledge of results.

In any event, the important matter at this stage is not the form any particular matrix takes so much as it is the powerful analysis of retention that is possible once we expand the study of learning and retention curves to include, in addition to the usual mean values, variances and intertrial correlations. In two instances in this chapter, we have seen the role that study of intertrial correlations can play in the analysis of processes in perceptual-motor learning and retention. That analysis can easily be extended to the study of verbal learning and recall, and we may expect some new insights to arise when such application is made.

EPILOGUE

There is a reason for making the chapter on perceptual-motor learning the last chapter in a book on learning, though perhaps it is not immediately obvious. This reason is that the study of perceptual-motor learning depends upon nearly every other process that can be investigated in the study of learning. Reinforcement analysis, generalization (both stimulus generalization and response generalization), discrimination, rote learning, concept learning, grammatical analysis, and schematic memory all play a role in perceptual-motor learning. We have seen that perceptual-motor learning does depend upon verbal components, and the most sophisticated analysis of the processes in perceptual-motor learning makes the assumption that what is learned is schematic representation of the actual movements required to execute some task.

Students of perceptual-motor learning have drawn upon other aspects of the study of learning for theories and experimental paradigms. Thus, one theory of extinction has dominated ideas about work-produced decrements in performance, and investigators of forgetting in perceptual-motor learning have often cast their studies in the familiar retroaction-proaction paradigms. It is only fairly recently that students of perceptual-motor learning have begun to make methodological advances of their own. It is gratifying to see, therefore, that many of the techniques they have devised have utility beyond the study of purely perceptual-motor problems. Most important in this respect is the general structural analysis of the learning process through correlational methods. This approach brings the whole study of learning closer to the traditional techniques for the study of human abilities, and we may expect, in the next few years, wider appreciation of the work of Tucker (1960), DuBois (1961), and others on the application of factor-analytic and general correlational techniques to the study of learning. The realization of the general utility of these techniques may well be the most important contemporary move in the study of human learning.

REFERENCES

ADAMS, J. A. (1954) Multiple vs. single problem training in human concept problem solving. *J. exp. Psychol.*, 48, 15-19.

ADAMS, J. A. (1955) A source of decrement in psychomotor performance. *J. exp. Psychol.*, 49, 390-394.

ADAMS, J. A. (1961) The second facet of forgetting: A review of warm-up decrement. *Psychol. Bull.*, 58, 257-273.

ADAMS, J. A. (1964) Motor skills. *Annu. Rev. Psychol.*, 15, 181-202.

ADAMSON, R. E. (1952) Functional fixedness as related to problem solving: A repetition of three experiments. *J. exp. Psychol.*, 44, 288-291.

ADELMAN, H. M., & MAATSCH, J. L. (1955) Resistance to extinction as a function of the type of response elicited by frustration. *J. exp. Psychol.*, 50, 61-65.

AHLSTRÖM, K. (1961) *Transfer and communality, an experimental study of learning.* Studia Scientiae Paedagogicae Upsaliensia. Norstedts, Sweden: Svenska Bokförlaget.

AMMONS, R. B. (1950) Acquisition of motor skill: III. Effects of initially distributed practice on rotary pursuit performance. *J. exp. Psychol.*, 40, 777-787.

AMSEL, A. (1958) The role of frustrative nonreward in noncontinuous reward situations. *Psychol. Bull.*, 55, 102-119.

AMSEL, A. (1962) Frustrative nonreward in partial reinforcement and discrimination learning: Some recent history and a theoretical extension. *Psychol. Rev.*, 69, 306-328.

AMSEL, A., & COLE, K. F. (1953) Generalization of fear-motivated interference with water intake. *J. exp. Psychol.*, 46, 243-247.

AMSEL, A., & MALTZMAN, I. (1950) The effect upon generalized drive strength of emotionality as inferred from the level of comsummatory response. *J. exp. Psychol.*, 40, 563-569.

AMSEL, A., & ROUSSEL, J. (1952) Motivational properties of frustration: I. Effect on a running response of the addition of frustration to the motivational complex. *J. exp. Psychol.*, 43, 363-368.

ANDERSON, N. H. (1963) Comparison of different populations: Resistance to extinction and transfer. *Psychol. Rev.*, 70, 162-179.

ANNAU, Z., & KAMIN, L. J. (1961) The conditioned emotional response as a function of intensity of the US. *J. comp. physiol. Psychol.*, 54, 428-432.

APPEL, J. B. (1963) Punishment and shock intensity. *Science,* 141, 528-529.

ARCHER, E. J. (1960) Re-evaluation of the meaningfulness of all possible CVC trigrams. *Psychol. Monogr.*, 74, No. 497.

ARCHER, E. J., BOURNE, L. E., JR., & BROWN, F. G. (1955) Concept identification as a function of irrelevant information and instructions. *J. exp. Psychol.*, **49**, 153–164.

ARNOULT, M. D. (1957) Stimulus predifferentiation: Some generalizations and hypotheses. *Psychol. Bull.*, **54**, 339–350.

ASCH, S. E., & EBENHOLTZ, S. M. (1962) The principle of associative symmetry. *Proc. Amer. Phil. Soc.*, **106**, 135–163.

ATKINSON, J. W. (1964) *An introduction to motivation.* Princeton, N.J.: Van Nostrand.

ATKINSON, R. C. (1957) A stochastic model for rote serial learning. *Psychometrika*, **22**, 87–96.

AUTOR, S. M. (1960) The strength of conditioned reinforcers as a function of frequency and probability of reinforcement. Unpublished doctoral dissertation, Harvard University.

AVERBACH, E., & CORIELL, A. S. (1961) Short-term memory in vision. *Bell Sys. tech. J.*, **40**, 309–328.

AZRIN, N. H. (1956) Some effects of two intermittent schedules of immediate and non-immediate punishment. *J. Psychol.*, **42**, 3–121.

AZRIN, N. H. (1960) Effects of punishment intensity during variable-interval reinforcement. *J. exp. Anal. Behav.*, **3**, 123–142.

AZRIN, N. H., HAKE, D. F., HOLZ, W. C., & HUTCHINSON, R. R. (1965) Motivational aspects of escape from punishment. *J. exp. Anal. Behav.*, **8**, 31–44.

AZRIN, N. H., HOLZ, W. C., & HAKE, D. F. (1963) Fixed-ratio punishment. *J. exp. Anal. Behav.*, **6**, 141–148.

BACON, W. E. (1962) Partial-reinforcement extinction effect following different amounts of training. *J. comp. physiol. Psychol.*, **55**, 998–1003.

BAHRICK, H. P. (1964) Retention curves: Facts or artifacts? *Psychol. Bull.*, **61**, 188–194.

BAKER, R. A., & LAWRENCE, D. H. (1951) The differential effects of simultaneous and successive stimuli presentation on transposition. *J. comp. physiol. Psychol.*, **44**, 378–382.

BARCH, A. M., & LEWIS, D. (1954) The effect of task difficulty and amount of practice on proactive transfer. *J. exp. Psychol.*, **48**, 134–142.

BARNES, J. B., & UNDERWOOD, B. J. (1959) "Fate" of first-list associations in transfer theory. *J. exp. Psychol.*, **58**, 97–105.

BARON, M. R. (1965) The stimulus, stimulus control, and stimulus generalization. In D. I. Mostofsky (Ed.), *Stimulus generalization.* Stanford, Calif.: Stanford.

BARRY, H., III (1958) Effects of strength of drive on learning and extinction. *J. exp. Psychol.*, **55**, 473–481.

BARTLETT, F. C. (1932) *Remembering: A study in experimental and social psychology.* New York: Cambridge.

BARTLETT, F. C. (1948) The measurement of human skill. *Occup. Psychol.*, **22**, 31–38.

BASS, M. J., & HULL, C. L. (1934) The irradiation of a tactile conditioned reflex in man. *J. comp. Psychol.*, **17**, 47–65.

BATTIG, W. F. (1961) Comparison of anticipation and recall methods of paired-associate learning. *Psychol. Rep.*, **9**, 59–65.

BATTIG, W. F. (1962) Paired-associate learning under simultaneous repetition and nonrepetition. *J. exp. Psychol., 64,* 87–93.

BATTIG, W. F., & BRACKETT, H. R. (1963) Transfer from verbal-discrimination to paired-associate learning: II. Effects of intralist similarity, method, and percentage occurrence of response members. *J. exp. Psychol., 65,* 507–514.

BATTIG, W. F., WILLIAMS, J. M., & WILLIAMS, J. G. (1962) Transfer from verbal-discrimination to paired-associate learning. *J. exp. Psychol., 63,* 258–268.

BAUM, M. H. (1954) Simple concept learning as a function of intralist generalization. *J. exp. Psychol., 47,* 89–94.

BEHREND, E. R., & BITTERMAN, M. E. (1961) Probability-matching in the fish. *Amer. J. Psychol., 74,* 542–551.

BEVAN, W., & ADAMSON, R. (1960) Reinforcers and reinforcement: Their relation to maze performance. *J. exp. Psychol., 59,* 226–232.

BILODEAU, E. A., & BILODEAU, I. McD. (1958) Variation of temporal intervals among critical events in five studies of knowledge of results. *J. exp. Psychol., 55,* 603–612.

BILODEAU, E. A., & BILODEAU, I. McD. (1961) Motor skills learning. *Annu. Rev. Psychol., 12,* 243–280.

BILODEAU, E. A., JONES, M. B., & LEVY, C. M. (1964) Long-term memory as a function of retention time and repeated recalling. *J. exp. Psychol., 67,* 303–309.

BILODEAU, E. A., & LEVY, C. M. (1964) Long-term memory as a function of retention time and other conditions of training and recall. *Psychol. Rev., 71,* 27–41.

BILODEAU, E. A., SULZER, J. L., & LEVY, C. M. (1962) Theory and data on the interrelationships of three factors of memory. *Psychol. Monogr., 76,* No. 20.

BITTERMAN, M. E., & COATE, W. B. (1950) Some new experiments on the nature of discrimination learning in the rat. *J. comp. physiol. Psychol., 43,* 198–210.

BITTERMAN, M. E., FEDDERSON, W. E., & TYLER, D. W. (1953) Secondary reinforcement and the discrimination hypothesis. *Amer. J. Psychol., 66,* 456–464.

BLACK, A. H. (1958) The extinction of avoidance responses under curare. *J. comp. physiol. Psychol., 51,* 519–524.

BLACKWELL, H. R., & SCHLOSBERG, H. (1943) Octave generalization, pitch discrimination, and loudness thresholds in the white rat. *J. exp. Psychol., 33,* 407–419

BLODGETT, H. C. 1929) The effect of the introduction of reward upon the maze performance of rats. *Univ. Calif. Publ. Psychol., 4,* 113–134.

BLOUGH, D. S. (1965) Definition and measurement in generalization research. In D. I. Mostofsky (Ed.), *Stimulus generalization.* Stanford, Calif.: Stanford.

BOLLES, R., & PETRINOVICH, L. (1954) A technique for obtaining rapid drive discrimination in the rat. *J. comp. physiol. Psychol., 47,* 378–380.

BOOK, W. F. (1925) *Learning to typewrite.* New York: Gregg.

BOREN, J. J. (1961) Resistance to extinction as a function of the fixed ratio. *J. exp. Psychol., 61,* 304–308.

BOURNE, L. E., JR. (1963) Some factors affecting strategies used in problems of concept formation. *Amer. J. Psychol., 76,* 229–238.

BOURNE, L. E., JR. (1966) *Human conceptual behavior.* Boston: Allyn and Bacon.

BOURNE, L. E., JR., & HAYGOOD, R. C. (1959) The role of stimulus redundancy in concept identification. *J. exp. Psychol.,* **58,** 232–238.

BOURNE, L. E., JR., & RESTLE, F. (1959) Mathematical theory of concept identification. *Psychol. Rev.,* **66,** 278–296.

BOUSFIELD, W. A. (1953) The occurrence of clustering in the recall of randomly arranged associates. *J. gen. Psychol.,* **49,** 229–240.

BOUSEFIELD, W. A. (1961) The problem of meaning in verbal learning. In C. N. Cofer (Ed.), *Verbal learning and verbal behavior.* New York: McGraw-Hill.

BOUSFIELD, W. A., COHEN, B. H., & SILVA, J. G. (1956) The extension of Marbe's law to the recall of stimulus words. *Amer. J. Psychol.,* **69,** 429–433.

BOUSFIELD, W. A., COHEN, B. H., & WHITMARSH, G. A. (1958) Associative clustering in the recall of different taxonomic frequencies of occurrence. *Psychol. Rep.,* **4,** 39–44.

BOWER, G. H. (1961) Application of a model to paired-associate learning. *Psychometrika,* **26,** 255–280.

BOWER, G. H. (1962) The influence of graded reductions in reward and prior frustrating events upon the magnitude of the frustration effect. *J. comp. physiol. Psychol.,* **55,** 582–587.

BOWER, G. H., & MILLER, N. E. (1958) Rewarding and punishing effects from stimulating the same place in the rat's brain. *J. comp. physiol. Psychol.,* **51,** 669–674.

BOWER, G. H., STARR, R., & LAZAROVITZ, L. (1965) Amount of response-produced change in the CS and avoidance learning. *J. comp. physiol. Psychol.,* **59,** 13–17.

BRADY, J. V., & HUNT, H. F. (1955) An experimental approach to the analysis of emotional behavior. *J. Psychol.,* **40,** 313–324.

BREGMAN, A. S., & CHAMBERS, D. W. (1966) The all-or-none learning of attributes. *J. exp. Psychol.,* **71,** 785–793.

BRIGGS, G. E. (1954) Acquisition, extinction and recovery functions in retroactive inhibition. *J. exp. Psychol.,* **47,** 285–293.

BRIGGS, G. E. (1957) Retroactive inhibition as a function of the degree of original and interpolated learning. *J. exp. Psychol.,* **53,** 60–67.

BROADBENT, D. E. (1958) *Perception and communication.* New York: Pergamon.

BROGDEN, W. J., LIPMAN, E. A., & CULLER, E. (1938) The role of incentive in conditioning and extinction. *Amer. J. Psychol.,* **51,** 109–117.

BROWN, J. S. (1961) *The motivation of behavior.* New York: McGraw-Hill.

BROWN, J. S., KALISH, H. I., & FARBER, I. E. (1951) Conditioned fear as revealed by magnitude of startle response to an auditory stimulus. *J. exp. Psychol.,* **41,** 317–328.

BROWN, J. S., MARTIN, R. C., & MITCHELL, W. M. (1964) Self-punitive behavior in the rat: Facilitative effects of punishment on resistance to extinction. *J. comp. physiol. Psychol.,* **57,** 127–133.

BROWN, W. L., & McDOWELL, A. A. (1963) Response shift learning set in rhesus monkeys. *J. comp. physiol. Psychol.,* **56,** 335–336.

BRUNER, J. S., GOODNOW, J. J., & AUSTIN, G. A. (1956) *A study of thinking.* New York: Wiley.

BRUNSWICK, E. (1939) Probability as a determiner of rat behavior. *J. exp. Psychol.,* **25,** 175–197.

BRUNSWICK, E. (1956) *Perception and the representative design of psychological experiments.* Berkeley, Calif.: Univ. Calif. Press.

BRUSH, F. R., GOODRICH, K. P., TEGHTSOONIAN, R., & EISMAN, E. H. (1963) Dependence of learning (habit) in the runway on deprivation under three levels of sucrose incentive. *Psychol. Rep.,* **12,** 375–384.

BRYAN, W. L., & HARTER, N. (1897) Studies in the physiology and psychology of the telegraphic language. *Psychol. Rev.,* **4,** 27–53.

BRYAN, W. L., & HARTER, N. (1899) Studies on the telegraphic language: The acquisition of a hierarchy of habits. *Psychol. Rev.,* **6,** 345–375.

BUGELSKI, B. R. (1962) Presentation time, total time, and mediation in paired-associate learning. *J. exp. Psychol.,* **63,** 409–412.

BUGELSKI, B. R., & CADWALLADER, T. C. (1956) A reappraisal of the transfer and retroaction surface. *J. exp. Psychol.,* **52,** 360–366.

BUGELSKI, B. R., & RICKWOOD, J. (1963) Presentation time, total time and mediation in paired-associate learning: Self-pacing. *J. exp. Psychol.,* **65,** 616–617.

BURTT, H. (1941) An experimental study of early childhood memory. *J. genet. Psychol.,* **58,** 435–439.

BUSH, R. R., & MOSTELLER, F. (1955) *Stochastic models for learning.* New York: Wiley.

BUTLER, R. A. (1953) Discrimination by rhesus monkeys to visual-exploration motivation. *J. comp. physiol. Psychol.,* **46,** 95–98.

BUTLER, R. A. (1954) Incentive conditions which influence visual exploration. *J. exp. Psychol.,* **48,** 19–23.

BUTTER, C. M., & THOMAS, D. R. (1958) Secondary reinforcement as a function of the amount of primary reinforcement. *J. comp. physiol. Psychol.,* **51,** 346–348.

CALLANTINE, M. R., & WARREN, J. M. (1955) Learning sets in human concept formation. *Psychol. Rep.,* **1,** 363–367.

CALVIN, A. D., CLIFFORD, L. T., CLIFFORD, B., BOLDEN, L., & HARVEY, J. (1956) Experimental validation of conditioned inhibition. *Psychol. Rep.,* **2,** 51–56.

CAMPBELL, B. A. (1955) The fractional reduction in noxious stimulation required to produce "just noticeable" learning. *J. comp. physiol. Psychol.,* **48,** 141–148.

CAMPBELL, B. A. (1956) The reinforcement difference limen (RDL) function for shock reduction. *J. exp. Psychol.,* **52,** 258–262.

CAMPBELL, B. A. (1958) Absolute and relative sucrose preference thresholds for hungry and satiated rats. *J. comp. physiol. Psychol.,* **51,** 795–800.

CAMPBELL, B. A., & KRAELING, D. (1954) Response strength as a function of drive level and amount of drive reduction. *J. exp. Psychol.,* **47,** 101–103.

CAPEHART, J., VINEY, W., & HULICKA, I. M. (1958) The effect of effort upon extinction. *J. comp. physiol. Psychol.,* **51,** 505–507.

CARTERETTE, E. C. (1963) A replication of free recall and ordering of trigrams. *J. exp. Psychol.,* **66,** 311–313.

CHAMPION, R. A. (1964) The latency of the conditioned fear-response. *Amer. J. Psychol.,* **77,** 75–83.

CHURCH, R. M. (1963) The varied effects of punishment on behavior. *Psychol. Rev.,* **70,** 369–402.

CIEUTAT, V. (1962) Replication report: Implicit verbal chaining in paired-associate learning. *Percept. mot. Skills.,* 14, 45–46.

CLIFFORD, T. (1964) Extinction following continuous reward and latent extinction. *J. exp. Psychol.,* 68, 456–465.

COFER, C. N. (1960) Experimental studies of the role of verbal processes in concept formation and problem solving. *Ann. N.Y. Acad. Sci.,* 91, 94–107.

COFER, C. N. (1961) Comment on Professor Deese's paper. In C. N. Cofer (Ed.), *Verbal learning and verbal behavior.* New York: McGraw-Hill.

COFER, C. N. (1965) On some factors in the organizational characteristics of free recall. *Amer. Psychologist,* 20, 261–272.

COFER, C. N., & APPLEY, M. H. (1964) *Motivation: Theory and research.* New York: Wiley.

COFER, C. N., & FOLEY, J. P., JR. (1942) Mediated generalization and the interpretation of verbal behavior: I. Prolegomena. *Psychol. Rev.,* 49, 513–540.

COFER, C. N., & MUSGRAVE, B. S. (1963) *Verbal behavior and learning.* New York: McGraw-Hill.

COFER, C. N., & YARCZOWER, M. (1957) Further study of implicit verbal chaining in paired-associate learning. *Psychol. Rep.,* 3, 453–456.

COHEN, B. H. (1963a) An investigation of recoding in free recall. *J. exp. Psychol.,* 65, 368–376.

COHEN, B. H. (1963b) Recall of categorized word lists. *J. exp. Psychol.,* 66, 227–234.

COLE, M., & ABRAHAM, F. (1962) Extinction and spontaneous recovery as a function of amount of training and extinction intertrial interval. *J. comp. physiol. Psychol.,* 55, 978–982.

COLEMAN, E. B. (1962) Sequential interferences demonstrated by serial reproduction. *J. exp. Psychol.,* 64, 46–51.

COLEMAN, E. B. (1963) Approximations to English: Some comments on the method. *Amer. J. Psychol.,* 76, 239–247.

COLEMAN, E. B. (1964) Verbal concept learning as a function of instructions and dominance level. *J. exp. Psychol.,* 68, 213–214.

COLLIER, G., & MARX, M. H. (1959) Changes in performance as a function of shifts in the magnitude of reinforcement. *J. exp. Psychol.,* 57, 305–309.

COLLIER, G., & MYERS, L. (1961) The loci of reinforcement. *J. exp. Psychol.,* 61, 57–66.

CONRAD, R. (1959) Errors of immediate memory. *Brit. J. Psychol.,* 50, 349–359.

CONRAD, R. (1960) Very brief delay of immediate recall. *Quart. J. exp. Psychol.,* 12, 45–47.

CONRAD, R., & HILLE, B. A. (1958) The decay theory of immediate memory and paced recall. *Canad. J. Psychol.,* 12, 1–6.

COTTON, J. W. (1953) Running time as a function of amount of food deprivation. *J. exp. Psychol.,* 46, 188–198.

COWLES, J. T., & NISSEN, H. W. (1937) Reward-expectancy in delayed responses of chimpanzees. *J. comp. Psychol.,* 24, 345–358.

CRESPI, L. P. (1942) Quantitative variation of incentive and performance in the white rat. *Amer. J. Psychol.,* 55, 467–517.

CRESPI, L. P. (1944) Amount of reinforcement and level of performance. *Psychol. Rev.,* 51, 341–357.

CROSSMAN, E. R. F. (1959) A theory of acquisition of speed-skill. *Ergonomics,* 2, 153–166.

CROTHERS, E. J. (1962) Paired-associate learning with compound responses. *J. verb. Learn. verb. Behav.,* 1, 66–70.

DALLETT, K. M. (1962) The transfer surface re-examined. *J. verb. Learn. verb. Behav.,* 1, 91–94.

D'AMATO, M. R. (1955) Secondary reinforcement and magnitude of primary reinforcement. *J. comp. physiol. Psychol.,* 48, 378–380.

D'AMATO, M. R., & SCHIFF, D. (1965) Overlearning and brightness-discrimination reversal, *J. exp. Psychol.,* 69, 375–381.

D'AMATO, M. R., SCHIFF, D., & JAGODA, H. (1962) Resistance to extinction after varying amounts of discriminative or nondiscriminative instrumental training. *J. exp. Psychol.,* 64, 526–532.

DARBY, C. L., & RIOPELLE, A. J. (1959) Observational learning in the rhesus monkey, *J. comp. physiol. Psychol.,* 52, 94–98.

DATTMAN, P. E., & ISRAEL, H. (1951) The order of dominance among conceptual capacities: An experimental test of Heidbreder's hypothesis. *J. Psychol.,* 31, 147–160.

DAVIS, R., SUTHERLAND, N. S., & JUDD, B. R. (1961) Information content in recognition and recall. *J. exp. Psychol.,* 61, 422–429.

DEESE, J. (1951) Extinction of a discrimination without performance of the choice response. *J. comp. physiol. Psychol.,* 44, 362–366.

DEESE, J. (1957) Serial organization in the recall of disconnected items. *Psychol. Rep.,* 3, 577–582.

DEESE, J. (1959a) Influence of inter-item associative strength upon immediate free recall. *Psychol. Rep.,* 5, 305–312.

DEESE, J. (1959b) On the prediction of occurrence of particular verbal intrusions in immediate recall. *J. exp. Psychol.,* 58, 17–22.

DEESE, J. (1960) Frequency of usage and number of words in free recall: The role of association. *Psychol. Rep.,* 7, 337–344.

DEESE, J. (1961) From the isolated unit to connected discourse. In C. N. Cofer (Ed.), *Verbal learning and verbal behavior.* New York: McGraw-Hill.

DEESE, J. (1965) *The structure of associations in language and thought.* Baltimore: The Johns Hopkins Univ. Press.

DEESE, J., & CARPENTER, J. A. (1951) Drive level and reinforcement. *J. exp. Psychol.,* 42, 236–238.

DEESE, J., & KAUFMAN, R. A. (1957) Serial effects in recall of unorganized and sequentially organized verbal material. *J. exp. Psychol.,* 54, 180–187.

DEESE, J., & KRESSE, F. H. (1952) An analysis of errors in rote serial learning. *J. exp. Psychol.,* 43, 199–202.

DEESE, J., & MARDER, V. J. (1957) The pattern of errors in delayed recall of serial learning after interpolation. *Amer. J. Psychol.,* 60, 594–599.

DELGADO, J. M. R., ROBERTS, W. W., & MILLER, N. E. (1954) Learning motivated by electrical stimulation of the brain. *Amer. J. Physiol.,* 179, 587–593.

DEUTSCH, J. A. (1963) Learning and electrical self-stimulation of the brain. *J. theoret. Biol.,* **4,** 193–214.

DEUTSCH, J. A., & HOWARTH, C. I. (1963) Some tests of a theory of intracranial self-stimulation. *Psychol. Rev.,* **70,** 444–460.

DEWEY, J. (1896) The reflex arc concept in psychology. *Psychol. Rev.,* **3,** 357–370.

DOWLING, R. M., & BRAUN, H. W. (1957) Retention and meaningfulness of material. *J. exp. Psychol.,* **54,** 213–217.

DUBOIS, P. H. (1961) The design of correlational studies of training. In R. Glaser (Ed.), *Training research and education.* Pittsburgh, Pa.: Univ. of Pitt. Press.

DUNCAN, C. P. (1960) Description of learning to learn in human subjects. *Amer. J. Psychol.,* **73,** 108–114.

DUNCAN, C. P. (1964) Learning to learn in response-discovery and in paired-associate lists. *Amer. J. Psychol.,* **77,** 367–379.

DUNCKER, K. (1945) On problem solving. (Trans. from 1935 original.) *Psychol. Monogr.,* **58,** No. 270.

DYAL, J. A. (1964) Latent extinction as a function of placement-test interval and irrelevant drive. *J. exp. Psychol.,* **68,** 486–491.

EBBINGHAUS, H. (1885) *Über das Gedächtnis: Untersuchungen zur experiment-elen Psychologie,* Leipzig: Duncker und Humbolt.

EBENHOLTZ, S. M. (1963) Serial learning: Position learning and sequential associations. *J. exp. Psychol.,* **66,** 353–362.

EDWARDS, W. (1956) Reward probability, amount, and information as determiners of sequential two-alternative decisions. *J. exp. Psychol.,* **52,** 177–188.

EHRENFREUND, D. (1948) An experimental test of the continuity theory of discrimination learning with pattern vision. *J. comp. physiol. Psychol.,* **41,** 408–422.

EHRENFREUND, D. (1952) A study of the transportation gradient. *J. exp. Psychol.,* **43,** 83–87.

EHRLICH, S., FLORES, C., & LE NY, J. (1960) Rappel et reconnaissance d'éléments appartenant a des ensembles definis. *Année psychol.,* **60,** 29–37.

EIMAS, P. D., & ZEAMAN, D. (1963) Response speed changes in an Estes' paired-associate "miniature" experiment. *J. verb. Learn. verb. Behav.,* **1,** 384–388.

ELLSON, D. G. (1938) Quantitative studies of the interaction of simple habits: I. Recovery from specific and generalized effects of extinction. *J. exp. Psychol.,* **23,** 339–358.

ENTWISLE, D. R., & HUGGINS, W. H. (1964) Interference in meaningful learning. *J. educ. Psychol.,* **55,** 75–78.

EPSTEIN, A. N. (1960) Water intake without the act of drinking. *Science,* **131,** 497–498.

EPSTEIN, A. N., & TEITELBAUM, P. (1962) Regulation of food intake in the absense of taste, smell, and other oropharyngeal sensations. *J. comp. physiol. Psychol.,* **55,** 753–759.

EPSTEIN, W. (1961) The influence of syntactical structure on learning. *Amer. J. Psychol.,* **74,** 80–85.

Estes, W. K. (1944) An experimental study of punishment. *Psychol. Monogr.,* **57,** No. 263.

Estes, W. K. (1950) Toward a statistical theory of learning. *Psychol. Rec.,* **57,** 94–107.

Estes, W. K. (1955) Statistical theory of spontaneous recovery. *Psychol. Rev.,* **62,** 145–154.

Estes, W. K. (1958) The statistical approach to learning theory. In S. Koch (Ed.), *Psychology: A study of a science.* Vol. 2. New York: McGraw-Hill.

Estes, W. K. (1960) Learning theory and the new "mental chemistry." *Psychol. Rev.,* **67,** 207–223.

Estes, W. K. (1961) New developments in statistical behavior theory: Differential tests of axioms for associative learning. *Psychometrika,* **26,** 73–84.

Estes, W. K. (1964a) All-or-none processes in learning and retention. *Amer.-Psychol.,* **19,** 16–25.

Estes, W. K. (1964b) Probability learning. In A. W. Melton (Ed.), *Categories of human learning.* New York: Academic.

Estes, W. K. & Burke, C. J. (1953) A theory of stimulus variability in learning. *Psychol. Rev.,* **60,** 276–286.

Estes, W. K., Hopkins, B. L., & Crothers, E. J. (1960) All-or-none and conservation effects in the learning and retention of paired associates. *J. exp. Psychol.,* **60,** 329–339.

Estes, W. K., & Skinner, B. F. (1941) Some quantitative properties of anxiety. *J. exp. Psychol.,* **29,** 390–400.

Felsinger, J. M., Gladstone, A. I., Yamaguchi, H. G., & Hull, C. L. (1947) Reaction latency $(_st_r)$ as a function of the number of reinforcements (n). *J. exp. Psychol.,* **37,** 214–228.

Ferster, C. B. (1953) Sustained behavior under delayed reinforcement. *J. exp. Psychol.,* **45,** 218–224.

Ferster, C. B., & Skinner, B. F. 1957 *Schedules of reinforcement.* New York: Appleton-Century-Crofts.

Fitts, P. M. (1962) Factors in complex skill training. In R. Glaser (Ed.), *Training research and education.* Pittsburgh, Pa.: Univ. of Pitt. Press.

Fitts, P. M. (1964) Perceptual-motor skill learning. In A. W. Melton (Ed.), *Categories of human learning.* New York: Academic.

Fleishman, E. (1962) The description and prediction of perceptual-motor learning. In R. Glaser (Ed.), *Training research and education.* Pittsburgh: Univ. Pittsburgh Press.

Fleishman, E. A., & Hempel, W. E., Jr. (1954) Changes in factor structure of a complex psychomotor test as a function of practice. *Psychometrika,* **19,** 239–252.

Fowler, R. L., & Kimmel, H. D. (1962) Operant conditioning of the GSR. *J. exp. Psychol.,* **63,** 563–567.

Freibergs, V., & Tulving, E. (1961) The effect of practice on utilization of information from positive and negative instances in concept identification. *Canad. J. Psychol.,* **15,** 101–106.

Fries, C. C. (1952) *The structure of English.* New York: Harcourt, Brace & World.

GAGNÉ, R. M. (1941) The effect of spacing trials on the acquisition and extinction of a conditioned operant response. *J. exp. Psychol.,* **29,** 201–216.

GAGNÉ, R. M., & BAKER, R. E. (1950) Stimulus pre-differentiation as a factor in transfer of training. *J. exp. Psychol.,* **40,** 439–451.

GARNER, W. R. (1962) *Uncertainty and structure as psychological concepts.* New York: Wiley.

GARNER, W. R., & WHITMAN, J. R. (1965) Form and amount of internal structure as factors in free recall learning of nonsense words. *J. verb. Learn. verb. Behav.,* **4,** 257–266.

GELFAND, S. (1958) Effects of prior associations and task complexity upon the identification of concepts. *Psychol. Rep.,* **4,** 567–574.

GIBSON, E. J. (1940) A systematic application of the concepts of generalization and differentiation to verbal learning. *Psychol. Rev.,* **47,** 196–229.

GIBSON, E. J., PICK, A., OSSER, H., & HAMMOND, M. (1962) The role of grapheme-phoneme correspondence in the perception of words. *Amer. J. Psychol.,* **75,** 554–570.

GIBSON, J. J. (1960) The concept of the stimulus in psychology. *Amer. Psychologist,* **16,** 694–703.

GLANZER, M. (1953) Stimulus satiation: An explanation of spontaneous alternation and related phenomena. *Psychol. Rev.,* **60,** 257–268.

GLANZER, M. (1962) Grammatical category: A rote learning and word association analysis. *J. verb. Learn. verb. Behav.,* **1,** 31–41.

GLANZER, M., & CLARK, W. H. (1962) Accuracy of perceptual recall: An analysis of organization. *J. verb. Learn. verb. Behav.,* **1,** 289–299.

GLANZER, M., & PETERS, S. C. (1962) Re-examination of the serial position effect. *J. exp. Psychol.,* **64,** 258–266.

GLAZE, J. A. (1928) The association value of non-sense syllables. *J. genet. Psychol.,* **35,** 255–269.

GOGGIN, J. (1963) Influence of the written recall measure on first-list associations. *J. exp. Psychol.,* **65,** 619–620.

GONZALEZ, R. C., & COFER, C. N. (1959) Exploratory studies of verbal context by means of clustering in free recall. *J. genet. Psychol.,* **95,** 293–320.

GOODRICH, K. P. (1959) Performance in different segments of an instrumental response chain as a function of reinforcement schedule. *J. exp. Psychol.,* **57,** 57–63.

GOODWIN, W. R., & LAWRENCE, D. H. (1955) The functional independence of two discrimination habits associated with a constant stimulus situation. *J. comp. Physiol. Psychol.,* **48,** 437–443.

GORMEZANO, I., MOORE, J. W., & DEAUX, E. (1962) Supplementary report: Yoked comparisons of classical and avoidance eyelid conditioning under three UCS intensities. *J. exp. Psychol.,* **64,** 551–552.

GRANT, D. A. (1964) Classical and operant conditioning. In A. W. Melton (Ed.), *Categories of human learning.* New York: Academic.

GRANT, D. A., HAKE, H. W., & HORNSETH, J. P. (1951) Acquisition and extinction of a verbal conditioned response with differing percentages of reinforcement. *J. exp. Psychol.,* **42,** 1–5.

GREEN, R. T. (1958) The attention-getting value of structural change. *Brit. J. Psychol.,* **49,** 311–314.

GRICE, G. R. (1948) The relation of secondary reinforcement to delayed reward in visual discrimination learning. *J. exp. Psychol.,* **38,** 1–16.

GRICE, G. R. (1949) Visual discrimination learning with simultaneous and successive presentation of stimuli. *J. comp. physiol. Psychol.,* **42,** 365–373.

GRICE, G. R., & SALTZ, E. (1950) The generalization of an instrumental response to stimuli varying in the size dimension. *J. exp. Psychol.,* **40,** 702–708.

GUTHRIE, E. R. (1935) *The psychology of learning.* New York: Harper & Row.

GUTHRIE, E. R. (1952) *The psychology of learning.* (Rev. ed.) New York: Harper & Row.

GUTHRIE, E. R. (1958) Association by contiguity. In S. Koch (Ed.), *Psychology: A study of a science.* Vol. II. New York: McGraw-Hill.

GUTHRIE, E. R., & HORTON, G. P. (1946) *Cats in a puzzle box.* New York: Holt.

GUTTMAN, N. (1953) Operant conditioning, extinction and periodic reinforcement in relation to concentration of sucrose used as a reinforcing agent. *J. exp. Psychol.,* **46,** 213–224.

GUTTMAN, N., & KALISH, H. I. (1956) Discriminability and stimulus generalization. *J. exp. Psychol.,* **51,** 79–88.

HABER, R. N. (Ed.) (1966) *Current research in motivation.* New York: Holt.

HAKE, H. W. (1955) The perception of frequency of occurrence and the development of "expectancy" in human experimental subjects. In H. Quastler (Ed.), *Information theory in psychology; problems, and methods.* New York: Free Press.

HALL, J. F. (1954) Learning as a function of word-frequency. *Amer. J. Psychol.,* **67,** 138–140.

HALL, J. F. (1961) *Psychology of motivation.* New York: Lippincott.

HAMMERTON, M. (1963) Transfer of training from a simulated to a real control situation. *J. exp. Psychol.,* **66,** 450–453.

HANSON, H. M. (1959) Effects of discrimination training on stimulus generalization. *J. exp. Psychol.,* **58,** 321–334.

HARCUM, H. R. (1953) Verbal transfer of overlearned forward and backward associations. *Amer. J. Psychol.,* **66,** 622–625.

HARLOW, H. F. (1949) The formation of learning sets. *Psychol. Rev.,* **56,** 51–65.

HARLOW, H. F. (1950) Performance of catarrhine monkeys on a series of discrimination reversal problems. *J. comp. physiol. Psychol.,* **43,** 231–239.

HARLOW, H. F. (1958) Learning set and error factor theory. In S. Koch (Ed.), *Psychology: A study of a science.* Vol. II. New York: McGraw-Hill.

HARLOW, H. F., & HICKS, L. H. (1957) Discrimination learning theory: Uniprocess vs. duoprocess. *Psychol. Rev.,* **64,** 104–109.

HATTON, G. I. (1965) Drive shifts during extinction: Effects on extinction and spontaneous recovery of bar-pressing behavior. *J. comp. physiol. Psychol.,* **59,** 385–391.

HEATHERS, G. L. (1940) The avoidance of repetition of a maze reaction in the rat as a function of the time interval between trials. *J. Psychol.,* **10,** 359–380.

HEBB, D. O. (1949) *The organization of behavior.* New York: Wiley.

HEBERT, J. A., & KRANTZ, D. L. (1965) Transposition: A reevaluation. *Psychol. Bull.*, **63**, 244–257.

HEIDBREDER, E. (1946) The attainment of concepts: II. The problem. *J. gen. Psychol.*, **35**, 173–189.

HEIDBREDER, E. (1947) The attainment of concepts: III. The process. *J. gen. Psychol.*, **24**, 93–138.

HERRICK, R. M. (1964) The successive differentiation of a lever displacement response. *J. exp. Anal. Behav.*, **7**, 211–215.

HILGARD, E. R. (1956) *Theories of learning.* (2d ed.) New York: Appleton-Century-Crofts.

HILGARD, E. R., & BOWER, G. H. (1966) *Theories of learning.* (3d ed.) New York: Appleton-Century-Crofts.

HILGARD, E. R., & MARQUIS, D. M. (1940) *Conditioning and learning.* New York: Appleton-Century-Crofts.

HILL, W. F. (1963) *Learning: A survey of psychological interpretations.* San Francisco: Chandler.

HILL, W. F., COTTON, J. W., & CLAYTON, K. N. (1962) Effect of reward magnitude, percentage of reinforcement, and training method on acquisition and reversal in a T maze. *J. exp. Psychol.*, **64**, 81–86.

HILL, W. F., & SPEAR, N. E. (1962) Resistance to extinction as a joint function of reward magnitude and the spacing of extinction trials. *J. exp. Psychol.*, **64**, 636–639.

HILL, W. F., & SPEAR, N. E. (1963) Extinction in a runway as a function of acquisition level and reinforcement percentage. *J. exp. Psychol.*, **65**, 495–500.

HILLMAN, B., HUNTER, W. S., & KIMBLE, G. A. (1953) The effect of drive level on the maze performance of the white rat. *J. comp. physiol. Psychol.*, **46**, 87–89.

HOFFMAN, H. S., & FLESHLER, M. (1965) Stimulus aspects of aversive controls: The effects of response contingent shock. *J. exp. Anal. Behav.*, **8**, 89–96.

HOLZ, W. C., & AZRIN, N. H. (1961) Discriminative properties of punishment. *J. exp. Anal. Behav.*, **4**, 225–232.

HOMME, L. E. (1956) Spontaneous recovery and statistical learning. *J. exp. Psychol.*, **51**, 205–212.

HONIG, W. K. (1961) Generalization of extinction on the spectral continuum. *Psychol. Rec.*, **11**, 269–278.

HONIG, W. K. (1962) Prediction of preference, transposition, and transposition-reversal from the generalization gradient. *J. exp. Psychol.*, **64**, 239–248.

HONIG, W. K., THOMAS, D. R., & GUTTMAN, N. (1959) Differential effects of continuous extinction and discrimination training on the generalization gradient. *J. exp. Psychol.*, **58**, 145–152.

HOROWITZ, L. M. (1961) Free recall and ordering of trigrams. *J. exp. Psychol.*, **62**, 51–57.

HOROWITZ, L. M. (1962) Associative matching and intralist similarity. *Psychol. Rep.*, **10**, 751–757.

HOROWITZ, L. M., BROWN, Z. M., & WEISSBLUTH, S. (1964) Availability and the direction of associations. *J. exp. Psychol.*, **68**, 541–549.

HOROWITZ, L. M., & IZAWA, C. (1963) Comparison of serial and paired-associate learning. *J. exp. Psychol.*, **65**, 352–361.

HOROWITZ, L. M., & LARSEN, S. R. (1963) Response interference in paired-associate learning. *J. exp. Psychol.,* 65, 225–232.

HOROWITZ, L. M., LIPPMAN, L. G., NORMAN, S. A., & McCONKIE, G. W. (1964) Compound stimuli in paired-associate learning. *J. exp. Psychol.,* 67, 132–141.

HORTON, D. L., & KJELDERGAARD, P. M. (1961) An experimental analysis of associative factors in mediated generalizations. *Psychol. Monogr.,* 75, No. 11.

HOVLAND, C. I. (1936) "Inhibition of reinforcement" and phenomena of experimental extinction. *Proc. Nat. Acad. Sci. Wash.,* 22, 430–433.

HOVLAND, C. I. (1937a) The generalization of conditioned responses: I. The sensory generalization of conditioned responses with varying frequencies of tone. *J. gen. Psychol.,* 17, 125–148.

HOVLAND, C. I. (1937b) The generalization of conditioned responses: II. The sensory generalization of conditioned responses with varying intensities of tone. *J. genet. Psychol.,* 51, 279–291.

HOVLAND, C. I. (1937c) The generalization of conditioned responses: IV. The effects of varying amounts of reinforcement upon the degree of generalization of conditioned responses. *J. exp. Psychol.,* 21, 261–276.

HOVLAND, C. I. (1938) Experimental studies in rote-learning theory: II. Reminiscence with varying speeds of syllable presentation. *J. exp. Psychol.,* 22, 338–353.

HOVLAND, C. I. (1952) A "communication analysis" of concept learning. *Psychol. Rev.,* 59, 461–472.

HOVLAND, C. I., & HUNT, E. B. (1960) Computer simulation of concept attainment. *Behavioral Science,* 5, 265–267.

HOVLAND, C. I., & WEISS, W. (1953) Transmission of information concerning concepts through positive and negative instances. *J. exp. Psychol.,* 45, 175–182.

HUGHES, C. L., & NORTH, A. J. (1959) Effect of introducing a partial correlation between a critical cue and a previously irrelevant cue. *J. comp. physiol. Psychol.,* 52, 126–128.

HUGHES, L. H. (1957) Saccharine reinforcement in a T maze. *J. comp. physiol. Psychol.,* 50, 431–435.

HULL, C. L. (1921) Quantitative aspects of the evolution of concepts: An experimental study. *Psychol. Monogr.,* 28, No. 123.

HULL, C. L. (1930) Knowledge and purpose as habit mechanisms. *Psychol. Rev.,* 37, 511–525.

HULL, C. L. (1931) Goal attraction and directing ideas conceived as habit phenomena. *Psychol. Rev.,* 38, 487–506.

HULL, C. L. (1943) *Principles of behavior.* New York: Appleton-Century-Crofts.

HULL, C. L. (1951) *Essentials of behavior.* New Haven, Conn.: Yale.

HULL, C. L. (1952) *A behavior system.* New Haven, Conn.: Yale.

HULSE, S. H. (1958) Amount and percentage of reinforcement and duration of goal confinement in conditioning and extinction. *J. exp. Psychol.,* 56, 48–57.

HULSE, S. H. (1962) Partial reinforcement, continuous reinforcement, and reinforcement shift effects. *J. exp. Psychol.,* 64, 451–459.

HULSE, S. H., & BACON, W. E. (1962) Supplementary report: Partial reinforcement and amount of reinforcement as determinants of instrumental licking rates. *J. exp. Psychol.,* **63,** 214–215.

HULSE, S. H., & FIRESTONE, R. J. (1964) Mean amount of reinforcement and instrumental response strength. *J. exp. Psychol.,* **67,** 417–422.

HULSE, S. H., SNYDER, H. L., & BACON, W. E. (1960) Instrumental licking behavior as a function of schedule, volume, and concentration of a saccharine reinforcer. *J. exp. Psychol.,* **60,** 359–364.

HULSE, S. H., & STANLEY, W. C. (1956) Extinction by omission of food as related to partial and secondary reinforcement. *J. exp. Psychol.,* **52,** 221–227.

HUMPHREYS, L. G. (1939) Acquisition and extinction of verbal expectations in a situation analogous to conditioning. *J. exp. Psychol.,* **25,** 294–301.

HUNT, E. B. (1962) *Concept learning.* New York: Wiley.

HUNT, H. F., & BRADY, J. V. (1955) Some effects of punishment and intercurrent "anxiety" on a simple operant. *J. comp. physiol. Psychol.,* **48,** 305–310.

HURWITZ, H. M. B. (1955) Response elimination without performance. *Quart. J. exp. Psychol.,* **7,** 1–7.

HUTT, P. J. (1954) Rate of bar pressing as a function of quality and quantity of food reward. *J. comp. physiol. Psychol.,* **47,** 235–239.

HYMAN, R. (1953) Stimulus information as a determinant of reaction time. *J. exp. Psychol.,* **45,** 188–196.

IRION, A. L. (1948) The relation of "set" to retention. *Psychol. Rev.,* **55,** 336–341.

IRION, A. L., & GUSTAFSON, L. M. (1952) "Reminiscence" in bilateral transfer. *J. exp. Psychol.,* **43,** 321–323.

ISON, J. R. (1962) Experimental extinction as a function of number of reinforcements. *J. exp. Psychol.,* **64,** 314–317.

JAHNKE, J. C., & DUNCAN, C. P. (1956) Reminiscence and forgetting in motor learning after extended rest intervals. *J. exp. Psychol.,* **52,** 273–282.

JENKINS, H. M. (1962) Resistance to extinction when partial reinforcement is followed by regular reinforcement. *J. exp. Psychol.,* **64,** 441–450.

JENKINS, H. M., & HARRISON, R. H. (1960) Effect of discrimination training on auditory generalization. *J. exp. Psychol.,* **59,** 246–253.

JENKINS, J. J. (1963) Mediated associations. In C. N. Cofer, & B. S. Musgrave (Eds.) *Verbal behavior and learning.* New York: McGraw-Hill.

JENKINS, J. J., MINK, W. D., & RUSSELL, W. A. (1958) Associative clustering as a function of verbal association strength. *Psychol. Rep.,* **4,** 127–136.

JENKINS, J. J., & RUSSELL, W. A. (1952) Associative clustering during recall. *J. abnorm. soc. Psychol.,* **47,** 818–821.

JENKINS, W. O. (1950) A temporal gradient of derived reinforcement. *Amer. J. Psychol.,* **63,** 237–243.

JENKINS, W. O., McFANN, H., & CLAYTON, F. L. (1950) A methodological study of extinction following aperiodic and continuous reinforcement. *J. comp. physiol. Psychol.,* **43,** 155–167.

JENKINS, W. O., PASCAL, G. R., & WALKER, R. W., JR. (1958) Deprivation and generalization. *J. exp. Psychol.,* **56,** 274–277.

JENKINS, W. O., & STANLEY, J. C., JR. (1950) Partial reinforcement: A review and critique. *Psychol. Bull.,* **47,** 193–234.

JENSEN, A. R. (1961) On the reformulation of inhibition in Hull's system. *Psychol. Bull.*, **58**, 274–298.

JENSEN, A. R. (1962) Temporal and spatial effects of serial position. *Amer. J. Psychol.*, **75**, 390–400.

JONES, M. B. (1962) Practice as a process of simplification. *Psychol. Rev.*, **69**, 274–294.

JUDSON, A. I., & COFER, C. N. (1956) Reasoning as an associative process: I. "Direction" in a simple verbal problem. *Psychol. Rep.*, **2**, 469–476.

KARSH, E. (1962) Effects of number of rewarded trials and intensity of punishment on running speed. *J. comp. physiol. Psychol.*, **55**, 44–51.

KELLEHER, R. T. (1956) Discrimination learning as a function of reversal and nonreversal shifts. *J. exp. Psychol.*, **51**, 379–384.

KELLEHER, R. T., & GOLLUB, L. R. (1962) A review of positive conditioned reinforcement. *J. exp. Anal. Behav.*, **5**, 543–597.

KELLER, F. S. (1958) The phantom plateau. *J. exp. Anal. Behav.*, **1**, 1–13.

KELLER, F. S., & SCHOENFELD, W. N. (1950) *Principles of psychology.* New York: Appleton-Century-Crofts.

KENDLER, H. H. (1945) Drive interaction: II. Experimental analysis of the role of drive in learning theory. *J. exp. Psychol.*, **35**, 188–198.

KENDLER, H. H. (1964) The concept of the concept. In A. W. Melton (Ed.) *Categories of human learning.* New York: Academic.

KENDLER, H. H., & D'AMATO, M. F. (1955) A comparison of reversal shifts and nonreversal shifts in human concept formation behavior. *J. exp. Psychol.*, **49**, 165–174.

KENDLER, H. H., & KENDLER, T. S. (1962) Vertical and horizontal processes in problem solving. *Psychol. Rev.*, **69**, 1–16.

KENDLER, T. S. (1950) An experimental investigation of transposition as a function of the difference between training and test stimuli. *J. exp. Psychol.*, **40**, 552–562.

KENDLER, T. S., & KENDLER, H. H. (1959) Reversal and nonreversal shifts in kindergarten children. *J. exp. Psychol.*, **58**, 56–60.

KENDLER, T. S., KENDLER, H. H., & WELLS, D. (1960) Reversal and nonreversal shifts in nursery school children. *J. comp. physiol. Psychol.*, **53**, 83–88.

KENDRICK, D. C. (1958) Inhibition with reinforcement (conditioned inhibition). *J. exp. Psychol.*, **56**, 313–318.

KEPPEL, G., & UNDERWOOD, B. J. (1962) Proactive inhibition in short-term retention of single items. *J. verb. Learn. verb. Behav.*, **1**, 153–161.

KIENTZLE, M. J. (1946) Properties of learning curves under varied distributions of practice. *J. exp. Psychol.*, **39**, 187–211.

KIERNAN, C. C. (1964) Positive reinforcement by light: Comments on Lockard's article. *Psychol. Bull.*, **62**, 351–357.

KIMBLE, G. A. (1961) *Hilgard and Marquis' conditioning and learning.* (2nd ed.) New York: Appleton-Century-Crofts.

KIMBLE, G. A., & KENDALL, J. R., JR. (1953) A comparison of two methods of producing experimental extinction. *J. exp. Psychol.*, **45**, 87–90.

KIMBLE, G. A., MANN, L. I., & DUFORT, R. H. (1955) Classical and instrumental eyelid conditioning. *J. exp. Psychol.*, **49**, 407–417.

KING, D. J., & COFER, C. N. (1960) Retroactive interference in meaningful material as a function of the degree of contextual constraint in the original and interpolated learning. *J. gen. Psychol.,* 63, 145–158.

KIRKPATRICK, D. R., PAVLIK, W. B., & REYNOLDS, W. F. (1964) Partial-reinforcement extinction effect as a function of size of goal box. *J. exp. Psychol.,* 68, 515–516.

KISH, G. B. (1955) Learning when the onset of illumination is used as reinforcing stimulus. *J. comp. physiol. Psychol.,* 48, 261–264.

KLING, J. W. (1952) Generalization of extinction of an instrumental response to stimuli varying in the size dimension. *J. exp. Psychol.,* 44, 339–346.

KLING, J. W. (1956) Speed of running as a function of goal-box behavior. *J. comp. physiol. Psychol.,* 49, 474–476.

KOHN, M. (1951) Satiation of hunger from food injected directly into the stomach versus food ingested by mouth. *J. comp. physiol. Psychol.,* 44, 412–422.

KONORSKI, J. (1950) *Mechanisms of learning.* Vol. 4. *Society for Experimental Biology Symposium on physiological mechanisms in animal behavior.* New York: Academic.

KRASNER, L. (1958) Studies of the conditioning of verbal behavior. *Psychol. Bull.,* 55, 148–170.

KRECHEVSKY, I. (1932a) "Hypotheses" in rats. *Psychol. Rev.,* 38, 516–532.

KRECHEVSKY, I. (1932b) "Hypotheses" versus "chance" in the pre-solution period in sensory discrimination learning. *Univ. Calif. Publ. Psychol.,* 6, 27–44.

KRUEGER, W. C. F. (1929) The effect of overlearning on retention. *J. exp. Psychol.,* 12, 71–78.

KRUEGER, W. C. F. (1934) The relative difficulty of nonsense syllables. *J. exp. Psychol.,* 17, 145–153.

KUENNE, M. R. (1946) Experimental investigation of the relation of language to transposition behavior in young children. *J. exp. Psychol.,* 36, 471–490.

LAMBERT, W. W., & SOLOMON, R. L. (1952) Extinction of a running response as a function of distance of block point from the goal. *J. comp. physiol. Psychol.,* 45, 269–279.

LASHLEY, K. S. (1930) The mechanism of vision: I. A method for rapid analysis of pattern-vision in the rat. *J. genet. Psychol.,* 37, 453–460.

LASHLEY, K. S. (1938) The mechanism of vision: XV. Preliminary studies of the rat's capacity for detail vision. *J. gen. Psychol.,* 18, 123–193.

LASHLEY, K. S. (1942) An examination of the "continuity theory" as applied to discriminative learning. *J. gen. Psychol.,* 26, 241–265.

LASHLEY, K. S., & WADE, M. (1946) The Pavlovian theory of generalization. *Psychol. Rev.,* 53, 72–87.

LAWRENCE, D. H. (1949) Acquired distinctiveness of cues: I. Transfer between discriminations on the basis of familiarity with the stimulus. *J. exp. Psychol.,* 39, 770–784.

LAWRENCE, D. H. (1950) Acquired distinctiveness of cues: II. Selective association in a constant stimulus situation. *J. exp. Psychol.,* 40, 175–188.

LAWRENCE, D. H. (1955) The applicability of generalization gradients to the transfer of a discrimination. *J. gen. Psychol.,* 52, 37–48.

LAWRENCE, D. H. (1958) Learning. *Annu. Rev. Psychol.,* **9,** 157–188.

LAWRENCE, D. H. (1963) The nature of a stimulus: Some relationships between learning and perception. In S. Koch (Ed.), *Psychology: A study of a science.* Vol. V. New York: McGraw-Hill.

LAWRENCE, D. H., & DE RIVERA, J. (1954) Evidence for relational discrimination. *J. comp. physiol. Psychol.,* **47,** 465–471.

LAWRENCE, D. H., & FESTINGER, L. (1962) *Deterrents and reinforcement.* Stanford, Calif.: Stanford.

LAWRENCE, D. H., & HOMMEL, L. (1961) The influence of differential goal boxes on discrimination learning involving delay of reinforcement. *J. comp. physiol. Psychol.,* **54,** 552–555.

LAWRENCE, D. H., & MASON, W. A. (1955) Systematic behavior during discrimination reversal and change of dimension. *J. comp. physiol. Psychol.,* **48,** 267–271.

LEAF, R. C., & MULLER, S. A. (1965) Simple method for CER conditioning and measurement. *Psychol. Rep.,* **17,** 211–215.

LEARY, R. W. (1958) Homogeneous and heterogeneous reward of monkeys. *J. comp. physiol. Psychol.,* **51,** 706–710.

LEVIN, G. R., & BAKER, B. L. (1963) Item scrambling in a self-instructional program. *J. educ. Psychol.,* **54,** 138–143.

LEVIN, H., WATSON, J. S., & FELDMAN, M. (1964) Writing as pretraining for association learning. *J. educ. Psychol.,* **55,** 181–184.

LEVINE, M. (1959) A model of hypothesis behavior in discrimination learning set. *Psychol. Rev.,* **66,** 353–366.

LEVINE, M. (1965) Hypothesis behavior. In A. M. Schrier, H. F. Harlow, & F. Stollnitz (Ed.), *Behavior of nonhuman primates.* Vol. I. New York: Academic.

LEVINE, M., LEVINSON, B., & HARLOW, H. F. (1959) Trials per problem as a variable in the acquisition of discrimination learning set. *J. comp. physiol. Psychol.,* **52,** 396–398.

LEWIS, D., & LOWE, W. F. (1956) Retention of skill on the SAM complex coordinator. *Proc. Iowa Acad. Sci.,* **63,** 591–599.

LEWIS, D. J. (1960) Partial reinforcement: A selective review of the literature since 1950. *Psychol. Bull.,* **57,** 1–28.

LEWIS, D. J., & COTTON, J. W. (1959) The effect of intertrial interval and number of acquisition trials with partial reinforcement on performance. *J. comp. physiol. Psychol.,* **52,** 598–601.

LEWIS, M. (1964) Some nondecremental effects of effort. *J. comp. physiol. Psychol.,* **57,** 367–372.

LLOYD, K. E., REID, L. S., & FEALLOCK, J. B. (1960) Short-term retention as a function of the average number of items presented. *J. exp. Psychol.,* **60,** 201–207.

LOCKARD, R. B. (1963) Some effects of light upon the behavior of rodents. *Psychol. Bull.,* **60,** 509–529.

LOCKHEAD, G. R. (1962) Methods of presenting paired associates. *J. verb. Learn. verb. Behav.,* **1,** 62–65.

LOGAN, F. A. (1956) A micromolar approach to behavior theory. *Psychol. Rev.,* **63,** 63–73.

LOGAN, F. A. (1960) *Incentive*. New Haven, Conn.: Yale.

LOGAN, F. A. (1965) Decision making by rats: delay versus amount of reward. *J. comp. physiol. Psychol.,* 59, 1–12.

LOGAN, F. A., BEIER, E. M., & ELLIS, R. A. (1955) Effect of varied reinforcement on speed of locomotion. *J. exp. Psychol.,* 49, 260–266.

LOGAN, F. A., BEIER, E. M., & KINCAID, W. D. (1956) Extinction following partial and varied reinforcement. *J. exp. Psychol.,* 52, 65–70.

LONGNECKER, E. G., KRAUSKOPF, J., & BITTERMAN, M. E. (1952) Extinction following alternating and random reinforcement. *Amer. J. Psychol.,* 65, 580–587.

LONGO, N. (1964) Probability-learning and habit-reversal in the cockroach. *Amer. J. Psychol.,* 77, 29–41.

LORGE, I. (1930) Influence of regularly interpolated time intervals upon subsequent learning. *Teach. Coll. Contr. Educ.,* No. 438.

LORGE, I., & THORNDIKE, E. L. (1935) The influence of delay in the aftereffect of a connection. *J. exp. Psychol.,* 18, 186–194.

LUCE, R. D., BUSH, R. R., & GALANTER, E. (1963a) *Readings in mathematical psychology.* Vol. 1. New York: Wiley.

LUCE, R. D., BUSH, R. R., & GALANTER, E. (Eds.) (1963b) *Handbook of mathematical psychology.* Vols. I & II. New York: Wiley.

LUCHINS, A. S. (1942) Mechanization in problem solving. The effect of einstellung. *Psychol. Monogr.,* 54, No. 248.

LUH, C. W. (1922) The conditions of retention. *Psychol. Monogr.,* 31, No. 142.

LYON, D. O. (1917) *Memory and the learning process.* Baltimore: Warwick and York.

MacCORQUODALE, K., & MEEHL, P. E. (1948) On a distinction between hypothetical constructs and intervening variables. *Psychol. Rev.,* 55, 95–107.

MACKINTOSH, N. J. (1965) Selective attention in animal discrimination learning. *Psychol. Bull.,* 64, 124–150.

MAHER, W. B., & WICKENS, D. D. (1954) Effect of differential quantity of reward on acquisition and performance of a maze habit. *J. comp. physiol. Psychol.,* 47, 44–46.

MALTZMAN, I., EISMAN, E., BROOKS, L. O., & SMITH, W. M. (1956) Task instructions for anagrams following different task instructions and training. *J. exp. Psychol.,* 51, 418–420.

MALTZMAN, I., & MORRISETT, L. (1953) Effects of task instruction on solution of different classes of anagrams. *J. exp. Psychol.,* 45, 351–354.

MANDLER, G. (1955) Associative frequency and associative prepotency as response measures of nonsense syllables. *Amer. J. Psychol.,* 68, 662–665.

MANDLER, G. (1963) Comments on Professor Jenkins' paper. In C. N. Cofer & B. S. Musgrave (Eds.), *Verbal behavior and learning.* New York: McGraw-Hill.

MANDLER, G., & COWAN, P. H. (1962) Learning of simple structures. *J. exp. Psychol.,* 64, 177–183.

MARX, M. H., & MURPHY, W. W. (1961) Resistance to extinction as a function of the presentation of a motivating cue in the startbox. *J. comp. physiol. Psychol.,* 54, 207–210.

MASSERMAN, J. H., & PECHTEL, C. (1953) Neurosis in monkeys: A preliminary report of experimental observations. *Ann. N. Y. Acad. Sci.,* 56, 253–265.

McCRARY, J. W., JR., & HUNTER, W. S. (1953) Serial position curves in verbal learning. *Science,* 117, 131–134.

McGEHEE, N. E., & SCHULZ, R. W. (1961) Mediation in paired-associate learning. *J. exp. Psychol.,* 62, 565–570.

McGEOCH, J. A. (1930) The influence of associative value upon the difficulty of non-sense syllable lists. *J. genet. Psychol.,* 37, 421–426.

McGEOCH, J. A. (1936) The direction and extent of intra-serial associations at recall. *Amer. J. Psychol.,* 48, 221–245.

McGEOCH, J. A., & IRION, A. L. (1952) *The psychology of human learning.* New York: Longmans.

McGUIGAN, F. J. (1956) The logical status of Hull's principle of secondary reinforcement. *Psychol. Rev.,* 63, 303–309.

MECHANIC, A. (1962) Effects of orienting task, practice, and incentive on simultaneous incidental and intentional learning. *J. exp. Psychol.,* 64, 393–399.

MEDNICK, S. A. & FREEDMAN, J. L. (1960) Stimulus generalization. *Psychol. Bull.,* 57, 169–200.

MEEHL, P. E. (1950) On the circularity of the law of effect. *Psychol. Bull.,* 47, 52–75.

MELTON, A. W. (1963) Implications of short-term memory for a general theory of memory. *J. verb. Learn. verb. Behav.,* 2, 1–21.

MELTON, A. W., & IRWIN, J. McQ. (1940) The influence of degree of interpolated learning on retroactive inhibition and the overt transfer of specific responses. *Amer. J. Psychol.,* 53, 173–203.

MELTON, A. W., & VON LACKUM, W. J. (1941) Retroactive and proactive inhibition in retention: Evidence for a two factor theory of retroactive inhibition. *Amer. J. Psychol.,* 54, 157–173.

MILES, R. C. (1956) The relative effectiveness of secondary reinforcers throughout deprivation and habit-strength parameters. *J. comp. physiol. Psychol.,* 49, 126–130.

MILES, R. C. (1965) Discrimination-learning sets. In A. M. Schrier, H. F. Harlow, & F. Stollnitz (Eds.), *Behavior of nonhuman primates.* New York: Academic.

MILLER, G. A. (1956) The magical number seven, plus or minus two: Some limits on our capacity for processing information. *Psychol. Rev.,* 63, 81–97.

MILLER, G. A. (1958) Free recall of redundant strings of letters. *J. exp. Psychol.,* 56, 485–491.

MILLER, G. A., GALANTER, E., & PRIBRAM, K. H. (1960) *Plans and the structure of behavior.* New York: Holt.

MILLER, G. A., & McGILL, W. J. (1952) A statistical description of verbal learning. *Psychometrika,* 17, 369–396.

MILLER, G. A., & SELFRIDGE, J. A. (1950) Verbal context and the recall of meaningful material. *Amer. J. Psychol.,* 63, 176–185.

MILLER, G. R. (1963) Extra experimental transfer in serial recall. *J. verb. Learn. verb. Behav.,* 2, 494–497.

MILLER, N. E. (1935) A reply to "sign—Gestalt or conditioned reflex?" *Psychol. Rev.,* **42,** 280–292.

MILLER, N. E. (1948) Studies of fear as an acquirable drive: I. Fear as motivation and fear-reduction as reinforcement in the learning of new responses. *J. exp. Psychol.,* **38,** 89–101.

MILLER, N. E. (1951) Learnable drives and rewards. In S. S. STEVENS (Ed.), *Handbook of experimental psychology.* New York: Wiley.

MILLER, N. E. (1958) Liberalization of basic S–R concepts: Extensions to conflict behavior, motivation and social learning. In S. Koch (Ed.), *Psychology: A study of a science.* Vol. II. New York: McGraw-Hill.

MILLER, N. E. (1963) Some reflections on the law of effect produce a new alternative to drive reduction. In M. R. Jones (Ed.), *Nebraska symposium on motivation.* Lincoln, Nebr.: Univ. Nebraska Press.

MILLER, N. E., & DOLLARD, J. (1941) *Social learning and imitation.* New Haven, Conn.: Yale.

MILLER, N. E., & KESSEN, M. L. (1952) Reward effects of food via stomach fistula compared with those of food via mouth. *J. comp. physiol. Psychol.,* **45,** 555–564.

MOELLER, G. (1954) The CS–UCS interval in GSR conditioning. *J. exp. Psychol.,* **48,** 162–166.

MOLTZ, H. (1955) Latent extinction and the reduction of secondary reward value. *J. exp. Psychol.,* **49,** 395–400.

MOLTZ, H. (1957) Latent extinction and the fractional anticipatory response mechanism. *Psychol. Rev.,* **64,** 229–241.

MONTGOMERY, K. C. (1954) The role of exploratory drive in learning. *J. comp. physiol. Psychol.,* **47,** 60–64.

MOOK, D. G. (1963) Oral and postingestional determinants of the intake of various solutions in rats with esophageal fistulas. *J. comp. physiol. Psychol.,* **56,** 645–659.

MOORE, J. W. & GORMEZANO, I. (1961) Yoked comparisons of instrumental and classical eyelid conditioning. *J. exp. Psychol.,* **62,** 552–559.

MORAY, N., & TAYLOR, A. (1958) The effect of redundancy in shadowing one of two dichotic messages. *Language and Speech,* **1,** 102–109.

MORGAN, C. T. (1964) *Physiological psychology.* (3d ed.) New York: McGraw-Hill.

MOSTOFSKY, D. I. (Ed.) (1965) *Stimulus generalization.* Stanford, Calif.: Stanford.

MOWBRAY, G. H., & RHOADES, M. V. (1959) On the reduction of choice reaction times with practice. *Quart. J. exp. Psychol.,* **11,** 16–23.

MOWRER, O. H. (1947) On the dual nature of learning—a reinterpretation of "conditioning" and "problem-solving." *Harvard educ. Rev.,* **17,** 102–148.

MOWRER, O. H. (1960) *Learning theory and behavior.* New York: Wiley.

MOWRER, O. H., & JONES, H. (1943) Extinction and behavior variability as functions of effortfulness of task. *J. exp. Psychol.,* **33,** 369–386.

MOWRER, O. H., & JONES, H. (1945) Habit strength as a function of the pattern of reinforcement. *J. exp. Psychol.,* **35,** 293–311.

MOWRER, O. H., & LAMOREAUX, R. R. (1942) Avoidance conditioning and signal duration—a study of secondary motivation and reward. *Psychol. Monogr.,* **54,** No. 247.

MUELLER, C. G. (1950) Theoretical relationships among some measures of conditioning. *Proc. Nat. Acad. Sci. Wash.,* **36,** 123–130.

MUENZINGER, K. F. (1934) Motivation in learning. I. Electric shock for correct response in the visual discrimination habit. *J. comp. Psychol.,* **17,** 267–277.

MURDOCK, B. B., JR. (1956) "Backward" learning in paired associates. *J. exp. Psychol.,* **51,** 213–215.

MURDOCK, B. B., JR. (1957) Transfer designs and formulas. *Psychol. Bull.,* **54,** 313–326.

MURDOCK, B. B., JR. (1960) The immediate retention of unrelated words. *J. exp. Psychol.,* **60,** 222–234.

MURDOCK, B. B., JR. (1961) The retention of individual items. *J. exp. Psychol.,* **62,** 618–625.

MURDOCK, B. B., JR. (1962) The serial position effect of free recall. *J. exp. Psychol.,* **64,** 482–488.

MURILLO, N. R., & CAPALDI, E. J. (1961) The role of overlearning trials in determining resistance to extinction. *J. exp. Psychol.,* **61,** 345–349.

MUSGRAVE, B. S. (1962) The effect of nonsense-syllable compound stimuli on latency in a verbal paired-associate task. *J. exp. Psychol.,* **63,** 499–504.

MYERS, A. K., & MILLER, N. E. (1954) Failure to find a learned drive based on hunger: Evidence for learning motivated by "exploration." *J. comp. physiol. Psychol.,* **47,** 428–440.

MYERS, J. L. (1958) Secondary reinforcement: A review of recent experimentation. *Psychol. Bull.,* **55,** 284–301.

NAPALKOV, A. V. (1959) Chains of motor conditioned reactions in pigeons. *Zh. vyssh. nervn. Deiatel.,* **9,** 615–621.

Nebraska symposium on motivation. M. R. Jones (Ed.), Vols. 1–13, *et seq.* Lincoln, Nebr.: Univ. Nebraska Press.

NOBLE, C. E. (1952) An analysis of meaning. *Psychol. Rev.,* **59,** 421–430.

NORTH, A. J., & STIMMEL, D. T. (1960) Extinction of an instrumental response following a large number of reinforcements. *Psychol. Rep.,* **6,** 227–234.

OAKLEY, B., & PFAFFMAN, C. (1962) Electrophysiologically monitored lesions in the gustatory thalamic relay of the albino rat. *J. comp. physiol. Psychol.,* **55,** 155–160.

OLDS, J. (1958) Satiation effects in self-stimulation of the brain. *J. comp. physiol. Psychol.,* **51,** 675–678.

OLDS, J., & MILNER, P. (1954) Positive reinforcement produced by electrical stimulation of septal area and other regions of the rat brain. *J. comp. physiol. Psychol.,* **47,** 419–427.

OSGOOD, C. E. (1949) The similarity paradox in human learning: A resolution. *Psychol. Rev.,* **56,** 132–143.

PAUL, I. H. (1959) Studies in remembering: The reproduction of connected and extended verbal material. *Psychol. Issues,* **1,** 152 pp.

PAVLOV, I. P. (1927) *Conditioned reflexes.* (Translated by G. V. Anrep) London: Oxford.

PERIN, C. T. (1942) Behavior potentiality as a joint function of the amount of training and degree of hunger at the time of extinction. *J. exp. Psychol.,* **30,** 93–113.

PERIN, C. T. (1943) A quantitative investigation of the delay-of-reinforcement gradient. *J. exp. Psychol.,* 32, 37–51.

PERKINS, C. C. (1947) The relation of secondary reward to gradients of reinforcement. *J. exp. Psychol.,* 37, 377–392.

PETERSON, C. R., & ULEHLA, Z. J. (1965) Sequential patterns and maximizing. *J. exp. Psychol.,* 69, 1–4.

PETERSON, L., & PETERSON, M. J. (1959) Short-term retention of individual verbal items. *J. exp. Psychol.,* 58, 193–198.

PFAFFMANN, C. (1960) The pleasures of sensation. *Psychol. Rev.,* 67, 253–268.

PFAFFMANN, C. (1964) Taste, its sensory and motivating properties. *Amer. Scientist,* 52, 187–206.

PFAFFMANN, C. (1965) De gustibus. *Amer. Psychol.,* 20, 21–33.

PIMSLEUR, P., & BONKOWSKI, R. J. (1961) Transfer of verbal material across sense modalities. *J. educ. Psychol.,* 52, 104–107.

POSTMAN, L. (1947) The history and present status of the law of effect. *Psychol. Bull.,* 46, 489–563.

POSTMAN, L. (1954) Learned principles of organization in memory. *Psychol. Monogr.,* 68, No. 374.

POSTMAN, L. (1962a) Retention as a function of degree of overlearning. *Science,* 135, 666–667.

POSTMAN, L. (1962b) Repetition and paired-associate learning. *Amer. J. Psychol.,* 75, 372–389.

POSTMAN, L. (1962c) Transfer of training as a function of experimental paradigm and degree of first-list learning. *J. verb. Learn. verb. Behav.,* 1, 109–118.

POSTMAN, L. (1963) Does interference theory predict too much forgetting? *J. verb. Learn. verb. Behav.,* 2, 40–48.

POSTMAN, L. (1964) Short-term memory and incidental learning. In A. W. Melton (Ed.), *Categories of human learning.* New York: Academic.

POSTMAN, L., & ADAMS, P. A. (1957) Studies in incidental learning: VI. Intra-serial interference. *J. exp. Psychol.,* 54, 153–167.

POSTMAN, L., & ADAMS, P. A. (1960) Studies in incidental learning: VII. The effects of contextual determination. *J. exp. Psychol.,* 59, 153–164.

POSTMAN, L., & RAU, L. (1957) Retention as a function of the method of measurement. *Univ. Calif. Publ. Psychol.,* 8, 217–270.

PRACHTL, H. F. R. (1953) Zur Physiologie der angeboren auslösenden Mechanism. *Behav.,* 5, 32–50.

PREMACK, D., & COLLIER, G. (1962) Analysis of nonreinforcement variables affecting response probability. *Psychol. Monogr.,* 76, No. 524.

PRIMOFF, E. (1938) Backward and forward associations as an organizing act in serial and in paired-associate learning. *J. Psychol.,* 5, 375–395.

PROKASY, W. F. (1960) Postasymptotic performance decrements during massed reinforcements. *Psychol. Bull.,* 57, 237–247.

PUBOLS, B. H., JR. (1956) The facilitation of visual and spatial discrimination reversal by overtraining. *J. comp. physiol. Psychol.,* 49, 243–248.

PUBOLS, B. H., JR. (1960) Incentive magnitude, learning, and performance in animals. *Psychol. Bull.,* 57, 89–115.

REED, H. B. (1946) Factors influencing learning and retention of concepts. II. Influence of length of series. *J. exp. Psychol.,* **36,** 166–181.

REID, L. S. (1953) The development of noncontinuity behavior through continuity learning. *J. exp. Psychol.,* **46,** 107–112.

REID, L. S., LLOYD, K. E., BRACKETT, H. R., & HAWKINS, W. F. (1961) Short-term retention as a function of average storage load and average load reduction. *J. exp. Psychol.,* **62,** 518–522.

RESTLE, F. (1957) Theory of selective learning with probable reinforcements. *Psychol. Rev.,* **64,** 182–191.

RESTLE, F. (1958) Toward a quantitative description of learning set data. *Psychol. Rev.,* **65,** 77–91.

RESTLE, F. (1962) The selection of strategies in cue learning. *Psychol. Rev.,* **69,** 329–343.

REYNOLDS, B. (1945) A repetition of the Blodgett experiment on "latent" learning. *J. exp. Psychol.,* **35,** 504–516.

REYNOLDS, B. (1949) The relationship between strength of habit and the degree of drive present during acquisition. *J. exp. Psychol.,* **39,** 296–305.

REYNOLDS, G. S. (1961) Attention in the pigeon. *J. exp. Anal. Beh.,* **4,** 203–208.

REYNOLDS, R. W. (1958) The relationship between stimulation voltage and rate of hypothalamic self-stimulation in the rat. *J. comp. physiol. Psychol.,* **51,** 193–198.

RILEY, D. A. (1962) Memory for form. In L. Postman (Ed.), *Psychology in the making.* New York: Knopf.

RILEY, D. A., GOGGIN, J. P., & WRIGHT, D. C. (1963) Training level and cue separation as determiners of transposition and retention in rats. *J. comp. physiol. Psychol.,* **56,** 1044–1049.

RIOPELLE, A. (1953) Transfer suppression and learning sets. *J. comp. physiol. Psychol.,* **46,** 108–114.

ROBERTS, C. L., MARX, M. H., & COLLIER, G. (1958) Light onset and light offset as reinforcers for the albino rat. *J. comp. physiol. Psychol.,* **51,** 575–579.

ROCK, I. (1957) The role of repetition in associative learning. *Amer. J. Psychol.,* **70,** 186–193.

ROCK, I., & HEIMER, W. (1959) Further evidence of one-trial associative learning. *Amer. J. Psychol.,* **72,** 1–16.

ROTHKOPF, E. Z., & ZEAMAN, D. (1952) Some stimulus controls of alternation behavior. *J. Psychol.,* **34,** 235–255.

RUSSELL, W. A., & JENKINS, J. J. (1954) *The complete Minnesota norms for responses to 100 words from the Kent-Rosanoff Association Test.* Tech. Rep. No. 11, Contract N80NR-66216 between Office of Naval Research and Univ. Minnesota.

RUSSELL, W. A., & STORMS, L. H. (1955) Implicit verbal chaining in paired-associate learning. *J. exp. Psychol.,* **49,** 287–293.

SALTZ, E., & NEWMAN, S. E. (1959) The von Restorff isolation effect: Test of the intralist association assumption. *J. exp. Psychol.,* **58,** 445–451.

SALTZMAN, I. J. (1949) Maze learning in the absence of primary reinforcement: A study of secondary reinforcement. *J. comp. physiol. Psychol.,* **42,** 161–173.

SAPORTA, S., BLUMENTAL, A., & REIFF, D. G. (1963) Grammatical models and language learning. *Monograph Series on Language and Linguistics,* 16, 133–142.

SCHLOSBERG, H. (1937) The relationship between success and the laws of conditioning. *Psychol. Rev.,* 44, 379–394.

SCHRIER, A. M. (1958) Comparison of two methods of investigating the effect of amount of reward on performance. *J. comp. physiol. Psychol.,* 51, 725–731.

SEWARD, J. P., & LEVY, N. (1949) Sign learning as a factor in extinction. *J. exp. Psychol.,* 39, 660–668.

SHARP, H. C. (1958) Effect of contextual constraint upon recall of verbal passages. *Amer. J. Psychol.,* 71, 568–572.

SHEFFIELD, F. D. (1948) Avoidance training and the contiguity principle. *J. comp. physiol. Psychol.,* 41, 165–177.

SHEFFIELD, F. D. (1966) A drive-induction theory of reinforcement. In R. N. Haber (Ed.), *Current research in motivation.* New York: Holt.

SHEFFIELD, F. D., & JENKINS, W. O. (1952) Level of repetition in the "spread of effect." *J. exp. Psychol.,* 44, 101–107.

SHEFFIELD, F. D., ROBY, T. B., & CAMPBELL, B. A. (1954) Drive reduction versus consummatory behavior as determinants of reinforcement. *J. comp. physiol. Psychol.,* 47, 349–354.

SHEFFIELD, F. D., & TEMMER, H. W. (1950) Relative resistance to extinction of escape training and avoidance training. *J. exp. Psychol.,* 40, 287–298.

SHEFFIELD, F. D., WULFF, J. J., & BACKER, R. (1951) Reward value of copulation without sex drive reduction. *J. comp. physiol. Psychol.,* 44, 3–8.

SHEPARD, R. N. (1957) Stimulus and response generalization: A stochastic model relating generalization to distance in psychological space. *Psychometrika,* 22, 325–345.

SHEPARD, R. N. (1958) Stimulus and response generalization: Tests of a model relating generalization to distance in psychological space. *J. exp. Psychol.,* 55, 509–523.

SHEPARD, R. N. (1965) Approximation to uniform gradients of generalization by monotone transformations of scale. In D. I. Mostofsky (Ed.), *Stimulus generalization.* Stanford, Calif.: Stanford.

SIEGEL, S., & WAGNER, A. R. (1963) Extended acquisition training and resistance to extinction. *J. exp. Psychol.,* 66, 308–310.

SKINNER, B. F. (1935) Two types of conditioned reflex and a pseudo type. *J. gen. Psychol.,* 12, 66–77.

SKINNER, B. F. (1938) *The behavior of organisms.* New York: Appleton-Century-Crofts.

SKINNER, B. F. (1948) Superstition in the pigeon. *J. exp. Psychol.,* 38, 168–172.

SKINNER, B. F. (1950) Are theories of learning necessary? *Psychol. Bull.,* 57, 193–216.

SLAMECKA, N. J. (1959) Studies of retention of connected discourse. *Amer. J. Psychol.,* 72, 409–416.

SMODE, A. F. (1958) Learning and performance in a tracking task under two levels of achievement information feedback. *J. exp. Psychol.,* 56, 297–304.

SMOKE, K. L. (1933) Negative instances in concept learning. *J. exp. Psychol.,* 16, 583–588.

SNODDY, G. S. (1926) Learning and stability. *J. Appl. Psychol.,* **10**, 1–36.

SNYDER, H. L. (1962) Saccharine concentration and deprivation as determinants of instrumental and consummatory response strengths. *J. exp. Psychol.,* **63**, 610–615.

SNYDER, H. L., & HULSE, S. H. (1961) Effect of volume of reinforcement and number of consummatory responses on licking and running behavior. *J. exp. Psychol.,* **61**, 474–479.

SOLOMON, R. L., (1964) Punishment. *Amer. Psychol.,* **19**, 239–253.

SOLOMON, R. L., KAMIN, L. J., & WYNNE, L. C. (1953) Traumatic avoidance learning: The outcomes of several extinction procedures with dogs. *J. abnorm. soc. Psychol.,* **48**, 291–302.

SOLOMON, R. L., & WYNNE, L. C. (1953) Traumatic avoidance learning: Acquisition in normal dogs. *Psychol. Monogr.,* **67**, No. 354.

SOLOMON, R. L., & WYNNE, L. C. (1954) Traumatic avoidance learning: The principles of anxiety conservation and partial irreversibility. *Psychol. Rev.,* **61**, 353–385.

SPENCE, K. W. (1936) The nature of discrimination learning in animals. *Psychol. Rev.,* **43**, 427–449.

SPENCE, K. W. (1937a) The differential response in animals to stimuli varying within a single dimension. *Psychol. Rev.,* **44**, 430–444.

SPENCE, K. W. (1937b) Analysis of formation of visual discrimination habits in the chimpanzee. *J. comp. Psychol.,* **23**, 77–100.

SPENCE, K. W. (1940) Continuous versus non-continuous interpretations of discrimination learning. *Psychol. Rev.,* **47**, 271–288.

SPENCE, K. W. (1947) The role of secondary reinforcement in delayed reward learning. *Psychol. Rev.,* **54**, 1–8.

SPENCE, K. W. (1948) The postulates and methods of behaviorism. *Psychol. Rev.,* **55**, 67–78.

SPENCE, K. W. (1951) Theoretical interpretations of learning. In S. S. Stevens (Ed.), *Handbook of experimental psychology.* New York: Wiley.

SPENCE, K. W. (1952) The nature of the response in discrimination learning. *Psychol. Rev.,* **59**, 89–93.

SPENCE, K. W. (1956) *Behavior theory and conditioning.* New Haven, Conn.: Yale.

SPENCE, K. W. (1958) A theory of emotionally based drive (D) and its relation to performance in simple learning situations. *Amer. Psychol.,* **13**, 131–141.

SPENCE, K. W. (1960) *Behavior theory and learning.* Englewood Cliffs, N.J.: Prentice-Hall.

SPENCE, K. W., & RUNQUIST, W. H. (1958) Temporal effects of conditioned fear on the eyelid reflex *J. exp. Psychol.,* **55**, 613–616.

SPERLING, G. (1960) The information available in brief visual presentations. *Psychol. Monogr.,* **74**, No. 498.

SPERLING, S. E. (1965a) Reversal learning and resistance to extinction. *Psychol. Bull.,* **63**, 281–297.

SPERLING, S. E. (1965b) Reversal learning and resistance to extinction: A supplementary report. *Psychol. Bull.,* **64**, 310–312.

SPIELBERGER, C. D. (1965) Theoretical and epistemological issues in verbal conditioning. In S. Rosenberg (Ed.), *Directions in psycholinguistics.* New York: Macmillan.

SPOONER, A., & KELLOGG, W. N. (1947) The backward conditioning curve. *Amer. J. Psychol.*, **60**, 321–334.

STANER, B. J. (1956) Transfer as a function of simultaneous stimulus and response generalization. M.A. thesis, Northwestern Univ., cited in B. J. Underwood. An evaluation of the Gibson theory of verbal learning. In C. N. Cofer (Ed.), *Verbal learning and verbal behavior.* New York: McGraw-Hill.

STANLEY, W. C., & AAMODT, M. S. (1954) Force of responding during extinction as a function of force requirement during conditioning. *J. comp. physiol. Psychol.*, **47**, 462–464.

STANLEY, W. C., & ROWE, M. I. (1954) Extinction by omission of food as a function of goal-box confinement. *J. exp. Psychol.*, **48**, 271–274.

STEIN, L. (1958) Secondary reinforcement established with subcortical stimulation. *Science,* **127**, 466–467.

STELLAR, E., (1954) The physiology of motivation. *Psychol. Rev.*, **61**, 5–22.

STEPHENS, J. M. (1934) Further notes on punishment and reward. *J. genet. Psychol.*, **44**, 464–472.

STEPHENS, J. M. (1942) Expectancy vs. effect-substitution as a general principle of reinforcement. *Psychol. Rev.*, **49**, 102–116.

STEVENSON, H. W., ISCOE I., & McCONNELL, C. (1955) A developmental study of transposition. *J. exp. Psychol.*, **49**, 278–280.

STOLLNITZ, F. (1965) Spatial variables, observing responses, and discrimination learning sets. *Psychol. Rev.*, **72**, 247–261.

STONE, G. R. (1948) A note on Postman's review of the literature on the law of effect. *Psychol. Bull.*, **45**, 151–160.

SUTHERLAND, N. S. (1959) Stimulus analysing mechanisms. In *Proceedings of a symposium on the mechanization of thought processes.* Vol. 2. London: H.M.S.O.

SUTHERLAND, N. S., MACKINTOSH, N. J., & WOLFE, J. B. (1965) Extinction as a function of the order of partial and consistent reinforcement. *J. exp. Psychol.*, **69**, 56–59.

TAYLOR, A., & MORAY, N. (1960) Statistical approximations to English and French. *Lang. & Speech,* **3**, 7–10.

TAYLOR, J. A. (1951) The relationship of anxiety to the conditioned eyelid response. *J. exp. Psychol.*, **41**, 81–92.

TAYLOR, J. A. (1956) Drive theory and manifest anxiety. *Psychol. Bull.*, **53**, 303–320.

TEICHNER, W. H. (1952) Experimental extinction as a function of the intertrial intervals during conditioning and extinction. *J. exp. Psychol.*, **44**, 170–178.

TEITELBAUM, P., & CYTAWA, J. (1965) Spreading depression and recovery from lateral hypothalamic damage. *Science,* **147**, 61–63.

TEITELBAUM, P., & EPSTEIN, A. N. (1962) The lateral hypothalamic syndrome: Recovery of feeding and drinking after lateral hypothalamic lesions. *Psychol. Rev.*, **69**, 74–90.

TERRACE, H. S. (1964) Wavelength generalization after discrimination learning with and without errors. *Science,* **144**, 78–80.

THEIOS, J. (1962) The partial reinforcement effect sustained through blocks of continuous reinforcement. *J. exp. Psychol.*, **64**, 1–6.

Theios, J. (1963) Drive stimulus generalization increments. *J. comp. physiol. Psychol.,* 56, 691–695.

Theios, J., & Brelsford, J. (1964) Overlearning-extinction effect as an incentive phenomenon. *J. exp. Psychol.,* 67, 463–467.

Thistlethwaite, D. (1951) A critical review of latent learning and related experiments. *Psychol. Bull.,* 48, 97–130.

Thorndike, E. L. (1898) Animal intelligence. *Psychol. Monogr.,* 2, No. 8.

Thorndike, E. L. (1903) *Educational psychology.* New York: Lemcke & Buechner.

Thorndike, E. L. (1911) *Animal intelligence.* New York: Macmillan.

Thorndike, E. L. (1923) The influence of first-year Latin upon the ability to read English. *School. & Soc.,* 17, 165–168.

Thorndike, E. L. (1932a) Reward and punishment in animal learning. *Comp. Psychol. Monogr.,* 8, No. 39.

Thorndike, E. L. (1932b) *The fundamentals of learning.* New York: Teachers College.

Thorndike, E. L. (1933) An experimental study of rewards. *Teach. Coll. Contr. Educ.,* No. 580.

Thorndike, E. L. (1935) *The psychology of wants, interests and attitudes.* New York: Appleton-Century-Crofts.

Thorndike, E. L., & Lorge, I. (1944) *The teacher's word book of 30,000 words.* New York: Teachers College.

Thorndike, E. L., & Woodworth, R. S. (1901) The influence of improvement in one mental function upon the efficiency of other functions. *Psychol. Rev.,* 8, 247–267, 384–395, 553–564.

Thurstone, L. L. (1930a) The learning function. *J. gen. Psychol.,* 3, 469–493.

Thurstone, L. L. (1930b) The relation between learning time and length of task. *Psychol. Rev.,* 37, 44–53.

Tinbergen, N. (1951) *The study of instinct.* Fair Lawn, N.J.: Oxford.

Tinklepaugh, O. L. (1928) An experimental study of representative factors in monkeys. *J. comp. Psychol.,* 8, 197–236.

Tolman, E. C. (1932) *Purposive behavior in animals and men.* New York: Appleton-Century-Crofts.

Tolman, E. C. (1948) Cognitive maps in rats and men. *Psychol. Rev.,* 55, 189–208.

Tolman, E. C. (1949) There is more than one kind of learning. *Psychol. Rev.,* 56, 144–155.

Tolman, E. C. (1951) *Collected papers in psychology.* Berkeley, Calif.: Univ. Calif. Press.

Tolman, E. C. (1958) Principles of purposive behavior. In S. Koch (Ed.), *Psychology: A study of a science.* Vol. II. New York: McGraw-Hill.

Tolman, E. C., & Honzik, C. H. (1930) Introduction and removal of reward and maze performance in rats. *Univ. Calif. Publ. Psychol.,* 4, 257–275.

Torgerson, W. S. (1965) Multidimensional scaling of similarity. *Psychometrika,* 30, 379–393.

Troland, L. T. (1928) *The fundamentals of human motivation.* Princeton, N.J.: Van Nostrand.

Tucker, L. R. (1960) Determination of generalized learning curves by factor analysis. *Technical Report.* Princeton, N.J.: Educational Test Services.

TULVING, E., & PATKAU, J. E. (1962) Concurrent effects of contextual constraint and word frequency on immediate recall and learning of verbal material. *Canad. J. Psychol.,* **16,** 83–95.

TURNER, L. H., & SOLOMON, R. L. (1962) Human traumatic avoidance learning: Theory and experiments on the operant-respondent distinction. *Psychol. Monogr.,* **76,** No. 40.

TYLER, D. W., WORTZ, E. C., & BITTERMAN, M. E. (1953) The effect of random and alternating partial reinforcement on resistance to extinction in the rat. *Amer. J. Psychol.,* **66,** 57–65.

UNDERWOOD, B. J. (1948) Retroactive and proactive inhibition after 5 and 48 hours. *J. exp. Psychol.,* **38,** 29–38.

UNDERWOOD, B. J. (1954) Speed of learning and amount retained: A consideration of methodology. *Psychol. Bull.,* **51,** 276–282.

UNDERWOOD, B. J. (1961) Ten years of massed practice on distributed practice. *Psychol. Rev.,* **68,** 229–247.

UNDERWOOD, B. J. (1964) Degree of learning and the measurement of forgetting. *J. verb. Learn. verb. Behav.,* **3,** 112–129.

UNDERWOOD, B. J., & KEPPEL, G. (1962) One-trial learning? *J. verb. Learn. verb. Behav.,* **1,** 1–13.

UNDERWOOD, B. J., & POSTMAN, L. (1960) Extraexperimental sources of interference in forgetting. *Psychol. Rev.,* **67,** 73–95.

UNDERWOOD, B. J., REHULA, R., & KEPPEL, G. (1962) Item-selection in paired-associate learning. *Amer. J. Psychol.,* **75,** 353–371.

UNDERWOOD, B. J., & RICHARDSON, J. (1956a) Some verbal materials for the study of concept formation. *Psychol. Bull.,* **53,** 84–95.

UNDERWOOD, B. J., & RICHARDSON, J. (1956b) Verbal concept learning as a function of instructions and dominance level. *J. exp. Psychol.,* **51,** 229–238.

UNDERWOOD, B. J., RUNQUIST, W. N., & SCHULZ, R. W. (1959) Response learning in paired-associate lists as a function of intralist similarity. *J. exp. Psychol.,* **58,** 70–78. ∘

UNDERWOOD, B. J., & SCHULZ, R. W. (1960) Meaningfulness and verbal learning. Philadelphia: Lippincott.

VON RESTORFF, H. (1933) Über die Wirkung von Bereichsbildungen im Spurenfeld. *Psychol. Forsch.,* **18,** 299–342.

VON WRIGHT, J. M. (1959a) Forgetting and interference. *Societas Scientarium Fennica Commentationes Humanorum Litterarum,* **26,** No. 1

VON WRIGHT, J. M. (1959b) The effect of systematic changes of context stimuli on repeated recall. *Acta Psychologica,* **16,** 59–68 (also in *Nordisk Psykologi,* 1959, **11,** 59–68).

WAGNER, A. R. (1959) The role of reinforcement and nonreinforcement in an "apparent frustration effect." *J. exp. Psychol.,* **57,** 130–136.

WAGNER, A. R. (1961) Effects of amount and percentage of reinforcement and number of acquisition trials on conditioning and extinction. *J. exp. Psychol.,* **62,** 234–242.

WALLACH, M. A. (1963) Perceptual recognition of approximations to English in relation to spelling achievement. *J. educ. Psychol.,* **54,** 57–62.

WARREN, J. M. (1954) An analysis of the formation of visual discriminative habits of rhesus monkeys. *Amer. J. Psychol.,* **67,** 517–520.

WARREN, J. M. (1965) The comparative psychology of learning. *Annu. Rev. Psychol.,* **16,** 95–118.

WATSON, J. B., & RAYNOR, R. (1920) Conditioned emotional reactions. *J. exp. Psychol.,* **3,** 1–4.

WAUGH, N. C. (1961) Free versus serial recall. *J. exp. Psychol.,* **62,** 496–502.

WAUGH, N. C. (1962) Length of series and the learning curve. *Amer. J. Psychol.,* **75,** 177–192.

WEINGARTNER, H. (1963) Associative structure and serial learning *J. verb. Learn. verb. Behav.,* **2,** 476–479.

WEINSTOCK, S. (1954) Resistance to extinction of a running response following partial reinforcement under widely spaced trials. *J. comp. physiol. Psychol.,* **47,** 318–323.

WEINSTOCK, S. (1958) Acquisition and extinction of a partially reinforced running response at a 24-hour intertrial interval. *J. exp. Psychol.,* **56,** 151–158.

WELFORD, A. T. (1951) *Skill and age.* Fair Lawn, N.J.: Oxford.

WELFORD, A. T. (1960) The measurement of senso-motor performance: Survey and reappraisal of twelve years progress. *Ergonomics,* **3,** 189–230.

WHITMAN, J. R., & GARNER, W. R. (1962) Free recall learning of visual figures as a function of form of internal structure. *J. exp. Psychol.,* **64,** 558–564.

WHITING, J. W. M., & MOWRER, O. H. (1943) Habit progression and regression—a laboratory study of some factors relevant to human socialization. *J. comp. Psychol.,* **36,** 229–253.

WILLIAMS, J. P. (1962) A test of the all-or-none hypothesis for verbal learning. *J. exp. Psychol.,* **64,** 158–165.

WILLLAMS, S. B. (1938) Resistance to extinction as a function of the number of reinforcements. *J. exp. Psychol.,* **23,** 506–522.

WILSON, W., WEISS, E. J., & AMSEL, A. (1955) Two tests of the Sheffield hypothesis concerning resistance to extinction, partial reinforcement, and distribution of practice. *J. exp. Psychol.,* **50,** 51–60.

WIMER, R. (1964) Osgood's transfer surface: Extension and test. *J. verb. Learn. verb. Behav.,* **3,** 274–279.

WISCHNER, G. J. (1947) The effect of punishment on discrimination learning in a non-correction situation. *J. exp. Psychol.,* **37,** 271–284.

WISCHNER, G. J., FOWLER, H., & KUSHNICK, S. A. (1963) The effect of strength of punishment for "correct" and "incorrect" responses on performance. *J. exp. Psychol.,* **65,** 131–138.

WOLFE, J. B. (1934) The effect of delayed reward upon learning in the white rat. *J. comp. Psychol.,* **17,** 1–21.

WOLFE, J. B. (1936) Effectiveness of token-rewards for chimpanzees. *Comp. Psychol. Monogr.,* **12,** No. 60.

WOLFLE, H. M. (1930) Time factors in conditioning finger-withdrawal. *J. gen. Psychol.,* **4,** 372–378.

WOLFLE, H. M. (1932) Conditioning as a function of the interval between the conditioned and the original stimulus. *J. gen. Psychol.,* **7,** 80–103.

WOLLEN, K. A. (1962) One-trial versus incremental-paired associate learning. *J. verb. Learn. verb. Behav.,* 1, 14–21.

WOODROW, H. (1927) The effect of type of training upon transference. *J. educ. Psychol.,* 18, 159–172.

WYCKOFF, L. B., JR. (1952) The role of observing responses in discrimination learning. Part I. *Psychol. Rev.,* 59, 431–442.

YAMAGUCHI, H. (1961) The effect of continuous, partial, and varied magnitude reinforcement on acquisition and extinction. *J. exp. Psychol.,* 61, 319–321.

YNTEMA, D. B., & TRASK, F. P. (1963) Recall as a search process. *J. verb. Learn. verb. Behav.,* 2, 65–74.

YOUNG, P. T. (1961) *Motivation and emotion. A survey of the determinants of human and animal activity.* New York: Wiley.

YOUNG, P. T., & SHUFORD, E. H., JR. (1954) Intensity, duration, and repetition of hedonic processes as related to acquisition of motives. *J. comp. physiol. Psychol.,* 47, 298–305.

YOUNG, P. T., & SHUFORD, E. H., JR. (1955) Quantitative control of motivation through sucrose solutions of different concentrations. *J. comp. physiol. Psychol,* 48, 114–118.

YOUNG, R. K. (1959) A comparison of two methods of learning serial associations. *Amer. J. Psychol.,* 72, 554–559.

YUM, K. S. (1931) An experimental test of the law of assimilation. *J. exp. Psychol.,* 14, 68–82.

ZANGWILL, O. L. (1937) An investigation of the relationship between the process of reproducing and recognizing simple figures with special reference to Koffka's trace theory. *Brit. J. Psychol.,* 27, 250–276.

ZEAMAN, D. (1949) Response latency as a function of the amount of reinforcement. *J. exp. Psychol.,* 39, 466–483.

ZEAMAN, D., & HOUSE, B. J. (1951) The growth and decay of reactive inhibition as measured by alternation behavior. *J. exp. Psychol.,* 41, 177–186.

ZEAMAN, D., & HOUSE, B. J. (1963) The role of attention in retardate discrimination learning. In N. R. Ellis (Ed.), *Handbook of mental deficiency.* New York: McGraw-Hill.

INDEX

INDEX

Page numbers in italics are in the Reference section